INSIDE SERVLETS

INSIDE SERVLETS

Server-Side Programming for the Java™ Platform

Second Edition

Dustin R. Callaway

Addison-Wesley

Boston • San Francisco • New York • Toronto • Montreal
London • Munich • Paris • Madrid
Capetown • Sydney • Tokyo • Singapore • Mexico City

The publisher offers discounts on this book when ordered in quantity for special sales. For more information, please contact:

Pearson Education Corporate Sales Division
One Lake Street
Upper Saddle River, NJ 07458
(800) 382-3419
corpsales@pearsontechgroup.com

Visit us on the Web at www.awl.com/cseng/

Library of Congress Cataloging-in-Publication Data

Callaway, Dustin R., 1970-
    Inside servlets: server-side programming for the Java platform / Dustin R. Callaway.—2nd ed.
        p. cm.
    Includes bibliographical references and index.
    ISBN 0-201-70906-6
    1. Java (Computer program language) 2. Client/server computing. 3. Servlets (Computer programs) I. Title.
    QA76.73.J38 C35 2001
    005.2'762—dc21   2001018181

ServletExec™ files on CD-ROM copyright © New Atlanta Communications, LLC. All rights reserved.
JRun™ files copyright © Allaire Corporation. All rights reserved.
Resin™ copyright Caucho Technology, Inc. All rights reserved.
JBuilder™ copyright Borland Software Corporation. All rights reserved.

ISBN 0-201-70906-6

Text printed on recycled paper.
1234567890 —MA—0504030201
First printing, April 2001

This book is dedicated to my beautiful wife, Erin, and my three wonderful children, Tyler, Madison, and Reagan.

CONTENTS

Part III   Advanced Servlet Concepts   **279**

FOREWORD

The release of the Java programming language in 1995 in many ways took the world of computing by surprise. So great was the initial excitement about a language that had started as a research project at Sun Microsystems that people did not quite know how to react. They immediately recognized, however, that it was going to be important. A frenzy began that could not have been anticipated: formerly static Web sites became enriched with animated and interactive Java applets; daily news stories followed the initial dramas of the release of the technology; companies scrambled to establish a position on the technology; and the media had a field day trying to make sense of a phenomenon that was, after all, only a programming language.

During 1995, James Gosling and his team began work on a piece of the technology puzzle that was to take Java into a new venue: the server. The increasing importance of the Internet as a way of gathering, sharing, and personalizing information and services meant that the role of the server was rising quickly. Under the internal name of "Jeeves" and badged as the familiar Java mascot "Duke" dressed as a butler carrying a serving platter, the project defined a component model somewhat akin to applets, but for running components on a Web server. As components for generating dynamic and interactive Web pages, servlets were a simple embodiment of the HTTP request/response paradigm, and they were easy to understand. They promised to bring to Web developers the cost-benefits and ease-of-deployment features of Java as a cross-platform/cross-server technology. They promised to improve on the familiar CGI model by being both quicker by design and easier to glue into existing systems using APIs like JDBC. They promised to bring a new community of developers, intrigued by Java applets and the extensive and appealing Java platform APIs, into a new style of programming on the server side.

When Jeeves was released as a technology preview on the JavaSoft Web site in late 1996, initial interest was great. Jeeves contained what is usually known as the 1.0 version of the Servlet API. It soon morphed into a product known as the Java Web Server, which was released the following July. This release of a fully functioning Web server written on the Java platform and incorporating support for Java servlets contained all the building blocks of the servlet technology that exist in the API today. Aside from the definition of the component model, the API contained facilities to give servlets a view into the Web server that was running them, and facilities to encapsulate user sessions that were essential to personalizing Web content for each user requesting it.

Meanwhile, other companies became interested in this technology and started to build support into their products, quickly seeing the benefit of these cross-platform Web components as a way to add great value to their offerings. As the Java Web Server and associated Java Servlet Development Kit matured through versions, developers and their companies who wished to establish a presence on the Internet started to shift their focus from dancing Duke to this simple, intuitive, and flexible model of HTTP interaction.

As companies and organizations from Allaire to Zeus released servlet-enabled products, it became clear that the technology needed a more formal footing. Release 2.0 of the Servlet API with the Java Servlet Development Kit 2.0 included a specification document that described the API classes and some of the conventions for their use. JSDK 2.0 acted as a reference implementation, a kind of reality check for the specification of Java servlets in order to guide the development of servlet support in the ever-growing number of Web servers, and to keep the "cross-server" promise of servlets intact. During this time, several technologies sprang up—for example, JavaServer Pages (JSP), WebMacro, and other templating languages that built on the servlet framework and semantics, while extending the ease of development of servlet applications. By focusing on writing small pieces of logic into a static page that would be interpreted by a specially enabled servlet engine and complied into a servlet, these derived technologies were aimed at the armies of Web designers who didn't want to learn a programming language to enrich their Web sites. They wanted a technology that extended what they were best at: authoring appealing Web sites.

An early adopter and champion of servlet technology was the open source community at the Apache Software Foundation, best known for its Apache Web Server, which remains the market leader in Web servers. With a Java extension called JServ, this highly successful Web server could be extended easily to support servlets. Continued work within JavaSoft on the reference implementation, in parallel with ever-stronger ties with the Apache development community, resulted in the donation of the JSDK code in the summer of 1999 to the Apache Software Foundation. Thus, the Tomcat Web server, developed under the Apache umbrella, was born and continues to provide the open source reference implementation of the Servlet API.

While servlet components were pioneering the debut of Java on the server side, they soon found they were not the only kids on the block. Traditional enterprise information system providers began to move from two-tier client/ server architectures to more scalable and flexible three-tier and multitier architectures. With the first release of Enterprise JavaBeans technology in 1997, which defined a component model for the middle tier in these large-scale systems, it was becoming clear that Java had a highly respected position as a leading technology for writing server-side applications. The merging of EJB, servlet, and JSP teams within JavaSoft following this release resulted in the birth of a technology called Java 2, Enterprise Edition (J2EE). J2EE was to unite EJB, Java servlets, and JavaServer Pages into a common platform, which would include APIs to manage database access and transactions for naming and directory services. Soon after its release in late 1999, rapid adoption of this application server standard quickly made J2EE a de facto platform for server-side applications. Incorporation of servlets as first-class components acting as the "mouthpiece" of a J2EE application has taken servlets from great popularity in the Web server market into nearly every application server on the planet.

Development of the Servlet API in the time since its early days as a fledgling technology in its version 1.0 guise has been rapid. Version 2.0 is the version most developers experienced first. Moving through versions 2.1 and 2.2, the notion of the request dispatcher, somewhat akin to a server-side include mechanism, has been added, as well as the introduction of standardized file format for Web applications. In order to keep pace with the development of a popular standard, the servlet specification is now developed and maintained by a team of experts in servlet technology drawn from leading areas in the industry, and by listening to the needs of the developer community. At the time of this writing, the version of the API about to mature is version 2.3. The new release, described in this book, adds the notion of servlet filtering and Web application events, and is fully developed in this community manner. In this way, the future of the API is guaranteed to keep up the often bewildering pace of new ideas in Web technology.

Today Java servlets stand as a highly successful and well-maintained technology that has found its home squarely on the server side. Servlets have become an essential weapon in the armory of the Web developer. Dozens of special-interest groups and mailing lists, as well as a large volume of literature, focus solely on the technology. A highly fertile developer community means that there are frameworks available for developers that either build on the Servlet API or use the servlet model for specialized applications. These applications run the gamut from traditional Web development to wireless service development, from XML messaging applications to Internet telephony. Now more than ever, since the quiet beginning of Java servlets as a research project, programmers with a desire to understand and use servlets are assured of being at the forefront of the Internet revolution.

Readers of this book will find everything they need to help them on their quest to learn and understand Java servlets. If they are new to Web technologies, they will find themselves thoroughly grounded in the basic pieces that form the Internet. Readers will be led through a comprehensive and clear exposition of all aspects of the servlet programming model. Along the way, they will add to their toolkit numerous useful tips, tricks, and examples that they will come back to again and again.

Danny Coward,
Specification Lead for the Java Servlet API
Sun Microsystems, Inc.

PREFACE

Future generations will likely rank the Internet alongside the printing press, the airplane, and the personal computer as one of the most revolutionary technologies in history. After seemingly lying dormant for more than two decades, the Internet has emerged from obscurity to capture the interest and imagination of people around the world. One of the primary factors driving this phenomenon is the astounding popularity of the World Wide Web. Globally accessible via the Internet, the Web has forever changed the way information is published and distributed. The first goal of this book is to familiarize you with the underlying technologies that drive the Internet and the World Wide Web.

The Java programming language is another emerging technology whose potential is just beginning to be recognized. Due to its platform-independent nature, standard network interfaces, and many other advantages, Java is the ideal language for Internet programming. Although initially popularized by applets capable of running on any client, the true power of Java is being realized on the server. Among other things, server-side Java allows developers to build dynamic Web sites using a powerful, object-oriented language that is completely portable across virtually all operating systems and hardware. By writing programs for the Java platform, you are in essence developing applications for all existing platforms—from mobile phones to mainframes and everything in between. This kind of portability and cross-platform functionality is unprecedented.

The Internet relies on open standards to ensure that all clients have equal access to the vast amount of information it provides. Similarly, standards are essential to the advancement of the Java platform. Sun Microsystems, Inc., in cooperation with many industry partners and other interested parties, has created a standard for developing server-side Java programs that extend and enhance the functionality of the server. Known as the Java Servlet API, this standard ensures that all servlets will run properly on all platforms for which a Java virtual machine is available.

By conforming to the Servlet API specification, you can guarantee that all of your server-side programs will run on any platform that fully supports Java. After presenting Web development fundamentals, the second and primary goal of this book is to provide an in-depth understanding of Java servlets and the Servlet API through discussion and example.

What's New in This Edition

This edition of _Inside Servlets_ both revises and expands upon the first edition. Primarily, the bulk of the revisions update the text and source code to conform to version 2.2 of the Java Servlet Specification. In addition to conforming to the new specification, the breadth and depth of the book has been greatly expanded. The second edition of _Inside Servlets_ provides comprehensive coverage of several new topics, including security, JavaServer Pages, packaging and deployment, and servlet troubleshooting. The chapter on database access has also been greatly expanded. Finally, this edition includes improved sample servlets, an updated quick reference section, and a complete review of version 2.3 of the Java Servlet Specification.

Intended Audience

In general, this book was written for anyone interested in using server-side Java to build dynamic, data-driven Web sites or other networked applications. To this end, _Inside Servlets: Server-Side Programming for the Java™ Platform_, Second Edition, presents an in-depth review of the Servlet API as well as advanced programming concepts essential for successful servlet development. These concepts include writing thread-safe servlets, session management, database access, and security.

More specifically, the book is intended for programmers and consultants who desire to learn Web development fundamentals in addition to server-side Java programming. Much of this audience likely consists of current client/server programmers. After all, in an increasingly Internet-centric world, many client/server programs are being redeveloped as Web applications. This decision is often driven by the fact that Web applications offer significant distribution and maintenance advantages over traditional client/server systems.

Because Java servlets may represent your first foray into Web development, the first part of the book is dedicated to teaching the basics of the Internet and the World Wide Web. Although basic Web concepts are presented, the Java programming language is not taught. This book assumes a basic knowledge of object-oriented programming and the Java language. If you are not familiar with Java, I recommend reading the Java primer in _Java in a Nutshell_ by David

Flanagan. This primer is especially well suited to C programmers. Another personal favorite for learning about Java is *Thinking in Java* by Bruce Eckel. If you do not already know Java, you may want to have one of these books available as a reference while reading this book.

Acknowledgments

Above all, I would like to thank my wife, Erin, for her enduring patience and support throughout this project. I would also like to express my appreciation to all of the reviewers at Sun Microsystems and elsewhere for the help and feedback that made this book possible. Specifically, I would like to thank Danny Coward, Jim Inscore, Todd Gee, Debbie Fleming, Eddy Boite, Michael Wynholds, and Svetlana Khawaja.

INTRODUCTION

Organization of This Book

This book is partitioned into the following six parts, each of which consists of multiple chapters.

Part I: Introduction to Web Development

Part I introduces basic Web development concepts. These concepts include fundamentals such as firewalls, proxy servers, HTTP protocol, MIME types, and HTML forms.

Part II: Introduction to Servlets

Part II introduces the reader to Java servlets and the Servlet API. The information presented here includes the advantages of servlets over traditional CGI programming, basic servlet structure, writing your first servlet, running servlets, debugging servlets, and a preview of the Servlet API.

Part III: Advanced Servlet Concepts

Part III presents advanced concepts essential for building more complex servlets. These concepts include writing thread-safe servlets, HTTP redirects, cookies, session management, server-side includes, request forwarding, servlet chaining, database access, security, JavaServer Pages, packaging and deployment, and servlet troubleshooting.

Part IV: Sample Servlets

Part IV presents several real-world examples of servlets in action. The function of each sample servlet is explained and the entire source code is given. Sample servlets include a Form Mailer servlet, a File Upload servlet, and a complete servlet-based template framework.

Part V: Servlet API Quick Reference

Part V provides a comprehensive reference for Servlet API 2.2 as well as a chapter that presents the alterations and enhancements introduced in version 2.3. Every method defined by all classes and interfaces in the Servlet API is presented.

Part VI: Appendices

Part VI provides useful information in the form of several appendices. Additional information documented here includes a Java port scanner, a Java HTTP server, HTTP response status codes, HTTP request header fields, common MIME types, Servlet API class hierarchy diagram, and much more.

How to Use This Book

If you are new to Web development, I recommend that you start with Chapter 1 of Part I and read each chapter in order (skimming or skipping material with which you are already familiar). If you know all about Web development concepts (perhaps you're a CGI programmer), you may choose to skip Part I and proceed to Part II. Finally, if you already have servlet development experience, you may choose to jump directly to Part III, IV, or V to learn advanced servlet concepts or to review the Servlet API reference material.

Because of the pace at which Internet and Java technologies are evolving, it is possible that a portion of this text may be outdated by the time you read it. For this reason, in addition to the fact that some errors always seem to find their way into a publication this size, a companion Web site has been created for this book. Please visit the Web site for book updates and corrections in addition to the latest servlet news and answers to frequently asked questions. You can find the companion Web site at the following URL:

http://www.InsideServlets.com/

Conventions Used in This Book

A `fixed-width` font is used for

- Anything that might appear in a Java program
- Command lines and other text that should be typed
- Tags that appear in an HTML document
- Any sample program output
- Java class names and packages
- Anything that appears in an HTTP header or other protocol communication

An *italic* font is used for

- New terms where they are first defined
- Pathnames, filenames, and program names (except when a program name is a Java class)
- Internet addresses such as domain names and URLs

A **bold** font is used for

- Keys on a computer keyboard
- Names of user interface elements such as text fields, buttons, menus, dialog boxes, and windows displayed by an application or HTML page

Contents of the CD-ROM

The CD-ROM that accompanies this book contains the following material.

- The source code and compiled class files for all sample code presented in the text and appendices
- JRun 3.0 from Allaire for Windows, Solaris, HP-UX, AIX, IRIX, Tru64 UNIX, and Linux (servlet container)
- ServletExec 3.0 from New Atlanta Communications for Windows, Solaris, HP-UX, AIX, and Linux (servlet container)
- Apache Tomcat 3.1 and 3.2 (servlet container)
- Resin 1.2 from Caucho Technology (servlet container)
- MySQL 3.23 database and JDBC driver for Windows, UNIX, and Linux
- JBuilder 4, Foundation Edition, from Borland for Windows, Solaris, and Linux
- SourceStream Template Server (servlet-based template framework)
- *Protocol Explorer* application used to examine all types of Internet protocol communications (e.g., http headers, ftp sessions)

Many of the directories that contain the software described here also contain a file called *readme.txt*. This file includes additional information and/or instructions about the software in the current directory. Whenever present, please read this file before using the software.

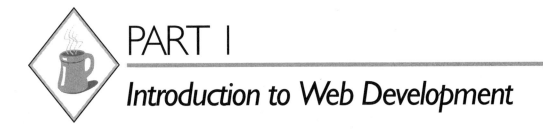

PART I

Introduction to Web Development

CHAPTER 1

Internet Basics

In virtually any field of endeavor, a sound understanding of the fundamentals is essential before tackling more complex tasks. This "learn to walk before you run" strategy is especially important in the area of Web development. Perplexing problems are often quickly resolved once the underlying concepts are understood. So, before jumping into servlet development with both feet, let's review the basics.

This chapter will teach you the basic networking concepts and terminology that you need to know when developing networked applications. The following topics are covered:

- Networks
- Protocols
- TCP/IP
- Brief history of the Internet
- Internet addresses
- Ports
- Sockets
- Name resolution
- Firewalls
- Protocol tunneling
- Proxy servers
- Internet standards

Although many important topics are presented, this chapter is only a primer and not intended to replace a comprehensive study of networking. (For more detailed information on this subject, an excellent resource is the *Networking Basics Series* from Addison-Wesley.) If you are familiar with networks and networking concepts, however, feel free to skim or skip this chapter.

Networks

At its core, a *network* is simply a group of computers and other devices connected in a manner that promotes communication among them. Networked computers are most commonly connected by wire of some sort (often coaxial cable or a twisted-pair wire similar to a phone line); however, machines on a network can be linked by virtually any medium. Some networks communicate via radio waves, infrared light, or fiber-optic cable. The only absolute requirement of a network is that there must be some way for devices to communicate.

To begin our discussion on networking, let's define a few new words. A *node* is any addressable device connected to a network. This could be a computer, printer, fax machine, or even a network-enabled toaster. In contrast, the term *host* is a more specific descriptor that refers to a networked general-purpose computer rather than a single-purpose device (such as a printer). The relationship between a host and a node is asymmetric. Every host is a node, but not every node is a host.

Let's take a closer look at one of the elements in the definition of a node. The definition states that a node must be addressable, but what does that mean? In short, it means that there must be some way to locate each node individually on a network. To facilitate this, every node is assigned a unique address. Without a unique address, there would be no way to communicate with the device.[1] For example, you cannot send someone a letter unless he has a valid address. Therefore, each node on a network is assigned a unique number to identify it. When a message is packaged and transmitted across the network (this package of information is called a *packet*), the source and destination addresses are included with the message's data. This address information is used by network hardware to route the packet to its proper destination.

The network hardware (usually devices known as *routers*) operates like electronic postal workers that evaluate and forward packets between networks. They send the packet directly to the addressed node or to another router that will, in turn, pass the packet along. Eventually, the packet will arrive at its final destination. Thanks to unique addressing, it is possible to communicate with every node on the network. We will take a closer look at addresses later in this chapter.

Now that we have figured out how nodes on a network send each other messages, there is still one more question. How can we guarantee that a node

---

1. Actually, through a transmission called a *broadcast message,* it is possible to send information to all devices on the network without specifically addressing a particular one. However, a device that responds only to broadcast messages (that is not uniquely addressable) is not a considered a node.

will understand the messages it receives? Good question! The answer is something called protocols.

Protocols

One of the fundamentals of network communications is the concept of a protocol. Simply put, a *protocol* is a formal set of rules that must be followed in order to communicate. Though you may not realize it, you use protocols every day. Imagine the confusion generated by someone who did not follow commonly accepted protocols for speaking with others.

You approach a stranger in the mall . . .

You: "Excuse me sir, but do you have the time?"
Stranger: "Yeah, it's 2000."
You: "No. I was wondering if you know what time it is."
Stranger: "July."
You: "Uhh, thanks. Goodbye."

Not a lot of communication took place during that conversation because the stranger did not follow a common protocol for exchanging the time of day. Now, let's try it again.

You approach a stranger in the mall . . .

You: "Excuse me sir, but do you have the time?"
Stranger: "Yeah, it's 2:30."
You: "Thank you."

Now we're talking! Once both sides of the conversation were using the same protocol, communication began to take place. A computer protocol is very similar to this example, but a bit more structured. For instance, when you ask for the time, the response could be in any number of formats. A person might say, "Yep, it's half past two." She could also use commonly accepted shorthand such as, "It's noon." Or she may respond, "No, but there's a clock just down the hall." Regardless, you will be able to process the information that is delivered. There is no predefined set of options that must be spoken in response to the phrase, "Do you have the time?" Computer protocols, on the other hand, cannot afford to be so loosely structured. Though our minds are perfectly adapted to processing and responding to extremely varied input, computers are not. An extremely complex program is required to process even the simplest natural-language sentence. For this reason, networked computers usually converse using an extremely rigid protocol.

For example, when a computer requests that a file be downloaded, it expects either the file to be transmitted or an error condition to be returned. The computer would not understand if the host machine responded with, "Please try back when I'm not so busy" or "It's been a long day, try back tomorrow." However, a properly constructed error message could be construed as "server busy" by the requesting application. At this point, the application may be programmed to wait for a predefined timeout period and then try again. The computer understands the error condition, but not the randomly constructed sentence.

In the context of computer networks, there are many protocol levels. A low-level protocol might define details such as the rate at which bits are transmitted or the voltage levels required to interpret a signal as a zero or a one. Alternatively, a high-level protocol defines the format of the data as well as the sequence and syntax of messages. The following is an example of the high-level HTTP protocol in action.

```
Web Browser:     GET /index.html HTTP/1.0

Web Server:      HTTP/1.0 200 OK
                 Server: Apache/1.3.9 (Win32)
                 Content-type: text/html
                 Content-length: 70

                 <HTML><HEAD><TITLE>Example</TITLE></HEAD>
                 <BODY>It works!</BODY></HTML>
```

The example demonstrates an actual conversation between a Web browser and server. The HTTP protocol defines the format of all requests that are recognized by the server and how the server should respond to these requests. In this case, the browser requested a file called *index.html* and the server returned the contents of the file as well as some additional information to help the browser render the page. We will discuss the HTTP protocol in detail in Chapter 3.

TCP/IP

TCP/IP is a collection, or suite, of protocols used to communicate across a network. The entire protocol suite is named TCP/IP after the two original protocols: Transmission Control Protocol (TCP) and Internet Protocol (IP). Typically, the TCP/IP suite is broken down into four layers,[2] as shown in Figure 1.1.

---

2. The most common network model, known as the OSI model, actually consists of seven layers. However, very few network implementations strictly adhere to the OSI model. The TCP/IP model, for instance, combines several OSI layers into a single layer.

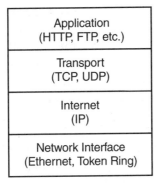

Figure 1.1   The Four Layers of the TCP/IP Model

Why are the protocols layered? The answer is that layering protocols simplifies the task of communicating over the network and it allows reuse of layers that are not specific to a particular application. Each layer is responsible for a different aspect of the transmission and each layer insulates the layers above it from some detail of network communication. For instance, whether a program is using the HTTP or FTP protocol in the application layer, they both use the same underlying protocols—TCP, IP, and Ethernet. The combination of all layers is referred to as a *protocol stack*. As information is transmitted, data flows down through the protocol stack at the source, across the network, and up the protocol stack at the destination.

As data moves down the protocol stack at the source, each layer attaches its information. The information added by each layer is called a *header*. Once all layers have attached their headers to the data, the information is ready to be transmitted across the network. This package of information is called a *packet*. At the destination, each layer removes its header as the packet moves up the protocol stack. Attaching a header to a packet is similar to putting an envelope inside another envelope. To illustrate, let's follow this envelope analogy all the way through. Imagine that you have a message that you would like to send to a coworker in one of your company's foreign offices.

First, you print the message that you would like to send (this is analogous to the data portion of a packet). You then place the message inside an interoffice envelope and address it to your coworker by specifying his name and the office at which he works (the envelope is analogous to a header). When the mailroom receives the envelope, a worker places it in a larger envelope and addresses it with more specific information, such as country, city, and street address (this is similar to attaching a second header). This additional information is required to route the letter to the office in Japan.

Finally, when the envelope arrives at the mailroom of the office in Japan, a worker removes the inner envelope (strips off the outer header) and sends it via interoffice mail. When your coworker receives the interoffice envelope, he opens it and removes the message (strips off the inner header). This process is very similar to the manner in which data is transmitted across the network.

Let's take a look at an actual network transmission (see Figure 1.2). A program wants to send some data to an application running on another computer. The data is packaged in the application layer and a header is applied. As the data moves down the protocol stack, each layer adds its header. Placing data inside a package of headers is known as *encapsulation*. Once the data has been encapsulated inside a packet, it is transmitted across the network. At the destination, each layer removes its header from the packet and passes it up the stack. This process continues until the data is handed back to the application at the highest layer. The application was not interested in the headers attached by

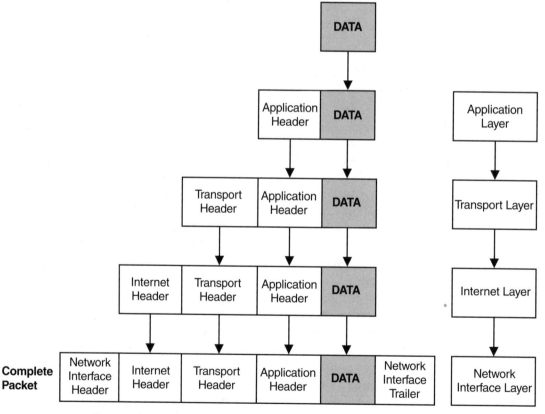

Figure 1.2   Each Layer Adds Its Own Header

other layers; it was simply looking for data. However, these headers were necessary in order to properly transport the information across the network.

Now that we have established that TCP/IP is a collection of layered protocols, let's examine each of the layers: network interface, Internet, transport, and application.

Network Interface Layer

The network interface layer handles the lowest-level details of communicating across a network. This layer consists of the network device driver (software) and the network interface card (hardware). An Ethernet device driver and network card is a good example of an implementation of the network interface layer. These two pieces together ensure the proper transmission of data across whatever medium is being used (coaxial cable, twisted pair, fiber optics, etc.). The network interface layer insulates all layers above it from the complexities of interfacing with various network hardware and transmission mediums. It is interesting to note that the network interface layer adds a trailer to the header (see Figure 1.2). The trailer carries Cyclic Redundancy Check (CRC) information used for error detection.

Internet Layer

The Internet layer is responsible for transmitting packets around the network. The Internet layer uses a protocol called IP (Internet Protocol). This protocol defines exactly how a packet must be structured if it is to be understood by an IP network. The Internet layer's job is to build a packet that conforms to the IP standard. An IP packet, also called a *datagram,* contains a great deal of information. This information includes the length of the header, the total length of the packet, the type of service (Telnet, FTP, etc.), time to live (how many times routers will forward the packet), checksum (for error detection), source address, destination address, and much more.

Transport Layer

The transport layer manages the manner in which data flows between hosts. Although the Internet layer does an excellent job routing network packets, it does not provide a mechanism to ensure their arrival or guarantee the order in which the packets are delivered. If this functionality is desired, it must be provided by the transport layer (or, possibly, in the application layer). Within the TCP/IP model, there are two extremely different transport protocols—TCP and UDP (User Datagram Protocol).

TCP is a reliable protocol that guarantees the arrival of network packets. This guarantee is possible due to the connection-oriented approach implemented by the Transmission Control Protocol. Before any data is sent via the TCP protocol, a connection between the two hosts must first be established. This connection verifies that the destination host is listening and that there is a valid network path whereby the data can reach the destination. The source machine waits for an acknowledgment from the destination host for every group of packets that is sent. If no acknowledgment is received or the destination requests a retransmission, the packet is sent again. In addition to verifying that no packets are lost, TCP also ensures that the packets are in the proper sequence before passing them up the protocol stack.

To understand the connection-oriented nature of the TCP protocol better, imagine the difference between making a telephone call and mailing a letter. When you speak to someone on the phone, you are sure that she received your message. Why? Because you first established a connection with her and she responded to (i.e., acknowledged) your message. Alternatively, consider mailing a letter. Once you address an envelope and drop it in the mail, you have no guarantee that the letter will arrive. The address may have been incorrect or the letter could have been lost in the mail. Since a connection was not established beforehand, you may never know if the letter was delivered unless you receive a reply. Of course, if a reply does come, there is no telling how long you will have to wait for it.

User Datagram Protocol is the second protocol employed in the transport layer. UDP is an unreliable, connectionless protocol. UDP is referred to as "connectionless" because, similar to mailing a letter, no connection is established between the source and destination when a packet is sent. Unlike TCP, this protocol does not automatically ensure a valid network path through which the packet can be delivered. UDP packets are not guaranteed to arrive at their intended destinations.

It might seem as if an unreliable protocol would be useless. However, this is far from the truth. A connection-oriented protocol like TCP requires much more overhead in order to keep track of packets and manage the connection. Thus, a connectionless protocol is able to transmit information much faster. Another advantage to a connectionless protocol is the ability to broadcast messages without specifying the address of a particular recipient. With UDP, it is possible to send a broadcast message to all nodes on a network without knowing the exact address of any of the recipients.[3] A single message is transmitted over the network and all nodes receive it. Of course, some of the packets may

---

3. Fortunately, it is not possible to send a broadcast message to the entire Internet. Broadcast messages are not forwarded by routers and are, therefore, isolated to a local network. Otherwise, the network traffic generated by thousands of broadcast messages could cripple the entire Internet.

not arrive at the destination, but for a broadcast message, this is seldom a concern. TCP, on the other hand, would be required to establish a connection with each node individually and transmit the information separately to each. The network traffic would be much greater and the performance much worse.

Streaming audio and video is another example of a network application that is well suited to a connectionless protocol. By its very nature, streaming information is time sensitive. The additional performance gained by using UDP is well worth settling for less than 100 percent reliability. In fact, if a streaming audio or video transmission lost a few packets, you probably would not even notice. In addition, even if there were no performance penalty for using a connection-oriented protocol, retransmitting lost packets during streaming transmissions is not desirable. If a lost packet were retransmitted while a user was listening to a streaming audio broadcast, the packet would arrive out of sequence. The sound information that the packet carried should have been played long ago and the packet would now be useless. The retransmission would have only increased network traffic.

Application Layer

The application layer is responsible for providing services particular to an application. HTTP is an excellent example of an application-level protocol. As we saw before, HTTP defines how a Web client (or browser) communicates with a Web server. In addition to HTTP, some examples of application-layer protocols include FTP for file transfers, Telnet for remote login, NNTP for newsgroups, SMTP for sending and receiving e-mail, and POP3 for retrieving e-mail.

Now let's look at something a little more interesting to the developer. Figure 1.3 shows the communication protocols employed when a Web client makes a request to a Web server. The *logical connections* convey the idea that when writing software for the application layer (where servlet developers spend most of their time) the developer is not concerned with any other layer or protocol. The logical connection between the application layer of his machine and the application layer of the server insulates the developer from the details of network transmission. The TCP/IP protocol stack manages all lower layers. Likewise, a developer working on the transport layer need not concern himself with the complexities of the Internet and network interface layers. The logical connection between layers simplifies the development process. For additional information on TCP/IP, see RFC 1180 "A TCP/IP Tutorial" (for information about RFCs and where to find them, see the "Internet Standards" section later in this chapter).

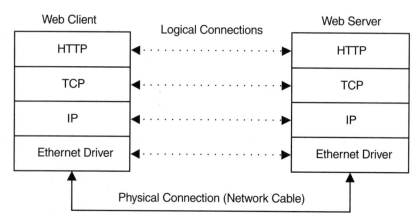

Figure 1.3   Protocols Used for Communication between a Browser and a Web Server

Brief History of the Internet

The *Internet* is a TCP/IP based, global network that connects millions of computers around the world. In order to get an idea of where the Internet is headed, it may be useful to know where it has been. This section presents a brief history of the Internet.

The precursor to the Internet, known as the *ARPAnet*, was originally developed in the late 1960s by the U.S. Department of Defense's Advanced Research Projects Agency (ARPA) in conjunction with a number of universities and military contractors. The ARPAnet project was intended to produce a fail-safe network capable of functioning even in the case of global nuclear war. With the end of the cold war, the Department of Defense's interest in the ARPAnet cooled. However, the private sector was just starting to investigate the vast possibilities of a global network. In 1983 the transition of the ARPAnet to the TCP/IP suite of protocols was completed and the Internet was born.

In 1985 a new IP-based high-speed network funded by the National Science Foundation, known as *NSFnet,* succeeded the ARPAnet as the primary network linking universities and research facilities. These organizations quickly adopted the Internet as a medium through which to send and receive e-mail and electronically publish findings. The usefulness of this new communications medium caught on quickly and the Internet spread to countries around the world. In 1995, NSFnet was replaced by a commercial Internet backbone and the evolution of the Internet from government-funded project to commercial success was complete. If you are interested in reading more about the Internet and its origins, see RFC 1462.

Today, the Internet is well on its way to being as ubiquitous as the telephone. Virtually every major corporation has staked its claim in cyberspace and household access to the Internet is increasing rapidly. People are using the Internet for activities ranging from shopping for cars to purchasing books to playing games. As the phenomenal growth of the Internet continues, those with the knowledge and skills to build Internet applications will be poised to take advantage of the great opportunities that arise.

Internet Addresses

Each computer connected to the Internet is identified by a unique numeric address. IP requires that this address consist of four bytes (each byte ranging from 0 to 255). For example, the IP address of this book's companion Web site is currently *216.250.230.28* (however, IP addresses are frequently subject to change). To ensure uniqueness, Internet addresses are assigned by accredited registrars and all address information is submitted to the same authoritative database. Domain registrars are accredited by the Internet Corporation for Assigned Names and Numbers (ICANN). Although the four-byte address standard, known as *IPv4*, seemed more than sufficient when IP was first developed, ICANN is rapidly running out of unique addresses. Fortunately, a new sixteen-byte addressing scheme, known as *IPv6*, is currently being tested.

NOTE: The manner in which domain names and IP addresses are assigned and managed has recently changed. Until recently, an organization established by the U.S. government known as the Internet Assigned Numbers Authority (IANA) had granted a company called Network Solutions the exclusive right to administer all *.com*, *.org*, and *.edu* domain names. However, in order to increase competition and allow greater participation from other nations, the responsibility of managing IP addresses and domain names has been transitioned from the IANA (and Network Solutions) to a nonprofit corporation known as the Internet Corporation for Assigned Names and Numbers (ICANN). Network Solutions is now one of many accredited registrars. For more information, see *http://www.icann.org/*.

Although numeric addresses are easy for a computer to work with, they are extremely difficult for humans to remember. For this reason, it is possible to assign an alias, known as a *hostname,* to an IP address. For instance, this book's companion Web site is currently accessible on the Internet using the IP address of *216.250.230.28* or the hostname *www.insideservlets.com.* Certainly, the latter is much easier to remember.

Let's take a moment to dissect this hostname and look at its parts individually. The first portion of the hostname (*www* in this case) is arbitrary. Its meaning is interpreted by the server. Regardless, *www* is the standard convention for sites that serve HTML pages using the HTTP protocol (*www* stands for World Wide Web). Another common value for this position is *ftp* for file transfer services, for example, *ftp.insideservlets.com*. Although terms like *www* and *ftp* are commonly used, the server does not use this data to determine the type of service to provide. The type of service (e.g., HTTP, FTP, Telnet) is determined by the port on which the connection was established (ports are discussed in the next section). It is common to designate a service to begin a hostname, but any string can occupy this location. For example, *sales.insideservlets.com* or *service.insideservlets.com* is permissible and might direct users to different portions of a Web site (or a different Web site altogether).

The final string, *.com* (pronounced "dot com"), is referred to as the *top-level domain*. The top-level domain defines the type of organization (see Table 1.1) or the country of origin (*.ca* = Canada, *.uk* = United Kingdom, etc.) if outside of the United States. (For more information on the structure of the domain name system, see RFC 1591.) Lastly, the middle string combined with the top-level domain (*insideservlets.com*) creates a unique *domain name* that allows Internet users around the world to locate a site. In addition to assigning Internet addresses, ICANN registrars are also responsible for registering unique domain names.

It is worth noting that, beyond being easier to remember, there is another advantage to using domain names rather than IP addresses. Hostnames are usually much less likely to change than the underlying IP address. What if, for instance, a commercial Internet Service Provider (ISP) hosted your Web site. Service providers essentially "rent" you a static IP address so that your site can be located via your domain name. However, what if you decided to move to

Table 1.1   Common Top-Level Domains

Domain	Description
.com	For-profit companies, corporations, partnerships, and so forth (e.g., *www.sun.com*)
.edu	Educational institutions such as universities and technical colleges (e.g., *www.byu.edu*)
.gov	Nonmilitary government organizations (e.g., *www.ustreas.gov*)
.mil	Military organizations (e.g., *www.navy.mil*)
.net	Network facilities such as ISPs and network integrators (e.g., *www.internic.net*)
.org	Nonprofit organizations (e.g., *www.pbs.org*)

another provider or chose to host your own site? The answer is that nothing would happen as long as Internet users reference your site using your domain name rather than your IP address. Simply update the Domain Name Service (DNS) entry for your domain and the transition will be seamless. DNS and the process of converting hostnames into their proper numeric IP addresses are discussed in the "Name Resolution" section later in this chapter.

Ports

Host machines are uniquely identified by IP addresses[4] but the applications running on them are identified by port numbers. A *port* is a two-way logical channel to an application running on a host. Keep in mind that we are referring to logical ports, not physical ports like the serial or parallel port on your computer. Ports provide a means of routing requests to the applications that service them. They ensure that e-mail is not sent to a Web server and that ftp requests are not sent to a mail server.

To illustrate, Web servers typically "listen" for connections on port 80. This port has been reserved for HTTP transactions (the protocol used on the World Wide Web). Though it is possible for an HTTP server to be listening on another port, this is somewhat unusual and would require the port to be explicitly specified by the user. By default, a Web browser requests all HTTP connections on port 80. To issue an HTTP request to port 81, for example, the user must explicitly specify the port by typing something like `http://www.insideservlets.com:81/` into the browser's address field. Similarly, an FTP client application would, by default, connect to port 21 (reserved for FTP) or, if designated by the user, another port on which an FTP server was listening. Unlike the server, the client uses any available port for its side of the connection (rather than a specific port each time).

Port numbers can range from 1 to 65535; however, ports 1 to 1023 are reserved. These reserved ports are referred to as "well-known ports" because the applications that use them are publicly documented by the Internet Corporation for Assigned Names and Numbers (ICANN). Table 1.2 lists several of the well-known ports in use today (also provided in Appendix A).

NOTE: On UNIX systems, ports under 1024 are privileged. Only the root user can bind (i.e., connect) to these ports.

---

4. Although an IP address uniquely identifies a host, it is possible (and common) for a host to have more than one IP address.

It is possible to write a simple Java application, called a port scanner, that will scan all ports on a host and display the ports on which a server is responding. For example, a port scanner can determine if an ftp server is running on a particular host or if a server is responding on the echo port. See Appendix B for the source code and sample output for a Java port scanner.

Sockets

A *socket* insulates the programmer from the complexities of network programming by making network communications appear identical to reading or writing to a file or any other standard stream. Network sockets interface Java's standard IO with its network communication facilities. The abstraction of network functionality provided by sockets is similar to the manner in which one layer of the TCP/IP protocol stack insulates another layer from some complexity of network communications. A socket connection is established between any available port on the client and a specified port and IP address of a server.[5] Figure 1.4 illustrates this point, depicting a client establishing a socket connection to port 80 of a Web server. In fact, the primary functions of a Web browser are

Table 1.2   Common Well-Known Port Assignments

Name	Port	Description
echo	7	Echo is used to test the connection between hosts. Any data sent to port 7 is echoed back to the sender.
daytime	13	Responds to any connection with the time of day on the server.
ftp	21	Used for transferring files.
telnet	23	Allows for remote login to a host machine.
smtp	25	Simple Mail Transfer Protocol is used to send and receive email.
whois	43	A directory service for looking up names of users on a remote server.
finger	79	Displays information about a user or all users logged in to a server.
http	80	Responds to HyperText Transfer Protocol requests. HTTP is the protocol used for communicating on the World Wide Web.
pop3	110	Post Office Protocol 3 allows users to retrieve stored e-mail messages.
nntp	119	Network News Transfer Protocol provides access to thousands of newsgroups for the exchange of information. Commonly known as "Usenet."
https	443	Secure HTTP protocol. This is the HTTP protocol running on top of the Secure Sockets Layer (SSL) for encrypted HTTP transmissions.

5. Once a connection is established, the server reassigns its end of the socket to an available port above 1023 so that the original port can resume listening.

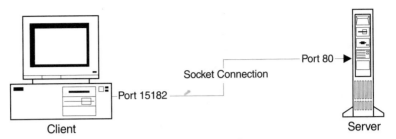

Figure 1.4 Simple Socket Connection from the Client to the Server's HTTP Port

to open a socket connection to the server, request an HTML page, receive a response, interpret the HTTP headers, and render a view of the HTML.

Sockets were originally developed for Berkeley UNIX but the simplicity of treating network connections like any other standard input/output attracted the attention of people working with many operating systems and programming languages. For instance, a sockets API called WinSock has been developed for the Windows environment. Similarly, Java implements a sockets API that makes reading and writing to the network no more difficult than reading and writing a file on the local hard drive. The Java code in Listing 1.1 demonstrates a simple application that uses a socket connection to retrieve the time of day on a specified host. If no host is indicated on the command line, the local host is presumed.

Listing 1.1 Opens a socket connection to a host's daytime port to retrieve the time on the server.

```java
import java.io.*;
import java.net.*;

/**
 * Queries a server's daytime port for the time of day.
 */
public class GetTime
{
  //main is invoked by the JVM at execution
  public static void main(String[] args)
  {
    Socket socket;
    String host = "localhost"; //default host

    if (args.length > 0)
    {
      //host was passed on command line, set host value
      host = args[0];
    }
```

```
          try
          {
            //open socket connection to daytime port 13
            socket = new Socket(host, 13);

            //get handle to input stream to read the time
            BufferedReader in = new BufferedReader(
              new InputStreamReader(socket.getInputStream()));

            //read the first line of the host's response
            String time = in.readLine();

            //print time to standard out
            System.out.println("The time on host " + host + " is " +
              time);
          }
          catch (UnknownHostException e) //host not found
          {
            System.out.println("Host is invalid.");
          }
          catch (IOException e) //problem opening socket
          {
            System.out.println("Error opening socket: " + e);
          }
        }
      }
```

The output looks like this:

```
C:\>java GetTime www.mit.edu
The time on host www.mit.edu is Fri Jan 7 12:32:17 2000
```

NOTE: Similar to the manner in which a domain name resolves to an IP address, the term *localhost* resolves to the "loopback" IP address of *127.0.0.1,* which refers to the local machine. This term is often used in network programming as an alias for the local machine's IP address.

Name Resolution

As discussed earlier, Internet addresses can be referenced by hostname or IP address. Hostnames are provided to make it easier for us to remember addresses. Unfortunately, the computer does not understand hostnames, only numeric IP addresses. Therefore, every time an Internet address is requested using a hostname, the computer must look up its associated IP address. *Name resolution* is the process of mapping a hostname to its corresponding IP address.

One way to translate a hostname to an IP address is to look it up in a simple text file. This text file, usually called *HOSTS* (or something similar), contains hostnames and their corresponding IP addresses. For example, a mapping to this book's companion Web site in a *HOSTS* file might look like this:

```
216.250.230.28  www.insideservlets.com
```

Whenever a hostname is referenced, the computer determines its IP address by locating the name in the *HOSTS* file and retrieving its IP address.

This method is simple and straightforward, but there are several major drawbacks. First, every site that you reference by name would need to be stored in this text file (it could get rather large). Second, you would have to copy this file to every computer on which you use named references. Lastly, you would be required to maintain and update this file to see that it remains current. There has to be a better way. Luckily, there is. It is called the Domain Name Service.

The *Domain Name Service* (DNS) is a distributed database that contains all registered hostnames on the Internet and their IP addresses. Using DNS to resolve names to IP addresses is vastly different from using a *HOSTS* file. Rather than looking in a local text file for a hostname's IP address, the computer queries a DNS server for the information. This approach frees the user from maintaining a constantly growing *HOSTS* file and, because any computer can reference a DNS server, all hosts on the network can share the same information.

In addition, a DNS server is normally configured to use a sequence of name servers when resolving a hostname. DNS servers on the Internet are organized in a hierarchical fashion in order to process requests most efficiently. For instance, if your company's local DNS server does not contain a particular hostname, it can query the next higher DNS server for the translation, and so on. If properly registered, the hostname will eventually be found and the IP address returned to the host that requested it. If the hostname cannot be found, an error message indicating that the host does not have a DNS entry will be returned. For additional information on DNS, see RFCs 1034 and 1035.

Firewalls

A *firewall* is a combination of network hardware and software that serves as a secure gateway between an internal network and the Internet. It protects the internal network from unauthorized access or activity. Often, a firewall is just an ordinary server running specialized software through which all network traffic between the internal network and the Internet must flow. The firewall examines each packet passing through it and verifies that the packet does not violate established security policies. To illustrate, a firewall can deny access to all hosts within a specified IP range. It may allow outgoing FTP connections but block all incoming FTP requests. It could refuse external connections to a Web server's administration port. In essence, a properly configured firewall allows network administrators to sleep at night.

Protocol Tunneling

Protocol tunneling is the process of encapsulating one protocol in another that operates on the same layer of the protocol stack. Tunneling is commonly used to circumvent firewall restrictions. For example, if a firewall allows HTTP connections but blocks all FTP requests, HTTP tunneling can be implemented to encapsulate FTP protocol commands within an HTTP message. In this way, FTP operations can be performed through the unblocked HTTP port. Note that HTTP and FTP are both application-layer protocols.

Proxy Servers

A *proxy server* is a host that makes Internet requests on behalf of other machines on the network. Proxy servers are often used to monitor Internet use in a corporation. Some companies prefer that each employee not have direct access to the Internet. Rather, these employees can request Internet services from the proxy server. Rules set on the proxy server can either grant or deny these service requests. In addition, proxy servers can cache frequently requested files. Thus, when a user requests a file from a proxy server, the server first looks in its own cache for the file. If found, the server returns the file. Otherwise, the file is requested from the source. In this manner, performance is improved and network traffic is reduced. Lastly, proxy servers provide some degree of security for an internal network. Because the proxy server makes all external requests, external hosts cannot learn the name or IP address of computers on the internal network. Only the proxy server shares this information with the outside world. Firewalls and proxy servers are commonly used in conjunction to provide a comprehensive network security strategy.

Internet Standards

Assembling a global network of compatible protocols is no small task. You may wonder how such an enormous effort was coordinated and how new standards are determined. The whole process centers around documents known as Internet Drafts (IDs) and Requests for Comments (RFCs). These documents are the driving force behind current and proposed Internet standards. They are also the most current and accurate references for information on Internet standards and protocols. Unfortunately, they are often a bit lengthy and esoteric.

There are numerous locations on the Internet where RFCs and IDs can be found. A few locations that are not likely to change are listed here.

- For RFCs:

  http://www.rfc-editor.org/
  http://info.internet.isi.edu/1/in-notes/rfc

- For Internet standards:

  http://info.internet.isi.edu/1/in-notes/std

- For IDs:

  http://info.internet.isi.edu/1/in-drafts

Many RFCs are of particular interest to the servlet developer. Table 1.3 shows several important RFCs of which you should be aware. For more detail on the Internet standardization process, see Appendix C.

Table 1.3   Small Sampling of Important RFCs

RFC	Status	Title	Description
821	Draft Standard	SMTP	Defines the Simple Mail Transfer Protocol for sending e-mail
1034, 1035	Standard	Domain Names	Describe the Domain Name System
1462	Informational	FYI on "What is the Internet?"	Describes the Internet and its origins
2045, 2046, 2047, 2048, 2049	Draft Standard	MIME Parts 1–5	Specification for MIME
1866	Proposed Standard	Hypertext Markup Language—2.0	Specification for HTML 2.0
1942	Experimental	HTML Tables	Specification for adding table support to HTML
1945	Informational	Hypertext Transfer Protocol	Specification for HTTP/1.0
2068	Proposed Standard	Hypertext Transfer Protocol—HTTP/1.1	Specification for HTTP/1.1
2200	Standard	Internet Official Protocol Standards	Often updated to give the current status of many protocols

Summary

A firm understanding of networking basics is essential to developing robust Internet applications. The information in this chapter provides a good foundation in basic networking concepts that can be applied to servlet development. In Chapter 2, we will focus on fundamental concepts pertaining to the World Wide Web.

Chapter Highlights

- A *network* is a group of computers and other devices connected in a manner that promotes communication among them.
- A *protocol* is a formal set of rules that must be followed in order to communicate.
- *TCP/IP* is a collection of protocols used to communicate across a network.
- The *Internet* is a TCP/IP-based, global network that connects millions of computers around the world.
- Each computer connected to the Internet is identified by a unique IP address. In addition, aliases known as hostnames can often be used in place of numeric IP addresses.
- A *port* is a logical channel to an application running on a host.
- A *socket* insulates the programmer from the complexities of network programming by making network communication appear identical to reading or writing to a file or any other standard stream.
- *Name resolution* is the process of mapping a hostname to its corresponding IP address.
- A *firewall* is a piece of network hardware that serves as a secure gateway between an internal network and the Internet.
- *Protocol tunneling* is the process of encapsulating one protocol within another protocol that operates on the same layer (for TCP/IP, this usually takes place at the transport layer).
- A *proxy server* is a host that makes Internet requests on behalf of other machines on the network.
- Internet standards are proposed, documented, and revised in documents called Internet Drafts and Requests for Comments.

CHAPTER 2

Web Basics

Java is an extremely powerful language for developing Web applications that run on the client or the server. However, until you understand the basics behind communicating on the World Wide Web, your network programming projects may be confined to writing animated applets to enhance your Web site. On the other hand, with the proper background, you will be able to build complex sites ranging from order entry to customer tracking to decision support systems. Although these projects may not provoke the same "that's cool!" response, they can certainly make a positive impact on your company's bottom line.

This chapter describes the basic concepts behind the World Wide Web. The following topics are covered:

- Brief history of the Web
- URLs and URL encoding
- Web browsers and browser/server communication
- Web servers
- Introduction to the Common Gateway Interface (CGI)

If you are already familiar with this material, you may prefer to skim or skip this chapter.

Brief History of the Web

The humble beginnings of the World Wide Web go way back to 1989 (about 100 years ago in "Web time"). During that year, Tim Berners-Lee of the European Laboratory of Particle Physics (CERN) proposed a new network composed of files that contain links to related files. These links, called *hypertext*, allow the reader to find additional information by simply clicking on any hypertext word or phrase in a document. In 1990 the first text-only hypertext clients, known as *browsers,* were developed and implemented at CERN and other research facilities. For the first time, a network of linked documents was available for publishing research worldwide. This network proved to be successful, but the Web was still very young and required refinement and standardization. In order to standardize the format of hypertext documents, Tim Berners-Lee drafted the first HTML specification. As more and more browsers began to support this new specification, HTML quickly became the *de facto* standard for publishing documents on the Web.

The growth of the Web was relatively modest until the National Center for Supercomputing Applications (NCSA) developed the first "killer" Web application in 1993. Its new browser, called Mosaic, allowed users to view graphical images on the World Wide Web for the first time. The popularity of this browser increased rapidly as the Web started to grow at a dizzying rate.

In the fall of 1994, Netscape Communications Corporation released the first browser that added unique, nonstandard extensions to the HTML language. These extensions, such as HTML tables, became wildly popular and made Netscape's browser, known as Navigator, the most popular on the Internet (at one point, Navigator owned about 90 percent of the Web browser market). Netscape's practice of implementing the latest features at a breakneck pace spawned a vicious race among several companies to be the first to reach the market with newer and better browser features. At times, new browser versions were released every month or two. The rate at which this new technology advanced was unprecedented.

Today, the World Wide Web is still the fastest growing sector of the Internet. From its beginnings as a simple method for sharing research, the Web has captured the imagination of Internet users and businesses around the world.

URLs

A *Uniform Resource Identifier* (URI) is a generic term that refers to all types of names and addresses that identify objects on the Internet (formerly known as Universal Resource Identifier). Today there are two types of URIs—the Uniform Resource Locator and the Uniform Resource Name.

A *Uniform Resource Locator* (URL) is a specification for identifying an object, such as a file, newsgroup, CGI program, or e-mail address, by indicating its exact location on the Internet. URLs are the most common type of URI and are fully supported by today's software.

A *Uniform Resource Name* (URN) is a method of referencing an object without declaring the full path to the object. The idea behind a URN is that rather than a resource being specified by its location, it is referenced by an alias (similar to the way a hostname serves as an alias for an IP address). In this manner, even if the resource is moved, it can still be located via its URN. In addition, several copies of a single resource can be stored on different servers in different parts of the world. When a request is made for a particular URN, the browser can locate the nearest copy of the resource and return it—increasing performance and reducing network traffic. For more information on the syntax of URNs, see RFC 2141. Though URNs sound promising, they are not currently supported by most software. Because of the current lack of support for URNs, this section focuses on the widely implemented URL specification.

The syntax of a URL depends on the protocol (referred to as the "scheme" in the RFC) required to access the object. Though the syntax of URLs varies, most URLs assume one of these two forms:

```
protocol://host[:port]/url-path
protocol://username:password@host[:port]/url-path
```

For instance, the standard syntax of an HTTP URL is:

```
http://host[:port]/path/resource_name[#section][?query_string]
```

Here are a few examples of valid HTTP URLs:

http://www.insideservlets.com/
http://www.ietf.org/tao.html#What_Is_IETF
http://www.awl.com/index.html
http://www.webcrawler.com:80/cgi-bin/WebQuery?searchText=servlets

Let's further examine the last URL. An HTTP URL consists of a host and an optional port, path, filename, section, and query string. A query string is a set of parameters listed as key/value pairs (key=value format) with each pair separated by an ampersand (&) character. In the sample URL, the *http* string specifies that the URL should be accessed using the HTTP protocol. *www.webcrawler.com* is the hostname pointing to the server on which the resource resides and *:80* explicitly indicates that the connection will be on port 80 (this is, however, unnecessary since port 80 is the default for HTTP transactions). The string */cgi-bin/WebQuery* states that there is a CGI application called *WebQuery* in a directory named *cgi-bin* (CGI is discussed later in this chapter). Finally, the query string *?searchText=servlets* passes a parameter called searchText with a value of servlets. As you might have guessed, this URL queries the WebCrawler Internet search engine for sites related to servlets.

NOTE: Although URLs can be constructed using both upper- and lowercase letters, the URL specification for a hostname does not differentiate based on case. Therefore, *http://WWW.AWL.COM/* is the same as *http://www.awl.com/*. Though hostnames are not case-sensitive, they are usually displayed in lowercase letters. Additionally, though the hostname is not case-sensitive, the path information that follows may be (depending on the server). For example, though *http://WWW.AWL.COM/* and *http://www.awl.com/* are the same, *http://www.awl.com/INDEX.HTML* and *http://www.awl.com/index.html* may not be the same (if the server uses case-sensitive resource names). Typically, UNIX filenames are case-sensitive and Windows filenames are not.

In contrast to the previous examples, the URL format for FTP is different. The syntax for an FTP URL is as follows:

```
ftp://username:password@host[:port]/path
```

Here are a few examples of FTP URLs:

> *ftp://anonymous@ftp.netscape.com/*
> *ftp://guest:password@ftp.insideservlets.com/incoming*
> *ftp://ftp.sun.com:21/*

As you can see, the syntax of the URL varies greatly depending on the protocol (or "scheme") in use. Appendix D shows the URL syntax for many common protocols (for more detail, see RFC 1738).

URLs are commonly used in links within an HTML document, to request files from a browser, or to retrieve network resources from within a Java application. For example, the Java code in Listing 2.1 uses an HTTP URL to retrieve an HTML file and print it to standard out (e.g., the console screen).

Listing 2.1   Downloads an HTML file using the Java URL object.

```java
import java.io.*;
import java.net.*;

/**
 * This class downloads data from the specified URL and prints
 * it to standard out.
 */
public class GetURLData
{
  //main is invoked by the JVM at execution
  public static void main(String[] args)
  {
```

```
URL url=null;
String nextLine; //string to store the HTML output

try
{
  //create the URL object from a valid URL
  url = new URL("http://java.sun.com/index.html");

  //open an input stream from the URL
  BufferedReader in = new BufferedReader(
    new InputStreamReader(url.openStream()));

  //get data, line by line
  while((nextLine = in.readLine()) != null)
  {
    System.out.println(nextLine); //print to standard out
  }
}
catch (MalformedURLException e) //this catch required
{
  System.err.println("Invalid URL: " + e);
}
catch (Exception e) //catch all other errors here
{
  System.err.println("Error: " + e);
}
}
}
```

The first few lines of output from GetURLData look like this:

```
<!DOCTYPE HTML PUBLIC "-//W3C//DTD HTML 3.2//EN">
<HTML>
<HEAD>
<TITLE>java.sun.com - The Source for Java(TM) Technology</TITLE>
```

Up to this point, every URL we have seen has been fully qualified. That is, all information necessary to find the object was completely specified in the URL.

This type of URL is called an *absolute* URL. An absolute URL designates the protocol, host, path, and name of a resource. When a Web browser references an absolute URL, it stores the protocol, host, and path information in order to support another type of URL. A *relative URL* is not fully qualified, but rather it inherits the protocol, host, and path information from its parent document (the document that links to it). To illustrate, let's look at an example of each type of URL in an HTML document. Listing 2.2 shows a simple HTML document, called *test.html,* with two hyperlinks—one using an absolute path and the other using a relative path.

Listing 2.2   An example of an absolute and a relative URL.

```
<HTML>
<HEAD>
<TITLE>Absolute vs. Relative URLs</TITLE>
</HEAD>
<BODY>

<A HREF="http://www.awl.com/index.html">Absolute URL</A><BR>

<A HREF="link.html">Relative URL to link.html</A>

</BODY>
</HTML>
```

Notice how the absolute URL fully specifies the protocol, host, path, and resource name. On the other hand, the relative URL designates only the resource name. For the relative URL, the browser will "fill in the blanks" and assume that the protocol, host, and path information are the same as the document that linked to it. Thus, the *link.html* file referenced in the relative URL would need to be in the same directory as the *test.html* file shown in Listing 2.2.

Relative URLs offer two advantages over absolute URLs. The first advantage is that they are much shorter to type. The second and most important advantage is the portability provided by relative URLs. Since a host and path are not specified, a directory, or even an entire directory tree, of HTML files can be moved to a new directory or server without having to change any of the internal links. For instance, assume that Listing 2.2 is stored at the location *http://www.insideservlets.com/test/*. If only relative URLs are used in the HTML, all files in the *test* directory can be moved to *http://www.awl.com/examples/* without modification. For additional information on relative URLs, see RFC 1808.

URL Encoding

URLs are comprised of a string of printable characters within the US-ASCII coded character set. Any unsafe or nonprintable characters within a URL must be encoded. *URL encoding* involves replacing all unsafe and nonprintable characters with a percent sign (%) followed by two hexadecimal digits corresponding to the character's ASCII value. Control characters are a good example of nonprintable characters. Unsafe characters are those that may be misinterpreted or altered by network software or hardware. Within URLs, there are many unsafe characters. A good rule of thumb is that any character not described in the following list should be encoded:

- Upper- and lowercase letters
- Numbers

- Underscores
- Periods
- Hyphens

Thus, any character other than those listed must be used according to the URL specification or it must be encoded. For instance, within a URL the characters ";", "/", "?", ":", "@", "=", and "&" have special meanings (see Appendix E). If these characters are used in a manner that is not consistent with the URL specification, they must be encoded. For example, if a filename contains a question mark, the question mark must be encoded or the URL will construe this character as the beginning of the query string. According to the URL specification, a question mark is used to separate the name of a resource from a list of parameters (the query string) being passed to the server.

One special case worth noting is the space character. Because they are so common, spaces can be encoded using a single plus sign (+) rather than the normal encoding scheme (%20). Since the plus sign designates a space, the plus sign itself must be encoded using %2B. See Appendix F for the hexadecimal encoding of many nonprintable and unsafe URL characters.

There are a number of reasons that some characters are considered unsafe and must be encoded in a URL. Spaces are encoded because blank spaces may disappear or be introduced when transcribing the URL from code to print or when modifying it with a text editor. Similarly, some network software may consider extra spaces insignificant and simply remove them. In addition, some systems may use other characters, such as "<", ">", and the quotation mark ("), as delimiters. If these characters are not encoded, they could cause confusion and produce errors during transport. The URL specification itself uses characters "#", "/", "?", "=", and "&" to delimit sections of the URL. Finally, some unsafe characters may be modified by gateways or other transport agents.

Let's look at an example to make sure that we have a good handle on URL encoding. Assume that we would like to reference a resource called *java's great.html* stored on the server *java.sun.com*. According to the rules, the apostrophe (') and the space are unsafe and must be encoded. The encoded URL would look like this:

http://java.sun.com/java%27s+great.html

It is as simple as that. The apostrophe is encoded using %27 (see Appendix F) and the space is encoded with a plus sign. Encoding makes the URL more difficult to read, but it allows the request to travel across the Internet safely without being mangled by network hardware or varying operating systems.

Fortunately for the servlet developer, Java includes a class to help convert resource names and other references into URL-safe strings. The URLEncoder class in the java.net package contains a single static method for encoding strings for use in URLs. The method, called encode(), accepts a standard Java string and returns the URL-encoded equivalent. Likewise, a class called URLDecoder contains a single static method, called decode(), that can be used to decode URL-encoded strings. Listing 2.3 demonstrates the URLEncoder and URLDecoder classes by outputting several URL-encoded and -decoded strings.

Listing 2.3   URLEncoder and URLDecoder demonstration.

```
import java.net.URLEncoder;
import java.net.URLDecoder;

/**
 * Demonstrates URL encoding and decoding.
 */
public class EncodeDemo
{
  //main is invoked by the JVM at execution
  public static void main(String[] args) throws Exception
  {
    String text1 = "Inside Servlets";
    String text2 = "Java's here to stay!";
    String text3 = "Velocity Formula: v = d/t";

    System.out.println("NORMAL STRING\t\t\tURL ENCODED STRING");

    String encoded1 = URLEncoder.encode(text1);
    System.out.println(text1 + "\t\t\t" + encoded1);

    String encoded2 = URLEncoder.encode(text2);
    System.out.println(text2 + "\t\t" + encoded2);

    String encoded3 = URLEncoder.encode(text3);
    System.out.println(text3 + "\t" + encoded3);

    System.out.println("\n\n"); //separate encoding from decoding

    System.out.println("URL ENCODED STRING\t\tDECODED STRING");

    System.out.println(encoded1 + "\t\t\t" + URLDecoder.decode(
      encoded1));

    System.out.println(encoded2 + "\t" + URLDecoder.decode(
      encoded2));

    System.out.println(encoded3 + "\t" + URLDecoder.decode(
      encoded3));
  }
}
```

The output from Listing 2.3 looks like this:

```
NORMAL STRING                    URL ENCODED STRING
Inside Servlets                  Inside+Servlets
Java's here to stay!             Java%27s+here+to+stay%21
Velocity Formula: v = d/t        Velocity+Formula%3A+v+%3D+d%2Ft


URL ENCODED STRING               DECODED STRING
Inside+Servlets                  Inside Servlets
Java%27s+here+to+stay%21         Java's here to stay!
Velocity+Formula%3A+v+%3D+d%2Ft  Velocity Formula: v = d/t
```

Web Browsers

A *Web browser* is a client application that requests, receives, and displays HTML pages. However, current browsers do much more than just render HTML pages. Today's browsers display animated images, play sound and video, cache pages for improved performance, provide secure connections through encryption, and much more. Browsers are the "window to the Web" for Internet users around the world.

Current Web Browsers

Currently, two browsers enjoy the vast majority of the browser market. Netscape Navigator and Microsoft Internet Explorer are the most popular browsers on the Web and both implement many of the latest HTML extensions. This additional functionality is referred to as "extensions" because many new HTML features supported by these browsers have not been adopted as official Internet standards. Features such as frames, blinking and scrolling text, background sounds, and cookies are just a few of the exciting but nonstandard extensions implemented by these browsers.[1] For the servlet developer, testing your new Web site using both of these browsers is essential. If your site supports both, you can feel confident that more than 90 percent of Web users can successfully view your site. It should also be noted that the latest version of Netscape is based on the Mozilla open source browser developed by Netscape and a host of volunteer programmers. Mozilla is a full-featured browser that strictly adheres to open Internet standards. To participate in the development of Mozilla or just to learn more about it, see the Mozilla Web site at *http:// www.mozilla.org/*.

---

1. Although you might expect basic features such as frames and cookies to be Internet standards, these technologies have not been officially recognized as standards. They are, however, on a standards track that may lead to their eventual adoption as official Internet standards.

HotJava from Sun is another browser worth mentioning. Written entirely in Java, the HotJava browser provides an excellent "proof of concept" for the power of a Java application. HotJava supports many of the latest HTML extensions including tables, frames, and cookies. In contrast to a stand-alone Web browser, Sun has recently repositioned HotJava as a software component that can be incorporated into existing Java applications. Though its popularity languishes in relation to the other two browsers, HotJava is a remarkably interesting and impressive implementation of the Java language.

Browser/Server Communication

To develop, debug, and deploy servlet-driven Web sites, it is imperative to understand the process by which a browser communicates with a Web server. Fortunately, the process is simple. The specifics of the language used by browsers and servers to communicate, however, will be covered in Chapter 3. This section discusses, at a high level, the manner in which a browser sends a request to a server and receives a response.

The first step in the process involves the browser requesting a file from the Web server. A common scenario in which the browser requests a file called *index.jsp* is described in the following lines.

You type this URL into your browser:

```
http://www.insideservlets.com/index.jsp
```

Your browser resolves *www.insideservlets.com* to a valid IP address using DNS (as described in Chapter 1) and sends this HTTP request to the host (simplified):

```
GET /index.jsp HTTP/1.0
```

You may remember this command from the first chapter. The browser uses this very basic HTTP request to instruct the server that it wants a file called *index.jsp*. (See Chapter 3 for a detailed discussion about the format of this request.) If the file is available and the client has proper authorization, the server will return the requested file. The response might look like Listing 2.4.

Listing 2.4   Sample Web server response including HTTP header and HTML.

```
HTTP/1.0 200 OK
Server: Apache/1.3.9 (Win32)
Content-type: text/html
Content-length: 478

<html>
<head>
```

```
<TITLE>Inside Servlets</TITLE>
</head>
<body BGCOLOR="#FFFFFF">

<center>
<table width="660" height="60" border="0" bgcolor="#002754"
  cellpadding="0" cellspacing="0">
<tr>
<td width="10" bgcolor="#FFFFFF" align="right">
  <img src="/images/title_small_left.gif">
</td>
<td>
  <img src="/images/title_small_is.gif">
</td>
<td align="right" valign="bottom">
  <a href="mailto:dustin@insideservlets.com"
    target="content"><font size="2" color="#FFFFFF"
    face="ARIAL,SANS SERIF"><b>CONTACT AUTHOR</b></font></a>
  <font size="3" color="#FFFFFF"><b>|</b></font>
  <a href="main.jsp" target="content">
  <font size="2" color="#FFFFFF" face="ARIAL,SANS SERIF">
  <b>HOME</b></font></a>
</td>
<td width="20" bgcolor="#FFFFFF" align="left">
  <img src="/images/title_small_right.gif" width="10">
</td>
</tr>
</table>
</center>

</body>
</html>
```

The server returned the contents of the requested HTML page. But what about the images referenced in the HTML? If you examine the HTML in Listing 2.4, you will see that three images, *title_small_left.gif, title_small_is.gif,* and *title_small_right.gif,* are referenced (the <IMG> tags). After receiving the contents of the requested file, the browser parses the HTML looking for other information that may need to be downloaded. This information can be images, Java applets, background sounds, or any other format that the browser supports. Upon locating an image tag, the browser opens a new connection to the server using the URL provided in the tag and downloads the image data. The image is then displayed in its appropriate location on screen. This process is repeated for all images referenced in the HTML (see Figure 2.1).

You have probably often noticed that when a Web page is downloaded, the text is displayed first, followed by the images. This is because the browser does indeed receive the text first (embedded in the HTML), which it displays,

Figure 2.1   Simple Transaction between a Web Browser and a Web Server

and then proceeds to "fill in the blanks" with images, applets, or whatever. Each new image is downloaded separately using a new connection.[2]

NOTE: For some browsers to render a page properly before the image files are downloaded, all image tags must include height and width information. For example, the following tag includes the necessary information to allow the browser to reserve space on the page for the image.

```
<IMG SRC="/images/logo.gif" HEIGHT="85" WIDTH="370" ALT="Logo">
```

Without the height and width information, the browser would not know how much space to reserve for each image. Thus, the browser would have to either wait until all images were downloaded before displaying the page or rebuild the page after each new image was received. To avoid the performance penalty this incurs, it is good practice to include the HEIGHT and WIDTH attributes in every image tag. It is also a good idea to include the ALT attribute in each image tag. The ALT attribute specifies an alternative display message in case the browser does not support images or image rendering has been turned off.

Web Servers

A *Web server,* also known as an HTTP server, responds to requests from a Web browser by returning HTML, images, applets, or other data. The Web server is also responsible for enforcing security policies, storing frequently requested files in cache, logging requests, and much more. These servers are the workhorses of the Web that sit quietly behind the scenes waiting to fulfill any valid request.

---

2. Modern browsers that support HTTP/1.1 connection persistence may not always create a new connection to download images referenced by the HTML page. Rather, these browsers may reuse the current connection to download images.

The market for Web servers is much more open than that for browsers. There are many popular servers in use today. A few of the most popular servers include the following:

- Netscape FastTrack Server
- iPlanet Web Server
- Microsoft Internet Information Server
- Apache Web Server
- Java Web Server

FastTrack is the "personal edition" Web server from Netscape (owned by America Online) intended for low-traffic sites with fewer functionality requirements. Alternatively, *iPlanet Web Server* (formerly Netscape Enterprise Server) is a heavy-duty Web server employed to service some of the most active sites on the Web. iPlanet Web Server is a product of the Sun-Netscape Alliance. This server is programmable via NSAPI (Netscape Server Application Programming Interface), Server-Side JavaScript, and CGI (Common Gateway Interface). In addition, iPlanet Web Server provides robust native support for Java servlets (as well as JavaServer Pages). iPlanet Web Server runs on Windows NT 12000, Macintosh, and numerous flavors of UNIX.

Microsoft Internet Information Server (IIS) is Microsoft's offering in the Web server market. The biggest drawback to IIS is that it is available only on the Windows platform. If you are only deploying on Windows, however, this can be an advantage because of its tight integration with Windows security. IIS provides several simple scripting options for customizing a Web site as well. Development on IIS can be accomplished using the Active Server Pages (ASP), ISAPI (Internet Server Application Programming Interface), or CGI.

The *Apache Web Server* is an industrial-strength, public-domain HTTP server for UNIX and Windows NT 12000. It is based on many of the innovations found in the original NCSA httpd server. Since its inception, the Apache Web Server has evolved to become arguably the fastest, most functional, and most popular HTTP server on the Web. It is also the cheapest. The Apache Web Server is available free of charge for Windows and many flavors of UNIX. Apache is programmable via CGI and now supports Java servlets via the Apache Tomcat servlet container (Tomcat replaces JServ as the standard Apache servlet container). Tomcat is the servlet and JavaServer Pages (JSP) portion of the larger Apache Jakarta project. In addition to servlet and JSP support, the Jakarta project aims to support additional functionality defined by the Java 2 Platform, Enterprise Edition (J2EE) such as Enterprise JavaBeans. Jakarta and Tomcat are discussed in detail later in the book. For additional information, see *http://jakarta.apache.org/*.

Although it has been phased out, the Java Web Server still deserves some attention. Originally code-named *Jeeves,* the *Java Web Server* is an HTTP server implemented in Java. The Java nature of this server allows it to be run on a wide array of platforms. The Java Web Server was the first HTTP server to support servlets and served as the initial reference implementation for this new technology. Unfortunately, the Java Web Server is a casualty of the Sun-Netscape Alliance. Due to product overlap, the Java Web Server is in its final release (version 2.0) and is no longer be supported. Though its life span was relatively short, this product had a profound impact on the industry. With the introduction of Java servlets, it spawned a new era in dynamic Web site development where, for the first time, server-side Web applications could be completely portable.

This cross-server and cross-platform portability is a result of the fact that, like the Java Web Server itself, servlets are written in pure Java. (Servlets are introduced in more detail in Chapter 4.) It should also be noted that servlet support can be added to current versions of servers from Netscape, Microsoft, and Apache using third-party extensions such as JRun from Allaire or ServletExec from New Atlanta Communications.

Although Web servers can be very complex, the basic service they provide is simple. A Web server listens on a port for a connection and a request from a client. The Web server interprets the request according to the HTTP protocol specification and fulfills the request accordingly. Most often, this simply involves returning an HTML or an image file from the file system or running a CGI application. To demonstrate the basic concepts behind a generic Web server, Appendix G shows a basic Java HTTP server that accepts requests from clients and returns HTML and image files from the local file system.

The output from the HTML in Listing 2.4 looks like the browser rendering illustrated in Figure 2.2. With verbose mode enabled (-v switch), the HttpServer application shown in Appendix G can give you a good idea of how the browser requests files and how the server responds. After fulfilling the browser's request, the output generated in the HttpServer console window looks like the following:

```
C:\>java HttpServer -v

Listening for connections on port 80...

Connection opened. (Mon Jan 10 18:27:12 GMT+00:00 2000)
File /index.jsp of type text/html returned.
Connection closed.

Connection opened. (Mon Jan 10 18:27:13 GMT+00:00 2000)
File /images/title_small_left.gif of type image/gif returned.
Connection closed.

Connection opened. (Mon Jan 10 18:27:14 GMT+00:00 2000)
File /images/title_small_is.gif of type image/gif returned.
Connection closed.
```

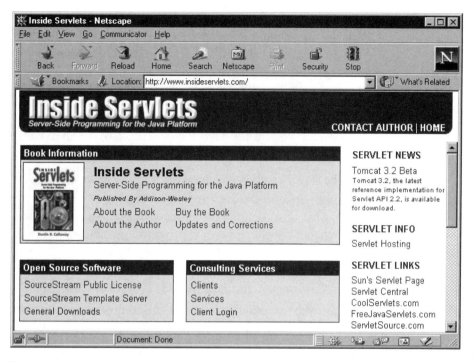

Figure 2.2 Browser Rendering of Listing 2.4 (Top Frame)

```
Connection opened. (Mon Jan 10 18:27:15 GMT+00:00 2000)
File /images/title_small_right.gif of type image/gif returned.
Connection closed.
```

From this output generated by the HttpServer application, you can clearly see the browser opening a new connection for each request. The browser issues a new request for every image referenced within the HTML page.

Common Gateway Interface

The Common Gateway Interface, or CGI, is a standard interface between an HTTP server and an application. CGI enables the Web server to generate dynamic content rather than just return static HTML files. In addition, because CGI can accept and process information submitted by the user, it can provide two-way interaction between the client and the Web server. For example, CGI is commonly used to create dynamic HTML pages from information in a database or to process user input such as validating a credit card when a product is ordered online. Many popular Internet search engines use CGI. These engines receive search criteria from a user, process the input, and return the search results. CGI was the first and continues to be among the most popular methods of building dynamic Web sites. Typically, CGI scripts are written in Perl, Tcl, C, or a UNIX shell, but almost any language can be used, including Java.

A CGI application works in the following manner. The Web server receives a request that maps to a CGI application, the Web server executes a CGI program that runs in a separate process space, the CGI program returns HTML to the Web server, and the Web server returns the HTML to the client. To illustrate, a typical CGI transaction might go like this:

1. The server receives a request for a resource called */cgi-bin/guestbook.cgi*.
2. Either because the file has a *.cgi* extension or because it is located in the */cgi-bin* directory, the server recognizes the file as a CGI request and launches the *guestbook.cgi* program, passing any parameters received from the client via environment variables.
3. The *guestbook.cgi* program executes, processing any information passed as a parameter, and returns an HTML document to the Web server.
4. The Web server returns the HTML to the client.

To the user, this process is invisible. The user simply requested a resource using a URL and received an HTML document in return. Other than the format of the URL, the user would have no way of knowing that the document was created dynamically on the server rather than simply stored in a static file. Using this process, the Web server can vary its response based on user input. Prior to CGI, this kind of two-way interaction on the Web was not possible.

One important note is that all CGI applications run as independent processes. Creating a new process for every CGI request is resource intensive and incurs a large performance penalty. We will discuss this issue further in Chapter 4, where we learn that servlets take a much different approach. For more information about CGI, see the CGI specification at *http://web.golux.com/coar/cgi/*.

Summary

This chapter provides a basic foundation in several important areas of Web technology. Understanding URLs and the way browsers and servers communicate is essential to servlet development. In Chapter 3, we will discuss advanced Web topics including the HTTP protocol, MIME, and HTML forms.

Chapter Highlights

- *The Web* got its start in 1989 when Tim Berners-Lee of the European Laboratory of Particle Physics proposed a new network composed of files containing links to related files. Shortly thereafter, the first text-only browsers were developed and the Web was born.

- A *Uniform Resource Locator* is a specification for identifying an object such as a file, newsgroup, CGI program, or e-mail address by indicating its exact location on the Internet (see RFC 1738).

- URL encoding is the process of replacing all unsafe and nonprintable characters with a percent sign followed by two hexadecimal digits corresponding to the character's ASCII value.

- A *Web browser* is a client application that requests, transfers, and displays HTML pages.

- A *Web server,* also known as an HTTP server, responds to requests from a Web browser by returning HTML, images, applets, or other data.

- *CGI* is a standard interface between an HTTP server and an application.

CHAPTER 3

Beyond Web Basics

This chapter covers critical topics designed to give you a stronger foundation in Web development. Much of this chapter will serve as a brief tutorial and reference for HTTP, MIME, and HTML forms. I hope this information will save you the frustration of searching through hundreds of pages of RFCs. However, the RFCs referenced in this chapter are the authoritative documents on the subject and contain additional detail. Please refer to the appropriate RFC if you desire more information.

The following topics are covered in this chapter:

- HyperText Transfer Protocol (HTTP)
- Multipurpose Internet Mail Extensions (MIME)
- HTML forms

Of course, if you are already familiar with these topics, feel free to jump ahead to the next chapter, where servlets are introduced.

HTTP

The HyperText Transfer Protocol is a stateless, TCP/IP-based protocol for communicating on the World Wide Web. HTTP defines the precise manner in which Web clients communicate with Web servers. HTTP/1.0 is the most widely supported version because it is recognized by both HTTP/1.0 and HTTP/1.1 servers and clients. HTTP/1.0 is documented in the informational RFC 1945. Every HTTP server and client supports HTTP/1.0, and the vast majority of modern HTTP servers and clients also support its successor, HTTP/1.1. HTTP/1.1 is documented in RFC 2068.

HTTP Basics

The HTTP protocol follows a very simple request/response paradigm. In short, a conversation between a Web browser and Web server operates like this: the client opens a connection to the server, the client makes a request to the server, the server responds to the request, and the connection is closed (see Figure 3.1). To illustrate an HTTP conversation between a browser and a server, let's walk through the four steps of a simple Web transaction.

1. *The client opens a connection to the server.* The transaction begins when the client opens a TCP connection (i.e., a socket) to the server. Since TCP connections are established down in the transport layer of the protocol stack, there is not a lot of HTTP-specific activity in this step. (Remember that HTTP is an application-layer protocol.) By default, the connection to the server is made on port 80 (the well-known HTTP port), unless otherwise specified. For its side of the connection, the client uses any available port.

2. *The client sends a request to the server.* This is where we get our first look at HTTP syntax. Let's assume that the Web browser makes a very basic request to retrieve an HTML file. The URL entered into the Web browser might look like *http://www.awl.com/index.html*. However, the HTTP request sent by the browser to the server (minus additional informational headers for simplicity) would look something like this:

```
GET /index.html HTTP/1.0
```

This request can be broken into three parts: the request method, the resource name, and the protocol. GET is an HTTP method that requests a resource from the server. (HTTP methods are discussed in detail later in this chapter.) */index.html* is a relative path to the requested resource. Because a TCP connection to the server was established in step 1, it is not necessary to fully qualify the resource name using *http://www.awl.com/index.html* (though this would have worked as well). It is assumed that the requested resource re-

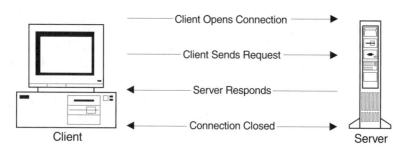

Figure 3.1   Request/Response Nature of HTTP

sides on the server to which the browser is currently connected. HTTP/1.0 is the name and version of the protocol implemented by the client. Finally, the request is terminated by a blank line (created by a pair of carriage return/ linefeeds).

In addition to the GET command, the browser may send other information about itself to the server. We will take a closer look at the other information that a browser may send later in this chapter.

3. *The server responds to the request.* The server responds with a status code, various header fields, and, if possible, the contents of the requested resource. If the resource requested in step 2 is available and the client has proper authorization, the server's response may look something like this:

```
HTTP/1.0 200 OK
Server: Apache/1.3.9 (Win32)
Content-Type: text/html
Content-Length: 94

<HTML>
<HEAD>
<TITLE>HTTP Request Successful</TITLE>
</HEAD>
<BODY>
It Worked!
</BODY>
</HTML>
```

The first line of the response indicates the server's protocol and returns a status code stating that the request was fulfilled successfully. The OK message on this line simply provides a brief, human-readable description of the status code 200. This message, called a *Reason-Phrase*, is only for our benefit and is actually not required since the browser evaluates only the status code number. However, it is recommended that a brief description of the status always be included.

Every HTTP response includes a status code. Possible status codes for HTTP/1.0 are documented in Appendix H. The other lines above the blank line are called *header fields* (though perhaps not technically correct, header fields are often referred to simply as *headers*). The combination of the status code line plus all header fields is known as the *HTTP header*. Header fields convey information about the server or the requested resource (see Appendix I for a list of header fields).

The header fields in the response designate the type of Web server that serviced the request, the MIME type of document being returned (see the section on MIME later in this chapter), and the length of the document content. The lines below the blank line are the content of the resource that was requested. All HTTP responses consist of a status code line followed by a series of header fields followed by an empty line. In many cases, a block of data immediately follows the empty line.

4. *The connection is closed.*   The TCP connection may be closed by either the server or the client or both. Usually, it is the server that terminates the connection after the response has been sent. Similarly, a browser will often close the connection once the complete response has been received. Regardless, the connection is closed and the HTTP transaction is complete. If the client wishes to make another request, the whole process starts again (see Figure 3.1).

NOTE: There is a method, known as *persistent connections* or *HTTP keep-alive*, whereby a single connection can service multiple HTTP requests. In fact, this is the default behavior of all HTTP/1.1 transactions. Similarly, some HTTP/1.0 clients and servers also implement a form of persistence. Persistent connections are discussed later in this chapter.

Connectionless Protocol

HTTP is a connectionless protocol. As you may have guessed, the difference between a connectionless and a connection-oriented protocol is in the way they handle connections. Using a *connectionless* protocol, the client opens a connection to the server, sends a request, receives a response, and closes the connection. Each request requires its own connection.[1] With a *connection-oriented* protocol, the client connects to the server, sends a request, receives a response, and then holds the connection open in order to service all future requests.

The connectionless nature of HTTP is both a strength and a weakness. Because it holds a connection open only long enough to service the request, very few server resources are required to service large numbers of users. In fact, many popular Web sites service millions of users in a single day. The drawback to a connectionless protocol is that a connection must be established with every request. Opening a new connection with each request increases network traffic and incurs a performance penalty that translates into additional delays for the user.

Alternatively, a connection-oriented protocol such as FTP has a strong performance advantage over a connectionless protocol like HTTP. This is because the overhead required to open a new connection is incurred only once rather

---

1. Persistent connections do allow a single connection to service multiple HTTP requests. However, since there is no guarantee how many requests a single connection will service (and since a single persistent connection usually services only a few requests), HTTP/1.1 is still considered a connectionless protocol. As far as the developer is concerned, each request is being serviced by a new connection.

than with every request. Unfortunately, each open connection consumes some amount of server resources. These finite resources, such as memory and disk space, limit the number of concurrent users the server can handle. In contrast to a Web site, an FTP site can rarely support more than a few hundred simultaneous users.

Stateless Protocol

As stated earlier, HTTP is a stateless protocol. A protocol is said to be *stateless* if it has no memory of prior connections and cannot distinguish one client's request from that of another. That is, the server has no way of knowing if a series of requests all came from the same client. In contrast, FTP is a *stateful* protocol because the connection is not opened and closed with every request. After the initial login, the FTP server maintains the user's credentials throughout the session. On the other hand, due to its stateless nature, there is no inherent method in HTTP for tracking a client's traversal of a Web site.[2] To the server, every connection is a new request from an anonymous client.[3] In Chapter 14, State and Session Management, we will discuss strategies for adding state to HTTP. State and session allows the server to identify the client and is extremely useful for secure sites where a user must log in or for electronic commerce sites that provide customers with a virtual shopping cart. Additionally, HTTP authentication can also convey client identity to the server (see Chapter 17 for information about HTTP authentication).

The stateless nature of HTTP is both a strength and a weakness. It is a strength in that the protocol is kept simple and straightforward since state information need not be managed. It also consumes fewer resources on the server and can support more simultaneous users since there are no client credentials and connections to maintain. The disadvantage is in the overhead required to create a new connection with each request and the protocol's inability to track a single user as he traverses a Web site.

HTTP/1.0

As previously mentioned, HTTP/1.0 is the most widely supported version of HTTP since all HTTP/1.1-compliant browsers and servers also support

---

2. It is possible to track a user's traversal of a Web site in a very rudimentary way (not sufficient for most Web applications) using the `Referer` HTTP header field.

3. Actually, the server can often distinguish one client from another using the source IP address transmitted along with the request. However, this IP address cannot guarantee a unique identification. For instance, many Internet Service Providers dynamically assign IP addresses to users. Each time a user logs in, he may receive a new IP address. In addition, if a proxy server is being used, requests from many users will be generated from the same IP address.

HTTP/1.0. However, most of today's Web software supports the newer HTTP/1.1 specification in addition to HTTP/1.0. Since HTTP/1.1 simply builds on the 1.0 foundation, the following information applies equally to both HTTP versions.

Status Codes

Every HTTP response returned from the server begins with a status code. These codes convey important information if you know what they mean. Table 3.1 documents the meaning behind different ranges of HTTP/1.0 status codes. For a complete list of HTTP/1.0 status codes and their meanings, see Appendix H.

Due to the large number of response status codes, it is much easier to just remember the ranges instead. Status codes in the 200 through 299 range indicate success, 300 through 399 indicate redirection, 400 through 499 indicate client error, and 500 through 599 indicate server error.

The status code line may be followed by any number of HTTP header fields. These fields convey additional information to the client, such as the time and date of the response, the type and version of server, when the file was last

Table 3.1   HTTP Status Code Category Descriptions

Code Range	Category	Description
1xx	Informational	A provisional status code for use in experimental applications only. HTTP/1.0 does not define informational status codes, but HTTP/1.1 does.
2xx	Successful	The request was successfully received, understood, and accepted.
3xx	Redirection	The server is requesting the Web client to redirect to another URL. The Web client can automatically redirect only in response to a GET or HEAD request. Redirection of a POST request requires user confirmation. To prevent an infinite loop, the client should not automatically redirect more than five times.
4xx	Client Error	The request is improperly formatted or cannot be fulfilled. Unless responding to a HEAD request, the server should return information in the response body that describes the error and whether it is a temporary or permanent condition. The client must immediately stop sending the request to the server.
5xx	Server Error	A valid request was received but the server cannot fulfill it. Unless responding to a HEAD request, the server should return information in the response body that describes the error and whether it is a temporary or permanent condition.

modified, the length of the requested file, and the file type (e.g., plain text, HTML, GIF image, JPEG image). The following sample HTTP response illustrates the status code line followed by several HTTP header fields.

```
HTTP/1.0 200 OK
Date: Tue, 18 Jan 2000 01:10:32 GMT
Server: Apache/1.3.9 (Win32)
Last-Modified: Fri, 14 Jan 2000 05:31:49 GMT
Content-Length: 359
Content-Type: text/html
```

As we saw earlier, every HTTP request begins with a request method (e.g., GET, HEAD, POST). A request method indicates the operation the client is asking the server to perform. Now that we have seen what a simple HTTP transaction looks like, let's explore a little deeper and examine the various HTTP/1.0 methods.

The GET Method

GET is the most common HTTP method. It is used to request a resource from the server. Containing no body content, a GET request is comprised of only a method statement and various request header fields. An example GET request follows.

```
GET /login.html HTTP/1.0
User-Agent: Mozilla/4.51 [en] (WinNT; I)
Accept: image/gif, image/jpeg, image/pjpeg, */*
```

You can see from the method statement (first line) of this request that the GET method is being employed to request the *login.html* file using the HTTP/1.0 protocol. The User-Agent header field conveys the type of browser that initiated the request. In this case, the browser is the English version of Netscape Navigator 4.51 running on Windows NT (Mozilla was the original code name for Navigator). The Accept header field indicates the content types supported by the client (see the MIME section later in this chapter). Even though a GET request does not send information in the body of the message, data can be passed as part of the GET statement itself. The following example passes username and password information to the server:

```
GET /login.html?username=dustin&password=servlets HTTP/1.0
User-Agent: Mozilla/4.51 [en] (WinNT; I)
Accept: image/gif, image/jpeg, image/pjpeg, */*
```

This GET request is identical to the first example except that it passes two parameters called username and password with values of dustin and servlets, respectively. This information can be passed to the server by manually appending the query string to the URL or by an HTML form. For example, the preceding GET request may be generated by the browser in response to a user requesting this URL:

http://www.insideservlets.com/login.html?username=dustin&password=servlets

It is somewhat uncommon, however, for users to create their own query strings and append them to a URL. More often, the preceding GET request would have been generated by the browser in response to the user clicking the **Submit** button on an HTML form. Figure 3.2 is an example of such a form. The HTML code used to build this form is presented in the "HTML Forms" section later in this chapter.

NOTE: Traditionally, the GET method is used to request static data. Responses to GET requests are often cached by proxy servers for use in future requests. In contrast, the POST method is usually used to request dynamic data. Therefore, responses to POST requests should not be cached.

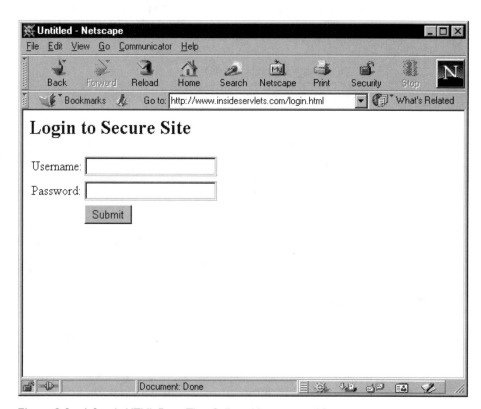

Figure 3.2   A Simple HTML Form That Collects Username and Password

A drawback to using a GET method for login transactions is that the information entered by the user is appended to the URL and displayed in plain text in the browser's address field. Therefore, if a user enters login information and clicks **Submit**, the username and password will be visible in the URL displayed in the browser's window. Another disadvantage is that a limited amount of data can be passed as part of the URL in a GET request. For example, earlier versions of Microsoft Internet Explorer could pass no more than 255 characters in the URL. This is because HTTP servers traditionally store GET parameters in system environment variables that can be accessed by CGI programs and other out-of-process applications. Unfortunately, the amount of information that can be stored in environment variables is limited and varies among operating systems. Both of these disadvantages are remedied in another HTTP method called POST.

NOTE: If a GET request includes an If-Modified-Since header field, the request becomes a *conditional GET.* This means that the content of the requested resource is returned only if the information has changed since the date specified in the If-Modified-Since header field. This allows the browser to display a cached copy of the page if it has not been modified since it was last downloaded. A conditional GET statement might look like this:

```
GET /login.html HTTP/1.0
If-Modified-Since: Mon, 17 Jan 2000 20:43:07 GMT
User-Agent: Mozilla/4.51 [en] (WinNT; I)
Accept: image/gif, image/x-xbitmap, image/jpeg, */*
```

In the conditional GET request shown here, the server will return the *login.html* file only if the page has been modified since January 17, 2000. Otherwise, a status code of "304 Not Modified" will be returned by the server without a message body, indicating that the browser should load the page from cache. This technique reduces network traffic and improves performance.

The POST Method

POST is an HTTP method commonly used for passing user input to the server. The POST method differs from GET in that all parametric information is stored in the body of the request rather than in the URL portion of the method statement. This approach has two advantages. First, the information submitted by the user is not visible in the URL. Second, there is no limit to the amount of information that can be passed when it is stored in the body of the request.

This is because the name/value pairs passed in a POST request are accessed via the client's input stream rather than the server's environment variables.

Unlike the GET method, there is no way to issue a POST by altering the URL in the browser's address field. A POST is typically generated by the browser in response to the user clicking the **Submit** button on an HTML form that uses the POST method. Such an HTML form might look identical to the one shown in Figure 3.2. An actual POST request looks like the following:

```
POST /login.html HTTP/1.0
User-Agent: Mozilla/4.51 [en] (WinNT; I)
Accept: image/gif, image/jpeg, image/pjpeg, */*
Content-Length: 34
Content-Type: application/x-www-form-urlencoded

username=dustin&password=servlets
```

Notice that the user input is passed in the body of the request rather than in the method statement (i.e., the first line of the HTTP request). This is the primary difference between the GET and POST methods. HTTP/1.0 requires that a valid Content-Length header field accompany all POST requests.

The HEAD Method

The HEAD method is identical to the GET method except that it returns only the HTTP header—the body content is excluded. The HTTP header returned by the server in response to a HEAD request should be identical to the header that would have been returned in response to a GET. This method is very useful for debugging, verifying hypertext links, and checking the status of a file before attempting to retrieve it. For instance, the HEAD method makes it possible to check when a file was last modified or to check the length of the file without actually having to download it. If included in the HEAD request, the If-Modified-Since header field is ignored.

Other Methods

Four additional methods are implemented either inconsistently or by few HTTP/1.0 implementations. These nonstandard methods include PUT for file uploads, DELETE for deleting resources on the server, LINK for establishing relationships between resources, and UNLINK for breaking relationships between resources. In contrast to HTTP/1.0, PUT and DELETE are standard methods in the HTTP/1.1 specification (LINK and UNLINK are not directly supported in the Servlet API).

HTTP/I.I

HTTP/1.1 is the heir to the rapidly aging HTTP/1.0 protocol. Unlike version 1.0, HTTP/1.1 is being developed in conjunction with the Internet Engineering Task Force (IETF) and is currently a proposed Internet Standard (see RFC 2068). (For more information on the IETF and the Internet standardization process, see Appendix C.) HTTP/1.1 adds many new and powerful request methods and response status codes. In addition to the GET, HEAD, and POST methods introduced in HTTP/1.0, HTTP/1.1 adds support for the methods described in Table 3.2.

Persistent connections are another important feature of HTTP/1.1. *Persistent connections*, often called *HTTP keep-alive*, allow an HTTP client to use the same connection for multiple requests. Persistent connections improve performance by reducing the network overhead required to create a new connection with each request. Unlike standard HTTP/1.0, a server that implements the HTTP/1.1 specification does not close the connection after servicing each request from an HTTP/1.1 client. Rather, both the client and the server hold the connection open for use with future requests. The number of requests that a server will accept on a single connection is configurable on the server. Since persistent connections are the default for HTTP/1.1 messages, the following header field must be sent in the request if persistent connections are not desired:

```
Connection: close
```

It should also be noted that even though there is no official specification for it, some HTTP/1.0 clients and servers implement a form of persistent connections. However, since persistent connections are not the default for HTTP/1.0 transactions, they must be explicitly negotiated. An HTTP/1.0 client

Table 3.2   Methods That HTTP/1.1 Adds to the Standard HTTP/1.0 Request Methods

Method	Description
DELETE	Requests that the server delete the resource specified in the URL.
OPTIONS	Requests information regarding the communication options supported by the server.
PUT	Requests that a new resource be created on the server at the specified URL using the data included in the request.
TRACE	Returns the request to the client for debugging purposes, thus allowing the client to see the request received by the server at the end of the calling chain. This information can be useful for testing or diagnostic purposes.

may indicate to the server that it wishes to use persistent connections by passing the following header field in each request:

```
Connection: Keep-Alive
```

This header field instructs the server that the HTTP/1.0 client wishes to use the current connection for future requests. If the server supports persistent connections, it will include the same `Connection: Keep-Alive` header field in its response, and will keep the connection active.

It may appear that the use of persistent connections converts HTTP into a stateful, connection-oriented protocol. This is not the case. Since an HTTP server does not associate clients or requests with a connection (even when multiple requests are made across the same connection), HTTP is still stateless, regardless of whether persistent connections are used. Similarly, since the connection is not preserved throughout the entire session, HTTP can still be considered connectionless even when connection persistence techniques are employed. In fact, there is no guarantee regarding the number of requests that a single connection will service (a single persistent connection usually services only a few requests).

NOTE: Because there was no official specification for persistent connections in HTTP/1.0, many previous experimental implementations of persistence are incompatible or faulty. For instance, many HTTP/1.0 proxy servers do not properly handle the `Connection` header field and erroneously forward it to the next server. Due to this errant handling, an HTTP/1.0 client should never send a `Connection: Keep-Alive` header field to a proxy server.

HTTP-NG

HTTP-NG (Next Generation) is a protocol that was being developed to address many of the performance problems inherent in the HTTP specification. HTTP-NG proposes the transformation of HTTP into a stateful, connection-oriented protocol. Similar to FTP, HTTP-NG would not open a new connection with each request, but would use a single shared connection across all requests. Of course, the trade-off would be that each client connection would require additional server resources. At the time of publication, HTTP-NG protocol research had been halted and its future is unclear. Regardless, HTTP-NG is an interesting proposal and may be worth reviewing for educational purposes. For more information see the World Wide Web Consortium at *http://www.w3.org/*.

SSL and S-HTTP

SSL (Secure Sockets Layer) is a protocol developed by Netscape for establishing secure connections between two hosts. Security is provided through a combination of public key and symmetric key encryption methods applied to all data sent over the SSL connection (see Chapter 17 for more information about SSL). Secure Sockets is supported by both Netscape and Microsoft browsers. SSL is commonly used on the Web to ensure the privacy of confidential information, such as a customer's credit card number. By convention, the URL for an HTTP resource that implements SSL begins with *https://* rather than *http://*. SSL includes the following security measures:

- Encrypts data before transmission
- Prevents the unauthorized modification of data during transit
- Can guarantee the client that it is communicating with the correct server and vice versa
- Can prevent unauthorized clients from accessing the server

S-HTTP (Secure HTTP) is an extension of the HTTP protocol and can be used to transmit data securely over the Web. While SSL creates a secure connection between two hosts across which any amount of data can be sent, S-HTTP is used to securely transfer individual messages. S-HTTP is far less popular than SSL and does not enjoy the same support from browsers. Both SSL and S-HTTP have been approved by the IETF as official Internet standards.

Examining HTTP Header Fields

In view of the importance of headers when debugging HTTP transactions, it is fortunate that there are a number of ways in which the developer can view these headers. Examining the header fields returned by a server or sent by a client is one of the primary methods of troubleshooting problems in a Web conversation. This section presents two methods of viewing the HTTP header returned by the server or sent by the browser.

The simplest way to view the HTTP header returned by a server is to use a standard Telnet client. By simply connecting to the HTTP port with a Telnet client, the entire data stream returned by the server, including the header, can be viewed. The steps required to accomplish this are as follows:

1. Start your Telnet client. This is usually accomplished by typing `telnet` at the command console.
2. Establish a connection to the server using the standard HTTP port 80 (or whatever port on which the HTTP server is listening).

3. Send the server a valid HTTP request such as "GET /index.html HTTP/1.0"
   followed by two carriage return/linefeeds (press **ENTER** twice). If you are
   interested only in the HTTP header returned by the server and not the
   contents of a file, send a request like "HEAD /index.html HTTP/1.0". Recall
   that HEAD returns the same header as the GET method but that no content is
   included with the response.

4. The server's HTTP header, followed by the data requested, will be returned
   and the connection closed by the server. The header displayed in Figure 3.3
   shows that the server is running an Apache Web Server version 1.3.12
   implementing the HTTP/1.1 protocol and that the length of the file
   requested is 1358 bytes.

NOTE: The HTTP request described in step 3 should be entered rather quickly
because many Web servers have a very short timeout period between the time the
connection is established and the time the request is received. This timeout ensures
that the server is not wasting resources by holding connections open longer than
necessary. If supported by your Telnet client, it is advisable to copy the request
onto the clipboard and paste it into the Telnet session once a connection has been
established.

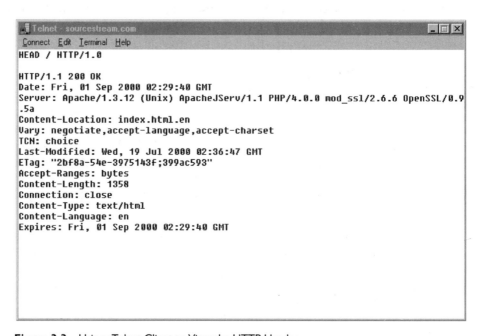

Figure 3.3   Using aTelnet Client to View the HTTP Header

There is another, less primitive, method for checking a Web server's response header. Included on the accompanying CD-ROM is a program that allows the user to query a server for the HTTP header and data. It can serve as an excellent diagnostic tool. The program, called *Protocol Explorer*, is documented in Chapter 20 and contains online documentation accessible via the **Help** menu. A sample request using *Protocol Explorer* is shown in Figure 3.4.

Using *Protocol Explorer*, examining the HTTP header generated by a browser is just as simple as viewing the server's header. When *Protocol Explorer* is used in receive mode, the client request is visible in the browser as well as in *Protocol Explorer*'s **Request** window. Figure 3.5 shows the response from *Protocol Explorer* (listening on port 80) when it is queried by a Netscape browser.

Lastly, a browser's HTTP header can be viewed with the diagnostics servlet presented in Chapter 20. This servlet is a comprehensive diagnostic tool that shows all browser header fields as well as many additional browser and server properties.

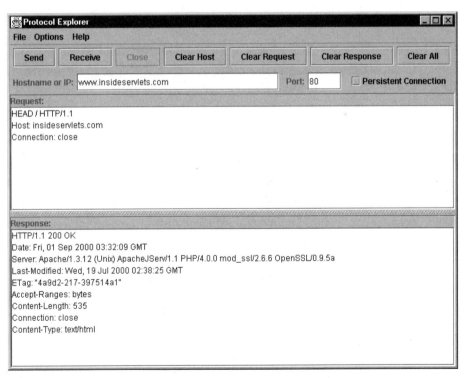

Figure 3.4 Using *Protocol Explorer* to Retrieve a Server's HTTP Header

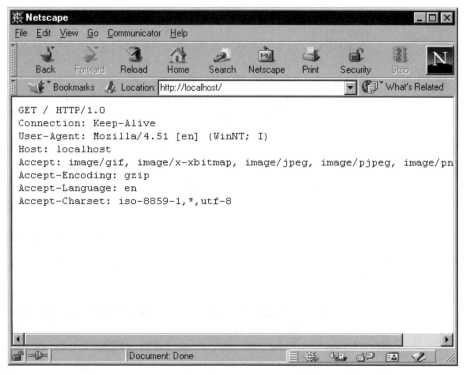

Figure 3.5   Using *Protocol Explorer* to View the HTTP Headers Generated by the Browser

MIME

Multipurpose Internet Mail Extensions, *MIME*, is an extension to the electronic mail format originally defined by RFC 822. Most notably, MIME provides three important Internet services. These services include the following:

- Provides a standard mechanism for encoding binary data into the ASCII format
- Defines a standard for specifying the type of content stored in the body of a message
- Describes a standard method for defining a multipart mail message containing heterogeneous body parts

Let's take a look at how each of these services is of interest to the Web developer.

The original Internet mail system did not provide services to support rich content, such as images or sound. Rather than upgrade the entire Internet mail system to support these new content types, the MIME specification was developed. MIME defines a method for converting binary data into standard ASCII characters for transmission over the Internet. In this manner, MIME-encoded e-mail looks like a standard RFC 822 message to mail transport agents that are not MIME compliant. Only the source and the destination need to understand MIME. All other hosts should simply route the message as if it were a normal RFC 822 mail message. For detailed information on MIME, see RFC 2045 through RFC 2049.

MIME specifies two formats for encoding binary data into ASCII characters—Base64 and Quoted Printable. *Base64,* the most common encoding scheme, is used to encode pure binary data into standard ASCII. Though MIME was originally developed for e-mail, it is now commonly used by many different Internet technologies and protocols. For example, binary data transferred over the Web, such as downloading a JPEG image on a Web page, may use Base64 encoding. *Quoted Printable* encoding is used primarily for documents that comprise mostly standard ASCII characters but still contain a small number of non-ASCII characters. This might include a document defining scientific or mathematical formulas. In contrast to Base64, a Quoted Printable document is largely readable without decoding.

The MIME method for describing a resource's contents is used by Web browsers in addition to e-mail clients. For instance, a Web browser uses the MIME specification to determine if a file is an HTML document, a JPEG image, or just plain text. In this way, the client knows how to handle the data it just received. Each MIME type consists of two parts—type and subtype. The *type* is a general description of the information the data contains. It defines whether the data represents text, image, video, or some other type of information. The *subtype* defines the exact kind and format of the data such as whether an image is JPEG or GIF. The MIME type is communicated from the server to the browser via an HTTP header field called Content-Type. The MIME type assumes a *type/subtype* format. For example, the content type of an HTML document is text/html and for a GIF image it is image/gif. Table 3.3 shows some basic MIME types. See Appendix K for a more comprehensive list of common MIME types.

MIME is also used to define nonstandard or proprietary subtypes. These subtypes are always prefaced by x-. For example, Table 3.3 shows an audio type of audio/x-wav. This type represents a Microsoft WAV (pronounced "wave") sound file. Because the WAV format is proprietary, it begins with x-. Since these x- subtypes are not industry standards, they may be readable only by a single application (such as FrameMaker or MacPaint) or may be interpreted differently by different programs. See Appendix K for a list of commonly used x- subtypes. For a more complete list of MIME media types, see the following URL:

http://www.isi.edu/in-notes/iana/assignments/media-types/media-types

Table 3.3   Basic MIME Types

Type	Description	Example
application	Binary data that is read or executed by another program	application/java application/zip
audio	Sound file that can be played by another program	audio/basic audio/x-wav
image	Picture file that can be displayed by another program	image/gif image/jpeg
message	Encapsulated mail message	message/rfc822 message/news
multipart	Data consisting of multiple, possibly heterogenous, parts	multipart/mixed multipart/digest
text	Data consisting of printable text	text/html text/plain
video	Video file that can be played by another program	video/mpeg video/quicktime
x-world	Experimental data types	x-world/x-vrml

Lastly, MIME defines the manner in which boundaries are placed around heterogeneous parts of a mail message. This specification allows a text e-mail message to contain attachments such as an HTML document or binary image data.

HTML Forms

HTML, or HyperText Markup Language, is the language used to create hypertext documents on the World Wide Web. HTML describes the semantic value of a document such as the layout of the page or the relative size of fonts. HTML has evolved through a number of specifications, including HTML 1.0, HTML 2.0, HTML 3.0, HTML 3.2, and HTML 4.0. However, version 4.0 is the last step in the evolution of HTML. The Worldwide Web Consortium (W3C) has proposed XHTML (Extensible HyperText Markup Language) as a replacement for HTML. Another language known as XML (Extensible Markup Language), in conjunction with XSL (Extensible Stylesheet Language), is rapidly gaining popularity and may replace HTML and XHTML as the standard markup language for Web pages. For the latest HTML specification or for more information regarding XHTML and XML, see the World Wide Web Consortium home page at *http://www.w3.org/*.

Because of the size and scope of a comprehensive introduction to HTML, this book does not attempt to familiarize the reader with the many facets of HTML page design. Rather, it focuses on HTML forms. After all, HTML forms are the most common method of providing user interaction over the Web. They are also the most common method for communicating with servlets. For a complete review of HTML, see RFC 1866 or one of the many good books on the subject.

NOTE: As a result of the explosive growth of the Web and the relatively slow Internet standards process, many companies have jumped the gun and implemented experimental features into their products. For instance, both Netscape Navigator and Microsoft Internet Explorer supported HTML tables when they were still considered experimental extensions to HTML (RFC 1942). However, the latest HTML specifications (3.2 and 4.0) include tables, frames, and many other common extensions.

Implementing features before they become standards may not always be bad. After all, if we always waited for an official standard to emerge, the Web would not exist today (HTTP is still not an official Internet standard). Unfortunately, vendors do not always agree on which experimental extensions should be implemented. For example, Netscape Navigator supported form-based file uploads (RFC 1867) several versions earlier than Microsoft Internet Explorer. Similarly, Internet Explorer provided strong support for Cascading Style Sheets and XML before Netscape. However, Netscape recently leap-frogged Internet Explorer with the release of *Netscape 6*. Netscape 6, based on the Mozilla open source project, currently provides the best browser support for accepted Internet standards. As you can see, varying support for Web specifications by these browsers contributes to making cutting-edge Web design a moving target.

Introduced in HTML 2.0, *HTML forms* provide a simple way to prompt a user for input via a formatted HTML page and allow the user to "submit" the information to the server. Forms were the first mechanism to allow true two-way interaction on the Web. See Figure 3.2 for an example of a basic HTML form used to collect username and password information from a user.

The <FORM> Tag

Each HTML form consists of a block of code beginning with the <FORM> tag and ending with the </FORM> tag. Any standard HTML body tags may be included within this block. Though forms cannot be nested, multiple forms can be defined in a single HTML document. The <FORM> tag specifies these three attributes:

- The HTTP method to be used to submit the form
- The action to be performed when the form is submitted
- The type of encoding to be used when submitting the form

The following <FORM> tag will post the data entered on the form to the resource at the relative URL */cgi-bin/login.cgi* using the application/x-www-form-urlencoded MIME encoding.

```
<FORM METHOD="POST" ACTION="/cgi-bin/login.cgi"
    ENCTYPE="application/x-www-form-urlencoded">
```

NOTE: Although it is good practice to place all values inside an HTML tag within quotation marks, most browsers do not require them unless there is a space within the value. For example, the preceding <FORM> tag could have been written as:

```
<FORM METHOD=POST ACTION=/cgi-bin/login.cgi
    ENCTYPE=application/x-www-form-urlencoded>
```

However, for consistency, it is a good idea to always enclose HTML tag values in quotation marks (in addition, HTML 4.0, XHTML, and XML require quotation marks).

The METHOD Attribute

The METHOD attribute specifies the HTTP method to use when the form is submitted. The two possible methods are GET and POST. As discussed earlier, when a GET method is specified, any form data input by the user is passed to the server as a query string appended to the URL (following the ? character). If a POST method is used, the user's input is passed within the body of the request. Due to the length constraints of the GET method, in most circumstances it is preferable to use a POST. If no METHOD is defined in the <FORM> tag, the GET method is used by default.

The ACTION Attribute

The ACTION attribute specifies the action that is to be performed when the HTML form is submitted. Usually, the ACTION attribute indicates the URL of the CGI script or servlet that will process the user's input (see the <FORM> tag shown in the previous section). In addition to the ubiquitous http URL scheme, `mailto` is also commonly specified in a form's `ACTION` attribute. The `mailto` scheme is used to e-mail the form data to a specified e-mail address. A `<FORM>` tag using the `mailto` directive looks like this:

```
<FORM METHOD="POST" ACTION="mailto:dustin@insideservlets.com">
```

Listing 3.1 shows a simple form that performs the `mailto` action. When the form is submitted, the user's input is URL encoded and e-mailed to the specified recipient. When the e-mail is retrieved, the data appears in the body of the message as a URL-encoded string.

Listing 3.1   A simple HTML form utilizing the `mailto` action.

```
<HTML>
<HEAD><TITLE>Mailing List</TITLE></HEAD>
<BODY>
<FORM METHOD="POST" ACTION="mailto:dustin@insideservlets.com"
  ENCTYPE="application/x-www-form-urlencoded">
<P>Name: <INPUT TYPE="TEXT" NAME="name" SIZE="25"></P>
<P>Email Address: <INPUT TYPE="TEXT" NAME="email" SIZE="25"></P>
<P><INPUT TYPE="SUBMIT" VALUE="Submit">
</FORM>
</BODY>
</HTML>
```

A sample of the body of the e-mail message generated by Listing 3.1 follows. Notice that the URL-encoded message associates the name of each input element with the value entered by the user (known as a name/value pair). To receive e-mail generated by the `mailto` action, it may be helpful to write a simple program that parses the name/value pairs and URL decodes them for easy viewing (using the `URLDecoder` class demonstrated in Chapter 2).

```
name=Dustin+Callaway&email=dustin@insideservlets.com
```

If not specified, all three of the `<FORM>` tag attributes presented here are assigned default values. The `METHOD` attribute defaults to `GET`, the `ACTION` attribute defaults to the URL from which the HTML form was requested, and the `ENCTYPE` attribute defaults to `application/x-www-form-urlencoded`.

The ENCTYPE Attribute

The `ENCTYPE` attribute specifies the MIME content type used to encode the form data. Though helpful for clarification, `application/x-www-form-encoded` is the default encoding type and need not be declared (it will be assumed if no encoding type is specified). `application/x-www-form-encoded` is the same as standard URL encoding. Though other MIME types may be used (such as `text/plain` or `multipart/form-data`), `x-www-form-encoded` is a safer encoding because it is designed to prevent characters from being lost or transposed in transit. For more information about why x-www-form-urlencoded is a safe method, see the "URL Encoding" section in Chapter 2.

The <INPUT> Tag

An HTML form only becomes useful once the appropriate input elements are added to it. Within a form block, input components such as text boxes, radio buttons, and check boxes can be added to the HTML page by using special tags. For example, Listing 3.2 shows the HTML code used to generate the Web page shown in Figure 3.6.

Listing 3.2   A simple HTML form.

```
<HTML>
<HEAD>
<TITLE>Login</TITLE>
</HEAD>
<BODY>
<H2>Login to Secure Site</H2>
<FORM METHOD="POST" ACTION="/cgi-bin/login.cgi">

Username: <INPUT TYPE="TEXT" NAME="username" SIZE="25"><BR>
Password: <INPUT TYPE="PASSWORD" NAME="password" SIZE="25"><P>

<INPUT TYPE="SUBMIT" VALUE="Submit">
<INPUT TYPE="RESET" VALUE="Clear">
</FORM>
</BODY>
</HTML>
```

Specifically designed for forms, the <INPUT> tag defines some type of input component. The exact type of component is specified with the TYPE attribute. The elements of the <INPUT> tag are described next.

The TYPE Attribute

The TYPE attribute defines the type of component represented by the <INPUT> tag. For example, the <INPUT> tag that follows specifies a text box component that is 25 characters wide.

```
<INPUT TYPE="TEXT" NAME="username" SIZE="25">
```

Table 3.4 shows the valid values for the TYPE attribute.

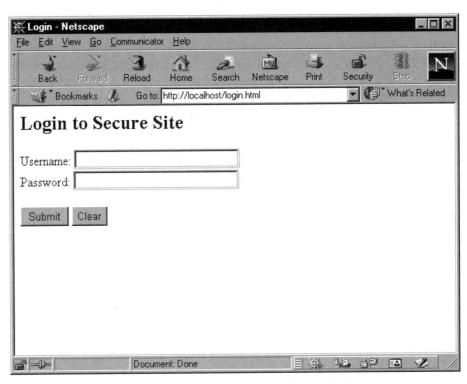

Figure 3.6 Browser Rendering of a Simple HTML Form

Table 3.4 Values for the TYPE Attribute

Type	Description
TEXT	Standard text box. Can be used in conjunction with the SIZE and MAXLENGTH attributes to specify the width of the text box and the maximum number of characters allowed, respectively. The VALUE attribute specifies the text shown in the text box when the form is first loaded. `<INPUT TYPE="TEXT" NAME="username" SIZE="25" MAXLENGTH="25">`
CHECKBOX	Standard check box. Used for simple boolean values (on or off, true or false). Can be used in conjunction with the CHECKED attribute to specify whether it is initially selected. Unselected check boxes are not included with the name/value pairs when the form is submitted. `<INPUT TYPE="CHECKBOX" NAME="active">`

RADIO	Standard radio button. Accepts a single value from a group of choices. Can be used in conjunction with the CHECKED attribute to specify whether it is initially selected. Unselected radio buttons are not included with the name/value pairs when the form is submitted.
	`<INPUT TYPE="RADIO" NAME="gender" VALUE="Male">`
	`<INPUT TYPE="RADIO" NAME="gender" VALUE="Female">`

continued

Table 3.4   Values for the TYPE Attribute *(continued)*

HIDDEN	No field is visible to the user, but its name/value pair is submitted with the other form data. Useful for transmitting state information from page to page (such as a username or session ID). `<INPUT TYPE="HIDDEN" NAME="sessionID" VALUE="4839204294575934">`
PASSWORD	Same as the TEXT attribute except that the text is not displayed as the value is entered (usually shows spaces or asterisks instead). The fact that text is not displayed as it is typed does not affect the value of the field when the form is submitted. Can be used in conjunction with the SIZE and MAXLENGTH attributes to specify the width of the text box and the maximum number of characters allowed, respectively. `<INPUT TYPE="PASSWORD" NAME="password" SIZE="25" MAXLENGTH="25">`
SUBMIT	A button that submits the form. The VALUE attribute specifies the label displayed on the button. If a NAME attribute is specified, the SUBMIT button will contribute a name/value pair to the form data when submitted. Otherwise, the SUBMIT button does not contribute to the form data. `<INPUT TYPE="SUBMIT" NAME="save" VALUE="Submit Form">`
RESET	A button that resets all form fields to their initial values. The VALUE attribute specifies the label displayed on the button. `<INPUT TYPE="RESET" VALUE="Clear All Values">`
IMAGE	An image button that, when clicked, submits the form (same as the SUBMIT button). Similar to a standard HTML <IMG> tag, the SRC attribute specifies the URL of the image to display. Any VALUE attribute is ignored. When the image is clicked, the IMAGE type contributes two name/value pairs to the form data—one indicating the X coordinate of the mouse click and the other indicating the Y coordinate. For instance, the following IMAGE type would submit two name/value pairs such as "Save.x=10&Save.y=5" depending on where the image was clicked. `<INPUT TYPE="IMAGE" NAME="save" SRC="/images/savebutton.gif">`
FILE	An experimental type supported by Netscape Navigator and Microsoft Internet Explorer (see RFC 1867) that facilitates the selection of a file from the file system by supplying a text box and a **Browse** button. The ACCEPT attribute specifies file patterns that are accepted by the field. For file uploads, the ENCTYPE of the HTML form should be set to multipart/form-data. If multipart/form-data encoding is not used, the FILE type contributes a name/value pair containing the full path and filename of the file selected. (See Chapter 22 for more information about multipart/form-data encoding.) `<INPUT TYPE="FILE" NAME="filename" SIZE="50" MAXLENGTH="255">`

Other Attributes

In addition to the TYPE attribute, several other important attributes are used within the <INPUT> tag. Table 3.5 describes each of these attributes.

The <SELECT> *and* <OPTION> *Tags*

The <SELECT> and <OPTION> tags are used to create a selectable list or drop-down list of items. Each item is added to the list using a series of <OPTION> tags that are embedded between the <SELECT> and </SELECT> tags. To illustrate, the syntax for a list containing three items that allows multiple items to be selected (with item1 selected by default) looks like this:

```
<SELECT NAME="items" SIZE="3" MULTIPLE>
  <OPTION VALUE="item1" SELECTED>Item 1 Text</OPTION>
  <OPTION VALUE="item2">Item 2 Text</OPTION>
  <OPTION VALUE="item3">Item 3 Text</OPTION>
</SELECT>
```

Each <SELECT> block contributes one or more name/value pairs to the form data (unless no items are selected). The name portion of the name/value pair comes from the NAME attribute of the <SELECT> tag. The value portion comes from the VALUE attribute of the <OPTION> tag that corresponds to the selected item. The information nested between the <OPTION></OPTION> tags contains the

Table 3.5   <INPUT> Tag Attributes in Addition to TYPE

Attribute	Description
ALIGN	Used with the IMAGE type for vertical alignment. Alignment values are the same as with the <IMG> tag.
CHECKED	Indicates that a check box or radio button is initially selected. This attribute is not set to any value. It is simply either present or absent.
MAXLENGTH	Specifies the maximum number of characters that can be entered into a text field. This may be larger than the width specified by the SIZE attribute, in which case the text field will scroll.
NAME	Provides a unique identifier for a field. The NAME attribute is submitted with the form data as part of the name/value pair. Allows the program that processes the data to match fields with their appropriate values.
SIZE	Specifies the visible width, in characters, of a text field.
SRC	Used with the IMAGE type; specifies the URL where the image data is located.
TYPE	Specifies the specific type of input element represented by the <INPUT> tag.

text that is displayed in the list. The SELECTED attribute can be added to any <OPTION> tag to have it selected by default when the page is displayed.

The SIZE attribute of the <SELECT> tag indicates the maximum number of rows to display at a time. If the <SELECT> tag contains more items (<OPTION> tags) than rows (SIZE attribute), a vertical scroll bar appears allowing the user to scroll through all options.

The MULTIPLE attribute in the <SELECT> tag serves as a flag to indicate that the user may select multiple items. This is accomplished by holding down the **Control, Option,** or **Meta** key (depending on the operating system) while clicking multiple items in the list. If the MULTIPLE attribute is not present, no more than one item can be selected at a time.

The <SELECT> block submits one name/value pair for each selected item. These name/value pairs all share the same name (from the <SELECT> tag's NAME attribute) but have different values (based on the item selected). For example, if the user selects both "Item 1 Text" and "Item 2 Text" from the <SELECT> block shown previously, the browser will include the following name/value pairs in the request when the form is submitted:

```
items=item1&items=item2
```

In addition to standard lists, the <SELECT> tag can be used to create drop-down lists. Drop-down lists are created by simply setting the SIZE attribute of the <SELECT> tag to "1". Unlike standard lists, drop-down lists do not support multiple selections.

The <TEXTAREA> Tag

The <TEXTAREA> tag displays a multiline text box that is useful for collecting large amounts of text from the client. The syntax for the <TEXTAREA> tag is as follows:

```
<TEXTAREA NAME="name" COLS="x" ROWS="y">Initial Text</TEXTAREA>
```

The <TEXTAREA> element allows you to specify not only the number of columns, such as the TEXT input type, but also the number of rows. Listing 3.3 shows HTML that demonstrates a typical application of the <TEXTAREA> tag. Figure 3.7 shows Listing 3.3 when rendered by a browser.

Listing 3.3 A simple HTML form using the <TEXTAREA> tag.

```
<HTML>
<HEAD>
<TITLE>Suggestion Box</TITLE>
</HEAD>
```

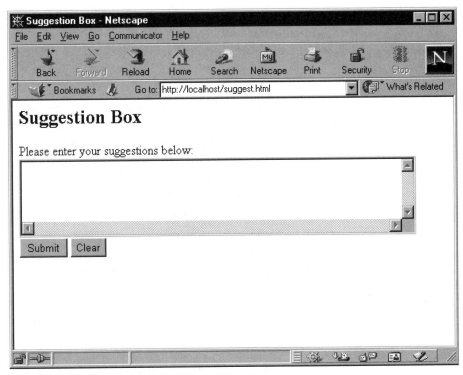

Figure 3.7 Sample HTML Form Using a TEXTAREA Input Element

```
<BODY>
<H2>Suggestion Box</H2>
<FORM METHOD="POST" ACTION="/cgi-bin/login.cgi">

Please enter your suggestions below:
<BR>
<TEXTAREA NAME="suggestion" COLS="60" ROWS="4"></TEXTAREA>
<BR>

<INPUT TYPE="SUBMIT" VALUE="Submit">
<INPUT TYPE="RESET" VALUE="Clear">
</FORM>
</BODY>
</HTML>
```

Summary

This chapter presents an introduction to the HTTP protocol, MIME, and HTML forms. A thorough understanding of these topics will help the reader know how communication takes place on the Web and can assist with trouble-shooting when things go wrong. Combined with the appendices referred to in the text, this chapter may serve as a useful reference during your servlet development projects. The next chapter introduces servlets—at last!

Chapter Highlights

- The *HyperText Transfer Protocol* is a stateless, TCP/IP-based protocol used for communicating on the World Wide Web. HTTP defines the precise manner in which Web clients communicate with Web servers.

- The HTTP protocol follows a very simple request/response paradigm.

- HTTP is a connectionless protocol. In a *connectionless* protocol, the client opens a connection with the server, sends a request, receives a response, and closes the connection.

- HTTP is a stateless protocol. A protocol is *stateless* if it has no memory of prior connections and cannot distinguish one client's request from that of another client.

- *SSL* is a protocol developed by Netscape for establishing secure connections between two hosts.

- *MIME* is an extension to the electronic mail format originally defined by RFC 822. It provides a standard mechanism for encoding binary data into ASCII characters, defines a standard for specifying the type of content stored in the body of a message, and describes a standard method for defining a multi-part mail message that contains heterogeneous body parts.

- Introduced in HTML 2.0, *HTML forms* provide a simple way to prompt a user for input via a formatted HTML page and to allow the user to "submit" the information to the server.

PART II

Introduction to Servlets

CHAPTER 4

Why Servlets?

Originally, Web sites were comprised of only static HTML documents stored in the server's file system. This approach provided no way for the client to transmit information to the server in order to customize the information returned or store data in a database. These were the days before Internet search engines, online order processing, and interactive Web-based games. Fortunately, the introduction of CGI breathed life into the static World Wide Web.

In combination with HTML forms, CGI provided a mechanism for true two-way interaction between the client and the server. This new technology paved the way for new ideas such as online customer support and electronic commerce. As CGI begins to show its age in areas of performance and flexibility, new technologies are vying to replace CGI as the standard interface for building dynamic Web sites. With industry momentum building rapidly, Java servlets are likely to succeed CGI as the most popular Internet development technology.

This chapter provides a high-level introduction to servlets by answering the following basic questions:

- What is a servlet?
- Where do servlets fit in?
- What can servlets do?
- Why are servlets better than CGI?

On completion of this chapter, you should have a good grasp of what a servlet is used for and the advantages of servlets over competing technologies.

What Is a Servlet?

A *servlet* is a server-side software component, written in Java, that dynamically extends the functionality of a server (usually an HTTP server). Similar to the manner in which applets run within a Java-enabled Web browser on the client, servlets execute on a Java-enabled server. Unlike applets, servlets do not display a graphical interface to the user. A servlet's work is done "behind the scenes" on the server and only the results of the servlet's processing are returned to the client (usually in the form of HTML).

Specifically, servlets are Java classes that conform to a specific interface that can be invoked by the server. Note that the functionality provided by servlets is not restricted to Web servers. Servlets can enhance any server that supports Java and the Servlet API. Common examples include FTP, Telnet, mail, and news servers. The *Servlet API* is a specification developed by Sun Microsystems and many other contributors that defines the classes and interfaces used to create and execute servlets.

Servlets provide a framework for creating applications that implement the request/response paradigm. For example, when a browser sends a request to the server, the server may forward the request to a servlet. At this point the servlet can process the request (through database access or any other means) and construct an appropriate response (usually in HTML) that is returned to the client.

Servlets have many advantages over competing technologies, including the following:

- Capable of running in-process
- Compiled
- Crash resistant
- Cross platform
- Cross server
- Durable
- Dynamically loadable across the network
- Easily deployed
- Extensible
- Multithreaded
- Object oriented
- Protocol independent
- Secure
- Written in Java

Let's briefly discuss each of these points.

Capable of Running In Process

Servlets are capable of running in the same process space as the server. This capability offers significant performance advantages over many competing technologies. For instance, server-side programming methods like CGI require programs to run as separate processes when servicing client requests. The overhead involved with creating a new process for every request incurs a large performance penalty. Because servlets run in process, they need to be loaded only once (at server start-up or when first invoked). Due to the multithreaded nature of servlets, all client requests can be serviced by separate threads within the server's process space. Lightweight context switching between threads is far faster than heavyweight context switching between processes. In addition, since servlets are tightly integrated with the server, it is possible for a servlet to instruct the server to log errors, translate file paths, perform user authorization, or other tasks that are not possible with CGI.

Compiled

Unlike scripting languages, servlets are compiled into Java bytecodes. By virtue of their compilation, Java servlets can execute much more quickly than common scripting languages can. Bytecode compilation improves servlet performance over scripting languages through compile-time code optimization. Server-side just-in-time and dynamic compilers also dramatically improve servlet performance.

In addition, compilation offers the advantages of strong error checking and type checking. Many critical errors are flushed out during compilation. This compilation stage makes servlets more stable and easier to develop and debug than traditional scripting solutions. Lastly, compiled code is more compact and secure than noncJava virtual machineompiled options.

Crash Resistant

Although it can't be said that any application is completely crash proof, servlets come much closer to this ideal than native applications. This is primarily because servlets are written in Java and executed by a *Java virtual machine* (JVM). The JVM does not allow servlets direct access to memory locations, thereby eliminating crashes that result from invalid memory accesses (e.g., errant pointers in C). In addition, before execution, the JVM verifies that compiled Java class files are valid and do not perform illegal operations (e.g., forged pointers, access restriction violations, illegal object casting). Finally, rather than crashing, the JVM will propagate an exception up the calling chain until it is caught (if not caught in the code, the JVM itself will handle the error without crashing). Thus, a poorly written or malicious servlet cannot crash the server.[1]

Cross Platform

Because servlets are written completely in Java, they enjoy the same cross-platform support as any Java program. This "write once, run anywhere" capability allows servlets to be distributed easily throughout an enterprise without rewriting for each platform. Servlets operate identically without modification whether they are running on UNIX, Windows, or any other Java-enabled operating system.

NOTE: Currently, there are some areas in which Java falls short of the "write once, run anywhere" promise. For instance, the GUI is a common area wherein some Java programs may require modification in order to run on different platforms. However, since they do not present a graphical interface to the user, servlets provide more consistent cross-platform support than graphics-intensive Java applications.

Cross Server

Servlets can be run on virtually every popular Web server in use today. Dozens of major software vendors currently provide native support for servlets in their products, including the IBM WebSphere Application Server, Bluestone Sapphire Web, Apache Tomcat, ATG Dynamo Application Server, BEA WebLogic Application Server, Inprise Application Server, Oracle Application Server, SilverStream Application Server, and iPlanet Web Server (see *http://java.sun.com/ products/servlet/runners.html* for a more comprehensive list). For those servers that do not currently offer native servlet support, there are many third-party add-ons that allow these servers to load and run servlets. For example, servlet containers such as JRun from Allaire and ServletExec from New Atlanta Communications add servlet support to many popular Web servers, including Microsoft Internet Information Server, Netscape Enterprise Server, and Apache Web Server.

---

1. Creating a crash-proof servlet environment requires a properly configured Java security manager. For instance, the security manager used by the servlet container should not allow servlets to call the System.exit() method.

Durable

Servlets are durable objects. *Durable* means that they remain in memory until there is a specific instruction to destroy them. In this way, servlets need to be instantiated only once in order to service many requests. In addition, a servlet can create other objects that also endure across multiple requests. For instance, it is common for a servlet to create a pool of database connections when it is first loaded. These connections can then be shared across all requests.

Dynamically Loadable across the Network

Similar to applets, servlets can be dynamically loaded either locally or from across the network. Dynamic loading ensures that unused servlets do not consume precious server resources. They are loaded only when needed. Fortunately, for performance reasons it is also possible to instruct the server to load a servlet at start-up rather than when it is first invoked.

The ability to load servlets across the network is a great advantage for distributed computing environments. Rather than having to copy each servlet and all modifications to every server, servlets can be dynamically loaded from a remote location on the network. And similar to applets, servlets can run in a secure sandbox on the server to ensure security and stability.

Easily Deployed

Unlike many competing technologies, servlets have a standard deployment model that allows a servlet application to essentially install itself (by automatically conveying all necessary installation parameters to the server). Introduced in Servlet API 2.2, this new deployment model greatly simplifies and standardizes the packaging and deployment of servlets through a concept known as Web applications. A *Web application* is a collection of servlets, JavaServer Pages, HTML documents, utility classes, images, and other resources that comprise a Web site or other networked application. An entire Web application can be packaged in a single *Web application archive* file ending with a .war extension. By using a Web application archive, step-by-step user installation instructions can be replaced by a *deployment descriptor* file that instructs the Java-enabled server exactly how to install the application without user assistance. Web archives allow an entire application, including the deployment descriptor, to be distributed easily within a single file. Simply drop the .war file in the right directory and register it with an administration utility, and the application is ready to service requests. For more information on servlet packaging and deployment, see Chapter 19.

Extensible

Because servlets are written in Java, there is a wealth of third-party support for writing and extending them. New development tools, Java class libraries, and database drivers are constantly becoming available and they all can be utilized by servlets.

Multithreaded

Java was designed to be a multithreaded language. Unlike C or C++, threading mechanisms are inherent in the Java language and the thread synchronization syntax is consistent across platforms. Since servlets are written in Java, they support multithreaded functionality. The multithreaded nature of servlets allows client requests to be handled by separate threads within a single process. This approach requires far less overhead and executes much more quickly than the alternative—creating a new process for every request.

Object Oriented

Servlets provide an extremely simple and elegant architecture in which to develop networked applications. This is primarily due to the fact that the Servlet API encapsulates all essential information and functionality into well-designed objects. For example, the Servlet API provides classes that conveniently abstract objects such as requests, responses, sessions, and cookies. These objects provide simple access to information and functionality through basic method calls.

Protocol Independent

Though servlets are commonly used to extend HTTP server functionality, they are by no means limited to this protocol. On the contrary, servlets are completely protocol independent. Protocol independence allows a servlet to be constructed to support FTP commands, SMTP or POP3 e-mail functionality, Telnet sessions, NNTP newsgroups, or any other protocol (whether standard or created by the servlet developer). The Servlet API provides strong support for common HTTP functionality without sacrificing the ability to support other protocols.

Secure

Servlets are secure in several ways. In particular, three important features ensure servlet security. First, because servlets are written in Java, invalid memory access calls and strong typing violations are not possible. Second, servlets use the server's *security manager* for the customization and enforcement of specific security policies. For instance, a properly configured security manager can restrict network or file access for an untrusted servlet. On the other hand, the security manager may grant full rights to a local or digitally signed and trusted servlet. Third, a servlet has access to all information contained in each client request. This information includes HTTP authentication data. When used in conjunction with secure protocols like SSL, servlets can positively verify the identity of every client. These three features combine to make servlets more secure than API server extensions or CGI.

Written in Java

Because servlets are written in Java, they are afforded many advantages provided by the Java language and Java virtual machine. A few of these advantages include support for true object-oriented programming (providing extensibility and simplified code maintenance), strong type checking, full multithreading support, built-in security, optimized code compilation, automatic garbage collection, internationalization through Unicode support, built-in network support, and "write once, run anywhere" cross-platform and cross-server support. And since Java does not support pointers, difficult-to-find pointer bugs, along with the security and stability risks they present, are eliminated from your code. Lastly, servlets can use any of the existing Java APIs. Just a few of these APIs include JDBC for database access, RMI for remote method calls, JNDI for directory services, JavaMail for sending e-mail, and JavaIDL for calling CORBA services.

Where Do Servlets Fit In?

You may be wondering where servlets fit in with regard to the standard Java classes. The answer is that the Servlet API is considered a *Java standard extension* to the Java 2 Platform, Standard Edition (J2SE). All Java standard extensions are located in the `javax` package. The servlet packages include `javax.servlet` and `javax.servlet.http` (as well as `javax.servlet.jsp` and `javax.servlet.jsp.tagext` for JavaServer Pages). In contrast to the core Java packages, standard extensions are not required to be supported by every Java environment. The Servlet API is available as a stand-alone Java library from Sun Microsystems and is also distributed as part of the open source Apache Tomcat project. Tomcat is the official reference implementation for the Servlet API and JavaServer Pages. You can download the Servlet API library from *http://java.sun.com/products/servlet/*. Similarly, the Servlet API can be downloaded as a part of Tomcat from *http://jakarta.apache.org/tomcat/*.

On the other hand, unlike the Standard Edition, the Servlet API is a required member of the Java 2 Platform, Enterprise Edition (J2EE), and is included in the Java 2 SDK, Enterprise Edition, distribution (see *http://java.sun.com/j2ee/* for more information). All J2EE-compliant servers must provide full support for Java servlets.

What Can Servlets Do?

Servlets extend a server's functionality in almost any way imaginable. Similar to CGI, they allow true two-way interaction between the client and server. The following are just a few of the many possibilities provided by servlets:

- Dynamically build and return an HTML file based on the nature of the client's request
- Process user input passed by an HTML form and return an appropriate response
- Facilitate communication among groups of people by publishing information submitted by many clients (e.g., an online bulletin board system)
- Provide user authentication and other security mechanisms
- Interact with server resources such as databases, other applications, and files to return useful information to the client
- Process input from many clients for interaction among peers for applications such as multiplayer games
- Allow the server to communicate with a client applet via a custom protocol and keep the connection open throughout the conversation
- Automatically attach Web page design elements, such as headers or footers, to all pages returned by the server
- Forward requests from one server to another for load-balancing purposes
- Partition a single logical service across servers or between servlets in order to process a task most efficiently
- Virtually any other way you can imagine to enhance or extend a server

Why Are Servlets Better Than CGI?

Servlets offer advantages over CGI in the areas of performance, portability, and security. Each of these advantages will be discussed in turn.

Performance is perhaps the most visible difference between servlets and CGI. Since servlets typically run in the same process space as the server and are loaded only once, they are able to respond much more quickly and efficiently to client requests. In contrast, CGI must create a new process to service each new request. The overhead involved with creating a new process incurs a significant performance penalty.

Figure 4.1 illustrates how a Java-enabled server spawns a new thread within its process space for each request and a CGI-based server creates a new process for every request. In addition, the majority of Web sites today are database driven. Since a new process must be created for each request, database-driven pages require a new database connection with every request. Unlike servlets, CGI cannot share a single database connection or pool of connections across multiple requests.

Portability is another strong advantage enjoyed by servlets. Unlike many CGI applications, servlets can run on different servers and platforms without modification (similar to many Perl scripts). This characteristic can be extremely important when building enterprise-wide distributed applications.

Lastly, servlets are much more secure than CGI. Although CGI scripts can be written in Java, they are often written in more error-prone languages such as C. Since C programs can inadvertently or maliciously access invalid memory

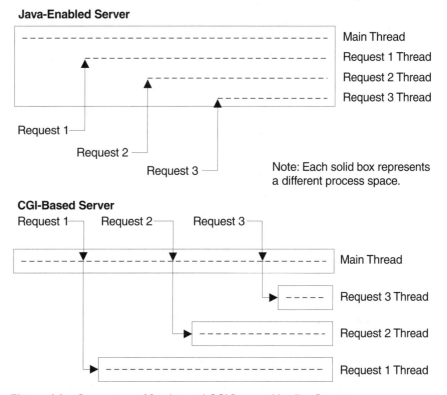

Figure 4.1   Comparison of Servlets and CGI Request-Handling Process

locations, CGI programs are less secure. In addition, similar to the manner in which applets run in a browser, untrusted servlets run inside a sandbox on the server. This *sandbox* is a protected memory space wherein a program cannot access outside resources such as file or network services. Of course, these restrictions can be lifted according to the security policies set by the Java security manager.

FastCGI

FastCGI is an innovation originally developed by a company called Open Market that addresses some of CGI's most serious performance flaws. For instance, in contrast to traditional CGI, FastCGI creates a single persistent process for each FastCGI application (see Figure 4.2). This process endures between requests, thus eliminating the excessive overhead of creating a new process for every request. Though it's better than CGI, FastCGI suffers from some performance problems of its own. For example, unlike servlets, FastCGI requires at least one process for every program and each process can service only one request at a time. To service concurrent requests, a pool of processes must be created (one for each request). As you can imagine, the number of processes required to support a popular FastCGI-based Web site can grow rather quickly. Though FastCGI improves upon standard CGI, it still cannot match the performance and efficiency of single-process, multithreaded Java servlets.[2]

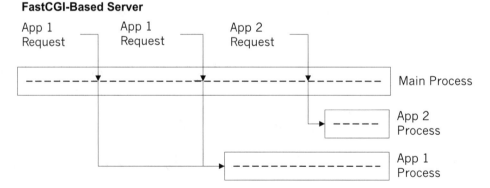

FastCGI-Based Server

Note: Each dotted line represents a single thread.

Figure 4.2   FastCGI Request-Handling Process

---

2. Actually, though many servers run servlets within their own process space, this is not always the case. Some multiprocess servers may run servlets in a JVM outside their own process. This method requires a heavyweight context switch, but it is still more efficient than FastCGI because all servlets share the same external process.

NSAPI/ISAPI

Nestcape Server API (NSAPI) and Microsoft's Internet Server API (ISAPI) are both proprietary application programming interfaces for extending the functionality of an HTTP server. These APIs provide better performance and are much more tightly integrated with the Web server than CGI. Applications written to these APIs usually perform comparably to servlets or even faster. The primary drawback to these proprietery extensions is the fact that they are tied to particular HTTP servers or platforms. For instance, ISAPI is supported primarily by the Microsoft Internet Information Server (IIS) running on the Windows NT/2000 platform.[3] Similarly, NSAPI applications are compatible with only a few select Web servers from Netscape/iPlanet. In addition, even though NSAPI servers are available on both Windows and UNIX, since most NSAPI programs are written in C or another language that requires compilation to native code, these applications must be recompiled for each new platform.

Servlets have a couple of strong advantages over proprietary APIs like NSAPI and ISAPI. First, the Servlet API is an industry standard that has been adopted by many server vendors. These vendors have developed numerous Servlet API–compatible servers running on multiple platforms. Second, since Java bytecodes are executed by a virtual machine, compiled servlets can be deployed across servers and platforms without recompilation.

Summary

The purpose of this chapter is to present an introduction to servlets: what they are and how they can be used. In the coming chapters, we will abandon the "high-level" descriptions and move into the specifics of servlet implementation. In the next chapter, we will see exactly what a servlet looks like and start writing code—beginning with your first "Hello World" servlet.

Chapter Highlights

- A *servlet* is a server-side software component, written in Java, that dynamically extends the functionality of a server.
- Unlike applets, servlets do not display a graphical interface to the user.

---

3. In fact, a few companies other than Microsoft have added ISAPI support to their Web servers. However, Microsoft's IIS running under Windows is far and away the dominant ISAPI-compatible server and platform.

- Servlets offer many advantages over traditional Web development technologies. They are capable of running in-process, compiled, cross-platform, cross-server, dynamically loadable across the network, multithreaded, protocol independent, secure, crash resistant, and written in Java.

- Beginning with Java 2, servlets are considered *Java standard extensions*.

- Servlets offer advantages over CGI in the areas of performance, portability, and security.

- Though FastCGI improves upon standard CGI, it still cannot match the performance and efficiency of single-process, multithreaded Java servlets.

- Servlets have a couple of strong advantages over proprietary APIs like NSAPI and ISAPI. First, the Servlet API is an industry standard that has been adopted by many server vendors. Second, since Java bytecodes are executed by a virtual machine, compiled servlets can be deployed across servers and platforms without recompilation.

CHAPTER 5

Servlet Basics

Once you begin writing them, you will quickly notice that servlets handle request/respond operations in an extremely clean, simple, and efficient manner. The Servlet API interface provides an intuitive framework for extending the functionality of Java-enabled servers. Although learning to use servlets can be relatively quick and easy, do not be fooled by their simplicity. Servlets offer significant power and flexibility for building networked applications.

This chapter focuses on the structure and syntax of servlets and the manner in which they are invoked. Specifically, the following topics are covered:

- Basic servlet structure
- Servlet lifecycle
- Servlet reloading
- Dissecting two sample servlets

On completion of this chapter you should understand the structure of a simple servlet and the process by which it is called.

Basic Servlet Structure

Before we examine our first functional servlet, let's take a moment to discuss the basic structure of a servlet. As we begin examining servlets, you will quickly notice that they are basic Java classes similar to others you may have written. The only difference is that they extend new classes and implement some unfamiliar methods. Fortunately, servlets are as simple to write as any other Java program. You just have to learn the servlet structure and a new class library.

Practically all servlets that perform some useful function have two things in common. First, they all extend one of two servlet classes—`GenericServlet` or HttpServlet.[1] Extending these classes provides a framework for creating a servlet as well as significant default functionality. We will discuss these classes in more detail later in this chapter. Second, all servlets override at least one method wherein custom functionality is implemented. The method that is automatically called by the server in response to each client request is called service(). This method may be overridden to provide custom functionality. However, for servlets that extend HttpServlet, the servlet developer may choose not to override the service() method. In this case, the default service() implementation will automatically invoke another method in response to a client request (based on the type of HTTP request received). We will discuss these methods a little later.

In addition to the classes and methods mentioned previously, two other methods are implemented by most servlets—init() and destroy(). The init() method is called a single time when the servlet is first loaded. It is similar to a constructor in that it provides a method wherein initialization code is guaranteed to be run. The destroy() method is executed when the servlet is unloaded. It is used to free any resources held by the servlet.

Based on this brief description concerning the structure of a servlet, let's construct the skeleton of a common servlet. For simplicity, the skeleton servlet that follows does not include parameters passed to the methods or exceptions that are thrown. These details will be presented shortly.

```
public class SkeletonServlet extends HttpServlet
{
  public void init()
  {
    //initialization code goes here
  }

  public void service()
  {
    //meaningful work happens here
  }

  public void destroy()
  {
    //resources are released here
  }
}
```

Now that doesn't look too difficult. Of course, the actual implementation of different servlets may vary widely. For example, servlets may or may not

1. Actually, a servlet is not required to extend GenericServlet or HttpServlet. An advanced developer can create a servlet by implementing the Servlet interface and thus bypass the need to extend one of these two classes. Extending GenericServlet or HttpServlet is, however, the simplest and most common way to build a servlet.

implement the init() or destroy() methods. Implementation of these methods is not mandatory for servlets that extend GenericServlet or HttpServlet (since GenericServlet and HttpServlet provide default implementations of these methods). Likewise, if the servlet extends HttpServlet, the servlet developer may choose not to override the service() method and opt to implement another method that is automatically called by the inherited service() method. Similar to service(), this method would implement the servlet's unique functionality. The method automatically called by service() depends on the type of HTTP request received (e.g., doGet() is called for GET requests and doPost() for POST requests). However, regardless of these differences, the basic structure is similar to almost any servlet you might see or write. More details regarding these classes and methods (including the methods' parameters) are presented later in this chapter.

NOTE: The terms *server, Java-enabled server,* and *servlet container* are often used interchangeably throughout the text. Therefore, we'd better define these terms.

A *servlet container* (formerly known as a *servlet engine*) is the software that actually executes servlets. All servers that support servlets include a servlet container (either integrated or via an add-on). The term *Java-enabled server* is often used to denote a servlet-enhanced HTTP server (i.e., it includes a servlet container for running servlets). Finally, the term *server* may be used occasionally with the understanding that it supports servlets via an integrated or add-on servlet container.

Servlet Lifecycle

Now that you have seen the basic structure of a servlet, let's review the process by which a server invokes a servlet. This process can be broken down into these eight steps.

1. The server loads the servlet when it is first requested by a client or, if configured to do so, at server start-up. The servlet may be loaded from either a local or a remote location using a custom Java class-loading facility (designed to allow automatic servlet reloading). This step is equivalent to the following Java code:

```
Class c = Class.forName("com.sourcestream.MyServlet");
```

Note that, when referring to servlets, the term *load* often refers to the process of both loading and instantiating the servlet.

2. The server creates one instance of the servlet class to service all requests.[2] Utilizing multiple threads, concurrent requests can be serviced by a single servlet instance. The only exception to this rule is that, for servlets that implement the `SingleThreadModel` interface (see Chapter 11), the server may create a pool of instances from which one is chosen to service each new request. This step is equivalent to the following Java code:

```
Servlet s = (Servlet)c.newInstance();
```

3. The server calls the servlet's `init()` method, which is guaranteed to finish execution prior to the servlet processing of the first request. If the server has created multiple servlet instances (step 2), the `init()` method is called one time for each instance.

4. The server constructs a `ServletRequest` or `HttpServletRequest` object from the data included in the client's request. It also constructs a `Servlet-Response` or `HttpServletResponse` object that provides methods for returning a response. The parameter type depends on whether the servlet extends `GenericServlet` or `HttpServlet`, respectively. Note that this step, along with steps 5 through 7, may never occur if the server does not receive a request for this servlet.

5. The server calls the servlet's `service()` method (which, for HTTP servlets, may call a more specific method such as `doGet()` or `doPost()`), passing the objects constructed in step 5 as parameters. When concurrent requests arrive, multiple `service()` methods can run simultaneously in separate threads (unless the servlet implements the `SingleThreadModel` interface).

6. The `service()` method processes the client's request by evaluating the `ServletRequest` or `HttpServletRequest` object, and it responds using the `ServletResponse` or `HttpServletResponse` object.

7. If the server receives another request for this servlet, the process begins again at step 5.

8. Whenever the servlet container determines that a servlet should be unloaded, perhaps to reclaim some resources or because it is being shut down, the server calls the servlet's `destroy()` method after allowing all of the sevlet's `service()` threads to complete (or after a server-defined time limit). The servlet is then eligible for garbage collection. The servlet container is not required to keep a servlet loaded for any specific amount of time.

---

2. Prior to version 2.2, the Servlet API did not specify the number of servlet instances that should be created when a servlet is loaded. This detail was left to the server, which may have created a single instance (most common) or a pool of instances. Servlets that implement the `SingleThreadModel` interface are an exception to this rule.

These eight steps illustrate the entire lifecycle of a servlet. Though the lifecycle described here is consistent across all Java-enabled servers, specifics not defined in the Java Servlet Specification may be implemented by different servers in a slightly different way. For instance, the manner in which servers are administrated may differ greatly. Regardless, the steps listed previously should give you a good understanding of the servlet lifecycle. Figure 5.1 shows the flow of the servlet lifecycle.

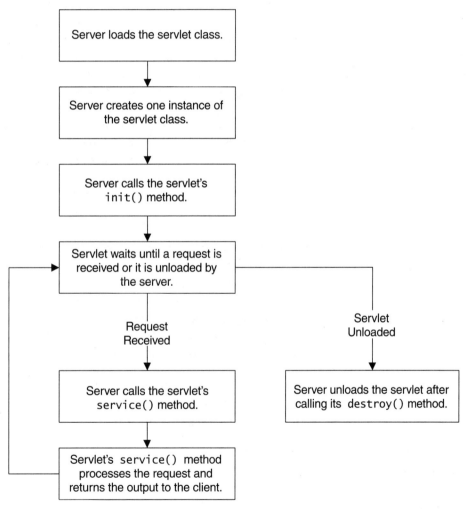

Figure 5.1 The Servlet Lifecycle

Servlet Reloading

Many servlet containers support a feature known as automatic servlet reloading. *Servlet reloading* is the process of detecting changes to servlets and automatically reloading any that have changed. This feature can be very useful during the development and test phases of a project because it allows you to recompile and test servlets without having to shut down and restart the server each time.

Servlet reloading can be extremely useful, but there are two caveats. First, detecting changes to a servlet each time it is called can incur a significant performance penalty. To avoid this performance degradation, it is recommended that servlet reloading be disabled in a production environment. Second, servlet reloading is accomplished by using a new Java `ClassLoader` object to load the altered servlet. In some cases, loading a class from a new `ClassLoader` can result in cast errors when utilizing the reloaded classes.

Finally, though we usually think of servlets when discussing the process of servlet reloading, some servlet servers will also reload any support classes as long as they reside in the servlet directory (if they have changed). Classes that reside in the system or the server's CLASSPATH are not automatically reloaded. For example, the Apache Tomcat server standard installation places a number of sample servlets in the following directory:

/jakarta-tomcat/webapps/examples/WEB-INF/classes

In addition to */WEB-INF/classes*, any classes added to the */jakarta-tomcat/classes* directory are also included in the Tomcat CLASSPATH. However, the difference between these two directories is the fact that any support classes contained in the */jakarta-tomcat/webapps/examples/WEB-INF/classes* directory are automatically reloaded when changed (if servlet reloading is enabled). On the other hand, Tomcat 3.1 does not detect changes to classes in the */jakarta-tomcat/classes* directory and will not automatically reload them. Any changes to these classes require shutting down the server and restarting it. Since servlet reloading is implementation specific, be sure to examine the documentation included with your server or servlet container regarding the rules governing the servlet reloading process.

Dissecting Two Sample Servlets

By this point you are probably anxious to see what a real servlet looks like. Let's alleviate your anxiety right now by looking at two examples.

Generic Servlet

Unlike HTTP servlets, generic servlets are not specific to a particular protocol. Generic servlets, or servlets that extend the `GenericServlet` class, are most often used to build networked applications that employ a custom protocol or some other non-HTTP protocol such as FTP or POP3. Listing 5.1 demonstrates a simple generic servlet that returns the current time of day at the server.

Listing 5.1   Time servlet returns time of day.

```
import javax.servlet.*;

/**
 * Time Servlet
 *
 * This servlet returns the time of day at the server.
 */
public class TimeServlet extends GenericServlet
{
   /**
    * The server calls the service() method in response to each
    * servlet request.
    */
   public void service(ServletRequest request,
      ServletResponse response) throws ServletException,
      java.io.IOException
   {
      //get a handle to the client output stream
      java.io.PrintWriter out = response.getWriter();

      //print the current time and date to the output stream
      out.println(new java.util.Date());
   }
}
```

If you would like to run this servlet right now, feel free to jump ahead briefly to Chapter 8, Running Servlets. The servlet can be tested using a browser (as described in Chapter 8) or you might want to try the `GetTime` class presented in Listing 1.1 of Chapter 1. The output from this servlet, as rendered by a browser, is shown in Figure 5.2.

The servlet can be compiled just like any other Java application as long as the `servlet.jar` file is in the CLASSPATH. The `servlet.jar` file contains all of the classes and interfaces that make up the Servlet API. This file is part of the Apache Tomcat project available at *http://jakarta.apache.org/tomcat/* and is also included in the Java 2 SDK, Enterprise Edition, available at *http://java.sun.com/j2ee/*. To illustrate, this servlet can be compiled from the command line using a command similar to the following:

```
javac -classpath /tomcat/lib/servlet.jar TimeServlet.java
```

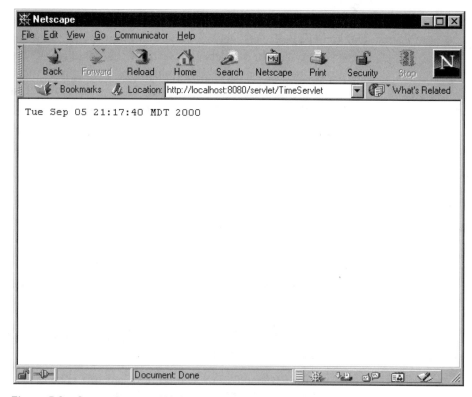

Figure 5.2   Output Generated by Servlet Presented in Listing 5.1

Now that you know what a simple servlet looks like, let's examine a basic HTTP servlet in much more detail.

Http Servlet

HTTP servlets, or servlets that extend the HttpServlet class, are used to build Web applications that typically return HTML, XHTML, WML, or XML documents in response to browser requests (though images or any other type of content may also be returned). The HttpServlet class extends GenericServlet and, therefore, inherits all of its functionality. In addition, HttpServlet adds HTTP-specific functionality and provides a framework in which to build HTTP applications. The HTTP servlet in Listing 5.2 returns HTML containing the canonical phrase "Hello World" and the number of times it has been requested. When unloaded, it writes to a file the number of times it has been called in order to keep a running count even when the server is restarted. The servlet response is shown in Figure 5.3.

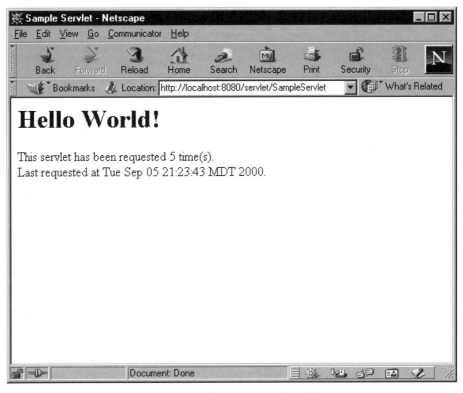

Figure 5.3   Output Generated by Servlet Presented in Listing 5.2

Listing 5.2   A simple "Hello World" servlet.

```
import javax.servlet.*;
import javax.servlet.http.*;
import java.io.*;
import java.util.*;

/**
 * Sample Servlet
 *
 * This servlet returns "Hello World" and the number of times
 * the servlet has been requested.
 */
public class SampleServlet extends HttpServlet
{
  int numRequests = 0; //number of times servlet requested
  String lastRequest = (new Date()).toString(); //last request
  Properties prop = null;
```

```java
/**
 * init() is called when the servlet is first loaded. Use this
 * method to initialize resources.
 *
 * This method reads (from a properties file) the number of
 * times the servlet has been requested and initializes the
 * numRequests variable.
 */
public void init() throws ServletException
{
  prop = new Properties(); //create new Properties object

  try
  {
    //create a file object pointing to the properties file
    File file = new File("SampleServlet.properties");

    //determine if the properties file exists
    if (file.exists())
    {
      //get an input stream to the properties file
      FileInputStream fileIn = new FileInputStream(file);

      prop.load(fileIn); //load the properties object from file

      //initialize the numRequests variable, default to zero
      numRequests = Integer.parseInt(
        prop.getProperty("RequestCount", "0"));

      //initialize lastRequest, default to current date/time
      lastRequest = prop.getProperty("LastRequest",
        (new Date()).toString());
    }
    else
    {
      //properties file doesn't exist, use default values
    }
  }
  catch (Exception e)
  {
    //if unable to read file, use default values
  }
}


/**
 * service() is called with each client request.
 */
public void service(HttpServletRequest request,
  HttpServletResponse response) throws ServletException,
  IOException
{
  //set MIME type for HTTP header to HTML
  response.setContentType("text/html");
```

```
//get a handle to the output stream
PrintWriter out = response.getWriter();

//send HTML response to client
out.println("<HTML>");
out.println("<HEAD><TITLE>Sample Servlet</TITLE></HEAD>");
out.println("<BODY>");
out.println("<H1>Hello World!</H1>");
out.println("<P>This servlet has been requested " +
  numRequests++ + " time(s).");
out.println("<BR>Last requested at " + lastRequest + ".");
out.println("</BODY></HTML>");

lastRequest = (new Date()).toString(); //update last request

out.close(); //always close the output stream
}


/**
 * getServletInfo() allows the server to query this servlet for
 * information regarding its name, version, and brief
 * description.
 */
public String getServletInfo()
{
  return "Sample Servlet version 1.0";
}


/**
 * Destroy is called before the server unloads the servlet. Use
 * this method to release any resources held by the servlet and
 * other housekeeping chores.
 *
 * This method stores (in a properties file) the number of
 * times the servlet has been requested.
 */
public void destroy()
{
  try
  {
    //create a file object pointing to the properties file
    File file = new File("SampleServlet.properties");

    //get an output stream to the properties file
    FileOutputStream fileOut = new FileOutputStream(file);

    //store the request count in the properties object
    prop.put("RequestCount", Integer.toString(numRequests));

    //store the last request date/time in the properties object
    prop.put("LastRequest", lastRequest);
```

```
      //write the properties object data to the properties file
      prop.store(fileOut, "SampleServlet Storage File");
    }
    catch (Exception e)
    {
      //if there is an error writing to file, ignore it
    }
  }
}
```

Let's take a closer look at each part of the sample servlet, starting with the imports:

```
import javax.servlet.*;
import javax.servlet.http.*;
import java.io.*;
import java.util.*;
```

The entire Servlet API is contained in two packages: `javax.servlet` and `javax.servlet.http`. You will use classes from both of these packages in every one of your HTTP servlets. Non-HTTP servlets do not require classes from the `javax.servlet.http` package.

The simplest way to ensure that you have imported the proper servlet classes is to use the "`*`" wildcard as shown in the preceding imports (this style is used regularly throughout the book). However, in order to provide better code documentation and simplify debugging, it is often a good idea to specifically import each class. In this way, there is no question concerning which classes are being imported or which package contains a particular class. The following import statements document the package in which each class is contained.

```
import javax.servlet.ServletConfig;
import javax.servlet.ServletException;
import javax.servlet.http.HttpServlet;
import javax.servlet.http.HttpServletRequest;
import javax.servlet.http.HttpServletResponse;
import java.io.PrintWriter;
import java.io.IOException;
import java.io.File;
import java.io.FileInputStream;
import java.io.FileOutputStream;
import java.util.Properties;
import java.util.Date;
```

The class declaration is the next important part of this servlet:

```
public class SampleServlet extends HttpServlet
```

Every servlet that you write will either extend the `GenericServlet` or

HttpServlet class or implement the Servlet interface. Although it is possible to write servlets by implementing the Servlet interface, this practice is rarely necessary. Almost any servlet that you care to write can be implemented more easily by extending either GenericServlet or HttpServlet, each of which implements the Servlet interface. As previously mentioned, the HttpServlet class contains methods specific to the HTTP protocol. The GenericServlet class is useful when building non-HTTP servlets such as those that implement FTP, POP3, SMTP, or any custom protocol. In this book we focus primarily on developing HTTP servlets through extending the HttpServlet class.

The sample servlet's superclass, HttpServlet, provides a number of methods that may be overridden in order to implement custom functionality. Four of the most basic methods defined by HttpServlet are used in Listing 5.1: init(), service(), getServletInfo(), and destroy().

init() Method

```
public void init() throws ServletException
```

When the servlet is first loaded, the server executes the init() method exactly once. The init() method is guaranteed to be exectued prior to the servlet receiving its first request. After instantiation, the servlet resides in memory until explicitly unloaded by the server. Although only one instance is created, the servlet is capable of servicing multiple concurrent requests.[3] This is due to the fact that the server spawns a new thread (or retrieves one from a thread pool) for each call to the service() method (allowing multiple service() methods to execute simultaneously).

The init() method is ideal for initializing resources that are shared by servlet requests. For instance, it is common to establish database or network connections within the init() method. Once opened, these connections can be shared across all requests and the overhead required to open the connection is incurred only once. All shared resources, such as instance and class variables, are accessible by every servlet invocation and visible to all requests. Keep in mind, however, that a servlet's service() method (including methods called by service() such as doGet() and doPost()) may be executed simultaneously by multiple threads. Therefore, any shared objects created in the init() method must either be inherently thread safe or be used in a thread-safe manner. (See Chapter 11 for more information on writing thread-safe servlets.)

In the case of an error, ServletException is thrown by the init() method and is handled by the parent class (ServletException is discussed in Chapter 10).

---

3. There is a way to prevent the server from spawning a new thread for each request. This is accomplished by implementing the SingleThreadModel interface, in which case the server will create a pool of servlet instances to service concurrent requests. When multiple instances are created, the server calls the init() method of each servlet instance. The SingleThreadModel is discussed in Chapter 11.

Since the server must be able to call the init() method when the servlet is first loaded, the method is declared public.

NOTE: If an error occurs during initialization that prevents the servlet from properly responding to client requests, UnavailableException should be thrown. All errors should be handled in the servlet or thrown to the parent class. The System.exit() method should never be called. If a properly configured security manager is used, the container will throw a SecurityException whenever System.exit() is invoked by a servlet. Conversely, calling System.exit() within a servlet container that does not enforce strict security policies may shut down the Java virtual machine and disable the container.

Actually, there are two init() methods defined by GenericServlet (and inherited by HttpServlet). Early versions of the Servlet API defined only one init() method, which has the following signature:

```
public void init(ServletConfig config) throws ServletException
```

Originally, the reason that this method existed was to allow the servlet access to the ServletConfig object (used to retrieve initialization parameters and other information about the servlet's environment). However, this method is somewhat inconvenient to use because once the the ServletConfig object is received, it must then be passed to the servlet's parent class. This is due to the fact that the GenericServlet object's init(ServletConfig) method stores the Servlet-Config object and makes it accessible via the getServletConfig() method. Therefore, if the ServletConfig object is not passed to the GenericServlet parent class, it will not be accessible to the service() or destroy() methods and getServletConfig() will always return null (unless the servlet developer stores the ServletConfig object and implements the getServletConfig() method himself). Consequently, when using the init(ServletConfig) method, it is recommended that the ServletConfig object always be passed to the parent class by using code similar to the following.

```
public void init(ServletConfig config) throws ServletException
{
  super.init(config); //pass the ServletConfig object to parent
}
```

Passing the ServletConfig object along doesn't require a lot of typing, but it can become tedious and can lead to errors if omitted. Fortunately, Servlet API 2.1 added a parameterless init() method that makes the developer's job a little easier. This convenience method frees the developer from having to store the ServletConfig object (and implement the getServletConfig() method) or call super.init(config).

NOTE: The server always calls the servlet's init(ServletConfig) method regardless of which init() method is overridden by the developer. If the developer chooses to override the init() method rather than init(ServletConfig), the servlet's init(ServletConfig) method inherited from GenericServlet will still be executed. This method stores the ServletConfig object (making it accessible via the getServletConfig() method) and then calls the parameterless init() method. Since init() is always called (even if not overridden by the developer), the GenericServlet itself defines a parameterless init() method but provides no implementation for it (it performs no work). Of course, if the developer overrides init(), this method will be called rather than the default implementation provided by the GenericServlet object. The following code illustrates how these methods are implemented by GenericServlet.

```
private transient ServletConfig config;

public void init(ServletConfig config) throws ServletException
{
  this.config = config;
  log("init");
  this.init();
}

public void init() throws ServletException
{
}

public ServletConfig getServletConfig()
{
  return config;
}
```

Although two init() methods exist, the parameterless version is recommended. There is really no reason to use the init(ServletConfig) method, unless backward compatability with prior versions of the Servlet API is required.

NOTE: It is possible to retrieve the ServletConfig object (i.e., an object that implements the ServletConfig interface) using the getServletConfig() method, but this is not really necessary since the GenericServlet class implements the

ServletConfig interface itself. Therefore, any method defined by the Servlet-Config interface can be called directly without first having to obtain a reference to the ServletConfig object. For example, the following code reads an initialization parameter (defined by the ServletConfig interface) within the parameterless init() method.

```
public void init() throws ServletException
{
  String rootPath = getInitParameter("Root");
}
```

Now that we have thoroughly covered the init() method, let's take a look at its implementation in the sample servlet. The whole init() method from SampleServlet looks like this:

```
public void init() throws ServletException
{
  prop = new Properties(); //create new Properties object

  try
  {
    //create a file object pointing to the properties file
    File file = new File("SampleServlet.properties");

    //determine if the properties file exists
    if (file.exists())
    {
      //get an input stream to the properties file
      FileInputStream fileIn = new FileInputStream(file);

      prop.load(fileIn); //load the properties object from file

      //initialize the numRequests variable, default to zero
      numRequests = Integer.parseInt(
        prop.getProperty("RequestCount", "0"));

      //initialize lastRequest, default to current date/time
      lastRequest = prop.getProperty("LastRequest",
        (new Date()).toString());
    }
    else
    {
      //properties file doesn't exist, use default values
    }
  }
  catch (Exception e)
  {
    //if unable to read file, use default values
  }
}
```

The code within the `init()` method begins by instantiating a `Properties` object that is used to store the number of times the servlet has been requested and the date and time of the last request. `Properties` objects have the ability to load their values from a basic text file known as a *properties file*. Likewise, after they have been populated with information, `Properties` objects can store their contents to a properties file to ensure data persistence. The contents of the properties file, called *SampleServlet.properties,* created by this servlet looks like this (the spaces and colons are escaped to maintain their literal value):

```
#SampleServlet Storage File
#Tue Sep 05 19:44:19 MST 2000
LastRequest=Tue\ Sep\ 05\ 19\:44\:19\ MST\ 2000
RequestCount=5
```

Next, the `init()` method creates a `File` object that represents the properties file and verifies that the file exists (if not, the `numRequests` and `lastRequest` variables will simply retain their default values). A `FileInputStream` is then created, and it is used by the `Properties` object to load its values from the properties file. Finally, the `numRequests` and `lastRequest` variables are initialized using the values read from the properties file.

`service()` Method

```
public void service(HttpServletRequest request,
   HttpServletResponse response) throws ServletException,
   java.io.IOException
```

The server calls the `service()` method whenever it has a request for the servlet to process. This method accepts two parameters. The first parameter is an object that implements the `HttpServletRequest` interface. This parameter is an object representation of the client's request. All relevant data in the request (such as HTTP headers) is encapsulated within the `HttpServletRequest` object. This data is accessible via the methods defined by `HttpServletRequest`.

The second parameter is an object that implements the `HttpServletResponse` interface. This parameter is an object representation of the server's response to the client. The servlet can customize the response by calling the appropriate `HttpServletResponse` methods. When working with network requests and responses, an `IOException` might occur at any time. This exception should not be caught by the servlet. Rather, it should be thrown by the `service()` method. An `IOException` should always be handled by the server.

Since the server must be able to call the `service()` method whenever a servlet request is received, the method is declared `public`. In addition to `service()`, more specific methods may be called when a servlet request is received. In fact, when writing HTTP servlets, it is advisable to use the specific

HTTP request methods, such as doGet() or doPost(), rather than override the generic service() method. (These specific methods are discussed in the next chapter.) The service() method is used in this example to familiarize the reader with its function; however, it is used sparingly in future HTTP servlet examples.

NOTE: Be sure to examine the difference between the service() methods for both types of servlets—generic and HTTP. The syntax of the service() methods for the generic servlet and the HTTP servlet, respectively, are shown here:

```
public void service(ServletRequest request, ServletResponse
    response) throws ServletException, java.io.IOException
```

```
public void service(HttpServletRequest request,
    HttpServletResponse response) throws ServletException,
    java.io.IOException
```

The difference lies in the parameters. A generic servlet receives ServletRequest and ServletResponse parameters rather than HttpServlet-Request and HttpServletResponse. HttpServletRequest and HttpServlet-Response are subinterfaces of ServletRequest and ServletResponse, respectively.

The following lines are executed inside the service() method.

```
//set MIME type for HTTP header to HTML
response.setContentType("text/html");

//get a handle to the output stream
PrintWriter out = response.getWriter();

//send HTML response to client
out.println("<HTML>");
out.println("<HEAD><TITLE>Sample Servlet</TITLE></HEAD>");
out.println("<BODY>");
out.println("<H1>Hello World!</H1>");
out.println("<P>This servlet has been requested " +
    numRequests++ + " time(s).");
out.println("<BR>Last requested at " + lastRequest + ".");
out.println("</BODY></HTML>");

lastRequest = (new Date()).toString(); //update last request

out.close(); //always close the output stream
```

The first line of code sets the MIME type for the response to text/html using the setContentType() method. This line will add the Content-Type: text/html HTTP header to the response. The content type, or any other HTTP header values, should be set before accessing the output stream using the getWriter() or getOutputStream() method of HttpServletResponse. This is because the HTTP headers may be flushed to the client at any time after the output stream is accessed.[4]

The next line of code gets a handle to the output stream using the get-Writer() method. Use getWriter() when you are returning text data to the client. The PrintWriter object returned by getWriter() is specially constructed for outputting text and provides Unicode support for international languages. For responses consisting of binary data, use the getOutputStream() method to create a ServletOutputStream object, as follows:

```
ServletOutputStream out = response.getOutputStream();
```

Once the PrintWriter object has been acquired, you can use its print() and println() methods to return information to the client. The println() method is used in the sample servlet because it makes the HTML source easier to read by adding a linefeed to the end of each line of output. The sample servlet returns an HTML-formatted document.

In addition to sending the phrase "Hello World" to the client, the number of times the servlet has been requested and the date and time of the last request is also displayed. This is accomplished by incrementing numRequests and updating lastRequest each time the service() method is executed. Since numRequests and lastRequest are declared as instance variables (outside of any method), they are visible to every invocation of SampleServlet and their values persist between requests. Lastly, the output stream of the PrintWriter object is closed. Always close the output stream once the response is complete (in order to flush the output buffer and close the stream). Normally, the close() method should be invoked within a finally block to ensure that it is always called. For simplicity, no exception handling is included in the sample servlet.

getServletInfo() Method

```
public String getServletInfo()
{
   return "Sample Servlet version 1.0";
}
```

---

4. It is possible for the developer to determine when the output will be flushed by checking the size of the output buffer using the ServletResponse object's getBufferSize() method. Addition- ally, the buffer size can be set using the setBufferSize() method of the ServletResponse object.

The Servlet interface (implemented by GenericServlet) defines a method called getServletInfo() that accepts no parameters and returns a String. The purpose of this method is to provide a simple way for a server to request information about a servlet. It is good practice to override this method, returning a short description of your servlet.

destroy() Method

The servlet continues to process requests until explicitly unloaded by the server. The server always calls the destroy() method before unloading the servlet. The servlet developer should use this method to free resources, such as closing database and socket connections, or to perform any other housekeeping chores that should be completed before the servlet is removed from service (such as saving the current state of the servlet). Once the destroy() method has been called, the servlet object is eligible for garbage collection.

```
public void destroy()
{
  try
  {
    //create a file object pointing to the properties file
    File file = new File("SampleServlet.properties");

    //get an output stream to the properties file
    FileOutputStream fileOut = new FileOutputStream(file);

    //store the request count in the properties object
    prop.put("RequestCount", Integer.toString(numRequests));

    //store the last request date/time in the properties object
    prop.put("LastRequest", lastRequest);

    //write the properties object data to the properties file
    prop.store(fileOut, "SampleServlet Storage File");
  }
  catch (Exception e)
  {
    //if there is an error writing to file, ignore it
  }
}
```

The destroy() method implemented by the sample servlet stores the number of times the servlet has been requested (numRequests variable) and the date and time of the last request (lastRequest variable) in the Properties object, and then writes its data to a properties file called *SampleServlet.properties*. Consequently, the request count and last access time information will persist after the servlet is unloaded. When loaded again, the servlet will pick up where it left off. In addition to freeing resources, saving state information prior to the servlet being unloaded is a common use for the `destroy()` method.

NOTE: If the state information is critical, it is a good idea to intermittently write the information to disk in addition to storing it when the servlet is unloaded. In this way, even if the server crashes, you will not lose all of your data (though you will lose everything since your last update). For example, writing the number of requests to disk every 10 requests will ensure that you will not lose count of more than 10 requests even if the server crashes. This can be accomplished by adding the following code to the `service()` method of `SampleServlet`.

```
if ((numRequests % 10) == 0) //save every 10 requests
{
  destroy();
}
```

Although the previous code will effectively save the request count and last access time every 10 requests, it is not customary for the servlet to call its own `destroy()` method (though it is possible). This method is normally called only by the server before unloading the servlet. So, in this case, it is recommended that the code from the `destroy()` method be placed in a separate `storeData()` method. `storeData()` could then be called from the `destroy()` method as well as from within the `service()` method.

Finally, you may notice that the manner in which every tenth request is determined is not completely thread safe. Under certain conditions, this lack of thread safety could result in the information not being saved after every 10 requests. However, it is sufficient for our purposes since occasionally missing an update is not significant. For more information about thread safety, see Chapter 11.

This concludes our examination of two sample servlets. You should now have a pretty good idea of what a basic servlet looks like and be familiar with several common methods used in servlet development. Of course, now that you have been exposed to these concepts, more detailed information will be presented in the coming chapters.

Summary

This chapter exposes you to the basic syntax and structure of a generic and HTTP servlet. The examples presented here demonstrate the fact that although servlets can be very powerful and complex, their basic structure is simple and straightforward. This simplicity facilitates quick learning and application of various servlet features. In addition, you learn the basic steps by which a servlet is created, invoked, and destroyed by the servlet container.

The next chapter introduces the most common classes and interfaces used to build servlets.

Chapter Highlights

- Nearly all servlets extend one of two servlet classes—GenericServlet or HttpServlet. Extending these classes provides a framework for creating a servlet as well as significant default functionality.

- The HttpServlet class contains methods specific to the HTTP protocol.

- The GenericServlet class is useful when building non-HTTP servlets such as those that implement FTP, POP3, SMTP, or any custom protocol.

- Servlets override at least one method wherein custom functionality is implemented. The method that is automatically called by the server in response to a client request is called service(). This method may be overridden to provide custom functionality.

- In addition to the service() method, there are two other methods that are implemented by most servlets—init() and destroy().

- The init() method is called a single time when the servlet is first loaded. It is similar to a class constructor in that it provides a location wherein initialization code is guaranteed to be run.

- The destroy() method is executed when the servlet is unloaded. It is used to free any resources held by the servlet.

- The process of creating, invoking, and destroying a servlet is known as the servlet lifecycle.

CHAPTER 6

Servlet API Basics

All of the classes and interfaces required to create and execute servlets are contained in two packages—javax.servlet and javax.servlet.http. This collection of classes and interfaces is known as the *Java Servlet API*. Though the Servlet API is considered a standard Java extension, it is not included in the Java™ 2 SDK, Standard Edition (J2SE). Rather, the Servlet API is available as a stand-alone library, as part of the Apache Tomcat project (the official Servlet API reference implementation), or as a required member of the Java 2 SDK, Enterprise Edition (J2EE). Therefore, if you are currently using J2SE, you will need to download the Servlet API library, Apache Tomcat (which includes the Servlet API) and its accompanying documentation, or J2EE separately. You can find this material at *http://java.sun.com/products/servlet/*, *http://jakarta.apache.com/tomcat/*, and *http://java.sun.com/j2ee/*, respectively. In addition to the information presented in this book, I recommend reviewing the Servlet API documentation provided by Sun Microsystems (also available at *http://java.sun.com/products/servlet/*).

In this chapter, we introduce several of the most common classes and interfaces, as well as their most implemented methods, including the following:

- HttpServlet class
- GenericServlet class
- ServletRequest interface
- HttpServletRequest interface
- ServletResponse interface
- HttpServletResponse interface

These classes and interfaces are essential components of the Servlet API. You will certainly use many of these components in every one of your servlet projects. This chapter prepares you for the next chapter, where we actually build a fully functional servlet. The classes and interfaces presented here are used in the upcoming servlet exercise. Chapter 10 continues this preview of the Servlet API with additional classes and interfaces used in more advanced servlets (such as those presented in Part III, Advanced Servlet Concepts, and Part IV, Sample Servlets). The objects and methods described here are based on Servlet API 2.2 (see Chapter 26 for an update regarding Servlet API 2.3).

Before we dive into individual classes, methods, and interfaces of the Servlet API, take a moment to examine the class hierarchy diagram in Figure 6.1. This diagram is also in Appendix M.

Now that you've seen the Servlet API from a high level, let's get a little more detailed. The rest of this chapter dissects specific objects within the Servlet API.

NOTE: Although the material presented in this chapter is extremely important, it is also a bit terse and can be rather dry. Therefore, due to the type and volume of information presented here, you may choose to skim portions of this chapter, referring back to it as needed. The important thing is that you familiarize yourself with the common interfaces, classes, and methods defined by the Servlet API.

HttpServlet Class

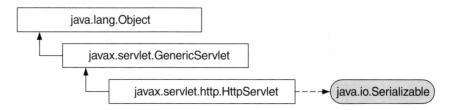

HttpServlet is an abstract class that resides in the javax.servlet.http package. Because it is abstract, it cannot be instantiated. Rather, when building an HTTP servlet, you should extend the HttpServlet class and implement at least one of its methods. A functional HTTP servlet must override *at least one* of the methods described in Table 6.1 (typically service(), doGet(), or doPost()). Although HttpServlet provides only a very basic implementation for most of its methods, it does provide a framework for the HTTP protocol.

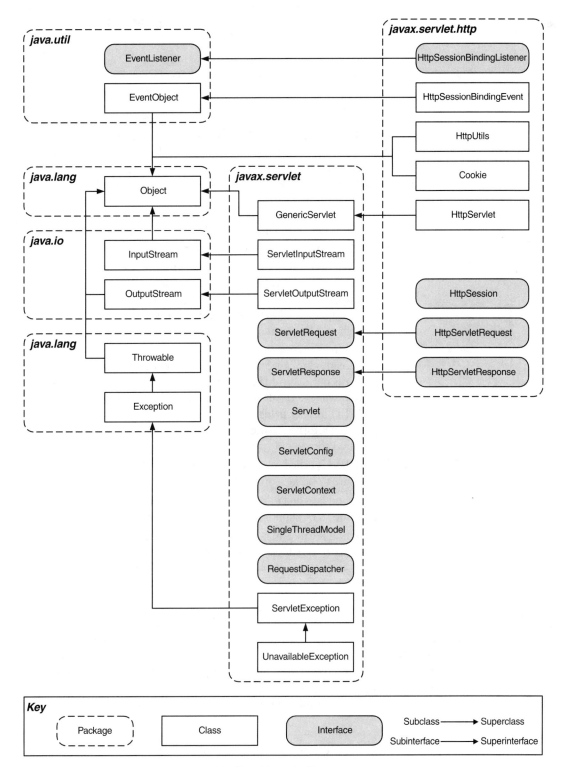

Figure 6.1 Servlet API Class Hierarchy Diagram

Table 6.1   Methods Required to Create a Functional HTTP Servlet

Method	Description
service()	The server calls this method whenever a servlet request is received. For HTTP servlets, this method usually should not be overridden. Rather, a request-specific method should be implemented (e.g., doGet() or doPost()). If not overridden, the default functionality of the service() method is to call one of the following methods according to the type of HTTP request received. If service() is overridden, these methods are not automatically called (but may be called explicitly by the servlet developer from within the service() method).
doGet()	This method is called in response to an HTTP GET request (including conditional GET requests). Overriding this method automatically provides support for HEAD requests (if the doHead() method is not overridden by the servlet developer). If GET requests are to be supported, this method should be overridden.
doHead()	Removed from version 2.2 of the Servlet API but reinstated in version 2.3, this method is called in response to an HTTP HEAD request. If doHead() is not overridden by the servlet developer, the default implementation will call the doGet() method in order to generate the appropriate HTTP header fields. A response containing only HTTP header fields is then returned to the client (body content is excluded). Normally, this method should not be overridden.
doPost()	This method is called in response to an HTTP POST request. If POST requests are to be supported, this method should be overridden.
doPut()	This method is called in response to an HTTP PUT request. If PUT requests are to be supported, this method should be overridden.
doDelete()	This method is called in response to an HTTP DELETE request. If DELETE requests are to be supported, this method should be overridden.

NOTE: Because doHead() was supported in Servlet API versions prior to 2.2, was removed from Servlet API 2.2, and has returned in version 2.3, the doHead() method is presented here. Regardless, keep in mind that doHead() is not supported by version 2.2–compliant servlet containers. You can, however, add rudimentary support for the doHead() method, by overriding the doGet() method, as shown here.

```
public class HeadServlet extends HttpServlet
{
```

```
protected void doGet(HttpServletRequest request,
  HttpServletResponse response) throws ServletException,
  IOException
{
  if (request.getMethod().equalsIgnoreCase("HEAD"))
  {
    doHead(request, response);
  }
}

protected void doHead(HttpServletRequest request,
  HttpServletResponse response) throws ServletException,
  IOException
{
  //Generate HTTP header fields here (no body content)
}
}
```

In addition, the methods described in Table 6.2, though not required, are commonly implemented. If you examine the Servlet API documentation, you may notice that the methods described in Table 6.2 are not defined by the HttpServlet class. HttpServlet inherits these methods from the Generic-Servlet class, which it extends. Let's take a closer look at each of the methods described in the Table 6.1.

Table 6.2   Common Servlet Methods

Method	Description
init()	This method is called only once by the server when the servlet is first loaded. It is commonly used to initialize resources to be used by the servlet when requests are received. For example, database or network connections may be established in this method.
destroy()	This method is called by the server immediately before the servlet is unloaded. This method should be overridden by the servlet developer in order to free any resources being used by the servlet. For example, database or network connections may be closed in this method. This method may also be used to save the current state of the servlet.
getServletInfo()	It is good practice to implement this method so your servlet can identify itself when queried by the server.

service()

```
protected void service(HttpServletRequest request,
    HttpServletResponse response) throws ServletException,
    java.io.IOException
```

As mentioned in Table 6.1, the service() method is not normally over-ridden. This is due to the fact that the HttpServlet class defines methods that are called in response to specific types of HTTP requests (e.g., GET, POST, PUT). Since all of these request methods begin with "do," we will often refer to them as do*Xxx*() methods (e.g., doGet(), doPost(), doPut(), doDelete()). If the HttpServlet object's service() method is not overridden, its default implementation is to call the do*Xxx*() method that corresponds to the type of request received (e.g., GET, POST, PUT). If the service() method is overridden and some do*Xxx*() methods are implemented, it is up to the servlet developer to evaluate each HTTP request and call the appropriate do*Xxx*() method. Remember that the servlet container does not actually call any of the do*Xxx*() methods. When a servlet request is received, the servlet container always calls the servlet's service() method, which may then call one of the do*Xxx*() methods.

Although it is possible to implement all of a servlet's functionality in the service() method, the default implementation of this method used in conjunction with the do*Xxx*() methods makes for cleaner code and provides useful default functionality. For example, the default implementation of each do*Xxx*() method, if not overridden, returns an HTTP 400 "Bad Request" message to the client. Therefore, the client will automatically receive an error message for any HTTP request type that is not supported (meaning that the corresponding do*Xxx*() method was not implemented).

NOTE: You may be wondering why an HTTP 400 "Bad Request" message is returned rather than HTTP 501 "Not Implemented" when a servlet doesn't support a particular HTTP method. The reason is that the "Not Implemented" or "Not Supported" HTTP 501 response indicates a server condition. That is, the server does not support this particular method. However, a server can host multiple servlets that support different HTTP methods. Consequently, stating that the server does not support a specific method is inaccurate. Therefore, HTTP 400 "Bad Request" is returned to indicate a servlet-specific limitation as opposed to a server limitation.

If, for instance, the client attempts to issue a POST request to a servlet that does not override the doPost() method, the default implementation of doPost() will discard the request and return an HTTP 400 "Bad Request" message to the client. This functionality is lost when the service() method is overridden, unless each of the doXxx() methods is specifically called by the overriding code. Listing 6.1 illustrates the use of the service() method. Each of the methods used in Listing 6.1 is discussed later in this chapter.

The service() method throws two exceptions. ServletException indicates a problem with the servlet. The server chooses how to handle this exception when it occurs. An IOException may occur at any time during socket communications (often a result of the user's clicking the browser's **Stop** button or following another link). This exception should always be thrown to the server for proper handling.

Listing 6.1   Sample servlet that overrides the service() method.

```
import javax.servlet.http.*;
import javax.servlet.ServletException;
import java.io.PrintWriter;
import java.io.IOException;

public class ServiceServlet extends HttpServlet
{
  public void service(HttpServletRequest request,
    HttpServletResponse response) throws ServletException,
    IOException
  {
    //set MIME type for HTTP header
    response.setContentType("text/plain");

    //get a handle to the output stream
    PrintWriter out = response.getWriter();

    //determine type of request
    if (request.getMethod().equalsIgnoreCase("GET"))
    {
      out.println("GET request handled by the service() method");
    }
    else //not a GET request
    {
      //send an error to the client since only GET is supported
      response.sendError(HttpServletResponse.SC_BAD_REQUEST);
    }

    out.close(); //always close the output stream
  }
}
```

The service() method in Listing 6.1 is executed in response to every type of HTTP request (e.g., GET, HEAD, POST). This servlet sets the Content-Type HTTP header to text/plain and returns a success message if a GET request is received; otherwise, it returns an HTTP 400 "Bad Request" error (it is up to the browser to display text describing this error). Again, HTTP servlets usually do not override the `service()` method, opting to implement the do*Xxx*() methods instead.

doGet()

```
protected void doGet(HttpServletRequest request,
    HttpServletResponse response) throws ServletException,
    java.io.IOException
```

The `doGet()` method is called by the default implementation of the `service()` method in response to an HTTP GET request. This is the most overridden do*Xxx*() method because GET is the most common HTTP request (followed by POST). If an HTTP GET request is received and the `doGet()` method (as well as the `service()` method) is not overridden, the default implementation of this method will return an HTTP 400 "Bad Request" message.

Additionally, implementing the `doGet()` method provides automatic support for HTTP HEAD requests as long as the `doHead()` method is not overridden. "Automatic support" means that if the `doGet()` method is implemented, no other special coding is required to support HEAD requests. This is due to the fact that the default implementation of `doHead()` automatically calls the `doGet()` method and allows it to generate the proper HTTP header fields. Any output other than header fields that is generated by `doGet()` is discarded. Since all content generated by `doGet()` is ignored by the `doHead()` method, you may wish to check if a HEAD request was received and, in that case, bypass generating body content (to conserve resources since all content is buffered). To illustrate, the following code will ensure that the request is a GET before sending body content to the client.

```
if (request.getMethod().equalsIgnoreCase("GET"))
{
    out.println("Body content goes here...");
}
```

Like all of the do*Xxx*() methods, the `doGet()` method is passed an object representation (or encapsulation) of the client's request and the server's response. Reading from the `request` object and customizing the `response` object is the primary function of a servlet. Listing 6.2 demonstrates a sample servlet that implements the `doGet()` method.

Listing 6.2   Sample servlet that implements the doGet() method.

```
import javax.servlet.http.*;
import javax.servlet.ServletException;
import java.io.PrintWriter;
import java.io.IOException;
```

```
public class GetServlet extends HttpServlet
{
  /**
   * Returns a brief message to the client.
   */
  protected void doGet(HttpServletRequest request,
    HttpServletResponse response) throws ServletException,
    IOException
  {
    //set MIME type for HTTP header
    response.setContentType("text/plain");

    //get a handle to the output stream
    PrintWriter out = response.getWriter();

    out.println("Request handled by the doGet() method");

    out.close(); //always close the output stream
  }
}
```

The doGet() method in the preceding sample servlet is called in response to any HTTP GET request. The doGet() method is declared protected because it is not called from outside of the servlet class. Remember that the server actually calls the servlet's service() method whenever a request is received. The default implementation of the service() method calls the doGet() method in response to a GET request. This sample servlet sets the HTTP Content-Type header to text/plain and returns a message to the client.

doPost()

```
protected void doPost(HttpServletRequest request,
  HttpServletResponse response) throws ServletException,
  java.io.IOException
```

The doPost() method is called whenever an HTTP POST request is received by the servlet. This method is commonly used to process information collected from an HTML form. The information entered by the user into an HTML form is encapsulated in an HttpServletRequest object and passed to the doPost() method (we will discuss the HttpServletRequest object in detail later in this chapter). If a POST request is received and the doPost() method is not implemented, an HTTP 400 "Bad Request" message is returned to the client.

Listing 6.3 uses both the doGet() and doPost() methods to create a functional servlet. The doGet() method is used to create a simple HTML form. When the user clicks the **Submit** button, the form data is posted to the servlet and processed by the doPost() method. In this case, the doPost() method simply constructs an HTML document that contains the data that was submitted

and returns it to the client. When building a servlet to collect information from
the client, using the doGet() method to create an HTML form and subse-
quently handling the submission with the doPost() method is very common.

Listing 6.3   Sample servlet that implements the doGet() and doPost()
methods.

```
import javax.servlet.http.*;
import javax.servlet.ServletException;
import java.io.PrintWriter;
import java.io.IOException;

public class PostServlet extends HttpServlet
{
  /**
   * Returns an HTML form to the client prompting for their name
   * and e-mail address.
   */
  public void doGet(HttpServletRequest request,
    HttpServletResponse response) throws ServletException,
    IOException
  {
    //set MIME type for HTTP header
    response.setContentType("text/html");

    //get a handle to the output stream
    PrintWriter out = response.getWriter();

    out.println("<HTML><HEAD>");
    out.println("<TITLE>Sample POST Servlet</TITLE>");
    out.println("</HEAD>");
    out.println("<BODY>");
    out.println("<H1>GUEST BOOK</H1>");
    out.println("<P>Please enter your name and e-mail " +
      "address below:</P>");
    out.println("<FORM METHOD=\"POST\" ACTION=" +
      "\"http://localhost:8080/servlet/PostServlet\">");
    out.println("<P>Name: <INPUT TYPE=\"TEXT\" NAME=\"name\" " +
      "SIZE=\"20\"><BR>");
    out.println("E-mail: <INPUT TYPE=\"TEXT\" NAME=\"email\" " +
      "SIZE=\"30\"></P>");
    out.println("<INPUT TYPE=\"SUBMIT\" VALUE=\"Submit\">" +
      "<INPUT TYPE=\"RESET\" VALUE=\"Clear\">");
    out.println("</FORM></BODY></HTML>");

    out.close(); //always close the output stream
  }


  /**
   * Processes the data received from the HTML form and returns
   * an HTML document that displays the submitted information.
   */
```

```
      public void doPost(HttpServletRequest request,
        HttpServletResponse response) throws IOException
      {
        //set MIME type for HTTP header
        response.setContentType("text/html");

        //get data from request object
        String name = request.getParameter("name");
        String email = request.getParameter("email");

        //get a handle to the output stream
        PrintWriter out = response.getWriter();

        out.println("<HTML><HEAD>");
        out.println("<TITLE>Sample POST Servlet</TITLE>");
        out.println("</HEAD>");
        out.println("<BODY>");
        out.println("<H1>Thank You</H1>");
        out.println("<P>The following information was submitted:");
        out.println("<P>Name: " + name + "<BR>");
        out.println("E-Mail: " + email + "</P>");
        out.println("</BODY></HTML>");

        out.close(); //always close the output stream
      }
    }
```

Listing 6.3 uses a doGet() method to respond to the first GET request issued by the browser. The doGet() method builds an HTTP form and returns it to the client. When the user submits the form, the doPost() method is called to handle the POST request. We can tell that this form generates a POST request by evaluating the <FORM> tag in the HTML document constructed in the doGet() method (FORM METHOD="POST"). Finally, using a method from the HttpServlet-Request object, getParameter(), the data input by the user is extracted from the request and added to the HTML document that is returned to the client. At this point, don't worry about the HttpServletRequest methods. They will be discussed in detail shortly.

doPut()

```
      protected void doPut(HttpServletRequest request,
        HttpServletResponse response) throws ServletException,
        java.io.IOException
```

The doPut() method is called in response to an HTTP PUT request. PUT requests are used to upload data from the client to the server. If a PUT request is received and the doPut() method is not implemented, an HTTP 400 "Bad Request" message is returned to the client. If doPut() is overridden, all HTTP content headers must be respected, including Content-Base, Content-

Encoding, Content-Language, Content-Length, Content-Location, Content-MD5, Content-Range, and Content-Type. See Table 6.3 for a description of each of these HTTP content headers (see also RFC 2068). If the overridden method cannot honor all content header fields, it must return an HTTP 501 "Not Implemented" message and discard the request.

Although supported by the Servlet API, the doPut() method is currently not often implemented. This is largely due to the fact that the only specification for HTML form-based file uploads uses the POST method rather than PUT (see RFC 1867). The primary difference between the POST and PUT methods is the manner in which they interpret the URL specified in the request. The POST method interprets the URL as the resource that will process the request's content. Conversely, the PUT method interprets the URL as the name under which to store the request's contents on the server.

Table 6.3   Description of HTTP Content Headers

HTTP Header	Description
Content-Base	Indicates the base URL used to resolve relative URLs within a request (see RFC 1808). The Content-Base field must be an absolute URL. If Content-Base is not present, the base URL is constructed from the Content-Location (if it represents an absolute URL) or, secondly, the URL used to initiate the request.
Content-Encoding	Designates additional encoding (other than that specified by Content-Type) that has been applied to the entity body, thus conveying the decoding mechanisms that must be employed in order to obtain the media type specified by the Content-Type header. Content-Encoding is commonly used with compressed files.
Content-Language	Indicates the natural language of which the entity body is composed.
Content-Length	Designates the size of the entity body. In response to a HEAD request, this field designates the size of the message body that would have been returned if the request had been a GET.
Content-Location	Indicates the current location of the entity requested. Commonly used in conjunction with HTTP 301 "Moved Permanently" or HTTP 302 "Moved Temporarily" messages to specify the new location of the requested resource.
Content-MD5	Provides a type of checksum called a *message integrity check*. See RFC 1864 for more information.
Content-Range	Used if the server returns a partial response to the client's request. This header field designates the size of the full entity body as well as where this response fits within the entire body.
Content-Type	Designates the MIME type of the entity body. In response to a HEAD request, it contains the MIME type of the entity body that would have been returned if the request had been a GET.

Because a true Internet standard for file uploads does not yet exist, many browser and server vendors have yet to support this functionality. However, it should be noted that Netscape Navigator version 3 and higher and Microsoft Internet Explorer version 4 and higher both support HTML form-based file uploads according to the RFC 1867 specification. As the HTTP 1.1 protocol (which formally defines the PUT method) becomes prevalent, increasing numbers of browsers and servers will support the PUT method.

doDelete()

```
protected void doDelete(HttpServletRequest request,
    HttpServletResponse response) throws ServletException,
    java.io.IOException
```

The doDelete() method is called in response to an HTTP DELETE request. The DELETE method allows a client to request that the server delete the resource specified in the request. If a DELETE request is received and the doDelete() method is not implemented, an HTTP 400 "Bad Request" message is returned to the client. It is a good idea to require some type of user authentication in addition to storing a backup copy of any resource removed from the server in response to a DELETE request. In addition, it is common for the doDelete() method to simply move a resource to an inaccessible location in response to a DELETE request rather than actually delete it permanently. This method is not typically overridden.

doTrace()

```
protected void doTrace(HttpServletRequest request,
    HttpServletResponse response) throws ServletException,
    java.io.IOException
```

The doTrace() method is called in response to an HTTP TRACE request. A TRACE request is a diagnostic tool that allows the client to see exactly how its request appears to the server. A TRACE request should contain no body content, only headers. When a TRACE request is received, the server packages the entire request inside the entity body of an HTTP 200 "OK" message with Content-Type of message/http. This message is returned to the client. Using this method, the client can ensure that the proper request is arriving at the server. This type of request is commonly used to diagnose transmission problems involving gateways and routers. The default implementation of the doTrace() method responds according to the HTTP/1.1 TRACE specification. That is, the client's entire request is returned within the entity body of an HTTP 200 "OK" message. There is usually no reason to override this method.

doOptions()

```
protected void doOptions(HttpServletRequest request,
    HttpServletResponse response) throws ServletException,
    java.io.IOException
```

The doOptions() method is called in response to an HTTP OPTIONS request. An OPTIONS request is sent by the client to query the server for the supported protocol methods. The default implementation of this method automatically returns the HTTP options that are supported by the servlet. For instance, if a servlet implements the doGet() and doPost() methods, the server will return an HTTP ALLOWS header as follows:

```
ALLOWS: GET,HEAD,POST,TRACE,OPTIONS
```

The ALLOWS header informs the client of all HTTP methods that the server supports. The HEAD method is shown in the ALLOWS header because it is automatically supported by the doGet() implementation. Additionally, the Servlet API provides default implementations of the doTrace() and doOptions() methods, thereby providing default support for the TRACE and OPTIONS HTTP request types. It is not necessary to override the doOptions() method unless the servlet supports methods beyond those defined in HTTP/1.1. Thus, this method is rarely overridden.

getLastModified()

```
protected long getLastModified(HttpServletRequest request)
```

The getLastModified() method provides information required by the browser in order to intelligently cache data. Properly implementing this method can greatly improve the perceived performance of your application. However, before we implement this method, let's examine the process by which browsers can improve response time by caching data on the client.

When most Web servers return a static HTML document, their response includes a Last-Modified HTTP header field containing the date and time the file was last changed. This information is retrieved from the file's timestamp. Most browsers store copies of previously downloaded resources locally so that, if requested a second time, the resource need not be downloaded again. The Last-Modified header allows the browser to determine whether its cached copy of a resource is stale (i.e., it has an old version). A typical Last-Modified header field within the context of an HTTP response header looks like this:

```
HTTP/1.1 200 OK
Date: Wed, 12 Jan 2000 03:18:11 GMT
Server: Apache/1.3.9 (Unix)
Last-Modified: Mon, 03 Jan 2000 17:06:48 GMT
```

```
Content-Length: 4326
Content-Type: text/html
```

In addition to storing the requested resource (usually using the client's file system), the browser also records the time that the resource was last modified (using the `Last-Modified` header field). Once cached, the browser adds an `If-Modified-Since` header field to all future requests for this resource (this is known as a *conditional GET*). The `If-Modified-Since` header field contains the time the browser's copy of the resource was last modified. When a conditional GET request is received, the server uses the `If-Modified-Since` value to determine if the browser has the latest version of the resource. If not, the newer information is returned (along with an updated `Last-Modified` header field). Otherwise, the server returns a short HTTP 304 "Not Modified" message indicating that the resource has not changed and the browser should load the information from cache. The `If-Modified-Since` header field within an HTTP request header looks like this:

```
GET /index.html HTTP/1.0
User-Agent: Mozilla/4.51 [en] (WinNT; I)
If-Modified-Since: Mon, 03 Jan 2000 17:06:48 GMT
```

This method works fine for static files, but it becomes more complex when dealing with dynamic content such as the output produced by a servlet. Since it can't simply check the timestamp, how is the server to know if a servlet-generated page has changed? As you may have guessed, the answer is to implement the `getLastModified()` method. This method allows the server to query the servlet for the date and time its output last changed. Without this information, the server has no choice but to return the servlet-generated content in response to every request (thus defeating the browser's caching mechanisms).

NOTE: Though it has been stated that the server queries the servlet's `getLastModified()` method, this is not completely accurate. Actually, it is the default implementation of the `HttpServlet` object's `service()` method that calls the `getLastModified()` method and determines whether to call the `doGet()` method (to generate content) or return an HTTP 304 "Not Modified" message. However, since this functionality is transparently provided by the `HttpServlet` class, it can be viewed as if the server provided this functionality.

Again, the purpose of the `getLastModified()` method is to tell the server as well as other servlet methods the last time the servlet's output changed. The server can then include this information in the response's `Last-Modified` header field. In addition, the servlet can use the information from the getLast-Modified() method to determine whether to call the doGet() method in response to a conditional GET or simply return an HTTP 304 "Not Modified" message. Note that if the browser has a copy of the servlet's current content, the doGet() method may never be called. Again, this is due to the fact that the default implementation of the service() method verifies that the browser's cached copy of the resource is stale before calling the doGet() method to process the request. To illustrate, a portion of the default service() method implemented by the HttpServlet class looks something like this:

```
if ((now < ifModifiedSince) || (ifModifiedSince < lastModified))
{
  doGet(req, resp);
}
else
{
  // this is more of a message than an error, but
  // sendError does the job just fine.
  resp.sendError(HttpServletResponse.SC_NOT_MODIFIED);
}
```

Now that we know what the getLastModified() method is for, let's examine how to use it. The following sample code demonstrates a typical implementation of the getLastModified() method.

```
import javax.servlet.*;
import javax.servlet.http.*;
import java.io.*;
import java.util.*;

public class BulletinBoard extends HttpServlet
{
  Date lastModified = new Date(); //stores last modification date


  /**
   * Displays all bulletins posted to the bulletin board.
   */
  public void doGet(HttpServletRequest request,
    HttpServletResponse response) throws ServletException,
    IOException
  {
    //display bulletins here...
  }


  /**
   * Adds a new bulletin to the bulletin board.
   */
```

```
public void doPost(HttpServletRequest request,
  HttpServletResponse response) throws ServletException,
  IOException
{
  //add new bulletins here...

  //since the output changes with each new bulletin, update the
  //last modified variable
  lastModified = new Date();
}


/**
 * Returns the date and time the servlet's output was last
 * modified.
 */
protected long getLastModified(HttpServletRequest request)
{
  //round down to the nearest second
  return (lastModified.getTime() / 1000) * 1000;
}
}
```

The previous code example demonstrates the getLastModified() method in the context of a bulletin board servlet (see Chapter 7 for a complete bulletin board servlet). The doGet() method of this servlet builds an HTML document that contains a list of bulletins. When the first request is received from the browser (this request will not be conditional since the browser has not yet cached the page), the servlet-generated output is returned to the client within a response that includes a Last-Modified header field. In future GET requests, the browser will include an If-Modified-Since header field indicating that the servlet's output should be returned only if it has changed since the If-Modified-Since date and time. Therefore, all future requests for a list of bulletins will be served from the browser's local cache until a new bulletin is added in response to a POST request. The doPost() method resets the last modified date to reflect the most recent change (the addition of a bulletin). The next time the browser requests a list of bulletins, the servlet's last modified date will be later than the If-Modified-Since header. Therefore, the servlet content will be returned within a response that includes the new Last-Modified value.

NOTE: The Tomcat 3.1 implementation of Servlet API 2.2 does not properly set the Last-Modified header field in response to every GET request. Rather, the Last-Modified header field is included only in response to a *conditional* GET request (it erroneously fails to set this header in response to nonconditional GET requests). To remedy this problem, you can manually set the Last-Modified header within the doGet() method using the following code:

```
response.setDateHeader("Last-Modified", getLastModified());
```

What about the HttpServletRequest parameter passed to the getLast-Modified() method? This object is useful if the servlet generates different output based on the request. For example, if the bulletin board servlet supports several different bulletin boards, the list of bulletins generated by its doGet() method may vary based on the bulletin board that was requested. In order to allow the browser to properly cache each bulletin board's output, the servlet must store the last modified date and time for each bulletin board separately. Therefore, the getLastModified() method's return value depends on which bulletin board was requested. Fortunately, this information can be determined from the HttpServletRequest object (using its getParameter() method, perhaps).

You may have noticed that the getLastModified() method returns a long. This number indicates the time the resource was last modified expressed as the number of milliseconds since midnight January 1, 1970 GMT (this is how Java stores time internally). The default implementation of this method returns a negative number (usually -1) to convey that the method has not been properly implemented. The servlet developer must override this method to make it useful.

Though it returns the time in milliseconds, the sample getLastModified() method rounds the time down to the nearest second. This action is necessary because the Last-Modified and If-Modified-Since header fields convey the time in hours, minutes, and seconds (no milliseconds). If the time returned by the getLastModified() method is not rounded down, it might appear to always be a few milliseconds ahead of the time given by the browser in the If-Modified-Since header. If this occurs, the server will errantly return content when it should return an HTTP 304 "Not Modified" message that instructs the browser to load the page from its local cache.

NOTE: In addition to the Last-Modified response header field, another header field is often used in conjunction with client-side caching. The Expires response header field indicates the date and time after which a resource should be considered stale. This field allows the browser to display information from cache until it expires. The Expires header field uses the same format as Last-Modified. A typical HTTP header that includes the Expires header field looks like this:

```
HTTP/1.1 200 OK
Date: Wed, 12 Jan 2000 03:18:11 GMT
Server: Apache/1.3.9 (Unix)
Expires: Mon, 17 Jan 2000 17:06:48 GMT
Content-Length: 4326
Content-Type: text/html
```

GenericServlet Class

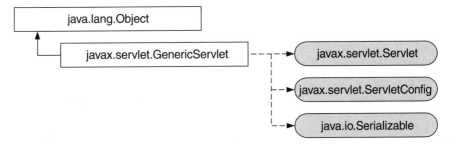

In addition to the methods described previously, `HttpServlet` inherits basic servlet functionality by extending `GenericServlet`. Some of the common methods inherited from `GenericServlet` are described here.

getInitParameter()

```
public String getInitParameter(String name)
```

The `getInitParameter()` method returns a `String` containing the value of the specified initialization parameter. *Initialization parameters* are configuration settings that are established by the developer or administrator at the time the servlet is defined (this process is often referred to as *registering* a servlet). Each servlet definition can have its own initialization parameters. If a single servlet class is defined multiple times using different initialization parameters, a separate instance will be created for each definition and the `init()` method will be called once for each instance.

Initialization parameters, often called *init* parameters, are stored in the Web application's deployment descriptor. The deployment descriptor file is named *web.xml* and resides in the Web application's */WEB-INF* directory (see Chapter 19 for more information about the deployment descriptor). Storing init parameters in a text file allows them to be changed easily without recompiling the servlet. The following portion of the *web.xml* file demonstrates how servlets are defined and init parameters are set.

```
<web-app>
  <servlet>
    <servlet-name>phonelist</servlet-name>
    <servlet-class>PhoneListServlet</servlet-class>
    <init-param>
      <param-name>maxRows</param-name>
      <param-value>100</param-value>
    </init-param>
    <init-param>
      <param-name>language</param-name>
      <param-value>English</param-value>
    </init-param>
  </servlet>
  <servlet-mapping>
    <servlet-name>phonelist</servlet-name>
    <url-pattern>/phone</url-pattern>
  </servlet-mapping>
</web-app>
```

The <servlet-name> element defines an alias (phonelist) to represent the servlet PhoneListServlet.class. The <init-param> elements define initialization parameters that the server passes to the phone list servlet. Finally, the <servlet-mapping> section maps the */phone* URL to the phonelist servlet (i.e., all requests directed to */phone* will be passed to PhoneListServlet). Please keep in mind that this example is simply meant to familiarize the reader with the manner in which initialization parameters are set. The process of defining servlets is discussed thoroughly in Chapter 8, Running Servlets, and Chapter 19, Packaging and Deployment.

Again, the getInitParameter() method returns a String that contains the value of the specified initialization parameter. These values are normally read in the servlet's init() method and used to perform some type of initialization. If the specified parameter does not exist, null is returned.

getInitParameter() is actually a convenience method. It retrieves initialization information from the ServletConfig object that is passed to the init(ServletConfig) method. The ServletConfig interface is discussed in detail in Chapter 10. The getInitParameter() method defined by Generic-Servlet provides a shortcut to the alternative method of getting initialization parameters—retrieving a reference to the ServletConfig object (using getServletConfig()) and calling its getInitParameter() method. The following sample code demonstrates how to retrieve initialization parameters.

```
public class InitParameterServlet extends HttpServlet
{
  int maxRows;        //maximum number of rows to display
  String language;    //default language
```

```
/**
 * Reads the maxRows and language initialization parameters.
 */
public void init() throws ServletException
{
  maxRows = Integer.parseInt(getInitParameter("maxRows"));
  language = getInitParameter("language");
}

//Implement doGet() or doPost() here...
}
```

getInitParameterNames()

```
public java.util.Enumeration getInitParameterNames()
```

The getInitParameterNames() method returns the names of all initialization parameters as an Enumeration of String objects. If no initialization parameters have been defined, an empty Enumeration is returned. Like getInit-Parameter(), described in the previous section, this method is implemented in GenericServlet for convenience. It actually gets the parameter names from the ServletConfig object that was passed to the init(ServletConfig) method. This method is often used in conjunction with getInitParameter() to retrieve the name and value of all initialization parameters. The following sample code demonstrates the getInitParameterNames() method.

```
public void init() throws ServletException
{
  String name, value;

  Enumeration enum = getInitParameterNames();

  while (enum.hasMoreElements())
  {
    name = (String)enum.nextElement();
    value = (String)getInitParameter(name);
    System.out.println("Name: " + name + ", Value: " +
      value);
  }
}
```

This init() method retrieves the names and values of all initialization parameters and prints them to standard out.

getServletConfig()

```
public ServletConfig getServletConfig()
```

The getServletConfig() method returns a ServletConfig object that contains servlet start-up configuration information. This information includes any

initialization parameters and a ServletContext object. The getInit-
Parameter(), getInitParameterNames(), and getServletContext() methods
described earlier are actually implemented by the ServletConfig object
(GenericServlet simply calls the ServletConfig object's implementation of
these methods). The ServletConfig and ServletContext objects are discussed
in detail in Chapter 10.

getServletContext()

```
public ServletContext getServletContext()
```

The getServletContext() method returns a ServletContext object that contains information regarding the environment in which the servlet is running.
This method is provided in the GenericServlet class for convenience. Actually,
it retrieves ServletContext from the ServletConfig object that was passed to
the servlet's init(ServletConfig) method.

getServletName()

```
public String getServletName()
```

getServletName() returns the name of the servlet instance according to the
<servlet-name> element in the servlet's definition. For example, this method
would return the value "phonelist" if called by the servlet defined previously
in the "getInitParameter()" section. getServletName() allows the servlet to
know the name by which it is referenced.

log()

```
public void log(String message)
public void log(String message, Throwable t)
```

The log(String) method writes the specified string along with the name of the
servlet class file to the servlet log file. The name and location of this log file are
server-specific. This method is often used to log events for administrative or
debugging purposes. The log(String, Throwable) method prints the stack
trace (error information) to the log file in addition to the string message.

ServletRequest Interface

> javax.servlet.ServletRequest

ServletRequest is an interface that resides in the `javax.servlet` package. This interface is used to convey request information to a servlet. When a request is received, the servlet container encapsulates vital request information in an object that implements the `ServletRequest` interface. This object is then passed to the servlet's `service()` method.

The `ServletRequest` interface is used by non-HTTP servers. HTTP servers encapsulate requests in objects that implement the `HttpServletRequest` interface (which extends `ServletRequest`). Some of the common methods of the `ServletRequest` object are described here.

getContentLength()

```
public int getContentLength()
```

The `getContentLength()` method returns an integer representing the total length of the request's data portion, or −1 if unknown. When using the HTTP protocol, this information can be useful when processing POST or PUT operations (file uploads).

getContentType()

```
public String getContentType()
```

The `getContentType()` method returns the MIME media type of the request's data portion, or `null` if the request contains only headers (no data). With this information the servlet can properly process or store the data portion of the request. To illustrate, Table 6.4 shows a few of the most common MIME types.

Table 6.4   Common MIME Types

MIME Type	Description
text/plain	Plain ASCII text; contains no formatting tags
text/html	HTML formatted document
image/gif	GIF image
image/jpeg	JPEG image

getInputStream()

```
public ServletInputStream getInputStream() throws
    java.io.IOException
```

The `getInputStream()` method returns an input stream in the form of a `ServletInputStream` object. The `ServletInputStream` class is discussed in Chapter 10. This input stream allows the servlet to read binary data from the body of the request (often used in conjunction with HTTP POST and PUT operations). For reading text information from the request, the `getReader()` method should be used.

getParameter()

```
public String getParameter(String name)
```

The `getParameter()` method returns the value of the specified parameter or `null` if the parameter does not exist. *Parameters* are name/value pairs that can be passed to a servlet in the URL's query string like this:

http://www.sourcestream.com/servlet/ShoppingCart?item=1234&quantity=2

Parameters can also be passed within the body of an HTTP request when an HTML form is submitted using the POST method. All form data from both the query string and the body of a POST request are aggregated into a single request parameter set that can be queried using `getParameter()` or `get-ParameterValues()`. By definition, the `getParameterValues()` method will list the query string parameters first followed by parameters passed in the POST request. Both query string parameters and POST request parameters may be received if the ACTION attribute of the <FORM> tag contains a query string. For example, the following HTML form submits two parameters. `param1` is submitted in the URL as a query string and `param2` is submitted within the body of the POST request.

```
<FORM METHOD="POST" ACTION="/servlet/ParamServlet?param1=query">
  <INPUT TYPE="HIDDEN" NAME="param2" VALUE="post">
  <INPUT TYPE="SUBMIT" VALUE="Submit">
</FORM>
```

Note that `getParameter()` returns only a single value. If a parameter might contain multiple values, use the `getParameterValues()` method instead. A single parameter can contain multiple values if an HTML form containing elements (e.g., text boxes or check boxes) having duplicate names is submitted. Multiple values for a single parameter can also be passed in the query string like this:

http://www.sourcestream.com/servlet/ShoppingCart?item=1234&item=2345

getParameterValues() returns a String array containing all values of a specified parameter.

getParameter() is actually a convenience method to use when you know that a parameter contains only a single value. In the event that a parameter does contain multiple values, the value returned by getParameter() is the same as the first value in the array returned by getParameterValues().

The sample code that follows demonstrates how to use getParameter().

```
public void service(HttpServletRequest request,
  HttpServletResponse response) throws ServletException,
  IOException
{
  String name;

  //set MIME type for HTTP header
  response.setContentType("text/plain");

  //get a handle to the output stream
  PrintWriter out = response.getWriter();

  //get the value of the name parameter
  name = request.getParameter("name");

  out.println("Thank you, " + name); //send message to client

  out.close(); //always close the output stream
}
```

This sample code could be called from an HTML form similar to the following.

```
<HTML>
<HEAD><TITLE>Guest Book</TITLE></HEAD>
<BODY>
<FORM METHOD="POST" ACTION="http://localhost/servlet/GuestBook">
Please sign our Guest Book.<BR>
<INPUT TYPE="TEXT" NAME="name" SIZE="20">
<INPUT TYPE="SUBMIT" VALUE="Save Name">
</FORM>
</BODY>
</HTML>
```

NOTE: There is an interesting side note concerning the getParameter() method. This method was actually deprecated in Servlet API 1.1 in favor of the getParameterValues() method. It was deemed by Sun that since a parameter could contain multiple values, multiple values should always be retrieved (if available). However, obtaining a single value from the getParameterValues() method requires a line of code that looks like this:

```
name = request.getParameterValues("name")[0];
```

Not nearly as simple or convenient as the getParameter() alternative. Fortunately, due to strong developer feedback, getParameter() became the first Java method ever to be removed from deprecation!

getParameterNames()

```
public java.util.Enumeration getParameterNames()
```

The getParameterNames() method returns the name of each name/value pair passed in the request. The names are returned as an Enumeration of String objects. If no parameters are passed in the request, this method returns an empty Enumeration. The following sample code demonstrates this method.

```
public void service(HttpServletRequest request,
  HttpServletResponse response) throws ServletException,
  IOException
{
  int numParams=0;

  //set MIME type for HTTP header
  response.setContentType("text/plain");

  //get a handle to the output stream
  PrintWriter out = response.getWriter();

  java.util.Enumeration enum = request.getParameterNames();

  if (!enum.hasMoreElements())
  {
    out.println("No parameters in this request");
  }
  else
  {
    while (enum.hasMoreElements())
    {
      numParams++;
      out.println("Parameter Name " + numParams + ": " +
        enum.nextElement());
    }
  }

  out.close(); //always close the output stream
}
```

If this code were invoked with this URL

http://localhost:8080/servlet/ParamNameServlet?age=4&name=Madison

the response would look like this:

```
Parameter Name 1: age
Parameter Name 2: name
```

getParameterValues()

```
public String[] getParameterValues(String name)
```

The getParameterValues() method returns all values of the specified parameter. The values are returned as an array of String objects or null if the parameter does not exist. Often, a parameter has only a single value. In this case, the value of this parameter can be determined using the following code (or using the getParameter() method):

```
Name = request.getParameterValues("name")[0];
```

The following sample code demonstrates how to extract parameter names and values from a request.

```
public void service(HttpServletRequest request,
  HttpServletResponse response) throws ServletException,
  IOException
{
  int numParams=0, loop;
  String name;
  String[] values;

  //set MIME type for HTTP header
  response.setContentType("text/plain");

  //get a handle to the output stream
  PrintWriter out = response.getWriter();

  java.util.Enumeration enum = request.getParameterNames();

  if (!enum.hasMoreElements())
  {
    out.println("No parameters in this request");
  }
  else
  {
    while (enum.hasMoreElements())
    {
      numParams++;
      name = (String)enum.nextElement();
      out.println("Parameter Name " + numParams + ": " +
        name);
      values = request.getParameterValues(name);
      for (loop=0; loop < values.length; loop++)
      {
        out.println(" Value: " + values[loop]);
      }
    }
  }

  out.close(); //always close the output stream
}
```

This `service()` method retrieves the name of all parameters passed in the request in addition to all values for each parameter. If this method were invoked by the following URL

http://localhost:8080/servlet/ParamServlet?drive=floppy&drive=zip&ram=128
&input=keyboard&input=mouse&computer=pentium

the output would look like this:

```
Parameter Name 1: drive
 Value: floppy
 Value: zip
Parameter Name 2: ram
 Value: 128
Parameter Name 3: input
 Value: keyboard
 Value: mouse
Parameter Name 4: computer
 Value: pentium
```

getProtocol()

```
public String getProtocol()
```

The `getProtocol()` method returns a `String` describing the protocol used by the servlet. The format of the protocol string looks like this:

<protocol>/<major_version>.<minor_version>

The following sample code demonstrates the use of the `getProtocol()` method.

```
public void service(HttpServletRequest request,
  HttpServletResponse response) throws ServletException,
  IOException
{
  //set MIME type for HTTP header
  response.setContentType("text/plain");

  //get a handle to the output stream
  PrintWriter out = response.getWriter();

  out.println(request.getProtocol());

  out.close(); //always close the output stream
}
```

The output from the preceding `service()` method looks like this:

```
HTTP/1.1
```

getReader()

```
public java.io.BufferedReader getReader() throws
    java.io.IOException
```

The getReader() method returns a BufferedReader for the purpose of reading text from the data portion of the request. The BufferedReader class translates character set encodings as required. This method is useful for protocols that include text data along with the protocol headers. For binary data, the get-InputStream() method should be used. The following code demonstrates how to read text information from the data portion of a request.

```
public void doGet(HttpServletRequest request,
    HttpServletResponse response) throws ServletException,
    IOException
{
  response.setContentType("text/html");

  BufferedReader br = request.getReader();
  PrintWriter out = response.getWriter();

  out.println("<HTML>");
  out.println("<HEAD><TITLE>getReader</TITLE></HEAD>");
  out.println("<BODY>");
  out.println("The content portion of your request included ");
  out.println("this information:<BR><BR>");

  String line = br.readLine();
  while (line != null)
  {
    out.println(line + "<BR>");
    line = br.readLine();
  }

  out.println("</BODY></HTML>");
}
```

getRemoteAddr()

```
public String getRemoteAddr()
```

The getRemoteAddr() method returns the IP address of the client that sent the request. Consider the following code:

```
public void service(HttpServletRequest request,
    HttpServletResponse response) throws ServletException,
    IOException
{
  //set MIME type for HTTP header
  response.setContentType("text/plain");
```

```
//get a handle to the output stream
PrintWriter out = response.getWriter();

out.println(request.getRemoteAddr());

out.close(); //always close the output stream
}
```

If a servlet containing this `service()` method were invoked from the local machine, the output would look like this:

```
127.0.0.1
```

You may recognize this as the local loopback address (meaning that the computer is communicating with itself).

getRemoteHost()

```
public String getRemoteHost()
```

This method returns the client's fully qualified hostname or the IP address if the hostname cannot be determined. Consider the following code:

```
public void service(HttpServletRequest request,
  HttpServletResponse response) throws ServletException,
  IOException
{
//set MIME type for HTTP header
response.setContentType("text/plain");

//get a handle to the output stream
PrintWriter out = response.getWriter();

out.println(request.getRemoteHost());

out.close(); //always close the output stream
}
```

If a servlet containing this `service()` method were invoked from the local machine, the output would look like this:

```
localhost
```

Localhost refers to a service running on the local machine.

getScheme()

```
public String getScheme()
```

The `getScheme()` method returns the scheme (which usually refers to the protocol) used by the request. For example, common schemes include "http," "https," "ftp," and "telnet." The URL requested by the client can be reconstructed by combining the scheme, hostname or IP address, port, request URL, and query string (request URL and query string are discussed in the HttpServletRequest Interface section). For more information about schemes, see RFC 1738.

getServerName()

```
public String getServerName()
```

The getServerName() method returns the hostname of the server on which the servlet is running.

getServerPort()

```
public int getServerPort()
```

The getServerPort() method returns an integer indicating the port on which the client's request was received (i.e., the port on which the server is listening).

isSecure()

```
public boolean isSecure()
```

The isSecure() method returns true if the request was made using a secure connection, such as HTTPS (HTTP over SSL).

HttpServletRequest Interface

HttpServletRequest is an interface that resides in the javax.servlet.http package. This interface extends ServletRequest and, therefore, supports all of its methods in addition to those presented here.

HttpServletRequest defines methods that describe an HTTP request. An object that implements the HttpServletRequest interface is passed to the servlet's service() method and all of the doXxx() methods. The request information encapsulated in this object includes information collected from the HTTP header such as the HTTP method (e.g., GET or POST), cookies, and authentication information. The name/value pairs passed by an HTML form or in a query string are also accessible via the HttpServletRequest object.

The `HttpServletRequest` object provides extensive information regarding the client's request. If you are an experienced CGI developer, Table 6.5 may be of assistance in retrieving request information from the `HttpServletRequest` object.

Now let's examine `HttpServletRequest` more closely. The following descriptions and sample code illustrate many of the most common methods of the `HttpServletRequest` object.

getAuthType()

```
public String getAuthType()
```

The `getAuthType()` method returns a string describing the authentication scheme employed by the client (e.g., "BASIC" or "SSL"). Using `Basic` authentication, when a request for a protected resource is received, the server usually responds with an HTTP 401 "Not Authorized" message. If authentication is required, the response will include a header like `WWW-Authenticate: Basic`. This type of response is known as an *authentication challenge*. Most browsers

Table 6.5   CGI Environment Variables and Their Equivalent `HttpServletRequest` Methods

CGI Environment Variable	HttpServletRequest Method
AUTH_TYPE	getAuthType()
CONTENT_LENGTH	getContentLength()
CONTENT_TYPE	getContentType()
DOCUMENT_ROOT	ServletContext.getRealPath("/")
HTTP_ACCEPT	getHeader("Accept")
HTTP_REFERER	getHeader("Referer")
HTTP_USER_AGENT	getHeader("User-Agent")
PATH_INFO	getPathInfo()
PATH_TRANSLATED	getPathTranslated()
QUERY_STRING	getQueryString()
REMOTE_ADDR	getRemoteAddr()
REMOTE_HOST	getRemoteHost()
REMOTE_USER	getRemoteUser()
REQUEST_METHOD	getMethod()
SERVER_NAME	getServerName()
SERVER_PORT	getServerPort()
SERVER_PROTOCOL	getProtocol()
SERVER_SOFTWARE	ServletContext.getServerInfo()

display a username and password dialog box when an authentication challenge is received. This allows the user to enter a name and password and resubmit the request with authentication information.

This new request will contain an authorization header like `Authorization: Basic` that includes the username and password. If the authentication information is correct, the requested resource will be returned. Otherwise, an HTTP 401 "Not Authorized" message will be sent again. The type of authentication scheme being employed by the client is returned by the `getAuthType()` method. If no authentication scheme is used, `null` is returned. See Chapter 17 on security for more information about HTTP authentication.

getCookies()

```
public Cookie[] getCookies()
```

This method returns the cookies from the request in the form of an array of `Cookie` objects. The `Cookie` object resides in the `javax.servlet.http` package. This is an extremely useful method that is discussed in detail in Chapter 13. For now, suffice it to say that a *cookie* is a mechanism whereby a server can send a small amount of data to a client, which, in turn, sends this information back to the server with each request.

getDateHeader()

```
public long getDateHeader(String name)
```

This method returns the value of the specified header field in the form of a long integer. The `long` integer represents the number of milliseconds since midnight, January 1, 1970 GMT. A Java `Date` object can be created using this `long`. The following sample code illustrates how this is done. Normally, a request's date field represents the date and time the request was sent. Usually, this header is simply called "Date". A -1 is returned if the request does not contain the specified date header field. If the specified header field's value cannot be converted to a date, an `IllegalArgumentException` is thrown.

```
public void service(HttpServletRequest request,
  HttpServletResponse response) throws ServletException,
  IOException
{
  long requestDate=0;
  java.util.Date date=null;

  //set MIME type for HTTP header
  response.setContentType("text/plain");

  //get a handle to the output stream
```

```
PrintWriter out = response.getWriter();

requestDate = request.getDateHeader("Date");
if (requestDate == -1)
{
  out.println("Date header not found");
}
else
{
  try
  {
    date = new java.util.Date(requestDate);
  }
  catch (IllegalArgumentException e)
  {
    out.println("Invalid request date");
  }

  out.println("Request Date: " + date);
}

out.close(); //always close the output stream
}
```

It may be rare that you need to know when a request was sent. Rather, this method is most often used to extract date information from cache-control header fields such as the If-Modified-Since header that accompanies conditional GET requests.

getHeader()

```
public String getHeader(String name)
```

The getHeader() method returns the value of the specified header field or null if it does not exist (the header name is not case-sensitive). If the header may contain multiple values, use getHeaders() instead. This is an extremely useful method for retrieving the value of any HTTP header. For instance, there is a handy HTTP header called Referer that designates the page from which the user linked to the currently running servlet. This information can be useful if you require users to follow a specific link to get to a page rather than recall a bookmark or type in the URL manually. The following code demonstrates how the getHeader() method can be used to retrieve the page that jumped the user to our servlet.

```
public void service(HttpServletRequest request,
  HttpServletResponse response) throws ServletException,
  IOException
{
```

```
//set MIME type for HTTP header
response.setContentType("text/plain");

//get a handle to the output stream
PrintWriter out = response.getWriter();

out.println("Referred by: " + request.getHeader("Referer"));

out.close(); //always close the output stream
}
```

In a more advanced servlet, rather than just display the page that referred the user to our servlet, we might check the Referer value to make sure that the user arrived via our home page. In this way, we could prevent other sites from linking to our internal resources and, thus, bypassing our main page (which may contain advertisements or other information). Of course, the Referer header is only one example. Any HTTP header field (or even nonstandard, custom headers in the HTTP request) can be retrieved with the getHeader() method.

getHeaders()

```
public java.util.Enumeration getHeaders(String name)
```

The getHeaders() method returns an Enumeration of String objects that contains all values of the specified header field. It is possible for the same header field to be included multiple times within the HTTP header (usually having different values). For instance, consider the following request where the browser indicates that it will accept the response in either English or Spanish:

```
GET / HTTP/1.1
Accept-Language: en
Accept-Language: es
Host: insideservlets.com
Connection: Keep-Alive
```

The name of the header field is not case-sensitive. If the specified header field does not exist, an empty Enumeration is returned.

getHeaderNames()

```
public java.util.Enumeration getHeaderNames()
```

The getHeaderNames() method returns an Enumeration of all headers in the HTTP request. The following sample code demonstrates how the names of the headers are extracted with getHeaderNames() and the header values are returned using the getHeader() method.

```
public void service(HttpServletRequest request,
  HttpServletResponse response) throws ServletException,
  IOException
{
  String headerName="";

  //set MIME type for HTTP header
  response.setContentType("text/plain");

  //get a handle to the output stream
  PrintWriter out = response.getWriter();

  java.util.Enumeration enum = request.getHeaderNames();

  while (enum.hasMoreElements())
  {
    headerName = (String)enum.nextElement();
    out.println(headerName + ": " +
      request.getHeader(headerName));
  }

  out.close(); //always close the output stream
}
```

Figure 6.2 shows the output from this program as rendered by a browser.

getIntHeader()

```
public int getIntHeader(String name)
```

The getIntHeader() method is identical to the getHeader() method except that it returns the value of the specified header as an integer (the header name is not case-sensitive). If the integer header field does not exist, a -1 is returned. If the value of the header field cannot be converted to an integer, a Number-FormatException is thrown.

getMethod()

```
public String getMethod()
```

The getMethod() method returns the HTTP method (e.g., GET, POST, PUT) used by the request. Though this method can be very useful, it is often not necessary. Rather, the servlet doXxx() methods (doGet, doPost, doPut) can be implemented. If the service() method is not overridden, its default functionality checks the method type of each request and calls the appropriate doXxx() method.

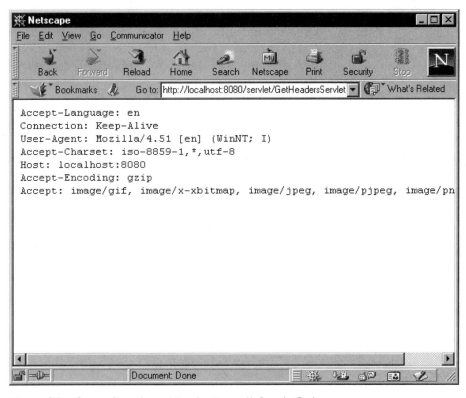

Figure 6.2 Output from the getHeaderNames() Sample Code

getPathInfo()

    public String getPathInfo()

The getPathInfo() method returns any path information following the servlet path but prior to the query string. It returns null if there is no path information following the servlet path. For example, if a servlet called GetPathServlet is invoked using this URL

http://localhost:8080/servlet/GetPathServlet/html/public?id=1234

the value returned by getPathInfo() is

    /html/public

getPathTranslated()

    public String getPathTranslated()

The getPathTranslated() method retrieves the path information following the servlet (excluding the query string) and translates it to a real path (according to the file system or network). It returns null if there is no path information following the servlet path. This method provides similar functionality to the getRealPath() method of the ServletContext object (see Chapter 10 for more information about the ServletContext object). For instance, getPathTranslated() is a convenience method that peforms the same function as this code:

```
String realPath = getServletContext().getRealPath(
    request.getPathInfo());
```

To illustrate the getPathTranslated() method, assume a servlet called Get-PathServlet is invoked using this URL:

http://localhost:8080/servlet/GetPathServlet/html/public?id=1234

The value returned by getPathTranslated() looks like this (on Windows):

```
C:\jakarta-tomcat\webpages\html\public
```

getQueryString()

```
public String getQueryString()
```

The getQueryString() method returns the query string of a URL. For example, if a servlet called GetQueryServlet is invoked using this URL

http://localhost:8080/servlet/GetQueryServlet?name=Tyler&age=6

the value returned by getQueryString() is

```
name=Tyler&age=6
```

getRemoteUser()

```
public String getRemoteUser()
```

The getRemoteUser() method returns the username submitted by HTTP authentication. For instance, if a resource on the server is protected using basic authentication, the browser is required to send a valid username and password to access the resource. The getRemoteUser() method returns the value of the username passed by the browser. Whether or not the username and password are passed on every subsequent request is browser dependent. If no username information exists in a request, getRemoteUser() returns null. For more information on HTTP authentication, see Chapter 17.

getRequestURI()

```
public String getRequestURI()
```

The getRequestURI() method returns the URI of the request. The URI includes all of the information in the URL up to the query string. This includes the protocol (if present), servlet path information, and additional path information (beyond the servlet path). For example, if a servlet called GetURIServlet is invoked using this URL

http://localhost:8080/servlet/GetURIServlet/html/public?name=Reagan&age=1

the value returned by getRequestURI() is

```
http://localhost:8080/servlet/GetURIServlet/html/public
```

getServletPath()

```
public String getServletPath()
```

The getServletPath() method returns the path to the servlet being invoked. For example, if a servlet called GetPathServlet is invoked using this URL

http://localhost:8080/servlet/GetPathServlet/html/public

the value returned by getServletPath() is

```
/servlet/GetPathServlet
```

ServletResponse Interface

> javax.servlet.ServletResponse

ServletResponse is an interface that resides in the javax.servlet package. This interface provides an object representation of the server's response to a client's request. When a servlet is invoked, the servlet container passes an object that implements the ServletResponse interface to the servlet's service() method. The servlet can then use this object to respond to the client's request. The ServletResponse object provides methods to acquire a handle to the server's output stream and set response headers.

The ServletResponse interface is used by non-HTTP servlets. HTTP servlets encapsulate responses in objects that implement the HttpServletResponse interface (which extends ServletResponse). Some of the most common methods of the ServletResponse object are described in the following pages.

getOutputStream()

```
public ServletOutputStream getOutputStream() throws
    java.io.IOException
```

The getOutputStream() method returns an output stream over which binary data can be transmitted back to the client. Actually, this method returns a specialized type of output stream object called ServletOutputStream. This object is discussed in detail in Chapter 10. This method should be used to transmit binary information to the client. For text responses, the getWriter() method is provided. Listing 6.4 demonstrates the getOutputStream() method as well as the getWriter() method described next.

Listing 6.4   Example of getOutputStream() and getWriter().

```java
import javax.servlet.http.*;
import javax.servlet.*;
import java.io.*;
import java.util.Date;

/**
 * GetOutputServlet
 *
 * Returns the requested file. It uses a ServletOutputStream to
 * return binary image data and a PrintWriter to return text
 * information.
 */
public class GetOutputServlet extends HttpServlet
{
  public void service(HttpServletRequest request,
    HttpServletResponse response) throws ServletException,
    IOException
  {
    File fileIn=null;
    FileInputStream streamIn=null;

    try
    {
      //get requested file after translating to file system path
      fileIn = new File(request.getPathTranslated());

      //open input stream
      streamIn = new FileInputStream(fileIn);
    }
    catch (FileNotFoundException e)
    {
      response.setContentType("text/plain");
      PrintWriter textOut = response.getWriter();
      textOut.println("File not found: " +
        request.getPathTranslated());
      textOut.close();
    }
```

```
     //create byte array to store file
     byte[] data = new byte[(int) fileIn.length()];

     streamIn.read(data); //read file into byte array
     streamIn.close(); //close file input stream

     if (request.getRequestURI().indexOf(".gif") > 0 ||
        request.getRequestURI().indexOf(".jpg") > 0 ||
        request.getRequestURI().indexOf(".jpeg") > 0) //image
     {
       //get output stream
       ServletOutputStream imageOut = response.getOutputStream();

       if (request.getRequestURI().indexOf(".gif") > 0 ) //gif
       {
         response.setContentType("image/gif");
       }
       else //not gif, so assume jpeg
       {
         response.setContentType("image/jpeg");
       }

       //write binary data to output stream
       imageOut.write(data);

       imageOut.close(); //close output stream
     }
     else //non-image request
     {
       if (request.getRequestURI().indexOf(".htm") > 0) //HTML
       {
         response.setContentType("text/html");
       }
       else //non-HTML file
       {
         response.setContentType("text/plain");
       }

       //get a handle to the output stream
       PrintWriter textOut = response.getWriter();

       //write text data to output stream using PrintWriter
       textOut.println(new String(data));

       textOut.close(); //always close the output stream
     }
   }
 }
}
```

getWriter()

```
public java.io.PrintWriter getWriter() throws
  java.io.IOException
```

The getWriter() method returns a PrintWriter object for the purpose of returning text information to the client. The PrintWriter object supports Unicode for providing international language support. Listing 6.5 demonstrates the getWriter() method. For binary data transmission, the getOutputStream() method should be used.

setContentLength()

```
public void setContentLength(int len)
```

The setContentLength() method sets the value of the Content-Length HTTP header in the response. The Content-Length header allows the client to determine when the entire response has been received. If the client wishes to use persistent connections, this information is required. Persistent connections (also called HTTP keep-alive) allow a single connection to support multiple requests. Persistent connections are the default behavior for HTTP/1.1 and will be employed if the Content-Length header is included in the response. The content length information is necessary so the client can determine when the response is complete and the next request can be issued (since the connection is not closed to indicate the end of the response). In addition, including the Content-Length header allows the client to accurately indicate progress as a response is received.

There are two important caveats to keep in mind when setting the content length. First, setContentLength() must be called before any output is sent to the client (as is the case with all HTTP header fields). Second, the content length value must be exact. The simplest way to ensure that the content length setting is accurate is to write the entire HTML output to a CharArrayWriter. The Content-Length can then be set based on the size of the CharArrayWriter and the HTML can be returned to the client by writing the CharArrayWriter to the client output stream (using the PrintWriter object returned from response.getWriter()) as shown here:

```
public void doGet(HttpServletRequest request,
  HttpServletResponse response) throws ServletException,
  IOException
{
  response.setContentType("text/html");

  //get CharArrayWriter to buffer the output
  CharArrayWriter htmlOutput = new CharArrayWriter();
```

```
//create a PrintWriter that writes to the CharArrayWriter
PrintWriter out = new PrintWriter(htmlOutput);

//write the HTML document to the CharArrayWriter
out.println("<HTML>");
out.println("<HEAD><TITLE>Sample</TITLE></HEAD>");
out.println("<BODY>");
out.println("Content-length header included.");
out.println("</BODY>");
out.println("</HTML>");

//set Content-Length based on the size of the CharArrayWriter
response.setContentLength(htmlOutput.size());

//GET request so send HTML (don't send HTML for HEAD requests)
if (request.getMethod().equals("GET"))
{
  //write HTML from CharArrayWriter to client output stream
  htmlOutput.writeTo(response.getWriter());
}
}
```

This doGet() method demonstrates how the exact content length can be determined before returning the response to the client. Note that the code does not return the content body (i.e., the HTML) in response to a HEAD request. Remember that, even though content is not returned in response to a HEAD request, the Content-Length header should be the same as if the request was a GET. Lastly, a ByteArrayOutputStream can be used in place of the CharArray-Writer if binary data is being returned (in which case response.getOutput-Stream() should be used in place of response.getWriter()).

setContentType()

```
public void setContentType(String type)
```

The setContentType() method sets the Content-Type HTTP header in the response. This header defines the format of the information returned in the data portion of the response and allows the client to properly process the information. If this method is called after the response has been committed (i.e., flushed to the client), an IllegalStateException is thrown. See Table 6.4 earlier in this chapter for examples of a few common MIME types. Since the HTTP/1.1 specification does not require this header to be set, servlet containers must not set a default content type if not explicitly set by the servlet.

HttpServletResponse Interface

HttpServletResponse is an interface that resides in the javax.servlet.http package. This interface extends ServletResponse and, therefore, supports all of its methods in addition to those presented here.

HttpServletResponse provides an object representation of the server's response to a client's request. Whenever an HTTP servlet is invoked, the servlet container passes an object that implements the HttpServletResponse interface to the servlet's service() method. The servlet can then use this object to respond to the client's request. The HttpServletResponse object provides methods to add cookies to the response, set response headers, send HTTP redirects, and more. The following descriptions and sample code illustrate many of the most common methods of the HttpServletResponse object.

addCookie()

```
public void addCookie(Cookie cookie)
```

The addCookie() method adds a cookie to the HTTP response. The Cookie object resides in the javax.servlet.http package. This method is discussed in detail in Chapter 13. As described previously, a *cookie* is a mechanism whereby a server can send a small amount of data to a client, which, in turn, sends this information back to the server with every request.

Cookies are transmitted within the HTTP header. They are very useful for setting user preferences and maintaining state on the Web. For instance, if a user logs into a protected site, the server may send the client a cookie containing a valid username and password or, more commonly, a unique *session ID* (usually a very large number or sequence of alphanumeric characters). The session ID that is transmitted back to the server inside every client request allows the server to verify that the request came from the same client that successfully logged into the site. In this manner security can be maintained and a user can be "tracked" throughout a site. See Chapters 13 and 14 for more information about cookies and session management.

containsHeader()

```
public boolean containsHeader(String name)
```

The containsHeader() method determines whether a specified header is contained in the response. If the header field exists in the response message, true is returned; otherwise, false is returned.

sendError()

```
public void sendError(int sc) throws java.io.IOException
public void sendError(int sc, String message) throws
    java.io.IOException
```

The sendError() methods return an error message to the client according to the specified status code. The HttpServletResponse object defines many status codes. These status codes are exposed as static constants. Just a few of the many status codes defined by HttpServletResponse are listed in Table 6.6.

The first sendError() method accepts an integer that specifies the HTTP status code to return to the client. The second sendError() method accepts an integer and a String. The integer represents the HTTP status code and the string should contain a descriptive message about the error. The status code is

Table 6.6 Common Status Codes Defined in HttpServletResponse

Status Code	Description
SC_BAD_GATEWAY	The server received an invalid response from an upstream server while acting as a proxy or gateway.
SC_BAD_REQUEST	The client's request used invalid syntax.
SC_CONFLICT	There was a conflict that prevented access to the requested resource.
SC_FORBIDDEN	The request was received and understood but the server refuses to fulfill it.
SC_GATEWAY_TIMEOUT	While serving as a proxy or gateway, the server did not receive a response from an upstream server within the timeout period.
SC_GONE	The resource is no longer available.
SC_HTTP_VERSION_NOT_SUPPORTED	The HTTP version used by the client is not supported by the server.
SC_INTERNAL_SERVER_ERROR	An unspecified error occurred on the server that prevented it from servicing the request.

part of the HTTP header but the descriptive message is contained in the message content and comprises the body of an HTML page returned to the client. If the status code was previously set by the setStatus() method (described shortly), it is reset to the error code specified in the call to sendError().

The sendError() method automatically calls the HttpServletResponse object's reset() method to clear any previously set headers, status codes, and body content. If sendError() is called after the response has been committed, this method throws an IllegalStateException. Therefore, it is good practice to use the HttpServletResponse.isCommitted() method before calling sendError() (discussed later in this chapter). The following sample code illustrates the use of the sendError() method.

```
public void service(HttpServletRequest request,
  HttpServletResponse response) throws ServletException,
  IOException
{
  if (!response.isCommitted())
  {
    response.sendError(response.SC_GONE,
      "Resource no longer available.");
  }
}
```

The response from the servlet that implements this simple service() method looks like this:

```
HTTP/1.1 410 Gone
Servlet-Engine: Tomcat Web Server/3.1
Content-Type: text/html
Content-Length: 119
Date: Tue, 25 Jan 2000 05:38:09 GMT

<html><head><title>410 Gone</title></head>
<h1>410 Gone</h1><body>
Resource no longer available.<p>
</body></html>
```

Notice how the string passed to the sendError() method is placed in the body of the HTML page returned to the client.

sendRedirect()

```
public void sendRedirect(String location) throws
  java.io.IOException
```

The sendRedirect() method sends a temporary redirect message to the client according to the specified location. If the location parameter represents a relative URL, it will be converted to an absolute URL before the response is returned. Upon receiving the redirect response, the browser should immediately request the resource from the new location. The sample code that follows demonstrates the `sendRedirect()` method.

```
public void service(HttpServletRequest request,
  HttpServletResponse response) throws ServletException,
  IOException
{
  response.sendRedirect("http://www.insideservlets.com/");
}
```

The servlet that implements this `service()` method sends the following HTTP redirect response to the client.

```
HTTP/1.1 302 Moved Temporarily
Content-Type: text/html
Location: http://www.insideservlets.com/
Content-Length: 161
Date: Tue, 25 Jan 2000 05:38:09 GMT

<head><title>Document moved</title></head>
<body><h1>Document moved</h1>
This document has moved <a href="http://www.insideservlets.com">
here</a>.<p>
</body>
```

The HTTP status code 302 "Moved Temporarily" instructs the browser to redirect to the URL specified in the `Location` header. HTTP redirects are discussed in more detail in Chapter 12.

setDateHeader() *and* addDateHeader()

```
public void setDateHeader(String name, long date)
public void addDateHeader(String name, long date)
```

The `setDateHeader()` method adds a new date header to the response—replacing any existing headers of the same name. The `addDateHeader()` method also adds a date header to the response but does not replace existing headers of the same name. `addDateHeader()` allows a response header to have multiple values. If the specified header does not already exist, `addDateHeader()` functions the same as `setDateHeader()` (it simply adds the new header). The `name` parameter sets the name of the header and the `date` parameter sets the date. The date is specified using the number of milliseconds since the epoch (midnight, January 1, 1970 GMT). The following sample code demonstrates these methods.

```
public void service(HttpServletRequest request,
  HttpServletResponse response) throws ServletException,
  IOException
{
  response.setContentType("text/plain");
```

```
        java.util.Date newDate = new java.util.Date();

        response.setDateHeader("MyDate", newDate.getTime());

        response.addDateHeader("MyDates", newDate.getTime());
        response.addDateHeader("MyDates", newDate.getTime());

        PrintWriter out = response.getWriter();

        out.println("This response includes three new date headers.");

        out.close();
    }
```

The HTTP response returned by the servlet that implements this `service()` method looks like this:

```
HTTP/1.1 200 OK
MyDate: Tue, 25 Jan 2000 05:38:09 GMT
MyDates: Tue, 25 Jan 2000 05:38:09 GMT
MyDates: Tue, 25 Jan 2000 05:38:09 GMT
Date: Tue, 25 Jan 2000 05:38:09 GMT
Content-Type: text/plain

This response includes three new date headers.
```

The new date headers, called `MyDate` and `MyDates`, are visible above the server's standard `Date` header.

NOTE: The `Date` header field that is automatically included in the HTTP response by the HTTP server cannot be replaced using the `setDateHeader()` method and, similarly, `Date` headers cannot be added using `addDateHeader()`. For instance, the following lines will not change the `Date` header or add `Date` headers. They will essentially be ignored by the server.

```
response.setDateHeader("Date", (new Date()).getTime());
response.addDateHeader("Date", (new Date()).getTime());
```

setHeader() *and* addHeader()

```
public void setHeader(String name, String value)
```

The `setHeader()` method is similar to the `setDateHeader()` method except that the value of the header is comprised of a `String` rather than a date. This method will replace any existing headers of the same name. Likewise, the `addHeader()` method functions the same as `addDateHeader()` except that it stores text rather than dates in the header. This method will add headers without replacing existing headers of the same name. If the specified header does not already exist, addHeader() functions the same as setHeader() (it simply adds the new header). The name parameter sets the name of the header and the value parameter specifies a String value. The following sample code sets the Cache-Control HTTP header to instruct the browser and proxy server that the response should not be cached.

```
public void service(HttpServletRequest request,
  HttpServletResponse response) throws ServletException,
  IOException
{
  response.setContentType("text/plain");

  response.setHeader("Cache-Control", "no-cache"); //for browser
  response.addHeader("Cache-Control", "no-store"); //for proxy

  PrintWriter out = response.getWriter();

  out.println("This response should not be cached.");

  out.close();
}
```

The HTTP response produced by the preceding service() method looks like this:

```
HTTP/1.1 200 OK
Cache-Control: no-store
Cache-Control: no-cache
Date: Tue, 25 Jan 2000 05:38:09 GMT
Content-Type: text/plain

This response should not be cached.
```

An HTTP/1.1-compliant browser or proxy server reads the Cache-Control header for instructions on how to cache the page. The no-cache value instructs the browser not to cache this page but to fetch it again from the server the next time it is requested. Similarly, the no-store value indicates that this page should not be stored by a proxy server (often for security reasons). HTTP/1.0 uses the Pragma: no-cache header to convey the same "do not cache" instructions. The counterpart to the setHeader() method is the getHeader() method of Http-ServletRequest, which can be used to read headers passed to the servlet.

setIntHeader() *and* addIntHeader()

```
public void setIntHeader(String name, int value)
```

The setIntHeader() method is identical to the setHeader() method except that the header value is comprised of an integer rather than a String. This method will replace any existing headers of the same name. Likewise, the add-IntHeader() method functions the same as addHeader() except that it stores an integer value rather than text in the header. This method will add headers without replacing existing headers of the same name. If the specified header does not already exist, addIntHeader() functions the same as setIntHeader() (it simply adds the new header). The name parameter sets the name of the header and the value parameter sets the integer value of the header. The counterpart to the setIntHeader() method is the getIntHeader() method of HttpServletRequest, which can be used to read integer headers passed to the servlet.

setStatus()

```
public void setStatus(int sc)
```

The setStatus() method is very similar to the sendError(int) method. It simply sets the HTTP status code to be included in the response according to the specified status code number. This sample code illustrates the use of this method.

```
public void service(HttpServletRequest request,
    HttpServletResponse response) throws ServletException,
    IOException
{
  response.setStatus(response.SC_OK); //HTTP 200 status code

  response.setContentType("text/plain");

  PrintWriter out = response.getWriter();

  out.println("Request serviced successfully.");

  out.close();
}
```

The preceding service() method returns the HTTP response shown here:

```
HTTP/1.1 200 OK
Content-Type: text/plain
Date: Tue, 25 Jan 2000 05:38:09 GMT

Request serviced successfully.
```

NOTE: Prior to Servlet API 2.1, a second setStatus() method was defined. This method accepted an integer as well as a String. The syntax of this method looked like this:

```
public void setStatus(int sc, String message)
```

The integer represented the HTTP status code and the `String` contained a brief description of the status code. This description replaced the *reason phrase* that normally accompanied an HTTP status code. For instance, HTTP status code 200 is normally accompanied by the phrase "OK" and HTTP status code 404 is usually accompanied by the message "Not Found" (both status code and reason phrase are on the first line of the HTTP header). This `status()` method enabled a servlet to replace a reason phrase with a message of its own (perhaps changing "OK" to "Success"). However, due to ambiguity regarding the proper use and purpose of the message parameter, this method was deprecated in Servlet API 2.1.

Response Buffering

Response buffering is routinely used by servers to improve performance and network efficiency. *Response buffering* is the process of storing a servlet's output in memory until a threshold amount is buffered or the servlet explicitly requests the buffer to be flushed. This allows the server to send information to the client in blocks of data rather than just a few bytes at a time. It also gives the servlet developer some additional flexibility.

Introduced in Servlet API 2.2, servlets can now control the amount of buffering performed by the server. Additionally, servlets now have the ability to query the server for the size of the output buffer, determine if any data has yet been returned to the client, and clear the buffer. The following methods allow a servlet to query and control many aspects of the response-buffering process.

flushBuffer()

```
public void flushBuffer() throws java.io.IOException
```

The `flushBuffer()` method forces the server to send all data in the buffer, including all response headers to the client. This method is useful if you would like to send data to the client at intervals rather than waiting for the entire response to be generated. Though less efficient, flushing the buffer at smaller intervals can give the perception that the response is being received faster. This is due to the fact that the user can immediately see the page start to load (a portion at a time) rather than receiving the entire page after some delay. To illustrate, the sample servlet presented in Listing 6.5 counts down from 5 to 1 by flushing the buffer after each number is written to the output stream.

Listing 6.5 Forcing the server to flush its buffer.

```
import javax.servlet.*;
import javax.servlet.http.*;
import java.io.*;
```

```
/**
 * CountdownServlet demonstrates how the server's buffer can be
 * flushed to the client at intervals.
 */
public class CountdownServlet extends HttpServlet
{
  /**
   * Sends a message to the client after counting down from 5.
   * Each number is flushed individually so the client will see
   * the numbers at 2 second intervals.
   */
  public void doGet(HttpServletRequest request,
    HttpServletResponse response) throws ServletException,
    IOException
  {
    response.setContentType("text/html");
    PrintWriter out = response.getWriter();

    out.println("<HTML>");
    out.println("<HEAD><TITLE>CountdownServlet</TITLE></HEAD>");
    out.println("<BODY>");

    //send countdown to client
    for (int x=5; x > 0; x--)
    {
      out.print(x + " . . . ");
      out.flush(); //flushes PrintWriter's buffer to the server
      response.flushBuffer(); //flushes server's buffer to client
      pause(2000); //pause for 2 seconds
    }

    //send message when countdown completes
    out.println("BUFFERING WORKS!");
    out.println("</BODY></HTML>");

    out.flush(); //flush the output stream
  }


  /**
   * Sleep for the specified number of milliseconds.
   *
   * @param interval Number of milliseconds to sleep.
   */
  private void pause(int interval)
  {
    try
    {
      Thread.sleep(interval);
    }
    catch (InterruptedException e)
    {
    }
  }
}
```

Note that the `PrintWriter` object has a buffer of its own. When the servlet writes to the `PrintWriter`, that data is not necessarily sent to the server's buffer immediately. It may be buffered by the `PrintWriter` object. Therefore, be sure to flush the `PrintWriter` object before flushing the server's buffer using `response.flushBuffer()`.

Flushing the buffer at intervals can also be used to show status while the client waits for the server to finish processing the request. For instance, if the server is performing a lengthy process, such as a credit card authorization, it may flush some type of progress indicator to the client every few seconds until the process is complete (at which point it informs the client that the card was either approved or rejected). Intermittent progress updates reassure the client that the server is still working on the request (even after a longer than expected wait).

getBufferSize()

```
public int getBufferSize()
```

The `getBufferSize()` method returns, in bytes, the size of the server's response buffer. This method is typically used when the proper processing of a request depends on the size of the server's buffer. For example, a servlet that alters its response if an error occurs can start writing the response to the output stream and, if there is an error while processing the response, it can clear the response buffer and send a new message. However, this behavior depends on the size of the response buffer since the server will automatically flush the buffer once it becomes full. The response cannot be altered after the buffer has been flushed. Therefore, in this case, checking the server's buffer size can guarantee expected results. `getBufferSize()` is often used in conjunction with `setBufferSize()`. In this way, if the response buffer is too small, the servlet can request that its size be increased.

isCommitted()

```
public boolean isCommitted()
```

A response is said to be *committed* once the first portion of it (including the response status code and headers) is sent to the client. The server commits the response when the response buffer is full or the servlet explicitly requests that the buffer be flushed (using the `flushBuffer()` method). Once committed, the headers cannot be altered and the response buffer cannot be cleared. Always check this method before attempting to clear the response buffer.

reset()

```
public void reset()
```

The reset() method clears all data in the response buffer as well as the response status code and all headers. reset() must be called before the response is committed or the method will throw an IllegalStateException. This method allows the servlet to alter the response even after it is partially complete (as long as the response has not been committed). For example, the following doGet() method alters its response when an error occurs.

```java
public void doGet(HttpServletRequest request,
  HttpServletResponse response) throws ServletException,
  IOException
{
  PrintWriter out = response.getWriter();

  try
  {
    response.setContentType("text/html");

    out.println("<HTML>");
    out.println("<HEAD><TITLE>Success</TITLE></HEAD>");
    out.println("<BODY>");

    //cause an error while generating response body
    int x = 1/0; //generate divide by zero error

    out.println("</BODY></HTML>");

    out.flush(); //flush the output stream
  }
  catch(Exception e) //catch divide by zero error
  {
    response.reset(); //clear the original response from buffer

    //create a new response that describes the error
    response.setContentType("text/html");

    out.println("<HTML>");
    out.println("<HEAD><TITLE>Error</TITLE></HEAD>");
    out.println("<BODY>");
    out.println("The following error occurred:<BR>" + e);
    out.println("</BODY></HTML>");

    out.flush(); //flush the output stream
  }
}
```

setBufferSize()
```
public void setBufferSize(int size)
```

The setBufferSize() method sets the preferred minimum reponse buffer size. The server may choose to use a larger buffer than that specified by setBuffer-Size(). Use getBufferSize() to determine the actual size of the response buffer. A larger buffer is more network efficient and often more flexible because it gives the servlet more time to set headers or alter the response. A smaller buffer size allows the user to receive data more quickly and consumes less memory on the server.

Summary

This chapter introduces some of the most used classes and interfaces in the Servlet API. Most likely, you will use many of these objects in every servlet you develop. In the next chapter, we will build a functional servlet from scratch.

Chapter Highlights

- HttpServlet class—Most HTTP servlets extend this class. HttpServlet defines methods that are called by the server whenever a servlet request is received. HttpServlet extends GenericServlet.

- GenericServlet class—Most non-HTTP servlets extend this class. GenericServlet defines the service() method that is called by the server whenever a servlet request is received.

- ServletRequest interface—For non-HTTP servlets, the information sent in the client request is encapsulated in a ServletRequest object. This object is passed to the servlet's service() method.

- HttpServletRequest interface—For HTTP servlets, the information sent in the client request is encapsulated in an HttpServletRequest object. This object is passed to the servlet's service() method (which, in turn, may pass it to the doGet() or doPost() method).

- ServletResponse interface—For non-HTTP servlets, the methods necessary to customize a response are contained in a ServletResponse object. This object is passed to the servlet's service() method.

- HttpServletResponse interface—For HTTP servlets, the methods necessary to customize a response are contained in an HttpServletResponse object. This object is passed to the servlet's service() method (which, in turn, may pass it to the doGet() or doPost() method).

CHAPTER 7

Writing Your First Servlet

In this chapter, we will construct a fully functional Bulletin Board servlet from scratch. This servlet will allow users to view posted comments and add their own thoughts. For the sake of simplicity, the bulletins will be stored in text files rather than a database. Adding database connectivity is an exercise left to the reader (see Chapter 16 for information about database connectivity). In the following chapters, we will explore how to test and debug your first servlet.

Servlet Requirements

As is critical with any project, we will begin with a brief analysis and design phase. For starters, let's take a look at the requirements for the servlet that we are going to build. The functionality of the Bulletin Board servlet can be described in the following five requirements.

1. The bulletins for each topic should be stored in a separate text file. A simple append operation can be used to add bulletins to the text file. No update, delete, or sorting operation is required. (A second phase of this project might allow the administrator to update, edit, and delete bulletins.)

2. The servlet should retrieve the location of the text files described in requirement 1 from an initialization parameter set on the server. In this way, the location of these files can be changed easily without recompiling the servlet.

3. The servlet must read a list of bulletin board topics from a properties file. In this manner, the administrator can dynamically add and remove topics by altering the properties file and reloading the servlet. (Again, a second phase of this project might add an administrative screen to allow the topics list to be reloaded without reloading the servlet.)

4. After selecting a topic of interest, users should be able to view the bulletins relating to that topic or append bulletins of their own. In addition, a large text area must be provided for typing bulletins that span several lines.

5. Every page must have a link back to the main page. In addition, on returning to the main page, the user's previously selected bulletin board topic should remain selected.

Now that we know the requirements, let's take a look at a few screen shots. A visual mock-up is often the best way to quickly convey an application's functionality.

Main Page

The main page of the Bulletin Board servlet allows the user to select a topic of interest from a drop-down list. The main page is shown in Figure 7.1.

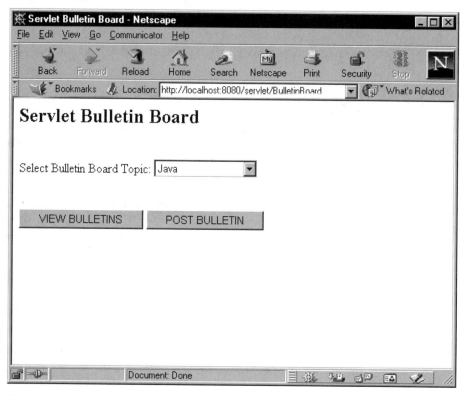

Figure 7.1   Bulletin Board Main Page

The drop-down list is populated with bulletin board topics that are read from a properties file. The **VIEW BULLETINS** button allows the user to view all bulletins for the selected bulletin board. The **POST BULLETIN** button displays an HTML form that allows users to add their own comments to the selected bulletin board.

Let's take a look at the code that generates this screen. First, the servlet must read the available topics from a properties file and retrieve the directory where the bulletins are stored from an initialization parameter. These operations are performed in the servlet's `init()` method.

```java
private String filePath; //stores root path for bulletin files
private Properties propTopics; //stores bulletin board topics

/**
 * init() method is called when the servlet is first loaded. It
 * reads the directory where the bulletin files are stored from
 * an initialization parameter.
 */
public void init() throws ServletException
{
  //get path to topics properties file and bulletin board files
  filePath = getInitParameter("FilePath");

  if (filePath == null)
  {
    //default to root directory if no FilePath init parameter
    filePath = File.separator;
  }
  else if (!filePath.endsWith(File.separator))
  {
    filePath += File.separator; //add separator if necessary
  }

  FileInputStream fileTopics = null;

  try
  {
    //open input stream to topics.properties file
    fileTopics = new FileInputStream(filePath +
      "topics.properties");

    propTopics = new Properties();
    propTopics.load(fileTopics); //load properties object
  }
  catch (FileNotFoundException e)
  {
    throw new ServletException("The topics.properties file " +
      "was not found at " + filePath + "<BR><BR>Error: " + e);
  }
```

```
catch (Exception e)
{
  throw new ServletException("Error: " + e);
}
finally
{
  try
  {
    fileTopics.close(); //close file input stream
  }
  catch (Exception ignored) {}
}
}
```

The getInitParameter() method is used to retrieve the value of the initialization parameter, FilePath. Notice how the filePath variable is declared as an instance variable outside of any method. In this way, all requests serviced by this servlet will have access to its value. Since the value of filePath is set in the init() method and does not change, the use of an instance variable is thread safe. As we will see in Chapter 11, storing volatile information in a class or instance variable is not thread safe and can lead to errors and inconsistent results. Many of these errors are subtle and very difficult to debug.

In addition to retrieving the FilePath initialization parameter, the init() method opens a stream to a properties file from which it loads a Properties object called propTopics. The servlet uses this Properties object to populate the drop-down list of bulletin board topics. The Properties object is declared as an instance variable so that it can be used by each servlet invocation. The Properties object is populated within the init() method so that the properties file need be read from disk only once.

The first line of the servlet's init() method retrieves the initialization parameter FilePath from the server environment and assigns its value to the filePath variable. If the FilePath initialization parameter was not set, the directory is set to the file system root by default (e.g., "/" or "\" depending on the operating system). The File.separator constant is used to determine the proper file separator for the current operating system. In addition, if the File-Path parameter does not end with a file separator (as expected), a separator is appended.

After processing the FilePath initialization parameter, a FileInput-Stream object called fileTopics is declared outside of the try/catch block. This object is declared outside the try/catch block because it is closed in the finally block. If it had been declared inside of the try/catch, it would have been out of scope within the finally block, resulting in a compile error.

```
try
{
  //open input stream to topics.properties file
  fileTopics = new FileInputStream(filePath +
    "topics.properties");

  propTopics = new Properties();
  propTopics.load(fileTopics); //load properties object
}
```

The preceding code represents the entire try block. The first line within the try block creates a FileInputStream to the *topics.properties* file located in the filePath directory (filePath is read from an initialization parameter). Before running the servlet, you must create this text file and place it in the filePath directory (unless altered by the FilePath init parameter, this will be the root of the file system). The contents of the *topics.properties* file used in this example are:

```
# Bulletin Board servlet topics
Topic1=Java
Topic2=Internet
Topic3=World Wide Web
```

NOTE: If you receive a java.io.FileNotFoundException exception when invoking the BulletinBoard servlet, make sure that you have created the *topics.properties* file and placed it in the directory specified by the FilePath init parameter (if no FilePath init parameter is explicitly set, the default is the root of the file system).

Next, a new Properties object is instantiated and, using the FileInput-Stream we just created, we load it with the bulletin board topics. The init() method concludes with several catch statements for catching errors and a finally block that closes the FileInputStream.

Now let's take a look at the next piece of functionality required to load the main page. The servlet must create an Enumeration using the propTopics object in order to populate the drop-down list of topics as well as generate the HTML to render the page. This functionality is located within the doGet() method. Recall that the doGet() method is invoked in response to any HTTP GET request.

```
/**
 * doGet() method is called in response to any GET request.
 * Returns an HTML form that allows the user to select a
```

```
 * bulletin board topic and choose to view bulletins or post
 * a new one.
 */
public void doGet(HttpServletRequest request,
  HttpServletResponse response) throws IOException
{
  response.setContentType("text/html"); //html output

  //get a handle to the output stream
  PrintWriter out = response.getWriter();

  try
  {
    //create HTML form to allow user to select a topic
    out.println("<HTML>");
    out.println("<HEAD>");
    out.println("<TITLE>Servlet Bulletin Board</TITLE>");
    out.println("</HEAD>");
    out.println("<BODY>");
    out.println("<H2>Servlet Bulletin Board</H2>");
    out.println("<BR><FORM METHOD=\"POST\">");
    out.println("Select Bulletin Board Topic: ");

    out.println("<SELECT NAME=\"Topic\">"); //begin SELECT tag

    String topic; //stores description of current topic

    //create enumeration from properties object
    Enumeration enumTopics = propTopics.propertyNames();

    //iterate through all topics in topics.properties file
    while (enumTopics.hasMoreElements())
    {
      //set topic variable to current topic in enumeration
      topic = (String)enumTopics.nextElement();

      //add each topic from properties file to drop-down list
      if (propTopics.getProperty(topic).equals(
        request.getParameter("Topic")))
      {
        //if user has selected a topic, keep it selected
        out.println("<OPTION SELECTED>" +
          propTopics.getProperty(topic) + "</OPTION>");
      }
      else
      {
        //not the selected topic, just add to drop-down list
        out.println("<OPTION>" +
          propTopics.getProperty(topic) + "</OPTION>");
      }
    }

    out.println("</SELECT><BR><BR><BR>"); //end SELECT tag
```

```
      //display View and Post buttons
      out.println("<INPUT TYPE=\"SUBMIT\" NAME=\"VIEW\" " +
        "VALUE=\"VIEW BULLETINS\"> ");
      out.println("<INPUT TYPE=\"SUBMIT\" NAME=\"POST\" " +
        "VALUE=\"POST BULLETIN\">");
      out.println("</FORM>");
      out.println("</BODY></HTML>");
    }
    catch (Exception e)
    {
      sendErrorToClient(out, e); //send stack trace to client
      log("Error occurred in doGet() method.", e); //log error
    }
    finally
    {
      try
      {
        //close output stream
        out.close();
      }
      catch (Exception ignored) {}
    }
  }
}
```

We will now dissect the doGet() method shown previously and evaluate its parts.

```
response.setContentType("text/html"); //html output

//get a handle to the output stream
PrintWriter out = response.getWriter();
```

This code is fairly straightforward. We begin the method by setting the content type of our response to HTML. The code then gets a handle to the output stream. Since we will be returning only ASCII text, a PrintWriter object is used.

```
try
{
  //create HTML form to allow user to select a topic
  out.println("<HTML>");
  out.println("<HEAD>");
  out.println("<TITLE>Servlet Bulletin Board</TITLE>");
  out.println("</HEAD>");
  out.println("<BODY>");
  out.println("<H2>Servlet Bulletin Board</H2>");
  out.println("<BR><FORM METHOD=\"POST\">");
  out.println("Select Bulletin Board Topic: ");
```

These lines of code open the try block and begin sending HTML to the client. An HTML form is created in order to send the user's selection back to the

server. Notice that the <FORM> tag does not contain an ACTION attribute. If no
ACTION is specified, the browser submits the form to the same URL from which
it was received (i.e., back to the Bulletin Board servlet).

```
out.println("<SELECT NAME=\"Topic\">"); //begin SELECT tag

String topic; //stores description of current topic

//create enumeration from properties object
Enumeration enumTopics = propTopics.propertyNames();

//iterate through all topics in topics.properties file
while (enumTopics.hasMoreElements())
{
  //set topic variable to current topic in enumeration
  topic = (String)enumTopics.nextElement();

  //add each topic from properties file to drop-down list
  if (propTopics.getProperty(topic).equals(
    request.getParameter("Topic")))
  {
    //if user has selected a topic, keep it selected
    out.println("<OPTION SELECTED>" +
      propTopics.getProperty(topic) + "</OPTION>");
  }
  else
  {
    //not the selected topic, just add to drop-down list
    out.println("<OPTION>" +
      propTopics.getProperty(topic) + "</OPTION>");
  }
}

out.println("</SELECT><BR><BR><BR>"); //end SELECT tag
```

The preceding code creates and populates the drop-down list of bulletin
board topics. After opening the <SELECT> HTML element, an Enumeration of
property names (e.g., Topic1, Topic2) is created. These property names, in conjunction with the Properties object's getProperty() method, are used to populate the drop-down list. The bulletin board topic selected by the user on the
main page is retrieved via the HttpServletRequest object's getParameter()
method. Since we know that the Topic parameter consists of a single value, it is
safe to use the getParameter() method rather than getParameterValues().

When a user is returning to the main page, the if/else statement in the
preceding code is used to maintain the user's topic selection. As we will see
shortly, this is accomplished by passing the currently selected topic from page
to page and finally passing it back to the main page in the query string of the
Return to Main Page hyperlink.

```
      //display View and Post buttons
      out.println("<INPUT TYPE=\"SUBMIT\" NAME=\"VIEW\" " +
        "VALUE=\"VIEW BULLETINS\"> ");
      out.println("<INPUT TYPE=\"SUBMIT\" NAME=\"POST\" " +
        "VALUE=\"POST BULLETIN\">");
      out.println("</FORM>");
      out.println("</BODY></HTML>");
    }
```

The preceding lines complete the HTML document that is returned to the client in response to a GET request. Two SUBMIT buttons are added to the HTML form to allow the user to select whether to view or post bulletins. When either of these buttons is clicked, the form values are transmitted to the server as name/value pairs. These name/value pairs allow the servlet to determine which bulletin board topic was selected by the user and which SUBMIT button was pressed. It is possible to determine which button was pressed by checking the named parameters passed to the server using the request object's getParameter() method. For example, if the **VIEW BULLETINS** button is pressed, a parameter named VIEW will be passed to the server (since this SUBMIT button's NAME attribute is set to VIEW). On the other hand, if the **POST BULLETIN** button is pressed, a parameter named POST is passed to the server.

```
      catch (Exception e)
      {
        sendErrorToClient(out, e); //send stack trace to client
        log("Error occurred in doGet() method.", e); //log error
      }
      finally
      {
        try
        {
          //close output stream
          out.close();
        }
        catch (Exception ignored) {}
      }
    }
```

The preceding code completes the doGet() method by catching all exceptions and closing the PrintWriter output stream. If an exception is thrown, the sendErrorToClient() method is called; it sends a simple error message to the client, and the error is logged. A second phase of the Bulletin Board servlet project might add more robust exception handling.

NOTE: Closing the client output stream (e.g., a `PrintWriter` or `ServletOutput-Stream` object) does not necessarily close the underlying socket connection. However, the server may choose to close the connection to the client when the output stream is closed by the servlet.

View Bulletins Page

The **View Bulletins** page displays bulletins for the selected topic. This page is displayed in response to the user's clicking the **VIEW BULLETINS** button on the main page. The **View Bulletins** page is shown in Figure 7.2.

The **View Bulletins** screen displays all bulletins for the selected topic in oldest-to-newest order. A link is also provided to return the user to the main page. Later we will see that a query string is appended to the **Return to Main Page**

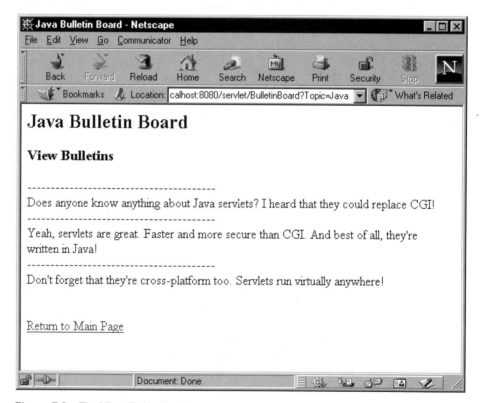

Figure 7.2   The **View Bulletins** Page

link, indicating the currently selected bulletin board topic. In this way, the current topic remains selected when the user returns to the main page.

The code that implements the functionality behind the **View Bulletins** screen is split between the doPost() and viewBulletins() methods. Remember that the doPost() method is called in response to an HTTP POST request. In this case, the doPost() method is called when the user clicks the **VIEW BULLETINS** button on the main page. However, this is not the only action that invokes the doPost() method. This method is also called when the user clicks the **POST BULLETIN** button on the main page as well as the **SAVE BULLETIN** button on the **Post Bulletin** page (which we'll discuss shortly). Let's start by examining the following doPost() method.

```java
/**
 * doPost() method is called in response to any POST request.
 * This method determines if it was called in response to the
 * user selecting to view bulletins, post a bulletin, or
 * save a bulletin and responds accordingly.
 */
public void doPost(HttpServletRequest request,
  HttpServletResponse response)
{
  PrintWriter out = null;

  //get bulletin board topic selected from drop-down list
  String currentTopic = request.getParameter("Topic");

  //get the name of file containing bulletins for this topic
  String file = filePath + currentTopic + ".txt";

  //get path to servlet for use in hyperlinks
  String servletPath = request.getContextPath() +
    request.getServletPath();

  response.setContentType("text/html"); //html output

  try
  {
    out = response.getWriter(); //get handle to output stream

    //send HTML tags common to show, post, and save pages
    out.println("<HTML>");
    out.println("<HEAD><TITLE>" + currentTopic +
      " Bulletin Board</TITLE></HEAD>");
    out.println("<BODY>");

    boolean showReturnLink = false;

    //display view, post, or save page
    if (request.getParameter("VIEW") != null) //view
    {
```

```
        //displays bulletins for the selected topic
        viewBulletins(out, file, currentTopic);

        showReturnLink = true;
      }
      else if (request.getParameter("POST") != null) //post
      {
        //allows user to enter bulletin and submit it
        postBulletin(out, currentTopic);
      }
      else if (request.getParameter("SAVE") != null) //save
      {
        //saves bulletin to file
        saveBulletin(out, file, request);

        showReturnLink = true;
      }
      else if (request.getParameter("CANCEL") != null) //cancel
      {
        response.reset(); //clear the response
        doGet(request, response); //pass request to doGet()
        return; //stop executing the doPost() method
      }
      else //error if no view, post, save, or cancel parameter
      {
        throw new ServletException("Expected Parameter Missing");
      }

      if (showReturnLink)
      {
        //create hyperlink to return to main page
        out.println("<BR><BR><A HREF=\"" + servletPath +
          "?Topic=" + java.net.URLEncoder.encode(currentTopic) +
          "\">Return to Main Page</A>");
      }

      out.println("</BODY></HTML>"); //close BODY and HTML tags
    }
    catch (Exception e)
    {
      sendErrorToClient(out, e); //send stack trace to client
      log("Error in doPost() method.", e); //log error
    }
  }
}
```

We will now dissect the doPost() method and evaluate its parts.

```
    PrintWriter out = null;

    //get bulletin board topic selected from drop-down list
    String currentTopic = request.getParameter("Topic");
```

```
        //get the name of file containing bulletins for this topic
        String file = filePath + currentTopic + ".txt";

        //get path to servlet for use in hyperlinks
        String servletPath = request.getContextPath() +
          request.getServletPath();

        response.setContentType("text/html"); //html output
```

Initially, a `PrintWriter` object is declared in order to store a handle to the output stream. This object is instantiated in the try block. The `PrintWriter` object is declared outside of the `try` block so that, if an error occurs, it can be referenced from within the `catch` block. In addition, a `String` variable, current-Topic, is declared in order to store the user's currently selected bulletin board topic. This value is passed to the **View Bulletins** page from the main page via a <SELECT> HTML form element named `Topic`. The value of the currently selected topic is assigned to `currentTopic` using the `HttpServletRequest` object's `getParameter()` method.

Next, a `String` object, `file`, is declared and assigned the value of the full path and filename of the text file that stores the bulletins for the currently selected topic. The `getContextPath()` and `getServletPath()` methods are then used to retrieve the URL path to the servlet's directory. The servlet path is stored in a `String` variable called `servletPath`. As we will see a little later, this variable is used to provide a hyperlink back to the main page. Lastly, the `setContentType()` method of the `HttpServletResponse` object is used to indicate that the response returned to the client will be in HTML format.

```
        try
        {
          out = response.getWriter(); //get handle to output stream

          //send HTML tags common to show, post, and save pages
          out.println("<HTML>");
          out.println("<HEAD><TITLE>" + currentTopic +
            " Bulletin Board</TITLE></HEAD>");
          out.println("<BODY>");
```

This code marks the beginning of the `try` block. The `getWriter()` method of the `HttpServletResponse` object is used to assign the output stream to the `PrintWriter` variable out that was declared earlier. This output stream is used to transmit HTML back to the client.

```
        boolean showReturnLink = false;

        //display view, post, or save page
        if (request.getParameter("VIEW") != null) //view
        {
          //displays bulletins for the selected topic
          viewBulletins(out, file, currentTopic);
```

```
      showReturnLink = true;
    }
    else if (request.getParameter("POST") != null) //post
    {
      //allows user to enter bulletin and submit it
      postBulletin(out, currentTopic);
    }
    else if (request.getParameter("SAVE") != null) //save
    {
      //saves bulletin to file
      saveBulletin(out, file, request);

      showReturnLink = true;
    }
    else if (request.getParameter("CANCEL") != null) //cancel
    {
      response.reset(); //clear the response
      doGet(request, response); //pass request to doGet()
      return; //stop executing the doPost() method
    }
    else //error if no view, post, save, or cancel parameter
    {
      throw new ServletException("Expected Parameter Missing");
    }
```

The `if/else` block is used to determine which action prompted the `doPost()` method to be called. By discovering which `SUBMIT` button's name/value pair was passed to the servlet, it can be determined which button was clicked. For example, if the **VIEW BULLETINS** button on the main page is clicked, a parameter named `VIEW` will be passed to the servlet (see the HTML form generated for the main page).

On the other hand, if the user clicks the **POST BULLETIN** button on the main page, a parameter named `POST` will be passed to the servlet. The `viewBulletins()`, `postBulletin()`, or `saveBulletin()` method will be called in response to the user's clicking the **VIEW BULLETINS, POST BULLETIN,** or **SAVE BULLETIN** button, respectively. The `showReturnLink` boolean variable indicates whether the **Return to Main Page** link should be added to the bottom of the page. Only the **View Bulletins** and **Save Bulletins** pages should include this link.

```
    if (showReturnLink)
    {
      //create hyperlink to return to main page
      out.println("<BR><BR><A HREF=\"" + servletPath +
        "?Topic=" + java.net.URLEncoder.encode(currentTopic) +
        "\">Return to Main Page</A>");
    }
```

```
      out.println("</BODY></HTML>"); //close BODY and HTML tags
    }
    catch (Exception e)
    {
      //send stack trace back to client
      sendErrorToClient(out, e);
      log("Error in doPost() method.", e); //log error
    }
  }
```

If the `showReturnLink` variable is `true`, the preceding code constructs the hyperlink that allows the user to return to the main page. Notice that a query string named `Topic` is passed in the URL. This query string allows the main page to "remember" which topic had been selected by the current user. The next line of code closes the HTML document. Finally, the `catch` block catches all exceptions, calls the `sendErrorToClient()` method to return an error message to the client, and logs the error.

The `viewBulletins()` method reads bulletins from disk and returns them to the client. If a text file does not exist for the selected bulletin board topic, the user is notified that the topic currently contains no bulletins. To complete our review of the **View Bulletins** page, let's look at the following code, which comprises the `viewBulletins()` method.

```
/**
 * viewBulletins() method reads bulletins from disk and sends
 * them to the client. If file does not exist, client is
 * informed that the selected topic contains no bulletins. This
 * method is synchronized for thread safety.
 *
 * @param out Client output stream
 * @param file File containing bulletins for selected topic
 * @param currentTopic User's currently selected topic
 */
private synchronized void viewBulletins(PrintWriter out,
  String file, String currentTopic)
{
  FileReader fr = null;
  BufferedReader br = null;

  try
  {
    File fileTopic = new File(file); //get handle to file

    //display page heading
    out.println("<H2>" + currentTopic +
      " Bulletin Board</H2>");
    out.println("<H3>View Bulletins</H3>");

    if (fileTopic.exists()) //file exists, display it
    {
```

```
      fr = new FileReader(file); //get file input stream
      br = new BufferedReader(fr);

      String line = br.readLine(); //read first line

      //iterate through each line of the bulletin board file
      while (line != null)
      {
        out.println(line + "<BR>\n"); //send bulletins
        line = br.readLine(); //read next line
      }
    }
    else //file doesn't exist, display no bulletins message
    {
      out.println("This topic currently contains no " +
        "bulletins.");
    }
  }
  catch (Exception e)
  {
    sendErrorToClient(out, e); //send stack trace to client
    log("Error in viewBulletins() method.", e); //log error
  }
  finally
  {
    try
    {
      br.close(); //close buffered reader
    }
    catch (Exception ignored) {}
    try
    {
      fr.close(); //close file reader
    }
    catch (Exception ignored) {}
  }
}
```

We will now break the viewBulletins() method into pieces and examine
its parts, starting with the definition for the viewBulletins() method.

```
private synchronized void viewBulletins(PrintWriter out,
  String file, String currentTopic)
{
  FileReader fr = null;
  BufferedReader br = null;
```

Notice that this method is synchronized (i.e., it is declared using the synchronized keyword) in order to guarantee thread safety. Synchronizing this method
keeps two threads from simultaneously accessing both the viewBulletins()
and saveBulletin() (which is also synchronized) methods. This strategy

ensures that one client cannot read from the bulletins file while another is writing to it. For more information on writing thread-safe code, see Chapter 11.

The `viewBulletins()` method accepts a `PrintWriter` object and two `String` parameters. The `PrintWriter` object, out, gives the method a handle to the output stream. The first `String` parameter, `file`, indicates the full file system path to the text file that stores the bulletins for the currently selected topic. The second `String` parameter, `currentTopic`, indicates which bulletin board topic was selected by the user and allows the method to display the bulletins that correspond to the selected topic. Finally, the first two lines of code simply declare a `FileReader` and a `BufferedReader` variable that will be used to read the bulletins from disk.

```
try
{
  File fileTopic = new File(file); //get handle to file

  //display page heading
  out.println("<H2>" + currentTopic +
    " Bulletin Board</H2>");
  out.println("<H3>View Bulletins</H3>");

  if (fileTopic.exists()) //file exists, display it
  {
    fr = new FileReader(file); //get file input stream
    br = new BufferedReader(fr);

    String line = br.readLine(); //read first line

    //iterate through each line of the bulletin board file
    while (line != null)
    {
      out.println(line + "<BR>\n"); //send bulletins
      line = br.readLine(); //read next line
    }
  }
  else //file doesn't exist, display no bulletins message
  {
    out.println("This topic currently contains no " +
      "bulletins.");
  }
}
```

The preceding code comprises the entire `try` block of the `viewBulletins()` method. Initially, a `File` object is created. This object points to the text file that stores the bulletins for the currently selected topic. The `if` statement uses the `File` object's `exists()` method to check for the existence of the file. If the file does not exist, a message conveying that no bulletins currently exist for the selected topic is returned to the client. Otherwise, a `BufferedReader` is chained to a `FileReader` object in order to read the file from disk. The `BufferedReader` provides a simple readLine() method for reading one line at a time from a file. The remaining lines of code generate the HTML required to render the **View Bulletins** page. A while loop is used to read all lines of text from the file.

```
catch (Exception e)
{
  sendErrorToClient(out, e); //send stack trace to client
  log("Error in viewBulletins() method.", e); //log error
}
finally
{
  try
  {
    br.close(); //close buffered reader
  }
  catch (Exception ignored) {}
  try
  {
    fr.close(); //close file reader
  }
  catch (Exception ignored) {}
}
}
```

The catch and finally blocks complete the viewBulletins() method. All exceptions are caught in this method. In the event an exception is thrown, the sendErrorToClient() method is called in order to return an error message to the client, and the error is logged. The finally block is critical in order to close the open input streams, FileReader and BufferedReader, even in the case of an exception. A finally block should always be used to release open resources.

This concludes the code necessary to implement the **View Bulletins** functionality. Keep in mind that the doPost() method presented above is also used by the **Post Bulletin** and **Save Bulletin** pages.

Post Bulletin Page

The **Post Bulletin** page displays an HTML form that allows the user to type a new bulletin into an HTML <TEXTAREA> field. This page is displayed in response to the user's clicking the **POST BULLETIN** button on the main page. The **Post Bulletin** page is shown in Figure 7.3.

When the **POST BULLETIN** button on the main page is clicked, the browser submits an HTTP POST request to the server, which, in turn, calls the doPost() method. As we saw in the **View Bulletins** page section, the button that the user pressed can be determined by checking for the existence of each button's name/value pair. The following if/then block from the doPost() method demonstrates how this is accomplished.

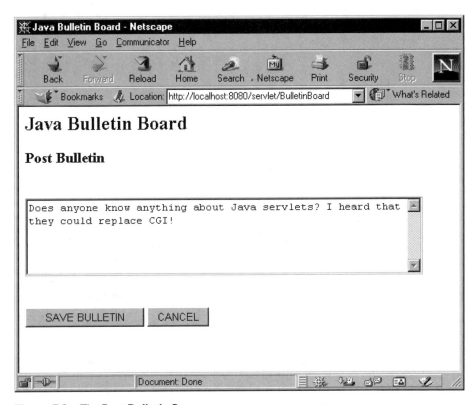

Figure 7.3   The **Post Bulletin** Page

```
//display view, post, or save page
if (request.getParameter("VIEW") != null) //view
{
  //displays bulletins for the selected topic
  viewBulletins(out, file, currentTopic);

  showReturnLink = true;
}
else if (request.getParameter("POST") != null) //post
{
  //allows user to enter bulletin and submit it
  postBulletin(out, currentTopic);
}
else if (request.getParameter("SAVE") != null) //save
{
  //saves bulletin to file
  saveBulletin(out, file, request);

  showReturnLink = true;
}
```

```
else if (request.getParameter("CANCEL") != null) //cancel
{
  response.reset(); //clear the response
  doGet(request, response); //pass request to doGet()
  return; //stop executing the doPost() method
}
else //error if no view, post, save, or cancel parameter
{
  throw new ServletException("Expected Parameter Missing");
}
```

As we can see from the preceding code, the postBulletin() method is called when the main page's **POST BULLETIN** button is clicked. Let's examine the postBulletin() method.

```
/**
 * postBulletin() method generates the HTML form that allows
 * the user to enter a new bulletin.
 *
 * @param out Client output stream
 * @param currentTopic User's currently selected topic
 */
private void postBulletin(PrintWriter out,
  String currentTopic)
{
  //create HTML form to allow user to enter new bulletin
  out.println("<H2>" + currentTopic + " Bulletin Board</H2>");
  out.println("<H3>Post Bulletin</H3><BR>");
  out.println("<FORM METHOD=\"POST\">");
  out.println("<P><TEXTAREA NAME=\"BULLETIN\" " +
    "COLS=\"60\" ROWS=\"5\" WRAP=\"VIRTUAL\"></TEXTAREA>");
  out.println("<BR><BR><BR><INPUT TYPE=\"SUBMIT\" " +
    "NAME=\"SAVE\" VALUE=\"SAVE BULLETIN\"> ");
  out.println("<INPUT TYPE=\"SUBMIT\" " +
    "NAME=\"CANCEL\" VALUE=\"CANCEL\">");
  //include current topic in hidden field
  out.println("<INPUT TYPE=\"HIDDEN\" " +
    "NAME=\"Topic\" VALUE=\"" + currentTopic + "\">");
  out.println("</FORM>");
}
```

The postBulletin() method generates the HTML form that allows a user to enter a new bulletin. Notice that a hidden field is created to store the name of the currently selected bulletin board topic. By passing this topic from screen to screen, the main page is able to maintain the user's selected topic. In addition, including the selected bulletin board topic when this form is submitted allows the saveBulletin() method to determine the topic to which the user's bulletin should be appended. Lastly, the <TEXTAREA> tag's WRAP attribute is set to VIRTUAL so that bulletins that exceed the width of the text area will automatically wrap to the next line.

Save Bulletin Page

The **Save Bulletin** page displays a confirmation message to users indicating that their bulletin has been saved successfully. It also provides a link back to the main page. This page is displayed in response to the user clicking the **SAVE BULLETIN** button on the **Post Bulletin** page. The **Save Bulletin** page is shown in Figure 7.4.

As with the **VIEW BULLETINS** and **POST BULLETINS** buttons, doPost() is the first method called in response to clicking the **SAVE BULLE-TIN** button. Again, the following if/then block determines which button was pressed and calls its corresponding method.

```
//display view, post, or save page
if (request.getParameter("VIEW") != null) //view
{
  //displays bulletins for the selected topic
  viewBulletins(out, file, currentTopic);
```

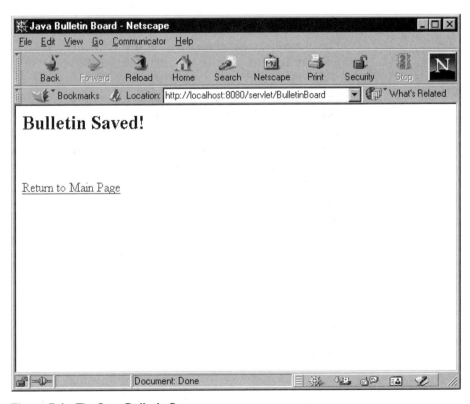

Figure 7.4   The **Save Bulletin** Page

```
      showReturnLink = true;
}
else if (request.getParameter("POST") != null) //post
{
   //allows user to enter bulletin and submit it
   postBulletin(out, currentTopic);
}
else if (request.getParameter("SAVE") != null) //save
{
   //saves bulletin to file
   saveBulletin(out, file, request);

   showReturnLink = true;
}
else if (request.getParameter("CANCEL") != null) //cancel
{
   response.reset(); //clear the response
   doGet(request, response); //pass request to doGet()
   return; //stop executing the doPost() method
}
else //error if no view, post, save, or cancel parameter
{
   throw new ServletException("Expected Parameter Missing");
}
```

The preceding code shows that in the event the **SAVE BULLETIN** button on the **Post Bulletin** page is clicked, the saveBulletin() method is called. Also notice that if the user clicks the **CANCEL** button on the **Post Bulletin** page, the response created by the doPost() method is cleared and the doGet() method is called in order to display the main page. The response must be cleared using the reset() method since the Content-Type header was set in the doPost() method and some HTML was written to the output stream. Once the response is cleared, the doGet() method is free to build its own response. Lastly, the doGet() method is able to "remember" the user's topic selection by reading it from the Topic hidden field contained in the request object that was passed to it.

If the request object does not contain any of the expected parameters (i.e., VIEW, POST, SAVE, or CANCEL), a ServletException is thrown. In turn, this exception is caught in the catch block and an error message is returned to the client. Fortunately, this error condition should never occur unless the client constructs an invalid request manually (e.g., issues a POST request using a custom HTML form). Again, the doPost() method calls the saveBulletin() method in response to the user clicking the **SAVE BULLETIN** button. Let's examine this method.

```
/**
 * saveBulletin() method saves the bulletin to disk. This
 * method is synchronized for thread safety.
 *
```

```
 * @param out Client output stream
 * @param file File containing bulletins for selected topic
 * @param request HttpServletRequest object
 */
private synchronized void saveBulletin(PrintWriter out,
  String file, HttpServletRequest request)
{
  FileWriter fw=null;
  PrintWriter pw=null;

  try
  {
    fw = new FileWriter(file, true); //get file output stream
    pw = new PrintWriter(fw);

    //writer separator to file
    pw.println("----------------------------------------");

    //write user's bulletin to file
    pw.println(request.getParameter("BULLETIN"));

    //inform user that the bulletin was saved successfully
    out.println("<H2>Bulletin Saved!</H2>");
  }
  catch (Exception e)
  {
    sendErrorToClient(out, e); //send stack trace to client
    log("Error in saveBulletin() method.", e); //log error
  }
  finally
  {
    try
    {
      pw.flush(); //flush output stream to file
      pw.close(); //close print writer
    }
    catch (Exception ignored) {}
    try
    {
      fw.close(); //close file writer
    }
    catch (Exception ignored) {}
  }
}
```

The purpose of the saveBulletin() method is to write the user's bulletin to disk. Let's break this method into three pieces and examine each
individually.

```
private synchronized void saveBulletin(PrintWriter out,
  String file, HttpServletRequest request)
{
  FileWriter fw=null;
  PrintWriter pw=null;
```

From the method definition we can see that `saveBulletin()` accepts three parameters—a `PrintWriter` object, a `String` object, and an `HttpServlet-Request` object. Also notice that, like `viewBulletins()`, this method is synchronized for thread safety (so that two threads cannot call it concurrently).

Similar to the previous methods we have explored, the `PrintWriter` object provides an output stream to the client. The `String` parameter, `file`, was defined in the `doPost()` method and represents the full path and filename of the currently selected topic (i.e., the text file that stores the topic's bulletins). Lastly, the `HttpServletRequest` parameter, `request`, is the object representation of the client's HTTP request. The `request` object's `getParameter()` method is used to retrieve the user's bulletin from the HTML form data. Following the method definition, `FileWriter` and `PrintWriter` objects are declared. Both of these objects are instantiated in the `try` block and closed in the `finally` block.

```
try
{
  fw = new FileWriter(file, true); //get file output stream
  pw = new PrintWriter(fw);

  //writer separator to file
  pw.println("---------------------------------------");

  //write user's bulletin to file
  pw.println(request.getParameter("BULLETIN"));

  //inform user that the bulletin was saved successfully
  out.println("<H2>Bulletin Saved!</H2>");
}
```

The code here represents the entire `try` block of the `saveBulletin()` method. The first line opens a `FileWriter` output stream to the file specified by the `file` parameter. The `true` parameter indicates that data written to the file should be appended. A `PrintWriter` object is then chained to the `FileWriter` object. The `PrintWriter` object is used because it implements a simple `println()` method for writing to a file a single line at a time. Next, a line of hyphens (to provide separation between bulletins) and the user's bulletin is written to the file. Finally, a confirmation message is returned to the client.

```
catch (Exception e)
{
  sendErrorToClient(out, e); //send stack trace to client
  log("Error in saveBulletin() method.", e); //log error
}
finally
{
  try
  {
```

```
      pw.flush(); //flush output stream to file
      pw.close(); //close print writer
    }
    catch (Exception ignored) {}
    try
    {
      fw.close(); //close file writer
    }
    catch (Exception ignored) {}
  }
}
```

The end of the `saveBulletin()` method consists of the `catch` and `finally` blocks. As we have seen before, all exceptions are caught by the `catch` block in which the `sendErrorToClient()` method is called and the error is logged. The `finally` block is used to close the `FileWriter` and `PrintWriter` output streams.

The `sendErrorToClient()` method that follows sends the stack trace to the client and also prints it to standard out. Returning the stack trace to the client is useful during debugging but should be replaced with a less cryptic error message in a production environment. The `sendErrorToClient()` method converts the stack trace generated by the error to a `String` and includes it in an HTML document that is returned to the client.

```
/**
 * Return stack trace to client. Useful for debugging but
 * not for use in a production environment.
 *
 * @param out Client output stream
 * @param e Exception
 */
private void sendErrorToClient(PrintWriter out, Exception e)
{
  //send stack trace back to client and to standard out
  StringWriter stringError = new StringWriter();
  PrintWriter printError = new PrintWriter(stringError);
  e.printStackTrace(printError);
  String stackTrace = stringError.toString();

  //send error message to client
  out.println("<HTML><TITLE>Error</TITLE><BODY>");
  out.println("<H1>Servlet Error</H1><H4>Error</H4>" + e +
    "<H4>Stack Trace</H4>" + stackTrace + "</BODY></HTML>");

  //print stack trace to standard out
  System.out.println("Servlet Error: " + stackTrace);
}
```

Complete Bulletin Board Servlet

Now that we have learned the purpose behind each line of code in the Bulletin Board servlet, let's examine the source code for the entire servlet, shown in Listing 7.1. You should be familiar with every object and method used in the Bulletin Board servlet. If necessary, turn back a few pages to review.

Listing 7.1   The complete Bulletin Board servlet source code.

```java
import javax.servlet.*;
import javax.servlet.http.*;
import java.io.*;
import java.util.*;

/**
 * The BulletinBoard servlet allows the user to view posted
 * bulletins as well as add bulletins of their own to be viewed
 * by others.
 *
 * @author Dustin R. Callaway
 */
public class BulletinBoard extends HttpServlet
{
  private String filePath; //stores root path for bulletin files
  private Properties propTopics; //stores bulletin board topics


  /**
   * init() method is called when the servlet is first loaded. It
   * reads the directory where the bulletin files are stored from
   * an initialization parameter.
   */
  public void init() throws ServletException
  {
    //get path to topics properties file and bulletin board files
    filePath = getInitParameter("FilePath");

    if (filePath == null)
    {
      //default to root directory if no FilePath init parameter
      filePath = File.separator;
    }
    else if (!filePath.endsWith(File.separator))
    {
      filePath += File.separator; //add separator if necessary
    }

    FileInputStream fileTopics = null;

    try
    {
```

```
      //open input stream to topics.properties file
      fileTopics = new FileInputStream(filePath +
        "topics.properties");

      propTopics = new Properties();
      propTopics.load(fileTopics); //load properties object
    }
    catch (FileNotFoundException e)
    {
      throw new ServletException("The topics.properties file " +
        "was not found at " + filePath + "<BR><BR>Error: " + e);
    }
    catch (Exception e)
    {
      throw new ServletException("Error: " + e);
    }
    finally
    {
      try
      {
        fileTopics.close(); //close file input stream
      }
      catch (Exception ignored) {}
    }
  }


  /**
   * doGet() method is called in response to any GET request.
   * Returns an HTML form that allows the user to select a
   * bulletin board topic and choose to view bulletins or post
   * a new one.
   */
  public void doGet(HttpServletRequest request,
    HttpServletResponse response) throws IOException
  {
    response.setContentType("text/html"); //html output

    //get a handle to the output stream
    PrintWriter out = response.getWriter();

    try
    {
      //create HTML form to allow user to select a topic
      out.println("<HTML>");
      out.println("<HEAD>");
      out.println("<TITLE>Servlet Bulletin Board</TITLE>");
      out.println("</HEAD>");
      out.println("<BODY>");
      out.println("<H2>Servlet Bulletin Board</H2>");
      out.println("<BR><FORM METHOD=\"POST\">");
      out.println("Select Bulletin Board Topic: ");

      out.println("<SELECT NAME=\"Topic\">"); //begin SELECT tag
```

```
            String topic; //stores description of current topic

            //create enumeration from properties object
            Enumeration enumTopics = propTopics.propertyNames();

            //iterate through all topics in topics.properties file
            while (enumTopics.hasMoreElements())
            {
              //set topic variable to current topic in enumeration
              topic = (String)enumTopics.nextElement();

              //add each topic from properties file to drop-down list
              if (propTopics.getProperty(topic).equals(
                request.getParameter("Topic")))
              {
                //if user has selected a topic, keep it selected
                out.println("<OPTION SELECTED>" +
                  propTopics.getProperty(topic) + "</OPTION>");
              }
              else
              {
                //not the selected topic, just add to drop-down list
                out.println("<OPTION>" +
                  propTopics.getProperty(topic) + "</OPTION>");
              }
            }

            out.println("</SELECT><BR><BR><BR>"); //end SELECT tag

            //display View and Post buttons
            out.println("<INPUT TYPE=\"SUBMIT\" NAME=\"VIEW\" " +
              "VALUE=\"VIEW BULLETINS\"> ");
            out.println("<INPUT TYPE=\"SUBMIT\" NAME=\"POST\" " +
              "VALUE=\"POST BULLETIN\">");
            out.println("</FORM>");
            out.println("</BODY></HTML>");
          }
          catch (Exception e)
          {
            sendErrorToClient(out, e); //send stack trace to client
            log("Error in doGet() method.", e); //log error
          }
          finally
          {
            try
            {
              //close output stream
              out.close();
            }
            catch (Exception ignored) {}
          }
        }
```

```
/**
 * doPost() method is called in response to any POST request.
 * This method determines if it was called in response to the
 * user selecting to view bulletins, post a bulletin, or
 * save a bulletin and responds accordingly.
 */
public void doPost(HttpServletRequest request,
  HttpServletResponse response)
{
  PrintWriter out = null;

  //get bulletin board topic selected from drop-down list
  String currentTopic = request.getParameter("Topic");

  //get the name of file containing bulletins for this topic
  String file = filePath + currentTopic + ".txt";

  //get path to servlet for use in hyperlinks
  String servletPath = request.getContextPath() +
    request.getServletPath();

  response.setContentType("text/html"); //html output

  try
  {
    out = response.getWriter(); //get handle to output stream

    //send HTML tags common to show, post, and save pages
    out.println("<HTML>");
    out.println("<HEAD><TITLE>" + currentTopic +
      " Bulletin Board</TITLE></HEAD>");
    out.println("<BODY>");

    boolean showReturnLink = false;

    //display view, post, or save page
    if (request.getParameter("VIEW") != null) //view
    {
      //displays bulletins for the selected topic
      viewBulletins(out, file, currentTopic);

      showReturnLink = true;
    }
    else if (request.getParameter("POST") != null) //post
    {
      //allows user to enter bulletin and submit it
      postBulletin(out, currentTopic);
    }
    else if (request.getParameter("SAVE") != null) //save
    {
      //saves bulletin to file
      saveBulletin(out, file, request);

      showReturnLink = true;
    }
```

```
        else if (request.getParameter("CANCEL") != null) //cancel
        {
          response.reset(); //clear the response
          doGet(request, response); //pass request to doGet()
          return; //stop executing the doPost() method
        }
        else //error if no view, post, save, or cancel parameter
        {
          throw new ServletException("Expected Parameter Missing");
        }

        if (showReturnLink)
        {
          //create hyperlink to return to main page
          out.println("<BR><BR><A HREF=\"" + servletPath +
            "?Topic=" + java.net.URLEncoder.encode(currentTopic) +
            "\">Return to Main Page</A>");
        }

        out.println("</BODY></HTML>"); //close BODY and HTML tags
      }
      catch (Exception e)
      {
        sendErrorToClient(out, e); //send stack trace to client
        log("Error in doPost() method.", e); //log error
      }
    }


    /**
     * viewBulletins() method reads bulletins from disk and sends
     * them to the client. If file does not exist, client is
     * informed that the selected topic contains no bulletins. This
     * method is synchronized for thread safety.
     *
     * @param out Client output stream
     * @param file File containing bulletins for selected topic
     * @param currentTopic User's currently selected topic
     */
    private synchronized void viewBulletins(PrintWriter out,
      String file, String currentTopic)
    {
      FileReader fr = null;
      BufferedReader br = null;

      try
      {
        File fileTopic = new File(file); //get handle to file

        //display page heading
        out.println("<H2>" + currentTopic +
          " Bulletin Board</H2>");
        out.println("<H3>View Bulletins</H3>");
```

```
    if (fileTopic.exists()) //file exists, display it
    {
      fr = new FileReader(file); //get file input stream
      br = new BufferedReader(fr);

      String line = br.readLine(); //read first line

      //iterate through each line of the bulletin board file
      while (line != null)
      {
        out.println(line + "<BR>\n"); //send bulletins
        line = br.readLine(); //read next line
      }
    }
    else //file doesn't exist, display no bulletins message
    {
      out.println("This topic currently contains no " +
        "bulletins.");
    }
  }
  catch (Exception e)
  {
    sendErrorToClient(out, e); //send stack trace to client
    log("Error in viewBulletins() method.", e); //log error
  }
  finally
  {
    try
    {
      br.close(); //close buffered reader
    }
    catch (Exception ignored) {}
    try
    {
      fr.close(); //close file reader
    }
    catch (Exception ignored) {}
  }
}


/**
 * postBulletin() method generates the HTML form that allows
 * the user to enter a new bulletin.
 *
 * @param out Client output stream
 * @param currentTopic User's currently selected topic
 */
private void postBulletin(PrintWriter out,
  String currentTopic)
{
  //create HTML form to allow user to enter new bulletin
  out.println("<H2>" + currentTopic + " Bulletin Board</H2>");
  out.println("<H3>Post Bulletin</H3><BR>");
```

```
        out.println("<FORM METHOD=\"POST\">");
        out.println("<P><TEXTAREA NAME=\"BULLETIN\" " +
          "COLS=\"60\" ROWS=\"5\" WRAP=\"VIRTUAL\"></TEXTAREA>");
        out.println("<BR><BR><BR><INPUT TYPE=\"SUBMIT\" " +
          "NAME=\"SAVE\" VALUE=\"SAVE BULLETIN\"> ");
        out.println("<INPUT TYPE=\"SUBMIT\" " +
          "NAME=\"CANCEL\" VALUE=\"CANCEL\">");
        //include current topic in hidden field
        out.println("<INPUT TYPE=\"HIDDEN\" " +
          "NAME=\"Topic\" VALUE=\"" + currentTopic + "\">");
        out.println("</FORM>");
    }


    /**
     * saveBulletin() method saves the bulletin to disk. This
     * method is synchronized for thread safety.
     *
     * @param out Client output stream
     * @param file File containing bulletins for selected topic
     * @param request HttpServletRequest object
     */
    private synchronized void saveBulletin(PrintWriter out,
      String file, HttpServletRequest request)
    {
      FileWriter fw=null;
      PrintWriter pw=null;

      try
      {
        fw = new FileWriter(file, true); //get file output stream
        pw = new PrintWriter(fw);

        //writer separator to file
        pw.println("--------------------------------------");

        //write user's bulletin to file
        pw.println(request.getParameter("BULLETIN"));

        //inform user that the bulletin was saved successfully
        out.println("<H2>Bulletin Saved!</H2>");
      }
      catch (Exception e)
      {
        sendErrorToClient(out, e); //send stack trace to client
        log("Error in saveBulletin() method.", e); //log error
      }
      finally
      {
        try
        {
          pw.flush(); //flush output stream to file
          pw.close(); //close print writer
        }
```

```
        catch (Exception ignored) {}
        try
        {
          fw.close(); //close file writer
        }
        catch (Exception ignored) {}
    }
}


/**
 * Return stack trace to client. Useful for debugging but
 * not for use in a production environment.
 *
 * @param out Client output stream
 * @param e Exception
 */
private void sendErrorToClient(PrintWriter out, Exception e)
{
    //send stack trace back to client and to standard out
    StringWriter stringError = new StringWriter();
    PrintWriter printError = new PrintWriter(stringError);
    e.printStackTrace(printError);
    String stackTrace = stringError.toString();

    //send error message to client
    out.println("<HTML><TITLE>Error</TITLE><BODY>");
    out.println("<H1>Servlet Error</H1><H4>Error</H4>" + e +
      "<H4>Stack Trace</H4>" + stackTrace + "</BODY></HTML>");

    //print stack trace to standard out
    System.out.println("Servlet Error: " + stackTrace);
  }
}
```

That's it. If you have followed along on your own, you have now written your first fully functional servlet. So what now? The next chapter will teach you how to run your servlet.

Summary

This chapter presents a full, although slightly simplified, servlet development process. We started by defining the requirements for the project at hand. Next, we designed the interface (HTML screens) and implemented functionality using the Servlet API object library. Of course, the servlet development process can differ greatly depending on the scope and complexity of the project. For instance, a more complex project may require extensive data modeling and object-oriented analysis and design before the first line of code is written. Fortunately, it is easy to alter the servlet development process presented here to conform to practically any development methodology. In Chapter 9, we will examine several options for testing and debugging servlets.

Chapter Highlights

- This chapter demonstrates a fully functional Bulletin Board servlet that allows users to view posted comments and append their own thoughts.

- The development process begins with a brief analysis and design phase that flushes out the servlet requirements. These requirements include support for multiple topics and the ability to view and create bulletins easily.

- A visual mock-up was created to convey the required functionality, and code was added to make the screens functional.

CHAPTER 8

Running Servlets

This chapter examines several options for running servlets. Fortunately, due to the cross-server and cross-platform nature of servlets, there is a wide array of options when it comes to running servlets. Some Web servers, such as iPlanet Web Server and W3C Jigsaw, natively support servlets. Other popular HTTP servers, such as Apache Web Server[1] and Microsoft Internet Information Server, support servlets through add-ons like Tomcat from Apache, JRun from Allaire, ServletExec from New Atlanta Communications, and Resin from Caucho Technology. Although several methods are presented, keep in mind that this chapter discusses only a few of the many options available for running servlets. This chapter covers the following products:

- Apache Tomcat
- JRun™
- ServletExec™
- Resin™

 NOTE: The Apache Tomcat section is recommended reading even if you are planning to use another servlet container. This section contains important information that applies to all Servlet API 2.2–compatible servers.

---

1. At the time of this writing, servlet support can be added to Apache Web Server using Tomcat from the Apache Software Foundation. However, in the future, in order to provide native servlet support within the Apache Web Server, Apache may release an integrated solution that combines both the Apache Web Server and the Tomcat servlet container.

Apache Tomcat

Perhaps the simplest way to run servlets is with the Tomcat server from the Apache Software Foundation. As a piece of the larger Apache Jakarta project, Tomcat is the official reference implementation for the Java Servlet and Java-Server Pages (JSP) specifications. In this section, we will examine how to run servlets using Tomcat 3.1, the reference implementation for Servlet API 2.2 and JSP 1.1.

> **NOTE:** Just before this book went to print, the final release of Tomcat 3.2 (the latest reference implementation for Servlet API 2.2 and JavaServer Pages 1.1) was made available. You can find this version on the accompanying CD or it can be downloaded from *http://jakarta.apache.org/tomcat/*. This chapter, however, demonstrates running servlets using the previous Tomcat release, version 3.1.

Installing Tomcat

To begin, you should install the Java Development Kit, also known as the Java 2 SDK, Standard Edition (JDK 1.1 or higher is required; JDK 1.2 or higher is recommended). The Java 2 SDK, Standard Edition, can be downloaded from *http://java.sun.com/j2se/*. After the JDK has been installed, you must locate a copy of the Tomcat 3.1 installation file. You can retrieve this file from the accompanying CD or you can download it from the Apache Web site. You can find Tomcat at the following URL:

> *http://jakarta.apache.org/tomcat/*

Though a Tar/GZIP installation file is available for UNIX systems, it is often easier to just use the ZIP file, regardless of your platform. This is due to the fact that JAR files use this same ZIP format. Therefore, the basic Java *jar* utility can be used to decompress the installation file on any platform.

Once you have acquired the ZIP file, copy it to the desired installation directory and install Tomcat by decompressing the installation file using the standard Java *jar* utility located in your JDK's */bin* directory (if the *jar* utility is not found, specify the absolute path to the file). The -x switch tells the JAR utility to extract (or decompress) the file, the -v switch enables verbose output, and the -f switch indicates that an archive file is specified on the command line. For example, the ZIP file can be decompressed like this on Windows (or any other standard ZIP utility, such as WinZIP, may be used):

```
C:\> cd \
C:\> jar -xvf jakarta-tomcat.zip
```

On UNIX, the installation file can be decompressed like this:

```
shell> cd /usr/local
shell> jar -xvf jakarta-tomcat.zip
```

Before starting Tomcat, you must indicate its location and the location of your JDK by setting the TOMCAT_HOME and JAVA_HOME environment variables. The simplest way to do this is to set these environment variables within the *startup.bat* file (on Windows) or the *startup.sh* file (on UNIX) located in the */jakarta-tomcat/bin* directory. Setting environment variables is platform and shell specific so you need to use the proper syntax according to your operating system. For example, on Windows, you can set the TOMCAT_HOME and JAVA_HOME environment variables by adding the following line to the top of the *startup.bat* file (be sure to use the location of your JDK).

```
set TOMCAT_HOME=C:\jakarta-tomcat
set JAVA_HOME=C:\jdk1.2.2
```

On UNIX, the settings might look something like this:

```
export TOMCAT_HOME=/usr/local/jakarta-tomcat
export JAVA_HOME=/usr/local/jdk1.2.2
```

Now that Tomcat is installed and the environment variables are set, you can start the Tomcat server by executing the *startup* batch/script file located in the */jakarta-tomcat/bin* directory. To illustrate, Tomcat can be run under Windows by executing the following two commands from the command prompt:

```
C:\> cd \jakarta-tomcat\bin
C:\> startup
```

You can run Tomcat on UNIX with these two commands:

```
shell> cd /usr/local/jakarta-tomcat/bin
shell> ./startup.sh
```

After executing the *startup* file, the Tomcat server will display several configuration parameters and a message indicating that it is starting (see Figure 8.1). To verify that Tomcat has started successfully, try requesting the following URL from your browser:

http://localhost:8080/

If Tomcat is running properly, it should reply with an HTML page similar to that shown in Figure 8.2. Click on the **Servlet Examples** link to verify that Tomcat is properly configured to run servlets (see Figure 8.2). If Tomcat fails to respond, check the */jakarta-tomcat/bin/logs/tomcat.log* file for clues regarding

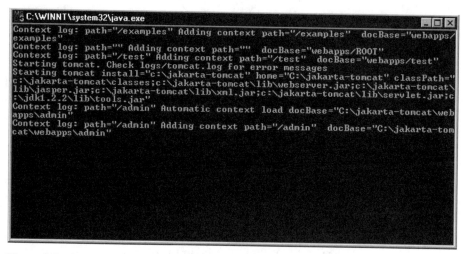

Figure 8.1   Server Output Indicates Tomcat Server Is Running

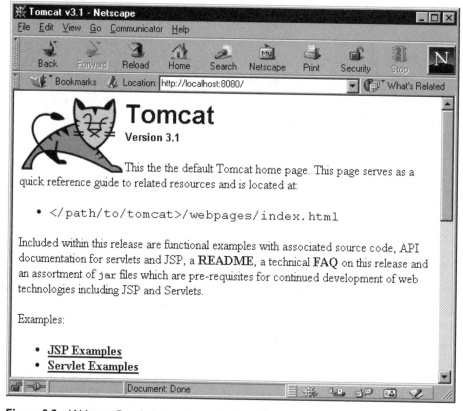

Figure 8.2   Welcome Page Indicates Tomcat Is Running

what went wrong. Also, notice that Tomcat listens on port 8080 by default (see the previous URL). Of course, this port is configurable. To alter the port on which Tomcat listens, edit the following portion of the *ljakarta-tomcat/conf/ server.xml* file.

```
<Connector className="org.apache.tomcat.service.
  SimpleTcpConnector">

  <Parameter name="handler" value="org.apache.tomcat.
    service.http.HttpConnectionHandler"/>

  <Parameter name="port" value="8080"/>
</Connector>
```

NOTE: Though it includes an HTTP server, Tomcat can also be integrated with existing servers such as Apache Web Server, Microsoft Internet Information Server, or Netscape/iPlanet Web Servers. For information on integrating Tomcat with other HTTP servers, see the documentation that accompanies Tomcat (contained on the included CD) or available at *http://jakarta.apache.org/tomcat/*.

Web Applications

All servlet containers that conform to the Servlet API 2.2 specification support the concept of a Web application. A *Web application* is the hierarchy of directories and files that together comprise an application. Web applications are commonly distributed in a *Web application archive* (WAR) file (either a compressed or uncompressed file having a .war extension). All Web applications use the same standard directory structure regardless of the server on which they are running (though each Web application can add its own directories to the standard ones). Though the directory structure of a Web application is server independent, the location of the installed Web applications varies among servers. For example, Tomcat stores all Web applications in the *ljakarta-tomcat/webapps* directory. In contrast, JRun stores Web applications for its default server (JRun can support multiple servers) in the *ljrun/servers/ default* directory. To illustrate, the following directory structure shows a Tomcat installation that includes three Web applications—*admin*, *examples*, and *ROOT*. Table 8.1 describes the purpose of each directory.

```
jakarta-tomcat
   |- bin
   |- conf
   |- doc
   |- lib
   |- logs
```

Table 8.1   Tomcat Directories

Directory	Description
bin	Contains batch files and shell scripts to start and stop the Tomcat server.
conf	Contains various configuration files, including *server.xml* and *web.xml*. *server.xml* is Tomcat's primary configuration file, containing settings such as logging information, Web application context definitions, and the port on which Tomcat listens for connections. *web.xml* contains default settings that are applied to all Web applications. In addition, each Web application has its own *web.xml* configuration file that may override any of the defaults provided by the */conf/web.xml* file.
doc	Contains various Tomcat documentation.
lib	Contains JAR files required by Tomcat. On UNIX, any file added to this directory is automatically added to Tomcat's CLASSPATH.
logs	Contains Tomcat's log files.
src	Contains Servlet API source files consisting of empty interfaces and abstact classes only (complete Tomcat source code can be downloaded separately).
webapps	Contains Tomcat Web applications.
work	Working directory automatically created by Tomcat to store temporary files.
classes	Optional directory that may be created by the developer. Any classes added to this directory will be added to Tomcat's CLASSPATH. Classes in this directory are not automatically reloaded when they are changed. Tomcat must be shutdown and restarted before changes to these classes take effect.

```
|- src
'- webapps
   |- admin
   |  |- contextAdmin
   |  |- META-INF
   |  '- WEB-INF
   |     '- classes
   |
   |- examples
   |  |- images
   |  |- jsp
   |  |- META-INF
   |  |- servlets
   |  '- WEB-INF
   |     |- classes
   |     '- jsp
   |
```

```
'- ROOT
   |- docs
   |- javadoc
   |- META-INF
   '- WEB-INF
      |- classes
      '- lib
```

NOTE: The directory structure shown here contains several nonstandard directories that are not required by the WAR format and are not part of every Web application. For instance, the *examples* Web application's */images*, */jsp*, and */servlets* directories were created by the developer and simply contain images, JSP, and HTML files (as opposed to servlets or other class files).

A Web application's top-level directory (e.g., */admin*, */examples*, */ROOT*) is known as the Web application's *document root*. This is where the server looks for HTML, JSP, and image files associated with the Web application (or in directories under the document root, if specified in the request URL).

When deployed, each Web application is assigned a unique *context path* by the system administrator. All requests to this context path will be routed to the appropriate Web application. For example, if the *examples* Web application is assigned the context path of */examples*, the following URL will display an *index.html* file located in the */jakarta-tomcat/webapps/examples* directory.

http://localhost:8080/examples/index.html

The context path for each Web application is specified in the *server.xml* file located in the */jakarta-tomcat/conf* directory. For instance, the following <Context> XML block from the *server.xml* file assigns the context path */examples* to the *examples* Web application (see Table 8.2 for a description of all <Context> attributes). Note that the context path is usually the same as the Web application's directory. In fact, Tomcat automatically assigns each new Web application a context path based on the name of its root directory.

```
<Context path="/examples" docBase="webapps/examples" debug="0"
  reloadable="true" >
</Context>
```

NOTE: Tomcat includes a simple browser-based utility for viewing, creating, and removing contexts. To run this utility, issue a request to the following URL:

http://localhost:8080/admin

Table 8.2   Attributes of the *server.xml* File's `<Context>` Element

Attribute	Description
`path`	Context path assigned to the Web application located at `docBase`.
`docBase`	Location of Web application's document root relative to the Tomcat server home directory.
`debug`	Indicates the level of logging to be employed for this Web application. Values range from `0` to `9`, with `0` indicating minimal logging and `9` representing most verbose.
`reloadable`	Indicates whether this Web application uses class reloading. Class reloading is the process of detecting changes to any classes in a Web application (either in the */WEB-INF/classes* directory or the */WEB-INF/lib* directory) and, if altered, automatically reloading them. Class reloading can be extremely useful during development because the Tomcat server need not be shut down and restarted in order for changes to take effect. On the other hand, detecting class changes can be time consuming and, in some instances, can cause class cast errors since a new `ClassLoader` object must be used to reload the servlet. For these reasons, servlet reloading is not recommended in a production environment. Set `reloadable` to `true` to enable servlet reloading; otherwise, set it to `false` (false is the default).

In addition, a default Web application can be defined by specifying an empty context path. For example, Tomcat installs the *ROOT* Web application as the default application by assigning it an empty context path as follows:

```
<Context path="" docBase="webapps/ROOT" debug="0"
  reloadable="true" >
</Context>
```

Since the *ROOT* Web application is defined with an empty context path, all requests that do not map to a defined context path will automatically be routed to *ROOT*. To illustrate, the following URL will return the *index.html* file located in the */jakarta-tomcat/webapps/ROOT* directory (notice that no context path is specified).

http://localhost:8080/index.html

As illustrated in the previous directory tree, notice that each of the Web applications contains a */META-INF* and */WEB-INF* directory. Though */META-INF* is optional, all Web applications must contain a */WEB-INF* directory directly under their document root. In addition to these directories, the developer can add any other application-specific directories to a Web application's document root. For instance, the developer of a particular Web application may choose to store all JSP files in a */jsp* directory and all image files in an */images* directory that resides under the document root. Of course, if a file is not located in the document root, its full directory path relative to the document root must be included whenever it is referenced (either from a hyperlink or typed into the browser's address field). For instance, the following URL could be used to reference the *examples* Web application's *code.gif* file located in the */jakarta-tomcat/webapps/examples/images* directory.

http://localhost:8080/examples/images/code.gif

The */META-INF* directory contains information (such as a manifest file) useful to Java archive tools. This directory and the files in it are created by the Java JAR utility and are of little concern to the developer. On the other hand, the */WEB-INF* directory is of significant interest to the servlet developer. This directory contains the following critical elements:

- *web.xml* file—The *web.xml* file is known as the deployment descriptor. The *Web application deployment descriptor* is an XML file that describes the servlets and other components that comprise a Web application, along with any initialization parameters, servlet names (a.k.a. aliases), servlet URL mappings, and security constraints. For a complete description of the *web.xml* file's format (i.e., its XML grammar), see the deployment descriptor DTD (Document Type Definition) in Appendix J.
- */classes* directory—This directory contains all of the Java class files required by a Web application. This includes all servlet and nonservlet classes. If any classes are in Java packages, the directory hierarchy under the */classes* directory must reflect the Java package structure. For instance, a class called `com.sourcestream.template.BaseServlet` must be located in the */classes/com/sourcestream/template* directory. If servlet reloading is enabled, class files in this directory are automatically reloaded when changed.
- */lib* directory—This directory contains any JAR files that are required by the Web application. This might include JDBC drivers or third-party class libraries. If servlet reloading is enabled, JAR files in this directory are automatically reloaded when changed.

The important thing to note is that all servlets should be stored in the Web application's */WEB-INF/classes* directory and that the *web.xml* file controls access to these servlets. We will discuss the *web.xml* file in more detail shortly.

Although we covered a lot of material here, this section was simply a preview to Web applications. See Chapter 19 for detailed information regarding how to package and deploy Web applications.

Servlet Names, Initialization Parameters, and Servlet Mappings

In this section, we will demonstrate the use of servlet names, initialization parameters, and servlet mappings. A *servlet name* (also called a *servlet alias*) is a user-defined logical name that can be used to reference a servlet in place of the fully qualified servlet class name. *Initialization parameters* allow the system administrator to alter servlet configuration settings without having to recompile the servlet. However, most servers must be restarted in order for initialization parameter changes to take effect. *Servlet mappings* (also known as *URL mappings*) associate a particular URL name or pattern to a specific servlet. For instance, a servlet mapping may route all requests for */login.html* to the Login-Servlet servlet. Additionally, the URL pattern `*.login` can map all requests having the `.login` extension to `LoginServlet`.

> **NOTE:** It is usually safe to assume that a servlet's instance variables are shared among all requests to that servlet. However, there are two exceptions to this rule. First, invocations to the same servlet via different servlet names (or aliases) do not share the same instance variables. Rather, the servlet container creates a separate servlet instance for each defined servlet name (even though these names may be referencing the same class). Second, servlets that implement the `SingleThreadModel` interface may be instantiated multiple times. Since instance variables are not shared between instances of a particular class, `static` class variables must be used if an object is to be shared across instances.

Servlet names, initialization parameters, and servlet mappings are all defined in the *web.xml* file. Listing 8.1 presents a typical *web.xml* file. Table 8.3 describes each of the XML elements presented in Listing 8.1. In a nutshell, this *web.xml* file creates a servlet name called `snoop` for the servlet `Snoop-Servlet`. In addition, two initialization parameters, named `name1` and `name2`, are defined. These parameters are passed to the `SnoopServlet` and can be read by the servlet via the `getInitParameter()` method. Lastly, two servlet URL mappings are defined. These mappings route all */snoop* requests to the `Snoop-Servlet` in addition to all requests having a `.snp` extension. Notice that servlet mappings can be created using either the servlet name or the servlet class name.

Listing 8.1   Sample *web.xml* file.

```
<?xml version="1.0" encoding="ISO-8859-1"?>

<!DOCTYPE web-app
  PUBLIC "-//Sun Microsystems, Inc.//DTD Web Application 2.2//EN"
  "http://java.sun.com/j2ee/dtds/web-app_2.2.dtd">
```

Table 8.3 XML Elements in the *web.xml* File

Element Name	Description
web-app	The root element for all *web.xml* files.
servlet	Defines a servlet name and initialization parameters for a single servlet. Contains servlet-name, servlet-class, and init-param elements.
servlet-name	Name of servlet alias.
servlet-class	Name of servlet class file. This name must be fully qualified. That is, if the servlet resides within a package, the full servlet class name, including package information, must be specified. For example, com.insideservlets.SnoopServlet is a fully qualified servlet class name.
init-param	Defines a single initialization parameter. Contains param-name and param-value elements.
param-name	Name of initialization parameter.
param-value	Value of initialization parameter.
servlet-mapping	Defines a single servlet mapping. Contains servlet-name and url-pattern elements.
servlet-name	Name of servlet alias or servlet class file.
url-pattern	URL path to map to the servlet. This can be either a directory such as */snoop* or a pattern like *.snp.

```
<web-app>
  <servlet>
    <servlet-name>snoop</servlet-name>
    <servlet-class>SnoopServlet</servlet-class>

    <init-param>
      <param-name>name1</param-name>
      <param-value>value1</param-value>
    </init-param>

    <init-param>
      <param-name>name2</param-name>
      <param-value>value2</param-value>
    </init-param>
  </servlet>

  <servlet-mapping>
    <servlet-name>snoop</servlet-name> <!-- servlet name -->
    <url-pattern>/snoop</url-pattern>
  </servlet-mapping>
```

```
<servlet-mapping>
  <servlet-name>SnoopServlet</servlet-name> <!-- class name -->
  <url-pattern>*.snp</url-pattern>
</servlet-mapping>
</web-app>
```

NOTE: Though not listed in Table 8.3, `<load-on-startup>` is another useful element that may be nested within the `<servlet>` block. The `<load-on-startup>` element instructs the servlet container to load the servlet when the server starts (as opposed to when the servlet is first requested). Loading a servlet at start-up improves the servlet's response time for the first request. If the order in which servlets are loaded is not important, the `<load-on-startup/>` empty element may be used. Otherwise, the `<load-on-startup>` element may contain a number that specifies the order in which each servlet should be loaded at start-up. For example, the following `<servlet>` blocks indicate that the SnoopServlet should be loaded first followed by the TestServlet.

```
<servlet>
  <servlet-name>snoop</servlet-name>
  <servlet-class>SnoopServlet</servlet-class>
  <load-on-startup>1</load-on-startup>
</servlet>
<servlet>
  <servlet-name>test</servlet-name>
  <servlet-class>TestServlet</servlet-class>
  <load-onstartup>2</load-on-startup>
</servlet>
```

Invoking Servlets

Now that we know where to store servlets in the file system and how to define servlet names and servlet mappings, let's examine how they are called. With Tomcat, a servlet can be invoked using the following URL format:

```
http://server:port/context_path/servlet/servlet_name
  [/path_info][?query_string]
```

The *context_path* portion of the URL represents the Web application under which the servlet is stored. Remember that every Web application is assigned a unique context path. Of course, a context path is not required to invoke the default Web application. The `/servlet` portion of the path tells Tomcat that a servlet is being referenced (as opposed to an HTML or JSP page). The *servlet_name* portion of the URL represents the servlet class name or servlet name (i.e., servlet alias). If a servlet class name is used, it must be fully qualified. That is, the full package information, if any, must be included in the class name.

For instance, if the `SnoopServlet` resides in the `com.insideservlets` package, the servlet class name is `com.insideservlets.SnoopServlet`.

NOTE: Though several examples in this chapter use the */servlet* path to indicate when a servlet is being requested, this convention is specific to Tomcat and may not be supported by every servlet container (i.e., it is not enforced by the Java Servlet Specification). Therefore, it is good practice to create a servlet mapping (see Listing 8.1) by which to invoke a servlet.

path_info and *query_string* are optional components of the URL. The *path_info* portion of the URL allows additional path information to be specified. This information can be extracted using the `getPathInfo()` method of the `HttpServletRequest` object. The `getPathInfo()` method returns any path information following the servlet path but prior to the query string. For example, if a servlet called `GetPathServlet` is invoked using this URL (assuming that the server is listening on port 8080):

http://localhost:8080/servlet/GetPathServlet/html/public?name=value

the value returned by `getPathInfo()` is

`/html/public`

Finally, the *query_string* portion of the URL allows additional information to be passed to the servlet in a name/value pair format. Query string names and values can be read using the `HttpServletRequest` object's `getParameterNames()`, `getParameter()`, and `getParameterValues()` methods. This URL demonstrates how name/value pairs can be passed to a servlet:

http://localhost:8080/servlet/GuestBook?name=Madison&age=4

NOTE: The examples throughout this chapter assume that the user is using the machine on which the server is running. Hence, `localhost` is used in most URLs. However, keep in mind that these services can be accessed from any machine on the network by specifying an IP address (or resolvable hostname) in place of `localhost` in the URL.

When you are ready to run your servlet, simply place it in the */WEB-INF/ classes* directory of one of the Web applications. Once it's in the right place, your servlet can be called by referencing the Web application's context path and the servlet class name while including the */servlet* path. For instance, if you placed a servlet named SnoopServlet.class in the */WEB-INF/classes* directory of the *examples* Web application (i.e., */jakarta-tomcat/webapps/examples/ WEB-INF/classes*), you could invoke it from a browser using the following URL:

http://localhost:8080/examples/servlet/SnoopServlet

Similarly, the SnoopServlet servlet could also be called using its servlet name (defined in Listing 8.1) rather than its class name like this:

http://localhost:8080/examples/servlet/snoop

NOTE: Although a servlet can be invoked using its class name or its servlet name, the servlet name must be used for any servlet that requires initialization parameters. This is due to the fact that initialization parameters are tied to the servlet name rather than to the servlet class file. Each servlet name receives its own servlet instance, allowing multiple instances of the same servlet to use different initialization parameters.

On the other hand, you can eliminate the context path by placing your servlet in the server's default Web application. On Tomcat, this is the *ROOT* Web application. Placing your servlet in the */WEB-INF/classes* directory of *ROOT* allows you to invoke it as follows:

http://localhost:8080/servlet/SnoopServlet

In addition to calling servlets using the */servlet* path, servlets can be invoked according to their servlet mappings. The URL format for requesting a servlet via a servlet mapping is as follows.

```
http://server:port/context_path/servlet_mapping[/path_info]
   [?query_string]
```

When invoking a servlet via one of its servlet mappings, the */servlet* path is not used. And since the */servlet* path may not be supported by all servlet containers, calling servlets by their servlet mappings is recommended. For example, according to the servlet mappings defined in Listing 8.1, the Snoop-Servlet servlet can be called using either of the following two URLs (assuming that SnoopServlet is in the *examples* Web application that is assigned the */examples* context path).

http://localhost:8080/examples/snoop
http://localhost:8080/examples/anything.snp

On the other hand, if `SnoopServlet` was placed in the *ROOT* Web application (which is assigned an empty context path), it could be called with the following URLs.

http://localhost:8080/snoop
http://localhost:8080/anything.snp

Now that we know how to invoke servlets, let's run the `BulletinBoard` servlet that we created in the last chapter. To begin, copy the *Bulletin-Board.class* file to the following directory:

/jakarta-tomcat/webapps/ROOT/WEB-INF/classes

This directory is under the Tomcat server's default Web application called *ROOT.* Remember that the default Web application has been defined as having an empty context path and, therefore, can be invoked without specifying a context path. To test the `BulletinBoard` servlet, make sure that the Tomcat server is running and issue a request to the following URL (remember that the `BulletinBoard` servlet requires the *topics.properties* file to be located at the root of the file system):

http://localhost:8080/servlet/BulletinBoard

If the Tomcat server has been installed properly and the servlet has been copied to the right directory, the `BulletinBoard` servlet should respond with the **Servlet Bulletin Board** page (see Figure 8.3). Now that we can invoke the `BulletinBoard` servlet, let's create a servlet name and URL mapping for it. To do so, add the following XML block to the *ROOT* Web application's *web.xml* file located in the */WEB-INF* directory. This block should be located between the <web-app> and </web-app> tags.

```
<servlet>
  <servlet-name>
    bboard
  </servlet-name>
  <servlet-class>
    BulletinBoard
  </servlet-class>
</servlet>
<servlet-mapping>
  <servlet-name>
    bboard
  </servlet-name>
  <url-pattern>
    /bulletins.html
  </url-pattern>
</servlet-mapping>
```

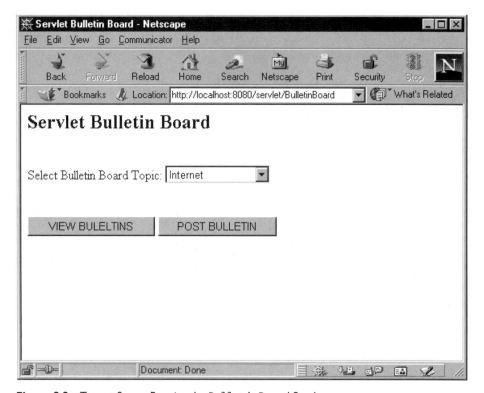

Figure 8.3   Tomcat Server Running the `BulletinBoard` Servlet

Once the servlet name and servlet mapping have been added to the *ROOT* Web application's *web.xml* file, the `BulletinBoard` servlet can be invoked via its servlet name like this:

http://localhost:8080/servlet/bboard

Or ir can be invoked by its servlet mapping like this:

http://localhost:8080/bulletins.html

This concludes our demonstration of the Apache Tomcat server. Although Tomcat may not be as robust as many commercial offerings, it is an excellent test platform because it is recognized as the official reference implementation for the Servlet API. All other servlet containers must conform to the Servlet API and Java Servlet Specification as strictly as Tomcat.

Before moving on to another servlet container, here are a few tips that may be useful when using Tomcat to test and debug servlets (see Chapter 9 for additional debugging information).

1. Use Tomcat's console window extensively. Placing `System.out.println()` statements throughout your servlet will aid the debugging process by printing variable values and location flags to the console window. In addition, it is often very useful to print the stack trace to standard out (for viewing in the console window). See Appendix L for instructions on converting the output of the `Exception` object's `printStackTrace()` method to a `String`. Additionally, you can use the `ServletContext` object's `log()` method to write information to the servlet log (see Chapter 10 for more information on the `log()` method).

2. If servlet reloading is not enabled or a support class outside of the _/WEB-INF/classes_ directory is changed, Tomcat must be restarted before any changes will take effect. To restart Tomcat, stop it by executing the _shutdown_ batch/script file located in the _/jakarta-tomcat/bin_ directory and start it again by running the _startup_ batch/script file.

3. All Servlet API 2.2–compatible servers are required to support Web application archive (`.war`) files. Use these `.war` files to simplify the process of distributing your Web application. See Chapter 19 for detailed information regarding the packaging and deployment of Web applications.

NOTE: Some servlet containers discard output sent to standard out (e.g., `System.out.println()`). To view this output, you may need to redirect standard out to a file like this:

```
try
{
  FileOutputStream fileOut = new FileOutputStream("/out.txt");
  PrintStream out = new PrintStream(fileOut);
  System.setOut(out); //redirect System.out to file
}
catch (FileNotFoundException ignored) {}

System.out.println("This text will be written to out.txt");
```

JRun

JRun™ is a leading third-party servlet and JSP container from Allaire Corporation[2] (formerly from Live Software) that adds servlet support to numerous Web servers running on various platforms. For example, JRun is available for

---

2. Allaire recently reached an agreement to be acquired by Macromedia, Inc.

Windows and various UNIX platforms, including SPARC Solaris, HP/UX, and Linux. JRun supports the following Web servers:

- Netscape Enterprise Server
- iPlanet Web Server
- Apache Web Server
- Microsoft Internet Information Server and Personal Web Server
- O'Reilly WebSite Pro
- Java Web Server
- Zeus Web Server

And, fortunately, the Developer version of JRun is free of charge for noncommercial use. You can find JRun on the CD accompanying this book or you can download it from:

http://www.allaire.com/Products/JRun/

In addition to supporting the Web servers listed above, JRun includes its own Web server. JRun Web Server is a simple HTTP server useful for developing and testing servlets when a more functional Web server is not required. For this demonstration, we will be using JRun version 3.0 and the integrated JRun Web Server.

First, if you're running UNIX, make sure that Java has been installed (JDK 1.2 or higher is required). The Windows version of JRun includes the Java Runtime Environment (JRE) so you are not required to provide your own JDK or JRE. Next, locate the correct JRun installation file for your platform (either from the CD or downloaded from Allaire's Web site) and execute it. On Windows, the installation file is a basic InstallShield executable. Simply double-click the installation file and the installation process will begin. On UNIX, the installation file consists of an executable shell script. Give this file execute permission with the following command:

```
chmod 755 jr30x.sh
```

The *x* in the filename should be replaced with the letter that represents your platform—h for HP/UX, 1 for Linux, s for Solaris, and g for all other UNIX platforms. Finally, execute the JRun installation script like this:

```
/bin/sh jr30x.sh
```

Once the script is running, follow the instructions to complete the installation. At the end of the installation, uncheck the box that states "I want to configure my Web server to connect to JRun." In this demonstration we will be using the

JRun Web server that is installed by default. However, if you wish, you can configure your Web server to connect to JRun at a later time.

JRun supports multiple servers with each server running its own Java virtual machine (JVM) within its own process space. By default, JRun installs two servers automatically—the JRun Admin Server and the JRun Default Server. The JRun Admin Server runs the *JRun Management Console* (JMC). *JMC* is an application that allows JRun services to be configured via a browser-based interface. The JRun Default Server is created to help the developer get up and running faster by providing a preconfigured server on which Web applications can be installed and servlets can be executed. In addition to freeing the developer from having to create a new JRun server, the JRun Default Server is used to run the *JRun Demo* application.

Before running the *JRun Management Console* and *JRun Demo* applications, the JRun Admin Server and the JRun Default Server must be started. To start these services, JRun includes a command-line utility called *jrun*. By default, this file is located at */Program Files/Allaire/JRun/bin* on Windows and in the */opt/jrun/bin* directory on UNIX. The *jrun* utility can be used to start and stop JRun servers in addition to many other functions (see Table 8.4). The syntax for this command is:

```
jrun [-admin | -demo | -install | -java | -remove | -restart |
      -start | -status | -stop] [parameters]
```

To illustrate, start the JRun Admin Server and the JRun Default Server by moving to JRun's */bin* directory and executing the following commands:

```
jrun -start admin
jrun -start default
```

Once the JRun Admin Server and the JRun Default Server are running, we can test them using a few simple techniques. To test the JRun Default Server, move to JRun's */bin* directory and type the following command:

```
jrun -demo default
```

This command should launch your browser and invoke the *JRun Demo* application. If this command does not work, you can start your browser manually and issue a request to the following URL (the JRun Default Server listens on port 8100 by default):

http://localhost:8100/demo/index.html

Table 8.4   The *jrun* Command-Line Utility

Option	Syntax/Description
admin	`jrun -admin` Starts the JRun Management Console.
demo	`jrun -demo server_name` Runs the JRun demo application from the specified server.

install	`jrun -install server_name service_name`
	`          server_directory [-quiet]`
	Installs JRun as a Windows NT/2000 service. `server_name` is the name of the JRun server to install as a service. `service_name` is the name that will be displayed in the services list. `server_directory` is the home directory for the specified JRun server. The `-quiet` parameter indicates that no dialog box should be displayed, even if the installation is unsuccessful.

java	`jrun -java program_name -classpath path [java_params]`
	`          class [class_params]`
	Launches a Java application.

remove	`jrun -remove server_name [-quiet]` Removes the specified server from the Windows NT/2000 services list. The `-quiet` parameter indicates that no dialog box should be displayed, even if the installation is unsuccessful.
restart	`jrun -restart [server_name]` Restarts the specified JRun server or, if not specified, restarts all JRun servers.
start	`jrun -start [server_name]` Starts the specified JRun server or, if not specified, starts all JRun servers.
status	`jrun -status [server_name]` Displays the status of the specified JRun server or, if not specified, displays the status of all JRun servers.
stop	`jrun -stop [server_name]` Stops the specified JRun server or, if not specified, stops all JRun servers.

If the JRun Default Server is running properly, it should respond with the **JRun Demos and Sample Pages** (see Figure 8.4). From this page, you can try out some sample servlets as well as test JavaServer Pages support.

To test the JRun Admin Server, invoke the *JRun Management Console* either from the command line like this:

```
jrun -admin
```

or request the following URL from within a browser (the JRun Admin Server listens on port 8000 by default):

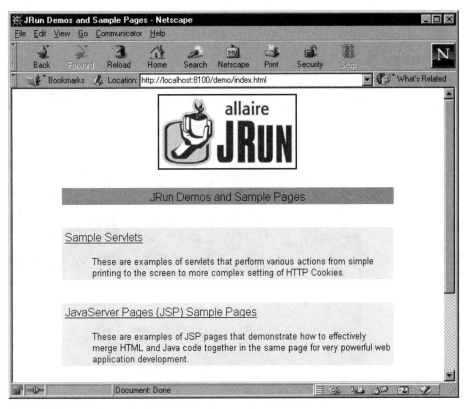

Figure 8.4   JRun Demo Application

http://localhost:8000/security/login.jsp

If the JRun Admin Server is running, it should respond with the *JMC* login page (see Figure 8.5).

If you can see the *JRun Management Console* login screen and the *JRun Demo* application is running properly, then you're ready to install and run a servlet. To begin, log in to the *JMC* using the username "admin" and the password that you provided during installation. If the login information is correct, you will see the *JMC* welcome screen. The *JMC* application consists of three frames (see Figure 8.6). The top and left-hand frames control what is displayed in the right-hand frame. The top frame contains information that is not specific to a particular JRun server. For instance, the top frame allows you to establish connections to various Web servers, change your password, manage users, and do other general maintenance tasks. The left-hand frame provides a tree view of the JRun object hierarchy (also called a *navigation*

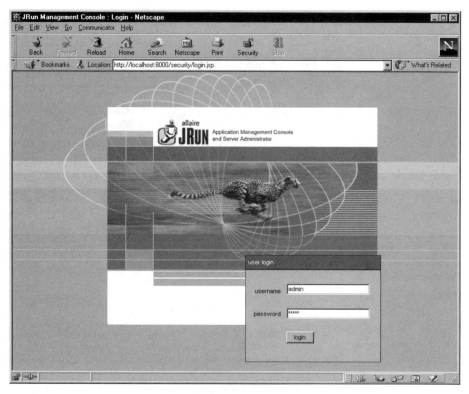

Figure 8.5   JRun Management Console Login Page

tree), starting with the machine on which JRun is installed. The currently configured JRun servers are displayed in the object hierarchy directly under the machine. By expanding the JRun server in the navigation tree (click on the "plus" sign next to the server name), the user can manage each server individually. Management activities may include viewing or altering Java settings, JDBC data sources, log file settings, and Web server settings, as well as installing new Web applications.

Now that we've reviewed the *JRun Management Console*, let's get back to the task at hand—installing and running a servlet. First, we have to decide which JRun server we will use to run the servlet and which Web application will contain it. For this demonstration, we will run the servlet using the JRun Default Server and store the servlet in the Web application called *Default User Application* (see Figure 8.7). Begin by copying the `BulletinBoard` servlet into the *Default User Application*'s */WEB-INF/classes* directory. By default, this

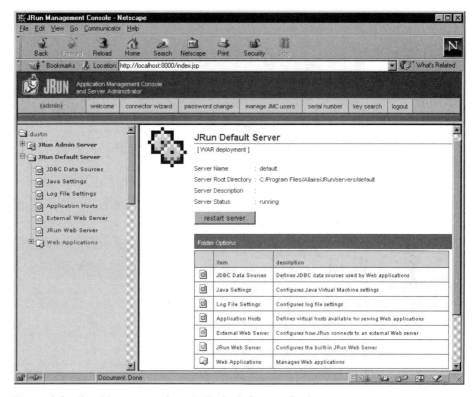

Figure 8.6 JRun Management Console **Default Server** Configuration

directory is located at */Program Files/Allaire/JRun/servers/default/default-app/ WEB-INF/classes* on Windows and at */opt/jrun/servers/default/default-app/ WEB-INF/classes* on UNIX.

Once the servlet has been copied to the right location, click on the **JRun Default Server** link in the navigation tree to view a list of administration options for this server (see Figure 8.6). Next, click on the **Web Applications** link in the navigation tree to view the list of Web applications currently installed under the JRun Default Server. Finally, to view the administration options for the *Default User Application*, click on the **Default User Application** link in the navigation tree (see Figure 8.7).

From Figure 8.7, you might notice that the **Application Mapping** for the *Default User Application* is simply "/". In JRun, application mapping is equivalent to Tomcat's context path. This mapping indicates that no context path is required in order to invoke the *Default User Application*. Therefore, any

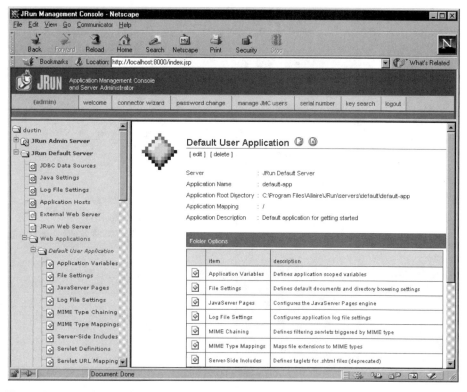

Figure 8.7   JRun Management Console Showing the **Default Server**'s Default Web Application

request to the JRun Default Server that does not include a context path is automatically mapped to the *Default User Application*. For example, once the
`BulletinBoard` servlet has been copied to the *Default User Application*'s
/WEB-INF/classes directory, it can be invoked with the following URL
(remember that the `BulletinBoard` servlet requires the *topics.properties* file to
be located at the root of the file system):

> *http://localhost:8100/servlet/BulletinBoard*

On the other hand, since the *JRun Demo* application defines an application
mapping of "*/demo*", if we were to place the `BulletinBoard` servlet in its */WEB-
INF/classes* directory (located at */jrun/servers/default/demo-app/WEB-INF/
classes*), the servlet could then be invoked using *http://localhost:8100/demo/
servlet/BulletinBoard*.

Now that we have installed the servlet and are able to reference it by class name, let's create a servlet name (known as a *servlet definition* within JRun) by which to reference the servlet. To do so, select the **Servlet Definitions** option in the navigation tree under the *Default User Application*. The **Servlet Definitions** page will be displayed in the right-hand frame (see Figure 8.8). Click the **edit** button to add a new servlet definition. The servlet definitions **Edit Window** will appear (see Figure 8.9). Type bboard in the top row of the **Name** column and BulletinBoard in the top row of the **Class Name** column. Click **update** to create the new servlet definition.

Once the servlet definition has been created, restart the JRun Default Server so that the new servlet name will take effect. To restart the default

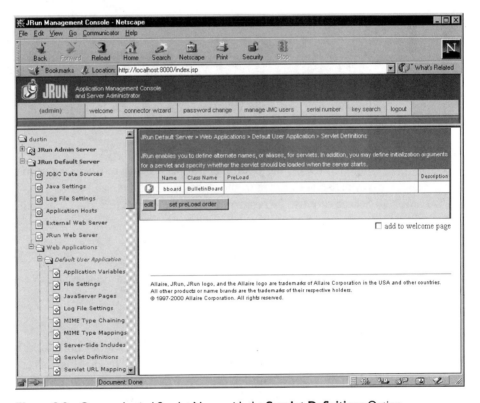

Figure 8.8 Create a Logical Servlet Name with the **Servlet Definitions** Option

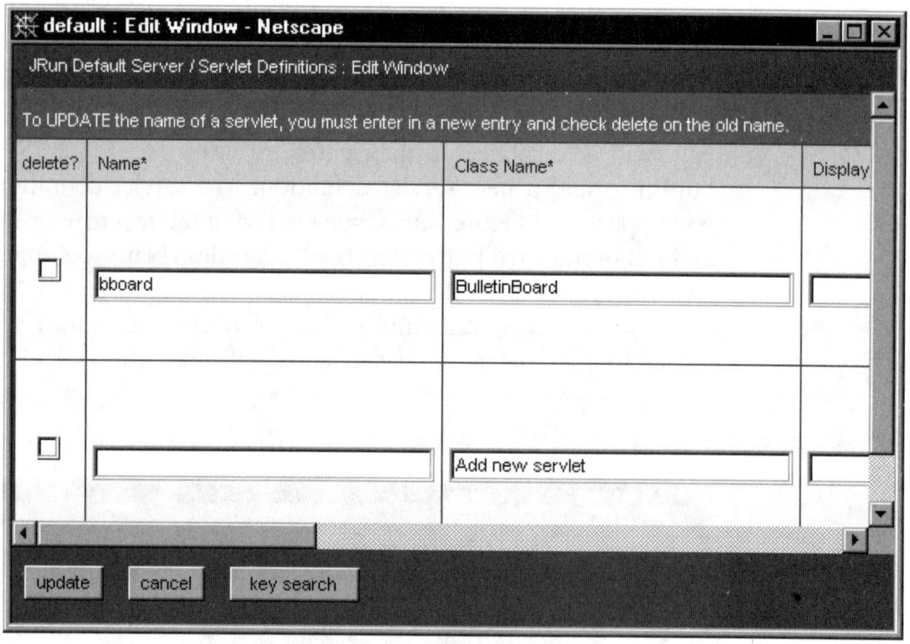

Figure 8.9   Use the **Edit Window** to Create a Servlet Definition

server, click on the **JRun Default Server** link in the navigation tree and click the **restart server** button in the right-hand frame (see Figure 8.6). The JRun Default Server can also be restarted from the command line by executing the following command from JRun's */bin* directory:

```
jrun -restart default
```

After restarting the JRun Default Server, test the new servlet name by requesting the following URL:

http://localhost:8100/servlet/bboard

Now that the servlet is installed and a servlet definition has been created, let's create a URL mapping to the servlet. To do this, select the **Servlet URL Mappings** option under the *Default User Application* in the navigation tree (see Figure 8.10). Click the **edit** button to create a new URL mapping. Type /bulletins.html in the top row of the **Virtual Path/Extension** column and bboard in the **Servlet Invoked** column (though we're using the servlet definition here, it is also legal to use the fully qualified servlet class name within the **Servlet Invoked** column). Click **update** when complete (see Figure 8.11). Again,

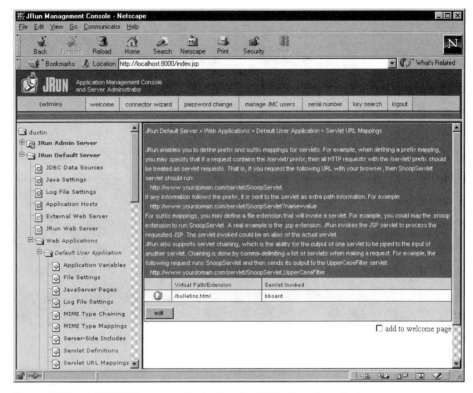

Figure 8.10   Add URL Mappings with the **Servlet URL Mappings** Option

restart the JRun Default Server in order for the changes to take effect. To test the new URL mapping, issue a request to the following URL:

> *http://localhost:8100/bulletins.html*

JRun offers many features beyond what has been presented here. To learn more about this product, try installing it from the accompanying CD and experiment on your own. In addition, see Chapter 19 for information regarding building Web applications and deploying them on JRun.

ServletExec

ServletExec™, from New Atlanta Communications,[3] is another leading third-party servlet and JSP container capable of adding servlet support to multiple

---

3. New Atlanta Communications was acquired by Unify Corporation in early 2000. However, that acquisition was rescinded near the end of that year. Therefore, the shortlived Unify eWave ServletExec product has been reinstated as ServletExec from New Atlanta Communications.

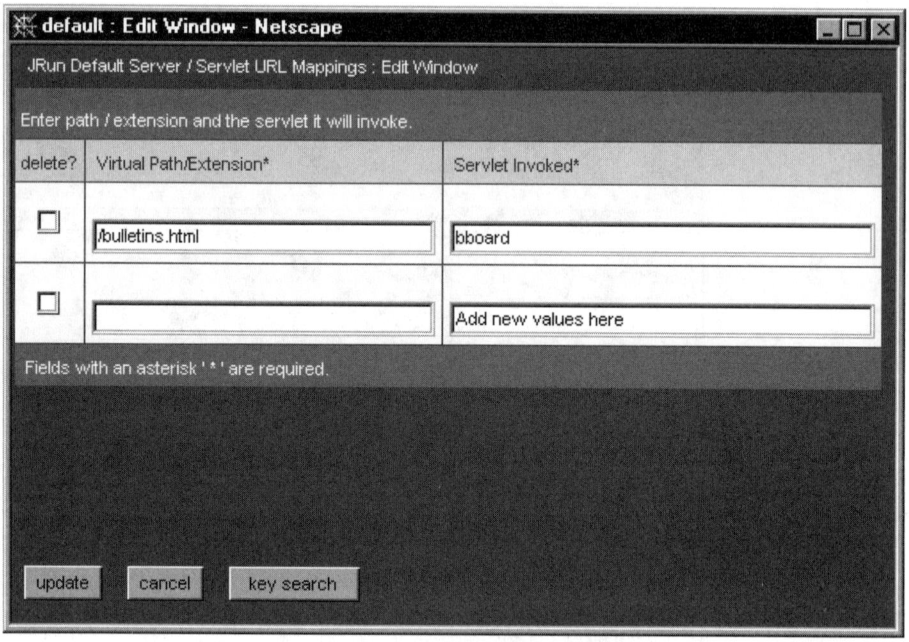

Figure 8.11   Create New URL Mappings with the **Edit Window**

platforms and Web servers. ServletExec is available for the Windows, SPARC Solaris, HP-UX, AIX, and Linux platforms and supports the following Web servers:

- Apache Web Server
- Netscape Enterprise Server
- iPlanet Web Server
- Microsoft Internet Information Server and Personal Web Server

In this section, we will demonstrate how to add servlet support to the Apache Web Server using ServletExec 3.0. Although integration with Apache is demonstrated here, the process is nearly identical for all Web servers. The only difference involves a few changes to each server's configuration file. For details regarding your specific Web server, see the ServletExec documentation provided with the installation program.

To install ServletExec, find the installation file for your platform on the accompanying CD or download the latest version from the following URL:

http://www.servletexec.com/

Once you have located the installation file, give it execution permission (if on UNIX) and run the file. You may then follow the instructions to complete the installation. When prompted to **Install a ServletExec AS Instance** or **Install a web server adapter**, select **Install a ServletExec AS Instance** and click **Next**. During the installation process, you may give the application server instance any name you wish. You may also choose any of the supported Web servers. In addition, you may want to note the port on which this ServletExec instance is running in case you choose to tie additional Web server adapters to it in the future (the port is displayed toward the end of the installation process).

Once ServletExec has been installed, stop and restart the Web server to allow any configuration changes to take effect. To test that your Web server is now serving servlets, issue a request to the following URL (assuming that the Web server is listening on port 80):

http://localhost/servlet/DateServlet

ServletExec installs the `DateServlet` sample servlet by default. If ServletExec is running properly, the date and time should be returned.

Now that our Web server supports basic servlet calls, let's see how we can register a new servlet with ServletExec and map a URL to it. To begin, start the *ServletExec Admin* utility by requesting the following URL:

http://localhost/servlet/admin

The *ServletExec Administration* utility allows the user to configure various settings for the servlet container. These settings include adding and configuring servlets and mapping URLs. Similar to JRun, ServletExec offers a browser-based administration utility that makes remote administration a snap.

To begin, copy the `BulletinBoard` servlet into the ServletExec default server's servlets directory. You can find the location of this directory by clicking on the **virtual servers** option in the left frame of the *ServletExec Administration* utility under the **Advanced** heading (see Figure 8.12) and then selecting the **default** virtual server. The **Servlets Directory** field contains the path to the default server's servlets directory (see Figure 8.12).

Once the `BulletinBoard` servlet has been copied to the correct servlets directory, you should be able to invoke it from a browser (remember that the `BulletinBoard` servlet requires the *topics.properties* file to be located at the root of the file system). To do so, issue a request to the following URL:

http://localhost/servlet/BulletinBoard

If everything is configured properly, the `BulletinBoard` servlet should respond with the **Servlet Bulletin Board** page (see Figure 8.3).

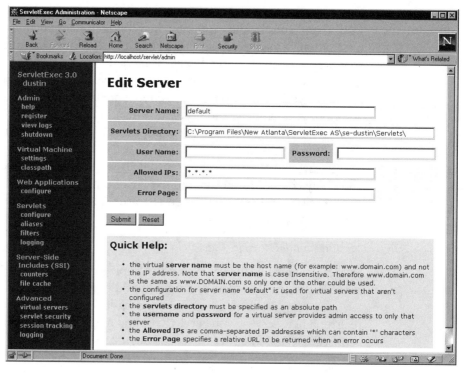

Figure 8.12   The **Edit Server** Page Indicates the Location of the Default Servlets Directory

Now let's define a servlet name for the `BulletinBoard` servlet. Start by clicking the **configure** option under the **Servlets** heading in the left frame of the admin utility. This option allows you to define any number of servlet names (see Figure 8.13).

To add a servlet, click the **Add Servlet . . .** button. On the **Add Servlet** page, enter bboard in the **Servlet Name** field and `BulletinBoard` in the **Servlet Class** field (see Figure 8.14). Click **Submit** when complete. See Table 8.5 for more information regarding the purpose of each field on the **Add Servlet** page. Once the servlet name has been created, you can test it by requesting the following URL:

http://localhost/servlet/bboard

Now that we have defined a servlet name by which to reference the `BulletinBoard` servlet, let's create a URL mapping to the servlet. To do this, click the **aliases** option under the **Servlets** heading in the left frame of the admin utility. The **Servlet Aliases** page allows you to create any number of servlet mappings. Create a mapping to the `BulletinBoard` servlet by typing

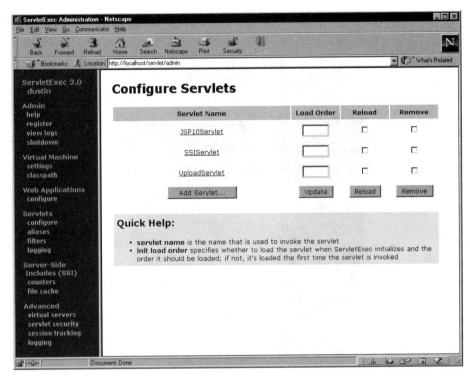

Figure 8.13   The **Configure Servlet's** Page Provides a Way to Define Servlet Names
(or Aliases)

/bulletins.html in the top field of the **Alias** column and bboard in the top
field of the **Servlet Name(s)** column (a servlet chain can be created by defining a comma-delimited list of servlet names). Click the **Submit** button when
complete (see Figure 8.15).

Once you have created the servlet mapping, notice the prominent note on
the **Servlet Aliases** page instructing you to make manual changes to your Web
server's configuration file (see Figure 8.15). Though a bit inconvenient, this
change is not difficult. To inform the Apache Web Server of the new servlet
mapping, add the /bulletins.html mapping to the end of the Servlet-
ExecAliases line and add a <Location> tag, as shown, to the *httpd.conf* file
located in the Apache Web Server's */conf* directory.

```
ServletExecAliases dustin /servlet .shtml .jsp /bulletins.html

<Location /bulletins.html>
    SetHandler servlet-exec
</Location>
```

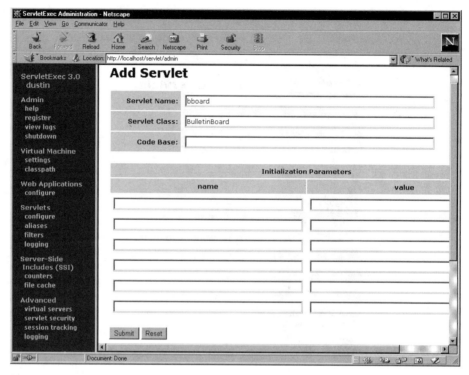

Figure 8.14   Define a New Servlet Name on the **Add Servlet** Page

Table 8.5   Servlet Configuration Fields

Field Name	Description
Servlet Name	Logical name (or alias) of servlet.
Servlet Class	Name of servlet class file. Must contain full package information.
Code Base	Contains the directory, `.jar` file, or `.zip` file containing the class files for remotely loaded servlets. For example: *http://www.insideservlets.com/servlets/*
Initialization Arguments	Name/value pairs passed to the servlet as initialization parameters.

Save the changes to the *httpd.conf* file and restart Apache. For detailed instructions on changing the configuration files for other Web servers, see the ServletExec documentation. Finally, test the servlet mapping by invoking the `BulletinBoard` servlet using the following URL:

http://localhost/bulletins.html

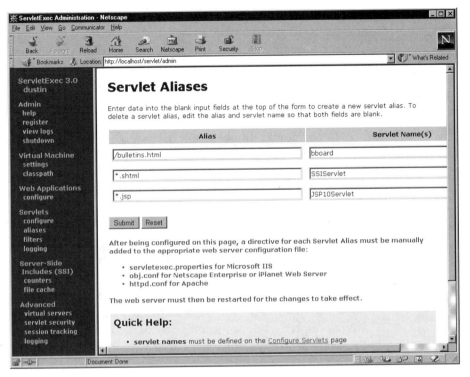

Figure 8.15 Servlet Mappings Can be Created on the **Servlet Aliases** Page

That's it! Install ServletExec, add a servlet, map a URL to it, and the servlet can be invoked from any Web browser. Of course, we have seen only a small portion of the full functionality offered by ServletExec. To learn more, install ServletExec from the accompanying CD and experiment on your own. Full documentation for this product is also included on the CD-ROM. In addition, see Chapter 19 for information regarding building Web applications and deploying them on ServletExec.

Resin

Resin™, from Caucho Technology, Inc., is a high-performance servlet and JSP container that is made available as an open source product. Resin's small size and excellent performance are particularly impressive. Resin includes a very fast integrated Web server or it can be used as the servlet container for Apache Web Server, Microsoft Internet Information Server, or Netscape/iPlanet Web Server. Resin is currently available for the Windows and UNIX platforms.

Despite its open source status, all funded entities are requested to purchase a license when deploying Resin. Since Caucho employs a paid engineering team, license revenue is essential for continued development of the Resin product. For licensing information or to download the latest version of Resin, visit the following URL:

http://www.caucho.com/

To begin, you should install the Java Development Kit, also known as the Java 2 SDK, Standard Edition (JDK 1.1 or higher is required, JDK 1.2 or higher is recommended). The Java 2 SDK, Standard Edition, can be downloaded from *http://java.sun.com/j2se/*. After the JDK has been installed, locate a copy of the Resin installation file. You can retrieve Resin 1.1 from the accompanying CD or you can download the latest version from the Caucho Web site. The Resin installation file consists of a single .zip file for Windows or a .tar.gz file for UNIX. To install Resin, simply decompress the installation file to the desired location on your file system.

Once installed, you can quickly test the Resin Web server by running the *httpd.exe* or *httpd.sh* file depending on whether you are using Windows or UNIX, respectively. For instance, to run the Resin Web server on Windows, use the following command (assuming that Resin was installed in the root of the C: partition):

```
C:>\resin1.1\bin\httpd
```

Running under Windows, the *httpd* executable displays the window shown in Figure 8.16. This window can be used to start and stop the Resin Web server. Similarly, under UNIX, start the Resin Web server using the following command (assuming that Resin was installed in the */usr/local* directory):

```
shell> /usr/local/resin1.1/bin/httpd.sh
```

Figure 8.16   Resin Web Server Control Panel

Once the server is running, test it by issuing a request to *http:// localhost:8080/* (like Tomcat, Resin Web server listens on port 8080 by default). If the server is running properly, a confirmation page will be returned indicating that the Resin Web server is working (see Figure 8.17). Likewise, it is just as easy to test Resin's servlet support by requesting the `HelloServlet` (one of Resin's sample servlets) using the following URL:

http://localhost:8080/servlet/HelloServlet

If the servlet executes successfully, you should see the immortal "Hello, World" message in your browser.

Running your own servlets with Resin is almost as easy as calling the sample servlets. To add a servlet to the default Web application, simply place it in the */resin1.1/doc/WEB-INF/classes* directory (where */resin1.1* is Resin's home directory—alter if necessary). Your servlet can then be invoked exactly like the

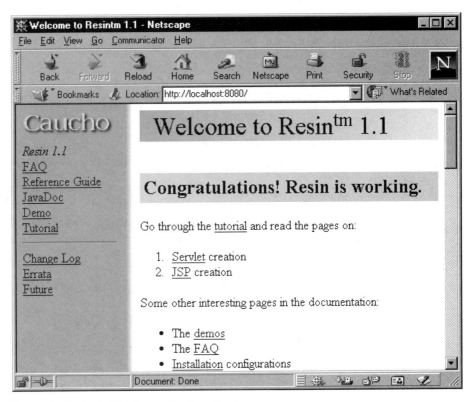

Figure 8.17 Resin Web Server Confirmation Screen

HelloServlet demonstration. For example, copy the BulletinBoard.class servlet file to */resin1.1/doc/WEB-INF/classes* and invoke it like this:

http://localhost:8080/servlet/BulletinBoard

Creating servlet aliases and URL mappings in Resin is very similar to performing these tasks in Tomcat. For starters, examine the *resin.conf* XML file in the */resin1.1/conf* directory. This file contains the majority of configuration settings for the Resin Web server and servlet container. For instance, this file stores configuration information such as the port on which the Resin Web server listens as well as default servlet settings like context paths (for mapping URLs to various Web applications), servlet names, URL mappings, and initialization parameters. To create a logical servlet name called bboard in addition to mapping all requests for */bulletins.html* to the BulletinBoard servlet, add the following XML to the default Web application section of the *resin.conf* configuration file. The default Web application section immediately follows the <web-app id='/'> tag.

```
<servlet servlet-name='bboard' servlet-class='BulletinBoard'/>
<servlet-mapping url-pattern='/bulletins.html'
    servlet-name='bboard'/>
```

Once the servlet name and URL mapping (i.e., servlet-mapping) are added to the *resin.conf* file, restart the server and invoke the BulletinBoard servlet with the following URL:

http://localhost:8080/bulletins.html

Before wrapping up our discussion, there are a few deployment tips of which you should be aware. First, if you are deploying Resin on UNIX, you should run the Web server using the *start* and *stop* scripts. These scripts improve reliability by automatically restarting the server should it ever exit. For example, to start the Web server use this command:

```
shell> /usr/local/resin1.1/bin/httpd.sh start
```

To stop the Web server, use this command:

```
shell> /usr/local/resin1.1/bin/httpd.sh stop
```

Second, if you are deploying Resin on Windows NT/2000, you will probably want to install it as a service so that it can be started automatically whenever the server starts. To install Resin as an NT service, use the following command:

```
C:\>\resin1.1\bin\httpd -install
```

To remove the service, use this command:

```
C:\>\resin1.1\bin\httpd -remove
```

Now that you know how to install Resin and invoke servlets, feel free to browse the documentation that is included under the */resin1.1/doc* directory for more information regarding Resin's features as well as instructions on integrating Resin with an existing Web server (Apache, IIS, or Netscape/iPlanet). Though we covered quite a bit, we have really only touched the surface of Resin's full capabilities.

Summary

This chapter presents a number of options for running servlets. Just from the small sampling examined here, we can see that servlets are capable of running on multiple platforms hosted by a variety of Web servers. It is this universal support for servlets that makes them so popular and powerful. In the next chapter, we will learn how to debug servlets using several popular Java development tools.

Chapter Highlights

- There are many ways in which to run a servlet. Some Web servers, such as iPlanet Web Server and W3C Jigsaw, natively support servlets. Other popular HTTP servers, such as Apache Web Server and Microsoft Internet Information Server, support servlets through add-ons like Tomcat from Apache, JRun from Allaire, or ServletExec from New Atlanta Communications.

- Perhaps the simplest way to run servlets is with the Tomcat server from the Apache Software Foundation. As a piece of the larger Apache Jakarta project, Tomcat is the official reference implementation for the Java Servlet and JavaServer Pages (JSP) specifications.

- A *Web application* is the hierarchy of directories and files that together comprise an application. Web applications are often distributed in a *Web application archive* (WAR) file (either a compressed or uncompressed file having a .war extension).

- When deployed, each Web application is assigned a unique *context path* by the system administrator. All requests to this context path will be routed to the appropriate Web application.

- The *web.xml* file is known as the deployment descriptor. The *Web application deployment descriptor* is an XML file that describes the servlets and other components that comprise a Web application, along with any initialization parameters, servlet names (or aliases), servlet URL mappings, and security constraints.

- A *servlet name* (also called a *servlet alias*) is a user-defined name that can be used to reference a servlet in place of the fully qualified servlet class name.

- *Initialization parameters* allow the system administrator to alter servlet configuration settings without having to recompile the servlet.

- *Servlet mappings* (also known as *URL mappings*) associate a particular URL name or pattern to a specific servlet.

- JRun is a leading third-party servlet container from Allaire Corporation (formerly from Live Software) that adds servlet and JSP support to numerous Web servers running on various platforms.

- ServletExec, from New Atlanta Communications, is another leading third-party servlet and JSP container capable of adding servlet support to multiple platforms and Web servers.

- Resin, from Caucho Technology, is a high-performance servlet and JSP container that is made available as an open source product.

CHAPTER 9

Debugging Servlets

In this chapter, we will demonstrate, step by step, how to debug servlets using several popular Java development tools, including JBuilder from Borland, Forte for Java from Sun Microsystems, and VisualCafé from WebGain. Specifically, this chapter covers the following topics:

- Servlet debugging process
- Servlet debugging with JBuilder
- Servlet debugging with Forte for Java
- Servlet debugging with VisualCafé

Though this chapter demonstrates how to debug servlets using three popular Java development tools, the debugging techniques presented here can be applied to almost any Java IDE (Integrated Development Environment).

Servlet Debugging Process

The servlet debugging process is virtually the same for all Java IDEs. To begin, a simple Java "stub" program is executed from within the development environment. This stub application starts a servlet-enabled server (i.e., a server that includes a servlet container, such as Tomcat). By running the stub application from within the IDE, the development tool is able to use its integrated debugger to set breakpoints and evaluate variables within servlets as they are invoked by the servlet container. Listing 9.1 demonstrates a simple stub application that starts the Tomcat server from within a Java IDE.

Listing 9.1   ServletDebug starts the Tomcat server from within an IDE.

```
/**
 * ServletDebug starts the Tomcat server to allow for debugging
 * from within an IDE. Be sure to set the -home command-line
 * argument to point to the root of the Tomcat server.
 */
public class ServletDebug
{
  public static void main(String[] args)
  {
    org.apache.tomcat.startup.Tomcat.main(args); //start server
  }
}
```

NOTE: You might be wondering how I created the ServletDebug application. Basically, I just examined the batch/script start-up files that are located in the /jakarta-tomcat/bin directory. If you evaluate these files, you will notice that the *startup* batch/script file calls the *tomcat* batch/script file. The *tomcat.bat* batch file (for Windows) then starts the Tomcat server with the following command:

```
start java %TOMCAT_OPTS% -Dtomcat.home="%TOMCAT_HOME%"
  org.apache.tomcat.startup.Tomcat %2 %3 %4 %5 %6 %7 %8 %9
```

Similarly, the *tomcat.sh* shell script file (for UNIX) starts the Tomcat server using this command:

```
$JAVACMD $TOMCAT_OPTS -Dtomcat.home=${TOMCAT_HOME}
  org.apache.tomcat.startup.Tomcat "$@" &
```

As you can see, the Tomcat server is started by executing the org.apache.tomcat.startup.Tomcat class. And as you probably already know, anytime that you execute a Java application, the virtual machine automatically calls the class's main() method. Therefore, by examining the start-up files, we discover that the Tomcat server can be started by calling the main() method of the org.apache.tomcat.startup.Tomcat class.

The process of debugging servlets from an IDE using the Tomcat server and the ServletDebug class involves the following nine basic steps.

1. Install Tomcat according to the instructions given in Chapter 8.
2. Add the ServletDebug program to the project in your Java IDE.
3. Add the *servlet.jar* (Servlet API), *webserver.jar* (Tomcat server), *xml.jar* (XML parsing functions), and *jasper.jar* (JSP classes) files to the project's CLASSPATH. These files are located in the /jakarta-tomcat/lib directory.

4. Set the project output path in your IDE to compile all classes to the */classes* directory of the desired Tomcat Web application. For example, to install the classes to the *ROOT* Web application, instruct your development tool to compile all classes to the */jakarta-tomcat/webapps/ROOT/WEB-INF/ classes* directory.

5. Set the `-home` command-line parameter for the `ServletDebug` application to point to the Tomcat home directory. For instance, on Windows, the `ServletDebug` command-line parameter might look like this: `-home c:\jakarta-tomcat`.

6. Add a servlet to the project and set a breakpoint somewhere within it.

7. Run the `ServletDebug` program in debug mode.

8. Invoke the servlet from a browser just like you would any other Tomcat servlet (see Chapter 8 for more information on invoking Tomcat servlets). For example, a servlet called `BulletinBoard` in the *ROOT* Web application can be called with a URL like this: *http://localhost:8080/ servlet/BulletinBoard*.

9. At this point, the development tool should halt execution at the servlet breakpoint and you should be able to evaluate variables and any other information your IDE makes available during debug (such as thread and call stack information).

Now that we've discussed, in a generic manner, the steps to debugging servlets using the Tomcat server, the following sections will demonstrate how this is accomplished using three specific Java IDEs. In this chapter, we examine JBuilder, Forte for Java, and VisualCafé.

NOTE: In addition to the `ServletDebug` application presented here, many servlet container manufacturers, such as Allaire (JRun) and New Atlanta Communications (ServletExec), provide servlet debugger applications that can start their servlet container from within an IDE. For example, New Atlanta Communications provides a free application called `ServletExecDebugger` that allows the ServletExec server to be started from within a Java IDE.

JBuilder

In this section we will demonstrate servlet debugging using JBuilder from Borland Software Corporation (formerly Inprise Corporation). JBuilder is a leading servlet development tool and, in my opinion, one of the strongest Java IDEs available. In addition, JBuilder is a cross-platform tool (written entirely in

Java) available for Windows, Linux, and Solaris. And best of all, the Foundation Edition of JBuilder 4 demonstrated here is completely free and included on the CD that accompanies this book. JBuilder Foundation can also be downloaded from Borland's Web site at the following URL:

http://www.borland.com/jbuilder/

Now let's examine how to debug servlets, step by step, in JBuilder Foundation. To begin, install the Tomcat server as discussed in Chapter 8. Next, install JBuilder Foundation from the CD (or download it from the Borland Web site) according to the installation instructions that accompany the install program. Launch JBuilder and close the current project by selecting **Close Projects** from the **File** menu. Create a new project by selecting **New Project** from the **File** menu. Choose a name and location for the project file using the **Project name** and **Root path** fields, respectively. Optionally, click the **Next** button twice to enter information that will be included in the project in the form of a "Project Notes" file containing the title of the project, author's name, and description. If you do not want to use the project notes file, clear the **Make project notes file** check box in Step 2 of the **Project Wizard** dialog box. Click **Finish** when complete (see Figure 9.1).

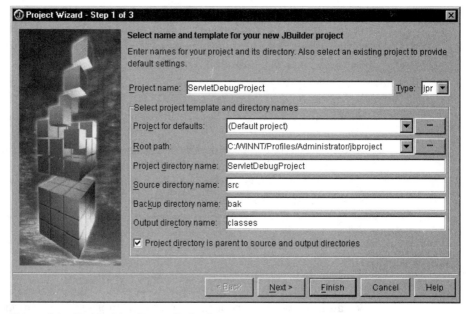

Figure 9.1   JBuilder New Project Dialog Box

Once the project is created, copy the `ServletDebug` program from the CD to your hard drive and add it to the project by selecting the **Add Files/Packages** option from the **Project** menu. Once `ServletDebug` has been added, select the **Project Properties** option from the **Project** menu in order to add the necessary JAR files to the project CLASSPATH. To add JAR files (or directories) to the CLASSPATH, select the **Required Libraries** tab located on the **Paths** tab and click **Add** (see Figure 9.2).

NOTE: The commercial versions of JBuilder provide built-in support for servlet debugging that does not depend on an external application such as the `ServletDebug` class presented earlier in this chapter. However, the JBuilder Foundation edition included on the accompanying CD does not include built-in servlet debugging and, therefore, requires a class like `ServletDebug` to perform this task.

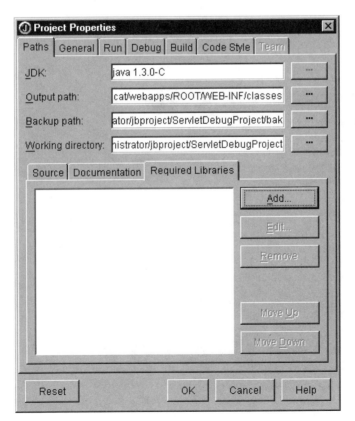

Figure 9.2   Required Libraries Tab Allows Items to Be Added to the CLASSPATH

After clicking the **Add** button, JBuilder displays a dialog box that allows you to add any of the available CLASSPATH libraries to your project or create a new one (see Figure 9.3). A CLASSPATH library is a collection of directories and/or JAR files that should be added to the CLASSPATH when the project is executed.

We must now create a CLASSPATH library that contains all of the JAR files required to compile servlets and run the Tomcat server. To accomplish this, click the **New** button on the dialog box titled **Select One or More Librar-ies**. In response, JBuilder displays a dialog box titled **New Library Wizard** that allows you to add directories and JAR files to a new CLASSPATH library and assign a name to it (see Figure 9.4). Click the **Add** button to add the following JAR files to a new CLASSPATH library entitled Servlet API 2.2.

> */jakarta-tomcat/lib/jasper.jar*
> */jakarta-tomcat/lib/servlet.jar*
> */jakarta-tomcat/lib/webserver.jar*
> */jakarta-tomcat/lib/xml.jar*

Once the required JAR files have been added, click **OK** twice to return to the **Project Properties** dialog box and point the output path to a directory

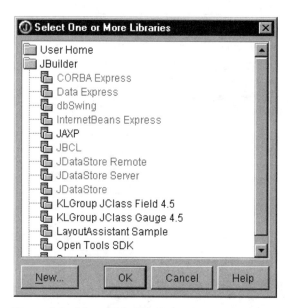

Figure 9.3   Library Selection Dialog Box

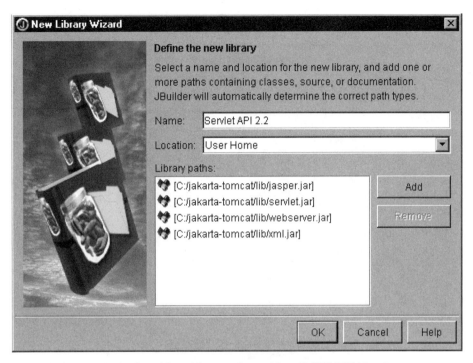

Figure 9.4 This Dialog Box Allows Users to Create New CLASSPATH Libraries

where the Tomcat server will be able to locate your new servlets. To compile
your servlet classes to Tomcat's default Web application, set the **Output path**
field to */jakarta-tomcat/webapps/ROOT/WEB-INF/classes* (see Figure 9.2). In
this way, Tomcat will be able to locate the compiled servlet when invoked like
this:

http://localhost:8080/servlet/DateServlet

To tell JBuilder which application should be run when the project is executed, select the **Run** tab on the **Project Properties** dialog box and click the **...**
button (three dots), as shown in Figure 9.6. This button displays the **Select
Main Class for Project** dialog box. Type `ServletDebug` into the **Class Name**
field to specify the class to be executed and click **OK** (see Figure 9.5).

Once the main class is selected, we must pass a parameter to the `Servlet-
Debug` application that specifies the root directory of the Tomcat server. Specify-
ing the root directory allows Tomcat to locate its Web applications. The root
directory is passed to `ServletDebug` using the `-home` command-line parameter.
To set this parameter, select the **Run** tab on the **Project Properties** dialog box

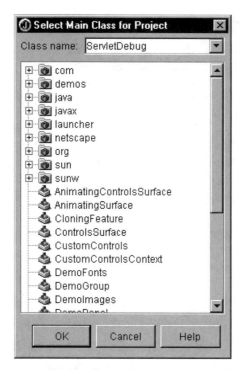

Figure 9.5   This Box Lets You Select the Class to Run When the Project Is Executed

and set the **application parameters** field to the value "-home /jakarta-tomcat" (assuming that Tomcat is installed at the root of the file system), as shown in Figure 9.6. We are now finished with the **Project Properties** dialog box. Click **OK** to close it.

The next step is to create a servlet to debug. To do this, select the **New Class** option from the **File** menu. JBuilder presents a dialog box titled **Class Wizard** that allows you to select the class name and package for the new class. For this example, clear the **Package** field (in order to use the default Java package), type DateServlet in the **Class name** field, and enter javax.servlet. HttpServlet in the **Base class** field. Also, clear all check boxes except for **Public** (see Figure 9.7).

The **Class Wizard** dialog box shown in Figure 9.7 simplifies the process of creating a new class. Upon completion of this dialog box, JBuilder automatically creates skeleton code for the new class. Once the skeleton of the new class has been created, complete the DateServlet as shown in Listing 9.2. Be sure to include the proper import statements.

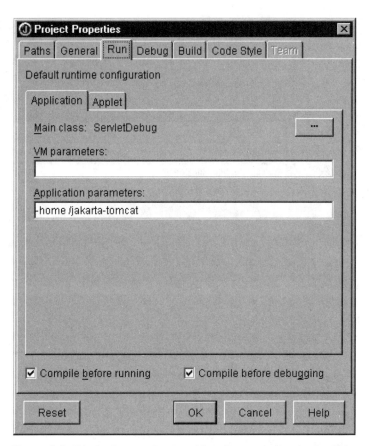

Figure 9.6 Set Application Command-Line Parameters on the Run Tab

Listing 9.2 DateServlet returns the date to the client.

```java
import javax.servlet.http.*;
import javax.servlet.*;
import java.io.*;

public class DateServlet extends HttpServlet
{
  public void doGet(HttpServletRequest request,
    HttpServletResponse response) throws ServletException,
    IOException
  {
    response.setContentType("text/plain");

    PrintWriter out = response.getWriter();

    out.println(new java.util.Date());
  }
}
```

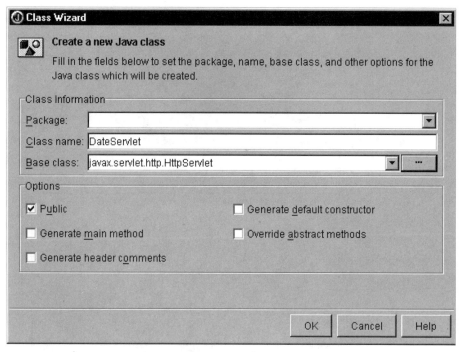

Figure 9.7   JBuilder Class Wizard Simplifies the Process of Creating a New Class

Now that the servlet has been created, let's try some debugging by adding a breakpoint. To set a breakpoint, move to any line within the doGet() method and press the **F5** key. Breakpoints can also be added by right-clicking on a line and selecting **Toggle Breakpoint** from the pop-up menu or by selecting the **Add Breakpoint** option under the **Run** menu. Breakpoint lines are highlighted in red and marked by a red circle in the margin (see Figure 9.8).

To start the Tomcat server running in debug mode, select **Debug Project** from the **Run** menu (see Figure 9.9). This action executes the ServletDebug application and activates the integrated debugger. In JBuilder's message window, you should see the output from the Tomcat server that includes a number of lines containing configuration information and the message "Starting Tomcat." This message indicates that the Tomcat server is running and ready to accept requests. You can invoke the DateServlet using the following URL:

http://localhost:8080/servlet/DateServlet

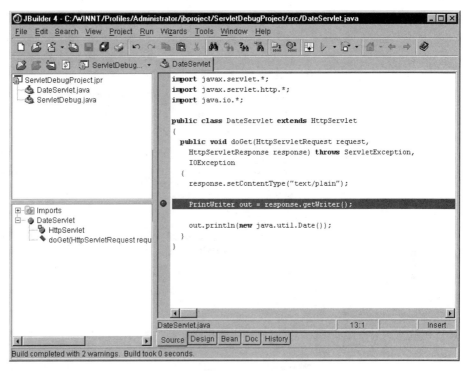

Figure 9.8 Breakpoints Are Highlighted in Red and Marked by a Red Circle

When Tomcat receives this request, the `DateServlet` is called and the servlet code begins to execute. The servlet will run until it reaches a breakpoint, at which time execution will pause and the JBuilder environment will automatically move to the foreground.[1] The current line at which execution is halted is highlighted in blue and marked by a green arrow in the margin (see Figure 9.9). Using the **Run** menu, you can step through execution line by line, evaluate variables, set watches, and much more. Providing an intuitive interface and integrated debugger, JBuilder makes servlet development and debugging a snap.

---

1. On some systems, JBuilder may not automatically move to the foreground. In this case, you will need to set focus back to JBuilder manually.

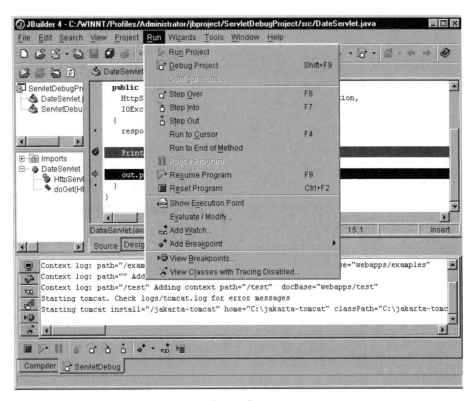

Figure 9.9   JBuilder Provides Numerous Debug Options

Forte for Java

Forte for Java (formerly NetBeans) is a powerful Java IDE from Sun Microsystems. Like JBuilder, Forte for Java is a cross-platform development tool
(written entirely in Java) available on the Windows, Linux, and Solaris platforms. And again similar to JBuilder, the Community Edition of Forte for Java
1.0 demonstrated here is completely free for download from Sun's Web site at
the following URL:

http://www.sun.com/forte/ffj/

With its single document interface (where each window floats indepen-
dently of the others), Forte for Java has a different look and feel from many
other Java IDEs. Though its interface is different, debugging servlets with Forte
for Java is similar to other development tools. To begin, be sure that the Tomcat server is installed as demonstrated in Chapter 8. Next, install Forte for Java

according to the installation instructions that accompany the install program. Once installed, launch Forte for Java and create a new project by clicking the **New Project** option under the **Project** menu. Select a name for the project and click **OK** (see Figure 9.10). When Forte for Java asks if you would like to "start with a new file system" click **New**. The file systems tab in Forte for Java contains the directories and JAR files that are added to the CLASSPATH when the project is run.

After creating a new project, copy the `ServletDebug` class from the CD to your hard drive and open it by selecting the **Open File** option from the **File** menu. Use the **Open** dialog box to locate and add the `ServletDebug` Java file. At this point, Forte for Java will ask you if the `ServletDebug` class should be in the default package. Respond by clicking **Accept**. Since no package information is included in the `ServletDebug` class, it should be placed in the default package.

Though the **Open File** dialog box opens the specified file and adds its directory to the CLASSPATH, it does not actually place the file in the project. To do this, select the **Project ServletDebug** tab (if you named your project "ServletDebug") in the Forte for Java **Explorer** window. Right-click on the **Project ServletDebug** icon in this tab and select the **Add Existing** option from the pop-up menu. The **Select Objects** dialog box will then allow you to find the `ServletDebug` program in the **Filesystems** directory that was added when you opened the `ServletDebug` file (see Figures 9.11 and 9.15). Notice that the icon

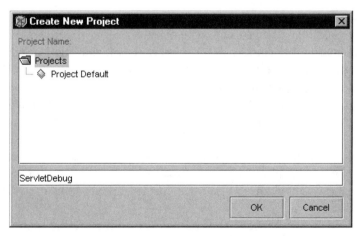

Figure 9.10   Create a New Project to Contain `DateServlet` and the `ServletDebug` Class

Figure 9.11   Add the `ServletDebug` Class to the Project

for the `ServletDebug` class contains a small green arrow. This arrow indicates the class that will be executed when the project is run. If you have more than one executable class within a project (i.e., classes that define a static `main()` method), be sure to indicate which class should be run by selecting the **Set Main Class** option from the **Project** menu.

Finally, we need to set the `-home` command-line parameter that allows the `ServletDebug` application to tell the Tomcat server the location of its home directory. To do this, click on the `ServletDebug` icon on the **Project** tab. Once the `ServletDebug` application is highlighted, select the **Execution** tab on the **Properties Window** and type `-home /jakarta-tomcat` in the **Arguments** field, as shown in Figure 9.12 (assuming that your Tomcat server is installed at */jakarta-tomcat*).

Once `ServletDebug` has been added to the project, we're ready to add the required JAR files in order to compile and run it. To do this, select the **Add**

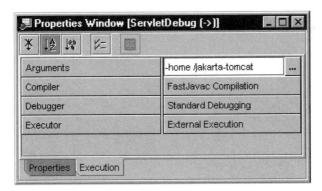

Figure 9.12 Add Command-Line Arguments on the Properties Window

JAR option under the **Tools** menu. Use this option to add the following four JARs to the CLASSPATH.

/jakarta-tomcat/lib/jasper.jar
/jakarta-tomcat/lib/servlet.jar
/jakarta-tomcat/lib/webserver.jar
/jakarta-tomcat/lib/xml.jar

The **Filesystems** tab of the Forte for Java **Explorer** window should now contain the four JAR files that were just added as well as the directory under which the ServletDebug file is stored (see Figure 9.13). The directory and JAR files shown on the **Filesystems** tab represent the items that will be added to the CLASSPATH when the project is run.

Once the necessary JAR files have been added to the CLASSPATH, create a servlet to debug by clicking the **New From Template** option under the **File** menu. On the **New From Template** dialog box, select the **Class** template under the **Classes** folder and click **Next** (see Figure 9.14).

After choosing the **Class** template, name the new class DateServlet and click **Finish** (see Figure 9.15). Forte for Java will ask if you would like Date-Servlet added to the current project. Click **Yes**.

At this point, you should have both the DateServlet and ServletDebug classes in your project (see Figure 9.16). Complete the DateServlet as shown in Listing 9.2 (presented in the "JBuilder" section). If the DateServlet code is not visible, double-click its icon on the **Project** tab.

Now we're ready to do some servlet debugging. Set a breakpoint in the DateServlet class by clicking on a line within the doGet() method and selecting

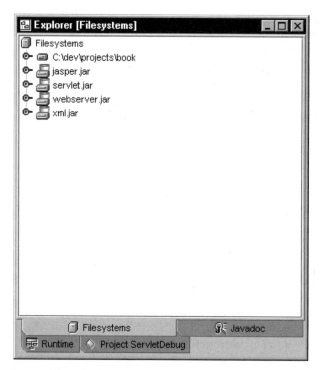

Figure 9.13   Explorer Window Shows the Items Added to the Project CLASSPATH

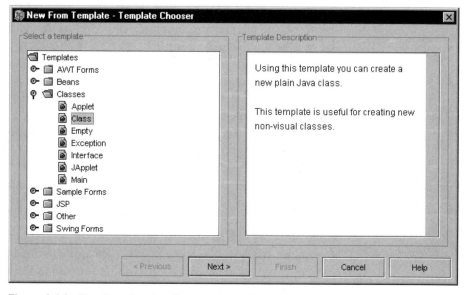

Figure 9.14   The Class Template Creates a New Class

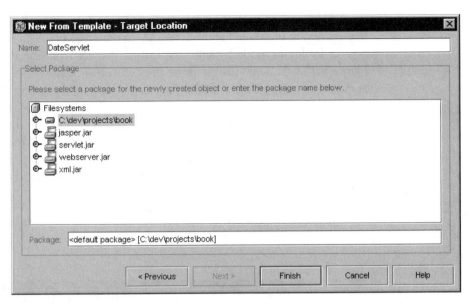

Figure 9.15 New From Template Dialog Box Allows New Items to Be Added to Project

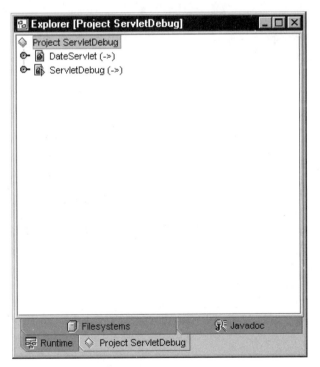

Figure 9.16 `DateServlet` and `ServletDebug` Should Appear on the Project Tab

the **Add/Remove Breakpoint** option from the **Debug** menu. Breakpoint lines are highlighted in blue (see Figure 9.18). Once the breakpoint has been set, run the project in debug mode by selecting **Debug Project** from the **Project** menu (see Figure 9.17). You can also execute the project in debug mode by selecting the ServletDebug application in the **Project** window and clicking **Start Debugging** under the **Debug** menu.

After starting the ServletDebug application, you should see output from the Tomcat server displayed in the Debugger **Output Window** (see Figure 9.18). The message that states "Starting Tomcat" indicates that the Tomcat server is running and ready to accept requests. Invoke the DateServlet from a browser by issuing a request to the following URL:

http://localhost:8080/servlet/DateServlet

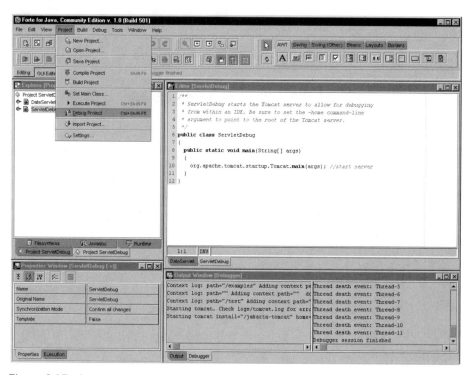

Figure 9.17   Run the Project in Debug Mode

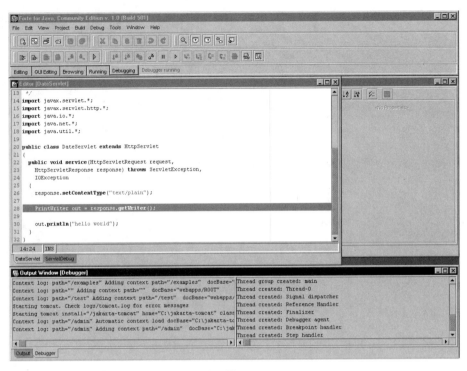

Figure 9.18   Breakpoints Are Highlighted in Blue

Once DateServlet is invoked, Tomcat will execute the servlet code until pausing at the breakpoint. Unlike JBuilder, Forte for Java does not automatically move to the foreground when a breakpoint is encountered. Therefore, after invoking the servlet, manually set the focus to the Forte for Java application. Execution should be halted at the breakpoint with the current line of execution highlighted in purple. At this point, you can step through the execution, add watches, and evalute variables using the options on the **Debug** menu (see Figure 9.19). To end the debugging process, select **Finish Debugging** from the **Debug** menu. As you can see, Forte for Java is a powerful Java development environment and well suited for developing and debugging servlets.

VisualCafé

VisualCafé is a popular Java IDE from WebGain (originally developed by Symantec). For more information about VisualCafé, see the following URL:

http://www.webgain.com/

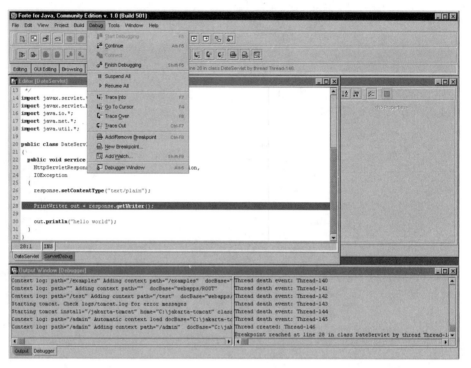

Figure 9.19   Step through Execution and Evaluate Variables Using the Debug Menu

Now let's examine how to debug servlets using VisualCafé 4. To begin, install the Tomcat server as demonstrated in Chapter 8. Next, install Visual-Café according to the installation instructions that accompany the install program. Once installed, launch VisualCafé and create a new project by clicking the **New Project** option under the **File** menu. When prompted to choose a project template, select **Empty Project** and click **OK** (see Figure 9.20).

Once an empty project is created, copy the ServletDebug class from the CD to your hard drive and select the **Files Into Project** option from the **Insert** menu. This option displays the **Project Files** dialog box, which can be used to add files to the project. To add ServletDebug to the project, locate it in the file system and click the **Add** button. ServletDebug will be added to the project (see Figure 9.21). After adding the file, click **OK**.

Once ServletDebug has been added to the project, add the following JAR files to the CLASSPATH.

> /jakarta-tomcat/lib/jasper.jar
> /jakarta-tomcat/lib/servlet.jar
> /jakarta-tomcat/lib/webserver.jar
> /jakarta-tomcat/lib/xml.jar

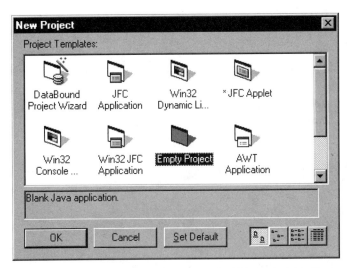

Figure 9.20   Select the Type of Project to Build from the New Project Dialog Box

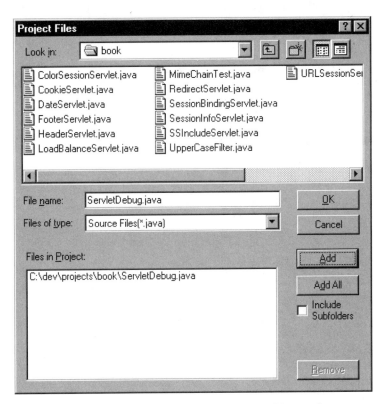

Figure 9.21   Use the Project Files Dialog Box to Add Files to a Project

To add these files to the CLASSPATH, click the **Options** item under the **Project** menu and select the **Directories** tab. Click the **New** toolbar icon to add an item to the CLASSPATH (hover over each toolbar icon and a tooltip will indicate its purpose). After clicking **New**, type in the full path to each JAR file (see Figure 9.22).

Once the required JAR files have been added, select **Output files** from the **Show directories for** drop-down list (see Figure 9.22). Type c:\jakarta-

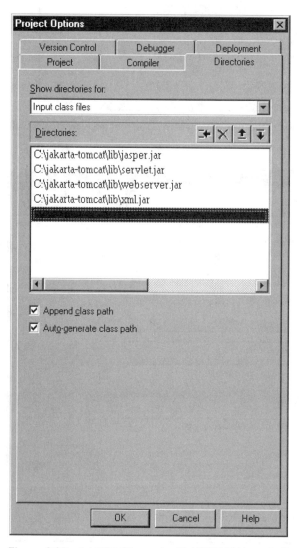

Figure 9.22   Add JAR Files to the CLASSPATH Using the Project Options Dialog Box

`tomcat\webapps\ROOT\WEB-INF\classes` in the **Output Directory** field (see Figure 9.23). Outputting the compiled class files to Tomcat's default Web application (*ROOT*) will allow Tomcat to locate compiled servlets when invoked in this manner:

http://localhost:8080/servlet/DateServlet

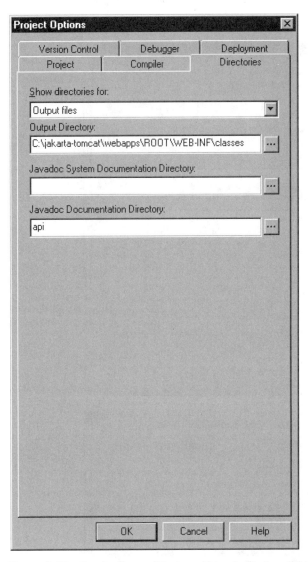

Figure 9.23 Set the Output Directory Using the Project Options Dialog Box

Lastly, select the **Project** tab on the **Project Options** dialog box. Type ServletDebug in the **Main Class** field and -home c:\jakarta-tomcat in the **Program Arguments** field (see Figure 9.24). These settings instruct VisualCafé to execute ServletDebug when the project is run and to pass it information regarding the root directory of the Tomcat server. Click **OK** when finished.

Now it's time to add a servlet to the project that we can debug. To create a new servlet, select the **Class** option from the **Insert** menu. On the **Insert**

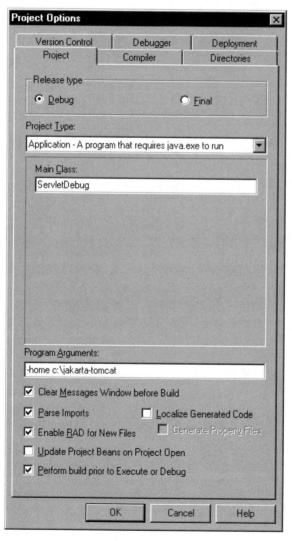

Figure 9.24   Set the Main Class and Program Arguments Using the Project Options Dialog Box

Class dialog box, type `DateServlet` in the **Name** field and click **Finish** (see Figure 9.25).

Now that the `DateServlet` class has been added to the project, double-click the `DateServlet` icon in the VisualCafé **Project** window to display the code for this class. Complete the `DateServlet` class according to Listing 9.2.

At last, we're ready to debug the servlet. Start by setting a breakpoint in `DateServlet` by clicking on a line in the `doGet()` method and selecting **Set Breakpoint** from the **Source** menu (or by pressing the F9 key). A red diamond marks the line with the breakpoint (see Figure 9.26).

Now start the project running in debug mode by selecting the **Run in Debugger** option under the **Project** menu. The VisualCafé **Messages** window will display output from the Tomcat server. The "Starting Tomcat" message indicates that Tomcat is running and ready to accept requests (see Figure 9.27). Invoke the `DateServlet` from a browser by issuing a request to the following URL:

http://localhost:8080/servlet/DateServlet

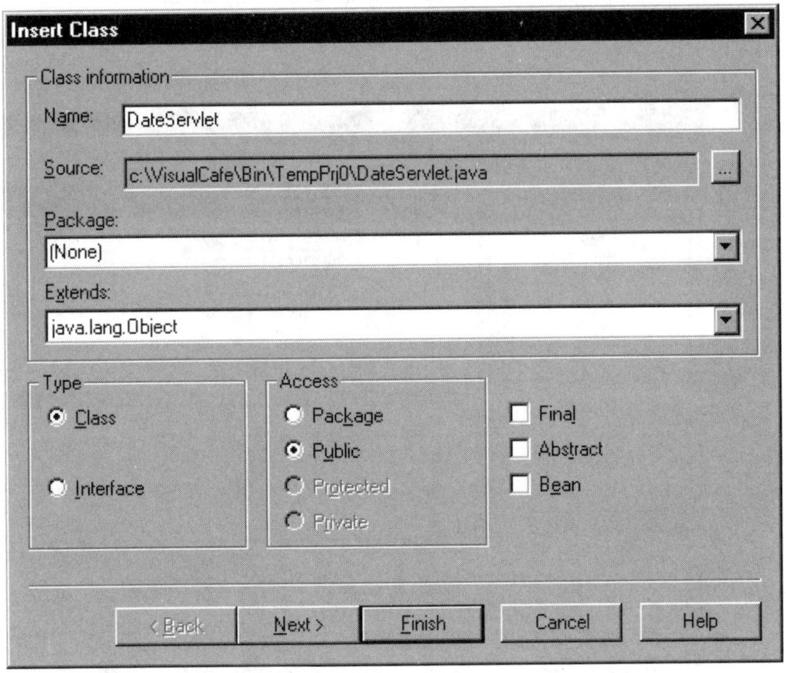

Figure 9.25 Create a New Class Using the Insert Class Dialog Box

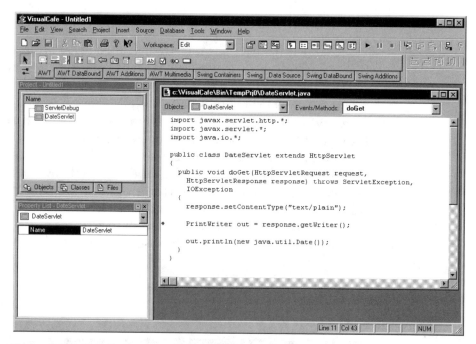

Figure 9.26   Set a Breakpoint to Pause Execution within the Servlet

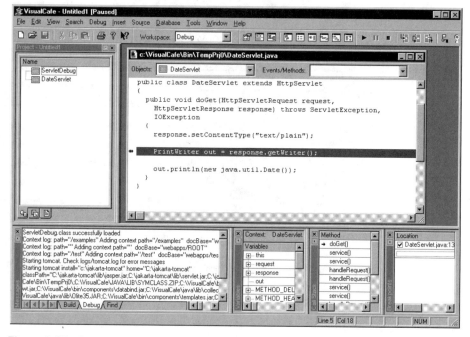

Figure 9.27   Servlet Execution Halts at the Breakpoint

Once `DateServlet` is invoked, Tomcat will execute the servlet code until pausing at the breakpoint. Like JBuilder, VisualCafé will automatically move to the foreground when the breakpoint is encountered. Execution should be halted at the breakpoint with the current line of execution highlighted in red with an arrow pointing to it (see Figure 9.27). At this point, you can step through the execution, add watches, and evalute variables using the options under the **Debug** menu and the many debug windows displayed while in debug mode. To end the debugging process, select **Stop** from the **Debug** menu. Similar to JBuilder in many respects, VisualCafé is a strong Java development environment for building and debugging servlets.

Summary

From this brief introduction to servlet debugging with a Java IDE, you may realize the enormous power and convenience of an integrated debugger when testing and debugging servlets. Though simple servlets can be debugged by sending messages to standard out or writing them to a log file (using `Servlet-Context.log()`), for more complex servlets, a fully functional debugger is a tremendous asset. In the next chapter, we will dig a little deeper into the Servlet API.

Chapter Highlights

- This chapter presents a simple Java class, called `ServletDebug`, that can be used to add servlet debugging functionality to most Java development tools. This class starts the Apache Tomcat server, allowing servlets processed by Tomcat to be debugged using the IDE's integrated debugger.

- The `ServletDebug` class can be used with almost any Java IDE, including the popular JBuilder, Forte for Java, and VisualCafé products. This chapter describes servlet debugging using each of these tools.

- There are a number of methods available for debugging servlets. In addition to the `ServletDebug` application presented here, there are several commercial products that add servlet debugging functionality to any Java development environment (e.g., servlet debuggers from Allaire and New Atlanta Communications). Additionally, some of these products include their own integrated servlet debugging framework.

CHAPTER 10

Beyond Servlet API Basics

In Chapter 6, we learned about the most basic classes and interfaces necessary to build a servlet. Many servlets can be developed using only the classes and interfaces previously described. However, other objects in the Servlet API provide the additional functionality necessary to build more advanced servlets. We explore these objects in this chapter.

Although not required by every servlet, the classes and interfaces presented here are commonly used to build servlets that are more functional and complex than anything we have seen so far. In this chapter, the following objects are presented:

- `ServletInputStream` class
- `ServletOutputStream` class
- `ServletConfig` interface
- `ServletContext` interface
- `ServletException` class
- `UnavailableException` class

They may not always be used, but these classes and interfaces are essential to building advanced servlets. Keep in mind that only the most common methods of each object are discussed in this chapter. For a complete list of methods supported by these objects, see Chapter 24. All of the classes and interfaces presented here reside in the `javax.servlet` package.

NOTE: Like Chapter 6, the material presented in this chapter is a bit terse and can be rather dry. Therefore, due to the type and volume of information presented here, you may choose to skim portions of this chapter, referring back to it only as needed. The important thing is that you familiarize yourself with the common interfaces, classes, and methods defined by the Servlet API.

ServletInputStream Class

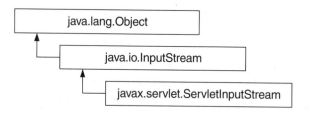

The `ServletInputStream` class provides an input stream for reading data from a client request. `ServletInputStream` directly extends `java.io.InputStream` and, therefore, supports all of its methods. In addition to the functionality inherited from `InputStream`, `ServletInputStream` provides a simple `readLine()` method for reading one line of text at a time from the request. The `ServletInputStream` is accessed through the `getInputStream()` method of the `ServletRequest` object. This class should be used for reading binary data from the content of the client request. A `BufferedReader` object, returned by the `getReader()` method of `ServletRequest` or `HttpServletRequest`, can be used for reading text data. Again, `ServletInputStream` defines only one method called `readLine()`.

readLine()

```
public int readLine(byte[] b, int off, int len) throws
    java.io.IOException
```

The `readLine()` method reads the number of bytes specified by the `len` parameter into the byte array `b` starting at the offset `off`. This method reads bytes into the byte array until the number of bytes specified by `len` has been read or a linefeed ("\n") is encountered. When read, the linefeed is added to the byte array and the read process is terminated. The `readLine()` method returns an integer representing the number of bytes actually read or -1 if the end of the stream is reached.

ServletOutputStream **Class**

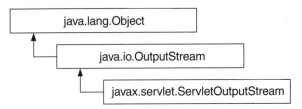

The ServletOutputStream class provides an output stream for sending data to the client. ServletOutputStream extends java.io.OutputStream and, therefore, supports all of its methods. In addition to the functionality inherited from OutputStream, ServletOutputStream provides many variations of the print() and println() methods that are used to write data to the output stream. The ServletOutputStream is accessed through the getOutputStream() method of the ServletResponse object. This class should be used for transmitting binary data. The PrintWriter object, returned by the getWriter() method of ServletResponse or HttpServletResponse, should be used for sending text data. Again, the methods defined by ServletInputStream are print() and println().

print()

```
print(String s)
print(boolean b)
print(char c)
print(int i)
print(long l)
print(float f)
print(double d)
```

The print() method supports seven different parameters—String, boolean, char, int, long, float, and double. This method simply prints the specified value to the client output stream. This method adds no white space, carriage return, or linefeed.

println()

```
println()
println(String s)
println(boolean b)
println(char c)
println(int i)
println(long l)
println(float f)
println(double d)
```

The print1n() method supports eight different parameters—none, String, boolean, char, int, long, float, and double. This method prints the value specified in the parameter to the output stream and appends a carriage return/linefeed ("\r\n"). Calling the print1n() method with no parameters sends only a carriage return/linefeed to the client.

ServletConfig Interface

```
javax.servlet.ServletConfig
```

The ServletConfig interface defines methods that provide configuration information to the servlet. The servlet container instantiates an object that implements the ServletConfig interface and passes it to the servlet's init(ServletConfig) method. ServletConfig defines four methods that servlets can use to acquire information regarding configuration settings and the environment in which they are running. The following methods are defined by the ServletConfig interface.

getInitParameter()

```
public String getInitParameter(String name)
```

The getInitParameter() method returns a String containing the value of the specified initialization parameter. Initialization parameters can be established before a servlet is started. These values are normally read in the servlet's init() method and used to perform some type of initialization. If the specified parameter does not exist, null is returned.

The following text demonstrates how initialization parameters are defined. For more information about setting initialization parameters, see Chapter 8.

```xml
<?xml version="1.0" encoding="ISO-8859-1"?>
<web-app>
  <servlet>
    <servlet-name>time</servlet-name>
    <servlet-class>TimeServlet</servlet-class>
    <init-param>
      <param-name>format</param-name>
      <param-value>24</param-value>
    </init-param>
    <init-param>
      <param-name>timeZone</param-name>
      <param-value>MST</param-value>
    </init-param>
```

```
      <init-param>
        <param-name>verbose</param-name>
        <param-value>true</param-value>
      </init-param>
    </servlet>
    <servlet-mapping>
      <servlet-name>time</servlet-name>
      <url-pattern>/time.html</url-pattern>
    </servlet-mapping>
  </web-app>
```

The preceding text is stored in a file called *web.xml*. This file is known as the *Web application deployment descriptor*. The <servlet-name> XML element defines a logical name (or alias) called time for the servlet (TimeServlet.class) defined in the <servlet-class> element (it is not necessary to include the .class extension). Three initialization parameters, format, time-zone, and verbose are defined within the <init-param> elements. Finally, the <servlet-mapping> element maps a specific URL, /time.html, to the time servlet. Therefore, the server will invoke the time servlet whenever a request for the resource /time.html is received. For more information about the Web application deployment descriptor, see Chapter 19, Packaging and Deployment.

The following code demonstrates how a servlet can retrieve initialization parameters. Note that the variables format, timeZone, and verbose are declared outside of the init() method so that they will be available in the service(), doGet(), or doPost() method.

```
int format;
String timeZone;
boolean verbose;

public void init() throws ServletException
{
  ServletConfig config = getServletConfig();

  //get initialization parameters format, timeZone, and verbose
  format = Integer.parseInt(config.getInitParameter("format"));

  timeZone = config.getInitParameter("timeZone");

  verbose = config.getInitParameter("verbose").equals("true");
}
```

getInitParameterNames()

```
public java.util.Enumeration getInitParameterNames()
```

As described in Chapter 6, the getInitParameterNames() method returns the names of all initialization parameters as an Enumeration of String objects. If no initialization parameters have been defined, an empty Enumeration is returned. This method is often used in conjunction with getInitParameter() to retrieve the name and value of all initialization parameters. The following sample code shows how the names and values of a servlet's initialization parameters can be retrieved.

```
public void init() throws ServletException
{
  String name, value;

  ServletConfig config = getServletConfig();

  //create Enumeration of initialization parameter names
  Enumeration enum = config.getInitParameterNames();

  //iterate through all initialization parameters
  while (enum.hasMoreElements())
  {
    name = (String)enum.nextElement();
    value = config.getInitParameter(name);
    System.out.println("Name: " + name + ", Value: " + value);
  }
}
```

The init() method shown above extracts all of the initialization parameter names and values from the ServletConfig object and prints them to standard out.

getServletContext()

```
public ServletContext getServletContext()
```

The getServletContext() method returns a ServletContext object. All servlets execute within an environment called the servlet context. The Servlet-Context object allows the servlet to communicate with its container. For example, this object provides methods that allow the servlet to write to the servlet log file, forward requests to other resources, and get or set attributes that can be shared among all servlets within the context.

getServletName()

```
public String getServletName()
```

The getServletName() method returns the registered name of this servlet instance. The registered name of a servlet instance is defined by the <servlet-name> element within the Web application deployment descriptor. For instance, the *web.xml* file presented under the "getInitParameter()" section indicates that "`time`" is the registered name for the `TimeServlet.class` servlet. Keep in mind that a single servlet class can be registered multiple times and, therefore, multiple instances of a servlet may exist (each having its own name). If an unregistered (and thus unnamed) servlet is called, this method will return the servlet's class name.

ServletContext Interface

> javax.servlet.ServletContext

The *servlet context* is the logical container in which servlets are run. Servlets in the same context share session information and attributes stored in the servlet context. The `ServletContext` interface provides information to servlets regarding the environment, or context, in which they are running. It also provides a standard way for servlets to write events to a log file. An object that implements the `ServletContext` interface can be retrieved using the `getServlet-Context()` method implemented by the `ServletConfig` object that is passed to the servlet's `init(ServletConfig)` method. For convenience, the `Generic-Servlet` class also supports the `getServletContext()` method (this method actually just calls the `ServletConfig` object's method). Many commonly used methods defined by the `ServletContext` interface are outlined in the following sections.

getMimeType()

```
public String getMimeType(String file)
```

The `getMimeType()` method returns the MIME type for the specified file, or `null` if the MIME type is unknown. MIME types are determined by the servlet container and may be specified within a Web application deployment descriptor. For example, the following deployment descriptor defines a set of MIME types for a specific Web application (Web applications are thoroughly discussed in Chapter 19).

```
<?xml version="1.0" encoding="ISO-8859-1"?>
<web-app>
  <servlet>
    <servlet-name>mime</servlet-name>
    <servlet-class>MimeServlet</servlet-class>
  </servlet>
  <servlet-mapping>
    <servlet-name>mime</servlet-name>
    <url-pattern>/mime.html</url-pattern>
```

```
    </servlet-mapping>
    <mime-mapping>
      <extension>class</extension>
      <mime-type>application/java</mime-type>
    </mime-mapping>
    <mime-mapping>
      <extension>pdf</extension>
      <mime-type>application/pdf</mime-type>
    </mime-mapping>
  </web-app>
```

This sample deployment descriptor defines two MIME types using the <mime-mapping> XML element. This deployment information is contained in the *web.xml* file. The following code illustrates this method.

```
public void service(HttpServletRequest request,
  HttpServletResponse response) throws ServletException,
  IOException
{
  //set MIME type for HTTP header
  response.setContentType("text/plain");

  //get a handle to the output stream
  PrintWriter out = response.getWriter();

  //get ServletContext object and get MIME type for Mime.class
  out.println(getServletContext().getMimeType("Mime.class"));

  out.close(); //always close the output stream
}
```

When the servlet that implements this `service()` method is invoked, the following output is returned to the client:

```
application/java
```

Notice that the MIME type designated for the `class` extension by the deployment descriptor was returned when the servlet passed `Mime.class` to the getMimeType() method.

getRealPath()

```
public String getRealPath(String path)
```

The getRealPath() method evaluates the virtual path passed as an argument and returns the actual path to the resource (according to the file system or network). If the translation is not possible, a `null` is returned. Passing a "/" to getRealPath() will return the server's document root. The following code demonstrates this method.

```
public void service(HttpServletRequest request,
  HttpServletResponse response) throws ServletException,
  IOException
{
  //set MIME type for HTTP header
  response.setContentType("text/plain");

  //get the ServletContext object
  ServletContext context = getServletContext();

  //get a handle to the output stream
  PrintWriter out = response.getWriter();

  //shows physical path for specified relative path
  out.println(context.getRealPath("/public/html"));

  //shows physical path to the requested resource (performs same
  //function as getPathTranslated() method of HttpServletRequest)
  out.println(context.getRealPath(request.getPathInfo()));

  out.close(); //always close the output stream
}
```

For example, if the preceding service() method were implemented by a servlet called GetPathServlet that was invoked using this URL

http://localhost:8080/servlet/GetPathServlet/index.html

the output of the servlet would look like this (under Windows OS):

```
C:\tomcat\webpages\public\html
C:\tomcat\webpages\index.html
```

getResource()

```
public java.net.URL getResource(String path) throws
  java.net.MalformedURLException
```

The getResource() method returns a java.net.URL object that provides access to the resource that is mapped to the specified path. The path information must begin with a forward slash ("/") and is interpreted relative to the context root. Each Web application defined under a Servlet API 2.2–compatible server is assigned a context root. For Tomcat, the context root for a Web application is normally located at */jakarta-tomcat/webapps/WEB_APP*, where *WEB_APP* is the name of the Web application. The exact location of the Web application relative to the Tomcat home directory is specified by the docBase attribute of the <Context> element in the */jakarta-tomcat/conf/server.xml* file.

The getResource() method is useful for insulating the servlet from details regarding a resource's physical location. This is known as *resource abstraction.*

Because no physical file paths are specified, the use of resource abstraction allows servlets to be moved easily between servers that have different directory structures. In addition, resources can be moved without updating the servlets that access them by simply altering the resource's mapping. Resource mapping is determined by the configuration of the servlet container and may be specified within the deployment descriptor. Lastly, getResource() allows remote servlets to access files via a URL mapping even if they do not have access to the file system on which the files are stored. The following sample code illustrates this method (it imports java.net.*).

```java
public void service(HttpServletRequest request,
  HttpServletResponse response) throws ServletException,
  IOException
{
  //get a handle to the output stream
  PrintWriter out = response.getWriter();

  //get a URL object that references the resource /index.html
  URL url = getServletContext().getResource("/index.html");

  //get a URLConnection object from the URL
  URLConnection conn = url.openConnection();

  String contentType = conn.getContentType();

  //determine if the requested resource is text
  if (contentType.startsWith("text"))
  {
    //set response MIME type to requested resource's MIME type
    response.setContentType(contentType);

    //get input stream from URLConnection
    InputStream in = conn.getInputStream();
    BufferedReader br = new BufferedReader(
      new InputStreamReader(in));

    //retrieve resource information one line at a time
    String line = br.readLine();

    while (line != null)
    {
      out.println(line); //send resource to client
      line = br.readLine(); //read next line
    }
  }
  else //resource is not text
  {
    response.setContentType("text/plain");
```

```
    //instruct client that the specified resource is not text
    out.println("Resource is not text.");
  }

  out.close(); //always close the output stream
}
```

This `service()` method reads the */index.html* file from the context root and returns it to the client. Keep in mind that the context root can be moved (perhaps to a different server) and as long as the URL mapping is updated, the servlet will still be able to access this resource without modification.

NOTE: The `URLConnection` object (accessible from the URL object returned by `getResource()`) contains extensive information regarding the requested resource. For instance, the content's length, type, and encoding can be accessed using the `getContentLength()`, `getContentType()`, and `getContentEncoding()` methods of the `URLConnection` object, respectively.

getResourceAsStream()

```
public java.io.InputStream getResourceAsStream(String path)
```

The `getResourceAsStream()` method returns a `java.io.InputStream` object that provides access to the resource that is mapped to the specified path. The path information must begin with a forward slash ("/") and is interpreted relative to the context root. Each Web application defined under a Servlet API 2.2–compatible server is assigned a context root.

`getResourceAsStream()` is a convenience method that provides the same functionality as the following code that uses the `getResource()` method.

```
URL url = getServletContext().getResource("/index.html");
InputStream in = url.openStream();
```

`getResourceAsStream()` allows the previous two lines to be condensed to one. However, if you require access to the specified resource's properties (such as content type and content length), use the `getResource()` method instead. The URL object returned by `getResource()` conveys information about the requested resource that cannot be obtained from the `InputStream` returned by `getResourceAsStream()`. The following code demonstrates the `getResource-AsStream()` method.

```
public void service(HttpServletRequest request,
  HttpServletResponse response) throws ServletException,
  IOException
  {
```

```
response.setContentType("text/html"); //return HTML

//get a handle to the output stream
PrintWriter out = response.getWriter();

//get input stream to requested resource
InputStream in = getServletContext().getResourceAsStream(
  "/index.html");
BufferedReader br = new BufferedReader(
  new InputStreamReader(in));

//retrieve resource information one line at a time
String line = br.readLine();

while (line != null)
{
  out.println(line); //send resource to client
  line = br.readLine(); //read next line
}

out.close(); //always close the output stream
}
```

NOTE: Java provides another way to abstract resources through the use of the java.lang.ClassLoader object's getResource() and getResourceAsStream() methods. These methods use the Java class loader to retreive the specified resource from anywhere in the CLASSPATH. This resource abstraction allows a Java application to be more portable since specific file paths need not be embedded in the code. The following code demonstrates how the getResourceAsStream() method can be used to load a configuration file (*config.xml*) located somewhere in the CLASSPATH.

```
import java.io.*;

public class ResourceAbstractor
{
  public static void main(String[] args)
  {
    ResourceAbstractor ra = new ResourceAbstractor();
    ra.getResource();
  }

  public void getResource()
  {
    try
    {
      InputStream in = this.getClass().getClassLoader().
        getResourceAsStream("config.xml");
```

```
BufferedReader br = new BufferedReader(
   new InputStreamReader(in));

String line = br.readLine();

while (line != null)
{
   System.out.println(line);
   line = br.readLine();
}
     }
     catch (IOException ignored) {}
   }
}
```

Thus, when used within a servlet, the ClassLoader.getResourceAsStream() method attempts to retrieve resources from a Web application's */WEB-INF/classes* directory or from any JAR files included in the servlet CLASSPATH. Conversely, the ServletContext.getResourceAsStream() method reads information from the root of the Web application (or WAR file) without regard to the servlet CLASSPATH.

getServerInfo()

```
public String getServerInfo()
```

The getServerInfo() method returns a String describing the name and version of the servlet container that is running the servlet. For example, while a servlet is running under the Apache Tomcat servlet container, this method returns the following string:

```
Tomcat Web Server/3.1 (JSP 1.1; Servlet 2.2; Java 1.2; Windows NT
   4.0 x86; java.vendor=Sun Microsystems Inc.)
```

log()

```
public void log(String message)
public void log(String message, Throwable throwable)
```

The first log() method accepts a String that is written to the servlet log file. The name and location of this file are server dependent. This method is useful for logging significant events. The second log() method accepts a Throwable object (i.e., an exception) and a String as parameters. This method writes the message and a stack trace to the servlet log file. This is useful for logging errors.

Context Attributes

Context attributes allow objects to be shared between all servlets running within the same servlet context. These objects, or attributes, can be stored in and retrieved from the servlet context by any servlet running within this context. Context attributes provide an elegent method of communicating between servlets and storing information common to all servlets (e.g., the name and e-mail address of the site administrator). In addition, context attributes are often used to store information common to all HTTP sessions. For instance, the page to which a user should be redirected if an error occurs could be stored in the servlet context so that this information would not have to be added to each client's session. Context attributes serve as a type of "global variable" to all servlets and sessions within the same context. The following methods provide access to context attributes.

setAttribute()

```
public void setAttribute(String name, Object object)
```

The `setAttribute()` method stores an object in the servlet context and binds it to the specified name. This object can be retrieved using the `getAttribute()` method. If an attribute of the specified name already exists, it will be removed from the context and the name will be bound to the new attribute. To reduce the chance of name collisions, it is recommended that attribute names follow the same naming convention as Java packages (if deployed in an existing Web application under which other servlets are running). The following code demonstrates how an administrator's information can be stored in the servlet context using the `setAttribute()` method.

```
Hashtable adminData = new Hashtable();

adminData.put("name", "Dustin Callaway");
adminData.put("email", "dustin@insideservlets.com");
adminData.put("web", "http://www.insideservlets.com/info.html");

getServletContext().setAttribute("com.insideservlets.Admin",
  adminData);
```

getAttribute()

```
public Object getAttribute(String name)
```

The `getAttribute()` method returns the object bound to the specified name from the servlet context. Because this method returns a generic `java.lang.Object`, the attribute should usually be cast to the expected type. If the specified attribute does not exist, `null` is returned. In addition to the attributes stored by servlets, the server itself may make additional information available to servlets via context attributes. For example, all servlet containers are required to provide a private temporary directory for each servlet context. This temporary directory is specified by a `java.io.File` object that is stored as a servlet context attribute under the name `javax.servlet.context.tempdir`. See your server documentation for a complete list of context attributes provided by the servlet container. The following line of code demonstrates how a `Hashtable` object can be retrieved from the servlet context.

```
Hashtable admin = (Hashtable)getServletContext().
  getAttribute("com.insideservlets.Admin");
```

getAttributeNames()

```
public java.util.Enumeration getAttributeNames()
```

The `getAttributeNames()` method returns an `Enumeration` of `String` objects containing the names of all attributes available in this servlet context. The `getAttribute()` method can be used to retrieve any of the named attributes. The following `service()` method demonstrates how the names of all available attributes can be returned to the client.

```
public void service(HttpServletRequest request,
  HttpServletResponse response) throws ServletException,
  IOException
{
  response.setContentType("text/plain"); //return plain text

  PrintWriter out = response.getWriter();

  //get an Enumeration of attribute names
  Enumeration enum = getServletContext().getAttributeNames();

  while (enum.hasMoreElements())
  {
    out.println("Attribute Name: " + enum.nextElement());
  }

  out.close(); //always close the output stream
}
```

removeAttribute()

```
public void removeAttribute(String name)
```

The `removeAttribute()` method removes the named attribute from the servlet context. Any future attempts to retrieve this object using `getAttribute()` will return `null`.

ServletException **Class**

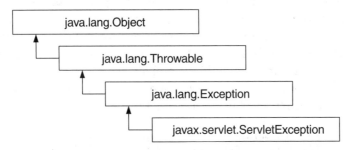

ServletException is thrown by the servlet in response to some type of servlet error. If ServletException is not caught or it is explicitly thrown by the servlet, the error will be handled by the servlet container. A well-written servlet should catch most exceptions and handle them in an elegant manner. However, both ServletException and IOException are usually thrown by the primary servlet methods (e.g., init(), service(), doGet(), doPost()). For example, the following code shows how the service() method is typically defined (notice the throws instruction):

```
public void service(HttpServletRequest request,
   HttpServletResponse response) throws ServletException,
   java.io.IOException
```

If a ServletException or IOException is caught, the servlet should log the event and explicitly throw the exception to the server (see the following sample service() method). If all exceptions are caught by the servlet, the error can be properly logged. Although many servers record servlet exceptions in an error log, this action is server dependent and not guaranteed. In addition to the functionality described here, ServletException extends java.lang.Exception and, therefore, inherits all of its methods.

ServletException defines the following four constructors:

```
public ServletException()
public ServletException(String msg)
public ServletException(String msg, Throwable rootCause)
public ServletException(Throwable rootCause)
```

The first constructor is the default constructor that accepts no parameters. The second constructor accepts a descriptive message about the error that has taken place. The third constructor accepts a String that describes the error as well as a Throwable object (an exception) that represents the root cause of the servlet error (i.e., the actual exception that resulted in this ServletException being thrown, such as a NullPointerException). Lastly, the fourth constructor accepts the Throwable object that caused this ServletException to be thrown. The following code demonstrates a typical situation in which ServletException may be thrown.

```
public void service(HttpServletRequest request,
  HttpServletResponse response) throws ServletException,
  IOException
{
  try
  {
    int x = 10/0; //divide by zero error to demonstrate exception
  }
  catch (Exception e)
  {
    log("Error Description: " + e.toString(), e);

    throw new ServletException(e.toString(), e);
  }
}
```

UnavailableException Class

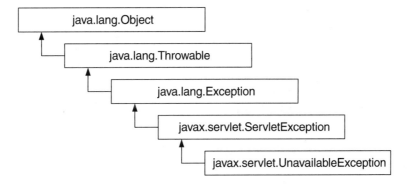

UnavailableException is an exception that extends ServletException and is thrown by the servlet to indicate that it is unavailable. Servlets may be unavailable for any number of reasons, including network problems, an error in the servlet configuration, or a lack of system resources (e.g., memory or disk space). A well-written servlet will throw an UnavailableException whenever a condition that makes it inaccessible occurs.

UnavailableException defines the following two constructors:

```
public UnavailableException(String message)
public UnavailableException(String message, int seconds)
```

The first constructor accepts a message describing the problem that is making the servlet unavailable. The second constructor is identical to the first except for the addition of the seconds parameter. The seconds parameter represents the number of seconds the servlet is anticipated to be unavailable. A zero or negative number indicates that no estimate is available.

The first constructor should be used if the servlet is permanently unavailable until some administrative action is taken to correct the problem. For instance, the servlet will not be available until an administrator resolves an issue with the server or network (e.g., servlet misconfiguration or network inaccessibility). Use the second constructor when the servlet is temporarily unavailable and an estimate can be made regarding when it will be accessible. A temporarily unavailable condition might be caused by excessive network congestion or server load. In other words, given time, a temporarily unavailable condition should correct itself.

Summary

This chapter introduces several important classes and interfaces that are commonly used to build robust servlets. A strong understanding of these objects, in addition to those presented in Chapter 6, will put you well on your way to writing powerful servlets.

Chapter Highlights

- The ServletInputStream class class provides an input stream for reading binary data from a client request.

- The ServletOutputStream class provides an output stream for writing binary data out to the client.

- The ServletConfig interface defines methods that provide configuration information to the servlet.

- The ServletContext interface allows servlets to communicate with their environment.

- A ServletException is thrown by the servlet in response to some type of servlet error.

- An UnavailableException is thrown if, for some reason, the servlet becomes unavailable.

This chapter concludes the Introduction to Servlets part of the book. In the next part, Advanced Servlet Concepts, we will examine more complex servlet development issues, including session management, thread safety, database access, security, and deployment.

PART III

Advanced Servlet Concepts

CHAPTER 11

Writing Thread-Safe Servlets

Thread safety is a common concern among Java programmers. Ensuring that multiple threads do not read or change data in a manner that may produce nondeterministic (i.e., inconsistent) results is a constant challenge. Writing servlets is no different. The Servlet API does not protect the developer against multiple threads accessing servlet class and instance variables simultaneously.

In this chapter, we will explore several techniques for achieving thread safety in your servlets. Specifically, the following five topics are covered:

- What is thread safety?
- Synchronization
- `service()`, `doGet()`, and `doPost()` local variables
- `SingleThreadModel` interface
- Background Threads

Although these topics will provide you with sufficient information to write thread-safe servlets, for an in-depth understanding of Java threads please see one of the many excellent books on the subject.

What Is Thread Safety?

An application is *thread safe* if it always behaves predictably regardless of the number of concurrent threads running in its process space. To achieve this predictable (or deterministic) behavior, the servlet writer must ensure that no thread can read a shared resource while another thread is in the process of changing it. Although this may sound simple, thread safety is often difficult to achieve. The following scenario illustrates a common mistake that can lead to inconsistent behavior within an application.

This example may be trite, but it does a good job of conveying the importance of thread safety. Consider the following sequence of events regarding the use of a bank's automatic teller machine (ATM). We are assuming that this ATM system does not properly enforce thread safety.

1. A bank customer with a balance of $1000 in checking withdraws $800. To process this transaction, the ATM program first checks the balance of the checking account to confirm that at least $800 exists. After verifying a sufficient balance, the checking account is debited $800 and the cash is dispensed to the customer.

2. At another ATM, the customer's spouse simultaneously attempts to withdraw $500 from checking. Since the ATM program is not thread safe, it is possible for the second ATM to read the balance of the checking account after the first ATM checked the balance but before it actually debited the account. Since the second ATM was able to verify a sufficient balance before the first ATM could debit the account, the account is debited another $500 and the cash is dispensed to the customer.

3. Because the ATM program is not thread safe, deductions of $500 and $800 were made from an account containing only $1000, leaving the account overdrawn.

This example contains a thread safety error known as a race condition. A *race condition* occurs when the proper behavior of the program relies on one thread completing execution before another. This timing requirement can result in inconsistent program behavior because there is usually no guarantee that one thread will finish before another (thread-scheduling strategies vary among operating systems). You may now understand the importance of enforcing thread safety in your own code. Listing 11.1 demonstrates a simple servlet that is not thread safe.

Listing 11.1   Example of a servlet that is not thread safe.

```
import javax.servlet.*;
import javax.servlet.http.*;
import java.io.*;

/**
 * The BankAccount servlet is an example of a servlet that
 * is not thread safe. A race condition is created between
 * the time the checking account balance is read and when it is
 * debited.
 */
public class BankAccount extends HttpServlet
{
    float checkingBalance;
```

```
/**
 * Initializes the checkingBalance variable.
 */
public void init() throws ServletException
{
  checkingBalance = 750; //start with $750 in checking
}


/**
 * Displays the current value of the checking and savings
 * account.
 */
public void service(HttpServletRequest request,
  HttpServletResponse response) throws ServletException,
  IOException
{
  response.setContentType("text/plain");
  PrintWriter out = response.getWriter();

  if (checkingBalance >= 100) //withdraw $100 with each request
  {
    //...some processing code may run here

    checkingBalance -= 100; //deduct $100 from checking

    out.println("Amount in Checking: " + checkingBalance);
    out.println("Reload this servlet to withdraw $100.");
  }
  else
  {
    out.println("You cannot withdraw $100. You only have $" +
      checkingBalance + " dollars in your account.");
  }

  out.close();
  }
}
```

The code that makes this servlet unsafe is shown here:

```
  if (checkingBalance >= 100) //withdraw $100 with each request
  {
    //...some processing code may run here

    checkingBalance -= 100; //deduct $100 from checking

    out.println("Amount in Checking: " + checkingBalance);
    out.println("Reload this servlet to withdraw $100.");
  }
```

A race condition occurs between the time the thread verifies sufficient funds (the `if` statement) and the time the `checkingBalance` variable is decremented. If another thread executes the `if` statement after the first thread checked the balance but before the balance is decremented, the servlet may perform improperly (allowing the account to become overdrawn).

NOTE: Race conditions only occur when reading or modifying shared objects. For example, since instance and `static` class variables are shared among all requests to a servlet (and all threads that service these requests), race conditions may occur when these variables are used. Later in the chapter, we will see that objects declared inside the `service()`, `doGet()`, or `doPost()` method are automatically thread safe because the objects are not shared among threads.

However, there are times when the use of shared objects is safe and appropriate (as long as the shared objects themselves are thread safe). For example, it is a common practice for servlets to create a shared database connection pool, usually created within the `init()` method, that is used by all threads (i.e., servlet invocations). As long as the database connection pool object itself is thread safe, the servlet can share it among invocations without thread safety concerns. Likewise, primitive class and instance variables (e.g., `int`, `float`, `char`) that are not modified by any thread present no thread safety concerns. Objects that are not thread safe must be used in a thread-safe manner (see the following section on synchronization).

So, the question remains: how do we make the preceding servlet thread safe? The Java `synchronized` keyword provides one answer. The next section describes the proper use of the `synchronized` keyword.

Synchronization

Synchronization in Java is the process of acquiring an exclusive lock, called a *monitor*, on an object so that it can be read and modified by only a single thread at a time. Synchronization allows the servlet container to call the `service()`, `doGet()`, or `doPost()` method without having to wait for all prior executions of these methods to finish.

The `synchronized` keyword eliminates race conditions by ensuring that a block of code can be executed only by a single thread at a time. Whenever a thread reaches a synchronized block, it must first obtain the monitor for the synchronized object before executing the code within the block (all Java objects have a monitor associated with them). After executing the code within the block, the thread releases the monitor. The following code demonstrates how it can be used to eliminate the race condition in the preceding servlet.

```
synchronized (this)
{
  if (checkingBalance >= 100) //withdraw $100 with each request
  {
    //...some processing code may run here...

    checkingBalance -= 100; //deduct $100 from checking

    out.println("Amount in Checking: " + checkingBalance);
    out.println("Reload this servlet to withdraw $100.");
  }
}
```

This code ensures that the `checkingBalance` variable cannot be read or altered by another thread while the synchronized block is executing. This eliminates the race condition and makes the servlet thread safe. Note that the previous sample code acquires the monitor associated with the servlet itself by calling `synchronized (this)`. This approach is used because it is not possible to acquire a monitor for primitive types (e.g., `int`, `char`, `long`, `float`). However, if the `checkingBalance` variable were an object, the previous synchronized block might look something like this:

```
synchronized (checkingBalance)
{
  if (checkingBalance.getValue() >= 100)
  {
    //...some processing code may run here...

    checkingBalance.setValue(checkingBalance.getValue() - 100);

    out.println("Checking: " + checkingBalance.getValue());
  }
}
```

All threads that execute this synchronized block must first obtain an exclusive lock on the `checkingBalance` object rather than on the servlet itself. It is customary to synchronize code using the object that represents the primary thread safety concern for the block. Synchronizing a block using the servlet object itself is not recommended if another synchronized block also requires the servlet's monitor. If two separate blocks are synchronized using the servlet object's monitor, only one block can execute at a time (the other has to wait).

NOTE: It is possible to synchronize the entire `service()` method rather than specific blocks of code within it. In this way, only one thread at a time can execute the method, ensuring that no other thread can read or modify shared objects. The declaration of a synchronized `service()` method looks like this:

```
public synchronized void service(HttpServletRequest
    request, HttpServletResponse response) throws
    ServletException, java.io.IOException
```

However, this approach is not recommended because it usually incurs a large performance penalty. Synchronized blocks of code create a performance bottleneck because all other threads must "wait in line" for the current thread to complete its execution of synchronized code. The more code that is synchronized, the greater the performance penalty. To avoid this penalty, minimize the amount of code that is synchronized by using the "`synchronized (object)`" technique shown in the text. This practice will reduce the bottleneck effect of synchronization by ensuring that objects remain locked for the least amount of time necessary.

When writing servlets, pay close attention to the way you handle class and instance variables. It is not necessary to synchronize shared primitive variables (e.g., `int`, `float`, `char`) if they are never modified by separate threads (e.g., separate servlet invocations). Similarly, an object reference that is defined as a class or instance variable need not be synchronized if the object being referenced is thread safe (i.e., concurrent calls cannot alter the object's state in a nondeterministic manner). For instance, if a shared database connection pool is instantiated in the `init()` method, it can be used by all threads without concern as long as the pool object itself is thread safe. If not, it must be used within a synchronized block. In summary, if a shared variable is both read and modified by separate threads or the variable itself is not thread safe, it may be a candidate for synchronization.

This concludes our very brief discussion about Java synchronization. Since this topic is not particular to writing servlets, this book does not attempt to fully educate the reader on writing thread-safe Java code. For a more in-depth review on the subject, please see one of the many books on the market that focus on Java threads.

service(), doGet(), and doPost() Local Variables

Normally, the servlet container does not instantiate multiple servlet objects. Rather, a single servlet instance usually services all requests.[1] This behavior explains how instance variables can often be shared.

So now you may be wondering, if a single servlet object services all requests, how are requests processed simultaneously? The answer is that each call to service(), doGet(), or doPost() acquires its own thread from the servlet thread pool. Though the servlet is instantiated only once, each request is processed by its own thread and all of these threads can execute concurrently.

NOTE: Although the text often refers to variables defined within the service(), doGet(), or doPost() methods as automatically thread safe, this fact also applies to all of the "do" method as well as any methods called by these methods. In addition to doGet() and doPost(), these methods include doDelete(), doOptions(), doHead(), doPut(), and doTrace().

Since every call to service(), doGet(), or doPost() is executed in its own thread, variables local to these methods are not shared among requests and are automatically thread safe. Objects that are not meant to be shared among requests should be declared in either the service(), doGet(), or doPost() method. These request-specific variables should then be passed to supporting functions in order to maintain thread safety. Methods that do not use shared objects but, rather, acquire all necessary information from the calling method are referred to as *reentrant*. Reentrant means that another flow of control (i.e., thread) can enter the method without thread safety concerns. To maintain thread safety, reentrant methods must not call non-reentrant methods. Consider the servlet in Listing 11.2. Can you find the thread safety problems in this code? The HTML form that invokes this servlet is shown in Listing 11.3.

Listing 11.2 This servlet's instance variable is not thread safe.

```
import javax.servlet.*;
import javax.servlet.http.*;
import java.io.*;

public class Greetings extends HttpServlet
{
    String userName; //instance variable
```

---

1. A possible exception to this rule is when the servlet implements the SingleThreadModel interface described later in this chapter.

```
/**
 * Retrieves the user's name from the request and calls the
 * printGreeting() method to send a greeting to the client.
 */
public void service(HttpServletRequest request,
    HttpServletResponse response) throws ServletException,
    IOException
{
    response.setContentType("text/plain");
    PrintWriter out = response.getWriter();

    userName = request.getParameter("Name");
    printGreeting(out);

    out.close();
}


/**
 * printGreeting sends a simple message to the client
 *
 * @param out Client output stream
 */
private void printGreeting(PrintWriter out)
{
    out.println("Hello, " + userName);
}
}
```

Listing 11.3   HTML form that sends the client's name to a servlet.

```
<HTML>
<HEAD><TITLE>Enter Your Name</TITLE></HEAD>
<BODY>
<FORM METHOD="POST" ACTION="/servlet/Greetings">
<P>Name: <INPUT TYPE="TEXT" NAME="Name" SIZE="25"></P>
<P><INPUT TYPE="SUBMIT" VALUE="Submit"></P>
</FORM>
</BODY>
</HTML>
```

In a single-user environment, this servlet would operate as expected. However, there is a thread safety concern when concurrent requests are received. Notice that the user's name is extracted from a Web variable that was submitted by the user. The problem arises when the user's name is assigned to the shared variable, userName. Because this variable is declared outside of the service() method, it is shared among all requests. You may now see the problem and the race condition that is created when multiple requests are received. Consider the following sequence of events.

1. A request is received from user "Tom" and the `service()` method is invoked to process the request.
2. The shared variable, `userName`, is assigned the value "Tom."
3. A second request is received from user "Jerry" and the `service()` method is invoked to process the request.
4. Before the thread for the first request is able to call the `printGreeting()` method, the second thread sets `userName` to "Jerry."
5. The first thread now calls the `printGreeting()` method, which returns the message "Hello, Jerry" rather than "Hello, Tom."
6. As long as no other request is processed between the time the second request sets the value of `userName` and when the greeting is returned to the client, the second request will receive the message "Hello, Jerry" as expected.

As you can see, a race condition is created between the time the value of `userName` is set and the time the greeting is returned to the client. Listing 11.4 demonstrates how this race condition can be eliminated by passing variables declared within the `service()` method.

Listing 11.4 Servlet is made thread safe by eliminating instance variable.

```
import javax.servlet.*;
import javax.servlet.http.*;
import java.io.*;

public class Greetings extends HttpServlet
{
  /**
   * Retrieves the user's name from the request and calls the
   * printGreeting() method to send a greeting to the client.
   */
  public void service(HttpServletRequest request,
    HttpServletResponse response) throws ServletException,
    IOException
  {
    String userName; //service() method local variable

    response.setContentType("text/plain");
    PrintWriter out = response.getWriter();

    userName = request.getParameter("name");

    printGreeting(out, userName); //pass local variable

    out.close();
  }
```

```
/**
 * printGreeting sends a simple message to the client
 *
 * @param out Client output stream
 * @param userName Name of user
 */
private void printGreeting(PrintWriter out, String userName)
{
  out.println("Hello, " + userName);
}
}
```

This servlet eliminates the race condition by eliminating the shared variable. Notice that userName is now declared inside the service() method. Because each call to service() is processed by its own thread, this variable is protected (each request has its own copy) and cannot be read or modified by other requests. However, since userName is no longer globally visible, it must now be passed as a parameter to the printGreeting() function. The practice of declaring request-specific variables in the service(), doGet(), or doPost() method and passing them to other functions is a powerful technique that ensures servlet thread safety.

SingleThreadModel Interface

The simplest way to ensure that a servlet is thread safe is to implement the SingleThreadModel interface. This interface defines no methods; it simply serves as a flag to the server. If a servlet implements the SingleThreadModel interface, the servlet container guarantees that no more than one thread can execute the service(), doGet(), or doPost() method at a time for a particular servlet instance. This restriction effectively guarantees that your servlet will be thread safe.

NOTE: Actually, the SingleThreadModel does not completely guarantee thread safety. This is due to the fact that class variables (declared using the static keyword) can still be accessed concurrently by separate servlet instances. Therefore, even if a servlet implements the SingleThreadModel interface, it must still use class variables in a thread-safe manner. If possible, eliminating the use of class variables is a simple way to solve this problem.

Since the service() method cannot be executed concurrently, you may have concerns regarding the performance of servlets that implement the

SingleThreadModel interface. These concerns are valid. However, most servlet containers attempt to minimize these inherent performance problems by maintaining a pool of servlet instances. When the servlet container loads a servlet that implements SingleThreadModel, the container may automatically create a pool of servlet instances in order to service concurrent requests. The size of this pool is usually configurable on the server.

Though it is possible to ensure thread safety by synchronizing the service(), doGet(), or doPost() method, it is far better to implement the SingleThreadModel interface. This is due to the fact that, with a servlet that implements the SingleThreadModel interface, the servlet container may choose to create a pool of servlet instances. In this way, requests can be processed concurrently using separate instances of the same servlet. However, if the service() method is synchronized within a servlet that does not implement the SingleThreadModel interface, the servlet container can create only one servlet instance and is limited to servicing one request at a time. This is due to the fact that the Java Servlet Specification dictates that servlet containers can create only one servlet instance per servlet definition unless the servlet implements the SingleThreadModel interface. If SingleThreadModel is not implemented, the servlet container is forced to serialize (or queue) all requests to the servlet. Serialization can greatly reduce servlet performance.

Although the SingleThreadModel technique can be resource intensive (due to the creation of an instance pool), it is the simplest way to ensure thread safety and may be appropriate in some circumstances when servlet traffic is expected to be low. However, this technique should be used sparingly. Synchronizing only the parts of a servlet that contain thread safety issues is a much better method of writing high-performance, thread-safe servlets. The servlet that is shown in Listing 11.5 implements the SingleThreadModel interface to provide thread safety.

 NOTE: If excessive concurrent requests arrive such that the servlet instance pool is exhausted, the excess requests will be serialized (i.e., placed in queue) until an instance is available. This condition usually causes a strong negative impact on performance.

Listing 11.5 SingleThreadModel guarantees thread safety.

```
import javax.servlet.*;
import javax.servlet.http.*;
import java.io.*;
```

```
public class Greetings extends HttpServlet implements
  SingleThreadModel
{
  String userName; //instance variable

  /**
   * Retrieves the user's name from the request and calls the
   * printGreeting() method to send a greeting to the client.
   */
  public void service(HttpServletRequest request,
    HttpServletResponse response) throws ServletException,
    IOException
  {
    response.setContentType("text/plain");
    PrintWriter out = response.getWriter();

    userName = request.getParameter("Name");
    printGreeting(out);

    out.close();
  }


  /**
   * printGreeting sends a simple message to the client
   *
   * @param out Client output stream
   */
  private void printGreeting(PrintWriter out)
  {
    out.println("Hello, " + userName);
  }
}
```

It's that simple! Although earlier in the chapter we showed that the preceding servlet was not thread safe, thread safety can be achieved by simply implementing the `SingleThreadModel` interface.

Background Threads

Servlets are not required to remain idle while waiting for the next request. To the contrary, any thread started by a servlet will continue to execute even after the response has been sent. The ability to create threads that run in the background is a powerful feature that allows servlets to execute lengthy processes between requests.

The servlet presented in Listing 11.6 demonstrates how to create a background thread that continues to execute between requests. In response to each request, this servlet returns the current status of a mock election. The background thread simulates voting by randomly generating election results for each of the candidates.

Listing 11.6   Demonstrates servlet's ability to create background threads.

```
import javax.servlet.*;
import javax.servlet.http.*;
import java.io.*;
import java.util.*;

/**
 * VoteCheck demonstrates the ability of servlets to run threads
 * in the background that continue processing between servlet
 * calls. This servlet displays mock election results by adding
 * a random number to each candidate's vote count every second.
 * The servlet returns the current status of the election each
 * time it is called (conveyed by vote count and bar chart).
 */
public class VoteCheck extends HttpServlet implements Runnable
{
  long candidateA = 0;
  long candidateB = 0;
  long candidateC = 0;
  boolean stopFlag = false;
  Thread voteCount;

  /**
   * Creates a new thread to execute the run() method of this
   * servlet. The thread priority is set to minimum so that more
   * important tasks can preempt the vote counter.
   */
  public void init() throws ServletException
  {
    voteCount = new Thread(this); //instantiate a new thread
    voteCount.setPriority(Thread.MIN_PRIORITY); //set priority
    voteCount.start(); //start the new thread running
  }


  /**
   * Simulates an election by adding a random number between 0
   * and 10 to each candidates vote count every second. This
   * method stops executing when the destroy() method sets the
   * stopFlag variable to true.
   */
  public void run()
  {
    while (true)
    {
      //add a random number between 0 and 10 to each candidate
      candidateA += Math.random() * 10;
      candidateB += Math.random() * 10;
      candidateC += Math.random() * 10;
```

```java
    if (stopFlag) //exit run() method if stopFlag is true
    {
      return;
    }

    try
    {
      Thread.sleep(1000); //pause for 1 second
    }
    catch (InterruptedException e)
    {
    }
  }
}


/**
 * Sends the current election results to the client.
 */
public void doGet(HttpServletRequest request,
  HttpServletResponse response) throws ServletException,
  IOException
{
  response.setContentType("text/html");

  PrintWriter out = response.getWriter();

  //generate the HTML showing the election results
  out.println("<HTML>");
  out.println("<HEAD><TITLE>Election Results</TITLE></HEAD>");
  out.println("<BODY>");
  out.println("<B>ELECTION RESULTS</B><BR>");
  out.println(new Date() + "<BR><BR>");
  out.println("Candidate A: " + candidateA + "<BR>");
  showBar(out, candidateA, "red");
  out.println("Candidate B: " + candidateB + "<BR>");
  showBar(out, candidateB, "blue");
  out.println("Candidate C: " + candidateC + "<BR>");
  showBar(out, candidateC, "green");
  out.println("</BODY></HTML>");

  out.close(); //close the output stream
}


/**
 * Show a horizontal bar to visually illustrate the number of
 * votes received by this candidate.
 *
 * @param out Client output stream
 * @param votes Width of bar
 * @param color Color of bar
 */
```

```
private void showBar(PrintWriter out, long votes,
  String color)
{
  out.println("<TABLE BORDER=\"0\" BGCOLOR=\"" + color +
    "\" WIDTH=\"" + votes + "\">");
  out.println("<TR><TD> </TD></TR>");
  out.println("</TABLE><BR>");
}


/**
 * Sets a variable that tells the run() method to stop
 * executing. This stops the thread.
 */
public void destroy()
{
  stopFlag = true;
}
}
```

To execute its `run()` method in a separate thread, the `VoteCheck` servlet implements the `Runnable` interface. This interface defines only one method—a method called `run()` that returns nothing and accepts no parameters. The `run()` method is called automatically when the new thread is started. The `init()` method creates a new `Thread`, sets its priority to minimum (so that it may be preempted by more important threads), and starts it running. This thread will continue to run even after the servlet has processed the request and returned a response.

NOTE: The servlet container may enforce security restrictions that limit a servlet's functionality. For instance, some servlet containers may limit a servlet's ability to create new threads in order to ensure that other components in the container are not negatively affected. If they exist, these security restrictions are usually configurable by the administrator and, if necessary, may be removed.

The `run()` method adds a random number to each candidate's vote count every second in order to simulate election results. The new thread continually tallies votes (even between requests) until the servlet is unloaded and the `destroy()` method is called. The `destroy()` method stops the thread by setting the `stopFlag` variable to `true`. Notice that the `if` statement in the `run()` method executes a `return` when the `stopFlag` is set to `true`. Exiting from the `run()` method effectively stops the background thread. Background threads should always be stopped in this manner. If not explicitly killed, these threads will continue to run even after the servlet is unloaded.

Lastly, the doGet() and showBar() methods construct an HTML document that displays the current state of the election (see Figure 11.1). Variable-width tables having a background color of red, blue, and green are used to create a visual representation of each candidate's vote count. After initially invoking the VoteCheck servlet, repeatedly click the browser's **Reload** or **Refresh** button in order to watch the election results as they are tallied in the run() method. Keep in mind that the doGet() method can execute concurrently with the servlet's run() method because it is executed in a separate thread.

Summary

This chapter introduces you to the inherent dangers of running servlets that are not thread safe, as well as several techniques that ensure thread safety. Whenever you encounter seemingly random, infrequent, or otherwise perplexing bugs in your servlets, evaluate your servlet for code that may violate the rules

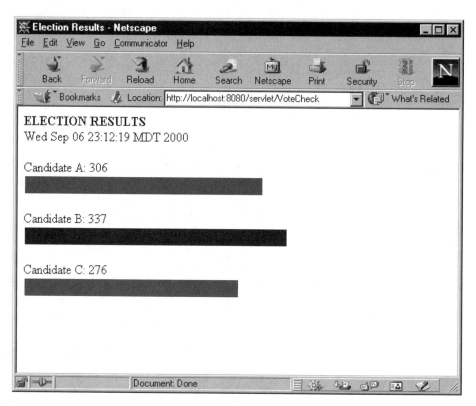

Figure 11.1   Sample Response from the VoteCheck Servlet

of thread safety. At first, if you are not used to dealing with threads, this may seem a bit unnatural. However, once you become accustomed to always asking yourself the question, "How will this portion of code respond to multiple concurrent calls?" you will be well on your way to writing thread-safe code.

In addition, remember that testing servlets in a single-user environment is not a true indication of how they will perform under load. If you develop servlets with multiple users in mind and simulate multiple users when testing, the aggravations resulting from race conditions and other thread safety violations will be greatly reduced.

Background threads are also presented in this chapter. These threads are created by the servlet and allow it to continue processing between requests. Just remember to explicitly stop all background threads when the servlet is unloaded. In the next chapter, we will explore a very useful mechanism known as an HTTP redirect.

Chapter Highlights

- An application is *thread safe* if it always behaves in a predictable manner regardless of the number of concurrent threads running in its process space.

- To achieve thread safety the servlet writer must ensure that no thread can read a variable while another thread is in the process of changing it.

- A *race condition* occurs when the proper behavior of the program relies upon one thread to complete execution before another. This timing requirement can result in inconsistent program behavior.

- *Synchronization* in Java is the process of locking variables so that they can only be read and modified by a single thread at a time. The synchronized keyword eliminates race conditions by locking variables for a specified duration.

- A new servlet object is not instantiated for each client request. Rather, a single servlet instance services all requests. Each call to service(), doGet(), or doPost() acquires its own thread from the servlet thread pool. Even though the servlet is instantiated only once, each request is processed by its own thread (allowing requests to be processed concurrently).

- Because every call to service(), doGet(), or doPost() is executed in its own thread, variables local to these methods are not shared among requests and are automatically thread safe.

- The simplest way to ensure that a servlet is thread safe is to implement the SingleThreadModel interface. If a servlet implements SingleThread-Model, the server guarantees that no more than one thread can execute the service(), doGet(), or doPost() method at a time. This restriction effectively guarantees thread safety in your servlet.

CHAPTER 12

HTTP Redirects

This chapter covers an important mechanism supported by the HTTP protocol—HTTP redirects. An HTTP redirect allows the server to respond to a client's request with instructions to load a resource at a different location. Most browsers will automatically request the new resource in response to a redirect. Specifically, the following topics are discussed:

- What is an HTTP redirect?
- HTTP header syntax for a redirect
- Sending a redirect from a servlet
- load-balancing Servlet using HTTP Redirects

What Is an HTTP Redirect?

An *HTTP redirect* is a set of instructions included in the header of an HTTP response that instructs the browser to issue a new request to a new URL. Although you may not notice them, redirects are extremely common on the Web and are useful in a number of different circumstances. For example, consider the following scenario.

The Web site for the SourceStream Company was hosted originally at *http://www.isp.com/~sourcestream/*. However, as SourceStream's Web site traffic and online sales increased, they decided to acquire their own domain name and host the site themselves. SourceStream's new URL is

  http://www.sourcestream.com/

But what about the people still referencing SourceStream's old URL? An obvious solution would be to display a page at the old URL that contained a hyperlink to the new URL. This method is effective but still requires the user to take action in order to visit the new site.

HTTP redirects offer a seamless way to transfer a user from one URL to another. Rather than simply display a page containing a hyperlink to the new URL, SourceStream decides to implement an HTTP redirect. Whenever a user references the old URL, the response will include the proper redirect instructions such that the browser will automatically request the page at the new location. Once the browser receives the redirect, the user is transferred seamlessly to the new site (most likely unaware that a redirect has taken place).

Although redirects are supported by virtually all current browsers, it is a good practice to include a hyperlink to the new URL in the body of the redirect response in case the user's browser does not support automatic HTTP redirects. The next two sections examine redirect syntax and how redirects can be issued from within a Java servlet.

HTTP Header Syntax for a Redirect

We have established that a redirect is an HTTP response from the server that instructs the client to request a resource at a different URL. There are two key elements in the header of an HTTP response that convey a redirect to the client. These elements are the HTTP status code and the Location header.

An HTTP redirect response uses an HTTP status code of either "301 Moved Permanently" or "302 Moved Temporarily" accompanied by a Location header containing a valid URL. If the client receives an HTTP response with status code 301 or 302, it will immediately request the resource at the URL designated by the Location header. If no Location header exists, the browser will display the status code message (indicating that the item has moved) and perhaps a more detailed description of the problem. The browser should respond identically to either HTTP status code 301 or 302 with one exception; in response to a "301 Moved Permanently" status code, the browser should update any bookmarks pointing to the old location. A typical redirect response (including all HTTP headers) is shown here:

```
HTTP/1.1 301 Moved Permanently
Date: Mon, 21 Feb 2000 19:45:12 GMT
Server: Apache/1.3.0 (Unix)
Location: http://www.sourcestream.com/
Content-Type: text/html

<HTML>
<HEAD><TITLE>301 Moved Permanently</TITLE></HEAD>
<BODY>
<H1>Moved Permanently</H1>
Document has moved <A HREF="http://www.sourcestream.com/">here.
</A>
</BODY>
</HTML>
```

Let's take a moment to examine this redirect response. First, the response indicates a "301 Moved Permanently" HTTP status code. At this point, the browser searches the response for a `Location` header. If found, the browser immediately requests the resource at the new URL (as specified by the `Location` header). In addition to the status code and `Location` header, notice that an HTML document is included in the response. This document provides an informative message and a hyperlink for browsers that do not support automatic redirects. Browsers that support automatic HTTP redirects do not display the information contained in the body of a redirect response even if it takes several seconds to load the resource at the new location. This behavior allows the redirect to appear seamless.

Finally, it should be noted that the URL stored in the `Location` header need not be fully qualified.[1] For instance, to redirect a request from the document `index.html` to `welcome.html` in the same directory, the value of the `Location` header may simply contain `welcome.html`. If no domain or path information is specified in the `Location` header, the domain and path of the originally requested resource are assumed.

Now that we understand how redirects are constructed at the HTTP header level, we will examine how to issue redirects from within a servlet. For more information on HTTP status codes and headers, see Appendices H and I, or RFC 2068.

Sending a Redirect from a Servlet

A servlet can send an HTTP redirect in several ways. One way is to manually set the HTTP status code and add the `Location` header to the response. The following `service()` method demonstrates this approach.

```
public void service(HttpServletRequest request,
  HttpServletResponse response) throws ServletException,
  IOException
{
  String newURL = "http://www.sourcestream.com/index.html";

  response.setContentType("text/html");

  response.setStatus(
    HttpServletResponse.SC_MOVED_PERMANENTLY);

  response.setHeader("Location", newURL);
```

---

1. Actually, HTTP 1.1 specifies that the URL in the `Location` header should be absolute. However, current browsers support relative URLs in the `Location` header field. Additionally, the servlet container converts relative URLs into absolute URLs when the `sendRedirect()` method is called.

```
PrintWriter out = response.getWriter();

out.println("<HTML>");
out.println("<HEAD>");
out.println("<TITLE>301 Moved Permanently</TITLE>");
out.println("</HEAD>");
out.println("<BODY>");
out.println("Document moved to <A HREF=\"" + newURL +
   "\">here</A>.");
out.println("</BODY>");
out.println("</HTML>");

out.close();
}
```

Let's examine this code. The `setStatus()` method of `HttpServletResponse` sets the HTTP response code to "301 Moved Permanently." This is the first step in issuing the redirect. Next, the `setHeader()` method of `HttpServletResponse` is used to add a `Location` header to the response that includes the new URL information. Finally, an HTML document is added to the body of the response for clients that do not support automatic redirects.

NOTE: Though not demonstrated in the sample code, it is a good practice to encode the URL when redirecting. URL encoding is necessary to maintain session whenever URL rewriting is employed as the session management mechanism (as opposed to cookies). The following code demonstrates how a URL can be encoded with session information using the `HttpServletResponse` object's `encodeRedirectURL()` method (see Chapter 14 for information on session management).

```
String newURL = response.encodeRedirectURL("/servlet/CheckOut");
response.sendRedirect(newURL);
```

The `encodeRedirectURL()` method adds session information to the redirect URL as shown here:

```
/servlet/CheckOut;jsessionid=xeha06ntz1
```

Another way to issue a redirect is from within the body of the HTML document itself using a special `META` tag. The `HTTP-EQUIV` tag can be embedded directly in the `<HEAD>` section of an HTML document. As its name suggests, this tag is the client-side equivalent to setting an HTTP header on the server by allowing the HTML document to convey HTTP header information to the browser. For example, the following server-side code instructs the browser not to cache the response:

```
response.setHeader("Cache-Control", "no-cache");
```

Likewise, this same "no cache" instruction can be conveyed in the HTML document itself like this:

```
<HEAD>
  <META HTTP-EQUIV="Cache-Control" CONTENT="no-cache">
</HEAD>
```

Now let's see how the HTTP-EQUIV tag can be used to issue a redirect. Since the HTTP-EQUIV tag cannot control the HTTP response code (i.e., it cannot set the response status code to 301 or 302), the standard Location HTTP header will not work in this case. Rather, the browser must be instructed to "refresh" the page using a new URL. The following HTML demonstrates an HTTP-EQUIV redirect.

```
<HEAD>
  <META HTTP-EQUIV="Refresh" CONTENT="0;URL=http://www.go.com/">
</HEAD>
```

Let's take a close look at this HTML. The HTTP-EQUIV attribute of the META tag instructs the browser to reload the page using the information specified in the CONTENT attribute. The first part of the CONTENT attribute (prior to the semicolon) indicates the number of seconds the browser should wait before reloading. This value is set to zero in order to issue an immediate redirect. The second part of the CONTENT attribute (following the semicolon) indicates the location of the new resource to load. The URL portion of the CONTENT attribute is optional. If excluded, the browser will continuously reload the current page according to the specified interval. This feature can be very useful when requesting data from a servlet that is frequently updated. For example, a servlet that displays the current status of an election may include an HTTP-EQUIV tag that instructs the browser to request new data every twenty seconds. In this way, the user is not required to refresh the page manually in order to view the latest information. Rather, the browser will do it automatically according to the instructions in the HTML page. The following service() method demonstrates how a redirect can be issued from within a servlet using the HTTP-EQUIV tag.

```
public void service(HttpServletRequest request,
  HttpServletResponse response) throws ServletException,
  IOException
{
  String newURL = "http://www.sourcestream.com/index.html";

  response.setContentType("text/html");

  PrintWriter out = response.getWriter();
```

```
out.println("<HTML>");
out.println("<HEAD>");
out.println("<META HTTP-EQUIV=\"Refresh\" CONTENT=\"0;URL=" +
    newURL + "\">");
out.println("</HEAD>");
out.println("<BODY>");

//leave body blank so transition looks seamless

out.println("</BODY>");
out.println("</HTML>");

out.close();
}
```

NOTE: In addition to the HTTP-EQUIV tag, the Refresh instruction can be sent in an HTTP header. For instance, the following code instructs the browser to refresh the page every ten seconds:

```
response.setHeader("Refresh", "10");
```

Of course, the value "10" can been replaced with "10;URL=http:// www.sourcestream.com/" in order to display the requested page for ten seconds and then automatically load the resource specified by the URL portion of the Refresh header.

There are yet other ways to issue a redirect from within an HTML document. For browsers that support JavaScript, a redirect can be accomplished by changing the value of the JavaScript location object in the <BODY> tag's onLoad event like this:

```
<BODY onLoad="location='http://www.sourcestream.com/'">
```

Likewise, the browser can be instructed to immediately load a new page using JavaScript code within the HTML document's <HEAD> block. The following JavaScript demonstrates how code within the <SCRIPT> block can instruct the browser to load a new page (using the document object to fully qualify the location object is optional).

```
<HEAD>
  <SCRIPT>
    document.location="http://www.sourcestream.com/";
  </SCRIPT>
</HEAD>
```

The previous techniques may have seemed pretty simple. However, using a specialized method, the Servlet API can make certain types of redirects even easier. The `HttpServletResponse` object includes the following method for sending temporary redirects:

```
public void sendRedirect(String location) throws
    java.io.IOException
```

This method accepts a single parameter—a `String` describing the new location of the requested resource. If the `location` parameter describes a relative URL, the servlet container will automatically convert it to an absolute URL before sending the response.

The `sendRedirect()` method automatically sets the HTTP status code of the response to "302 Moved Temporarily," adds the appropriate `Location` header, and generates a generic HTML message. Keep in mind that the `sendRedirect()` method sends temporary redirects only. For permanent redirects, use one of the manual redirect methods demonstrated previously. The following `service()` method illustrates the `sendRedirect()` method.

```
public void service(HttpServletRequest request,
  HttpServletResponse response) throws ServletException,
  java.io.IOException
{
  response.sendRedirect("http://www.sourcestream.com/");
  return; //good practice to exit immediately after redirect
}
```

One line is all it takes. The HTTP response (including headers) looks like this:

```
HTTP/1.0 302 Found
Location: http://www.sourcestream.com/
Date: Fri, 17 Mar 2000 04:11:37 GMT
Status: 302
Content-Type: text/html
Servlet-Engine: Tomcat Web Server/3.1 (JSP 1.1; Servlet 2.2; Java
1.2.2; Windows NT 4.0 x86; java.vendor=Sun Microsystems Inc.)
Content-Length: 161

<head><title>Document moved</title></head>
<body><h1>Document moved</h1>
This document has moved <a href="http://www.sourcestream.com/">
here</a>.<p>
</body>
```

Notice that the `sendRedirect()` method created all of the essential elements of an HTTP redirect. The "302 Moved Temporarily" status code was set (in this case, the server described a 302 status code using "Found"), the `Location` header was added to the response, and an HTML message was included for older browsers. For temporary redirects, the `HttpServlet-Response` object's `sendRedirect()` method is quick and easy.

NOTE: The sendRedirect() method should be executed before any data is sent to the output stream. Likewise, no data should be sent to the output stream after the sendRedirect() method is called. In fact, it is good practice to immediately exit the service(), doGet(), or doPost() method after execution of the sendRedirect() method.

Load-Balancing Servlet Using HTTP Redirects

In addition to forwarding clients to a Web site's new location, HTTP redirects can be used to provide a simple form of load-balancing. Figure 12.1 illustrates how client requests can be distributed across several servers by using a central redirection server. This strategy provides scalability by allowing a Web site to meet growing traffic demands by adding servers across which the load is shared. The following four steps describe this simple load-balancing process.

1. A client issues a request to the main URL of a Web site such as *http://www.insideservlets.com/*. This request is received by the load-balancing server.

2. The load-balancing server does not host the Web application. Rather, it simply redirects the client to the next server in a round-robin rotation. This ensures that all available servers handle a portion of the load.

3. The Web application duplicated on each server uses only relative URLs so that future requests from the same client are always received by the server to which the client was originally redirected. Since each client issues all of its requests to the same server, session information will be available for future requests and need not be shared among servers.

4. All of the servers hosting the load-balanced Web application share a single database for storing persistent information. In this way, if the client returns at a later time, any of the servers in the server pool can service the client's requests successfully by extracting previously stored information from the database (even if this information was stored by another server in the pool).

These four steps describe a simple method for adding load-balancing capabilities to your servlet applications. Listing 12.1 demonstrates a servlet that implements this process by distributing client requests evenly to any one of three servers based on a round-robin rotation. This is accomplished by requiring that each client issue an initial request to a load-balancing server, which will, in turn, redirect the client to the next server in the rotation.

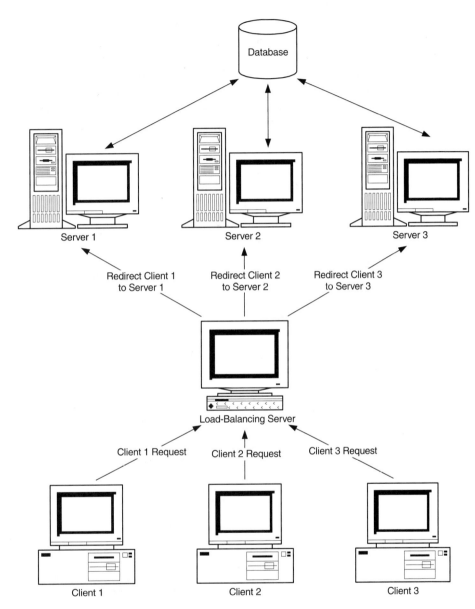

Figure 12.1   Load-Balancing Servlet Diagram

The load-balancing server does not generally require a very powerful computer because its only job is to issue redirects in response to each client request. In addition, the load-balancing server receives only a client's initial request. The client will send all future requests for this session directly to the server to which it was redirected. Lastly, don't forget that the Web application duplicated across each server in the server pool must use only relative URLs so that the client will be able to "remember" the server to which it was redirected. If an absolute URL is used, all future relative URLs will issue requests to the server referenced in the absolute URL (see Chapter 2 for more information about relative and absolute URLs). Of course, absolute URLs may be used if the HTML is altered for each server in the pool (such that each hyperlink or <FORM> tag uses an absoluate URL that points to the current machine). However, it is often much simpler to use only relative URLs rather than alter the HTML for each server in the pool.

Listing 12.1   load-balancing servlet redirects each client to a new server.

```
import javax.servlet.*;
import javax.servlet.http.*;

/**
 * LoadBalanceServlet provides load-balancing between servers by
 * redirecting each request to a new server using a round-robin
 * rotation.
 */
public class LoadBalanceServlet extends HttpServlet
{
  int nextServer = 0; //indicates the next server in the rotation

  //servers across which the load will be shared
  String[] servers = {"http://www1.insideservlets.com/",
                      "http://www2.insideservlets.com/",
                      "http://www3.insideservlets.com/"};

  /**
   * Redirects all requests to this servlet to the next server
   * in the round-robin rotation.
   */
  public void service(HttpServletRequest request,
    HttpServletResponse response) throws ServletException,
    java.io.IOException
  {
    synchronized(this)
    {
      response.sendRedirect(servers[nextServer]); //send redirect

      nextServer++; //increment server position

      //if past end of array, reset server position to zero
      if (nextServer >= servers.length)
      {
        nextServer = 0;
      }
    }

    return;
  }
}
```

The `LoadBalanceServlet` presented in Listing 12.1 is extremely simple. When the servlet is first loaded, a `String` array is created containing the URLs of all available application servers (i.e., servers that host the Web application to be load balanced). The servlet's `service()` method uses the `HttpServlet-Response` object's `sendRedirect()` method to redirect each client to the next application server in the rotation. After calling `sendRedirect()`, the `service()` method increments the `nextServer` variable. This variable indicates the server to which the next client should be redirected. If the `nextServer` variable is greater than the number of URLs in the array, its value is reset to zero so that the rotation can start again. Finally, the code in the `service()` method is contained in a `synchronized` block in order to guarantee thread safety.

Though the functionality currently provided by `LoadBalanceServlet` is extremely basic, this servlet can be enhanced easily. For instance, it would not be difficult to weight certain application servers more than others by placing them in the server array more than once. The servlet could also be altered to choose servers randomly rather than in a round-robin rotation. Lastly, the servlet could be enhanced to add servers dynamically and occasionally poll each server to ensure that it is still responding. If not responding, it could be removed from the rotation. This functionality could allow a server to be removed from service for maintenance and then added back into the rotation without interrupting the operation of the Web site.

Summary

This chapter introduces an extremely useful HTTP mechanism. HTTP redirects allow a server to seamlessly redirect clients to another location. Among other possibilities, redirects allow Web sites to temporarily or permanently change URLs without affecting users as well as provide a simple form of load-balancing. In the next chapter, we will examine another useful HTTP mechanism—cookies.

Chapter Highlights
- An HTTP redirect is a set of instructions included in the header of an HTTP response that instructs the browser to issue a new request to a new URL.
- There are two key elements in the header of an HTTP response that convey a redirect to the client. These elements are the HTTP status code and the `Location` header. An HTTP redirect response uses an HTTP status code of either "301 Moved Permanently" or "302 Moved Temporarily" accompanied by a `Location` header containing a valid URL.

- A servlet can send a redirect in two steps. First, set the HTTP status code of the response to 301 or 302 using the HttpServletResponse object's setStatus() method. Second, use the HttpServletResponse object's setHeader() method to add a Location header to the response that indicates the new URL.

- A redirect instruction can be conveyed to the client as embedded commands within an HTML document either using the HTTP-EQUIV command within a META tag or by changing the value of the location object via JavaScript.

- The Servlet API contains a shortcut method for sending temporary redirects. The sendRedirect() method of the HttpServletResponse object automatically sets the HTTP response status code to 302, adds the necessary Location header, and constructs a simple HTML message for browsers that do not support automatic redirects.

- HTTP redirects can be used to provide a simple form of load-balancing by redirecting client requests to an available Web application server.

CHAPTER 13

Cookies

A *cookie* is a small piece of information that is passed between an HTTP client and an HTTP server. This information can be used to add state to the stateless HTTP protocol. Sharing state information via cookies (known as state management) allows the server to uniquely identify each client and maintain user-specific settings. State management is necessary in order to "track" individual users as they traverse a Web site and store user-specific information such as the contents of a virtual shopping cart.[1] State management is covered in depth in the next chapter. This chapter discusses the following topics:

- What is a cookie?
- HTTP header syntax for a cookie
- Setting cookies with the Servlet API

What Is a Cookie?

Consider an electronic commerce Web site that allows users to order products from an online catalog. As customers browse the catalog, they are given the option of adding products to their virtual shopping cart. When they have completed shopping, they may then proceed to the virtual checkout line where their purchases are totaled and their credit card is charged.

You may be wondering how this sort of functionality is accomplished. After all, in Chapter 3 we learned that HTTP is a stateless protocol. Once a user issues a request and receives a response, the server has no memory of the transaction. Furthermore, when the same user makes another request, the

---

1. The ability to uniquely identify a client requires more than just state management. As we will see in the next chapter, an HTTP session must be established in order to maintain both state and client identity.

server has no way to distinguish this user from any other. So, how can the server remember the contents of each user's shopping cart? This is where the concept of a cookie comes to the rescue.

The cookie specification documents a simple method of storing and retrieving user-specific[2] information on the Web. This method requires a small piece of information, known as a cookie, to be passed between the client and the server as follows. When an HTTP server receives a request, in addition to the requested document, the server may choose to return some state information that should be stored by a cookie-enabled client. This state information includes a URL range that identifies when the information should be returned to the server. The URL range is composed of the server's domain and some path information. Whenever the client issues an HTTP request, it first checks the URL of the request against the URL ranges of all stored cookies. If a match is found, the state information received previously from the server is included in the client's request. The server essentially tells the client something like, "Here is a number to identify you. Please return it to me whenever you make a request so that I'll know who you are." In this way, the server can effectively overcome the stateless nature of the Web and track a client from request to request.

In the electronic commerce Web site example cited earlier, a cookie may have been used to store the items in a customer's shopping cart. When the customer requests to check out, the selected items (which are stored in a cookie) are transmitted back to the server for processing. Another common solution to the shopping cart problem is to store the contents of each customer's shopping cart on the server (either in memory or in a database) and send a cookie containing only a unique customer identification number. In this manner, when the customer attempts to check out, the database can be queried for the appropriate shopping cart contents using the customer's ID number that was returned in a cookie. We will discuss this type of state management in detail in the next chapter.

Before investigating how cookies are passed in the HTTP header, let's briefly examine the history of the cookie concept. Netscape Communications first proposed the idea of a cookie and proceeded to add cookie support to its popular browser, Netscape Navigator. Netscape states that this mechanism is

2. Cookies are often client specific rather than user specific. This means that they store information particular to a specific client (i.e., a Web browser running on a particular machine) without regard to which user is actually operating the client software. However, some browsers, such as Netscape Navigator, do support multiple user profiles. These profiles allow the browser to store cookie information for each user separately and distinguish among users. Profiles serve to make cookies user specific.

called a "cookie" for "no compelling reason." You may view the original cookie specification on Netscape's Web site at

http://home.netscape.com/newsref/std/cookie_spec.html

Since first proposed by Netscape, the cookie specification has been improved and expanded (see RFC 2109). Today, cookies are a very popular method of managing state on the Web.

HTTP Header Syntax for a Cookie

In this section, we will examine how cookies are passed in the header of HTTP requests and responses. Let's start with the server response that sets the cookie. The HTTP header syntax for setting a cookie is shown here (assume that the entire instruction is on one line).

```
Set-Cookie: NAME=VALUE; expires=DATE; domain=DOMAIN_NAME;
   path=PATH; secure
```

The Set-Cookie instruction is included in the header of the server's HTTP response to instruct the client to store a cookie. Multiple Set-Cookie headers can be included in a single HTTP response. When a cookie-enabled browser encounters the Set-Cookie header in the server's response, it stores the cookie for future use. An explanation of each attribute of the Set-Cookie header is given in Table 13.1.

A typical HTTP header for a response that sets a client-side cookie is shown here:

```
HTTP/1.0 200 OK
Server: Netscape-Enterprise/2.01
Content-Type: text/html
Content-Length: 87
Set-Cookie: customerID=1234; domain=.insideservlets.com;
   path=/orders
```

The cookie set by this HTTP header will be returned whenever the client makes a request to the /orders path of the .insideservlets.com domain. For instance, a request to the following URL returns the cookie:

http://www.insideservlets.com/orders/checkout.html

Now that we have discovered how the server stores a cookie on the client, let's take a look at how the cookie information is returned to the server. Similar to the manner in which the server sets a cookie, the client sends the cookie information in the HTTP header. However, rather than Set-Cookie, the header

Table 13.1   Attributes of the `Set-Cookie` Header

Attribute	Description
NAME=VALUE	The name/value pair for a cookie is similar to the name/value pair for a Web variable transmitted in an HTTP POST operation. NAME is the name of the cookie variable and VALUE is the value stored in this variable. This is the only required attribute of the `Set-Cookie` header. The following is an example of a name/value pair in a `Set-Cookie` header: `Set-Cookie: customerID=1234`.

expires=DATE	The `expires` attribute indicates when the cookie will no longer be valid. When a cookie expires, it should be removed from storage and no longer given out. If no `expires` attribute exists, then the cookie will expire at the conclusion of the user's session (when the browser is closed). The date should be in the following format (according to RFC 822): `Weekday, DD-Mon-YYYY HH:MM:SS GMT`.
	
	An example of setting a cookie with an `expires` attribute is
	
	`Set-Cookie: customerID=1234; expires=Saturday`
	`               08-Aug-2000 23:59:59 GMT`

domain=DOMAIN_NAME	The `domain` attribute indicates the domain to which the cookie should be returned. If the domain of a client request matches the `domain` attribute of a cookie, then the request's path is compared to the cookie's `path` attribute. If there is a match, the cookie is transmitted to the server along with the request. A successful domain match for the domain attribute *.insideservlets.com* would include the following: *www.insideservlets.com* *orders.insideservlets.com* *info.insideservlets.com* In addition, a server cannot arbitrarily set a cookie for any domain. It can only set cookies for its own domain. For the seven top-level domains including "COM", "EDU", "NET", "ORG", "GOV", "MIL", and "INT", the `domain` attribute must contain at least two periods. This prevents a server from setting a cookie using a generic domain such as ".com". The default value of the `domain` attribute is the hostname of the server that requested the cookie. An example `domain` attribute is shown here. `Set-Cookie: customerID=1234; domain=.insideservlets.com`
path=PATH	The `path` attribute indicates the URLs in a domain for which the cookie is valid. If a domain match is made, then the client compares the request's path information to the cookie's `path` attribute. If the request's path falls into the cookie's path range, the cookie is valid and is returned to the server with the request. If no `path` attribute is specified in the `Set-Cookie` header, the path is assumed to be the same as the resource that is being returned by the server. The most general, or root, path is specified by "/". Here is an example `path` attribute: `Set-Cookie: customerID=1234; domain=.insideservlets.com; path=/`
`secure`	The `secure` attribute indicates that this cookie should be sent across only a secure (i.e., encrypted) connection such as HTTPS. If a secure connection has not been established, the cookie is not sent.

field that returns state information is simply called Cookie. The syntax of the Cookie header is as follows:

```
Cookie: NAME1=VALUE1; NAME2=VALUE2; NAME3=VALUE3 ...
```

Whenever a client issues a request, it first attempts to match the domain and path information of the request against all stored cookies. If a match is found, the name/value pair of the cookie is added to the Cookie header field. A typical example of a client request that contains cookie information follows.

```
GET /login.html HTTP/1.0
User-Agent: Mozilla/4.02 [en] (Win95; I)
Accept: image/gif, image/x-xbitmap, image/jpeg, */*
Cookie: customerID=1234; color=blue
```

This cookie will allow the server to extract the user's customer ID number as well as his background color preference from the response. In this manner, the server can identify users, maintain user-defined preferences, and enforce security policies.

Here are a few other notes about cookies. To learn more about cookies, see Netscape's original cookie specification at *http://home.netscape.com/newsref/ std/cookie_spec.html* or RFC 2109, "HTTP State Management Mechanism."

- It is possible to have multiple Set-Cookie headers in a single HTTP response. If two cookies are set with identical names and paths, the second will overwrite the first. However, if two cookies with identical names but different paths are set, the two name/value pairs will coexist and the appropriate cookie will be returned when there is a path match.
- Cookies with more specific paths should be sent before cookies with more general paths. For instance, a cookie using the path "/orders" should be set before a cookie using the path "/".
- The Netscape cookie specification indicates that the client should store a maximum of 300 cookies, with each cookie having a maximum size of 4 kilobytes. Also, the client should store no more than 20 cookies per domain. This limit helps to ensure that cookies cannot exhaust the client's storage capacity.
- By default, cookies are returned only to the server from which they were sent. However, this behavior can be overridden by specifying a different domain. Domains within cookies must begin with a dot and contain at least two dots. Many browsers provide an option to allow cookies to be sent back only to the server from which they were created.

Setting Cookies with the Servlet API

Now that we understand the syntax for setting a cookie on the client, it becomes a rather simple task to add the Set-Cookie instruction to the HTTP response header. Let's first take a look at how this can be done manually using the Servlet API.

As we discovered in Chapter 6, the HttpServletResponse interface defines a method called setHeader() that allows a servlet to add HTTP headers to the response. The definition for the setHeader() method looks like this:

```
public void setHeader(String name, String value)
```

The name parameter sets the name of the header and the value parameter specifies a text value. The following sample code demonstrates how this method can be used to set cookies.

```
public void service(HttpServletRequest request,
  HttpServletResponse response) throws ServletException,
  IOException
{
  response.setContentType("text/plain");

  response.setHeader("Set-Cookie", "customerID=1234");
  response.setHeader("Set-Cookie", "color=blue");

  PrintWriter out = response.getWriter();

  out.println("You just received two cookies.");

  out.close();
}
```

The preceding code sends two cookies to the client—one named customerID having a value of 1234 and the other named color having a value of blue. These cookies may be used to identify the user and set user-defined preferences. Though the method shown here appears rather simple and straightforward, the Servlet API provides a cleaner, more object-oriented, way to send cookies.

Let's start by examining the javax.servlet.http.Cookie class. This class provides an object representation of a cookie. In essence, it encapsulates the state information contained in a cookie, thus allowing for easy modification and retrieval of this information. The Cookie class also simplifies the process of setting other cookie attributes such as domain and path.

The constructor for the `Cookie` class looks like this:

```
public Cookie(String name, String value)
```

Therefore, a `Cookie` object can be instantiated easily with the following line of code:

```
Cookie myCookie = new Cookie("customerID", "1234");
```

That was simple! Setting the rest of the attributes is just as easy. The following code demonstrates how a typical `Cookie` object may be created. Table 13.2 describes the methods of the `Cookie` class.

```
Cookie myCookie = new Cookie("password", "joshua");
myCookie.setDomain(".insideservlets.com");
myCookie.setPath("/");
myCookie.setSecure(true);
```

Once we have created a `Cookie` object, we need to send it to the client. Again, the Servlet API provides a simple method for accomplishing this task. The `HttpServletResponse` object (passed to the `service()`, `doGet()`, and `doPost()` methods) provides the following method for adding cookies to the response:

```
public void addCookie(cookie)
```

The `addCookie()` method can be called multiple times in order to add multiple `Cookie` objects. However, keep in mind that the original cookie specification indicates that no more than twenty cookies from any single domain should be stored. The `service()` method that follows demonstrates how multiple cookies can be set using `Cookie` objects and the `addCookie()` method.

```
public void service(HttpServletRequest request,
  HttpServletResponse response) throws IOException
{
  response.setContentType("text/plain");
  PrintWriter out = response.getWriter();

  Cookie customerID = new Cookie("customerID", "1234");
  Cookie color = new Cookie("color", "blue");

  response.addCookie(customerID);
  response.addCookie(color);

  out.println("You just received two cookies.");

  out.close();
}
```

Table 13.2   Methods of the `Cookie` Class

Method	Description
`setComment()`	Sends a comment describing the purpose of the cookie. Some clients may use this comment when advising the user that a cookie is being set.
`getComment()`	Returns the comment set by the `setComment()` method.
`setDomain()`	Sets the domain for which this cookie is valid. The domain must begin with a dot and contain at least two dots.
`getDomain()`	Returns the domain set by the `setDomain()` method.
`setMaxAge()`	Sets the maximum amount of time the cookie should persist. This method accepts an integer value representing the number of seconds before the cookie expires. A zero value will delete an existing cookie. A negative value indicates that the cookie should expire when the user session ends (the browser is closed).
`getMaxAge()`	Returns the number of seconds before the cookie expires as set by the `setMaxAge()` method.
`setPath()`	Sets the path portion of the URL in which the cookie is valid.
`getPath()`	Returns the path portion of the URL set by the `setPath()` method.
`setSecure()`	Specifies whether the cookie information should be transmitted across an unsecure connection. If `true` is passed to the `setSecure()` method, cookie information will be sent only if the client has established a secure link (such as HTTPS) with the server.
`getSecure()`	Returns the `boolean` value set by the `setSecure()` method.
`getName()`	Returns the name of the cookie set in the constructor when the cookie was first instantiated (this name cannot be changed). Represents the name portion of the name/value pair. For example, consider this cookie: `Cookie: customerID=1234` The name of this cookie is `customerID`.
`setValue()`	Sets the cookie's value. Represents the value portion of the name/value pair. For example, consider the cookie shown here: `Cookie: customerID=1234` The value of this cookie is `1234`.
`getValue()`	Returns the value of the cookie set in the constructor or by the `setValue()` method.
`setVersion()`	Sets the version of the cookie protocol being used.
`getVersion()`	Returns the version of the cookie protocol set by the `setVersion()` method.

NOTE: To delete a cookie, simply create a new `Cookie` object that has the same name as the cookie you wish to delete and set its maximum age to zero (0). Add this cookie to the response and the matching cookie on the client will be deleted. The sample code below demonstrates how to delete an existing cookie from the client's browser (assuming that a cookie named "customerID" already exists on the client).

```
Cookie customerID = new Cookie("customerID", "");
customerID.setMaxAge(0);
response.addCookie(customerID);
```

Note that when no domain or path information is specified for a cookie, the default is the domain of the server that sent the cookie and the path of the Web server's document root ("/"), respectively. After constructing your first servlet that uses cookies, you may need a way to test it. A simple way to test cookies generated by your servlet is to enable your browser's "Warn me before accepting cookies" option before requesting the servlet. This option should aid in troubleshooting cookies by displaying a dialog box similar to the one shown in Figure 13.1. This dialog box will be repeated for all cookies included in the response.

Another way to test a servlet that sets cookies is to use the *Protocol Explorer* utility demonstrated in Chapter 20 and provided on the accompanying CD. This utility allows you to view the entire HTTP header returned by a servlet (including the `Set-Cookie` headers). In the screen shot in Figure 13.2, you can see two cookies being set in the HTTP header.

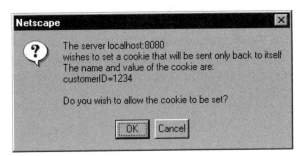

Figure 13.1 Dialog Box Warning the User That the Server Wishes to Set a Cookie

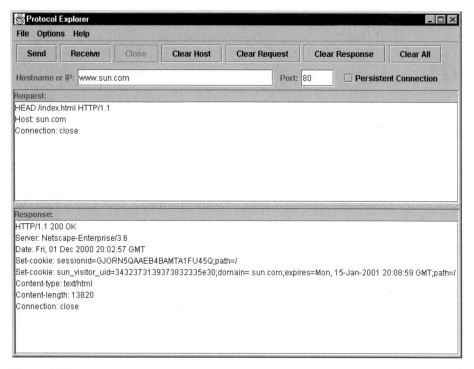

Figure 13.2   The Set-Cookie Header as Displayed by *Protocol Explorer*

Summary

Cookies provide a simple and efficient way to maintain state on the Web. Cookies can be used to enhance the Web experience by "remembering" user preferences and enabling other useful features such as electronic shopping carts, Web site tracking and statistics, and security. Although we touched on the topic of state management during our discussion on cookies, the next chapter will dig far deeper into this important subject. We will also examine the state and session management mechanisms included in the Servlet API.

Chapter Highlights

- A *cookie* is a small piece of information that is passed between an HTTP client and an HTTP server. This information can be used to add state to the stateless HTTP protocol.

- A cookie can be transmitted to the client by adding the Set-Cookie header to the HTTP response using the HttpServletResponse object's set-Header() method.

- The javax.servlet.http.Cookie class provides an object representation of a cookie. In essence, it encapsulates the state information contained in a cookie, thus allowing for easy modification and retrieval of this information.

- The addCookie() method of the HttpServletResponse object allows one or more Cookie objects to be added to the response.

CHAPTER 14

State and Session Management

We have already discussed the fact that HTTP is a stateless protocol. In the first section of this chapter, we will review what it means to be "stateless." Stateless protocols have many advantages over those that are stateful, but they also present some significant technical challenges. For instance, the lack of state prevents the server from uniquely identifying each user. This limitation inhibits the implementation of user-defined preferences because the server cannot distinguish one user from another. In addition, security policies cannot be enforced if the server cannot authenticate the client (i.e., determine the client's identity). Fortunately, several methods exist that effectively add state to the HTTP protocol. This chapter explores some of these methods as well as introduces the state and session management mechanisms built into the Servlet API.

At the end of this chapter, you should have a strong understanding of stateless protocols and some common methods that allow state to be added. You should also understand how state can be added to HTTP by using several specialized objects from the Servlet API. Specifically, the following topics are covered:

- What is a stateless protocol?
- What is a session?
- State and session management defined
- State and session management methods
- Session management with the Servlet API
- Session listeners and events

What Is a Stateless Protocol?

HTTP is a stateless protocol. A protocol is said to be *stateless* if it has no memory of prior connections and cannot distinguish one client's request from that

323

of another. In contrast, FTP (File Transfer Protocol) is a *stateful* protocol because the connection is not opened and closed with every request. After the initial login, the FTP server maintains the user's credentials throughout the session. In contrast, due to its stateless nature, there is no inherent method in HTTP for tracking a client's traversal of a Web site. Every request uses a new connection established by an anonymous client (from the server's perspective). State is extremely useful for secure sites that require user authentication or for electronic commerce sites that provide customers with a virtual shopping cart.

The stateless nature of HTTP is both a strength and a weakness. It is a strength in that its stateless nature keeps the protocol simple and straightforward. It also consumes fewer resources on the server and can support more simultaneous users since there are no client credentials and connections to maintain. The disadvantages are the increased overhead required to create a new connection with each request and the inability to track a single user as she traverses a Web site. The rest of this chapter discusses ways to overcome these disadvantages.

What Is a Session?

There is more than one definition of the term *session*. In the traditional sense, a *session* is a persistent network connection between two hosts (usually a client and a server) that facilitates the exchange of information. When the connection is closed, the session is over. However, we are not interested in this type of session. Rather, let's focus on another type of session known as an *HTTP session* or a *virtual session*. This type of session involves a virtual, rather than a physical, connection between the client and server. Let's first examine what is meant by a "virtual connection" as we attempt to understand an HTTP session.

In an HTTP transaction, each connection between the client and server is very brief. This is an inherent trait of a stateless protocol. To illustrate, a typical stateless protocol transaction goes like this: the client establishes a connection to the server, issues a request, receives a response, and then closes the connection. Because a persistent connection between the client and server is not maintained between requests, the server's tie to the client is severed once the connection is closed. If the same client issues a new request, the server cannot associate this connection with the client's previous one. The fact that the server "forgets" about the client after the connection is closed presents significant challenges to the HTTP protocol. If not remedied, this disconnect between client and server can lead to the following problems and limitations:

- If the server requires client authentication (e.g., a client must log in with a valid username and password), the client must reauthenticate with every request. The server does not realize that this client has already been authorized.

- Storing user-specific information, such as the contents of a shopping cart or user-defined preferences, is not possible because the server cannot distinguish one client from another.

Fortunately, these problems can be overcome by establishing a persistent "virtual connection" between the client and the server. A virtual connection associates each request received by the server with the client that issued it. This association is accomplished by requiring the client to return some specific piece of information with each new request. The server uses this information (usually called a *session ID*) to uniquely identify the client and associate the current request with the client's previous requests. By allowing the server to identify the client, virtual connections alleviate the problems just presented. These virtual connections are commonly referred to as HTTP sessions or simply sessions. Sessions are used to maintain state and client identity across multiple requests.

In a traditional session, all client requests are associated by virtue of the fact that they share a network connection. In contrast, an HTTP session associates client requests by virtue of the fact that they all share a session ID. A traditional session refers to the duration of time that a network connection is open. Similarly, an HTTP session refers to the duration of time that a virtual connection is active. In short, an *HTTP session* is a series of associated requests in which the client can be uniquely identified. This association between the HTTP client and the HTTP server persists across multiple requests and/or connections for a specific period of time.

We know that the traditional type of session expires when the network connection is closed. However, since an HTTP session persists between requests (with each request opening and closing a connection), you might be asking, "When does an HTTP session expire?" The duration of an HTTP session is configurable on the server. A common approach is to instruct the server to expire any sessions that have been inactive for more than a specified amount of time, say fifteen minutes. In this case, a particular client's session will persist between requests as long as they are received no more than fifteen minutes apart. If the client waits more than fifteen minutes before issuing a new request, the server will expire (i.e., end) the client's session and the client will be required to log in again (since the client's session ID is no longer valid). Automatically expiring sessions after a period of inactivity ensures that server resources are not consumed by old sessions. Session expiration also improves security by not allowing valid session IDs to remain active indefinitely.

Now let's consider the question, "What does it mean for an HTTP session to expire?" Essentially, this means that the unique session ID used to identify a client is removed from storage along with any associated data (e.g., shopping cart contents). Session IDs are usually stored in memory or in a database. Once a session ID expires and is removed from storage, the client that originally received this session ID must log in again in order to be assigned a new session ID.

NOTE: For security purposes, it is a good practice to allow users to immediately expire their sessions. This is usually accomplished by providing a logout option on the Web site's menu bar. When the user chooses to log out, the session ID should be deleted. In this way, if someone else uses the same browser before the session expires, he will not be able to use the previous user's session (and, therefore, the previous user's security privileges).

Likewise, the server should automatically expire sessions that are stale (inactive for a period of time) because many users may not log out properly. Rather, they may just close their browser or jump to another site. To prevent storing excess session information, old sessions should be purged regularly.

To illustrate, let's walk through a typical series of events that comprise the lifecycle of an HTTP session. Keep in mind that a network connection is opened before each client request and closed after each server response.[1]

1. The client requests a resource from the server.
2. The server returns an authentication challenge that results in the browser displaying a name/password dialog box.
3. The client returns a valid name and password.
4. The server returns a valid session ID that allows this client to be uniquely identified. In this case, the session ID is sent in a cookie that will be returned by the client with each request. THIS BEGINS THE HTTP SESSION.
5. The client issues any number of requests to the server. The server is able to identify the client and the client's security privileges based on the session ID that accompanies each request.

---

1. Actually, this is not completely accurate. HTTP/1.1 supports a strategy called persistent connections that allows the client to send multiple subsequent requests across a single connection. However, for the purpose of understanding HTTP sessions, it is simpler to imagine that a separate connection is employed for each request/response (which is often the case).

6. The client closes the browser without explicitly logging out (an explicit logout should immediately expire the session).

7. After fifteen minutes, the server expires the session by deleting the session ID (from memory or a database). THIS CONCLUDES THE HTTP SESSION.

This example used a cookie to communicate the session ID. In the next section, we will explore different ways that session information can be passed between client and server.

State and Session Management Defined

In this chapter, we often refer to state and session management. However, there is a distinct difference between state management and session management.

State management is the ability to maintain a client's current state (e.g., items in a shopping cart or user preferences) by passing client-specific information between the client and server. However, with simple state management, the server may not be able to uniquely identify each client. Allowing clients to select their background color is an example of state management. Once selected, the client will transmit this preferred color to the server with each request.

Although the server can determine the client's preferred background color, it cannot uniquely identify the client. For instance, assume that two clients select blue as their preferred background color. Each time either of these clients issues a request, the request will include a piece of state information, such as bcolor=blue, that will convey that preference. Although the server can determine the preferred background color for each of these clients, it cannot distinguish one client from the other. State management can be useful for storing small amounts of state information when the client's identity is not relevant.

In contrast, *session management* maintains both state and identity. Session management provides an association between the client and the server that allows the server to uniquely identify each client. This association persists across requests for a specified period of time. In essence, session management is a superset of state management (in fact, these two terms are often used interchangeably). However, in addition to managing state, sessions also keep track of client identity. For example, assume that two clients select blue as their preferred background color. Rather than send a piece of state information to the client (such as the preferred background color), the server will send a unique session ID and store all of the client's preferences on the server. This session ID, which uniquely identifies the client, is returned to the server with each request.

Once the client's identity is established, the server can determine the client's preferred background color, which may be stored in memory or in a database associated with the client's session ID.

Session management is useful for storing large amounts of state information because only a session ID is passed between the client and server. All other state information can be stored on the server. Additionally, session management can be used to enforce security policies because the client can be identified with every request.

State and Session Management Methods

Several methods facilitate the exchange of session IDs or state information between the client and the server. In this section, we will explore three of the most common techniques. These techniques include storing the session ID in the URL path, implementing rewritten URLs and hidden variables, and using cookies to pass session information.

Storing Session Information in the URL Path

When adding state to a stateless protocol like HTTP, every technique has one trait in common; the state-enabling mechanism must allow the server to send state information to the client with the guarantee that this information will be returned with every request. The URL path method of managing state accomplishes this two-way communication by embedding a session ID (or other state information) in the URL path. For instance, consider the following sequence of events.

1. The client requests the document located at *http://www.insideservlets.com/ login.html*. This screen includes an HTML form that allows the client to submit a name and password.

2. Upon receiving a valid name and password, the server generates a unique session ID, say 122893, and immediately redirects the client to *http:// www.insideservlets.com/sessionID/122893/welcome.html*.

3. The server parses the path portion of all requested URLs for a valid session ID. If no session ID exists or the session ID is invalid, the client is redirected to the login screen described in step 1.

4. From this point forward, the URLs in hyperlinks and <FORM> tags in all documents returned to the client use only relative URLs (rather than absolute URLs). Recall from Chapter 2 that the browser stores the protocol, host, and path information from the most recent absolute URL request. After requesting an absolute URL, every subsequent relative URL request

uses the same protocol, host, and path information as the absolute URL. The browser automatically fills in the missing protocol, host, and path information for every relative URL. Notice how this browser behavior will effectively return the client's session ID with every request.

5. Each time the client follows a relative URL hyperlink in the site, the browser will return the full path information (including the session ID) to the server. The server can then use this session information to identify the client, enforce security policies, and store client-specific information like personal preferences and shopping cart contents.

This procedure, as with all techniques for adding state to HTTP, has both advantages and disadvantages. The advantage of storing the session ID in the URL path is that no special browser features are required. This method will work with all browsers, including those that do not support cookies.

There are also several disadvantages to this approach. First, the requirement of using only relative URLs throughout an entire Web site can be limiting. Remember, if an absolute URL is ever used without explicitly including the session ID in the path, state information will be lost. Second, the client's unique session ID is visible in the browser's address field. This could present a security risk if another user were to copy the visible session ID. With this session ID a malicious user could violate security by referencing a resource on the server using the stolen session ID as follows:

http://www.insideservlets.com/sessionID/122893/catalog.html

Of course, the attacker would have to access the Web site in a timely manner before the session expired (a timeout period on the server automatically expires sessions after a period of inactivity).

NOTE: The servlet container allows you to specify the session timeout period. The timeout period can be set programmatically using the `setMax-InactiveInterval()` method of the `HttpSession` object. In addition, it is possible to set the default timeout period by altering one of the servlet container's configuration files or through the container's administration utility (this action is server dependent). For example, the following XML located in a Web application's *web.xml* file (or in Tomcat's default *web.xml* file located at */jakarta-tomcat/conf*) sets the default timout period to 30 minutes.

```
<web-app>
  <session-config>
    <session-timeout>30</session-timeout>
  </session-config>
<web-app>
```

Lastly, it can be more difficult to process URLs that contain session information. Every request must be parsed for session information and the appropriate resource (specified in the path after the session ID) must be returned. Cookies, for instance, do not require the URL to be parsed. In addition, when using cookies, the virtual path in the URL can be converted easily to the physical file-system path using the Servlet API (see the `getRealPath()` method of the `ServletContext` interface).

NOTE: Storing the session ID in the URL path can frustrate search engines. For example, when a search engine visits a site that stores the session ID in the URL path, it will index the Web site's pages using each page's full URL, including the session ID. If at a later time the search engine presents this URL to a user looking for your site, the link will not be valid because the session ID will have long since expired.

Rewritten URLs

Another popular method of managing state on the Web involves the use of rewritten URLs. Rewritten URLs pass state information between the client and server by embedding information in the URL of all hyperlinks and <FORM> tags in an HTML document. Recall from Chapter 2 that information can be passed in the query string of a URL in the form of name/value pairs, with each pair separated by an ampersand (&). For example, entering the following URL into your browser's address field will pass search criteria to the WebCrawler search engine:

```
http://www.webcrawler.com/cgi-bin/WebQuery?searchText=servlets
```

The query string immediately follows the question mark ("?") in the URL. The name/value pairs in the query string are passed to the server as Web variables. With the Servlet API, these variables can be read using the `getParameter()` or `getParameterValues()` method of the `HttpServletRequest` object.

Now that we understand that information can be passed in a URL, let's examine how we can use this behavior to pass state information between the client and the server. Let's start by demonstrating how hyperlinks in an HTML document can store client-specific state information. The following HTML document allows the client to select a preferred background color.

```
<HTML>
<HEAD>
<TITLE>Select Background Color</TITLE>
</HEAD>
<BODY>

<P>Please select your preferred background color:<BR>
<A HREF="ColorServlet?bcolor=white">White</A><BR>
<A HREF="ColorServlet?bcolor=black">Black</A><BR>
<A HREF="ColorServlet?bcolor=red">Red</A><BR>
<A HREF="ColorServlet?bcolor=green">Green</A><BR>
<A HREF="ColorServlet?bcolor=blue">Blue</A><BR>

</BODY>
</HTML>
```

Notice that each hyperlink requests the same resource (ColorServlet). However, each link passes a different color value. In order to maintain the specified background color for the client's future requests, this information must be transmitted between the client and server with each request and response. This can be accomplished with rewritten URLs. Rewriting URLs is a method whereby the server adds state information to the URL of every hyperlink and <FORM> tag in an HTML document before it is returned to the client. This process is accomplished in one of two ways. Either the developer explicitly adds state information to each URL as HTML is generated by servlet code or a servlet parses an HTML file, adding state information to every URL, before the document is sent to the client.

For example, the following HTML document is returned in response to the client selecting a background color of blue.

```
<HTML>
<HEAD>
<TITLE>Main Menu for Acme Company</TITLE>
</HEAD>
<BODY BGCOLOR="0000FF"> <!-- set background color to blue -->

<P>Please select from the choices below:<BR>
<A HREF="MenuServlet/catalog.html?bcolor=blue">Product
    Catalog</A><BR>
<A HREF="MenuServlet/info.html?bcolor=blue">Corporate Info
    </A><BR>
<A HREF="MenuServlet/press.html?bcolor=blue">Press Releases
    </A><BR>
<A HREF="MenuServlet/employment.html?bcolor=blue">Employment
    </A><BR>
<A HREF="MenuServlet/search.html?bcolor=blue">Search the Site
    </A>

</BODY>
</HTML>
```

Notice how the server added the query string `bcolor=blue` to the URL of every hyperlink in the document. In this way, no matter which option the client selects, the link will always return the preferred background color to the server. Of course, if this state information is to persist from page to page, the server must add the data to all URLs of every page that it returns to the client.

To this point, we have demonstrated only using rewritten URLs in hyperlinks. So, the question remains, "How is state information passed back to the server when an HTML form is submitted?" The answer is that, in addition to all URLs in hyperlinks, the URL specified by the `<FORM>` tag's `ACTION` attribute must also be rewritten to contain all desired state information. By rewriting the URL of the `<FORM>` tag's `ACTION` attribute, state information is returned to the servlet in the same manner as hyperlinks. This allows the servlet to extract state information from the request using the `HttpServletRequest` object's `getParameter()` and `getParameterValues()` methods. The following HTML document demonstrates a typical response to the client's selecting a background color of blue. This example illustrates the use of an HTML form instead of hyperlinks.

```html
<HTML>
<HEAD>
<TITLE>Main Menu for Acme Company</TITLE>
</HEAD>
<BODY BGCOLOR="0000FF"> <!-- set background color to blue -->

<FORM METHOD="POST" ACTION="MenuServlet?bcolor=blue">
<P>Please select from the choices below:<BR>
<INPUT TYPE="SUBMIT" NAME="menuitem" VALUE="Product Catalog">
   <BR>
<INPUT TYPE="SUBMIT" NAME="menuitem" VALUE="Corporate Info"><BR>
<INPUT TYPE="SUBMIT" NAME="menuitem" VALUE="Press Releases"><BR>
<INPUT TYPE="SUBMIT" NAME="menuitem" VALUE="Employment"><BR>
<INPUT TYPE="SUBMIT" NAME="menuitem" VALUE="Search the Site">
</FORM>

</BODY>
</HTML>
```

NOTE: In addition to rewritten URLs, hidden HTML form variables are commonly used to store state information. A hidden variable operates like an HTML input field (e.g., text fields, check boxes, radio buttons) in that when the page is submitted, the client transmits the field's name/value pair to the server. The difference between a hidden variable and a normal HTML input field is that the client cannot see or modify the value of a hidden HTML variable (however, hidden variables are visible in the HTML source). Remember that hidden variables work only when the client submits an HTML form. Following a hyperlink does not return hidden variables to the server. Though the use of hidden variables is not discussed in this chapter, you should be aware of them since they can be used to transparently pass state information between the client and the server. The following HTML demonstrates how the user's preferred background color can be passed from page to page within a hidden variable.

```
<HTML>
<HEAD>
<TITLE>What's Your Name?</TITLE>
</HEAD>
<BODY BGCOLOR="0000FF"> <!-- set background color to blue -->

<FORM METHOD="POST" ACTION="/servlet/NameServlet">
<P>Please enter your first name:<BR>
<INPUT TYPE="TEXT" NAME="name" SIZE="25"><BR>
<INPUT TYPE="HIDDEN" NAME="bcolor" VALUE="blue">
<BR>
<INPUT TYPE="SUBMIT" VALUE="Submit">
</FORM>

</BODY>
</HTML>
```

Although these simple examples allow state information (i.e., the user's preferred background color) to be shared between the client and server, they do not provide session management. A more efficient way of storing client-specific information is through the use of a session ID. In the case of rewritten URLs, the server typically generates a unique session ID and passes it to the client within the query string of each URL. In turn, the client returns the session ID to the server whenever a hyperlink is followed or an HTML form is submitted. In this way, client-specific state information can be stored on the server and only one piece of information (the session ID) need be exchanged. The following HTML document is a typical response from a server that uses rewritten URLs for both hyperlinks and HTML forms. Notice the sessionID variable in the query string of all URLs (in the hyperlinks as well as in the ACTION attribute of the <FORM> tag).

```
<HTML>
<HEAD>
<TITLE>Main Menu for Acme Company</TITLE>
</HEAD>
<BODY>

<P>Please select from the choices below:<BR>
<A HREF="MenuServlet/catalog.html?sessionID=122893">Catalog
  </A><BR>
```

```
<A HREF="MenuServlet/info.html?sessionID=122893">Corporate
   Info</A><BR>
<A HREF="MenuServlet/press.html?sessionID=122893">Press
   Releases</A><BR>

<FORM METHOD="POST" ACTION="MenuServlet?sessionID=122893">
<INPUT TYPE="SUBMIT" NAME="menuitem" VALUE="Employment"><BR>
<INPUT TYPE="SUBMIT" NAME="menuitem" VALUE="Search the Site">
</FORM>

</BODY>
</HTML>
```

Now that we've learned how they work, let's examine the advantages and disadvantages of using rewritten URLs for state and session management. Similar to placing the session ID in the URL path, the primary advantage of this method is that virtually all browsers support rewritten URLs. Specifically, cookie support is not required.

The primary disadvantage to this method is the amount of processing required on the server in order to implement rewritten URLs. To implement these features properly, the server must parse every HTML document that it serves, adding state information to all URLs. This increased overhead incurs a performance penalty and requires more complex code.

 NOTE: It is a good practice to keep the amount of information passed in a rewritten URL to a minimum. Some browsers enforce a limit on the length of URLs and will truncate those that are too long. For example, older versions of Microsoft Internet Explorer truncate URLs longer than 255 characters.

Cookies

Cookies provide the simplest way to store state information on the client. As discussed in Chapter 13, a *cookie* is a small piece of information that the server instructs the client to store. In turn, this information is returned to the server with each client request. See Chapter 13 for more detailed information about cookies.

The process of using cookies to manage state and session is very straightforward. To illustrate, let's return to the example of a user setting the preferred background color. Consider the following sequence of events.

1. The user selects a background color from a list of options on an HTML form and submits the form.

2. The server extracts the user's color selection from the HTML form submitted by the client.

3. To ensure that the user's color selection persists across multiple requests, the server instructs the client to set a cookie that stores the user's color preference. This information is returned to the server with each subsequent client request. (For more information on how to set cookies using the Servlet API, see Chapter 13.)

4. The server constructs an HTML document, setting its background color to the user's choice, and returns it to the client.

5. Each time the server receives a request, it extracts the user's color preference from the cookie information. The HTML document returned to the client is constructed according to the user's background color selection.

6. This process continues as long as the client issues requests and the cookie does not expire.

As you can see, using cookies to manage state is a very simple process. As in the previously discussed state management methods, cookies can also be used to manage sessions by storing a unique session ID rather than a background color. Session management with cookies allows client-specific information, such as color preference, to be stored on the server rather than the client. In turn, communication with the client is more efficient because only a single cookie (the session ID), rather than numerous client-specific preferences, is returned with each request.

Finally, let's examine the advantages and disadvantages to using cookies for state and session management. The advantages of using cookies are many. First, cookies are the simplest way to store state information on the client because this information need only be stored once. The server is not required to keep returning this information to the client, as is the case with rewritten URLs. And unlike storing the session ID in the URL path, either relative or absolute URLs may be used without losing state. Also, in contrast to either of the previous two methods, cookies do not require parsing of the requested URL or the HTML document. Cookie information can be extracted from the client request using a very simple Servlet API method (the HttpServletRequest object's getCookies() method). Thus, server-side processing is kept to a minimum. Cookies provide a simple method of maintaining state and session with very low overhead.

Despite the many benefits provided by cookies, there is one distinct disadvantage. The primary problem with cookies is that they are not supported by all browsers. This lack of cookie support may result from one of two conditions: either the client is using an older browser that does not support cookies or the user has instructed the browser not to accept cookies. Some users may, often out of ignorance, turn off cookie support in their browser for fear that cookies may somehow compromise security or exhaust their system's resources (or some other unfounded concern). Considering that virtually all current browsers support cookies, the chance that a user is running a browser that does not recognize cookies is small. The possibility that a user might manually disable cookie support and, in turn, disable a Web site's mechanism for state and session management is of greater concern. Therefore, some sites may choose to use an alternative session management mechanism because some users may not accept cookies. Fortunately, the Java Servlet Specification mandates that servlet containers support session management via cookies and rewritten URLs.

Session Management with the Servlet API

Although we could use any of the methods discussed previously to implement session management on our own, there is a simpler way. Session management support is built into the Servlet API and can be implemented using a few simple objects and methods. In this section, we explore how to manage sessions using the Servlet API.

The session management implementation in the Servlet API revolves around an interface called HttpSession. An HttpSession object encapsulates the essential information of an HTTP session, such as a unique session ID and other client-specific information. This client-specific information can include any Java object. For example, a String or an integer could be stored in the session during one request (using the setAttribute() method) and retrieved (using the getAttribute() method) when processing a future request from the same client.

NOTE: Whenever an attribute is retrieved from the session, it is returned as a java.lang.Object (the base object from which all Java classes extend). Therefore, when retrieving objects from the session, it is necessary to downcast the object back to its original class. Downcasting is the process of typecasting (or converting) an object to a class lower in the object hierarchy. For example, the following code stores a String in the session and then retrieves it as a String (by downcasting).

```
session.setAttribute("Username", "Reagan");
String username = (String)session.getAttribute("Username");
```

Every object stored in the session is assigned a unique name so that it can be retrieved at a later time. It is recommended that objects stored in the session be named according to the standard reverse package name convention. For instance, an object called `OrderList` might be stored in the session under the name `com.insideservlets.OrderList`. This naming convention is recommended in order to reduce the chance of name collisions as objects are stored in the session. Name collisions may occur often since all servlets within a servlet context (i.e., within the same Web application) share the same session. Therefore, care must be taken to ensure that another servlet (possibly written by another individual or company) does not overwrite your servlet's session objects. The use of the reverse package name convention minimizes the possibility of another servlet's interfering with your servlet's session objects. Of course, to eliminate this risk altogether, a new Web application can be created for each servlet (allowing each servlet to have its own session).

An object that implements `HttpSession` can be retrieved using the `HttpServletRequest` object's `getSession()` method. Table 14.1 briefly describes the methods defined by the `HttpSession` interface.

The `HttpSession` object contains the majority of the methods that you'll use to manage session. However, the `HttpServletRequest` object also contains several useful methods. Table 14.2 describes several methods implemented by the `HttpServletRequest` object that apply to session management.

By default, the session management mechanisms in the Servlet API use cookies. Servlet sessions are maintained using a cookie named `JSESSIONID`. Cookies are used because of the increased overhead required to implement rewritten URLs. However, the Servlet API does provide methods to determine if the client lacks cookie support, in which case rewritten URLs can be used instead (servlet containers are required to support both cookies and rewritten URLs). Listing 14.1 presents a servlet that uses cookies to establish a session with the client and returns session information in response to each request.

Listing 14.1 Servlet that displays session information.

```
import javax.servlet.*;
import javax.servlet.http.*;
import java.io.*;

/**
 * The SessionInfoServlet demonstrates the session management
 * mechanisms built into the servlet API.
 */
public class SessionInfoServlet extends HttpServlet
{
  /**
   * Builds an HTML document containing session information and
   * returns it to the client.
   */
  public void doGet(HttpServletRequest request,
    HttpServletResponse response) throws ServletException,
    IOException
  {
```

Table 14.1   Methods Defined by the HTTPSession Interface

Method	Description
getAttribute()	Returns a client-specific object that is bound to the current session. Objects are bound to a session using the setAttribute() method. Returns null if the named object does not exist.
getAttributeNames()	Returns an Enumeration containing the names of all objects bound to this session or an empty Enumeration if the session contains no objects.
getCreationTime()	Returns the time that the session was created. The time is returned as the number of milliseconds since midnight, January 1, 1970, GMT.
getId()	Returns the unique session ID assigned to this session.
getLastAccessedTime()	Returns the time of the client's last request using the current session ID. The time is returned as the number of milliseconds since midnight, January 1, 1970, GMT.
getMaxInactiveInterval()	Returns the maximum number of seconds that a session is guaranteed to be valid without a request from the client. After the maximum inactive interval expires, the session may be expired by the servlet container. If the session never expires, a -1 is returned.
getValue()	Deprecated as of Servlet API 2.2. Replaced by getAttribute().
getValueNames()	Deprecated as of Servlet API 2.2. Replaced by getAttributeNames().
invalidate()	Expires the current session.
isNew()	Returns true if this is a new session. When the getSession() method of HttpServletRequest is called, either it returns a valid session ID or, if the client has not yet established a session, it creates a new session.
putValue()	Deprecated as of Servlet API 2.2. Replaced by setAttribute().
removeAttribute()	Unbinds an object from the session and makes it available for garbage collection (removing the object from memory).
removeValue()	Deprecated as of Servlet API 2.2. Replaced by removeAttribute().
setAttribute()	Binds an object to the current session. This object can be retrieved during future requests using the getAttribute() method.
setMaxInactiveInterval()	Sets the maximum number of seconds that a session is guaranteed to be valid without a request from the client. After the maximum inactive interval expires, the session may be expired by the servlet container.

Table 14.2   Session Management Methods of `HttpServletRequest`

Method	Description
getRequestedSessionId()	Returns the session ID that accompanied the client's request. This may or may not be the same as the current session ID. For instance, if the client's session has expired, this method will return the expired session ID even if the client is issued a new session ID with this request.
getSession()	Returns a handle to the client's `HttpSession`. If the client has not yet established a session or the client's session is invalid, this method may return a handle to a new session. `getSession()` accepts a `boolean` parameter indicating whether to create a new session if one does not currently exist.
isRequestedSessionIdFromCookie()	Returns `true` if the session ID was returned by a cookie.
isRequestedSessionIdFromURL()	Returns `true` if the session ID was returned by a rewritten URL.
isRequestedSessionIdValid()	Returns `true` if the client's session ID represents a valid session. Returns `false` if the session is invalid (i.e., session has expired or never existed).

```
//get current session or, if necessary, create a new one
HttpSession mySession = request.getSession(true);

//MIME type to return is HTML
response.setContentType("text/html");

//get a handle to the output stream
PrintWriter out = response.getWriter();

//generate HTML document
out.println("<HTML>");
out.println("<HEAD>");
out.println("<TITLE>Session Info Servlet</TITLE>");
out.println("</HEAD>");
out.println("<BODY>");
out.println("<H3>Session Information</H3>");
out.println("New Session: " + mySession.isNew());
out.println("<BR>Session ID: " + mySession.getId());
out.println("<BR>Session Creation Time: " +
  new java.util.Date(mySession.getCreationTime()));
out.println("<BR>Session Last Accessed Time: " +
  new java.util.Date(mySession.getLastAccessedTime()));

out.println("<H3>Request Information</H3>");
out.println("Session ID from Request: " +
  request.getRequestedSessionId());
```

```
      out.println("<BR>Session ID via Cookie: " +
        request.isRequestedSessionIdFromCookie());
      out.println("<BR>Session ID via rewritten URL: " +
        request.isRequestedSessionIdFromURL());
      out.println("<BR>Valid Session ID: " +
        request.isRequestedSessionIdValid());

      out.println("</BODY></HTML>");

      out.close(); //close output stream
    }


    /**
     * Returns a brief description of this servlet.
     *
     * @return Brief description of servlet
     */
    public String getServletInfo()
    {
      return "Servlet returns session information.";
    }
}
```

Figure 14.1 displays the response to the client's first request to Session-InfoServlet, and Figure 14.2 shows the response to the client's second request to this servlet. Notice that a new session is created on the first request but not the second (see Figure 14.1).

The code in Listing 14.2 illustrates session management with a slightly more involved servlet. This servlet prompts a user to select a background color and enter his name. The servlet then demonstrates how, through session management techniques, it can remember each user's name, color preference, and the number of times the user has requested the servlet. Again, this example uses cookies for session management. A future example will demonstrate how rewritten URLs can be used if the client does not support cookies.

Listing 14.2   Using session management to remember client information.

```
import javax.servlet.*;
import javax.servlet.*;
import javax.servlet.http.*;
import java.io.*;

/**
 * The ColorSessionServlet demonstrates the session management
 * mechanisms built into the servlet API. A session is
 * established and the client's preferred background color
 * as well as the number of times they have requested the
 * servlet are stored.
 */
```

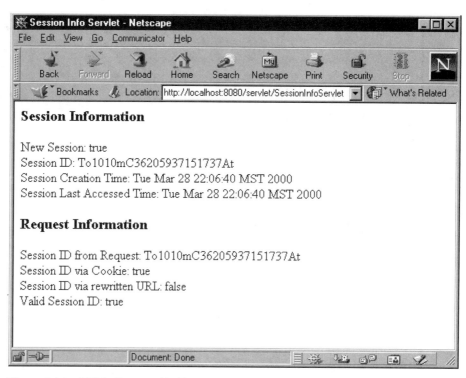

Figure 14.1 HTML Generated by First Request to SessionInfoServlet

```java
public class ColorSessionServlet extends HttpServlet
{
  /**
   * Generates HTML pages that allows the client to choose a
   * color and then remembers the color on future requests.
   */
  public void service(HttpServletRequest request,
    HttpServletResponse response) throws ServletException,
    IOException
  {
    String name; //name of user
    String color; //user's color preference
    Integer hitCount; //# of times user has requested servlet

    //get current session, create a new one if it doesn't exist
    HttpSession mySession = request.getSession(true);

    //MIME type to return is HTML
    response.setContentType("text/html");

    //get a handle to the output stream
    PrintWriter out = response.getWriter();
```

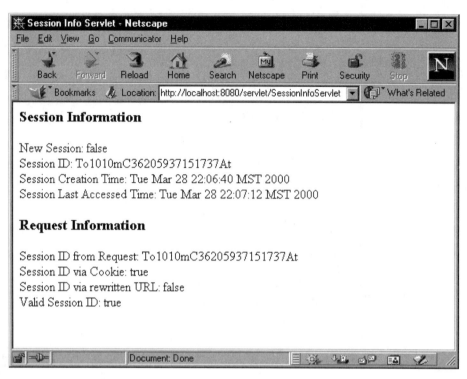

Figure 14.2   HTML Generated by Second Request to SessionInfoServlet

```
if (mySession.isNew()) //first time client requests page
{
  //generate HTML form requesting name and color preference
  out.println("<HTML>");
  out.println("<HEAD>");
  out.println("<TITLE>Color Selector</TITLE>");
  out.println("</HEAD>");
  out.println("<BODY>");
  out.println("<FORM METHOD=\"POST\" " +
    "ACTION=\"ColorSessionServlet\">");
  out.println("Please select background color:<BR>");
  out.println("<INPUT TYPE=\"RADIO\" NAME=\"bcolor\" " +
    "VALUE=\"white\">White<BR>");
  out.println("<INPUT TYPE=\"RADIO\" NAME=\"bcolor\" " +
    "VALUE=\"red\">Red<BR>");
  out.println("<INPUT TYPE=\"RADIO\" NAME=\"bcolor\" " +
    "VALUE=\"green\">Green<BR>");
  out.println("<INPUT TYPE=\"RADIO\" NAME=\"bcolor\" " +
    "VALUE=\"blue\">Blue<P>");
  out.println("Please enter your name:<BR>");
  out.println("<INPUT TYPE=\"TEXT\" NAME=\"name\" " +
    "SIZE=\"25\"><P>");
```

```
      out.println("<INPUT TYPE=\"SUBMIT\" VALUE=\"Submit\">");
      out.println("</BODY>");
      out.println("</HTML>");
}
else //client has already established a session
{
  if (request.getParameter("bcolor") != null)
  {
    //client is submitting the color preference form
    String bcolor; //for user's preferred background color
    bcolor = request.getParameter("bcolor");

    //get HEX code for color
    if (bcolor.equals("red"))
    {
      color = "#FF0000";
    }
    else if (bcolor.equals("green"))
    {
      color = "#00FF00";
    }
    else if (bcolor.equals("blue"))
    {
      color = "#0000FF";
    }
    else //if nothing selected, default to white
    {
      color = "#FFFFFF";
    }

    name = request.getParameter("name"); //get user name
    hitCount = new Integer(1); //requested 1 time so far

    mySession.setAttribute("bcolor", color); //store color
    mySession.setAttribute("hitCount", hitCount);
    mySession.setAttribute("name", name); //store user name
  }
  else //user has previously submitted HTML form
  {
    //get color, name, and hit count from session
    color = (String)mySession.getAttribute("bcolor");
    name = (String)mySession.getAttribute("name");
    hitCount = (Integer)mySession.getAttribute("hitCount");
  }

  //increment hit count and store in session
  mySession.setAttribute("hitCount",
    new Integer(hitCount.intValue() + 1));

  out.println("<HTML>");
  out.println("<HEAD>");
  out.println("<TITLE>Color Selected</TITLE>");
  out.println("</HEAD>");
  out.println("<BODY BGCOLOR=\"" + color + "\">");
```

```
      out.println("<H2>Hello " + name + "!</H2>");
      out.println("<H3>You have requested this page " +
        hitCount.toString() + " times.<BR>");
      out.println("Notice how session management allows me " +
        "to remember<BR>");
      out.println("who you are, how many times you've " +
        "requested this page,<BR>");
      out.println("and your preferred background color.<P>");
      out.println("<A HREF=\"ColorSessionServlet\">Reload " +
        "Page</A></H3>");
      out.println("</BODY>");
      out.println("</HTML>");
    }
    out.close();
  }


  /**
   * Returns a brief description of this servlet.
   *
   * @return Brief description of servlet
   */
  public String getServletInfo()
  {
    return "Servlet uses session management to maintain color.";
  }
}
```

Figure 14.3 shows the HTML form generated by Listing 14.2 that prompts users for their names and color preferences. When the form shown in Figure 14.3 is submitted, the page shown in Figure 14.4 is displayed. Each time the **Reload Page** hyperlink is clicked, the page hit counter increases by one.

So far, we have seen how cookies are used to manage state and session. Now let's examine how the Servlet API simplifies the process of using rewritten URLs to implement session management. The following servlet (see Listing 14.3) uses the encodeURL() method of the HttpServletResponse object to add a session ID (named jsessionid) to all URLs.

NOTE: Due to a few bugs, Tomcat 3.1 does not properly support URL rewriting. However, these problems have been remedied in Tomcat 3.2, which fully supports URL rewriting.

Listing 14.3   Using rewritten URLs for session management.

```
import javax.servlet.*;
import javax.servlet.http.*;
import java.io.*;
```

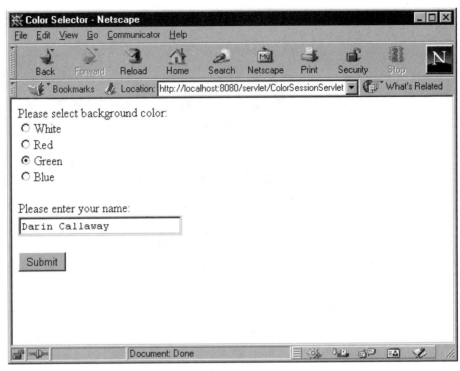

Figure 14.3   Generated by Listing 14.2, Prompts User for Name and Background Color

```
/**
 * The URLSessionServlet demonstrates how the servlet API makes
 * it easy to use rewritten URLs for session management rather
 * than cookies.
 */
public class URLSessionServlet extends HttpServlet
{
  /**
   * Tracks the number of times a user has requested this servlet
   * using rewritten URLs to maintain session.
   */
  public void service(HttpServletRequest request,
    HttpServletResponse response) throws ServletException,
    IOException
  {
    //get current session or, if necessary, create a new one
    HttpSession mySession = request.getSession(true);

    //get hit count from session
    Integer hits = (Integer)mySession.getAttribute("hitCounter");

    if (hits == null) //hitCounter value not in session
    {
      hits = new Integer(1); //start hit count at 1
    }
```

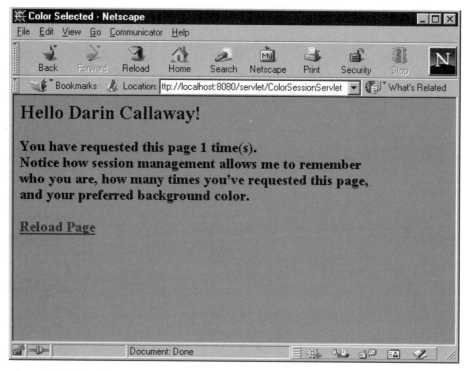

Figure 14.4   Page Demonstrates How Listing 14.2 Uses Session Management.

```
else //session contains hitCounter
{
  //increment hit counter
  hits = new Integer(hits.intValue() + 1);
}

//store hit count in session
mySession.setAttribute("hitCounter", hits);

//MIME type to return is HTML
response.setContentType("text/html");

//get a handle to the output stream
PrintWriter out = response.getWriter();

//generate HTML document to send to client
out.println("<HTML>");
out.println("<HEAD>");
out.println("<TITLE>Rewritten URLs Example</TITLE>");
out.println("</HEAD>");
out.println("<BODY>");
out.println("You have visited this page " + hits +
  " times.<P>");
```

```
            //create a hyperlink to reload the page
            out.println("<A HREF=\"" +
                response.encodeURL("/servlet/URLSessionServlet") +
                "\">Reload Page</A>");

            //create a submit button to reload the page
            out.println("<FORM METHOD=\"POST\" ACTION=\"" +
                response.encodeURL("/servlet/URLSessionServlet") + "\">");
            out.println("<INPUT TYPE=\"SUBMIT\" VALUE=\"Reload Page\">");
            out.println("</FORM>");

            out.println("</BODY>");
            out.println("</HTML>");

            out.close(); //close output stream
        }

        /**
         * Returns a brief description of this servlet.
         *
         * @return Brief description of servlet
         */
        public String getServletInfo()
        {
            return "Manages session using rewritten URLs.";
        }
    }
```

That's all there is to it. To encode the session ID into a hyperlink, simply pass the URL to the encodeURL() method of the HttpServletResponse object. Similarly, to maintain session when an HTML form is submitted, the URL within the ACTION attribute of the <FORM> tag must be encoded. Though intended to demonstrate rewritten URLs, the URLSessionServlet shown in Listing 14.3 works with either cookies or rewritten URLs. The implementation of the encodeURL() method checks to see if encoding is required. If URL rewriting is not required (e.g., the client supports cookies or session tracking is not enabled), the URL is returned unchanged. Otherwise, the session ID is added to the query string of the URL. For example, if cookie support on the client is turned off, the HTML generated by the URLSessionServlet looks like this:

```
<HTML>
<HEAD>
<TITLE>Rewritten URLs Example</TITLE>
</HEAD>
<BODY>
You have visited this page 3 times.<P>
<A HREF="/servlet/
    URLSessionServlet;jsessionid=xeha06ntz1">Reload Page</A>
```

```
<FORM METHOD="POST" ACTION="/servlet/
  URLSessionServlet;jsessionid=xeha06ntz1">
<INPUT TYPE="SUBMIT" VALUE="Reload Page">
</FORM>
</BODY>
</HTML>
```

Notice how a session ID named jsessionid is appended to the URL's query string. When using rewritten URLs for session management, all URLs (including those in hyperlinks and <FORM> tags) should be encoded using the encodeURL() method. This practice will ensure that no matter where the user travels in a Web site, session integrity will be maintained.

NOTE: The HttpServletResponse object also supports a method called encodeRedirectURL(). This method adds the session ID to the URL to which the client is being redirected. The following code demonstrates how a client can be redirected to a new URL without losing session:

```
response.sendRedirect(response.encodeRedirectURL(
  "http://www.insideservlets.com/orders.html"));
```

The implementation of the encodeRedirectURL() method determines whether session encoding is necessary. If encoding is unnecessary (e.g., the client supports cookies), the URL is returned unchanged. Since the rules regarding whether a URL requires encoding may differ between a redirect and a normal link, this method is provided separately. The following HTTP header illustrates how the session ID is passed in a redirect.

```
HTTP/1.1 302 Moved Temporarily
Date: Sat, 08 Apr 2000 04:24:35 GMT
Server: Apache/1.3.9 (Win32)
Location: http://www.insideservlets.com/
  orders.html;jsessionid=xeha06ntz1
Content-Type: text/html
```

Notice that the session ID is appended to the redirect URL designated by the Location header.

Although the Servlet API supports other methods of managing state and session, it is recommended that cookies be used when available. Since cookies require less coding and lower overhead, they are the preferred session management method.

Session Listeners and Events

The Servlet API provides a method of notifying an object whenever it is added to (i.e., bound) or removed from (i.e., unbound) a session. This notification allows an object to perform initialization tasks when it is bound to a session and to "clean up" after itself when unbound (perhaps releasing resources such as a database or network connection).

An object indicates that it wishes to be notified whenever it is bound to or unbound from a session by implementing the `javax.servlet.http.HttpSessionBindingListener` interface. The `HttpSession` object (the event source) automatically notifies all objects that implement this interface whenever they are added to or removed from the session (there is no need to call an `addListener()` method). The `HttpSession` object notifies an `HttpSessionBindingListener` object that it is being bound to or unbound from the session by calling its `valueBound()` and `valueUnbound()` methods. The `valueBound()` method is invoked when the object is added to the session and the `valueUnbound()` method is called when the object is removed from the session. Each of these methods receive an `HttpSessionBindingEvent` object that includes information about the binding event such as the name under which the object is stored and the session to which it is being added or removed. The two methods defined by the `HttpSessionBindingListener` interface are as follows:

```
public void valueBound(HttpSessionBindingEvent event)
public void valueUnbound(HttpSessionBindingEvent event)
```

NOTE: When a session expires or is invalidated, the `valueUnbound()` method is called on all objects stored within the session that implement the `HttpSessionBindingListener` interface.

The `HttpSessionBindingEvent` object implements two methods that convey information regarding the binding event. These methods are `getName()` and `getSession()`. The `getName()` method returns a `String` object containing the name under which the object is bound to the session. The `getSession()` method returns an `HttpSession` object representing the session to which the `HttpSessionBindingListener` object is being added or removed. The `SessionBindingServlet` presented in Listing 14.4 demonstrates the use of the `HttpSessionBindingListener` and `HttpSessionBindingEvent` objects.

Listing 14.4 Servlet notifies an object when it is added to the session.

```
import javax.servlet.*;
import javax.servlet.http.*;
import java.io.*;
```

```java
/**
 * The SessionBindingServlet demonstrates how an object that
 * implements HttpSessionBindingListener is notified when it is
 * bound to or unbound from the session.
 */
public class SessionBindingServlet extends HttpServlet
{
  /**
   * Generates an HTML form that allows the user to bind an
   * object to and unbind an object from the session.
   */
  public void service(HttpServletRequest request,
    HttpServletResponse response) throws ServletException,
    IOException
  {
    HttpSession session = request.getSession(true);
    PrintWriter out = response.getWriter();

    response.setContentType("text/html");

    //get the name of the session object as specified by user
    String sessionName = request.getParameter("Name");
    if (sessionName == null)
    {
      sessionName = ""; //default to empty string
    }

    //generate HTML form
    out.println("<HTML>");
    out.println("<HEAD>");
    out.println("<TITLE>Session Binding Servlet</TITLE>");
    out.println("</HEAD>");
    out.println("<BODY>");
    out.println("<FORM METHOD=\"POST\" ACTION=\"" +
      "/servlet/SessionBindingServlet\">");
    out.println("Name of session object: ");
    out.println("<INPUT TYPE=\"TEXT\" NAME=\"Name\" VALUE=\"" +
      sessionName + "\"> ");
    out.println("<INPUT TYPE=\"SUBMIT\" NAME=\"Bind\" " +
      "VALUE=\"Bind\"> ");
    out.println("<INPUT TYPE=\"SUBMIT\" NAME=\"Unbind\" " +
      "VALUE=\"Unbind\"><BR><BR>");
    out.println("</FORM>");

    //Binds or unbinds an object according to user instructions
    if (!sessionName.equals(""))
    {
      if (request.getParameter("Bind") != null) //bind object
      {
        SessionObject object = new SessionObject();
        object.setWriter(out);

        //bind SessionObject to the session
        session.setAttribute(sessionName, object);
      }
```

```
      else if (request.getParameter("Unbind") != null) //unbind
      {
        SessionObject object =
          (SessionObject)session.getAttribute(sessionName);

        if (object != null)
        {
          object.setWriter(out);

          //unbind SessionObject from the session
          session.removeAttribute(request.getParameter("Name"));
        }
      }
    }

  out.println("</BODY>");
  out.println("</HTML>");
}


/**
 * Inner class that implements the HttpSessionBindingListener
 * interface and will be notified whenever it is bound to or
 * unbound from the session.
 */
private class SessionObject implements
  HttpSessionBindingListener
{
  PrintWriter out;

  /**
   * Stores the output stream to the client.
   *
   * @param out Client output stream
   */
  public void setWriter(PrintWriter out)
  {
    this.out = out;
  }

  /**
   * Called when this object is bound to the session.
   *
   * @param event HttpSessionBindingEvent object
   */
  public void valueBound(HttpSessionBindingEvent event)
  {
    out.println("<B>Object Bound to Session</B><BR>");
    out.println("Name: " + event.getName() + "<BR>");
    out.println("Session ID: " + event.getSession().getId());
  }

  /**
   * Called when this object is unbound from the session.
   *
```

```
    * @param event HttpSessionBindingEvent object
    */
   public void valueUnbound(HttpSessionBindingEvent event)
   {
     out.println("<B>Object Unbound from Session</B><BR>");
     out.println("Name: " + event.getName() + "<BR>");
     out.println("Session ID: " + event.getSession().getId());
   }
 }
}
```

SessionBindingServlet defines an inner class called SessionObject that implements the HttpSessionBindingListener interface. This servlet allows the user to bind a new SessionObject to the session and to specify the name under which it should be bound. The user can also unbind objects from the session by name. Notice that SessionObject notifies the client (from within its value-Bound() method) when it is added to the session (see Figure 14.5). Likewise, SessionObject notifies the client (from within its valueUnbound() method) when it is removed from the session (see Figure 14.6).

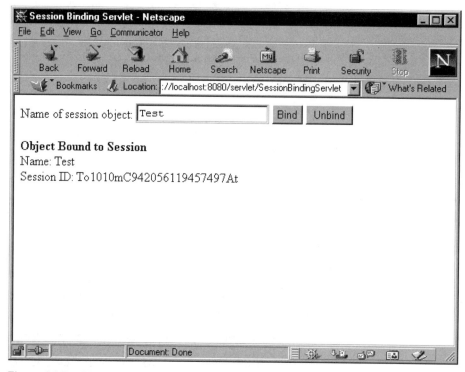

Figure 14.5   Object Notifies Client That It Was Added to the Session.

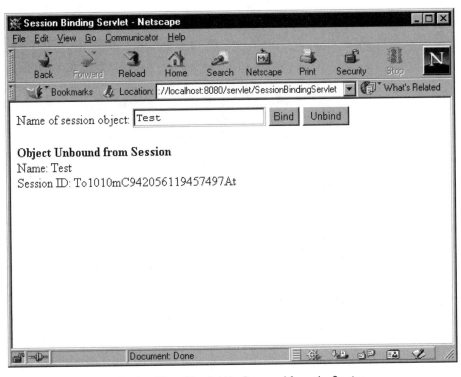

Figure 14.6 Object Notifies Client That It Was Removed from the Session.

Summary

As demonstrated in this chapter, the Servlet API provides a simple and straightforward method of implementing session management. With the addition of these mechanisms, the Servlet API allows the developer to build Web applications that provide an extraordinary level of user interaction. Session management provides a richer Web experience by enabling user-specific preferences, electronic shopping carts, enforcement of security policies, and much more.

This concludes our discussion of state and session management. In the next chapter, we will learn how to forward requests to other servlets, how to invoke a servlet from within an HTML document, and how to direct the output of one servlet to the input of another.

Chapter Highlights

- HTTP is a stateless protocol. A protocol is said to be *stateless* if it has no memory of prior connections and cannot distinguish one client's request from that of another.

- An HTTP session associates each request received by the server with the client that issued it. This association is accomplished by requiring the client to return some specific piece of information with each new request. This piece of information allows the server to identify the client. Sessions are used to maintain state and client identity across multiple requests.

- In this chapter, we often refer to "state/session" management. However, there is a distinct difference between state management and session management. *State management* is the ability to maintain a client's current state by passing client-specific information between the client and server. In contrast, *session management* maintains both state and identity. Session management provides an association between the client and the server that allows the server to uniquely identify each client. This association persists across requests for a specified period of time.

- There are several methods that facilitate the exchange of session IDs between the client and the server. These techniques include storing the session ID in the URL's path, implementing rewritten URLs, and using cookies to pass session information.

- The session management implementation in the Servlet API revolves around an interface called HttpSession. An HttpSession object encapsulates the essential information of an HTTP session, such as a unique session ID and other client-specific information.

- By default, the session management mechanisms in the Servlet API use cookies. Cookies are used by default because of the increased overhead required to implement rewritten URLs. However, the Servlet API does provide methods to determine if the client lacks cookie support, in which case rewritten URLs can be used instead.

- The Servlet API provides a method of notifying an object whenever it is bound to or unbound from a session. Objects that implement the HttpSessionBindingInterface are notified whenever they are added to or removed from the session by invoking their valueBound() or valueUnbound() methods.

CHAPTER 15

Request Forwarding, Server-Side Includes, Servlet Chaining

Using the RequestDispatcher object, the Servlet API defines a standard method of programmatically forwarding requests to and including content from other server resources. Additionally, though not defined by the Java Servlet Specification, many servlet containers support advanced functionality such as server-side includes and servlet chaining. In this chapter, we will examine all of these techniques. Specifically, the following topics are covered:

- Using the RequestDispatcher object
- Server-side includes
- Servlet chaining

Using the RequestDispatcher Object

The RequestDispatcher object allows requests to be forwarded to other server resources. In addition, this object allows the output generated by other server resources to be programmatically included within a servlet. Since the sole purpose of this object is to forward requests and include data, the RequestDispatcher object supports only two methods—forward() and include(). In this section, we will examine both of these methods.

RequestDispatcher is a Java interface. An object that implements this interface can be acquired using the ServletContext object's getRequestDispatcher() method, as demonstrated below. This example assumes that a servlet called AccountBalance already exists.

```
public void doGet(HttpServletRequest request,
  HttpServletResponse response) throws ServletException,
  IOException
{
  //create a string object with URL to the server resource
  String path = "/servlet/AccountBalance?cust_id=1234";

  //get a reference to the ServletContext object
  ServletContext context = getServletContext();

  //create a new RequestDispatcher object
  RequestDispatcher rd = context.getRequestDispatcher(path);
}
```

The getRequestDispatcher() method accepts a URL path that designates the server resource to which this request will be forwarded or from which content will be retrieved. The URL path references a local resource relative to the servlet's context root and, therefore, must begin with a forward slash ("/"). Fully qualified URLs are not permitted.

The RequestDispatcher object essentially serves as a "wrapper" around a server resource in order to provide request forwarding and server-side include functionality. Once you have created a RequestDispatcher object, you can use its forward() and include() methods to forward requests or include content generated by another server resource. Let's examine these methods now.

forward()

```
public void forward(ServletRequest request, ServletResponse
    response) throws ServletException, java.io.IOException
```

The forward() method of the RequestDispatcher object allows you to programmatically forward a request to another servlet (or other server resource) known as a *delegate*. Because forwarding passes all control to the new resource, you should not disrupt the delegate's communication with the client by retrieving a handle to the output stream (i.e., using the getWriter() or getOutputStream() method) or setting any HTTP headers (i.e., using the setHeader() or setStatus() method). These tasks should be left to the servlet to which the request is forwarded. However, the current servlet may do some preprocessing before the request is forwarded.

Let's take a look at a simple example of forwarding a request from one servlet to another. Again, this example assumes that a servlet called Account-Balance already exists.

```
public void doGet(HttpServletRequest request,
  HttpServletResponse response) throws ServletException,
  IOException
{
  //...execute all request preprocessing here...

  String path = "/servlet/AccountBalance?cust_id=1234";
  ServletContext context = getServletContext();
  RequestDispatcher rd = context.getRequestDispatcher(path);

  rd.forward(request, response); //forward request
}
```

The forward() method of the RequestDispatcher object passes the current request to the servlet designated by the path variable. Unlike the include() method, control will never return to the servlet that forwards the request. The forward() method permanently passes control to the delegate servlet, which will generate the response. Notice that both the request and response objects are passed to the delegate so that it may read from the request and generate an appropriate response.

NOTE: The request must be forwarded before the response has been committed (i.e., before the output buffer has been flushed to the client). If forward() is called after the response has been committed, an IllegalStateException is thrown.

You may have noticed that the URL path designated here includes a query string to pass information to the delegate servlet. This information can be read by the delegate using the request object's getParameter() method. (Parameters specified in the query string used to create the Request-Dispatcher take precedence over existing parameters.) However, there is a better way to pass information to a delegate servlet. The ServletRequest object's setAttribute() method allows any number of Java objects to be stored within the request object itself (which may be forwarded to another servlet). These stored objects can then be read by the delegate servlet using the request object's getAttribute() method. In addition, you may use the getAttributeNames() method to determine the names of all attributes stored in the request (it returns an Enumeration).

NOTE: Whenever an attribute is retrieved from the request, it is returned as a java.lang.Object (the base object from which all Java objects extend). Therefore, when retrieving objects from the request, it is necessary to downcast the object back to its original class. Downcasting is the process of typecasting (or converting) an object to a class lower in the object hierarchy. For example, the following code stores a Customer object in the session and then retrieves it as a Customer (by downcasting).

```
request.setAttribute("Customer", new Customer());
Customer cust = (Customer)session.getAttribute("Customer");
```

Therefore, rather than just passing string criteria using the URL path's query string, it is possible to pass actual Java objects to the delegate servlet. The following sample code demonstrates how attributes can be stored in the request rather than passing information in the query string.

```
public void doGet(HttpServletRequest request,
   HttpServletResponse response) throws ServletException,
   IOException
{
   //...execute all request preprocessing here...

   Customer cust = new Customer(1234); //create customer object
   request.setAttribute("Customer", cust);

   String path = "/servlet/AccountBalance";
   ServletContext context = getServletContext();
   RequestDispatcher rd = context.getRequestDispatcher(path);

   rd.forward(request, response); //forward request
}
```

Once the object is stored in the request using the setAttribute() method, the delegate servlet can extract the object using getAttribute ("*ATTRIBUTE _NAME*") and finish processing the request like this:

```
public void doGet(HttpServletRequest request,
   HttpServletResponse response) throws ServletException,
   IOException
{
   PrintWriter out = response.getWriter();

   //get Customer object out of request
   Customer cust = (Customer)request.getAttribute("Customer");

   out.println("Welcome, " + cust.getName()); //greet customer
}
```

include()

```
public void include(ServletRequest request, ServletResponse
    response) throws ServletException, java.io.IOException
```

The include() method of the RequestDispatcher object allows you to programmatically include content generated by another servlet (or other server resource) within the body of the calling servlet's response. Although both servlets cooperate in generating the response, only the original servlet can alter the response header. The included servlet cannot change the status of the response or set HTTP headers. Rather, setting the proper response status code and headers is the calling servlet's responsibility. Unlike the forward() method, control is returned to the calling servlet once the delegate servlet completes its processing. The delegate's output is then added to the body of the calling servlet's response. The following sample code demonstrates how a customer's balance is calculated by a delegate servlet and included in the output of the calling servlet.

```
public void doGet(HttpServletRequest request,
  HttpServletResponse response) throws ServletException,
  IOException
{
  PrintWriter out = response.getWriter();

  Customer cust = new Customer(1234); //create customer object
  request.setAttribute("Customer", cust);

  String path = "/servlet/AccountBalance";
  ServletContext context = getServletContext();
  RequestDispatcher rd = context.getRequestDispatcher(path);

  out.println("Your account balance is: ");

  rd.include(request, response); //get content from delegate

  out.println("<BR>Thank you for your business!");
}
```

At times, a delegate servlet may find it necessary to examine information about the servlet from which it was invoked rather than information about the origin of the original request. A delegate servlet can determine the servlet from which it was invoked by evaluating the request attributes presented in Table 15.1 (attributes can be retrieved using the request object's getAttribute() method).

Like forward(), the include() method passes the request and response objects to the delegate servlet so that it can process the request and generate a response (which is included in the calling servlet's response). The Request-

Table 15.1   Request Attributes Specify Information about the Servlet That Performed an Include

Attribute Name	Description
`javax.servlet.include.request_uri`	URI requested by the servlet that invoked the `include()` method
`javax.servlet.include.context_path`	Context path requested by the servlet that invoked the `include()` method
`javax.servlet.include.servlet_path`	Servlet path requested by the servlet that invoked the `include()` method
`javax.servlet.include.path_info`	Path information following the servlet path requested by the servlet that invoked the `include()` method
`javax.servlet.include.query_string`	Query string requested by the servlet that invoked the `include()` method

`Dispatcher` object's `include()` method makes it simple to generate server-side includes programmatically.

Server-Side Includes

Server-side includes (SSIs) allow servlet calls to be embedded in an HTML document using a special `<servlet>` tag. By convention, these documents use the `.shtml` file extension. This extension indicates to the server that the HTML document includes SSI directives and, therefore, should be passed to a specialized SSI servlet for processing. This specialized servlet, called `SSIncludeServlet` on the Java Web Server, parses the HTML document searching for `<servlet>` tags. When a `<servlet>` tag is encountered, `SSIncludeServlet` loads the servlet specified by the `<servlet>` tag (if not already loaded), executes it (passing any parameters included in the `<servlet>` tag), and includes the servlet's output in the HTML page that is returned to the client. The following sequence of events may help clarify the SSI process.

1. The server receives a request for the file *index.shtml*.
2. The Java-enabled server maps all `*.shtml` files to the SSI servlet. Thus, the client's request for *index.shtml* is passed to the SSI servlet for processing. (Although the extension `.shtml` is mapped to the SSI servlet by default, custom aliases may also be defined that map other extensions to the SSI servlet.)
3. The SSI servlet parses the requested HTML document searching for `<servlet>` tags. When a `<servlet>` tag is located, the SSI servlet reads any

initialization parameters (from the tag) and loads the servlet referenced by the tag (if necessary). It then reads any parameters included in the tag and, along with the request, passes them to the specified servlet.

4. The servlet specified by the `<servlet>` tag generates data that is included in the HTML page returned to the client. Essentially, the `<servlet>` tag is replaced by the specified servlet's output.

NOTE: Server-side include functionality is defined by the servlet container (i.e., it is not part of the Java Servlet Specification). Therefore, SSI functionality can vary among servlet containers (or not be supported at all). For example, the Java Web Server uses a servlet called `SSIncludeServlet` to process server-side includes. However, each servlet container that supports SSI implements its own Server-Side Include servlet and may name it something other than `SSIncludeServlet`. For example, the Server-Side Include servlet implemented by the JRun servlet container is called `JRunSSI`.

Now that you understand how the process works, let's take a look at the syntax of the `<servlet>` tag.

```
<servlet name="servlet_name"
  code="class_name"
  codebase="class_location_url"
  init_param1="value1"
  init_param2="value2"
  init_paramN="valueN">
<param name="servlet_param1" value="value1">
<param name="servlet_param2" value="value2">
<param name="servlet_paramN" value="valueN">
</servlet>
```

Using the `<servlet>` tag, servlets can be referenced by alias name or class name. To specify a servlet by alias, use the `name` attribute. To reference a servlet by class name (with or without the `.class` extension), use the `code` attribute instead of the `name` attribute. When a `<servlet>` tag is located, the SSI servlet attempts to load the servlet specified by the `name` attribute first. If the `name` attribute does not exist or the named servlet cannot be found, the servlet specified by the `code` attribute is loaded. The `codebase` attribute is optional but useful if the servlet must be loaded from a remote location.

All other name/value pairs in the `<servlet>` tag are passed as initialization parameters (i.e., they can be retrieved using the `ServletConfig` object's `getInitParameter()` method). Additionally, any number of `PARAM` tags may be included between `<servlet>` and `</servlet>`. These name/value pairs are passed to the specified servlet as parameters (i.e., they can be retrieved using the HttpServletRequest object's getParameter() method).

Now let's put server-side includes to work. Our goal is to standardize all of our company's Web pages by applying a standard header and footer to each. Listings 15.1 and 15.2 show two servlets that generate this header and footer.

Listing 15.1   Servlet that returns a standard header.

```
import javax.servlet.*;
import javax.servlet.http.*;
import java.io.*;
import java.util.Date;
import java.text.DateFormat;

/**
 * Header Servlet
 *
 * This servlet returns a standard header.
 */
public class HeaderServlet extends HttpServlet
{
  /**
   * Generates a page header and includes a message if one is
   * defined in the <servlet> tag's parameter list.
   */
  public void doGet(HttpServletRequest request,
    HttpServletResponse response) throws ServletException,
    IOException
  {
    response.setContentType("text/html"); //HTML output

    //get handle to output stream
    PrintWriter out = response.getWriter();

    //create a DateFormat object to format our Date object
    DateFormat longDate = DateFormat.getDateInstance(
      DateFormat.LONG);

    //generate header HTML
    out.println("<CENTER><FONT SIZE=6><B>SourceStream</B>" +
      "</FONT><BR>");
    out.println(longDate.format(new Date()));

    if (request.getParameter("message") != null)
    {
      out.println("<BR>" + request.getParameter("message"));
    }

    out.println("</CENTER><HR>");

    out.close(); //close output stream
  }
}
```

Listing 15.2   Servlet that returns a standard footer.

```
import javax.servlet.*;
import javax.servlet.http.*;
import java.io.*;

/**
 * Footer Servlet
 *
 * This servlet returns a standard footer.
 */
public class FooterServlet extends HttpServlet
{
  /**
   * Generates a page footer.
   */
  public void doGet(HttpServletRequest request,
    HttpServletResponse response) throws ServletException,
    IOException
  {
    response.setContentType("text/html"); //HTML output

    //get handle to output stream
    PrintWriter out = response.getWriter();

    //generate footer HTML
    out.println("<HR><CENTER><FONT SIZE=2>Copyright &copy 2000"+
      "SourceStream. All Rights Reserved.</FONT></CENTER>");

    out.close(); //close output stream
  }
}
```

Let's use these two servlets to add a consistent "look and feel" to the HTML document shown in Listing 15.3. Be sure to notice the placement of the <servlet> tags and the message passed to the header servlet from within a <param> tag. This HTML document, in conjunction with the header and footer servlets, produces the display shown in Figure 15.1.

Listing 15.3   Server-side includes used to add header and footer.

```
<HTML>
<HEAD>
<TITLE>Servlet API Support</TITLE>
</HEAD>
<BODY>

<servlet code="HeaderServlet">
  <param name="message" value="Welcome to SourceStream">
</servlet>
<BR>
Here is a small sample of the servers that support servlets:<P>
<LI>Allaire JRun
```

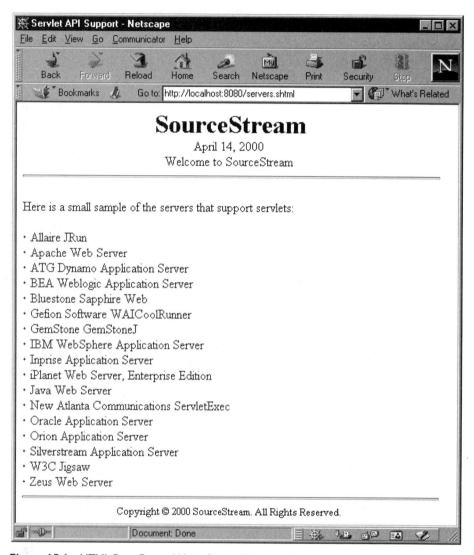

Figure 15.1   HTML Page Created Using Server-Side Includes

```
<LI>Apache Web Server
<LI>ATG Dynamo Application Server
<LI>BEA Weblogic Application Server
<LI>Bluestone Sapphire Web
<LI>Gefion Software WAICoolRunner
<LI>GemStone GemStoneJ
<LI>IBM WebSphere Application Server
<LI>Inprise Application Server
<LI>iPlanet Web Server, Enterprise Edition
```

```
<LI>Java Web Server
<LI>New Atlanta Communications ServletExec
<LI>Oracle Application Server
<LI>Orion Application Server
<LI>Silverstream Application Server
<LI>W3C Jigsaw
<LI>Zeus Web Server
<BR><BR>
<servlet code="FooterServlet"></servlet>

</BODY>
</HTML>
```

To test server-side includes on your machine, start by compiling the header and footer servlets and placing them in your server's servlet directory. Next, save the HTML presented in Listing 15.3 to a file called *servers.shtml* (remember to use the .shtml extension so that the server will know that this file should be parsed for <servlet> tags) and store this file in your servlet-enabled Web server's document root. Lastly, request the HTML file from your browser using a URL similar to the following:

```
http://localhost:8080/servers.shtml
```

You might be starting to recognize the power of server-side includes. The preceding example demonstrates that, through server-side includes, the standard header and footer displayed on all HTML pages can be changed by simply altering the servlets that generated them. This technique ensures a consistent "look and feel" across an entire Web site and greatly simplifies the task of changing headers and footers used by numerous pages. Better yet, the header and footer can include dynamic information since they are created by a servlet.

Of course, this example demonstrates only one possible application of server-side includes. In addition to establishing a consistent "look and feel," server-side includes can provide flexible customization. For example, an SSI servlet might check the time of day in order to include a "Good Morning," "Good Afternoon," or "Good Evening" message to users. Or perhaps after a user logs in, a server-side include servlet checks a database and displays a customized message if it is the user's birthday. As you can see, there are countless uses for this powerful feature.

Servlet Chaining

Servlet chaining is the process of passing the output of one servlet to the input of another. This feature is very similar to piping in UNIX or DOS. As shown in Figure 15.2, servlet chaining works as follows. The client request is sent to the

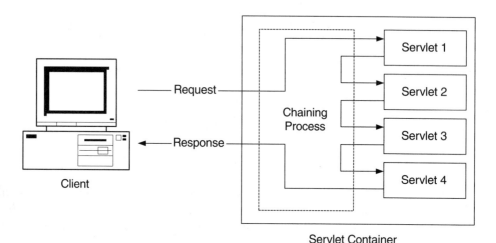

Figure 15.2   The Servlet Chaining Process

first servlet in the chain. Once the request has been processed by the servlet, it passes its output to the next servlet in the chain. This process continues through any number of servlets until the last servlet's output is returned to the client. The getWriter() or getInputStream() method of HttpServletRequest can be used to read the previous servlet's output.

In this chapter, we will examine how to create a servlet chain using the JRun servlet container. Though most servlet containers operate similarly, keep in mind that servlet chain configuration is container specific and may differ among servlet containers. Consult your servlet container's documentation for information regarding how to configure a servlet chain.

NOTE: Servlet API 2.3 defines functionality similar to servlet chaining that is known as servlet filtering. However, unlike servlet chaining, servlet filtering is part of the Java Servlet Specification and, therefore, it is completely portable among all Servlet API 2.3–compatible containers. See Chapter 26 for more information about servlet filtering.

Servlet chaining is most often used to filter a servlet's output. As a response moves through the servlet chain, each successive servlet alters (or filters) the response in some way and passes it along to the next servlet (eventually returning the response to the client). The UpperCaseFilter servlet shown in Listing 15.4 is a good example of this concept. This servlet reads the output generated by the previous servlet in the chain and converts all text to uppercase. It then passes the altered response along the chain or back to the client (if it is at the end of the chain).

Listing 15.4   Servlet that converts all input to uppercase.

```
import javax.servlet.*;
import javax.servlet.http.*;
import java.io.*;

/**
 * The UpperCaseFilter servlet is meant to be used within a
 * servlet chain. This servlet reads the output generated by a
 * previous servlet and converts all text to uppercase.
 */
public class UpperCaseFilter extends HttpServlet
{
  /**
   * Reads the output from a previous servlet and converts all
   * text to uppercase before passing the request along the
   * chain or returning it to the client.
   */
  public void doGet(HttpServletRequest request,
    HttpServletResponse response) throws ServletException,
    IOException
  {
    //set content type to the same as previous servlet
    response.setContentType(request.getContentType());

    PrintWriter out = response.getWriter();
    BufferedReader in = request.getReader();

    String line; //stores each line of previous servlet's output

    //read each line of previous servlet's output
    while ((line = in.readLine()) != null)
    {
      out.println(line.toUpperCase()); //convert line to upper
    }

    out.close(); //close output stream
  }
}
```

Now that we have a filtering servlet, let's add it to a servlet chain and see how it works. The simplest way to create a servlet chain using JRun is to use a comma-delimited servlet list in the URL. For example, to invoke a servlet chain that first calls SnoopServlet (a sample servlet that ships with JRun) and then passes its output to the UpperCaseFilter servlet, type the following URL into your browser's address field.

```
http://localhost:8080/servlet/SnoopServlet,UpperCaseFilter
```

Since all output produced by SnoopServlet is piped to the UpperCase-
Filter servlet, the response is completely converted to uppercase as shown in
Figure 15.3. In addition to using a comma-delimited list of servlets in the URL,
a servlet chain can also be created by adding a servlet mapping that references
a comma-delimited list of servlets (see Figure 15.4). Since only the servlet
mapping is required and not the entire list of chained servlets, this approach
can greatly simplify the URL. For example, the servlet mapping created in Figure 15.4 can be called using the following URL.

```
http://localhost:8080/snoop
```

In addition to the methods presented previously, there is yet another way to
chain servlets. Through a process known as *MIME chaining*, it is possible to
dynamically chain one servlet to another based on the MIME type of its output
(as designated by the Content-Type HTTP header). For example, it is possible to
configure the servlet container to direct all servlet output of content type text/
upper (or some other user-defined MIME type) through the UpperCaseFilter

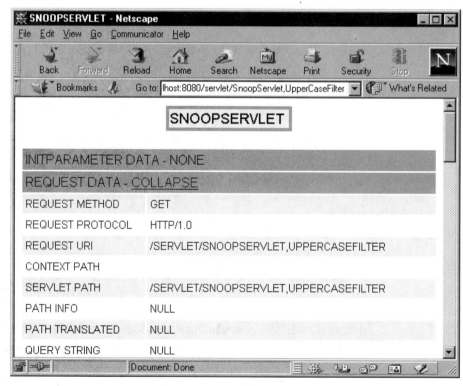

Figure 15.3   Output Produced by Chaining SnoopServlet to UpperCaseFilter

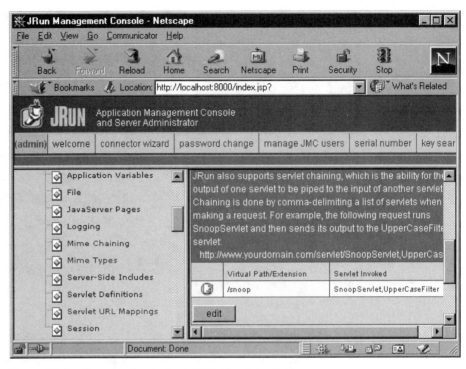

Figure 15.4 Creating a Servlet Chain URL Mapping with JRun

servlet (see Figure 15.5). In this way, whenever you wish to use `UpperCaseFilter`, you can simply set the `Content-Type` of the response to `text/upper` (using the `HttpServletResponse` object's `setContentType()` method) and the servlet's output will automatically be routed through the `UpperCaseFilter` servlet. For example, consider the servlet shown in Listing 15.5.

Listing 15.5 Servlet that sets its MIME content type to `text/upper`.

```
import javax.servlet.*;
import javax.servlet.http.*;
import java.io.*;

/**
 * MimeChainTest servlet sets the MIME content type of its
 * response to text/upper and returns a simple message.
 */
public class MimeChainTest extends HttpServlet
{
  /**
   * Generates a simple message.
   */
```

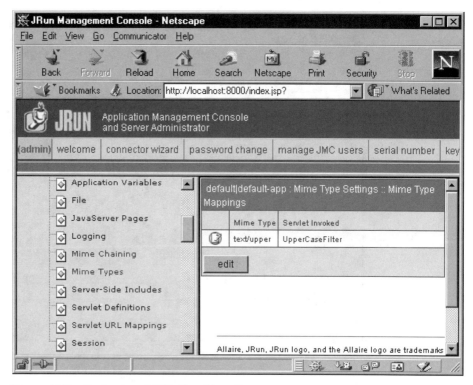

Figure 15.5   Configuring a MIME Chain Using JRun

```
public void doGet(HttpServletRequest request,
  HttpServletResponse response) throws ServletException,
  IOException
{
  //set to user-defined type that will trigger mime chain
  response.setContentType("text/upper");

  //get handle to output stream
  PrintWriter out = response.getWriter();

  //generate footer HTML
  out.println("The quick brown fox jumped over the lazy dog.");

  out.close(); //close output stream
  }
}
```

Listing 15.5 demonstrates a simple servlet that generates output of type text/upper. Since the servlet container has been configured to direct all text/upper output through UpperCaseFilter, this servlet will be dynamically chained to the UpperCaseFilter servlet. Of course, this MIME chain will convert all output generated by the `MimeChainTest` servlet to uppercase. However, there is one caveat. While using MIME chaining, you must alter the `UpperCaseFilter` servlet so that the content type of its output is set to `text/html` (or some MIME type other than `text/upper`). This is necessary for two reasons. First of all, `text/upper` is a user-defined MIME type that the browser will not understand. And second, if the MIME type is not altered, the servlet will enter an endless loop as its output is directed back to itself. In order to prevent continuous routing of a servlet's output to itself, the filtering servlet must alter the content type whenever MIME chaining is used.

Summary

This chapter demonstrates how the `RequestDispatcher` object can be used to programmatically forward requests to and include output from other server resources. In addition, this chapter presents a powerful technique called server-side includes that allows servlet calls to be embedded in an HTML document. Finally, the concept of servlet chaining is demonstrated. In the next chapter, we will learn how to add database connectivity to a servlet using JDBC.

Chapter Highlights

- The `RequestDispatcher` object allows you to forward requests to or include output from other server resources.
- The `forward()` method of the `RequestDispatcher` object allows you to programmatically forward a request to another servlet (or other server resource) known as a *delegate*.
- The `include()` method of the `RequestDispatcher` object allows you to programmatically include content generated by another servlet (or other server resource) within the body of the calling servlet's response.
- Though not defined by the Java Servlet Specification, many servlet containers support advanced functionality such as server-side includes and servlet chaining.
- *Server-side includes* allow you to embed servlet calls within an HTML document using a special `<servlet>` tag. By convention, these documents use the `.shtml` file extension. All `.shtml` files are passed to a special SSI servlet for processing.

- When a `<servlet>` tag is encountered, the SSI servlet loads the servlet specified in the `<servlet>` tag (if necessary), executes it (passing any parameters included in the `<servlet>` tag), and includes the servlet's output in the HTML page returned to the client.

- *Servlet chaining* is the process of passing the output of one servlet to the input of another.

- Servlet chaining works as follows: The client request is sent to the first servlet in the chain. Once the request has been processed by the servlet, it passes its output to the next servlet in the chain. This process continues through any number of servlets until the last servlet's output is returned to the client.

- Through a process known as *MIME chaining,* it is possible to dynamically chain one servlet to another based on the MIME type of its output (as designated by the `Content-Type` HTTP header).

CHAPTER 16

Database Access with JDBC

Storing and retrieving database information is one of the most common operations performed by servlets. In this chapter, we will examine the Java Database Connectivity (JDBC) API and demonstrate database connectivity from within a servlet. In addition, we will discuss some advanced database concepts, including prepared statements, transactions, stored procedures, and connection pooling. Finally, a sample JDBC servlet using the MySQL database will be presented.

This chapter provides a brief overview of a topic that could easily consume an entire book. In fact, many books currently focus completely on JDBC programming. Specifically, the following topics are covered in this chapter:

- JDBC architecture
- Accessing a database
- Advanced database concepts
- Database connection pooling
- Introduction to the MySQL database

JDBC Architecture

JDBC is an API specification developed by Sun Microsystems that defines a uniform interface for accessing various relational databases. JDBC is a core part of the Java platform and is included in the standard JDK distribution.

The primary function of the JDBC API is to provide a means for the developer to issue SQL statements and process the results in a consistent, database-independent manner. JDBC provides rich, object-oriented access to databases by defining classes and interfaces that represent objects such as:

- Database connections
- SQL statements

- Result sets
- Database metadata
- Prepared statements
- Binary Large Objects (BLOBs)
- Character Large Objects (CLOBs)
- Callable statements
- Database drivers
- Driver manager

The JDBC API uses a driver manager and database-specific drivers to provide transparent connectivity to heterogeneous databases. The *JDBC driver manager* ensures that the correct driver is used to access each data source. The driver manager is capable of supporting multiple concurrent drivers connected to multiple heterogeneous databases. The location of the driver manager with respect to the JDBC drivers and the servlet is shown in Figure 16.1.

A *JDBC driver* translates standard JDBC calls into a network or database protocol or into a database library API call that facilitates communication with

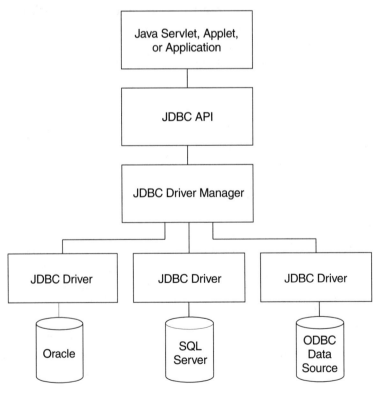

Figure 16.1   Layers of the JDBC Architecture

the database. This translation layer provides JDBC applications with database independence. If the back-end database changes, only the JDBC driver need be replaced with few code modifications required. There are four distinct types of JDBC drivers.

Type 1 *JDBC-ODBC Bridge.* Type 1 drivers act as a "bridge" between JDBC and another database connectivity mechanism such as ODBC. The JDBC-ODBC bridge provides JDBC access using most standard ODBC drivers. This driver is included in the Java 2 SDK within the sun.jdbc.odbc package. Finally, the JDBC-ODBC bridge requires that the native ODBC libraries, drivers, and required support files be installed and configured on each client employing a Type 1 driver. This requirement may present a serious limitation for many applications. (See Figure 16.2.)

Type 2 *Java to Native API.* Type 2 drivers use the Java Native Interface (JNI) to make calls to a local database library API. Type 2 drivers are usually faster than Type 1 drivers. Like Type 1 drivers, Type 2 drivers require native database client libraries to be installed and configured on the client machine. (See Figure 16.3.)

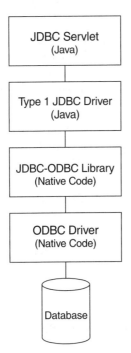

Figure 16.2   Type 1 JDBC Architecture

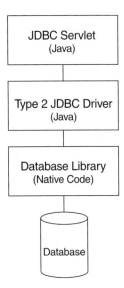

Figure 16.3   Type 2 JDBC Architecture

Type 3 *Java to Network Protocol.* Type 3 drivers are pure Java drivers that use a proprietary network protocol to communicate with JDBC middleware on the server. The middleware then translates the network protocol to database-specific function calls. Type 3 drivers are the most flexible JDBC solution because they do not require native database libraries on the client and can connect to many different databases on the back end. Type 3 drivers can be deployed over the Internet without client installation. (See Figure 16.4.)

Type 4 *Java to Database Protocol.* Type 4 drivers are pure Java drivers that implement a proprietary database protocol (like Oracle's SQL*Net) to communicate directly with the database. Like Type 3 drivers, they do not require native database libraries and can be deployed over the Internet without client installation. One drawback to Type 4 drivers is that they are database specific. Unlike Type 3 drivers, if your back-end database changes, you may have to purchase and deploy a new Type 4 driver (some Type 4 drivers are available free of charge from the database manufacturer). However, because Type 4 drivers communicate directly with the database engine rather than through middleware or a native library, they are usually the fastest JDBC drivers available. (See Figure 16.5.)

So, you may be asking yourself, "Which is the right type of driver for my application?" Well, that depends on the requirements of your particular project. If you do not have the opportunity or inclination to install and configure software on each client, you can rule out Type 1 and Type 2 drivers.

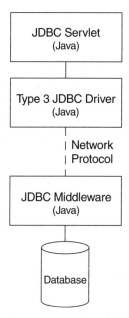

Figure 16.4 Type 3 JDBC Architecture

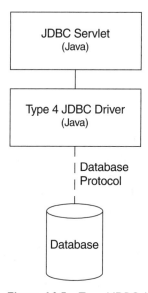

Figure 16.5 Type 4 JDBC Architecture

However, if the cost of Type 3 or Type 4 drivers is prohibitive, Type 1 and Type 2 drivers may become more attractive because they are usually available free of charge. Price aside, the debate will often boil down to whether to use a Type 3 or Type 4 driver for a particular application. In this case, you may need to weigh the benefits of flexibility and interoperability against performance. Type 3 drivers offer your application the ability to transparently access different types of databases, while Type 4 drivers usually exhibit better performance and, like Type 1 and Type 2 drivers, may be available free of charge from the database manufacturer. For more information, visit the following URL for a list of available JDBC drivers:

http://industry.java.sun.com/products/jdbc/drivers

Accessing a Database

The process of retrieving information from a database via JDBC involves these five basic steps:

1. Register the JDBC driver with the driver manager.
2. Establish a database connection.
3. Execute an SQL statement.
4. Process the results.
5. Close the database connection.

Let's examine how each of these steps is accomplished.

Register the JDBC Driver

Before a JDBC driver can be used to establish a database connection, it must first be registered with the driver manager. The driver manager's job is to maintain a reference to all driver objects that are available to JDBC clients. A JDBC driver automatically registers itself with the driver manager when it is loaded. To load a JDBC driver, use the `Class.forName().newInstance()` method call as demonstrated here:

```
Class.forName("sun.jdbc.odbc.JdbcOdbcDriver").newInstance();
```

`Class.forName()` is a static method that instructs the Java virtual machine to dynamically locate, load, and link the specified class (if not already loaded). If the class cannot be located, a `ClassNotFoundException` is thrown. The `newInstance()` method indicates that a new instance of this class should be created. (Alternatively, drivers can also be registered using the `DriverManager.registerDriver()` method.)

NOTE: In most cases, it is possible (and very common) to load a new JDBC driver using only the `Class.forName()` method call, excluding the `newInstance()` invocation, like this:

```
Class.forName("sun.jdbc.odbc.JdbcOdbcDriver");
```

This method usually works just fine. Unfortunately, some Java virtual machines do not properly call some static class initializers. On these virtual machines, driver registration will fail if the `newInstance()` method is not explicitly called. Therefore, to ensure that your JDBC driver will load regardless of the virtual machine in use, it is a good practice to always call the `newInstance()` method.

As you can see from this example, a JDBC driver is simply a Java class that resides in a valid CLASSPATH. In this case, we are loading the JDBC-ODBC bridge driver located in the `sun.jdbc.odbc` package.

Establish a Database Connection

Once the driver is loaded, we can use it to establish a connection to the database. A JDBC connection is identified by a *database URL* that tells the driver manager which driver and data source to use. The standard syntax for a database URL is shown here:

jdbc:*SUBPROTOCOL*:*SUBNAME*

The first part of the URL indicates that JDBC is being used to establish the connection. The *SUBPROTOCOL* is the name of a valid JDBC driver or other database connectivity solution. The *SUBNAME* is typically a logical name, or alias, that maps to a physical database. Though most database URLs closely follow the standard syntax, JDBC database URL conventions are flexible and allow each driver to define the information that should be included in its URL. To illustrate, Table 16.1 presents the syntax for three common JDBC database

Table 16.1 JDBC URLs for Common Data Sources

Database	JDBC Database URL
ODBC Data Source	`jdbc:odbc:`*DATA_SOURCE_NAME*
MySQL	`jdbc:mysql://`*SERVER*[:*PORT*]`/`*DATABASE_NAME*
Oracle	`jdbc:oracle:thin:@`*SERVER*:*PORT*:*INSTANCE_NAME*

URLs. Notice that each type of database driver requires different information within its URL.

To establish a database connection, use the `DriverManager` object's `get-Connection()` method. `getConnection()` is a `static` method that can be used like this:

```
Connection dbConn = DriverManager.getConnection(
  "jdbc:mysql://localhost/phonebook");
```

Or, for databases that require authentication, the connection can be established like this:

```
String username = "Erin", password = "secret";

Connection dbConn = DriverManager.getConnection(
  "jdbc:mysql://localhost/phonebook", username, password);
```

Within its `getConnection()` method, the `DriverManager` queries each registered driver until it finds one that recognizes the specified database URL. Once the correct driver is located, the `DriverManager` uses it to create the `Connection` object. The `DriverManager` and `Connection` objects (as well as all other JDBC objects) are contained in the `java.sql` package. Be sure to import this package when using JDBC.

NOTE: To improve performance of JDBC servlets, define your database connection as an instance variable and open the connection within the `init()` method (see sample code below). In this way, the database connection will be established only once (when the servlet is first loaded) and will be shared across all requests. However, this approach does raise some thread safety concerns. To avoid concurrency problems while maintaining high performance, use a database connection pool as demonstrated in the "Database Connection Pooling" section later in this chapter.

```
public class JdbcServlet extends HttpServlet
{
  //database connection is shared by all requests
  java.sql.Connection dbConn;

  public void init() throws ServletException
  {
    //...open database connection (dbConn) here...
  }
}
```

Execute an SQL Statement

Once established, the database connection can be used to submit SQL statements to the database. An SQL statement performs some operation on the database such as retrieving, inserting, updating, or deleting rows. To execute an SQL command, a `Statement` object must be created using the `Connection` object's `createStatement()` method. The `Statement` object provides methods to perform various operations against the database. A `Statement` object can be created as shown here:

```
Statement stmt = dbConn.createStatement();
```

Using the `Statement` object's `executeQuery()` method, information can be retrieved from the database. The `executeQuery()` method accepts an SQL SELECT statement and returns a `ResultSet` object containing the database rows extracted by the query. For inserts, updates, or deletes, use the `executeUpdate()` method. The `ResultSet` object can be created like this:

```
ResultSet rs = stmt.executeQuery("select * from employee");
```

Process the Results

To process the results, you can traverse the rows of the result set using the `ResultSet` object's `next()` and `previous()` methods (the `previous()` method is only available in JDBC 2.0 and later using certain types of result sets). The following sample code creates a `Statement` object, executes a query, and iterates through the result set. The `ResultSet` object's `getString()` method is used to extract the value of specific fields.

```
Statement stmt = dbConn.createStatement();
ResultSet rs = stmt.executeQuery("select * from employee");

while (rs.next())
{
  System.out.println(rs.getString("FIRST_NAME") + " " +
    rs.getString("LAST_NAME"));
}
```

It is important to keep in mind that the `ResultSet` object is tied to the `Statement` object that created it. If the `ResultSet` object's `Statement` is closed or used to execute another query, the `ResultSet` is closed automatically.

Close the Database Connection

Because database connections are a valuable and limited resource, you should close the connection when processing is complete. The Connection object provides a simple close() method for this purpose.

In addition to closing the database connection, you should also explicitly close all Statement and ResultSet objects using their close() methods. Although the Java virtual machine's garbage collector will eventually release resources that are no longer in scope, it is a good practice to manually release these objects as soon as they are no longer useful. To guarantee that database resources are always released (even in the case of an exception), database connections should be closed within a finally block as shown here:

```
try
{
  //...create statements and result sets here...

  rs.close();   //close ResultSet after use
  stmt.close(); //close Statement after use
}
catch (SQLException e)
{
  //...handle exception here...
}
finally
{
  try
  {
    if (dbConn != null)
    {
      dbConn.close(); //close Connection in finally block
    }
  }
  catch (SQLException e)
  {
    //...handle exception here...
  }
}
```

Of course, if you are sharing a database connection across all requests or using a connection-pooling strategy, you may not wish to close the database connection each time it is used. Holding a database connection open eliminates the overhead associated with creating a new connection for each request. For more information on database connection optimization, see the "Database Connection Pooling" section later in this chapter.

JDBC Basics

Creating Database Tables

The Structured Query Language (SQL) is a language used to create, manage, and query relational databases. SQL is largely comprised of two language subsets—the Data Definition Language (DDL) and the Data Manipulation Language (DML). The DDL defines the syntax for creating tables and indexes on an existing database. In contrast, the DML is used to retrieve, insert, delete, and modify data in database tables. This section demonstrates how to create database tables using the DDL. The rest of this chapter focuses on the DML.

The most common DDL statement is the CREATE TABLE command. As you may have guessed, this command is used to create new database tables. The basic syntax to create a database table looks like this:

```
CREATE TABLE table_name (
   column1_name   data_type   [NULL | NOT NULL],
   column2_name   data_type   [NULL | NOT NULL],
   column3_name   data_type   [NULL | NOT NULL]
)
```

The NULL and NOT NULL optional fields designate whether a column can be left blank when a row is inserted into the table. In addition to the basic syntax presented here, different databases support a wide variety of features. For instance, it is very common for databases to support syntax that describes additional features such as designating indexed fields, default values for columns, auto-incrementing fields, referential integrity constraints (primary and foriegn key definitions), and much more. Other database objects, such as triggers, sequences, and stored procedures, are also commonly supported in high-end relational database management systems (RDBMS).

Listing 16.1 presents the CREATE TABLE commands used to build the database utilized by the sample JDBC servlet presented at the end of this chapter (for improved readability, each column's data type is shown in lowercase). Notice that the ID fields for both tables are declared as auto-incrementing primary key fields. The PRIMARY KEY statement indicates that this column must always contain a unique value. The AUTO_INCREMENT statement indicates that this field will be automatically populated with an increasing sequential number whenever a new row is inserted. Since the database automatically populates AUTO_INCREMENT fields, INSERT statements should either pass these fields a value of NULL or not include them at all. For example, either of the following INSERT statements will allow MySQL to automatically populate the DEPARTMENT_ID field.

```
INSERT INTO DEPARTMENT VALUES (NULL, 'Human Resources');
INSERT INTO DEPARTMENT (NAME) VALUES ('Sales and Marketing');
```

For simplicity, no referential integrity constraints are defined between the EMPLOYEE and DEPARTMENT tables (e.g., a foreign key constraint enforcing the rule that any DEPARTMENT_ID in EMPLOYEE must exist in DEPARTMENT). Keep in mind that portions of Listing 16.1 are specific to the MySQL database (such as the AUTO_INCREMENT statement) and will not work on all databases. The logical database model is shown in Figure 16.6.

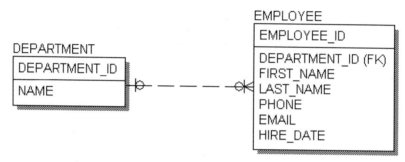

Figure 16.6   Logical Database Model

Listing 16.1   MySQL DDL script to create the sample servlet database.

```
CREATE TABLE DEPARTMENT (
  DEPARTMENT_ID  int NOT NULL AUTO_INCREMENT PRIMARY KEY,
  NAME           varchar(20) NULL
);

CREATE TABLE EMPLOYEE (
  EMPLOYEE_ID    int NOT NULL AUTO_INCREMENT PRIMARY KEY,
  DEPARTMENT_ID  int NULL,
  FIRST_NAME     varchar(20) NULL,
  LAST_NAME      varchar(20) NULL,
  PHONE          varchar(20) NULL,
  EMAIL          varchar(50) NULL,
  HIRE_DATE      date NULL
);
```

Each database defines its own data types and rules for column names. For instance, most databases allow, at a minimum, column names to consist of any sequence of letters, numbers, and underscores (no spaces or punctuation and often must begin with a letter). However, many databases provide more liberal naming rules (perhaps allowing spaces or some punctuation within column names). Likewise, each database defines its own set of data types. Though the names of data types can vary widely among databases, all databases provide some level of support for basic text and numeric data. High-end databases may support advanced data types like serialized objects or image data. Table 16.2 documents some of the most common data types supported by the MySQL database (see the MySQL documentation for a complete list). MySQL is presented later in this chapter.

In addition to creating tables, it is also possible to alter and drop (i.e., delete) tables using the ALTER TABLE and DROP TABLE commands. Check your database's documentation for a complete list of supported DDL commands.

Retrieving Data

Retrieving rows from the database using an SQL SELECT statement is the most common JDBC operation. As previously demonstrated, a ResultSet can be retrieved by passing an SQL SELECT statement to the Statement object's executeQuery() method. The definition for this method looks like this:

```
public java.sql.ResultSet executeQuery(String sql) throws
    java.sql.SQLException
```

Rows contained in a ResultSet object can be traversed using the next() and previous() methods. These methods return a boolean value indicating whether the current row is valid. For instance, next() returns false when it moves past the final row in the result set. Also keep in mind that ResultSet objects are always initially positioned before the first row. Therefore, the

Table 16.2 Common Data Types Supported by MySQL

Name	Description
INT	Normal integer. Signed range is –2147483648 to 2147483647. Unsigned range is 0 to 4294967295.
FLOAT	Signed floating-point number. Range is –1.175494351E–38 to 3.402823466E+38.
CHAR(n)	Fixed-length text information.
VARCHAR(n)	Variable-length text information.
DATE	Stores date information in the "YYYY-MM-DD" format.
TIME	Stores time information in the "HH:MM:SS" format.
DATETIME	Stores date and time information in the "YYYY-MM-DD HH:MM:SS" format.
TIMESTAMP	Adds an automatic timestamp to each row.
TEXT	Stores a large amount of text. Maximum capacity of 65535 characters.
BLOB	Stores a large amount of binary data. Maximum capacity of 65535 bytes.

ResultSet object's next() method must be called before any column values can be retrieved.

The previous() method allows you to move backward through a result set, but this method often does not work. For instance, since previous() was introduced in JDBC 2.0, older JDBC drivers do not support this functionality. Additionally, the previous() method works only with scrollable result sets (many result sets are defined as forward only). Therefore, when using previous(), you should always verify that your JDBC driver supports the JDBC 2.0 or later specification. And if your JDBC driver does support JDBC 2.0 functionality, you must also verify that the ResultSet object is scrollable by calling its getType() method like this:

```
if (set.getType() != ResultSet.TYPE_FORWARD_ONLY)
{
  //...set.previous() may be safely called here...
}
```

After retrieving a database row using the next() or previous() method, the values of each column in the row can be extracted using the ResultSet object's getObject() method or any of the data type–specific method calls. For example, the getString() method returns a String object and can be used with most data types, including dates and numeric values (of course, the date or numeric value will be returned as a String). Similarly, methods such as getInt(), getLong(), getFloat(), and getDouble() return the Java primitives int, long, float, and double, respectively. Lastly, special methods like getDate(), getTime(), and getTimestamp() return Java objects of type java.sql.Date, java.sql.Time, and java.sql.Timestamp. Table 16.3 documents the appropriate ResultSet method call for each SQL data type as well as the type of object returned when a column's value is retrieved using the getObject() method.

The getObject() method and all of the data type–specific "get" methods accept a single parameter—either a String containing the column name or an integer representing the index number corresponding to the column whose value should be returned. Since specifying the column name makes for more readable code, that method is used most often throughout this book. However, there are times that you may need to iterate through all of the columns of a result set. In this case, being able to specify a column by index number can be very useful.

The following sample code demonstrates how rows can be retrieved from the EMPLOYEE and DEPARTMENT tables defined in Listing 16.2. Notice how the HIRE_DATE field is retrieved as a java.sql.Date object. Figure 16.7 shows the output produced by the ShowEmployees servlet.

Table 16.3 Methods Defined by the `ResultSet` Object for Retrieving Data

SQL Data Type	Method Name	getObject() Return Type
TINYINT	`byte getByte()`	`Integer`
SMALLINT	`short getShort()`	`Integer`
MEDIUMINT	`int getInt()`	`Integer`
INT or INTEGER	`int getInt()`	`Integer`
BIGINT	`long getLong()`	`Long`
REAL	`float getFloat()`	`Float`
FLOAT	`float getFloat()`	`Float`
DOUBLE	`double getDouble()`	`Double`
DECIMAL	`java.math.BigDecimal getBigDecimal()`	`java.math.BigDecimal`
NUMERIC	`java.math.BigDecimal getBigDecimal()`	`java.math.BigDecimal`
NUMBER	`java.math.BigDecimal getBigDecimal()`	`java.math.BigDecimal`
BIT	`boolean getBoolean()`	`Boolean`
CHAR or CHARACTER	`String getString()`	`String`
VARCHAR	`String getString()`	`String`

LONGVARCHAR	`java.io.InputStream getAsciiStream()`
	`java.io.Reader getCharacterStream()`
	`java.sql.Clob getClob()`
		`String`

TEXT	`java.io.InputStream getAsciiStream()`
	`java.io.Reader getCharacterStream()`
	`java.sql.Clob getClob()`
		`String`

BINARY	`byte[] getBytes()`	`byte[]`
VARBINARY	`byte[] getBytes()`	`byte[]`
LONGVARBINARY	`java.io.InputStream getBinaryStream()` `java.sql.Blob getBlob()`	`byte[]`
DATE	`java.sql.Date getDate()`	`java.sql.Date`
DATETIME	`java.sql.Date getDate()`	`java.sql.Date`
TIME	`java.sql.Time getTime()`	`java.sql.Time`
TIMESTAMP	`java.sql.Timestamp getTimestamp()`	`java.sql.Timestamp`

Listing 16.2 ShowEmployees servlet retrieves rows from a database.

```
import javax.servlet.*;
import javax.servlet.http.*;
import java.io.*;
import java.sql.*;
import java.text.DateFormat;

/**
 * ShowEmployees creates an HTML table containing a list of all
```

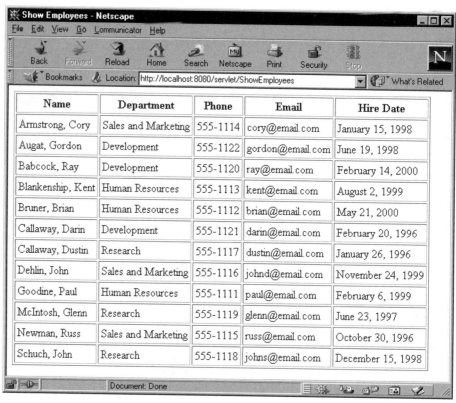

Figure 16.7   Output from the ShowEmployees Servlet

```
 * employees (sorted by last name) and the departments to which
 * they belong.
 */
public class ShowEmployees extends HttpServlet
{
  Connection dbConn = null;

  /**
   * Establishes a connection to the database.
   */
  public void init() throws ServletException
  {
    String jdbcDriver = "org.gjt.mm.mysql.Driver";
    String dbURL = "jdbc:mysql://localhost/phonebook";

    try
    {
      Class.forName(jdbcDriver).newInstance(); //load driver
      dbConn = DriverManager.getConnection(dbURL); //connect
    }
```

```
        catch (ClassNotFoundException e)
        {
          throw new UnavailableException("JDBC driver not found:" +
            jdbcDriver);
        }
        catch (SQLException e)
        {
          throw new UnavailableException("Unable to connect to: " +
            dbURL);
        }
        catch (Exception e)
        {
          throw new UnavailableException("Error: " + e);
        }
      }


      /**
       * Displays the employees table.
       */
      public void service(HttpServletRequest request,
        HttpServletResponse response) throws ServletException,
        IOException
      {
        response.setContentType("text/html");

        PrintWriter out = response.getWriter();

        try
        {
          //join EMPLOYEE and DEPARTMENT tables to get all data
          String sql = "select * from EMPLOYEE,DEPARTMENT where " +
            "EMPLOYEE.DEPARTMENT_ID = DEPARTMENT.DEPARTMENT_ID " +
            "order by LAST_NAME,FIRST_NAME,DEPARTMENT.NAME";

          Statement stmt = dbConn.createStatement();
          ResultSet rs = stmt.executeQuery(sql);

          out.println("<HTML>");
          out.println("<HEAD><TITLE>Show Employees</TITLE></HEAD>");
          out.println("<BODY>");
          out.println("<TABLE BORDER=\"1\" CELLPADDING=\"3\">");
          out.println("<TR>");
          out.println("<TH>Name</TH>");
          out.println("<TH>Department</TH>");
          out.println("<TH>Phone</TH>");
          out.println("<TH>Email</TH>");
          out.println("<TH>Hire Date</TH>");
          out.println("</TR>");

          while (rs.next())
          {
            out.println("<TR>");
```

```
        out.println("<TD>" + rs.getString("LAST_NAME") + ", " +
          rs.getString("FIRST_NAME") + "</TD>");
        out.println("<TD>" + rs.getString("NAME") + "</TD>");
        out.println("<TD>" + rs.getString("PHONE") + "</TD>");
        out.println("<TD>" + rs.getString("EMAIL") + "</TD>");

        java.sql.Date hireDate = rs.getDate("HIRE_DATE");
        DateFormat longDate = DateFormat.getDateInstance(
          DateFormat.LONG);
        out.println("<TD>" + longDate.format(hireDate) +
          "</TD>");

        out.println("</TR>");
      }

      out.println("</TABLE>");
      out.println("</BODY></HTML>");

      rs.close();
      stmt.close();
    }
    catch (SQLException e)
    {
      out.println("<H2>Database currently unavailable.</H2>");
    }

    out.close();
  }
}
```

If you do not know beforehand if your SQL statement will retrieve rows or perform an insert/update/delete operation, you can use the Statement object's execute() method. The definition for this method looks like this:

```
public boolean execute(String sql) throws SQLException
```

The execute() method returns true if the SQL statement generated a result set. If true, use the Statement object's getResultSet() method to retrieve the ResultSet object; otherwise, use getUpdateCount() to determine the number of rows affected by the SQL operation.

In addition to supporting a wide array of SQL commands, the execute() method can be useful when receiving multiple result sets. If an SQL statement generates multiple result sets, the first set can be retrieved using the get-ResultSet() method. All subsequent result sets can be acquired by first calling getMoreResults() followed by the getResultSet() method. Each time getMoreResults() is called, it makes the next result set available via the getResultSet() method. When no more result sets are available, getMore-Results() returns false.

Inserting Rows

Rows can be inserted into a database table using the ResultSet object's executeUpdate() method. This method is also used to update and delete rows. The definition for executeUpdate() looks like this:

```
public int executeUpdate(String sql) throws SQLException
```

The executeUpdate() method returns the number of rows that were affected by the insert, update, or delete operation. Listing 16.3 presents a Java application that demonstrates how a row can be inserted into a database table using executeUpdate().

Listing 16.3 InsertExample inserts a row into the database.

```java
import java.sql.*;
import java.text.DateFormat;

public class InsertExample
{
  public static void main(String[] args)
  {
    String jdbcDriver = "org.gjt.mm.mysql.Driver";
    String dbURL = "jdbc:mysql://localhost/phonebook";
    Connection dbConn = null;

    try
    {
      Class.forName(jdbcDriver).newInstance();
      dbConn = DriverManager.getConnection(dbURL);
      Statement stmt = dbConn.createStatement();

      String sql = "insert into EMPLOYEE values (NULL, 1, " +
        "'John', 'Public', '555-2222', 'johnp@email.com', " +
        "'2000-12-28')";

      stmt.executeUpdate(sql);

      stmt.close();
    }
    catch (ClassNotFoundException e)
    {
      System.out.println("JDBC driver not found: " + jdbcDriver);
    }
    catch (SQLException e)
    {
      System.out.println("Error retrieving data from: " + dbURL);
    }
    catch (Exception e)
    {
      System.out.println("Error: " + e);
    }
```

```
      finally
      {
        try
        {
          if (dbConn != null)
          {
            dbConn.close();
          }
        }
        catch (SQLException ignored) {}
      }
    }
  }
```

In addition to manually executing an SQL INSERT statement, JDBC 2.0 defines a new, more object-oriented way to insert rows into a database. This new method involves retrieving a ResultSet object, moving to the insert row of the result set, updating the insert row's fields, and inserting the row into the result set and the database. The *insert row* is a special row that serves as a buffer for new information until the row can be committed to the database. The following sample code demonstrates how to insert rows into a database table using the special insert row.

```
String sql = "select * from EMPLOYEE";

Statement stmt = dbConn.createStatement();
ResultSet rs = stmt.executeQuery(sql);

rs.moveToInsertRow(); //move to insert row

//update all columns in insert row
rs.updateString("EMPLOYEE_ID", null);
rs.updateInt("DEPARTMENT_ID", 1);
rs.updateString("FIRST_NAME", "John");
rs.updateString("LAST_NAME", "Public");
rs.updateString("PHONE", "555-2222");
rs.updateString("EMAIL", "johnp@email.com");
rs.updateString("HIRE_DATE", "2000-12-28");

rs.insertRow(); //insert row into ResultSet and database
```

That's all there is to it. The insert row makes it extremely easy to add rows to an existing result set. However, remember that this functionality is available only when using a JDBC 2.0–compliant driver and an updatable result set.

Updating Rows

Database rows can be updated using the Statement object's executeUpdate() method. This method returns the number of rows affected by the update operation. Listing 16.4 presents a Java application that demonstrates how database rows can be updated using executeUpdate().

Listing 16.4 UpdateExample updates rows in the database.

```
import java.sql.*;
import java.text.DateFormat;

public class UpdateExample
{
  public static void main(String[] args)
  {
    String jdbcDriver = "org.gjt.mm.mysql.Driver";
    String dbURL = "jdbc:mysql://localhost/phonebook";
    Connection dbConn = null;

    try
    {
      Class.forName(jdbcDriver).newInstance();
      dbConn = DriverManager.getConnection(dbURL);
      Statement stmt = dbConn.createStatement();

      //move all employees in department 3 to department 4
      String sql = "update EMPLOYEE set DEPARTMENT_ID = 4 " +
        "where DEPARTMENT_ID = 3";

      int numRows = stmt.executeUpdate(sql);

      System.out.println(numRows + " rows updated.");

      stmt.close();
    }
    catch (ClassNotFoundException e)
    {
      System.out.println("JDBC driver not found: " + jdbcDriver);
    }
    catch (SQLException e)
    {
      System.out.println("Error retrieving data from: " + dbURL);
    }
    catch (Exception e)
    {
      System.out.println("Error: " + e);
    }
    finally
    {
      try
      {
        if (dbConn != null)
        {
          dbConn.close();
        }
      }
```

```
            catch (SQLException ignored) {}
        }
      }
    }
```

In addition to manually executing an SQL UPDATE statement, JDBC 2.0 defines a new, more object-oriented way to update rows in a database. This new method involves retrieving a ResultSet object, moving to the row to be updated, updating the row's fields, and committing the update to the result set and the database. The following sample code demonstrates this process.

```
String sql = "select * from EMPLOYEE";

Statement stmt = dbConn.createStatement();
ResultSet rs = stmt.executeQuery(sql);

//move all employees in department 3 to department 4
while (rs.next())
{
  if (rs.getInt("DEPARTMENT_ID") == 3)
  {
    rs.updateInt("DEPARTMENT_ID", 4);
    rs.updateRow();
  }
}
```

The previous example illustrates how the updateRow() method can be used to update rows in a database. However, in this case, this method is extremely slow. When performing a bulk update (i.e., you are making the same change to multiple records), it is much more efficient to send an SQL UPDATE command to the database and allow it to update multiple rows rather than to iterate through each row on the client. On the other hand, when the number of rows needing to be updated is small or the update criteria change with each row, this object-oriented method of updating database rows can be very convenient. Again, remember that this functionality is available only when using a JDBC 2.0-compliant driver and an updatable result set.

Deleting Rows

Database rows can be deleted using the Statement object's executeUpdate() method. This method returns the number of rows affected by the delete operation. Listing 16.5 presents a Java application that demonstrates how database rows can be deleted using executeUpdate().

Listing 16.5 `DeleteExample` deletes rows in the database.

```java
import java.sql.*;
import java.text.DateFormat;

public class DeleteExample
{
  public static void main(String[] args)
  {
    String jdbcDriver = "org.gjt.mm.mysql.Driver";
    String dbURL = "jdbc:mysql://localhost/phonebook";
    Connection dbConn = null;

    try
    {
      Class.forName(jdbcDriver).newInstance();
      dbConn = DriverManager.getConnection(dbURL);
      Statement stmt = dbConn.createStatement();

      //delete all employees in department 1
      String sql = "delete from EMPLOYEE where DEPARTMENT_ID=1";

      int numRows = stmt.executeUpdate(sql);

      System.out.println(numRows + " rows deleted.");

      stmt.close();
    }
    catch (ClassNotFoundException e)
    {
      System.out.println("JDBC driver not found: " + jdbcDriver);
    }
    catch (SQLException e)
    {
      System.out.println("Error retrieving data from: " + dbURL);
    }
    finally
    {
      try
      {
        if (dbConn != null)
        {
          dbConn.close();
        }
      }
      catch (SQLException ignored) {}
    }
  }
}
```

In addition to manually executing an SQL DELETE statement, JDBC 2.0 defines a new, more object-oriented way to delete rows from a database. This new method involves retrieving a ResultSet object, moving to the row to be deleted, and executing the `deleteRow()` method. The following sample code demonstrates this process.

```
String sql = "select * from EMPLOYEE";

Statement stmt = dbConn.createStatement();
ResultSet rs = stmt.executeQuery(sql);

//delete all employees in department 1
while (rs.next())
{
  if (rs.getInt("DEPARTMENT_ID") == 1)
  {
    rs.deleteRow();
  }
}
```

The previous example illustrates how the `deleteRow()` method can be used to delete rows from a database. However, in this case, this method is extremely slow. When performing a bulk delete (i.e., you are deleting multiple records based on the same criteria), it is much more efficient to send an SQL DELETE command to the database and allow it to delete multiple rows rather than iterate through each row on the client. In addition, the sample code shown here may not always work as expected. Deleting rows from an existing result set can disrupt the iteration process and result in some rows being skipped. These are important concerns to keep in mind when evaluating the `deleteRow()` method. Regardless, when the number of rows needing to be deleted is small or the delete criteria change with each row, this object-oriented method of deleting database rows may come in handy. Again, remember that this functionality is available only when using a JDBC 2.0–compliant driver and an updatable result set.

SQL Exceptions

Every method defined by the `Connection`, `Statement`, and `ResultSet` objects throws `java.sql.SQLException`. Therefore, whenever these objects are used, you must either catch `SQLException` or throw it. In most cases, as demonstrated throughout this chapter, you should simply catch this exception and handle it in some manner. This may involve returning an error message to the client, logging the error, or just throwing a `javax.servlet.Unavailable-Exception` indicating that your servlet is not available.

`SQLException` is similar to other exceptions, except for the fact that it can store a vendor-specific error code, an "SQLState" string (following the XOPEN SQLstate conventions), and nested exceptions. This additional information can be very useful when attempting to troubleshoot database connectivity issues.

When a database error occurs, the SQLException object is populated with a vendor-specific error code indicating the error returned by the underlying database. This error code can be retrieved using the getErrorCode() method. The SQLState string can be obtained with the getSQLState() method. See the XOPEN SQL specification for more information regarding the format of the SQLState string. Lastly, a chain of nested exceptions can be encapsulated in an SQLException object. The getNextException() method returns the next SQLException object or null if the end of the chain has been reached. The getNextException() method can be used like this:

```
catch (SQLException e)
{
  int count = 1; //exception counter

  //first exception
  out.println("Exception " + count + ": " + e.getMessage());

  //chained exceptions
  while ((e = e.getNextException()) != null)
  {
    count++;
    out.println("Exception " + count + ": " + e.getMessage());
  }
}
```

The previous code returns the first SQLException as well as all chained exceptions to the client. Though each exception in the chain can offer clues as to the root cause of the database error, the first exception usually contains the most specific information.

When extracting data from an SQLException object, keep in mind that it is up to the JDBC driver and the database to return relevant error information (including an error code, SQLState information, and chained exceptions). Different drivers may provide various amounts of error information.

Advanced Database Concepts

Prepared Statements

A *prepared statement* is an SQL statement that is precompiled by the database. Through precompilation, prepared statements improve the performance of SQL commands that are executed multiple times (given that the database supports prepared statements). Once compiled, prepared statements can be customized prior to each execution by altering predefined SQL parameters.

A PreparedStatement object is created using the Connection object's prepareStatement() method. Question marks ("?") in the SQL are used as placeholders for dynamic parameters that may change each time the prepared statement is executed. Use the appropriate setXxx() method (based on the parameter's SQL data type) to set the value of each parameter prior to executing the statement (see Table 16.4). The following code demonstrates how to create and execute a prepared statement.

Table 16.4　Typical setXxx() Methods of the PreparedStatement Object

Method Name	Description
setAsciiStream()	Sets a prepared statement parameter to the given java.io.InputStream object. This method is useful for inputting large amounts of text data into a database field. The database will read data from the InputStream as necessary, until reaching the end of the stream or until the specified number of bytes have been read.
setBinaryStream()	Sets a prepared statement parameter to the given java.io.InputStream object. This method is useful for inputting large amounts of binary data into a database field. The database will read data from the InputStream as necessary, until reaching the end of the stream or until the specified number of bytes have been read.
setBoolean()	Sets the prepared statement parameter to the given boolean value.
setByte()	Sets the prepared statement parameter to the given byte value.
setBytes()	Sets the prepared statement parameter to the given array of bytes.
setCharacterStream()	Sets a prepared statement parameter to the given java.io.Reader object. This method is useful for inputting large amounts of text data into a database field. The database will read data from the Reader as necessary, until reaching the end of the stream or until the specified number of bytes have been read.
setDate()	Sets the prepared statement parameter to the given java.sql.Date value.
setDouble()	Sets the prepared statement parameter to the given double value.
setFloat()	Sets the prepared statement parameter to the given float value.
setInt()	Sets the prepared statement parameter to the given int value.
setLong()	Sets the prepared statement parameter to the given long value.
setNull()	Sets the prepared statement parameter to SQL NULL.
setObject()	Sets the prepared statement parameter using the given Java object. The JDBC specification defines a standard mapping between Java objects and SQL data types. Use the Java object that corresponds to the parameter's SQL data type.
setString()	Sets the prepared statement parameter to the given String value.
setTime()	Sets the prepared statement parameter to the given java.sql.Time value.
setTimestamp()	Sets the prepared statement parameter to the given java.sql.Timestamp value.

```
String sql = "insert into EMPLOYEE (DEPARTMENT_ID, " +
  "FIRST_NAME, LAST_NAME, PHONE, EMAIL, HIRE_DATE) " +
  "values (?, ?, ?, ?, ?, ?)";

//create the prepared statement
PreparedStatement pstmt = dbConn.prepareStatement(sql);

//get java.sql.Date for HIRE_DATE field
GregorianCalendar cal =
  (GregorianCalendar)Calendar.getInstance();
cal.set(2000, Calendar.DECEMBER, 28);
java.sql.Date hireDate = (java.sql.Date)cal.getTime();

pstmt.clearParameters(); //clear previous parameter values
pstmt.setInt(1, 1);
pstmt.setString(2, "John");
pstmt.setString(3, "Public");
pstmt.setString(4, "555-2222");
pstmt.setString(5, "johnp@email.com");
pstmt.setDate(6, hireDate);
pstmt.executeUpdate(); //execute the prepared statement
```

The previous code inserts a new row into the EMPLOYEE table using the PreparedStatement object. The clearParameters() method clears all previously set parameter values. The six setXxx() methods set the value of each of the insert parameters according to the specified parameter index. Each parameter is indexed, starting at one, according to the order in which it appears in the SQL statement (moving from left to right). Finally, the prepared statement is executed using the executeUpdate() method. In contrast, if the SQL statement had represented a SELECT query, the PreparedStatement object's executeQuery() method would have been used.

In addition to improving the performance of frequently executed SQL statements, prepared statements are useful in other areas. For instance, prepared statements allow large amounts of text and binary data to be stored in the database using the setXxxStream() methods. To illustrate, consider the EMPLOYEE_PHOTO database table, defined as follows:

```
CREATE TABLE EMPLOYEE_PHOTO (
    EMPLOYEE_ID     int NOT NULL,
    FIRST_NAME      varchar(20) NULL,
    LAST_NAME       varchar(20) NULL,
    PHOTO           blob NULL);
```

Notice that the EMPLOYEE_PHOTO table contains a field called PHOTO that is defined as type blob. The MySQL database presented in this chapter supports a BLOB data type for the storage of binary data. The following code demonstrates how a binary image file can be stored in the EMPLOYEE_PHOTO table using the PreparedStatement object's setBinaryStream() method and then extracted from the database using the `ResultSet` object's `getBinaryStream()` method (`java.io.*` and `java.sql.*` are imported).

```
//INSERT ROW INTO EMPLOYEE_PHOTO TABLE (including photo)
String sql = "insert into EMPLOYEE_PHOTO values (?, ?, ?, ?)";

//create the prepared statement
PreparedStatement pstmt = dbConn.prepareStatement(sql);

//get handle to the image file to be sent to the database
File file = new File("/photo.gif");
FileInputStream fileIn = new FileInputStream(file);

//initialize prepared statement parameters
pstmt.setInt(1, 1);
pstmt.setString(2, "John");
pstmt.setString(3, "Public");
pstmt.setBinaryStream(4, fileIn, (int)file.length());
pstmt.executeUpdate(); //execute prepared statement

fileIn.close(); //close input stream

//EXTRACT PHOTO FROM DATABASE AND WRITE TO LOCAL FILE
sql = "select PHOTO from EMPLOYEE_PHOTO where EMPLOYEE_ID = 1";

Statement stmt = dbConn.createStatement();
ResultSet rs = stmt.executeQuery(sql);

if (rs.next())
{
  //get input stream for reading binary data from the PHOTO field
  InputStream in = rs.getBinaryStream("PHOTO");

  //get output stream used to write photo to the file system
  FileOutputStream fileOut = new FileOutputStream("/copy.gif");

  int bytesRead = 0;
  byte[] buffer = new byte[4096]; //4k buffer for reading image
  while ((bytesRead = in.read(buffer)) != -1)
  {
    fileOut.write(buffer, 0, bytesRead); //write image to file
  }

  fileOut.close(); //close output stream
}
```

NOTE: While reading information from the database using the `ResultSet` object's `getAsciiStream()`, `getCharacterStream()`, or `getBinaryStream()` method, you should not call any other `ResultSet.get`*Xxx*`()` method. This is due to the fact that retrieving data from any other database field will close the `InputStream`.

Prepared statements are also useful for writing text containing special characters to the database without having to convert the characters to their appropriate escape sequences. For example, the apostrophe (') is commonly used to convey text field boundaries within an SQL statement as shown here:

```
insert into COMPANY values ('Sun Microsystems');
```

Imagine that this SQL was dynamically constructed by a servlet in response to a user entering his company name on a Web page. Now imagine the problem that would result if the company name included an apostrophe. The resulting SQL might look like this:

```
insert into COMPANY values ('Crazy Bob's Software Shack');
```

Since apostrophes are used as string delimiters in SQL, the database will assume that the quoted string was not terminated properly (since it appears to terminate twice), resulting in a syntax error. One way to resolve this problem would be to replace the apostrophe with its escape sequence. Most databases recognize two consecutive apostrophes as the escape sequence for a single embedded apostrophe (i.e., embedded in a text field). Therefore, the following rewritten SQL statement solves this problem.

```
insert into COMPANY values ('Crazy Bob''s Software Shack');
```

The database will automatically convert the double apostrophe into a single apostrophe and there is no ambiguity regarding the text field boundaries. Listing 16.6 presents a simple Java class containing a single `static` method that converts all single apostrophes within a `String` to double apostrophes.

Listing 16.6 DBQuote converts single apostrophes to double apostrophes.

```
public class DBQuote
{
  /**
   * Replaces all single quotes (') with double quotes ("). This
   * method is useful when dynamically building SQL statements.
   *
   * @param text String to check for single quotes
   * @return String after converting single quotes to double
   *   quotes
   */
  public static String parse(String text)
  {
    StringBuffer textBuffer = new StringBuffer();

    int pos = 0;
```

```
      while (true)
      {
        int quoteIndex = text.indexOf("'", pos);

        if (quoteIndex == -1)
        {
          textBuffer.append(text.substring(pos));
          break;
        }

        textBuffer.append(text.substring(pos, quoteIndex));
        textBuffer.append("''");

        pos = quoteIndex + 1;
      }

      return textBuffer.toString();
  }
}
```

Passing all SQL text fields to the parse() method of the DBQuote class resolves the problem created by apostrophes within text fields that are used to construct an SQL statement. The DBQuote class can be used like this:

```
String name = "Crazy Bob's Software Shack";
String sql = "insert into COMPANY values ('" +
  DBQuote.parse(name) + "')";
```

The only problem with the DBQuote class is that it escapes only the apostrophes in a String. What about other special characters (such as ")? We could write a class that would search for every special character and replace it with its escape sequence, but fortunately, there is a simpler way. As mentioned earlier, prepared statements allow text to be sent to the database without escaping special characters. This characteristic of prepared statements can greatly simplify the database code within your servlets by automatically solving the problems normally associated with inserting special characters into the database. To illustrate, the following code uses a prepared statement to insert text into a database without concern for any special characters that may be included.

```
String sql = "insert into COMPANY values (?)";
PreparedStatement pstmt = dbConn.prepareStatement(sql);
pstmt.setString(1, "Crazy Bob's Software Shack");
pstmt.executeUpdate();
```

Transactions

There are times when a set of SQL statements must all be executed as one atomic action (i.e., as a single unit) in order to ensure database integrity. For instance, consider a banking example similar to the one presented in Chapter 11. Imagine a transfer between two bank accounts that requires two rows in a database table to be updated using the SQL UPDATE command. The first UPDATE debits some amount from one account and the second UPDATE credits a separate account for the same amount. Now imagine that an error occurs in the system between the first and second update operations that prevents the second update from completing successfully. If this happens, the database will be left in an invalid state. One account was debited but the other account was not credited. Therefore, the money that was to be transferred is lost. Fortunately, this type of database integrity problem can be remedied using database transactions.

A *transaction* is a set of SQL statements that are grouped such that all statements are guaranteed to be executed or the entire operation will fail. If all statements execute successfully, the results are committed to the database; otherwise, all changes are rolled back. Thus, the indeterminate state resulting from the partial execution of a group of SQL statements is avoided.

NOTE: Transactions are available only when using a database and JDBC driver that supports them. Fortunately, most commercial databases provide full transaction support. Before using transactions, check your database documentation to ensure that they are supported. For instance, the MySQL database demonstrated in this chapter does not support transactions, but the Oracle database does. For this reason, Listing 16.7 uses an Oracle database to demonstrate transactions via JDBC.

When created, a JDBC connection begins in autocommit mode. This mode treats each SQL statement as an individual transaction, committing the action as soon as it is performed. To execute multiple SQL statements as an atomic transaction, the autocommit feature must be deactivated by passing false to the Connection object's setAutoCommit() method. Once autocommit is disabled, all SQL statements executed against this connection are automatically added to a transaction. Once all statements have been executed, the Connection object's commit() method is called to commit the results to the database. If an error occurs while executing any of the SQL statements, the entire transaction can be rolled back using the Connection object's rollback() method. Though it is a good practice to explicitly call rollback() if an error occurs, this is not absolutely necessary. Any transaction that is not explicitly committed (using the commit() method) is automatically rolled back. Listing 16.7 demonstrates how transactions can be employed to guarantee that both of the SQL statements are committed to the database or neither is committed.

Listing 16.7   Servlet using transactions to enforce database integrity.

```java
import javax.servlet.*;
import javax.servlet.http.*;
import java.io.*;
import java.sql.*;

/**
 * FundsTransfer transfers $1000 from one account to another.
 * Transactions are employed to guarantee that the appropriate
 * amount is debited from or credited to each account. If an
 * error occurs during the transfer, the entire process is rolled
 * back.
 */
public class FundsTransfer extends HttpServlet
{
  private static final long TRANSFER_AMOUNT = 1000;
  private static final long FROM_ACCOUNT = 100001;
  private static final long TO_ACCOUNT = 100002;

  Connection dbConn = null;

  /**
   * Creates a persistent connection to an Oracle database.
   */
  public void init() throws ServletException
  {
    String jdbcDriver = "oracle.jdbc.driver.OracleDriver";
    String dbURL = "jdbc:oracle:thin:@localhost:1521:orcl";

    try
    {
      Class.forName(jdbcDriver).newInstance();

      dbConn = DriverManager.getConnection(dbURL, "transfer",
        "transfer");
    }
    catch (ClassNotFoundException e)
    {
      throw new UnavailableException("JDBC driver not found:" +
        jdbcDriver);
    }
    catch (SQLException e)
    {
      throw new UnavailableException("Unable to connect to: " +
        dbURL);
    }
  }
```

```java
/**
 * Alters two rows within a database table in order to transfer
 * funds from one account to another. Both SQL UPDATE commands
 * are executed within a transaction in order to guarantee that
 * both commands succeed or both fail.
 */
public void doGet(HttpServletRequest request,
    HttpServletResponse response) throws ServletException,
    IOException
{
    response.setContentType("text/plain");

    PrintWriter out = response.getWriter();

    try
    {
        dbConn.setAutoCommit(false); //disable auto-commit mode

        Statement stat = dbConn.createStatement(); //get statement

        //create SQL to debit the FROM account
        String debitSQL = "update ACCOUNT set ACCOUNT_VALUE = " +
            "(ACCOUNT_VALUE - " + TRANSFER_AMOUNT + ") where " +
            "ACCOUNT_ID = " + FROM_ACCOUNT;

        stat.executeUpdate(debitSQL); //debit FROM_ACCOUNT

        //create SQL to credit the TO account
        String creditSQL = "update ACCOUNT set ACCOUNT_VALUE = " +
            "(ACCOUNT_VALUE + " + TRANSFER_AMOUNT + ") where " +
            "ACCOUNT_ID = " + TO_ACCOUNT;

        stat.executeUpdate(creditSQL); //credit TO_ACCOUNT

        dbConn.commit(); //commit transaction

        //inform client that the money was transferred successfully
        out.println("$" + TRANSFER_AMOUNT + " transferred from " +
            "account " + FROM_ACCOUNT + " to " + TO_ACCOUNT);

        out.close();
    }
    catch (Exception e)
    {
        try
        {
            dbConn.rollback(); //rollback transaction if error occurs
        }
        catch (SQLException ignored) {}
    }
}
}
```

NOTE: For simplicity, Listing 16.7 shows one database connection being shared among all requests. This is safe when running in a single-user environment and sufficient for this demonstration. However, in a multi-user environment, this approach can result in some serious thread safety problems. For production applications, be sure to use a database connection pool, as demonstrated later in this chapter.

Stored Procedures

A *stored procedure* is an SQL operation that is stored on the database server. Stored procedures are usually written in an SQL dialect that has been expanded to include conditional statements, looping constructs, and other procedural programming features. Oracle's PL/SQL and SQL Server's Transact-SQL are examples of SQL languages in which stored procedures are commonly written. Stored procedures are used for a number of reasons, including the following:

- Stored procedures are precompiled on the server so they have a performance advantage over dynamic SQL.
- Because stored procedures are stored on the database server, they are available to all clients.
- Encapsulating business rules within a stored procedure allows business logic to be altered in one place (on the server) without requiring modification to any client.
- A stored procedure may execute any number of SQL operations without requiring the client to transmit each statement to the server.

Listing 16.8 presents an Oracle stored procedure written in PL/SQL. This procedure accepts three input parameters—the transfer amount (transfer_amount), the account from which funds should be debited (from_account), and the account to which funds should be credited (to_account). Lastly, an output parameter (transfer_date) is defined. This procedure transfers the specified amount (transfer_amount) from from_account to to_account. The transfer_date output parameter returns the date (according to the database) that the transaction took place.

Listing 16.8   Oracle PL/SQL stored procedure used to transfer funds.

```
CREATE or REPLACE procedure SP_TRANSFER
(transfer_amount IN  INTEGER,
 from_account    IN  INTEGER,
```

```
to_account       IN  INTEGER,
transfer_date    OUT VARCHAR) IS
BEGIN

update ACCOUNT set ACCOUNT_VALUE = (ACCOUNT_VALUE -
  transfer_amount) where ACCOUNT_ID = from_account;

update ACCOUNT set ACCOUNT_VALUE = (ACCOUNT_VALUE +
  transfer_amount) where ACCOUNT_ID = to_account;

select SYSDATE into transfer_date from DUAL;

END;
```

JDBC provides support for calling stored procedures via the `Callable-Statement` object. `CallableStatement` extends `PreparedStatement` and, therefore, inherits its functionality. In addition, `CallableStatement` provides methods to define input parameters and output parameters and retrieve return values. `CallableStatement` uses the following syntax to call a stored procedure:

```
{call PROCEDURE_NAME(?, ?, ?, ?)}
```

Or, for stored procedures that return a value:

```
{? = call PROCEDURE_NAME(?, ?, ?, ?)}
```

Similar to prepared statements, the question marks represent input and output parameters. The input parameters can be set using the `CallableStatement` object's `setXxx()` methods. Output parameters that have been registered using the `CallableStatement` object's `registerOutParameter()` method can be retrieved using the appropriate `getXxx()` method. The `registerOutParameter()` method defines the output parameter's type (see Listing 16.9). Since the SP_TRANSFER stored procedure presented in Listing 16.8 defines four parameters, the `{call PROCEDURE_NAME()}` statement shown previously contains four question marks (one for each parameter).

Input and output parameters are referenced by an index number, starting with one, that corresponds to the order in which the parameters were defined in the stored procedure. For example, SP_TRANSFER defines four parameters (three input and one output). The first parameter, `transfer_amount`, is referenced by index number one, `from_account` is index number two, and so on. Listing 16.9 demonstrates how to call the SP_TRANSFER stored procedure from within a servlet.

Listing 16.9   Uses a stored procedure to transfer funds between accounts.

```java
import javax.servlet.*;
import javax.servlet.http.*;
import java.io.*;
import java.sql.*;

/**
 * StoredProcFundsTransfer transfers funds from one account to
 * another by calling a stored procedure.
 */
public class StoredProcFundsTransfer extends HttpServlet
{
  private static final long TRANSFER_AMOUNT = 1000;
  private static final long FROM_ACCOUNT = 100001;
  private static final long TO_ACCOUNT = 100002;

  Connection dbConn = null;

  /**
   * Creates a persistent connection to an Oracle database.
   */
  public void init() throws ServletException
  {
    String jdbcDriver = "oracle.jdbc.driver.OracleDriver";
    String dbURL = "jdbc:oracle:thin:@localhost:1521:orcl";

    try
    {
      Class.forName(jdbcDriver).newInstance();

      dbConn = DriverManager.getConnection(dbURL, "transfer",
        "transfer");
    }
    catch (ClassNotFoundException e)
    {
      throw new UnavailableException("JDBC driver not found:" +
        jdbcDriver);
    }
    catch (SQLException e)
    {
      throw new UnavailableException("Unable to connect to: " +
        dbURL);
    }
    catch (Exception e)
    {
      throw new UnavailableException("Error: " + e);
    }
  }


  /**
   * Calls a stored procedure that alters two rows within a
   * database table in order to transfer funds from one account
```

```
 * to another. The stored procedure returns the date (according
 * to the database) that the transfer occurred.
 */
public void doGet(HttpServletRequest request,
  HttpServletResponse response) throws ServletException,
  IOException
{
  response.setContentType("text/plain");

  PrintWriter out = response.getWriter();

  try
  {
    //create callable statement for stored procedure having
    //four parameters (three input and one output)
    CallableStatement cstmt = dbConn.prepareCall(
      "{call SP_TRANSFER(?, ?, ?, ?)}");

    //set values of stored procedure's input parameters
    cstmt.setLong(1, TRANSFER_AMOUNT);
    cstmt.setLong(2, FROM_ACCOUNT);
    cstmt.setLong(3, TO_ACCOUNT);

    //register stored procedure's output parameter
    cstmt.registerOutParameter(4, java.sql.Types.VARCHAR);

    cstmt.execute(); //execute stored procedure

    //return transaction summary (including date) to the client
    out.println("$" + TRANSFER_AMOUNT + " transferred from " +
      "account " + FROM_ACCOUNT + " to " + TO_ACCOUNT +
      " on " + cstmt.getString(4));

    out.close();
  }
  catch (Exception e)
  {
    out.println(e.getMessage());
  }
}
}
```

Database and Result Set Metadata

Metadata is defined as information (or data) about data. JDBC provides specific information about a database or a result set via metadata objects. A database metadata object, called `DatabaseMetaData`, can be retrieved using the `java.sql.Connection` object's `getMetaData()` method. Table 16.5 presents a small sample of the extensive amount of information that can be retrieved about the database from the `DatabaseMetaData` object.

Table 16.5   Small Sample of Information Available from the `DatabaseMetaData` Object

Method	Description
getDatabaseProductName()	Gets the name of the database.
getDatabaseProductVersion()	Gets the database's version number.
getDriverName()	Gets the JDBC driver's name.
getDriverVersion()	Gets the JDBC driver's version number.
getMaxColumnNameLength()	Gets the maximum column name length supported by this database.
getMaxColumnsInTable()	Gets the maximum number of table columns supported by this database.
getMaxConnections()	Gets the maximum number of concurrent connections supported by this database.
getMaxRowSize()	Gets the maximum row length, in bytes, supported by this database.
getMaxTableNameLength()	Gets the maximum table name length supported by this database.
getNumericFunctions()	Gets a comma-delimited list of the numeric functions supported by this database.
getPrimaryKeys()	Gets a description of the specified table's primary key columns.
getStringFunctions()	Gets a comma-delimited list of the string functions supported by this database.
getURL()	Gets the JDBC URL used to access this database.
getUsername()	Gets the current username according to the database.
isReadOnly()	Indicates if the database is in read-only mode.
supportsANSI92FullSQL()	Indicates if the database supports the full ANSI 92 SQL grammar.
supportsOuterJoins()	Indicates if the database supports some form of outer joins.
supportsStoredProcedures()	Indicates if the database supports stored procedures.
supportsTransactions()	Indicates if the database supports transactions.

Similar to the manner in which the `DatabaseMetaData` object describes a database, the `ResultSetMetaData` object describes a result set. The `ResultSet-MetaData` object can be retrieved using the `ResultSet` object's `getMetaData()` method. Table 16.6 illustrates some of the information about a result set that can be obtained from the `ResultSetMetaData` object.

In servlet programming, the `ResultSetMetaData` object is commonly used to dynamically construct an HTML table given any `ResultSet` object. For example, Listing 16.10 presents a servlet that queries the database for employee information and dynamically constructs an HTML table containing the results. This method of displaying database information is very flexible. If more information is desired, only the SQL statement that creates the result set

Table 16.6   Sample of Information Available from the `ResultSetMetaData` Object

Method	Description
`getColumnCount()`	Gets the number of columns in the result set.
`getColumnDisplaySize()`	Gets the column's maximum character width.
`getColumnLabel()`	Gets the suggested column title.
`getColumnName()`	Gets the name of the column.
`getColumnType()`	Gets the column's SQL data type (e.g., int, float, varchar). Returns an integer corresponding to the type constants defined within the `java.sql.Types` class.
`getColumnTypeName()`	Gets the database-specific SQL data type name.
`getTableName()`	Gets the column's table name.
`isAutoIncrement()`	Indicates if a column is set to auto-increment.
`isCaseSensitive()`	Indicates if a column is case-sensitive.
`isCurrency()`	Indicates if a column contains currency data.
`isDefinitelyWritable()`	Indicates if a write to the specified column will definitely succeed.
`isNullable()`	Indicates if a column can be set to `null`.
`isReadOnly()`	Indicates if a column is read-only (not writable).
`isSearchable()`	Indicates if a column can be used within an SQL `WHERE` clause.
`isWritable()`	Indicates if it is possible for a write to the specified column to succeed.

need be updated to include another database column. The HTML table will automatically adapt to accomodate the new `ResultSet`. This servlet reads from the database created by the script presented in Listing 16.1. Figure 16.8 displays the browser-rendered output created by Listing 16.10.

Listing 16.10   Dynamically builds an HTML table to show a `ResultSet`.

```
import javax.servlet.*;
import javax.servlet.http.*;
import java.io.*;
import java.sql.*;

/**
 * EmployeeInfo returns employee data presented in an HTML table
 * that is dynamically created with help from the
 * ResultSetMetaData object.
 */
public class EmployeeInfo extends HttpServlet
{
  Connection dbConn = null;
```

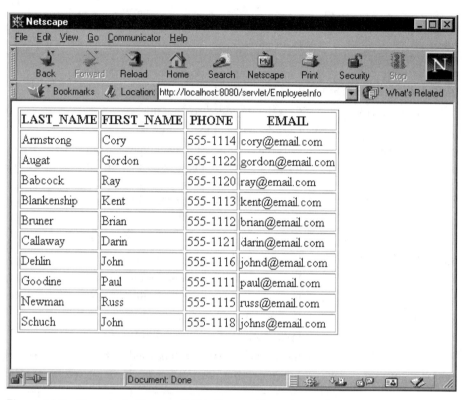

Figure 16.8   Dynamically Generated Table Returned from the `EmployeeInfo` Servlet

```
/**
 * Creates a persistent connection to a MySQL database.
 */
public void init() throws ServletException
{
  String jdbcDriver = "org.gjt.mm.mysql.Driver";
  String dbURL = "jdbc:mysql://localhost/phonebook";

  try
  {
    Class.forName(jdbcDriver).newInstance();

    dbConn = DriverManager.getConnection(dbURL);
  }
  catch (ClassNotFoundException e)
  {
    throw new UnavailableException("JDBC driver not found:" +
      jdbcDriver);
  }
  catch (SQLException e)
  {
```

```
      throw new UnavailableException("Unable to connect to: " +
        dbURL);
    }
    catch (Exception e)
    {
      throw new UnavailableException("Error: " + e);
    }
}


/**
 * Dynamically constructs an HTML table from a ResultSet object
 * containing employee information.
 */
public void doGet(HttpServletRequest request,
  HttpServletResponse response) throws ServletException,
  IOException
{
  response.setContentType("text/html");

  PrintWriter out = response.getWriter();

  try
  {
    Statement stmt = dbConn.createStatement();

    //create ResultSet containing employee information
    String sql = "select LAST_NAME, FIRST_NAME, PHONE, " +
      "EMAIL from EMPLOYEE order by LAST_NAME, FIRST_NAME";
    ResultSet rs = stmt.executeQuery(sql);

    //get ResultSetMetaData object from ResultSet
    ResultSetMetaData rsMeta = rs.getMetaData();

    //get number of columns in ResultSet
    int cols = rsMeta.getColumnCount();

    out.println("<TABLE BORDER=\"1\">"); //begin dynamic table

    //create header row containing column titles
    out.println("<TR>");
    for (int i = 1; i <= cols; i++)
    {
      out.println("<TH>" + rsMeta.getColumnLabel(i) + "</TH>");
    }
    out.println("</TR>");

    //create a row for each row in result set
    while (rs.next())
    {
      out.println("<TR>");
      for (int i = 1; i <= cols; i++)
      {
```

```
            out.println("<TD>" + rs.getString(i) + "</TD>");
          }
          out.println("</TR>");
        }

        out.println("</TABLE>"); //end dynamic table

        out.close();
      }
      catch (Exception e)
      {
        System.out.println(e.getMessage());
      }
    }
  }
```

SQL Escape Syntax

JDBC enables cross-database development by defining a single database API capable of interfacing with any database for which a JDBC driver is available. This ability to support numerous vendor's databases from a single codebase helps database applications realize Java's "Write Once, Run Anywhere" promise. Unfortunately, strictly adhering to the JDBC API does not, in itself, guarantee cross-database compatability. This is due to the fact that although most databases share a common SQL syntax for simple functions, they are not consistent when specifying more advanced functionality. One way to solve the problems presented by inconsistent SQL syntax is to use database-specific SQL in your JDBC applications. However, writing database-specific SQL into a JDBC application destroys its database independence by tying it to a particular vendor's product. Fortunately, there is a way to take advantage of many advanced database functions while maintaining database independence. This is accomplished through the use of JDBC escape clauses. An *escape clause* defines a standard JDBC syntax for common SQL features whose syntax may vary among databases. Escape clauses are translated into the proper database-specific SQL by the JDBC driver. Proper use of escape clauses can help ensure that your JDBC application will run using any JDBC-compliant database.

The JDBC escape syntax consists of a keyword followed by any number of parameters. The entire escape clause is always enclosed within braces as follows:

```
{KEYWORD PARAMETERS}
```

You might recognize this syntax from the section on stored procedures. This section demonstrated how to use a JDBC escape clause to call a stored procedure in a database-independent way. Again, the escape syntax for calling a stored procedure looks like this:

```
{call PROCEDURE_NAME(?, ?, ?, ?)}
```

Or, for stored procedures that return a value:

```
{? = call PROCEDURE_NAME(?, ?, ?, ?)}
```

In addition to stored procedures, there are many other areas where database-specific SQL diverges. For example, the syntax used to specify dates and times varies widely among databases. Fortunately, there is a very simple escape syntax for specifying dates and times within SQL statements. For example, the following escape clauses specify a date, a time, and a timestamp, respectively.

```
{d 'yyyy-mm-dd'}
{t 'hh:mm:ss'}
{ts 'yyyy-mm-dd hh:mm:ss'}
```

To illustrate, the following UPDATE statement updates a customer's birth date in a database-independent way.

```
update CUSTOMER set BIRTHDAY = {d '1970-01-26'} where ID = 1;
```

JDBC defines an escape syntax for performing numeric, string, time, date, system, and conversion functions. These escape clauses use the fn keyword followed by the function name and any function parameters like this:

```
{fn FUNCTION(PARAM1, PARAM2, ..., PARAMn)}
```

Not all databases support all of the functions defined by the JDBC specification. To determine which functions are supported by a particular database, use the DatabaseMetaData object's getNumericFunctions() and getString-Functions() methods. These methods return a comma-delimited list of all supported numeric or string functions, respectively.

JDBC escape functions can be used in place of their database-specific counterparts rather easily. For example, the following SQL statements demonstrate a database-specific SQL statement (using Oracle syntax) followed by its database-independent equivalent (using JDBC escape syntax).

```
update CUSTOMER set LAST_VISIT = SYSDATE where ID = 1;
update CUSTOMER set LAST_VISIT = {fn CURDATE()} where ID = 1;
```

The following paragraphs present the functions supported by the JDBC escape syntax.

JDBC defines the following numeric functions: ABS(number), ACOS(float), ASIN(float), ATAN(float), ATAN2(float1,float2), CEILING(number), COS(float), COT(float), DEGREES(number), EXP(float), FLOOR(number), LOG(float), LOG10(float), MOD(integer1,integer2), PI(), POWER(number, power), RADIANS(number), RAND(integer), ROUND(number,places), SIGN (number), SIN(float), SQRT(float), TAN(float), and TRUNCATE(number, places).

JDBC defines the following string functions: ASCII(string), CHAR(code), CONCAT(string1,string2), DIFFERENCE(string1,string2), INSERT(string1, start,length,string2), LCASE(string), LEFT(string,count), LENGTH (string), LOCATE(string1,string2,start), LTRIM(string), REPEAT(string, count), REPLACE(string1,string2,string3), RIGHT(string,count), RTRIM (string), SOUNDEX(string), SPACE(count), SUBSTRING(string,start, length), and UCASE(string).

JDBC defines the following date and time functions: CURDATE(), CURTIME(), DAYNAME(date), DAYOFMONTH(date), DAYOFWEEK(date), DAYOFYEAR (date), HOUR(time), MINUTE(time), MONTH(date), MONTHNAME(date), NOW(), QUARTER(date), SECOND(time), TIMESTAMPADD(interval,count,timestamp), TIMESTAMPDIFF(interval,timestamp1,timestamp2), WEEK(date), and YEAR (date).

JDBC defines the following system and conversion functions: DATABASE(), IFNULL(expression,value), USER(), and the conversion function CONVERT (value,SQLtype), where SQLtype is BIGINT, BINARY, BIT, CHAR, DATE, DECIMAL, DOUBLE, FLOAT, INTEGER, LONGVARBINARY, LONGVARCHAR, REAL, SMALLINT, TIME, TIMESTAMP, TINYINT, VARBINARY, or VARCHAR.

Outer joins are another area where SQL syntax varies widely among databases. The escape syntax for an outer join is as follows:

```
{oj TABLE_NAME LEFT OUTER JOIN TABLE_NAME ON SEARCH_CRITIRIA}
```

Use the DatabaseMetaData object's supportsOuterJoins(), supportsLimited-OuterJoins(), and supportsFullOuterJoins() to determine the extent to which outer joins are supported by a particular database.

Lastly, JDBC escape syntax allows special characters to be escaped so that they are interpreted literally rather than according to some special meaning. For example, the characters "%" and "_" have special meaning within an SQL LIKE clause. To interpret these characters literally, precede them with an escape character defined by this JDBC escape clause:

```
{escape 'ESCAPE_CHARACTER'}
```

For example, the following SQL statement searches for any rows where the customer's first name begins with an underscore.

```
select * from CUSTOMER where FIRST_NAME like '\_%' {escape '\'}
```

Database Connection Pooling

As previously discussed, database connections should usually not be created within the servlet's `service()`, `doGet()`, or `doPost()` method. Creating a new database connection to service each new request greatly reduces servlet performance. Of course, this performance penalty can be avoided by defining the database `Connection` object as a servlet instance variable and establishing the connection from within the servlet's `init()` method. This approach was first demonstrated in Listing 16.2. Though it may work well for low-traffic Web sites, there is a major disadvantage to this approach. The drawback is that all clients must share a single database connection. For heavy-traffic sites, any number of requests may arrive concurrently. If the first request grabs the database connection, all other requests are queued and forced to wait until the connection is available. In addition, this approach may present thread safety concerns. Fortunately, connection pooling provides a solution to these problems.

NOTE: Support for connection pooling was added to JDBC 2.0 as part of the JDBC 2.0 Optional Package. This package is based on the JDBC 2.0 Standard Extension API specification. The Standard Extension API allows JDBC 2.0 driver vendors to implement connection pooling in a standard way such that code written to take advantage of connection pools is portable across JDBC drivers and databases. The JDBC 2.0 Standard Extension API is contained within the `javax.sql` package as opposed to the basic `java.sql` package. Connection pooling and other advanced functionality was added as a standard extension in order to keep the core JDBC API as small and simple as possible. Unlike JDBC 2.0, the `javax.sql` package is included in the basic JDBC 3.0 distribution. Though available with many new drivers, connection pooling is demonstrated here for educational purposes (and is useful for older drivers).

Database connection pooling is the process of establishing a set, or *pool*, of database connections before they are needed. This pool of connections is often stored in a *connection broker* object that controls access to the connections. When a client requires a database connection, it simply asks the connection broker for an available (or free) connection. The broker selects a free connection from the pool, flags the connection as unavailable (or busy), and returns it to the client. Since it was created previously, the broker can return a connection almost instantly without the overhead required to establish a new connection. When the connection is no longer needed, the client returns it to the broker, who now flags it as available. In addition to handing out connections, the broker is responsible for all details regarding the maintenance of the connection pool. This may include occasionally refreshing database connections by dropping and recreating them or establishing new connections when the pool of available connections is exhausted by numerous concurrent requests. Listing 16.11 presents a connection broker object called ConnectionPool.

Listing 16.11 ConnectionPool manages a pool of database connections.

```
import java.sql.*;
import java.util.*;

/**
 * ConnectionPool creates a pool of connections of the specified
 * size to the specified database. The connection pool object
 * allows the client to specify the JDBC driver, database,
 * username, and password. In addition, the client can also
 * specify the number of connections to create when this class is
 * instantiated, the number of additional connections to create
 * if all connections are exhausted, and the absolute maximum
 * number of connections.
 *
 * @author Dustin R. Callaway
 */
public class ConnectionPool
{
  private String jdbcDriver = "";
  private String dbUrl = "";
  private String dbUsername = "";
  private String dbPassword = "";
  private String testTable = "";
  private int initialConnections = 10;
  private int incrementalConnections = 5;
  private int maxConnections = 50;
  private Vector connections = null;


  /**
   * Constructor stores the parameters passed by the calling
   * object.
   *
   * @param jdbcDriver String containing the fully qualified name
   *   of the jdbc driver (class name and full package info)
   * @param dbUrl String containing the database URL
   * @param dbUsername String containing the username to use when
   *   logging into the database
```

```
 * @param dbPassword String containing the password to use when
 *   logging into the database
 */
public ConnectionPool(String jdbcDriver, String dbUrl,
  String dbUsername, String dbPassword)
{
  this.jdbcDriver = jdbcDriver;
  this.dbUrl = dbUrl;
  this.dbUsername = dbUsername;
  this.dbPassword = dbPassword;
}


/**
 * Returns the initial number of connections to create.
 *
 * @return Initial number of connections to create.
 */
public int getInitialConnections()
{
  return initialConnections;
}


/**
 * Sets the initial number of connections to create.
 *
 * @param initialConnections Initial number of connections to
 *   create
 */
public void setInitialConnections(int initialConnections)
{
  this.initialConnections = initialConnections;
}


/**
 * Returns the number of incremental connections to create if
 * the initial connections are all in use.
 *
 * @return Number of incremental connections to create.
 */
public int getIncrementalConnections()
{
  return incrementalConnections;
}


/**
 * Sets the number of incremental connections to create if
 * the initial connections are all in use.
 *
 * @param incrementalConnections Number of incremental
```

```
 *  connections to create.
 */
public void setIncrementalConnections(
  int incrementalConnections)
{
  this.incrementalConnections = incrementalConnections;
}



/**
 * Returns the absolute maximum number of connections to
 * create. If all connections are in use, the getConnection()
 * method will block until one becomes free.
 *
 * @return Maximum number of connections to create.
 */
public int getMaxConnections()
{
  return maxConnections;
}



/**
 * Sets the absolute maximum number of connections to create.
 * If all connections are in use, the getConnection() method
 * will block until one becomes free.
 *
 * @param maxConnections Maximum number of connections to
 *   create.
 */
public void setMaxConnections(int maxConnections)
{
  this.maxConnections = maxConnections;
}



/**
 * Returns the name of the table that should be tested to
 * insure that the database connection is still open.
 *
 * @return Name of the database table used to test the
 *   connection.
 */
public String getTestTable()
{
  return testTable;
}



/**
 * Sets the name of the table that should be tested to insure
 * that the database connection is still open.
 *
```

```
 * @param testTable Name of the database table used to test the
 *   connection.
 */
public void setTestTable(String testTable)
{
  this.testTable = testTable;
}


/**
 * Creates a pool of connections. Number of connections is
 * determined by the value of the initialConnections property.
 */
public synchronized void createPool() throws Exception
{
  //make sure that createPool hasn't already been called
  if (connections != null)
  {
    return; //the pool has already been created, return
  }

  //instantiate JDBC driver object from init param jdbcDriver
  Driver driver = (Driver)
    (Class.forName(jdbcDriver).newInstance());

  DriverManager.registerDriver(driver); //register JDBC driver

  connections = new Vector();

  //creates the proper number of initial connections
  createConnections(initialConnections);
}


/**
 * Creates the specified number of connections, places them in
 * a PooledConnection object, and adds the PooledConnection to
 * the connections vector.
 *
 * @param numConnections Number of connections to create.
 */
private void createConnections(int numConnections) throws
  SQLException
{
  //create the specified number of connections
  for (int x=0; x < numConnections; x++)
  {
    //have the maximum number of connections been created?
    //a maxConnections value of zero indicates no limit
    if (maxConnections > 0 &&
      connections.size() >= maxConnections)
    {
```

```
      break; //break out of loop because we're at the maximum
    }

    //add a new PooledConnection object to connections vector
    connections.addElement(new PooledConnection(
      newConnection()));

    System.out.println("Database connection created...");
  }
}


/**
 * Creates a new database connection and returns it.
 *
 * @return New database connection.
 */
private Connection newConnection() throws SQLException
{
  //create a new database connection
  Connection conn = DriverManager.getConnection (dbUrl,
    dbUsername, dbPassword);

  //if this is the first connection, check the maximum number
  //of connections supported by this database/driver
  if (connections.size() == 0)
  {
    DatabaseMetaData metaData = conn.getMetaData();
    int driverMaxConnections = metaData.getMaxConnections();

    //driverMaxConnections value of zero indicates no maximum
    //or unknown maximum
    if (driverMaxConnections > 0 &&
      maxConnections > driverMaxConnections)
    {
      maxConnections = driverMaxConnections;
    }
  }

  return conn; //return the new connection
}


/**
 * Attempts to retrieve a connection from the connections
 * vector by calling getFreeConnection(). If no connection is
 * currently free, and more can not be created, getConnection()
 * waits for a short amount of time and tries again.
 *
 * @return Connection object
 */
public synchronized Connection getConnection() throws
  SQLException
{
```

```java
    //make sure that createPool has been called
    if (connections == null)
    {
      return null; //the pool has not been created
    }

    Connection conn = getFreeConnection(); //get free connection

    while (conn == null) //no connection was currently free
    {
      //sleep for a quarter of a second and then check to see if
      //a connection is free
      wait(250);

      conn = getFreeConnection(); //try again to get connection
    }

    return conn;
  }


  /**
   * Returns a free connection from the connections vector. If no
   * connection is available, a new batch of connections is
   * created according to the value of the incrementalConnections
   * variable. If all connections are still busy after creating
   * incremental connections, the method will return null.
   *
   * @return Database connection object
   */
  private Connection getFreeConnection() throws SQLException
  {
    //look for a free connection in the pool
    Connection conn = findFreeConnection();

    if (conn == null)
    {
      //no connection is free, create additional connections
      createConnections(incrementalConnections);

      //try again to find a free connection
      conn = findFreeConnection();

      if (conn == null)
      {
        //there are still no free connections, return null
        return null;
      }
    }

    return conn;
  }
```

```
/**
 * Searches through all of the pooled connections looking for
 * a free connection. If a free connection is found, its
 * integrity is verified and it is returned. If no free
 * connection is found, null is returned.
 *
 * @return Database connection object.
 */
private Connection findFreeConnection() throws SQLException
{
  Connection conn = null;
  PooledConnection pConn = null;

  Enumeration enum = connections.elements();

  //iterate through the pooled connections looking for free one
  while (enum.hasMoreElements())
  {
    pConn = (PooledConnection)enum.nextElement();

    if (!pConn.isBusy())
    {
      //this connection is not busy, get a handle to it
      conn = pConn.getConnection();

      pConn.setBusy(true); //set connection to busy

      //test the connection to make sure it is still valid
      if (!testConnection(conn))
      {
        //connection is no longer valid, create a new one
        conn = newConnection();

        //replace invalid connection with new connection
        pConn.setConnection(conn);
      }

      break; //we found a free connection, stop looping
    }
  }

  return conn;
}


/**
 * Test the connection to make sure it is still valid. If not,
 * close it and return FALSE.
 *
 * @param conn Database connection object to test.
 * @return True indicates connection object is valid.
 */
```

```java
private boolean testConnection(Connection conn)
{
  try
  {
    //determine if a test table has been designated
    if (testTable.equals(""))
    {
      //There is no table to test the database connection so
      //try setting the auto commit property. This verifies
      //a valid connection on some databases. However, the
      //test table method is much more reliable.
      conn.setAutoCommit(true);
    }
    else
    {
      //check if this connection is valid
      Statement stmt = conn.createStatement();
      stmt.execute("select count(*) from " + testTable);
    }
  }
  catch (SQLException e)
  {
    //connection is no longer valid, attempt to close it
    closeConnection(conn);

    return false;
  }

  return true;
}


/**
 * Turns off the busy flag for the current pooled connection.
 * All ConnectionPool clients should call returnConnection() as
 * soon as possible following any database activity (within a
 * finally block).
 *
 * @param conn Connection object
 */
public void returnConnection(Connection conn)
{
  //make sure that createPool has been called
  if (connections == null)
  {
    return; //the pool has not been created
  }

  PooledConnection pConn = null;

  Enumeration enum = connections.elements();
```

```java
//iterate through the pooled connections looking for the
//returned connection
while (enum.hasMoreElements())
{
  pConn = (PooledConnection)enum.nextElement();

  //determine if this pooled connection contains the returned
  //connection
  if (conn == pConn.getConnection())
  {
    //the connection has been returned, turn off busy flag
    pConn.setBusy(false);

    break;
  }
}
}


/**
 * Refreshes all of the connections in the connection pool.
 */
public synchronized void refreshConnections() throws
  SQLException
{
  //make sure that createPool has been called
  if (connections == null)
  {
    return; //the pool has not been created
  }

  PooledConnection pConn = null;

  Enumeration enum = connections.elements();

  while (enum.hasMoreElements())
  {
    pConn = (PooledConnection)enum.nextElement();

    if (!pConn.isBusy())
    {
      wait(10000); //wait 5 seconds
    }

    closeConnection(pConn.getConnection());

    pConn.setConnection(newConnection());

    pConn.setBusy(false);
  }
}
```

```
/**
 * Closes all of the connections and empties the connection
 * pool. Once this method has been called, the createPool()
 * method can again be called.
 */
public synchronized void closeConnections() throws SQLException
{
  //make sure that createPool has been called
  if (connections == null)
  {
    return; //the pool has not been created
  }

  PooledConnection pConn = null;

  Enumeration enum = connections.elements();

  while (enum.hasMoreElements())
  {
    pConn = (PooledConnection)enum.nextElement();

    if (!pConn.isBusy())
    {
      wait(5000); //wait 5 seconds
    }

    closeConnection(pConn.getConnection());

    connections.removeElement(pConn);
  }

  connections = null;
}


/**
 * Closes a database connection.
 *
 * @param conn Database connection to close.
 */
private void closeConnection(Connection conn)
{
  try
  {
    conn.close();
  }
  catch (SQLException e)
  {
  }
}
```

```java
/**
 * Sleeps for a specified number of milliseconds.
 *
 * @param mSeconds Number of seconds to sleep.
 */
private void wait(int mSeconds)
{
  try
  {
    Thread.sleep(mSeconds);
  }
  catch (InterruptedException e)
  {
  }
}


/**
 * Inner class encapsulating the properties of a pooled
 * connection object. These properties include a JDBC database
 * connection object and a flag indicating whether or not the
 * database object is currently in use (busy).
 */
class PooledConnection
{
  Connection connection = null;
  boolean busy = false;

  public PooledConnection(Connection connection)
  {
    this.connection = connection;
  }

  public Connection getConnection()
  {
    return connection;
  }

  public void setConnection(Connection connection)
  {
    this.connection = connection;
  }

  public boolean isBusy()
  {
    return busy;
  }

  public void setBusy(boolean busy)
  {
    this.busy = busy;
  }
}
}
```

The `ConnectionPool` class is a typical connection broker that provides methods to retrieve available connections, return connections to the pool, refresh connections, and close connections. Listing 16.12 presents a version of Listing 16.10 that has been adapted to use the `ConnectionPool` class to manage a database connection pool. The output created by this servlet is identical to that shown in Figure 16.8.

Listing 16.12   Servlet that employs database connection pooling.

```java
import javax.servlet.*;
import javax.servlet.http.*;
import java.io.*;
import java.sql.*;

/**
 * EmployeeInfo returns employee data presented in an HTML table
 * that is dynamically created with help from the
 * ResultSetMetaData object. This servlet utilizes the
 * ConnectionPool class to manage a pool of database connections.
 */
public class EmployeeInfo extends HttpServlet
{
  ConnectionPool connectionPool = null;

  /**
   * Creates a connection pool.
   */
  public void init() throws ServletException
  {
    String jdbcDriver = "org.gjt.mm.mysql.Driver";
    String dbURL = "jdbc:mysql://localhost/phonebook";

    try
    {
      //instantiate the connection pool object by passing the
      //jdbc driver, database URL, username, and password
      connectionPool = new ConnectionPool(jdbcDriver, dbURL,
        "", "");

      //specify the initial number of connections to establish
      connectionPool.setInitialConnections(5);

      //specify number of incremental connections to create if
      //pool is exhausted of available connections
      connectionPool.setIncrementalConnections(5);

      //specify absolute maximum number of connections to create
      connectionPool.setMaxConnections(20);

      //specify a database table that can be used to validate the
      //database connections (this is optional)
      connectionPool.setTestTable("EMPLOYEE");
```

```java
        connectionPool.createPool(); //create the connection pool
    }
    catch (Exception e)
    {
      System.out.println("Error: " + e);
    }
}


/**
 * Dynamically constructs an HTML table from a ResultSet object
 * containing employee information.
 */
public void doGet(HttpServletRequest request,
  HttpServletResponse response) throws ServletException,
  IOException
{
  Connection dbConn = null;

  response.setContentType("text/html");

  PrintWriter out = response.getWriter();

  try
  {
    //get free connection from pool
    dbConn = connectionPool.getConnection();

    Statement stmt = dbConn.createStatement();

    //create ResultSet containing employee information
    String sql = "select LAST_NAME, FIRST_NAME, PHONE, " +
      "EMAIL from EMPLOYEE order by LAST_NAME, FIRST_NAME";
    ResultSet rs = stmt.executeQuery(sql);

    //get ResultSetMetaData object from ResultSet
    ResultSetMetaData rsMeta = rs.getMetaData();

    //get number of columns in ResultSet
    int cols = rsMeta.getColumnCount();

    out.println("<TABLE BORDER=\"1\">"); //begin dynamic table

    //create header row containing column titles
    out.println("<TR>");
    for (int i = 1; i <= cols; i++)
    {
      out.println("<TH>" + rsMeta.getColumnLabel(i) + "</TH>");
    }
    out.println("</TR>");

    //create a row for each row in result set
    while (rs.next())
    {
```

```
            out.println("<TR>");
            for (int i = 1; i <= cols; i++)
            {
               out.println("<TD>" + rs.getString(i) + "</TD>");
            }
            out.println("</TR>");
         }

         out.println("</TABLE>"); //end dynamic table

         out.close();
      }
      catch (Exception e)
      {
         System.out.println(e.getMessage());
      }
      finally
      {
         //return connection to pool (always within a finally block)
         connectionPool.returnConnection(dbConn);
      }
   }
}
```

NOTE: It is imperative that you always return connections to the pool. Any connections that are not returned properly (using the `ConnectionPool` object's `returnConnection()` method) will become permanently unavailable. If connections are not returned, the entire pool can be quickly exhausted. In addition, connections should be returned as soon as possible to ensure that the maximum number of connections are available to service other requests. Finally, always return connections to the pool from within a `finally` block. This practice guarantees that all connections will be returned, even if an unexpected error occurs.

Introduction to the MySQL Database

Most of the samples presented in this chapter make use of the MySQL database server. *MySQL* (pronounced "My Ess Que Ell") was chosen because of its popularity and the fact that it is an open source product that is available free of charge on UNIX, Windows, and MacOS. The source code for MySQL is made available under the GNU General Public License (GPL). (To demonstrate functionality not provided by MySQL, Oracle was chosen because of its cross-platform availability.)

Despite the fact that MySQL is free, it is still a powerful industrial-strength database. For instance, the creators of MySQL describe running this product in a production environment comprised of more than 40 databases consisting of 10,000 tables. Of these tables, more than 500 contained more than 7 million rows. In addition, on some benchmarks, MySQL's performance has exceeded the performance of many commercial databases by an order of magnitude. As you can see, MySQL is a free database capable of handling many of your toughest mission-critical database requirements.

 NOTE: It should be noted that MySQL does not implement many of the functions that are commonly supported by commercial databases. For example, MySQL currently does not support database triggers, stored procedures, or transactions. Fortunately, however, the exclusion of these features does, in many areas, improve database performance by reducing processing overhead. For instance, triggers can greatly reduce a database's performance as they are executed for each row in an insert, update, or delete operation. Therefore, if you choose to deploy MySQL in your organization, you will need to consider these limitations as you design your systems.

The following sections describe where to get MySQL, how to install it, how to create a database that contains the sample tables (see Listing 16.1), and how to access the tables from a Java servlet using a freely available JDBC driver. Of course, this section is only a very brief tutorial. For full documentation and additional information regarding MySQL, visit *http://www.mysql.com/*.

Finding and Installing MySQL

You can locate the MySQL installation file for your platform on the accompanying CD or you can download the latest version from *http://www.mysql.com/*. The MySQL installation files are usually named using the following format:

```
mysql-VERSION-OS.extension
```

For example, a file containing MySQL version 3.22.32 for a Sun machine running Solaris 5 would look like *mysql-3.22.32-SunOS5.tgz*. And similarly, the installation file for MySQL running on Windows NT/2000/9x might look like *mysql-3.23.21-win.zip*.

After finding the appropriate file for your platform, install it according to the installation instructions contained on the CD or available at *http://www.mysql.com/*. On UNIX, installation involves expanding a compressed TAR file and following some additional simple instructions. On Windows,

MySQL is installed by simply running the executable installation file. Once MySQL is installed and running, you're ready to create a new database.

MySQL includes numerous useful utilities within its */bin* directory. These utilities include programs to import and export data, create and delete databases, and execute SQL statements. For example, to view all of the current databases, run the `mysqlshow` executable like this:

```
shell> mysqlshow
+--------------+
|  Databases   |
+--------------+
| mysql        |
| phonebook    |
| test         |
+--------------+
```

To create a new database, run the *mysqladmin* program using its `create` command while passing the name of the database as a command-line parameter. For instance, a database called phonebook can be created like this:

```
mysqladmin create phonebook
```

Similarly, a database can be dropped using the `drop` command like this:

```
mysqladmin drop phonebook
```

Once a database has been created, tables can be built using the *mysql* utility. In order to build the sample tables presented in Listing 16.1, retrieve the SQL script called *phonebook.sql* from the accompanying CD or use a text editor to create the *phonebook.sql* text file from Listing 16.1. Once you have the SQL script, build the tables by directing the SQL script instructions into the phonebook database using the *mysql* program like this:

```
mysql phonebook < phonebook.sql
```

The *mysql* utility is extremely useful for viewing data within database tables as well as creating, updating, and deleting rows. To perform these tasks, enter the *mysql* interactive shell and activate the phonebook database like this:

```
shell> mysql phonebook
Welcome to the MySQL monitor.  Commands end with ; or \g.
Your MySQL connection id is 9 to server version: 3.21.29a-gamma-
    debug

Type 'help' for help.

mysql>
```

Once you're at the `mysql>` prompt, you can perform a variety of tasks. For instance, you can examine a table within the database like this:

```
mysql> show columns from employee;
+---------------+-------------+------+-----+---------+----------+
| Field         | Type        | Null | Key | Default | Extra    |
+---------------+-------------+------+-----+---------+----------+
| EMPLOYEE_ID   | int(11)     |      | PRI | 0       | auto-inc |
| DEPARTMENT_ID | int(11)     | YES  |     | NULL    |          |
| FIRST_NAME    | varchar(20) | YES  |     | NULL    |          |
| LAST_NAME     | varchar(20) | YES  |     | NULL    |          |
| PHONE         | varchar(20) | YES  |     | NULL    |          |
| EMAIL         | varchar(50) | YES  |     | NULL    |          |
| HIRE_DATE     | date        | YES  |     | NULL    |          |
+---------------+-------------+------+-----+---------+----------+
7 rows in set (0.07 sec)

mysql>
```

You can also execute SQL SELECT, UPDATE, and DELETE commands like this:

```
mysql> select FIRST_NAME, LAST_NAME, PHONE, EMAIL from EMPLOYEE
    where EMPLOYEE_ID > 5;
+------------+-----------+----------+------------------+
| FIRST_NAME | LAST_NAME | PHONE    | EMAIL            |
+------------+-----------+----------+------------------+
| John       | Dehlin    | 555-1116 | johnd@email.com  |
| John       | Schuch    | 555-1118 | johns@email.com  |
| Ray        | Babcock   | 555-1120 | ray@email.com    |
| Darin      | Callaway  | 555-1121 | darin@email.com  |
| Gordon     | Augat     | 555-1122 | gordon@email.com |
+------------+-----------+----------+------------------+
5 rows in set (0.00 sec)

mysql> update EMPLOYEE set PHONE = 'UNLISTED';
Query OK, 10 rows affected (0.00 sec)

mysql> delete from EMPLOYEE where EMPLOYEE_ID <= 5;
Query OK, 5 rows affected (0.01 sec)

mysql>
```

Of course, we have only scratched the surface of the full array of configuration and database management utilities provided by MySQL. In addition, if you prefer a graphical interface, there are many useful GUI tools available for managing MySQL databases. Visit *http://www.mysql.com/* for a comprehensive list of free MySQL applications (many include source code).

Accessing MySQL from a Servlet

There are several free JDBC drivers available for MySQL. The driver used in this chapter is an open source JDBC driver called MM MySQL developed by Mark Matthews. This driver, along with its source code, is included on the accompanying CD or it can be downloaded from the following URL:

http://mmmysql.sourceforge.net/

The MM MySQL driver is packaged in a JAR file. Before using the `Class.forName().newInstance()` method to load the driver, its JAR file must be added to the CLASSPATH so that the Java class loader can locate the driver class file. The fully qualified class name (including package information) of the MM MySQL driver is `org.gjt.mm.mysql.Driver` and its JDBC URL uses this format:

```
jdbc:mysql://SERVER[:PORT]/DATABASE_NAME
```

Therefore, the URL for a database called phonebook residing on the local computer will look like `jdbc:mysql://localhost/phonebook`. To illustrate, the following code demonstrates how to establish a database connection using the MM MySQL JDBC driver from within a servlet's `init()` method.

```java
Connection dbConn = null;

/**
 * Creates a persistent connection to a MySQL database.
 */
public void init() throws ServletException
{
  String jdbcDriver = "org.gjt.mm.mysql.Driver";
  String dbURL = "jdbc:mysql://localhost/phonebook";

  try
  {
    Class.forName(jdbcDriver).newInstance();

    dbConn = DriverManager.getConnection(dbURL);
  }
  catch (ClassNotFoundException e)
  {
    throw new UnavailableException("JDBC driver not found:" +
      jdbcDriver);
  }
  catch (SQLException e)
  {
    throw new UnavailableException("Unable to connect to: " +
      dbURL);
  }
}
```

Summary

This chapter defines the purpose of the Java Database Connectivity API and illustrates the basic JDBC architecture. The four types of JDBC drivers are also described. In addition, the process of connecting to a database is discussed in detail and many advanced database concepts are presented. These advanced concepts include a discussion regarding prepared statements, stored procedures, transactions, and connection pooling. Finally, the MySQL database is introduced in order to provide the reader with a simple (and free) way to test the techniques presented in this chapter.

Chapter Highlights

- JDBC is an API specification developed by Sun Microsystems that defines a uniform interface for accessing different relational databases. The primary function of the JDBC API is to allow the developer to issue SQL statements and process the results in a consistent, database-independent manner.

- The JDBC API uses a driver manager and database-specific drivers to provide transparent connectivity to heterogeneous databases.

- The *JDBC driver manager* ensures that the correct driver is used to access each data source. The driver manager is capable of supporting multiple concurrent drivers connected to multiple heterogeneous databases.

- A *JDBC driver* translates standard JDBC calls into a network protocol or client API call that facilitates communication with the database. This translation provides JDBC applications with database independence.

- The basic process of connecting to a database via JDBC goes like this: register the JDBC driver, establish a database connection, execute an SQL statement, process the results, close the database connection.

- A *prepared statement* is an SQL statement that is precompiled by the database. Through precompilation, prepared statements improve the performance of SQL commands that are executed multiple times (given that the database supports prepared statements).

- A *transaction* is a set of SQL statements that are grouped such that all statements are guaranteed to be executed or the entire operation will fail. If all statements execute successfully, the results are committed to the database; otherwise, all changes are rolled back.

- A *stored procedure* is an SQL operation that is stored on the database server. Stored procedures are usually written in an SQL dialect that has been expanded to include conditional statements, looping constructs, and other procedural programming features.

- *Metadata* is defined as information (or data) about data. JDBC provides specific information about a database or a result set via metadata objects.

- *Database connection pooling* is the process of establishing a set, or *pool*, of database connections before they are actually needed.

CHAPTER 17

Security

In the early days of the World Wide Web, security was not a foremost concern. At that time, the Web was primarily used to publish information that was in the public domain. However, as the Web hosts increasing numbers of business transactions, the need for security increases accordingly. Today millions of people transmit credit card numbers and other sensitive information over the Internet. Fortunately, a number of security mechanisms can be employed to promote the confidentiality and integrity of this private information. In fact, without security, e-commerce would not exist.

In this chapter, four methods of securing information on the Web are presented. Specifically, the following topics are discussed:

- Basic authentication
- Form-based authentication
- Digest authentication
- Secure Sockets Layer (SSL)

Basic Authentication

Basic authentication is among the oldest and most common methods of securing documents on the Web. This section introduces basic authentication, presents a servlet that implements basic authentication, and demonstrates how to use basic authentication with Tomcat.

Introduction to Basic Authentication

The original HTTP specification (RFC 1945) describes a simple method, or "scheme," to perform client authentication before returning sensitive data. This method, called *basic authentication*, allows the client to authenticate itself by providing a valid username and password. To validate this information, the server maintains a list of usernames and associated passwords as well as a list of all protected resources. When a secure resource is requested, the server returns an authentication challenge indicating that the requested resource is protected and requires a valid username and password. At this point, most browsers display a dialog box in order to collect username and password information that can be returned to the server along with another request for the protected resource. The server then compares the username and password against its *access control list* (i.e., list of valid credentials) and, if valid, returns the protected resource. If invalid, the authentication challenge is returned again. The following six steps further illustrate the basic authentication scheme as implemented by the Apache Web Server.

1. The browser requests a resource called *salaries.html* using the following GET request.

   ```
   GET /protected/salaries.html HTTP/1.0
   ```

2. After receiving the request, the server determines that the requested resource requires basic authentication. Since the client's request did not include authorization information, the server responds with a "401 Unauthorized" status code as follows:

   ```
   HTTP/1.1 401 Unauthorized
   Server: Apache/1.2.6
   Date: Sat, 24 Jun 2000 02:29:07 GMT
   WWW-Authenticate: Basic realm="InsideServlets"
   Content-length: 223
   Content-type: text/html

   <HTML><HEAD><TITLE>Unauthorized</TITLE></HEAD>
   <BODY><H1>Unauthorized</H1>
   Proper authorization is required for this area. Either your
   browser does not perform authorization, or your authorization has
   failed.
   </BODY></HTML>
   ```

   In addition to the standard header fields, the server adds a field called WWW-Authenticate. This field indicates the authentication scheme employed by the server as well as the context, or "realm," in which the authentication is valid. This response is called an *authentication challenge*. In this example, the server is using basic authentication that is valid within the InsideServlets realm. The realm value is arbitrary and useful only in comparison to other realms on this server.

3. If the browser supports basic authentication, it displays a username/password dialog box when the "401 Unauthorized" response is received.

Otherwise, if basic authentication is not supported, it displays the HTML portion of the response indicating this fact.

4. After the username and password are entered, the original request is reissued to the server with the addition of an `Authorization` header field as shown here:

```
GET /protected/salaries.html HTTP/1.0
Authorization: Basic RHVzdGluOnNlcnZsZXRz
```

The `Authorization` field indicates the authentication scheme employed by the client (i.e., `Basic`) followed by the username and password represented as a Base64-encoded string. The `Authorization` header field here indicates that the client is using the basic authentication scheme. The username/password string "RHVzdGluOnNlcnZsZXRz" is the Base64-encoding of the string "Dustin:servlets," where "Dustin" is the username and "servlets" is the password. (Basic authentication encodes username and password information using the *username:password* format.)

5. If the username and password are valid, the server responds with the requested document. If invalid, the server responds with the same "401 Unauthorized" message. If challenged a second time, the browser may either display the username/password dialog box again or display the HTML portion of the server's response.

6. Once authenticated, most browsers continue to send the authentication information in the `Authorization` header with each subsequent request to this server. This allows the client to view other protected documents without having to reauthenticate with each new request.

The basic authentication scheme is actually not considered secure because the username and password are not encrypted before transmission. Basic authentication is most useful in low-security environments or in conjunction with a secure connection (e.g., https). However, more secure authentication schemes do exist. For instance, the HTTP/1.1 protocol includes support for the Digest Access Authentication scheme (see RFC 2069) that improves upon many of basic authentication's primary weaknesses.

Creating a Basic Authentication Servlet

As previously mentioned, basic authentication requires username and password information to be encoded in the Base64 format. Therefore, in order to implement basic authentication in a servlet, we must have some way to decode Base64-encoded messages (in order to extract username and password information from the encoded `Authorization` header). Fortunately, JDK 1.1, 1.2, and 1.3 all provide the `sun.misc.BASE64Decoder` class for decoding Base64 encoded text (BASE64Encoder is also provided). However, be aware that classes in the sun.* package are not part of the Java specification and may not exist in every Java implementation. Therefore, you may need to include this class when distributing applications that use it.

NOTE: *Base64* is the encoding scheme defined by MIME. This encoding scheme provides a format that is robust enough to preserve the original message in spite of the many transformations that can occur while data traverses the Internet. Base64 encodes information using a universally representable 64-character subset of US-ASCII (plus one special processing character). See RFC 1521 for more information regarding Base64 encoding.

Listing 17.1 presents a servlet that implements HTTP basic authentication to identify the client and grant access when appropriate.

Listing 17.1   Servlet uses basic authentication before showing salaries.

```
import javax.servlet.*;
import javax.servlet.http.*;
import java.io.*;
import sun.misc.BASE64Decoder;

/**
 * SalaryServlet uses HTTP basic authentication to authenticate
 * any request to this servlet. Salary information is only
 * returned if the user has been successfully authenticated.
 */
public class SalaryServlet extends HttpServlet
{
  private String validUsername = "Dustin";
  private String validPassword = "servlets";


  /**
   * Authenticate user and return confidential salary
   * information. Issue authentication challenge if username and
   * password is absent or invalid.
   */
  public void doGet(HttpServletRequest request,
    HttpServletResponse response) throws ServletException,
    IOException
  {
    response.setContentType("text/html");

    //get authorization header
    String authorization = request.getHeader("Authorization");
```

```
if (authorization == null)
{
  challenge(response); //no authorization so challenge
}
else
{
  //determine if client is using basic authentication
  if (!authorization.toLowerCase().startsWith("basic"))
  {
    challenge(response); //not basic so challenge
  }

  //strip off "basic " from Authorization line to get encoded
  //username and password
  String namePass = authorization.substring(6).trim();

  //instantiate Base64 decoder
  BASE64Decoder decode = new BASE64Decoder();

  //decode username and password
  namePass = new String(decode.decodeBuffer(namePass));

  int colon = namePass.indexOf(":");

  //get username and password from decoded authorization text
  String username = namePass.substring(0, colon);
  String password = namePass.substring(colon+1);

  //validate username and password (case-sensitive)
  if (!username.equals(validUsername) ||
    !password.equals(validPassword))
  {
    challenge(response); //invalid credentials so challenge
  }
  else
  {
    //authentication successful so return confidential data
    PrintWriter out = response.getWriter();

    out.println("<HTML>");
    out.println("<HEAD><TITLE>Salaries</TITLE></HEAD>");
    out.println("<BODY>");

    out.println("<H2>Confidential Salary Information</H2>");

    out.println("<TABLE BORDER=\"0\" CELLPADDING=\"4\" " +
      "CELLSPACING=\"2\">");
    out.println("<TR BGCOLOR=\"#E0E0E0\">");
    out.println("<TH>Employee</TH>");
    out.println("<TH>Position</TH>");
    out.println("<TH>Annual Salary</TH></TR>");
    out.println("<TR BGCOLOR=\"#E0E0E0\">");
    out.println("<TD>John Smith</TD>");
    out.println("<TD>Chief Executive Officer</TD>");
    out.println("<TD>$250,000</TD></TR>");
```

```
                    out.println("<TR BGCOLOR=\"#E0E0E0\">");
                    out.println("<TD>Dave Jones</TD>");
                    out.println("<TD>Chief Information Officer</TD>");
                    out.println("<TD>$200,000</TD></TR>");
                    out.println("<TR BGCOLOR=\"#E0E0E0\">");
                    out.println("<TD>Nancy Davis</TD>");
                    out.println("<TD>VP of Human Resources</TD>");
                    out.println("<TD>$150,000</TD></TR>");
                    out.println("<TR BGCOLOR=\"#E0E0E0\">");
                    out.println("<TD>Bob Johnson</TD>");
                    out.println("<TD>VP of Marketing</TD>");
                    out.println("<TD>$140,000</TD></TR>");
                    out.println("</TABLE>");

                    out.println("</BODY></HTML>");

                    out.close();
                }
            }
        }


        /**
         * Issues a basic authentication challenge.
         */
        private void challenge(HttpServletResponse response)
        {
            response.setStatus(response.SC_UNAUTHORIZED);
            response.setHeader("WWW-Authenticate", "Basic realm=\"" +
              "EmployeeData\"");
        }
    }
```

The SalaryServlet presented in Listing 17.1 secures its information by implementing basic authentication. This is accomplished in the doGet() method by first verifying that an Authorization header field is included with each request. If this header field does not exist, then the client is issued an authorization challenge by calling the challenge() method (see Figure 17.1). If

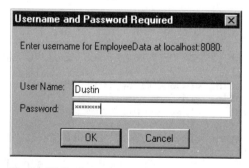

Figure 17.1   Browser Displays Dialog Box in Response to Authentication Challenge.

the request includes an Authorization header that uses basic authentication, a Base64 decoder is used to decode the username/password string that accompanies this header. The servlet then validates this information against a known username and password (see validUsername and validPassword in Salary-Servlet). If the validation fails, the user is issued another authentication challenge (see Figure 17.2). If successful, the requested document is returned to the client (see Figure 17.3).

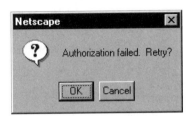

Figure 17.2   If Username/Password Is Invalid, Browser Prompts to Retry.

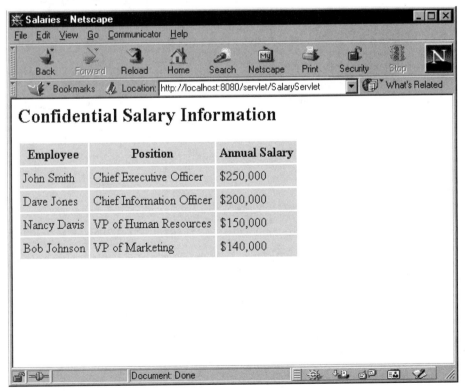

Figure 17.3   Once Client Is Authenticated, SalaryServlet Displays Confidential Salary Data.

Using Basic Authentication with Tomcat

Like most HTTP servers, Tomcat supports basic authentication. As previously discussed, basic authentication requires the Web server to maintain a list (known as the access control list) of valid usernames and passwords and the resources to which each username/password pair should be granted access. Although all basic authentication servers maintain an access control list, they may store this list in various ways. For example, a particular Web server may store access control information in a database, a directory service, or a text file. Tomcat uses the latter approach by storing a list of known usernames and passwords in a local text file called *tomcat-users.xml* located in the */jakarta-tomcat/conf* directory. Like all Tomcat configuration files, the *tomcat-users.xml* file is a well-formed XML document. Listing 17.2 shows a typical Tomcat access control list.

Listing 17.2   Sample *tomcat-users.xml* file.

```
<tomcat-users>
  <user name="tomcat"  password="tomcat"  roles="tomcat" />
  <user name="role1"   password="tomcat"  roles="role1" />
  <user name="both"    password="tomcat"  roles="tomcat,role1" />
  <user name="guest"   password="guest"   roles="guest" />
</tomcat-users>
```

Notice that, in addition to usernames and passwords, Tomcat users can be assigned roles. A *role* is an entity to which privileges are assigned. Each protected resource defines the roles that a user must possess in order to access it. These role assignments are made in each Web application's */WEB-INF/web.xml* file within the <security-constraint> block. To illustrate, here is the <security-constraint> block from the *examples* Web application installed with Tomcat 3.1:

```
<security-constraint>
  <web-resource-collection>
    <web-resource-name>Protected Area</web-resource-name>

    <!-- Define the context-relative URL(s) to be protected -->
    <url-pattern>/jsp/security/protected/*</url-pattern>

    <!-- Only these HTTP methods are protected -->
    <http-method>DELETE</http-method>
    <http-method>GET</http-method>
    <http-method>POST</http-method>
    <http-method>PUT</http-method>
  </web-resource-collection>
  <auth-constraint>
```

```
<!-- Anyone with one of these roles may access this area -->
  <role-name>tomcat</role-name>
  <role-name>role1</role-name>
</auth-constraint>
</security-constraint>
```

Let's evaluate each part of this sample `<security-constraint>` block. To begin, a `<web-resource-collection>` is defined. This element contains the `<web-resource-name>`, `<url-pattern>`, and `<http-method>` elements. The `<web-resource-name>` element indicates the logical name by which the protected area is known (`Protected Area`). The `<url-pattern>` element defines the URL pattern that is used to determine when a protected resource is being requested (`/jsp/security/protected/*`). Finally, the `<http-method>` element indicates the HTTP request methods that should be protected (`DELETE`, `GET`, `POST`, `PUT`). Following the `<web-resource-collection>` block, the `<auth-constraint>` (authentication constraint) block defines the roles (`tomcat`, `role1`) that grant a user access to the protected resource (the user must have one or more of the listed roles).

From this sample `<security-constraint>` block, we can see that all resources under the *examples* Web application's */jsp/security/protected* directory (including subdirectories) are protected. Without proper authorization, all HTTP `DELETE`, `GET`, `POST`, and `PUT` requests are denied. Proper authorization is defined by the `<auth-constraint>` block. The sample `<auth-constraint>` block indicates that only users possessing either the `tomcat` or `role1` roles will be granted access to the protected resources. Therefore, according to Listing 17.2, the `tomcat`, `role1`, and `both` users all have access to the protected resources under the */jsp/security/protected* directory, but `guest` does not.

NOTE: The security configurations specified in the *web.xml* file are defined by the Java Servlet Specification and are, therefore, portable between all servlet containers. However, other security configurations, such as mapping roles to users, are container specific. Though role mapping is demonstrated here using Tomcat, this mapping procedure varies with each servlet container.

In addition to security constraints, the *web.xml* file also defines the default authentication method used by each Web application. The default authentication method is contained within the `<login-config>` XML element. For example, the following `<login-config>` block indicates that the current Web application requires basic authentication.

```
<login-config>
  <auth-method>BASIC</auth-method>
  <realm-name>Example Basic Authentication Area</realm-name>
</login-config>
```

The `<auth-method>` element indicates the default authentication method. Tomcat 3.1 supports only two authentication methods—BASIC and EXPERIMENTAL_FORM (EXPERIMENTAL_FORM is discussed in the "Form-Based Authentication" section of this chapter). The `<realm-name>` element contains the name of an area that defines the scope within which a username and password are granted rights. Since each Web application can define its own security constraints, the realm usually refers to a particular Web application. The name of the realm is arbitrary and serves only to convey (to the client) the area to which they are attempting to gain access (see Figure 17.4).

To demonstrate the use of basic authentication, start the Tomcat server and request the following resource from your browser:

http://localhost:8080/examples/jsp/security/protected/

This request will attempt to load either the *index.html* or *index.jsp* file contained in the protected directory (Tomcat defines both of these as "default" files). Since the resource is requested using a protected URL pattern, Tomcat will issue an authentication challenge. Upon receiving the challenge, the browser displays a dialog box to collect username and password information (see Figure 17.4). Enter any of the usernames and passwords displayed in Listing 17.2 that are assigned the tomcat or role1 roles (e.g., use "tomcat" for both username and password) in order to access the protected *index.jsp* resource (*index.jsp* is automatically returned since there is no *index.html* file in the */protected* directory). Upon receiving an authorized username and password, Tomcat returns the protected file (see Figure 17.5).

Figure 17.4   Browser Displays Authentication Realm in Username and Password Required Dialog Box.

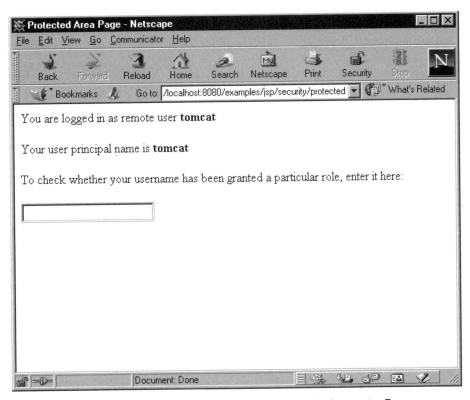

Figure 17.5 Tomcat Determines User Information from Basic Authentication Data.

NOTE: If you are using Tomcat 3.1, basic authentication does not work properly due to a bug in the code. To fix this problem, you can use Tomcat 3.2 provided on the accompanying CD (Tomcat 3.2 has fixed this bug), use the "patched" version of Tomcat 3.1 that is available on the accompanying CD, or manually apply the following patches to your copy of Tomcat 3.1.

To fix basic authentication in Tomcat 3.1, start by adding the following method to the org.apache.tomcat.core.Container class:

```
public boolean hasNonDefaultHandler()
{
  return handler != null;
}
```

Next, alter the org.apache.tomcat.request.SimpleMapper class by changing line 294 in the addContainer() method from this:

```
if( ct.getHandler() != null )
```

to this:

```
if( ct.hasNonDefaultHandler() )
```

Last, again alter the org.apache.tomcat.request.SimpleMapper class by changing line 390 in the getPrefixMatch() method from this:

```
if( wrapper != null && wrapper.getHandler() != null ) {
```

to this:

```
if( wrapper != null && wrapper.hasNonDefaultHandler () ) {
```

You may have noticed that once the client was authenticated, Tomcat was able to determine the client's username (see Figure 17.5). After authentication, the server makes the client's username available to the servlet via the Http-ServletRequest object's getRemoteUser() method. Similarly, it is possible to determine if a client has been assigned a particular role using the Http-ServletRequest object's isUserInRole() method. Table 17.1 documents several useful methods that return information regarding the user's authentication.

Now that we've seen some Tomcat samples in action, let's try securing our own custom servlet. Listing 17.3 presents a servlet that displays an authenticated user's login name and the roles to which the user has been assigned.

Listing 17.3   Retrieves information about the authenticated user.

```
import javax.servlet.*;
import javax.servlet.http.*;
import java.io.*;
```

Table 17.1   Methods That Return Information about an Authenticated User

Method	Description
getAuthType()	Returns the name of the security scheme used to authenticate the user (e.g., BASIC, DIGEST, CLIENT_CERT, or FORM).
getRemoteUser()	Returns the login name (username) if the user has been authenticated; otherwise, returns null. Whether authentication information will be returned with each request depends on the browser and type of authentication.
getUserPrincipal()	Returns a java.security.Principal object representing the currently authenticated user, or null if the user has not been authenticated.
isUserInRole()	Returns a boolean value of true if the authenticated user has been assigned the specified role. If the user is not included in the specified role or the user has not been authenticated, false is returned.

```java
/**
 * BasicAuthServlet displays information about an authenticated
 * user.
 */
public class BasicAuthServlet extends HttpServlet
{
  /**
   * Display the authenticated user's login name and the roles he
   * has been assigned.
   */
  public void doGet(HttpServletRequest request,
    HttpServletResponse response) throws ServletException,
    IOException
  {
    response.setContentType("text/html");

    PrintWriter out = response.getWriter();

    out.println("<HTML>");
    out.println("<HEAD>");
    out.println("<TITLE>Authentication Servlet</TITLE>");
    out.println("</HEAD>");
    out.println("<BODY>");

    out.println("<H2>Authentication Information</H2>");

    out.println("<TABLE BORDER=\"0\" CELLPADDING=\"5\" " +
      "CELLSPACING=\"2\">");

    out.println("<TR><TD BGCOLOR=\"#E0E0E0\">");
    out.println("Login Name:</TD>");
    out.println("<TD BGCOLOR=\"#E0E0E0\">" +
      request.getRemoteUser() + "</TD></TR>");

    out.println("<TR><TH BGCOLOR=\"#E0E0E0\" COLSPAN=\"2\">");
    out.println("ROLES");
    out.println("</TH></TR>");

    out.println("<TR><TD BGCOLOR=\"#E0E0E0\">tomcat:</TD>");
    out.println("<TD BGCOLOR=\"#E0E0E0\">" +
      request.isUserInRole("tomcat") + "</TD></TR>");

    out.println("<TR><TD BGCOLOR=\"#E0E0E0\">role1:</TD>");
    out.println("<TD BGCOLOR=\"#E0E0E0\">" +
      request.isUserInRole("role1") + "</TD></TR>");

    out.println("<TR><TD BGCOLOR=\"#E0E0E0\">guest:</TD>");
    out.println("<TD BGCOLOR=\"#E0E0E0\">" +
      request.isUserInRole("guest") + "</TD></TR>");

    out.println("</TABLE>");

    out.println("</BODY></HTML>");

    out.close();
  }
}
```

After you have typed in and compiled the `BasicAuthServlet` presented in
Listing 17.3 or located it on the accompanying CD, copy it to the *examples* Web
application's classes directory at */jakarta-tomcat/webapps/examples/WEB-INF/*
classes. Once in place, invoke the `BasicAuthServlet` using the following URL:

http://localhost:8080/examples/servlet/BasicAuthServlet

Figure 17.6 shows the output from the `BasicAuthServlet`. Notice that the
login name is `null`. This is due to the fact that the user is not authenticated. In
order to authenticate the user, we must instruct Tomcat to protect the `Basic-`
`AuthServlet`. To do this, assign security constraints to this servlet by changing
the URL pattern defined in the `<url-pattern>` element within the `<security-`
`constraint>` block in the *examples* Web application's *web.xml* file as follows:

```
<url-pattern>/servlet/BasicAuthServlet</url-pattern>
```

After the URL pattern has been altered and Tomcat has been restarted,
the `BasicAuthServlet` assumes the security constraints previously assigned to

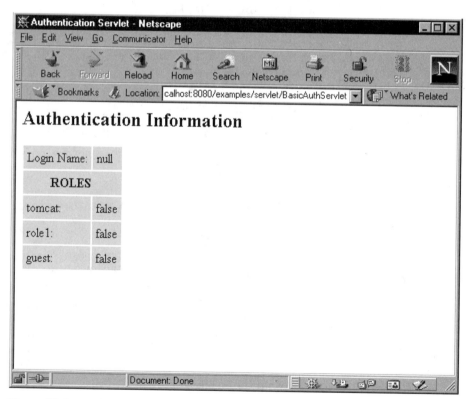

Figure 17.6   `BasicAuthServlet` Shows Data for a User That Has Not Been Authenticated.

the */jsp/security/protected* directory. For instance, it can be accessed only by users who have been assigned the `tomcat` or `role1` roles. Once protected, Tomcat will issue an authentication challenge to any client that requests the `BasicAuthServlet` that has not yet been authenticated. Now try accessing the servlet again using the following URL:

http://localhost:8080/examples/servlet/BasicAuthServlet

If the security constraints have been configured properly, Tomcat should respond to this request with an authentication challenge that causes your browser to display a dialog box used to collect your username and password (see Figure 17.4). Upon entering a valid username and password (try "both" for the username and "tomcat" for the password), the `BasicAuthServlet` will respond with much more information than what is returned to a user who has not been authenticated (see Figure 17.7).

Though basic authentication is quick and easy, remember that it is not really secure. The user credentials (name and password) are transmitted across the network in plain text and can be intercepted easily by someone monitoring

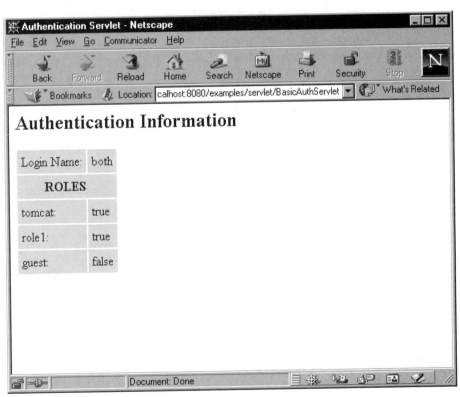

Figure 17.7 `BasicAuthServlet` Shows Data for a User That Has Been Authenticated.

network traffic. Then again, though it is not secure, basic authentication is often sufficient for many low-security tasks.

Form-Based Authentication

Form-based authentication is an extremely popular method of authenticating users on the Web. In short, *form-based authentication* consists of using an HTML form to query the user for his or her username and password. This information is then posted to the server where it is used to authenticate the user. Like basic authentication, form-based authentication on its own is not really secure. And since the username and password are not Base64 encoded, it can be considered even less secure than basic authentication. To be truly secure, form-based authentication must be combined with another security technology such as HTTP over SSL (i.e., https). However, like basic authentication, form-based authentication is oftentimes secure enough for low-security applications.

Creating a Form-Based Authentication Servlet

Form-based authentication is very simple to implement in a servlet. This authentication method usually includes two basic steps. First, the servlet must return an HTML form in response to all HTTP GET requests. This form should query the user for a username and a password. Second, the servlet must extract username and password information from any HTTP POST requests. This information can then be authenticated against a valid list of usernames and passwords and, if authentic, access can be granted. Listing 17.4 presents a servlet called FormAuthServlet that implements form-based authentication.

Listing 17.4   Authenticates a user using form-based authentication.

```
import javax.servlet.*;
import javax.servlet.http.*;
import java.io.*;

/**
 * FormAuthServlet queries the user for a username and password
 * using a basic HTML form. If the name and password is correct,
 * confidential salary information is returned.
 */
public class FormAuthServlet extends HttpServlet
{
  private String validUsername = "Dustin";
  private String validPassword = "servlets";
```

```java
/**
 * Build HTML form to query user for a username and password.
 * If the request object contains an attribute called
 * "loginMessage", this message is displayed in red directly
 * above the login button. A login message is added by the
 * doPost() method if authentication fails.
 */
public void doGet(HttpServletRequest request,
    HttpServletResponse response) throws ServletException,
    IOException
{
    response.setContentType("text/html");

    PrintWriter out = response.getWriter();

    out.println("<HTML>");
    out.println("<HEAD>");
    out.println("<TITLE>Authentication Servlet</TITLE>");
    out.println("</HEAD>");
    out.println("<BODY>");

    out.println("<H2>Form-Based Login</H2>");

    //no form action specified, so post back to this servlet
    out.println("<FORM METHOD=\"POST\">");

    out.println("<TABLE BORDER=\"0\">");

    out.println("<TR><TD>Username:</TD>");
    out.println("<TD><INPUT TYPE=\"TEXT\" NAME=\"Username\">");
    out.println("</TD></TR>");

    out.println("<TR><TD>Password:</TD><TD>");
    out.println("<INPUT TYPE=\"PASSWORD\" NAME=\"Password\">");
    out.println("</TD></TR>");

    String msg = (String)request.getAttribute("loginMessage");
    if (msg != null)
    {
        out.println("<TR><TD COLSPAN=\"2\" ALIGN=\"CENTER\">");
        out.println("<FONT COLOR=\"RED\">" + msg + "</FONT>");
        out.println("</TD></TR>");
    }

    out.println("<TR><TD COLSPAN=\"2\" ALIGN=\"CENTER\">");
    out.println("<INPUT TYPE=\"SUBMIT\" VALUE=\"Login\">");
    out.println("</TD></TR>");

    out.println("</TABLE>");

    out.println("</FORM></BODY></HTML>");

    out.close();
}
```

```
/**
 * Processes the login form when it is posted back the this
 * servlet. Authenticates the user using a hard-coded username
 * and password and, if authentication is successful, returns
 * confidential salary information. If authentication fails,
 * a message is added to the request via the setAttribute()
 * method and the doGet() method is called in order to display
 * the login form.
 */
public void doPost(HttpServletRequest request,
  HttpServletResponse response) throws ServletException,
  IOException
{
  String username = request.getParameter("Username");
  String password = request.getParameter("Password");

  //validate username and password (case-sensitive)
  if (username == null || password == null ||
    !username.equals(validUsername) ||
    !password.equals(validPassword))
  {
    request.setAttribute("loginMessage", "Invalid Login");
    doGet(request, response); //invalid password, show login
  }
  else
  {
    //user authenticated, show confidential salary information
    PrintWriter out = response.getWriter();

    out.println("<HTML>");
    out.println("<HEAD><TITLE>Salaries</TITLE></HEAD>");
    out.println("<BODY>");
    out.println("<H2>Confidential Salary Information</H2>");
    out.println("<TABLE BORDER=\"0\" CELLPADDING=\"4\" " +
      "CELLSPACING=\"2\">");
    out.println("<TR BGCOLOR=\"#E0E0E0\">");
    out.println("<TH>Employee</TH>");
    out.println("<TH>Position</TH>");
    out.println("<TH>Annual Salary</TH></TR>");
    out.println("<TR BGCOLOR=\"#E0E0E0\">");
    out.println("<TD>John Smith</TD>");
    out.println("<TD>Chief Executive Officer</TD>");
    out.println("<TD>$250,000</TD></TR>");
    out.println("<TR BGCOLOR=\"#E0E0E0\">");
    out.println("<TD>Dave Jones</TD>");
    out.println("<TD>Chief Information Officer</TD>");
    out.println("<TD>$200,000</TD></TR>");
    out.println("<TR BGCOLOR=\"#E0E0E0\">");
    out.println("<TD>Nancy Davis</TD>");
    out.println("<TD>VP of Human Resources</TD>");
    out.println("<TD>$150,000</TD></TR>");
    out.println("<TR BGCOLOR=\"#E0E0E0\">");
    out.println("<TD>Bob Johnson</TD>");
    out.println("<TD>VP of Marketing</TD>");
```

```
        out.println("<TD>$140,000</TD></TR>");
        out.println("</TABLE>");

        out.println("</BODY></HTML>");

        out.close();
      }
    }
  }
```

FormAuthServlet creates an HTML form in the doGet() method that collects the user's username and password (see Figure 17.8). Notice that the <FORM> tag in this HTML form does not specify an ACTION attribute. In the absence of an ACTION attribute, the browser submits the form data back to the same URL from which it received the form. Therefore, the username and password information will be posted back to the FormAuthServlet. The servlet's doPost() method then processes the form's input in order to authenticate the user. This simple servlet validates the user's credentials against a hard-coded username and password. Of course, in practice, this servlet typically reads

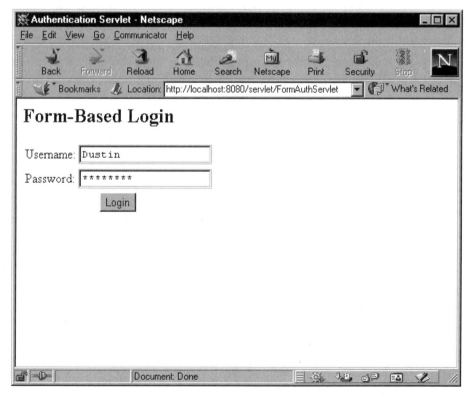

Figure 17.8 FormAuthServlet Returns a Login Form in Response to GET Requests.

username and password information from a database, directory service, or text file. If the user's credentials are vaild, the protected information is returned. Otherwise, a message is added to the request's attributes and the doGet() method is called in order to return the login screen along with a message indicating that the login information was incorrect.

Although this example used a single servlet, other variations are possible when implementing form-based authentication. For instance, some implementations may use two servlets—one that produces the HTML login form and a second servlet that authenticates the user's credentials. In this case, if the user's authentication fails, the second servlet redirects the user back to the first (using a RequestDispatcher.forward() or HttpServletResponse.sendRedirect() method). Of course, if the login form is not dynamic, you can skip the first servlet and simply allow the Web server to return an HTML document that submits username and password to the authentication servlet.

In addition, it is common to implement the authentication servlet such that when the user is authenticated, a special object is placed in the user's session indicating that the user is authorized. This "authorization" object may even contain the user's specific permissions. Using this approach, each protected servlet first checks the user's session for the authorization object before returning its confidential information. If the object exists and the user is authorized to access this servlet, the requested data is returned. Otherwise, the user is redirected to the login page. In this way, a single authentication servlet can pass authorization information to any number of protected servlets via the user's session.

Using Form-Based Authentication with Tomcat

In addition to basic authentication, Tomcat also includes built-in support for form-based authentication. When form-based authentication is enabled, Tomcat automatically returns the specified login page in response to any unauthorized request for a protected resource. To enable form-based authentication for a particular Web application, alter its /WEB-INF/web.xml file by commenting out any basic authentication instructions (if any exist) and add a <login-config> element indicating that form-based authentication should be used. For instance, the following example was extracted from the Tomcat 3.1 *examples* Web application's *web.xml* file.

```
<!--
<login-config>
  <auth-method>BASIC</auth-method>
  <realm-name>Example Basic Authentication Area</realm-name>
</login-config>
-->
```

```
<login-config>
  <auth-method>EXPERIMENTAL_FORM</auth-method>
  <realm-name>Example Form-Based Authentication Area
    </realm-name>
  <form-login-config>
    <form-login-page>/jsp/security/login/login.jsp
      </form-login-page>
    <form-error-page>/jsp/security/login/error.jsp
      </form-error-page>
  </form-login-config>
</login-config>
```

The form-based authentication `<login-config>` element is similar to the basic-authentication configuration except that the authentication method is set to `EXPERIMENTAL_FORM` and a `<form-login-config>` element is included. The `<form-login-config>` element contains information regarding the name and location of the login file that collects the client's username and password as well as an error page to display when a login attempt fails. The `<form-login-page>` tag specifies the name and location of the login page with respect to the current Web application's document root (e.g., /webapps/examples). Likewise, the `<form-error-page>` indicates the location of the login error page with respect to the Web application's document root.

You may be wondering about the `EXPERIMENTAL_FORM` value specified by the `<auth-method>` element. This value was chosen over the value of `FORM` in order to make it very clear that form-based authentication in Tomcat 3.1 is still considered experimental and has not been sufficiently tested. The implementation of form-based authentication is still incomplete. With Tomcat 3.1, this authentication method should not be used in a production environment and is presented here only to make you aware of its existence and function. Fortunately, Tomcat 3.2 includes complete and robust form-based authentication support. Therefore, the `<auth-method>` value has been changed from `EXPERIMENTAL_FORM` to simply `FORM` within Tomcat 3.2.

NOTE: Form-based authentication in Tomcat 3.1 is considered experimental and has not been sufficiently tested. In fact, there are several bugs in the implementation of this method. For example, when a user's login information is incorrect, Tomcat may respond with the login page rather than the error page as expected. However, as stated in the text, Tomcat 3.2 repairs all form-based authentication bugs and, therefore, uses the value `FORM` in the `<auth-method>` element rather than `EXPERIMENTAL_FORM`.

In this example, the `<form-login-page>` element indicates that the /jsp/security/login/login.jsp file will be returned whenever an unauthorized request is made for a protected resource in the *examples* Web application. Listing 17.5 shows the contents of the *login.jsp* file.

Listing 17.5   Contents of the *login.jsp* file.

```
<html>
<body>
<h1>Login page for examples</h1>

<form method="POST" action="j_security_check" >
 <input type="text" name="j_username">
 <input type="password" name="j_password">

 <input type="submit" name="j_security_check">
</form>

</body>
</html>
```

Notice that the *login.jsp* page simply contains an HTML form that prompts the user to enter a username and password (see Figure 17.9). The Servlet 2.2 Specification indicates that a form-based authentication login form must submit

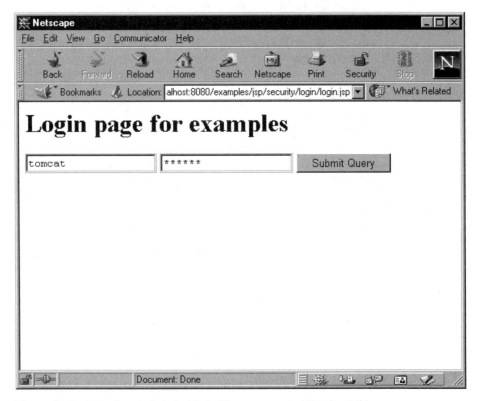

Figure 17.9   Login Page Included with the Tomcat *examples* Web Application

username and password variables named j_username and j_password using a form action called j_security_check. If the user's username and password credentials match one of those within the *tomcat-users.xml* file (and the user has been assigned the proper role), the user is authenticated and the protected resource is returned (see Figure 17.5). If the authentication check fails, the login error page, designated in the <form-error-page> element within the *web.xml* file, should be returned (see Figure 17.10).

Form-based authentication is a very popular method of securing Web sites. It allows the developer to build a more attractive and customized login screen than that provided by basic authentication (which involves the browser popping up a generic login dialog box as shown in Figure 17.1). However, remember that to be truly secure, form-based authentication must be coupled with an encryption technology, such as SSL, in order to protect the user's credentials as they are passed to the server.

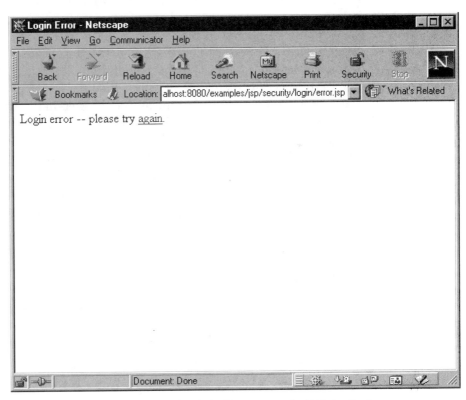

Figure 17.10 Error Page Included with the Tomcat *examples* Web Application

Digest Authentication

Like basic authentication, digest authentication is an HTTP authentication method that employs a challenge/response model to secure resources on the Web. Both of these methods require the server to maintain a user list and an access control list that includes a list of all users and passwords, as well as the privileges assigned to each user. Fortunately, however, digest authentication improves upon many of basic authentication's inadequacies.

For example, basic authentication transmits a client's username and password in plain text (using a thinly veiled Base64 encoding). In contrast, digest authentication never actually sends the client's password over the network. This eliminates the risk that the password may be intercepted during transit.

Now you may be asking, "If the password is not sent, how can the server authenticate the client?" The answer is that, rather than send the actual password, the client sends a "digest" representation of the password. This digest is derived from an irreversible computation (also known as a *one-way function*) that uses a random value received from the server (known as a *nonce*) and the password itself. The irreversible computation is performed by taking a hash of the password and nonce using the MD-5 (MessageDigest 5) or the SHA-1 (Secure Hashing Algorithm 1) hashing algorithms. The results of this computation are returned to the server, at which time the server performs the same digest computation in order to authenticate the user. In this manner, the client is able to prove to the server that it has the correct password without actually having to send the password. And since the server returns a different nonce value with each new request, the protected resources are secure even if someone intercepts the digest representation of the password (since the digest is invalid as soon as the request is serviced). To illustrate, the following five steps demonstrate a typical HTTP conversation using digest authentication.

1. Using the following GET request, the browser requests a resource called *salaries.html.*

   ```
   GET /protected/salaries.html HTTP/1.1
   ```

2. After receiving the request, the server determines that the requested resource requires digest authentication. Since the client's request did not include authorization information, the server responds with a "401 Unauthorized" status code as follows:

   ```
   HTTP/1.1 401 Unauthorized
   Date: Tue, 04 Jul 2000 17:54:04 GMT
   Server: SourceStreamServer/1.0
   Connection: close
   ```

```
WWW-Authenticate: Digest realm="InsideServlets",
   nonce="8288600389ca0ab110d0704c64c9b770630867a8b", domain="/",
   opaque="InsideServlets", stale=false, algorithm=MD5
```

```
401 Unauthorized
```

Table 17.2 explains each attribute of the WWW-Authenticate header.

3. If the browser supports digest authentication, it displays a username/password dialog box when the "401 Unauthorized" response is received. Otherwise, if digest authentication is not supported, it displays the HTML portion of the challenge response.

4. After the username and password are entered, the client calculates a digest representation of the password using the server's nonce value and the password itself. The original request is then reissued to the server with the addition of an Authorization header field as shown here:

```
GET /protected/salaries.html HTTP/1.1
Authorization: Digest username="digest", realm="InsideServlets",
   algorithm="MD5", uri="/",
   nonce="8f288600389ca0ab11b97f475a500d0704c64c9b770630867a8b",
   nc=00000001, cnonce="e2efc1677047449d7b87b22685e60275",
   opaque="InsideServlets", response="f3615df609bac9a0e3a281fad9"
```

The Authorization field indicates the authentication scheme employed by the client (i.e., Digest) followed by the username and a number of

Table 17.2 Attributes of a Digest Authentication WWW-Authenticate Header

Attribute	Description
Digest	Indicates that the server is requesting digest authentication.
realm	The scope in which this authentication is valid.
nonce	A randomly generated string created by the server. This value, along with the password, is used to produce the digest representation of the password (using the specified hashing algorithm). The contents of this string are server specific.
domain	A comma-delimited list of values indicating the URIs (Universal Resource Identifiers) that are associated with this authentication request.
opaque	Value specified by the server in order to identify this request further. This value should be returned unchanged by the client. The contents of this attribute are server specific.
stale	A boolean attribute indicating whether the nonce value was stale (i.e., old). If true, the client should reissue the request using the new nonce value. This attribute will be true only if the client's digest value was valid using the stale nonce. Otherwise, this attribute will be false.
algorithm	The algorithm used to perform the irreversible computation. If not specified, MD-5 is the default.

other attributes, including a checksum value (cnonce attribute) and the digest representation of the password (response attribute). The previous Authorization header field indicates that the client is using the digest authentication scheme.

5. The server extracts the client's username from the request and retrieves the password associated with this client (stored in a local user list). The server then performs the same computation as the client using its nonce value and its internal password for this user. If the server's calculation returns the same digest as the client's, authentication is successful and the requested document is returned. If unsuccessful, the server responds with the same "401 Unauthorized" message and a new nonce value. If challenged a second time, the browser may display either the username/password dialog box again or the HTML portion of the server's response.

Though digest authentication is much more secure than basic authentication, there aren't many browsers that support it. As of this writing, only Internet Explorer version 5.*x* provides full digest authentication support. Netscape browsers (version 4.7 and earlier) respond to a digest authentication challenge by sending a basic authentication header (hoping that, since they don't support digest, the server will accept basic authentication). Fortunately, RFC 2617 (documenting basic and digest authentication) allows the server to return WWW-Authenticate headers for both basic and digest authentication (if it supports both). In response, the browser should choose the most secure method that it supports. In this way, a more secure connection can be established when available, but this is not absolutely required if not supported by the client. The following server response demonstrates how this might look.

```
HTTP/1.1 401 Unauthorized
Date: Tue, 04 Jul 2000 17:54:04 GMT
Server: SourceStreamServer/1.0
Connection: close
WWW-Authenticate: Basic realm="InsideServlets"
WWW-Authenticate: Digest realm="InsideServlets",
  nonce="8288600389ca0ab110d0704c64c9b770630867a8b", domain="/",
  opaque="InsideServlets", stale=false, algorithm=MD5

401 Unauthorized
```

NOTE: Though RFC 2617 states that the browser must select the most secure authentication method that it supports, Internet Explorer 5.*x* does not seem to follow this rule. It supports digest communication, but it responds using basic authentication after receiving a response that includes both basic and digest authentication WWW-Authenticate headers.

This concludes the section on digest authentication. You may have noticed that we did not discuss how this authentication method is implemented by Tomcat. This is because Tomcat 3.1 does not support digest authentication. Therefore, the purpose of this section was to familiarize you with its use in case the server that you use supports this authentication method. This leads us to another security technology that is not yet supported by Tomcat, Secure Sockets Layer.

Secure Sockets Layer

Secure Sockets Layer (SSL) is a protocol developed by Netscape for establishing secure connections between two hosts. Security is provided through public key encryption methods applied to all data sent over the SSL connection. Secure Sockets is supported by most browsers, including those from Netscape and Microsoft. SSL is commonly used on the Web to ensure the privacy of confidential information, such as a customer's credit card number. By convention, the URL for an HTTP resource that implements SSL begins with *https://* rather than *http://*. SSL includes the following measures to ensure confidentiality, integrity, and authenticity:

- Encrypts data before transmission (confidentiality)
- Prevents the unauthorized modification of data during transit (integrity)
- Can guarantee the client that it is communicating with the correct server and vice versa (authenticity)

Now that we're familiar with the services SSL provides, let's discuss the technology that makes SSL possible. SSL is based on the principle of public key/private key cryptography. The following sections will introduce you to the world of cryptography and present the techologies upon which SSL is based.

Introduction to Cryptography

Cryptography is the process of transforming data (i.e., encrypting it) into an unreadable format (known as *cipher text*) as a means of keeping information confidential. Once encrypted, a secret key is required to decrypt (or decipher) the information back to its original form (known as *plain text*). A *key* is a sequence of bits used as input to an encryption algorithm in order to modify its output. If the same key is used for both encryption and decryption, it is known as a *symmetric key*. DES (Data Encryption Standard) is the most popular symmetric key encryption algorithm.

To use symmetric key cryptography, both the sender and receiver must possess the key in order to encrypt messages before sending and decrypt messages upon receipt. Therefore, the question is how do both sides get a copy of the symmetric key? The answer is that one side generates the symmetric key and sends it to the other. However, this begs the question, How can we ensure that the symmetric key will not be intercepted, allowing another party to decode our private messages? Public key cryptography is the solution.

Public Key Cryptography

Public key cryptography utilizes an asymmetric key algorithm. In contrast to symmetric keys, an *asymmetric key* is a value that can be used for encryption or decryption but not both. That is, decrypting a message requires a different key from that used to encrypt it. Though these two key values are mathematically related, one key cannot be derived from the other. One of the keys, known as the *public key*, is freely distributed to anyone who may request it. The other key, known as the *private key*, is kept secret. Together, these two keys can be used to securely exchange a symmetric key with another party, thus allowing both parties to decrypt each other's messages.

Here's how public key cryptography works. When I want to establish a secure conversation with you, I generate a symmetric key that we will both use to encrypt and decrypt our messages. Now, in order to securely send the symmetric key, I encrypt it using your public key and send it to you as cipher text. Anything encrypted with your public key can be decrypted only by using your private key (which you alone possess). In this way, I am able to securely send you the symmetric key that we will both use to communicate.

However, there are still some security problems here. Though the process just described does guarantee data confidentiality (since the data is encrypted) and integrity (since your private key will not be able to decrypt the information if it is altered in any way), it does not guarantee authenticity. That is, how do you know that this symmetric key really came from me? The answer is provided by the fact that public and private keys are asymmetrical. That is, either key can be used to encrypt a message and only the other key can be used to decrypt it. Therefore, before sending you my symmetric key, I can first encrypt it using my private key (that only my public key can decrypt) and then encrypt it again using your public key. In turn, when you receive my encrypted message, you decrypt the message once using your private key and then again using my public key. And since only my public key can decrypt a message encrypted with my private key, you are confident that the message came from me.

It may seem that we've covered everything, but there is one more security hole that must be addressed. That is, how can I tell that the public key that I just received really belongs to you? For instance, before sending data, I have to request your public key so that I can encrypt my secret symmetric key. However, what if someone interferes with this conversation and returns his public key instead of yours? Not knowing that I've received the wrong public key, I may send my symmetric key (encrypted with the wrong public key that the attacker can decrypt) and then proceed to transmit confidential information. Not good. Or what if someone simply masquerades as you on the Internet? Since we are not meeting face to face, it is difficult to make a positive identification before sharing confidential information. Again, this presents a formidable security risk. Fortunately, there is a solution to this problem. The solution is known as digital certificates.

Digital Certificates

Digital certificates provide a means whereby a trusted authority can vouch for your identity, thus guaranteeing the authenticity of a message. Digital certificates are issued by trusted entities known as *certificate authorities*. Digital certificates are analogous to passports. Similar to the manner that a customs officer may trust a passport issued by the United States government, you may choose to trust digital certificates that are issued by certain well-known certificate authorities (CA). VeriSign Corporation (*http://www.versign.com/*), Thawte Consulting (*http://www.thawte.com/*), and Entrust Technologies (*http://www.entrust.com/*) are three popular certificate authorities.

In order to receive a digital certificate, you must somehow prove your identity to the certificate authority. Depending on the certificate level (or class), this may involve something as simple as filling out a form on the Web and receiving an e-mail or something as complex as producing a birth certificate and various background checks. The higher the certificate level, the more confident you can be of the person's identity. Once the certificate authority is satisfied that your identity has been established, it will generate a public key for you and embed it in a digital certificate that is encrypted using its private key (this is also known as *signing* the certificate). This certificate is in the form of a file that can be saved on a disk or e-mailed to you. The corresponding private key is also generated and delivered to you. Using this process, a certificate authority can effectively "vouch" for your identity.

Now that we know what digital certificates are, let's see how they work. Again, let's assume that I want to send you a secure message. I first begin by requesting your public key. This, along with your identity, is returned in a digital certificate that has been signed by a certificate authority. Fortunately, my browser has already been programmed with the well-known public keys of several trusted certificate authorities. From the digital certificate, the browser is able to determine which certificate authority signed the certificate and, using the authority's well-known public key (hard-coded into the browser), decrypt the certificate to reveal the user's true identity and public key. In this way, it is possible to attach a positive identification to a public key before encrypting sensitive data and returning it. Once satisfied with your identity, I encrypt my symmetric key using my private key and then encrypt it again using your public key. Upon receipt, you request my public key, which is sent to you in a digital signature. After extracting my public key from my digital certificate, you first decrypt my symmetric key using your private key and then decrypt it again using my public key. We have now securely exchanged the symmetric key that can be used to encrypt and decrypt the rest of the conversation.

Although all secure servers have one, many individuals do not have a personal digital certificate (known as a *client certificate*) in order to positively establish their identities. However, most e-commerce Web sites do not require the customer to have a digital certificate when conducting an online transaction. Rather, most sites establish your identity by simply verifying that the name you entered matches the name on a valid credit card that you specified. However, for a much higher level of security, some servers may request a client's digital certificate. By exchanging certificates, both the client and server can be confident about the identity of the party with whom they are transacting business.

Though the server cannot positively identify you without a digital certificate, you can certainly verify the server's identity (since all secure sites use digital certificates). To examine the identity information contained in the server's digital certificate, select the menu option in your browser that allows you to view a site's security information. For example, in Netscape Navigator 4.*x*, select the **Communicator>Tools>Security Info** menu option and click the **View Certificate** button to examine the server's identity according to the digital certificate (see Figure 17.11). Typically, the browser will accept any digital certificate from a known certificate authority. However, if the browser receives a certificate from an unknown authority, it prompts the user whether to accept it or not. Once the server's public key has been retrieved from the digital certificate, the browser generates a symmetric key for this session, encrypts it using the server's public key, and sends it to the server. The server uses its private key to decrypt the symmetric key that is used to secure the rest of the conversation (i.e., session).

You may be wondering why a symmetric key is used at all if public key cryptography (using asymmetric keys) works so well. The primary reason is that symmetric encryption is much faster than asymmetric. Therefore, we use the slower asymmetric algorithms only on a small amount of data (i.e., the symmetric key) and then use the faster symmetric algorithms on a large amount of data (i.e., the rest of the secure conversation).

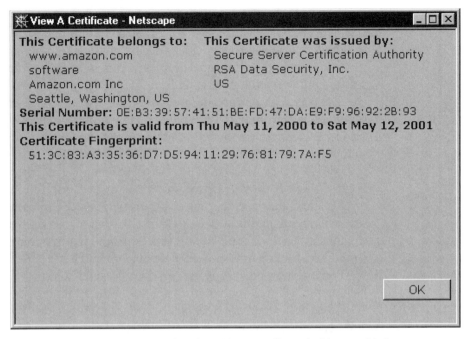

Figure 17.11 A Server's Digital Certificate Identity as Shown by Netscape Navigator

To this point, we have discussed a lot about public key cryptography and asymmetric keys. You may now be wondering exactly how this type of encryption works and how these keys are generated. Well, the answer is that this type of encryption is made possible by special mathematical algorithms known as one-way functions.

One-Way Functions

A *one-way function* is a process that is much easier to do than to undo. Breaking a mirror, for example, is a one-way function. It is easy to do and very difficult to undo. In cryptography, a one-way function involves a calculation that is very easy to perform but extremely difficult to reverse without an extra piece of information (i.e., the key).

Though other options exist, the most popular one-way functions in cryptography use prime numbers. As you know, a prime number is a number that can be divided evenly only by itself and one. For example, the numbers 2, 3, 5, and 7 are all prime because they can be divided evenly only by themselves and one. Another important characteristic of prime numbers is that one prime number multiplied by another always produces a number that can be divided evenly only by itself, the number 1, and the two prime numbers from which it was derived. For instance, $5 \times 3 = 15$. Since both 5 and 3 are prime numbers, we know that their product (15) is evenly divisible by only 15, 1, 3, and 5. In this calculation, the numbers 3 and 5 are known as *prime factors* and the process of finding them is called *factoring*.

The reason that prime numbers are often used to build one-way functions is that it is much easier to multiply two large prime numbers than it is to derive the prime factors from the result. For example, it is much easier for a computer to multiply the two prime numbers 61,001 and 93,139 and retrieve the result of 5,681,572,139 than it is to factor the number 5,681,572,139. This is because there is no known way to factor large numbers other than a brute-force method that may involve trying every possible combination. As you can see, when a number is very large (e.g., 200 digits), a trial-and-error approach can take a very long time. In fact, it is estimated that a number 200 digits long would take today's most powerful computers hundreds of years to factor.

Public key cryptography was first proposed by Whitfield Diffie and Martin Hellman in 1976. However, the original Diffie-Hellman algorithm proved to be not entirely secure. In 1980 three cryptographers, Ron Rivest, Adi Shamir, and Leonard Adelman, improved the original public key encryption algorithm by developing an algorithm called the *RSA cryptosystem*. The RSA cryptosystem is the most popular public key algorithm. The RSA algorithm creates a public and private key using a sophisticated mathematical function that involves a very large number and its two prime factors. SSL is based on the RSA cryptosystem.

SSL and Servlets

The great thing about SSL is that once a digital certificate is installed in your Web server, the encryption of all transmissions between the client and the server is completely transparent to the servlet. It is the SSL-enabled Web server's responsibility to encrypt all outgoing data (including output generated by a servlet) and decrypt incoming data (including any request information that is passed to a servlet). Since the process of installing a digital certificate is server specific, please see the documentation that accompanied your server for these instructions. Unfortunately, similar to digest authentication, Tomcat 3.1 does not support SSL. However, this feature is planned for a future release.

Since SSL operates just below the application protocol layer (such as HTTP), it can be coupled with any of the less secure HTTP authentication methods described in this chapter in order to provide a comprehensive security solution for servlets. Simply implement basic or form-based authentication in your servlet and let SSL guarantee the integrity and confidentiality of your communications. SSL provides state-of-the-art commercial-strength security without additional programming.

Accessing Secure Resources from Servlets

Although servlets can piggy-back on top of a Web server to return information securely to SSL clients, what if a servlet wishes to act as an SSL client itself in order to retrieve resources from a secure server? Fortunately, that is entirely possible, and very simple, using a relatively new Java API known as the Java Secure Socket Extension (JSSE). JSSE is an API specification that defines the objects and methods that allow a Java application to harness the power of SSL (or similar security technologies). Although Sun ships its own SSL implementation with the JSSE API, this is meant only as a reference implementation and is not recommended for use in a production environment. Though we use the reference implementation in this chapter, your code should be portable to any vendor's JSSE implementation as long as you adhere to the JSSE API. JSSE 1.0.2 is demonstrated here. You can download the latest version from Sun's Web site at the following URL:

http://java.sun.com/products/jsse/

To use JSSE, start by unzipping the installation file to the root of your file system, or wherever else you'd like to store it. The resulting JSSE directory includes a */doc* directory that contains the API documentation and a */lib* directory in which you will find the JAR files that contain the JSSE API and reference implementation. You will need to add these JAR files to your CLASS-PATH before compiling any servlets that use the JSSE API. The JSSE classes and interfaces are contained in the `javax.net` and `javax.net.ssl` packages. Next, you need to register the JSSE SSL implementation as a new security provider within the Java Runtime Environment. There are two ways to accomplish this task. One way is to edit the *java.security* text file that is located in the */jdk/jre/lib/ext/security* directory (where */jdk* is your Java installation directory, such as */jdk1.2.2*). Below the line that begins with "`security.provider.1=`", add the following line:

```
security.provider.2=com.sun.net.ssl.internal.ssl.Provider
```

The second way to add a security provider is to do it programmatically in your servlet, like this:

```
java.security.Security.addProvider(
  new com.sun.net.ssl.internal.ssl.Provider());
```

Once the JSSE JAR files have been added to your CLASSPATH and the JSSE SSL implementation has been registered as a new security provider, you're ready to start writing SSL code. The best part of writing secure network programs in Java using JSSE is that the process is almost identical to normal network programming in Java. For example, here is how you would normally open a socket to a server listening for connections on port 80:

```
Socket socket = new Socket("www.insideservlets.com", 80);
```

Pretty simple. With the resulting Socket object, you can easily acquire input and output streams that allow you to communicate with the *www.insideservlets.com* server on port 80. Now let's see how we can establish a secure connection to the *www.verisign.com* server on port 443:

```
Socket socket = SSLSocketFactory.getDefault().createSocket(
   "www.verisign.com", 443);
```

And that's it. It can't get much simpler than that. You are even given a standard java.net.Socket object with which to initiate your secure communications. The encryption taking place under the covers is transparent to the developer. A standard Socket is often all that you will need, but there may be times that you require additional security information that is provided by JSSE's javax.net.ssl.SSLSocket object. The SSLSocket object provides detailed information regarding the cipher systems that are currently supported and enabled (i.e., the cryptographic algorithms supported by this JSSE implementation) in addition to greater control over the SSL handshaking process. *SSL handshaking* is the stage of a secure conversation where the two sides agree on a method to encrypt their transmissions. (Note that, depending on your hardware and network connection, the handshaking process can take a considerable amount of time, commonly ranging from 10 seconds to approaching 1 minute.) The following code demonstrates how an SSLSocket can be acquired through typecasting.

```
SSLSocket sslSocket = (SSLSocket)SSLSocketFactory.getDefault().
   createSocket("www.verisign.com", 443);
```

Another common way to retreive data from the Internet is to use the java.net.URL object. A URL object can be created simply using a valid URL, like this:

```
URL url = new URL("http://www.insideservlets.com/");
```

Information can then be retrieved from the URL by reading from the Input-Stream returned by the URL object's openStream() method. Unfortunately, the

URL object does not automatically support SSL. For example, the following code would normally result in a MalformedURLException since the HTTPS protocol is not automatically supported.

```
URL url = new URL("https://www.verisign.com/");
```

However, once the JSSE SSL implementation has been registered as a security provider, we can add SSL support to the URL object by setting a simple System property, like this:

```
System.setProperty("java.protocol.handler.pkgs",
  "com.sun.net.ssl.internal.www.protocol");

URL url = new URL("https://www.verisign.com/");

InputStream in = url.openStream(); //open stream for reading data
```

And that's all there is to it. The System.setProperty() call tells the Java networking facilities how to handle the HTTPS protocol. Listing 17.6 demonstrates how to retrieve secure information from within a servlet using both the Socket and URL methods. The SSLClientServlet presented in Listing 17.6 prompts the user for a secure Web site (see Figure 17.12) and then proceeds to establish a secure connection to the URL and retrieve the requested information (see Figure 17.13).

Listing 17.6 Servlet that acts as an SSL client to retrieve secure data.

```
import javax.servlet.*;
import javax.servlet.http.*;
import java.io.*;
import java.net.*;
import javax.net.ssl.*;

/**
 * SSLClientServlet demonstrates how to connect to a secure
 * server via SSL using the Java Secure Socket Extension API.
 */
public class SSLClientServlet extends HttpServlet
{
  /**
   * Present the user with an HTML form that allows them to
   * choose a secured resource to access and the method by which
   * to access this resource (via Socket or URL object).
   */
  public void doGet(HttpServletRequest request,
    HttpServletResponse response) throws ServletException,
    IOException
  {
    response.setContentType("text/html");
```

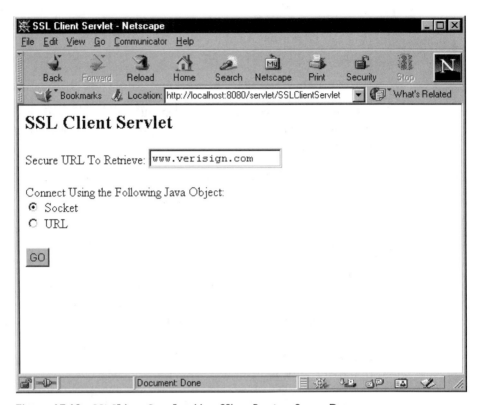

Figure 17.12   SSLClientServlet Uses SSL to Retrieve Secure Data.

```
PrintWriter out = response.getWriter();

out.println("<HTML>");
out.println("<HEAD>");
out.println("<TITLE>SSL Client Servlet</TITLE>");
out.println("</HEAD>");
out.println("<BODY>");

out.println("<H2>SSL Client Servlet</H2>");
out.println("<FORM METHOD=\"POST\">");
out.println("Secure URL To Retrieve: ");
out.println("<INPUT TYPE=\"TEXT\" NAME=\"SecureURL\" " +
    "VALUE=\"www.verisign.com\"><BR><BR>");
out.println("Connect Using the Following Java Object:<BR>");
out.println("<INPUT TYPE=\"RADIO\" NAME=\"SocketURLFlag\" " +
    "VALUE=\"Socket\" CHECKED> Socket<BR>");
out.println("<INPUT TYPE=\"RADIO\" NAME=\"SocketURLFlag\" " +
    "VALUE=\"URL\"> URL<BR><BR>");
out.println("<INPUT TYPE=\"SUBMIT\" VALUE=\"GO\">");
out.println("</FORM>");
```

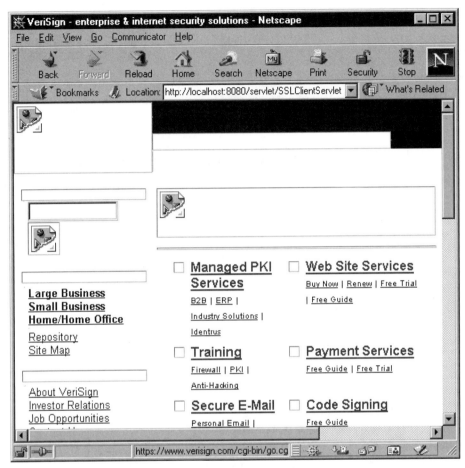

Figure 17.13 Secure HTML Document Retrieved from VeriSign Using SSL (No Images)

```java
    out.println("</BODY></HTML>");

    out.close();
}


/**
 * Requests the contents of a secure Web site and returns the
 * information non-secure back to the client.
 */
public void doPost(HttpServletRequest request,
    HttpServletResponse response) throws ServletException,
    IOException
{
    response.setContentType("text/html");
```

```
      PrintWriter out = response.getWriter();

      String secureURL = request.getParameter("SecureURL");
      String socketURLFlag = request.getParameter("SocketURLFlag");

      try
      {
        BufferedReader in = null;

        //register JSSE SSL implementation as new security provider
        java.security.Security.addProvider(
          new com.sun.net.ssl.internal.ssl.Provider());

        if (socketURLFlag.equals("Socket"))
        {
          in = getPageViaSocket(secureURL);
        }
        else
        {
          in = getPageViaURL(secureURL);
        }

        String nextLine; //read input from secure connection
        while ((nextLine = in.readLine()) != null)
        {
          out.println(nextLine); //return each line to client
        }

        in.close();
        out.close();
      }
      catch (Exception e)
      {
        out.println("<HTML>");
        out.println("<HEAD><TITLE>Network Error</TITLE></HEAD>");
        out.println("<BODY>");
        out.println("<H3>Connection Error</H3>");
        out.println(e.getMessage());
        out.println("</BODY></HTML>");
      }
    }


    /**
     * Establishes a secure socket connection to a secure resource.
     * The /index.html file is then requested and the HTTP headers
     * returned from the secure server are discarded before
     * returning the input stream to the calling method.
     *
     * @param secureURL URL of secure resource to retrieve
     * @return BufferedReader Input stream to secure resource
     */
```

```
private BufferedReader getPageViaSocket(String secureURL)
  throws Exception
{
  //open Socket to secure resource using SSLSocketFactory
  Socket socket = SSLSocketFactory.getDefault().createSocket(
    secureURL, 443);

  //send HTTP request for /index.html to secure server
  PrintWriter out = new PrintWriter(new BufferedWriter(
    new OutputStreamWriter(socket.getOutputStream())));
  out.println("GET http://" + secureURL +
    "/index.html HTTP/1.1");
  out.println();
  out.flush();

  //get input stream to secure resource
  BufferedReader in = new BufferedReader(new InputStreamReader(
    socket.getInputStream()));

  //discard all HTTP headers from input stream
  String nextLine;
  while ((nextLine = in.readLine()) != null)
  {
    if (nextLine.trim().equals(""))
    {
      break; //reached blank line following HTTP headers
    }
  }

  return in; //return input stream to secure resource
}


/**
 * Use the URL object to create an input stream to the secure
 * resource.
 *
 * @param secureURL URL of secure resource to retrieve
 * @return BufferedReader Input stream to secure resource
 */
private BufferedReader getPageViaURL(String secureURL) throws
  Exception
{
  //to avoid a MalformedURLException, this property must be set
  System.setProperty("java.protocol.handler.pkgs",
    "com.sun.net.ssl.internal.www.protocol");

  //create URL object representing the secure resource
  URL url = new URL("https://" + secureURL);

  //return an input stream to the secure resource
  return new BufferedReader(new InputStreamReader(
    url.openStream()));
}
}
```

NOTE: The ServletRequest interface defines a method called isSecure() that indicates if the client established a secure connection. If the request was issued over a secure connection (e.g., SSL), this method returns a boolean value of true; otherwise, it returns false. When security is critical, use this method to ensure a secure connection before returning sensitive data. The following code demonstrates this concept.

```
public void doGet(HttpServletRequest request,
  HttpServletResponse response) throws ServletException,
  IOException
{
  PrintWriter out = response.getWriter();

  if (!request.isSecure())
  {
    response.setContentType("text/plain");

    out.println("A secure connection is required.");

    return; //exit since connection is not secure
  }

  //...connection is secure, return sensitive information here...
}
```

Summary

This chapter introduces several strategies available to the servlet programmer for securing information on the Web. Specifically, this chapter covers HTTP basic authentication, form-based authentication, and HTTP digest authentication. Examples demonstrate how these security mechanisms can be applied to your own servlets. Lastly, an in-depth introduction to cryptography and SSL is presented. In the next chapter, we will learn about an exciting new technology, known as JavaServer Pages, that eliminates the need to embed HTML in your servlets.

Chapter Highlights

- The original HTTP specification (RFC 1945) describes a simple method, or "scheme," to perform client authentication before returning sensitive data. This method, called *basic authentication,* allows the client to authenticate itself by providing a valid username and password.

- Form-based authentication is an extremely popular method of authenticating users on the Web. In short, *form-based authentication* consists of using an HTML form to query the user for a username and password. This information is then posted to the server where it is used to authenticate the user.

- Like basic authentication, digest authentication is an HTTP authentication method that employs a challenge/response model to secure resources on the Web. However, digest authentication improves upon many of basic authentication's inadequacies. For example, basic authentication transmits a client's username and password in plain text (using a thinly veiled Base64 encoding). In contrast, digest authentication never actually sends the client's password over the network. This eliminates the risk that the password may be intercepted during transit.

- Secure Sockets Layer (SSL) is a protocol developed by Netscape for establishing secure connections between two hosts. Security is provided through public key encryption methods applied to all data sent over the SSL connection.

- *Digital certificates* provide a means whereby a trusted authority can vouch for your identity, thus guaranteeing the authenticity of a message. Digital certificates are issued by trusted entities known as *certificate authorities.*

- The great thing about SSL is that once a digital certificate is installed in your Web server, the encryption of all transmissions between the client and server is completely transparent to the servlet. It is the SSL-enabled Web server's responsibility to encrypt all outgoing data (including output generated by a servlet) and decrypt incoming data (including any request information that is passed to a servlet).

CHAPTER 18

JavaServer Pages

JavaServer Pages, commonly referred to as JSP, is a popular technology that simplifies and accelerates the process of creating dynamic Web applications. JSP accomplishes this task by separating the presentation of content (e.g., HTML pages) from the program implementation that generates the content (e.g., Java servlets). This chapter discusses the many advantages obtained by separating presentation and application logic. In addition, you will learn how JSP works and how to write your own JSP-based applications. Specifically, this chapter covers the following topics:

- Introduction to JSP
- Scope rules
- Implicit objects
- Directives
- Scripting elements
- Comments
- Actions
- Custom tag libraries
- Using JSP and servlets together

Although this chapter presents a comprehensive review of the JavaServer Pages technology, entire books have been devoted to this topic. If your interest in JSP exceeds the concepts discussed in this chapter, visit the following URL for a complete list of JSP tutorials, books, and articles:

http://java.sun.com/products/jsp/

Introduction to JSP

If you are at all familiar with Java servlets, you almost certainly have heard the buzz about JavaServer Pages and you may be wondering what all the excitement is about. The enthusiasm surrounding JSP stems from the fact that this technology provides a mechanism for building Web applications quickly and easily using the standard HTML that you're familiar with along with some new markup tags that add dynamic content to the page. And the great thing is that JSP is built on top of Java servlet technology. In fact, the JSP classes and interfaces are contained within the `javax.servlet.jsp` and `javax.servlet.jsp.tagext` packages. If you know how to program Java servlets, learning JavaServer Pages should be a snap. By way of introduction, this section tells you what JSP is, why it is used, and how it works.

What Is JSP?

JSP is a server-side technology that allows dynamic Web applications to be created by adding special markup tags to a standard HTML document (or any other markup language such as XML, WML, and XHTML). HTML pages that contain JSP markup tags (often referred to as *JSP pages*) usually end with a `.jsp` extension. At the time a JSP page is requested, the JSP tags are interpreted and, where appropriate, replaced with dynamic content before the page is returned to the client. For example, Listing 18.1 presents a simple JSP page that includes two dynamic pieces of data—the host name and IP address from which the request was received.

Listing 18.1   Simple JSP page that displays the origin of the request.

```
<HTML>
<HEAD>
<TITLE>Simple JSP Page</TITLE>
</HEAD>
<BODY>
<H2>Request Origin</H2>
Host Name: <%= request.getRemoteHost() %>
<BR>
IP Address: <%= request.getRemoteAddr() %>
</BODY>
</HTML>
```

Listing 18.1 demonstrates how simple it is to add dynamic content to an HTML page using a pair of JSP tags: `<%= request.getRemoteHost() %>` and `<%= request.getRemoteAddr() %>`. Both of these tags reference the `request` implicit object. JSP makes a number of implicit objects automatically available to the JSP developer. The `request` implicit object is an instance of the `HttpServletRequest` object that is passed to the servlet's `service()` method.

These two JSP tags invoke the `HttpServletRequest` object's `getRemoteHost()` and `getRemoteAddr()` methods to retrieve the client's host name and IP address (see Figure 18.1). The implicit objects created by JSP are discussed in detail later in this chapter.

Notice that through the use of a special tag syntax, objects can be called from within an HTML document. Once the method call is processed by the JSP container, the tag is replaced with the value returned by the method call. Whether or not JSP tags generate output, they are always processed on the server and removed from the HTML document before it is returned to the client. Since no JSP tags are visible in the HTML document returned to the client (not even in the HTML source), the `.jsp` extension is usually the client's only hint that a JSP page was used to generate the response.

As we will see later in this chapter, many JSP tags begin with "<%" and end with "%>" (as shown in Listing 18.1). Though many tags do follow this convention, JSP provides an equivalent XML tag, sometimes referred to as the XML alternate, for each "<% %>" formatted tag. The equivalent tag uses

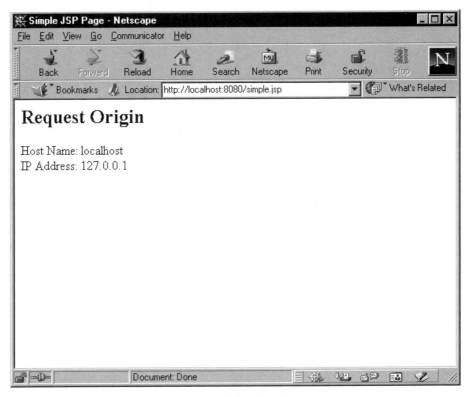

Figure 18.1 HTML Output Generated by JSP Page from Listing 18.1

well-formed XML and can be parsed by an XML parser. However, since the
"<% %>" format is older (dating back to the original JSP spec) and better supported, it is more common today (though this may change). To illustrate, Listing 18.2 demonstrates replacement of the two JSP tags in Listing 18.1 with their XML equivalents.

Listing 18.2   Simple JSP page that uses XML formatted tags.

```
<?xml version="1.0" encoding="ISO-8859-1"?>

<! DOCTYPE root PUBLIC
  "-//Sun Microsystems Inc.//DTD Java Server Pages Version 1.1//EN"
  "http://java.sun.com/products/jsp/dtd/jspcore_1_0.dtd">

<jsp:root xmlns:jsp=
  "http://java.sun.com/products/jsp/dtd/jsp_1_0.dtd">

<HTML>
<HEAD>
<TITLE>Simple JSP Page</TITLE>
</HEAD>
<BODY>
<H2>Request Origin</H2>
Host Name:
  <jsp:expression> request.getRemoteHost() </jsp:expression>
<BR>
IP Address:
  <jsp:expression> request.getRemoteAddr() </jsp:expression>
</BODY>
</HTML>
</jsp:root>
```

NOTE: Though JSP defines an XML equivalent for all tags, the basic "<% %>" formatted tags cannot simply be replaced by their XML equivalents. This is because a JSP page does not inherently subscribe to the rules required of well-formed XML documents. For instance, JSP pages do not mandate a single top element (i.e., root element) as required by an XML document. Similarly, unlike XML, JSP ignores all characters embedded between or outside of valid JSP tags. Conversely, characters that have significance within XML, such as "<", must be escaped within an XML document using a mechanism like CDATA. For example, the following code demonstrates the difference between a JSP declaration using the "<% %>" tag style and the XML equivalent.

```
<%! public boolean check(int i) { if (i < 10) return true; } %>
<jsp:declaration> <![CDATA[ public boolean check(int i) {
  if (i < 10) return true; ]]> </jsp:declaration>
```

As you can see, the XML equivalent requires a much more complex syntax in order to ensure that the XML parser can properly read the JSP page. Therefore, to use the XML equivalents for the JSP tags presented in this chapter, the following steps must be taken.

- A `<jsp:root>` element must be added as the single top element.
- All "*<% %>*" tags must be converted into their XML equivalents.
- All quotation mechanisms must be converted to valid XML (e.g., change quotation marks (") embedded within quotation marks to single quotes (')).
- All `taglib` directives must be specified as namespace attributes of the `<jsp:root>` element.
- All text that does not correspond to a JSP tag must be enclosed within CDATA elements.

Given the considerable effort required to convert a JSP page into valid XML, this chapter focuses on the original "*<% %>*" JSP tag format. However, the XML equivalent of all tags is also given for those brave enough to attempt the conversion. Although the JSP 1.1 specification does not fully define all aspects of converting standard JSP pages into valid XML documents, this topic will receive substantial emphasis in future JSP specifications.

Of course, so far we have caught only a glimpse of JSP's potential. JSP can do much more than replace a simple expression with a server-generated value. JSP is capable of performing much more advanced presentation tasks, such as including within the JSP page information generated by other server resources, forwarding control to another server resource, displaying conditional output, iterating through a loop to display repeating information, setting and retrieving information within Java components (i.e., JavaBeans), and elegant exception handling.

Why JSP?

So why would you want to use JSP? Well, there are a number of reasons but most of them boil down to the intrinsic advantages produced by separating presentation from implementation (also known as separating presentation from content). Once you're convinced of the necessity of separating presentation details and application logic, we will discuss why JSP is superior to the many alternative technologies that provide similar functionality.

Keeping the presentation of content separate from the application that creates the content produces three primary advantages—division of labor, reusability, and improved maintainability. The following sections discuss these three advantages in detail.

Division of Labor

By decoupling page design from Java programming, JSP provides a division of labor that allows people with different skill sets to contribute efficiently to the building of a Web application. For example, it is common for a company to employ a group of graphic designers and HTML developers (i.e., page designers) who are responsible for designing and building a Web application's user interface. On the other hand, these same companies may also employ a group of programmers who write the code that adds functionality to an application. For example, the functionality developed by programmers typically includes building components that access databases (to store and retrieve information), perform complex calculations (e.g., determine sales tax or shipping costs), and interface with back-end systems (e.g., instruct a bank's mainframe to transfer funds from one account to another). Of course, both of these skill sets are required to build a functional and intuitive Web application.

Because very few programmers possess graphic design skills and very few designers are expert programmers, separating these two responsibilities can greatly improve the speed and efficiency with which Web applications are built. With JSP, Java developers are responsible for building servlets and Java-Beans that can be accessed from a JSP page. In turn, graphic designers and HTML developers use the components created by Java developers in order to make their designs functional. As we will see, these components (e.g., servlets and JavaBeans) can be incorporated into a JSP application using standard JSP tags without requiring the user of the component to possess Java programming skills. This division of labor allows page designers to alter the presentation of an application without affecting the Java code that implements the application's functionality. Likewise, as long as they do not alter the component interface, developers are free to improve a component's implementation (e.g., for performance or maintainability) without affecting the application design.

Reusability

Reusability is another advantage obtained by separating presentation from implementation. Programmers are not concerned with the specifics of application presentation; their job is simply to create discrete components that can be invoked from a JSP page. Since the programmer is often not aware of exactly where and when these components will be employed by the page designer, the components must be built in such a manner that they can be used freely throughout an application. Because no presentation information (e.g., HTML) is embedded in the Java code, these Java components (usually servlets or Java-Beans) can be reused throughout an application and in entirely separate applications. Similarly, by confining application logic to Java components, this logic can be reused throughout an application without requiring the page designer to cut and paste portions of HTML from one page to another.

Maintainability

Separating presentation from implementation greatly improves the maintainability of an application. Without a clean separation, Java developers might be required to debug program logic embedded in an HTML page and page designers might be forced to scrutinize Java code that directly generates HTML. Imagine how much more difficult it would be for a Java developer to locate and fix a bug that might reside in a Java component or in any number of HTML pages that contain application-specific code. Similarly, imagine how difficult it would be for page designers to update an application's design if it required them to modify and recompile Java classes. Clearly, maintaining a clean separation between presentation and implementation simplifies the processes of fixing bugs and adding features.

Though we extoll the virtues of not adding Java code to your HTML pages, we will learn shortly that JSP allows you to do just that. If you choose to, it is possible to add a considerable amount of logic to a JSP page by embedding Java code directly into the page. This is quite common, but keep in mind that it does not maintain a clean separation between presentation and implementation and, therefore, suffers from many of the problems previously discussed (including fewer division-of-labor opportunities as well as decreased reusability and maintainability). However, after discussing the many ways in which to embed application logic into a JSP page, we will discuss how we can remove it using a fantastic JSP innovation known as *custom tags*.

NOTE: Remember that JSP is not exclusive to HTML. In fact, it can be used with just about any markup language including XML, WML, and XHTML. Though the text usually refers only to HTML, remember that JSP can be combined with virtually any markup language.

JSP versus Alternatives

You may be wondering why JSP is better than the many alternative server-side scripting technologies. The biggest reason is that JSP is based on Java and has full access to the rich Java API. Given its ability to use any of the many Java APIs, JSP is capable of performing extremely complex tasks including secure socket communications (JSSE API), accessing directory services (JNDI API), invoking Enterprise JavaBeans (EJB API), using transaction services (JTS API), accessing CORBA services (Java IDL API), retrieving database information (JDBC API), and using messaging services (JMS API). No other alternative offers so much functionality through such a comprehensive set of APIs.

Another reason that JSP is superior to many alternatives is again derived from the fact that it is based on Java. Unlike single-vendor, single-platform solutions like Microsoft's Active Server Pages (ASP) or Allaire's Cold Fusion, JSP is platform and server independent. JSP support can be added to various Web servers hosted on numerous platforms including Windows, UNIX, Linux, and MacOS. Its cross-platform and cross-server capability gives JSP a wide appeal by allowing companies to choose vendors of operating systems and servers without regard for whether they support a specific technology. The ability to run on virtually any hardware, operating system, and Web server, coupled with its ability to access the full power of the Java API, makes JSP stand out among server-side scripting technologies.

How Does JSP Work?

As we have already seen, JSP pages work by embedding special tags in the page. These tags are interpreted by the server at request time and replaced with the appropriate value. But how does the server know when a page should be parsed for JSP tags? The answer is that the developer can designate a special URL pattern that the server can use to recognize JSP pages and, thus, process them accordingly. The most commonly defined URL pattern (and the one that most servers support by default) involves mapping the pattern *.jsp (i.e., all requests for files having the .jsp extension) to an application that knows how to parse the page for JSP tags and process them appropriately. Though not required by the JSP specification, most servers process JSP pages by forwarding JSP requests to a special JSP processor servlet. For example, the following XML demonstrates how Tomcat defines the JSP processor servlet and URL pattern in the *ljakarta-tomcatlconflweb.xml* file. All settings in this file are inherited by each Tomcat Web application.

```
<servlet>
  <servlet-name>
    jsp
  </servlet-name>
  <servlet-class>
    org.apache.jasper.runtime.JspServlet
  </servlet-class>
</servlet>
<servlet-mapping>
  <servlet-name>
    jsp
  </servlet-name>
```

```
<url-pattern>
  *.jsp
</url-pattern>
</servlet-mapping>
```

Notice that these Tomcat settings indicate that all requests matching the *.jsp pattern are forwarded to the org.apache.jasper.runtime.JspServlet servlet. Of course, the vendor of another servlet container would map all JSP requests to its own implementation of the JSP processor servlet.

Now that we know how JSP requests are recognized by the server and forwarded to the appropriate servlet, let's examine how JSP pages are processed by the JSP servlet. In a nutshell, the JSP servlet processes a JSP page by parsing it, building a servlet representation of the page, compiling the servlet, loading the servlet, and invoking its service() method (passing it the HttpServletRequest and HttpServletResponse objects). Once the servlet is compiled and loaded into memory, it is used to service all future requests for the associated JSP page. All JSP page servlets must implement the javax.servlet.jsp.JspPage interface or, for pages that use the HTTP protocol, the javax.servlet.jsp.HttpJspPage interface.

Sounds pretty good, but there is a problem. If a previously requested JSP page is changed, its associated servlet is no longer current. To solve this problem, the server automatically detects when a JSP page has been altered. When this occurs, the page's servlet is rebuilt and recompiled automatically in order to incorporate changes (see Figure 18.2). Since JSP pages must be compiled into servlets the first time they are requested, the first request for a JSP page suffers a considerable performance penalty (because the page must be parsed and the servlet must be built, compiled, and loaded). Therefore, it is a good idea for the developer to issue the first request to all pages in a Web application so that they will have been compiled and loaded before the first client visits the site. Fortunately, most JSP containers provide administation tools that automatically compile all JSP pages in a Web application (saving the developer from having to manually requst each one).

NOTE: Though most JSP containers use a JSP processor servlet to build JSP page servlets, this is not actually required by the JSP specification. In fact, it is possible for a JSP container to be implemented entirely in native code (e.g., C or C++).

You might be wondering what a JSP page servlet looks like. Let's clear that up right here. Actually, the JSP page servlet is not a normal servlet. Rather than extend HttpServlet, JSP page servlets extend a JSP container-specific class. For

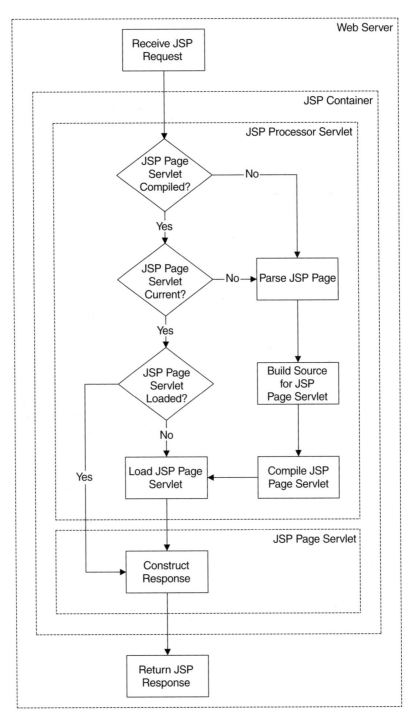

Figure 18.2 Process for Servicing JSP Requests

example, Tomcat page servlets extend a class called `HttpJspBase` and JRun page servlets extend a class called `HttpJSPServlet` (however, both of these classes extend from `HttpServlet`). When the JSP processor servlet receives a request, it invokes the appropriate page servlet's `service()` method. In turn, this `service()` method calls the container-specific class's `_jspService()` method. Most of the JSP page's functionality is created within this `_jspService()` method.

Basically, when the JSP page servlet is constructed, all literals in the JSP page are included in `out.print()` or `out.write()` statements in the `_jspService()` method. On the other hand, all JSP tags are interpreted, converted to their Java equivalents, and included in the page servlet in order to achieve the desired functionality. To illustrate, the following code is a greatly simplified illustration of how the page servlet's `_jspService()` method might look for Listing 18.1. Keep in mind that the exact style and syntax used by the page servlet are JSP container specific. However, most containers produce somewhat similar code.

```
public void _jspService(HttpServletRequest request,
  HttpServletResponse response) throws IOException,
  ServletException
{
  //implicit objects defined here

  try
  {
    out.print("<HTML>\r\n<HEAD>\r\n");
    out.print("<TITLE>Simple JSP Page</TITLE>\r\n");
    out.print("</HEAD>\r\n<BODY>\r\n");
    out.print("<H2>Request Origin</H2>\r\n");
    out.print("Host Name: ");
    out.print(request.getRemoteHost());
    out.print("\r\n<BR>\r\nIP Address: ");
    out.print(request.getRemoteAddr());
    out.print("\r\n</BODY>\r\n</HTML>\r\n");
  }
  catch (Exception e)
  {
    //page exceptions handled here
  }
  finally
  {
    //resources released here
  }
}
```

Understanding that JSP pages are compiled into servlets will greatly simplify the process of learning JSP. For instance, we will learn how JSP syntax can be used to add Java code directly into the page servlet's _jspService() method, or at the class level in order to define methods and instance variables. Your knowledge of how servlets work will help you understand the role that JSP plays in processing requests and generating responses.

Let's discuss for a moment the reasons behind compiling every JSP page into its own servlet. At first, this may appear to be a time-consuming and cumbersome process. After all, wouldn't it be easier to just parse the page each time it is requested, replace any JSP tags along the way, and return the output to the client? In this way, the lengthy process of generating source code and compiling servlets could be avoided. There are, however, some very compelling reasons behind the JSP architecture.

First, generating source code and compiling servlets is a one-time process that occurs when an application is placed into production (although repeated each time a JSP page is altered). And since many JSP containers provide administrative tools that allow the developer to precompile the entire project, no client need suffer the initial performance penalty invoked by the source code generation and compilation stage (without administrative tools, the developer can simply manually request each page in the application). The advantage gained by compiling all JSP pages when the application is first deployed is the fact that each page need be read from the file system and parsed only one time. This means that although the first request will be slow, each subsequent request will be serviced extremely fast by a compiled servlet. Compiled Java code can run much faster than interpreted scripting alternatives such as Active Server Pages, Cold Fusion, and PHP.

Second, since the response to every JSP request is generated by a servlet, the servlet container can use its built-in servlet-caching mechanisms to ensure that the necessary servlets are preloaded and ready to respond to incoming requests. In this manner, it is possible for an entire application to be serviced by invoking servlets that reside in memory rather than having to read from the much slower hard disk. The combination of single-page parsing, compilation, and caching makes the JSP approach superior to many alternatives.

How Are JSP Pages Invoked?

Now that you know what JSP is and why you'd use it, let's briefly discuss how to use it. First, you need to install a JSP container such as Tomcat, JRun, ServletExec, or Resin (see Chapter 8 for more information regarding installation of these products). This section describes how to invoke JSP pages using Apache Tomcat, but most JSP containers are very similar. Once your JSP container is installed, simply copy a JSP page to the document root of any Web application. For instance, to add the *simple.jsp* file shown in Listing 18.1 to

Tomcat's *ROOT* Web application, copy it to the */jakarta-tomcat/webapps/ROOT* directory and invoke it with a URL like this:

> *http://localhost:8080/simple.jsp*

Similarly, to add *simple.jsp* to the *examples* Web application, copy it to the */jakarta-tomcat/webapps/examples* directory and invoke it like this:

> *http://localhost:8080/examples/simple.jsp*

When the *simple.jsp* file is requested, Tomcat generates the servlet source code for the JSP page and compiles the servlet. It can be very educational to review the source code that Tomcat generates on behalf of your JSP page. You can find the source for the JSP page in one of the directories under the */jakarta-tomcat/work* directory. The */work* directory looks a bit strange but it contains your server name, port number, and Web application name, such as "localhost_8080%2Fexamples" for JSP pages in the *examples* Web application or just "localhost_8080" for the *ROOT* Web application. Within this directory, there is one copy of the servlet source code for each time that the JSP page was altered. The source code file name includes a number that is incremented with each successive compilation. For example, if you requested and altered the *simple.jsp* file several times, you may end up with a number of servlet source code versions within the Web application's */work* directory. These files may be named as follows:

```
_0002fsimple_0002ejspsimple_jsp_0.java
_0002fsimple_0002ejspsimple_jsp_1.java
_0002fsimple_0002ejspsimple_jsp_2.java
_0002fsimple_0002ejspsimple_jsp_3.java
```

The following code shows the Tomcat-generated servlet for the JSP page presented in Listing 18.1. As you can see, JSP containers may not produce the prettiest code, but performance is their primary goal.

```
import javax.servlet.*;
import javax.servlet.http.*;
import javax.servlet.jsp.*;
import javax.servlet.jsp.tagext.*;
import java.io.PrintWriter;
import java.io.IOException;
import java.io.FileInputStream;
import java.io.ObjectInputStream;
import java.util.Vector;
import org.apache.jasper.runtime.*;
import java.beans.*;
import org.apache.jasper.JasperException;
```

```java
public class _0002fsimple_0002ejspsimple_jsp_6 extends
  HttpJspBase {


  static {
  }
  public _0002fsimple_0002ejspsimple_jsp_6( ) {
  }

  private static boolean _jspx_inited = false;

  public final void _jspx_init() throws JasperException {
  }

  public void _jspService(HttpServletRequest request,
    HttpServletResponse  response) throws IOException,
    ServletException {

    JspFactory _jspxFactory = null;
    PageContext pageContext = null;
    HttpSession session = null;
    ServletContext application = null;
    ServletConfig config = null;
    JspWriter out = null;
    Object page = this;
    String  _value = null;
    try {

      if (_jspx_inited == false) {
        _jspx_init();
        _jspx_inited = true;
      }
      _jspxFactory = JspFactory.getDefaultFactory();
      response.setContentType("text/html;charset=8859_1");
      pageContext = _jspxFactory.getPageContext(this, request,
        response, "", true, 8192, true);

      application = pageContext.getServletContext();
      config = pageContext.getServletConfig();
      session = pageContext.getSession();
      out = pageContext.getOut();

      // HTML // begin [file="C:\\simple.jsp";from=(0,0);to=(6,
      11)]
      out.write("<HTML>\r\n<HEAD>\r\n<TITLE>Simple JSP Page
      </TITLE>\r\n</HEAD>\r\n<BODY>\r\n<H2>Request Origin</H2>
      \r\nHost Name: ");
      // end
      // begin [file="C:\\simple.jsp";from=(6,14);to=(6,39)]
      out.print( request.getRemoteHost() );
      // end
      // HTML // begin [file="C:\\simple.jsp";from=(6,41);to=(8,
      12)]
```

```
                  out.write("\r\n<BR>\r\nIP Address: ");
                  // end
                  // begin [file="C:\\simple.jsp";from=(8,15);to=(8,40)]
                  out.print( request.getRemoteAddr() );
                  // end
                  // HTML // begin [file="C:\\simple.jsp";from=(8,42);to=(
                  11,0)]
                  out.write("\r\n</BODY>\r\n</HTML>\r\n");
                  // end

              } catch (Exception ex) {
                  if (out.getBufferSize() != 0)
                    out.clearBuffer();
                  pageContext.handlePageException(ex);
              } finally {
                  out.flush();
                  _jspxFactory.releasePageContext(pageContext);
              }
          }
      }
```

As we have seen, invoking JSP pages from a properly installed JSP container couldn't be much simpler. Just place the JSP page in a Web application's document root and invoke it from any browser. The JSP container takes care of everything else.

Scope Rules

All objects created within a JSP page are assigned a scope within which they are valid. JSP applications recognize four well-defined scopes: page, request, session, and application. The following sections discuss these four scopes in detail.

page

Objects with *page scope* are accessible only within the page in which they are created. Once the response is returned to the client or the request is forwarded to another page, all references to page scope objects are released. Page scope objects are stored in and accessible from the pageContext implicit object.

request

Objects with *request scope* are accessible only while processing the request in which they were created. Once the request has been processed and the response returned to the client, all references to request scope objects are released. Unlike page scope, request scope objects are available to all pages to which the request is forwarded. Request scope objects are stored in and accessible from the request implicit object.

session

Objects with *session scope* are accessible only from pages that share the same session. Pages that are not session-aware (i.e., set the page directive's session attribute to false) do not have access to session scope objects. All references to session scope objects are released when the session ends. Session scope objects are stored in and accessible from the session implicit object.

application

Objects with *application scope* are accessible only from pages that reside in the same Web application. All references to application scope objects are released when the server environment ends the application (e.g., the server is shut down). Application scope objects are stored in and accessible from the application implicit object. The application object is an instance of the javax.servlet.ServletContext interface.

 NOTE: It is recommended that the name under which an object is stored be unique, regardless of its scope. That is, object-naming conventions should be prescribed as if all scopes shared a single namespace.

Implicit Objects

Implicit objects are variables that are defined automatically by the JSP container and are available to the JSP page without having to declare them first. Since the JSP developer can always assume that these objects are available under their specified name (as defined by the JSP specification), these objects are said to be *implicit*. Implicit objects are instantiated in the JSP page servlet's _jspService() method and are, therefore, available only to expressions and scriptlets—not to declarations. Table 18.1 presents the nine implicit objects that are automatically made available to each JSP page.

We have stated that implicit objects are always available, but there are two exceptions to this rule. First, the exception object is available only on an error page (i.e., a page that contains the <%@ page isErrorPage="true" %> directive). Second, the session object is available only on pages that participate in an

Table 18.1   The Nine Implicit Objects Automatically Available to Each JSP Page

Object Name	Object Type	Scope	Description
application	ServletContext	application	Represents the Web application in which the JSP page resides
config	ServletConfig	page	Contains configuration information relative to the page servlet
exception	Exception	page	Represents an uncaught exception or error
out	JspWriter	page	Buffered output stream for returning content to the client
page	HttpJspBase	page	Represents an instance of the JSP page servlet
pageContext	PageContext	page	Stores page-specific attributes
request	HttpServletRequest	request	Represents the request that invoked the JSP page
response	HttpServletResponse	page	Represents the response that is returned to the client
session	HttpSession	session	Represents the HTTP session in which the client is participating

HTTP session (i.e., a page that does not contain the `<%@ page session="false" %>` directive).

The following sections discuss in detail each of the implicit objects presented in Table 18.1. As you build your own JSP pages, you will almost certainly use most, if not all, of these implicit objects on a regular basis.

application

The `application` implicit object represents the Web application in which the JSP page resides. This object is an instance of the `javax.servlet.Servlet-Context` interface. Since the JSP `application` object is actually the `Servlet-Context` associated with the page servlet, it can be used to store objects that are shared among all servlets in the Web application. This can be accomplished using the `ServletContext` interface's `getAttribute()`, `getAttributeNames()`, `setAttribute()`, and `removeAttribute()` methods. In addition to sharing objects among all servlets in a Web application, the `application` object provides access to information about the servlet container (e.g., name and version numbers), aids the retrieval of server resources based on filename or URL, provides logging functions, supports request dispatching, and provides access to the servlet's initialization parameters. (See Chapter 10 for detailed information regarding the ServletContext interface.)

config

The config implicit object contains configuration information relative to the page servlet. The config object is an instance of javax.servlet.Servlet-Config interface. This object can be used to retrieve the servlet name as well as the names and values of the servlet's initialization parameters. (See Chapter 10 for detailed information regarding the ServletConfig interface.)

exception

The exception implicit object represents an uncaught exception or error. Unlike most of the other implicit objects, the exception object is not always available. Rather, this object is available only on JSP pages that have been flagged as error pages using the page directive's isErrorPage attribute. The exception object is an instance of the java.lang.Throwable class that was responsible for the request's being forwarded to the error page. In other words, the exception object contains information regarding the exception or error that caused control to be transferred to the error page.

The exception object provides methods for retrieving information about the error or exception. These methods include getMessage() and toString(). The getMessage() method returns a String that contains a descriptive error message. The toString() method returns a String that contains the class name of the error or exception and a descriptive error message. Lastly, the exception object's printStackTrace() method prints the complete stack trace to standard out or to the designated PrintStream or PrintWriter object. (See the Java documentation for the java.lang.Throwable class for more information.)

out

The out implicit object is a buffered output stream that is used to return information to the client. The out object is an instance of the javax.servlet.jsp.JspWriter class. This class implements most of the functionality provided by the java.io.PrintWriter class (i.e., the print() and println() methods) in addition to adding some methods of its own. Like PrintWriter, JspWriter extends the java.io.Writer class and, therefore, inherits all of its functionality. JspWriter buffers all JSP page output according to the page directive's buffer attribute. When the output buffer is flushed, the JspWriter instantiates the `PrintWriter` object retrieved from the page servlet's `Http-ServletResponse` object and writes its buffered output to it. In turn, the `PrintWriter` object sends the output to the client.

This method is used primarily by scriptlets because expressions are automatically added to the output stream. In addition to `print()` and `println()`, the `out` object supports the methods documented in Table 18.2.

page

The `page` implicit object represents an instance of the JSP page servlet. It is simply a synonym for the Java `this` variable. When Java is used as the scripting language (which is almost always the case), this object is practically useless. However, if another supported scripting language is being used, this object may be necessary in order to provide access to the page servlet's methods and variables.

pageContext

The `pageContext` implicit object stores page-specific attributes. The `pageContext` object is an instance of the `javax.servlet.jsp.PageContext` class. This `PageContext` class provides access to all other implicit objects, provides methods for forwarding requests and including output from other server resources, and provides methods for storing and retrieving attributes from any scope

Table 18.2   Methods Supported by the out Implicit Object (Excluding `print()` and `println()`)

Method	Description
`clear()`	Clears the buffer contents but throws an `IOException` if the buffer has been flushed
`clearBuffer()`	Clears the contents of the buffer without regard to whether it has been flushed
`close()`	Flushes any data in the output buffer, flushes the stream, and closes the stream
`flush()`	Flushes any data in the output buffer and flushes the output stream
`getBufferSize()`	Returns an integer that represents the size of the output buffer (in bytes)
`getRemaining()`	Returns an integer that represents the number of bytes available in the output buffer (i.e., the size of the output buffer minus the number of bytes stored in the buffer)
`isAutoFlush()`	Returns `true` if the output buffer is automatically flushed whenever it becomes full or `false` if an exception is thrown when the buffer becomes full
`newLine()`	Adds a platform-specific line separator to the output stream according to the `line.separator` system property

(i.e., page, request, session, and application scopes). This   can be accomplished using the pageContext object's getAttribute(), getAttributeNames-InScope(), getAttributesScope(), setAttribute(), and removeAttribute() methods. Unlike the request, session, and application objects, the pageContext object's getAttribute(), setAttribute(), and removeAttribute() methods accept a parameter that designates the scope in which the action should take place. This allows the pageContext object to retrieve not only page-specific attributes, but also request-specific, session-specific, and application-specific attributes. Table 18.3 documents some of the most important methods supported by the pageContext implicit object.

Table 18.3   Useful Methods of the pageContext Implicit Object

Method	Description
findAttribute()	Searches for the named attribute in the page, request, session (if valid), and application scopes, in that order, and returns the object or null if not found
forward()	Forwards the request to another server resource
getAttribute()	Returns the attribute associated with the specified name in the page scope or null if not found; also accepts a scope parameter for retrieving objects from a specified scope
getAttributeNamesInScope()	Returns an Enumeration that contains the names of all attributes within the specified scope
getAttributesScope()	Returns an integer that indicates the scope of the object associated with the specified name or zero if not found
getException()	Returns the exception implicit object
getOut()	Returns the out implicit object
getPage()	Returns the page implicit object
getRequest()	Returns the request implicit object
getResponse()	Returns the response implicit object
getServletConfig()	Returns the config implicit object
getServletContext()	Returns the application implicit object
getSession()	Returns the session implicit object
include()	Includes output from another resource in the JSP page
removeAttribute()	Removes the object associated with the specified name from the page scope; also accepts a scope parameter for removing objects from a specified scope
setAttribute()	Stores the specified object in the page scope and binds it to the specified name; also accepts a scope parameter for storing objects in a specified scope

NOTE: Since many of the pageContext object's methods expose objects that are available implicitly (e.g., getOut( ), getPage( ), and getRequest( ) methods), you may wonder why these methods are provided. Though not very useful in the context of a JSP page, these methods are essential when building custom tags.

request

The request implicit object represents the request that invoked the JSP page. Usually, the request object is an instance of the javax.servlet.http.Http-ServletRequest interface. However, it is possible that a specific JSP container implementation may support a request/response model that uses a protocol other than HTTP. In this rare circumstance, the request object would be an instance of the javax.servlet.ServletRequest interface. The request object is extremely useful because it provides access to the requested URL, the request type, the source of the request, and authentication information, in addition to all parameters and HTTP headers included in the request. (See Chapter 6 for detailed information regarding the ServletRequest and HttpServletRequest interfaces.)

response

The response implicit object represents the response that is returned to the client. Like the request object, this object is usually an instance of the javax.servlet.http.HttpServletResponse interface. However, a JSP container could support a request/response model using a non-HTTP protocol. In this rare case, the response object would be an instance of the javax.servlet.ServletResponse interface. The response object is useful for setting HTTP headers, adding cookies, setting the response content type and status, sending HTTP redirects, and encoding URLs (for use with URL rewriting session management). (See Chapter 6 for detailed information regarding the ServletResponse and HttpServletResponse interfaces.)

session

The session implicit object represents the HTTP session in which the client is participating. The session object is available only on session-aware pages (i.e., pages that have not turned off session support using the page directive's session attribute). The session object is an instance of the `javax.servlet.http.HttpSession` interface. This object is useful for adding, retrieving, and removing objects from the session using the `session` object's `getAttribute()`, `getAttributeNames()`, `setAttribute()`, and `removeAttribute()` methods. (See Chapter 14 for detailed information regarding the `HttpSession` interface.)

Directives

Directives are JSP tags that provide the JSP container with special instructions required to process the page. These instructions alter the structure of the servlet that is generated when the page is processed. For instance, directives can be used to import Java classes and packages, change the page servlet's superclass (i.e., the class from which it extends), include the contents of other files in the JSP page, specify tag libraries, and much more. All directives use the following basic syntax:

```
<%@ directive_type attribute1="value1"
                   attribute2="value2"
                   attributeN="valueN" %>
```

The white space following `<%@` and preceding `%>` is not required but is recommended to improve readability. The quotation marks around the attribute values, however, are mandatory (though they may be replaced by single quotes). As previously discussed, all JSP tags have an XML equivalent. The XML tag syntax for directives looks like this:

```
<jsp:directive.directive_type attribute1="value1"
                              attribute2="value2"
                              attributeN="valueN"/>
```

JSP 1.1 defines three directives: `page`, `include`, and `taglib`. Each of these directives will be presented in detail in the following sections.

page

Of the three directives, `page` is the most complex because of the wide array of attributes and functionality that it supports. The `page` directive includes page-specific processing instructions that are used by the JSP container when the page servlet is created. These instructions may involve importing Java classes and packages, specifying the parent class from which the page servlet should extend, indicating the MIME content type of the response, specifying the minimum size of the output buffer, and much more. Table 18.4 illustrates the eleven `page` directive attributes supported by the JSP 1.1 specification and a brief description of each attribute. As you examine Table 18.4, keep in mind that, with the exception of import, no page directive attribute can be specified more than once within a single JSP page.

autoFlush Attribute

The autoFlush attribute indicates whether the output buffer should be automatically flushed when it becomes full or whether an exception should be thrown. The type of exception thrown is implementation specific. The autoFlush attribute can be specified only once per JSP page. The tag syntax for this attribute looks like this:

```
<%@ page autoFlush="true|false" %>
```

For example, the following tags enable and disable the automatic flush option.

```
<%@ page autoFlush="true" %> (default)
<%@ page autoFlush="false" %>
```

The XML equivalent of this tag looks like this:

```
<jsp:directive.page autoFlush="true"/>
```

Table 18.4 The Eleven page Directive Attributes Supported by JSP 1.1

Attribute	Default Value	Description
autoFlush	true	Indicates whether the output buffer will be automatically flushed when full or whether an exception will be thrown
buffer	8kb	Conveys to the JSP container the minimum output buffer size for this page
contentType	text/html	Indicates the MIME type of the response generated by the JSP page
errorPage	server-specific	Specifies the JSP page to which the client should be forwarded if an uncaught exception occurs
extends	server-specific	Specifies the JSP page servlet's superclass
import	none	Specifies the packages and classes that are imported by the JSP page servlet
info	empty string	Specifies a brief desription of the page that is available by calling the page servlet's getServletInfo() method
isErrorPage	false	Indicates whether the current JSP page can serve as an error page
isThreadSafe	true	Indicates whether the servlet generated for this JSP page is thread safe or if it should implement the SingleThreadModel interface
language	java	Specifies the programming language used in the JSP page
session	true	Indicates whether the page participates in an HTTP session

The default value of true is usually the appropriate setting for this attribute. This setting ensures that if the response is larger than the output buffer, the user will receive the entire page rather than being forwarded to an error page. Basically, the output buffer will be flushed whenever it becomes full or upon reaching the end of the page. However, keep in mind that once the output buffer is flushed, response headers can no longer be set and the JSP page can no longer forward control to another resource. Therefore, response headers should be set and forward decisions should be made early within a page so as to ensure that the output buffer is not flushed prior to these actions. If one of these actions is requested anywhere within the page, setting the autoFlush property to false may ensure that the page is processed properly or not processed at all (since the request is forwarded to an error page if the output buffer becomes full). In this case, it is important to ensure that the page's typical response will fit within the prescribed minimum buffer size (so as to avoid returning an error page each time).

It is illegal to set the autoFlush attribute to false if the buffer attribute is set to none. This is due to the fact that if there is no buffer, setting autoFlush to false will raise an exception every time the page is requested. If there is no buffer, the page's output must always be flushed immediately to the client.

buffer Attribute

The buffer attribute specifies the minimum output buffer size. The JSP container may choose to use a buffer larger than that specified but it cannot select a smaller one. This allows the JSP page author to decide how much buffering the page requires. Setting the buffer attribute to none indicates that the page's output should be sent immediately to the client (no buffering should take place). The buffer attribute can be set only once per JSP page. The tag syntax for this attribute looks like this:

```
<%@ page buffer="buffer_size" %>
```

For example, the following tags set the buffer size to 8kb, 32kb, and none, respectively.

```
<%@ page buffer="8kb" %> (default)
<%@ page buffer="32kb" %>
<%@ page buffer="none" %>
```

The XML equivalent of this tag looks like this:

```
<jsp:directive.page buffer="8kb"/>
```

Buffering is important because it allows response headers to be added or altered even after the page has begun generating output. In addition, buffering allows a page's output to be retracted and the request forwarded to another page. For instance, if an error occurs halfway through a JSP page, the output generated by the first half of the page can be retracted and the request can be forwarded to a nicely formatted error page. However, once the buffer has been flushed to the client, response headers can no longer be added or altered and forwards are no longer permitted.

contentType Attribute

The `contentType` attribute indicates the MIME type of the response generated by the JSP page. This MIME type is communicated to the client by setting the `Content-Type` HTTP response header. (See Chapter 3 for more information on MIME types.) Common MIME types for JSP pages include `text/html`, `text/xml`, and `text/plain`. In addition to the MIME type, the `contentType` attribute can indicate the character set used by the JSP page. This setting facilitates content localization by allowing the page author to specify the encoding character set most appropriate for a particular language. The default character set is ISO-8859-1. The `contentType` attribute can be set only once per JSP page. The tag syntax for this attribute looks like this:

```
<%@ page contentType="mime_type" %>
<%@ page contentType="mime_type; charset=character_set" %>
```

The following tags set the page's content type to `text/html`, `text/xml`, and `text/plain`, respectively. The space following the semicolon is optional.

```
<%@ page contentType="text/html; charset=ISO-8859-1" %> (default)
<%@ page contentType="text/xml" %>
<%@ page contentType="text/plain" %>
```

The XML equivalent of this tag looks like this:

```
<jsp:directive.page contentType="text/html"/>
```

errorPage Attribute

The `errorPage` attribute specifies the JSP page to which the client should be forwarded if an uncaught exception occurs. This attribute does not accept absolute URLs (i.e., URLs that contain the protocol and hostname). Rather, a relative URL indicating a local resource should be used. Relative URLs beginning with a "/" are resolved relative to the Web application's document root, whereas relative URLs that do not begin with a "/" are resolved relative to the JSP page's current directory. In addition, the error page must exist on the same server as the requested JSP page. The `errorPage` attribute can be set only once per JSP page. The tag syntax for this attribute looks like this:

```
<%@ page errorPage="local_url" %>
```

For example, the following tags set the error page using both types of relative URLs.

```
<%@ page errorPage="invalid_login.jsp" %>
<%@ page errorPage="/errors/invalid_login.jsp" %>
```

The XML equivalent of this tag looks like this:

```
<jsp:directive.page errorPage="invalid_login.jsp"/>
```

Again, when a relative URL that does not begin with a "/" is used, the server looks for the specified error page relative to the directory that contains the JSP page that threw an uncaught exception. An error page specified using a relative URL that begins with a "/" is located relative to the Web application's document root. The errorPage attribute can be used only in conjunction with output buffering. If buffering is not used, the JSP container will not be able to forward the request to the error page in the event that an uncaught exception occurs. Likewise, if the page is flushed when the buffer becomes full, the JSP container will no longer be able to forward the request to the error page. Of course, if autoFlush is set to false, the request will be forwarded to the error page whenever the output buffer becomes full.

extends Attribute

The extends attribute indicates the parent class from which the JSP page servlet extends. The JSP page servlet inherits functionality from its parent class (also known as the superclass). The extends attribute can be set only once per JSP page. The tag syntax for this attribute looks like this:

```
<%@ page extends="package.Class" %>
```

For example, the following tag sets the JSP page servlet's superclass to com.insideservlets.jsp.JspPage.

```
<%@ page extends="com.insideservlets.jsp.JspPage" %>
```

The XML equivalent of this tag looks like this:

```
<jsp:directive.page extends="com.insideservlets.jsp.JspPage"/>
```

This attribute is rarely used because the JSP container usually specifies a custom superclass from which JSP page servlets extend. By not using this attribute, each JSP container is free to choose its own highly optimized version of the JSP page servlet's superclass.

`import` Attribute

The `import` attribute specifies the packages and classes that should be imported by the JSP page servlet. By default, each JSP page servlet imports `java.lang.*`, `javax.servlet.*`, `javax.servlet.http.*`, and `javax.servlet.jsp.*`. Therefore, any classes in these packages are made available to the JSP developer automatically, without having to specify a fully qualfied class name (i.e., include full package information). The `import` attribute is the only page directive attribute that can be set multiple times on a single JSP page. In addition to including multiple `import` attribute tags, multiple classes can be specified within a single `import` attribute tag by creating a comma-delimited list of packages and classes. For instance, the tag syntax for this attribute looks like this:

```
<%@ page import="package.*" %>
<%@ page import="package.Class" %>
<%@ page import="package.*, package.Class" %>
```

For example, the following tag imports the packages `java.net` and `java.util` as well as the `java.text.DateFormat` class. The space following the comma is optional.

```
<%@ page import="java.net.*, java.util.*" %>
<%@ page import="java.text.DateFormat" %>
```

The XML equivalent of these tags looks like this:

```
<jsp:directive.page import="java.net.*, java.util.*"/>
<jsp:directive.page import="java.text.DateFormat"/>
```

`info` Attribute

The `info` attribute specifies a brief description of the JSP page that is made available in the page servlet via the `getServletInfo()` method. If not specified, the default is an empty string. The `info` attribute can be set only once per JSP page. The tag syntax for this attribute looks like this:

```
<%@ page info="brief_description" %>
```

For example, the following tag indicates the page's function and copyright information.

```
<%@ page info="Guest List Page, Copyright (C) SourceStream" %>
```

The XML equivalent of this tag looks like this:

```
<jsp:directive.page info="Guest List Page"/>
```

isErrorPage Attribute

The isErrorPage attribute indicates whether this page can serve as an error page for other JSP pages. In other words, if isErrorPage is set to true, this page is a valid value for another JSP page's errorPage attribute. The isErrorPage attribute can be specified only once per JSP page. The tag syntax for this attribute looks like this:

```
<%@ page isErrorPage="true|false" %>
```

For example, the following tags indicate that the page can or cannot serve as an error page for other JSP pages, respectively.

```
<%@ page isErrorPage="true" %>
<%@ page isErrorPage="false" %> (default)
```

The XML equivalent of this tag looks like this:

```
<jsp:directive.page isErrorPage="true"/>
```

If the isErrorPage attribute is set to true, the implicit exception object is made available to the page. The implicit exception object is bound to the Java exception that caused the request to be forwarded to this error page. This implicit exception object is then accessible by the JSP page.

isThreadSafe Attribute

The isThreadSafe attribute indicates whether this page is capable of processing concurrent requests without thread safety concerns. If set to false, the resulting JSP page servlet implements the SingleThreadModel interface. The isThreadSafe attribute can be specified only once per JSP page. The tag syntax for this attribute looks like this:

```
<%@ page isThreadSafe="true|false" %>
```

For example, the following tags indicate that the page is or is not thread safe, respectively.

```
<%@ page isThreadSafe="true" %> (default)
<%@ page isThreadSafe="false" %>
```

The XML equivalent of this tag looks like this:

```
<jsp:directive.page isThreadSafe="true"/>
```

Setting the isThreadSafe attribute to false indicates that the page is not thread safe and requests should not be processed concurrently. Rather, all requests should be queued and processed one at a time. Setting the isThread-Safe attribute to true (its default value) indicates that the page servlet associated with this JSP page is capable of processing concurrent requests in a thread-safe manner (e.g., no race conditions). Therefore, requests can be processed concurrently in separate threads. (See Chapter 11 for more information regarding thread safety and the SingleThreadModel interface.)

language Attribute

The language attribute specifies the scripting language that is used in the JSP page. Java is the default value for this attribute as well as the only language currently supported by most JSP implementations (all implementations are required to support Java). Since Java is the default language and most implementations support only Java, this attribute is rarely used. The language attribute can be set only once per JSP page. The tag syntax for this attribute looks like this:

```
<%@ page language="scripting_language" %>
```

For example, the following tag indicates that the JSP page uses Java as its scripting language.

```
<%@ page language="java" %>
```

The XML equivalent of this tag looks like this:

```
<jsp:directive.page language="java"/>
```

session Attribute

The session attribute indicates whether the JSP page participates in an HTTP session. By default, this attribute is set to true. The session attribute can be specified only once per JSP page. The tag syntax for this attribute looks like this:

```
<%@ page session="true|false" %>
```

For example, the following tags indicate that the page does or does not participate in the session, respectively.

```
<%@ page session="true" %> (default)
<%@ page session="false" %>
```

The XML equivalent of this tag looks like this:

```
<jsp:directive.page session="true"/>
```

If the session attribute is true, the current session (if one exists) is bound to the implicit session object that can be accessed from within the JSP page. If the client does not belong to a session, then a new session is created and bound to the implicit session object. The implicit session object is not available on pages that set this attribute to false.

include

The include directive allows files to be included in a JSP page before the page is translated into a servlet. The include directive tag is essentially replaced by the contents of the included file. Similar to the page directive's errorPage attribute, the include directive can specify a local file using a relative URL. A relative URL beginning with a "/" is resolved relative to the Web application's document root, whereas a relative URL that does not begin with a "/" is resolved relative to the directory in which the JSP page is stored. There is no limit to the number of include directives that can appear in a JSP page. Likewise, there is no limit on nested include directives. For instance, a JSP page can include a JSP page that includes yet another JSP page (and so on). The syntax of the include directive looks like this:

```
<%@ include file="local_url" %>
```

For example, the following include directives include local files using both types of relative URLs.

```
<%@ include file="includes/footer.jsp" %>
<%@ include file="/resources/banner.jsp" %>
```

The XML equivalent of the include directive tag looks like this:

```
<jsp:directive.include file="includes/footer.jsp"/>
```

NOTE: The JSP include directive is analogous to the #include preprocessor instruction in C and C++.

In addition to static HTML or XML, included files may contain dynamic JSP tags. The static and dynamic content of all included files is compiled into the servlet associated with the original JSP page that contains the include directives. In this way, once the page servlet is created, the included files no longer need to be parsed with each successive request. This processing takes place only once when the JSP page's servlet source code is generated and compiled (usually when the page is first requested).

Though the JSP container automatically detects changes to a JSP page and recompiles the page servlet when necessary, the same is not usually true when included pages are altered. Some JSP implementations may be smart enough to recompile the page servlet when any of its included files have changed, but this functionality is not required by the JSP specification and, therefore, it cannot be assumed that the JSP container supports this functionality. The simplest way to ensure that the page servlet is recompiled is to alter the main JSP page whenever one of its included files is changed. This can be accomplished easily using a file utility (e.g., the UNIX touch command) or by including a timestamp comment in the main JSP page that can be updated whenever one of its included files is changed (see Listing 18.3).

To illustrate the `include` directive, Listing 18.3 presents a JSP page that includes two other JSP pages—*header.jsp* presented in Listing 18.4 and *footer.jsp* presented in Listing 18.5. These files are included in the original JSP page before translating it into a servlet. As you can see from Figure 18.3, the output generated by this page includes the contents of *header.jsp* and *footer.jsp*.

Listing 18.3   JSP page that uses the `include` directive to include files.

```
<!-- Last Modified: 07/24/2000 19:35 -->
<HTML>
<HEAD>
<TITLE>Include Directive Example</TITLE>
</HEAD>
<BODY>
<%@ include file="/includes/header.jsp" %>
This JSP page uses the include directive in order to include a
standard header and footer.
<%@ include file="/includes/footer.jsp" %>
</BODY>
</HTML>
```

Listing 18.4   The *header.jsp* file included by directive in Listing 18.3.

```
<CENTER>
<FONT SIZE=6><B>SourceStream</B></FONT>
<BR>
<%= new java.util.Date() %> <!-- display current date/time -->
<HR>
</CENTER>
```

Listing 18.4 contains a new type of JSP tag known as an expression (also presented in Listing 18.1). Expressions begin with <%= and end with %> and are used to generate dynamic output. In this case, the expression is used to display

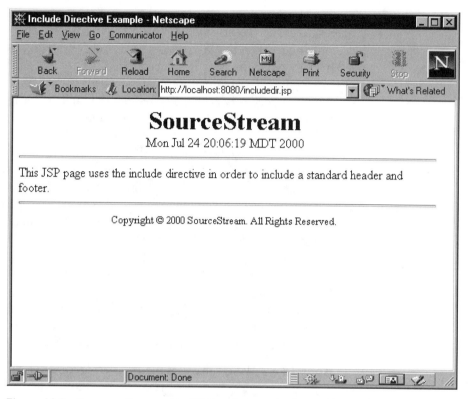

Figure 18.3   Response Generated by JSP Page Presented in Listing 18.3

the current date and time. Don't worry about this new tag right now. Expressions are presented in detail later in this chapter.

Listing 18.5   The *footer.jsp* file included by directive in Listing 18.3.

```
<HR>
<CENTER>
<FONT SIZE=2>Copyright &copy 2000 SourceStream. All Rights
   Reserved.</FONT>
</CENTER>
```

taglib

The `taglib` directive indicates that the JSP page references a custom tag library. A *custom tag library* is a collection of custom JSP tags that provide functionality beyond that provided by the standard JSP tags. (We will learn how to create custom tag libraries later in this chapter.) There is no limit to the number of `taglib` directives that can be specified in a JSP page. The syntax for the `taglib` directive looks like this:

```
<%@ taglib uri="taglib_uri" prefix="prefix" %>
```

The `uri` attribute specifies the location of the tag library descriptor (TLD) XML file. This file contains information regarding the tag library such as the tag library version, a short desription of the library, the name of each tag in the library, and the class file associated with each tag. Though the `uri` attribute always points to the TLD file, it may not always do so directly. Rather, it is possible to use the Web application's *web.xml* file to map specific URIs to local resources. For instance, imagine the following tag:

```
<%@ taglib uri="http://java.apache.org/tomcat/examples-taglib"
   prefix="tomcat" %>
```

Notice that this `uri` specifies an absolute URI pointing to a remote server. However, similar to the `include` directive, the JSP specification states that the `uri` attribute must resolve to a local TLD file (i.e., residing on the same machine as the requested JSP page) for security reasons. Fortunately, by specifying a `<taglib>` XML tag in the Web application's *web.xml* file, an absolute URI can easily be mapped to a local resource, as follows:

```
<taglib>
  <taglib-uri>
    http://java.apache.org/tomcat/examples-taglib
  </taglib-uri>
  <taglib-location>
    /WEB-INF/jsp/example-taglib.tld
  </taglib-location>
</taglib>
```

The `<taglib-location>` element specifies the local URL to which the URI contained in the `<taglib_uri>` element should be mapped. This layer of indirection can be extremely useful. For instance, if you acquire numerous JSP pages from a source whose `taglib` directives do not map to the appropriate directories on your system, you can simply provide the appropriate mapping in the Web application's *web.xml* file. Likewise, this URI mapping allows you to change the location of local resources without having to alter the `taglib` directives in every JSP page.

Whenever a `taglib` directive is evaluated by the JSP container, it will first look for a mapping in the Web application's *web.xml* file. If a mapping is found, then the relative URL specified by the `<taglib-location>` element is used to locate the TLD file. If a mapping does not exist and an absolute URI was specified in the `taglib` directive tag, a translation error is raised. If a mapping does not exist and a relative URI was specified, the JSP container attempts to locate the TLD file locally (i.e., the location of the local TLD file can be specified directly within the `taglib` directive tag). If the relative URI begins with a "/", its location is resolved relative to the Web application's document root. Otherwise, if the relative URI does not begin with a "/", it is resolved relative to the JSP page's current directory.

The `prefix` attribute specifies a unique XML namespace by which the tag library is identified. For example, the following `taglib` directives specify local tag libraries using a relative and absolute path, respectively.

```
<%@ taglib uri="sample.tld" prefix="isspjp" %>
<%@ taglib uri="/tld/sample.tld" prefix="isspjp" %>
```

The XML equivalent of the `taglib` directive looks like this:

```
<jsp:directive.taglib uri="sample.tld" prefix="isspjp"/>
```

These example `taglib` directives all use the `isspjp` namespace (standing for Inside Servlets: Server-Side Programming for the Java Platform). Therefore, if the *sample.tld* tag library descriptor contained a tag called `myCustomTag`, this tag could be referenced in the JSP page like this:

```
<isspjp:myCustomTag/>
```

Or, if `myCustomTag` expected some body text, it might be referenced like this:

```
<isspjp:myCustomTag> body text </isspjp:myCustomTag>
```

By specifying a unique prefix for each custom tag library, any number of tag libraries can be defined on a single JSP page without the possibility of name collisions. For example, even if two tag libraries contained a tag called `accountBalance`, there would be no ambiguity when this tag is referenced since all references to the `accountBalance` tag would include a unique prefix that indicates the tag library in which it resides. The following JSP sample demonstrates this concept.

```
<%@ taglib uri="checking.tld" prefix="chck" %>
<%@ taglib uri="savings.tld" prefix="save" %>

Check Account Balance: <chck:accountBalance/>
Savings Account Balance: <save:accountBalance/>
```

To this point, we have only briefly touched on the subject of custom tag libraries. However, we will dig much deeper into this topic later in this chapter when we discuss how to extend standard JSP functionality.

Scripting Elements

Scripting elements allow code to be embedded in a JSP page. When the JSP page is processed, the embedded code is inserted into the appropriate places in the JSP page servlet. As we will see, the placement of code in the JSP page servlet is controlled by the different types of scripting elements.

As you probably realized, embedding code in a JSP page essentially combines content presentation with the application logic that generates the content. However, earlier in this chapter, we discussed the virtues of keeping content presentation and implementation separate. So, why are we discussing how to embed code in a JSP page? The answer is that JSP is an extremely flexible technology that lets you choose your approach to building Web applications. For instance, if the same Java developer is both building the JSP pages and creating the JavaBeans and servlets, then you may choose to use scriptlets to embed code in the JSP pages (since the Java developer might be equally skilled with Java, JSP, and HTML). On the other hand, if you prefer a clean separation of presentation and implementation, JSP facilitates this approach by allowing developers to create custom tag libraries that JSP page designers can use. This approach makes it possible to replace all code in a JSP page with custom JSP tags by moving all code into the custom tag implementation.

Currently, there are three types of scripting elements: declarations, expressions, and scriptlets. Declarations define new instance variables and methods that are accessible by other scripting elements on the page. Expressions contain a single complete line of code that is evaluated for each request. The expression tag is then replaced with the expression's value. Similar to expressions, scriptlets consist of blocks of code that are executed at request time. Scriptlet code may or may not produce visible output. The following skeleton code illustrates the placement of declarations, expressions, and scriptlets in the JSP page servlet. The sections that follow discuss each of these three scripting elements in detail.

```
public class JspPageServlet extends HttpJspBase
{
  //declarations are inserted here

  public void _jspService(HttpServletRequest request,
    HttpServletResponse response) throws IOException,
    ServletException
  {
    //expressions and scriptlets are inserted here
  }
}
```

Declarations

Declarations are used to insert code into the JSP page servlet at the class level, outside of existing methods. Therefore, JSP declarations are used to define instance and class variables and methods that are accessible from anywhere on the page. Since declarations do not generate visible output, they are typically used in conjunction with expressions or scriptlets that do produce output. The syntax for a JSP declaration tag looks like this:

```
<%! declaration(s) %>
```

There is no limit to the number of declarations that can be defined on a single JSP page and a single declaration can include any amount of code. For example, a declaration can define several variables, like this:

```
<%! float farenheit=32.0, celsius=0.0; String tempScale="F"; %>
```

The XML equivalent of the declaration tag looks like this:

```
<jsp:declaration> declaration(s) </jsp:declaration>
```

Now that we know what a JSP declaration is, let's take a look at one. The following declaration defines a class variable called `hitCount`, a class variable called `startDate`, and a method called `getHitCount()`. These declarations will be used in the next section ("Expressions") in order to build a simple JSP page that tracks the number of times it has been accessed. The declaration looks like this:

```
<%! static private int hitCount = 1;
    static private java.util.Date start = new java.util.Date();

    private int getHitCount()
    {
      return hitCount++;
    }
%>
```

Notice that the `hitCount` and `start` variables are declared `static`. Under typical servlet circumstances, instance variables operate the same as class variables and can usually be used interchangeably (in practice, however, instance variables are used more often). This is due to the fact that the servlet container creates only one instance of any servlet that does not implement the `SingleThreadModel` interface (as required by the Java Servlet Specification). Therefore, if all requests are handled by the same servlet instance, class and instance variables operate identically. The only exception to this rule is when a servlet implements the `SingleThreadModel`. In JSP, this occurs when the JSP page includes the <%@ page isThreadSafe="false" %> directive. In this case, the servlet container is allowed to create a pool of servlet instances in order to service concurrent requests. Therefore, to ensure that the hitCount and start variables are shared across all class instances, static class variables are used.

Another important use of the declaration tag is to create the JSP lifecycle methods. Similar to servlets, JSP defines two lifecycle methods that are called when the servlet is created and destroyed. The jspInit() method is called by the JSP container when the page servlet is instantiated but before it processes the first request. The jspDestroy() method is called by the JSP container after all pending requests have been serviced but before the page servlet is unloaded. For example, the following declaration defines both of the JSP lifecycle methods.

```
<%! public void jspInit()
    {
       //perform initialization here
    }

    public void jspDestroy()
    {
       //release resources here
    }
%>
```

Expressions

Expressions are JSP tags that contain a single valid scripting language expression that is evaluated for every request. The expression tag is then replaced with the expression's value. The scripting language is whatever language has been specified for the page by the page directive's language attribute. Java is the default language and usually the only option. The syntax for the expression tag looks like this:

```
<%= expression %>
```

For example, the following expressions perform simple arithmetic and display the current date and time, respectively. Notice that JSP expressions never end with a semicolon. Rather, the JSP processor servlet adds the semicolon, where necessary, when it generates the page servlet source code.

```
<%= 5 + 5 %>
<%= new java.util.Date() %>
```

When the JSP processor servlet encounters these two expressions, it generates output by including them in out.print() statements in the page servlet's _jspService() method (which is called by the page servlet's service() method). To illustrate, Tomcat generates the following code in the page servlet's _jspService() method as it processes the previous two expressions.

```
out.print( 5 + 5 );
out.print( new java.util.Date() );
```

The XML equivalent of the expression tag looks like this:

```
<jsp:expression> expression </jsp:expression>
```

NOTE: Unlike scriptlets, expressions never include trailing semicolons. Rather, semicolons are added automatically when the page servlet is constructed.

Now that we have introduced expressions, let's put them to work. Listing 18.6 presents a JSP page that uses the declaration created in the previous section in conjunction with two expressions to inform the client how many times the servlet has been accessed since it was first loaded (see Figure 18.4).

Listing 18.6 JSP page tracks the number of times it has been accessed.

```
<%! static private int hitCount = 1;
    static private java.util.Date start = new java.util.Date();

    private int getHitCount()
    {
      return hitCount++;
    }
%>

<HTML>
<HEAD>
<TITLE>JSP Page Hit Counter</TITLE>
</HEAD>
<BODY>
<H2>JSP Page Hit Counter</H2>
This page has been hit <%= getHitCount() %> times since
<%= start %>.
</BODY>
</HTML>
```

Before ending our discussion regarding expressions, let's see how we can use Java's tertiary operator to generate conditional output. The Java tertiary operator (a.k.a., ternary operator) includes three expressions. If the boolean expression evaluates to true, then the true expression is evaluated and its value is returned. If the boolean expression evaluates to false, the false expression is

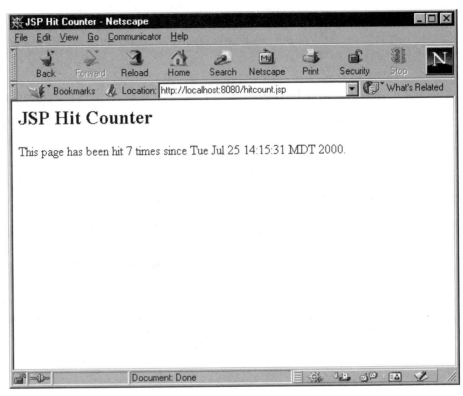

Figure 18.4   Output Generated by the JSP Page Presented in Listing 18.6

evaluated and its value is returned. The syntax of the tertiary operator looks like this:

```
boolean_expression ? true_expression : false_expression
```

Listing 18.7 demonstrates use of a tertiary operator within a JSP expression tag to generate conditional output. In this example, if the hit count is less than 10, a message to that effect is displayed. If it is more than or equal to 10, a different message is displayed.

Listing 18.7   JSP page uses tertiary operator to generate conditional output.

```
<%! static private int hitCount = 1;
    static private java.util.Date start = new java.util.Date();

    private int getHitCount()
    {
      return hitCount++;
    }
%>
```

```
<HTML>
<HEAD>
<TITLE>JSP Page Hit Counter</TITLE>
</HEAD>
<BODY>
<H2>JSP Page Hit Counter</H2>
<%= (hitCount < 10) ? "Less than 10 hits!":"10 or more hits!" %>
<BR>
This page has been hit <%= getHitCount() %> times since
<%= start %>.
</BODY>
</HTML>
```

Scriptlets

Scriptlets are used to insert arbitrary scripting code into the JSP page servlet. Like JSP expressions, scriptlet code is inserted into the page servlet's _jspService() method and, therefore, is executed upon each request. Unlike expressions, scriptlets do not automatically produce output that is returned to the client. Rather, scriptlets may perform application logic, such as conditional statements or looping constructs, that does not directly produce visible output. However, if desired, scriptlets can produce output using the out implicit object. The syntax for a scriptlet tag looks like this:

```
<% scriptlet %>
```

The XML equivalent looks like this:

```
<jsp:scriptlet> scriptlet </jsp:scriptlet>
```

Again, the scriptlet tag may contain any valid scripting code. For example, the following scriptlet extracts a numeric temperature value from the request, converts it from Farenheit to Celsius, and returns the results to the client.

```
<% float farenheit = Integer.parseInt(
    request.getParameter("temp"));

  float celsius = (farenheit - 32)*5/9;

  out.println(farenheit + " farenheit = " + celsius +
    " celsius");
%>
```

However, we can improve on this example by combining scriptlets and expressions in order to decouple the static text from the scriptlet code, like this:

```
<% float farenheit = Integer.parseInt(
    request.getParameter("temp"));
```

```
        float celsius = (farenheit - 32)*5/9;
%>

<%= farenheit %> farenheit = <%= celsius %> celsius
```

By adding this sample code to a JSP page called *conversion.jsp,* it can be invoked using a URL like this:

http://localhost:8080/conversion.jsp?temp=212

Unlike JSP expressions, scriptlets may contain complete statements or code fragments that must be combined with other fragments in order to be valid. Most code fragments are incomplete because they open a block of code that requires another fragment, which appears later in the page, to close the block. If the code block is not closed, the code is not valid and will result in a compilation error when the page servlet is compiled. In Java, code blocks are opened with an opening brace ("{") and closed with a closing brace ("}"). For instance, Listing 18.8 demonstrates how conditional output can be generated using the Java if and else statements within scriptlet fragments.

Listing 18.8 JSP page that generates conditional output.

```
<HTML>
<HEAD>
<TITLE>Farenheit to Celsius Conversion</TITLE>
</HEAD>
<BODY>
<% float farenheit =
    Integer.parseInt(request.getParameter("temp"));

    if (farenheit < -100)
    { %>

That's just too cold to even think about!

<% }
    else if (farenheit > 250)
    { %>

Now that's hot!

<% }
    else
    {
       float celsius = (farenheit - 32)*5/9; %>

<%= farenheit %> farenheit = <%= celsius %> celsius

<% } %>

</BODY>
</HTML>
```

Remember that when a JSP page is translated into a servlet, all static text is included in out.print() or out.write() statements within the _jspService() method. Likewise, all scriptlet code is simply added directly to the _jspService() method in the order that it appears in the page. Therefore, when Listing 18.8 is translated into a servlet, a portion of the code in its _jspService() method will look something like this:

```
float farenheit =
  Integer.parseInt(request.getParameter("temp"));

if (farenheit < -100)
{
  out.println("That's just too cold to even think about!");
}
else if (farenheit > 250)
{
  out.println("Now that's hot!");
}
else
{
  float celsius = (farenheit - 32)*5/9;

  out.println(farenheit + " farenheit = " + celsius +
    " celsius");
}
```

You may have noticed that Listing 18.8 does not include exception handling. Under these circumstances, if the client excluded the temp request parameter or included letters or other non-numeric text within the temp parameter, an ugly exception page would be returned by the JSP container (see Figure 18.5). Fortunately, using scriptlets, it is easy to add exception handling code to a JSP page. Listing 18.9 demonstrates this fact (see Figure 18.6). Also notice that Listing 18.9 uses a JSP declaration in order to move the temperature conversion calculation into a reusable method.

Listing 18.9 JSP page that elegantly handles a NumberFormat exception.

```
<%! private float f2c(float f)
    {
      return (f - 32)*5/9;
    }
%>

<HTML>
<HEAD>
<TITLE>Farenheit to Celsius</TITLE>
</HEAD>
<BODY>
<%
```

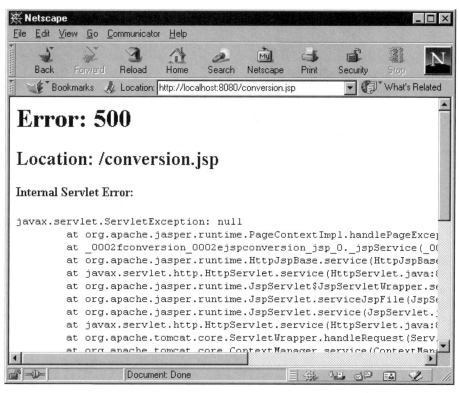

Figure 18.5 Ugly Error Page Resulting from No Exception Handling in Listing 18.8

```
try
{
  float farenheit =
    Integer.parseInt(request.getParameter("temp"));

  if (farenheit < -100)
  { %>

That's just too cold to even think about!

<% }
  else if (farenheit > 250)
  { %>

Now that's hot!

<% }
  else
  { %>
```

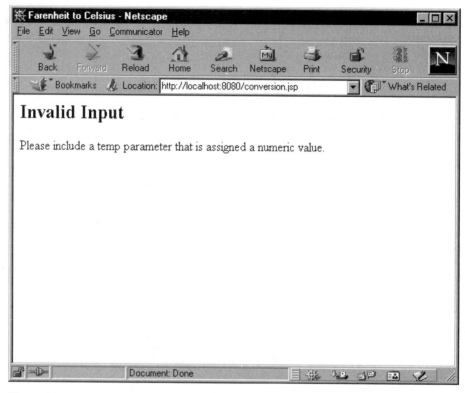

Figure 18.6   Friendly Error Page Resulting from Exception Handling in Listing 18.9

```
<%= farenheit %> farenheit = <%= f2c(farenheit) %> celsius

   <% }
   }
   catch (NumberFormatException e)
   { %>

<H2>Invalid Input</H2>
Please include a temp parameter that is assigned a numeric value.

<% } %>

</BODY>
</HTML>
```

Lastly, scriptlets can also be used to implement many types of looping constructs. Basically, any iterative statements supported by the scripting language
can be used in a JSP scriptlet. In Java, this includes the for, while, and do
while looping constructs. To illustrate, Listing 18.10 presents a JSP page that

uses a Java for loop to convert eleven Celsius temperatures into Farenheit (see Figure 18.7).

Listing 18.10 JSP page that uses a for loop to generate an HTML table.

```
<%! private float c2f(float c)
    {
        return c*9/5 + 32;
    }
%>

<HTML>
<HEAD>
<TITLE>C2F Conversion Loop</TITLE>
</HEAD>
<BODY>
<B>Celsius/Farenheit Comparison Chart</B><BR>
<TABLE BORDER="1">
<TR><TH>Celsius</TH><TH>Farenheit</TH></TR>
```

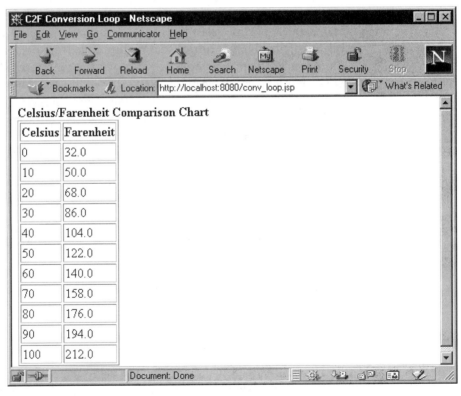

Figure 18.7 Output Produced by the JSP Page Presented in Listing 18.10

```
<% for (int c=0; c <= 100; c+=10)
   { %>

<TR><TD><%= c %></TD><TD><%= c2f(c) %></TD></TR>

<% } %>

</TABLE>
</BODY>
</HTML>
```

Before ending our discussion about scriptlets, let's briefly discuss the inherent problems associated with extensive use of scriptlet code. As you probably noticed from the code examples, scriptlets can result in JSP pages that are difficult to read and maintain. This is due primarily to the fact that scriptlets mix standard Java syntax with a markup language like HTML (thus combining presentation and application logic). Unfortunately, these two coding styles are not very compatible and don't seem to flow well on the page. Though this may not be much of a problem for a Java developer who is also creating JSP pages, the mixture of HTML and Java code can be extremely confusing to page designers and HTML programmers who don't understand the Java syntax. In addition, code embedded in a JSP page is not very reusable. Any reusability of scriptlets usually involves cutting and pasting code from one page into another.

Fortunately, there are ways to improve on the many shortcomings of scriptlets. For instance, later in this chapter we will discuss how to move application logic out of the JSP page and into JavaBeans, thus creating modular and reusable components. In addition, we will present an alternative to using scriptlets to produce conditional and iterative output. Through the use of special JSP tag extensions called custom tag libraries, we will see how it is possible to build custom XML-style JSP tags that can be used to produce conditional output, looping constructs, and a whole lot more.

NOTE: If you want the literal string " <% " or " %> " to be returned to the client from within a JSP page, you must escape the strings using "<\%" and "%\>", respectively.

Comments

There are a number of ways to comment a JSP page. First, you may use the standard comment syntax for the markup language being used on the page.

For example, the standard comment syntax for both HTML and XML looks like this:

```
<!-- comments -->
```

Therefore, you may include comments that begin with `<!--` and end with `-->` within a JSP page. Comments inserted into the page in this manner are added to the output stream and returned to the client. Of course, markup language comments do not produce visible output, but they are visible within the page source.

Second, you may include JSP comments in your pages using the following syntax:

```
<%-- comments --%>
```

Unlike HTML or XML comments, JSP comments are not returned to the client and are visible only in the original JSP page. How is this accomplished? Basically, the JSP processor servlet ignores all JSP comments as it constructs the JSP page servlet. Therefore, these comments are never added to the page servlet's `_jspService()` method. JSP comments are ideal for producing JSP page documentation that might include confidential or proprietary information. In addition, JSP comments are well suited for "commenting out" scripting code within a scriptlet. This is often useful while debugging JSP pages or if you would just like to remove portions of code from execution without deleting the code from the page.

Finally, JSP pages can include scripting comments in declarations, expressions, or scriptlets using the scripting language's standard comment syntax. Java supports the following two comment styles:

```
/* comments */
// comments
```

Unlike JSP comments, scripting comments are added to the JSP page servlet as comments within the source code. Of course, like JSP comments, these comments are not added to the output stream and are never visible to the client. Though both Java comment styles are supported, the "/* */" style is recommended. This is due to the fact that the "//" style requires an end-of-line character to mark the end of the comment. However, there may be instances when a JSP page flows from a scripting comment to scripting code without an end-of-line character. In this case, using the "//" comment style would effectively comment out the rest of the line following the comment (including any scripting code on that line). Therefore, it is often safer to explicitly delimit the beginning and end of all comments using "/*" and "*/".

Actions

Actions are JSP tags that can transfer control to other server resources, generate output, or create and modify objects. Unlike directives, scripting elements, and comments, the syntax for all action tags is based on XML. Though the current JSP specification supports only a handful of standard actions, the custom tags that we will discuss later are all based on JSP actions. These custom tags allow the developer to add any number of actions and define how they behave. In this section we will discuss the `jsp:include`, `jsp:forward`, `jsp:plugin`, and JavaBean-specific actions (i.e., `jsp:useBean`, `jsp:setProperty`, and `jsp:get-Property`).

`jsp:include`

The `jsp:include` action includes the output of a specified server resource (e.g., servlet, JSP page, CGI application) within a JSP page at request time. That is, the output from the specified resource is requested and inserted into the page each time the JSP page is invoked. When the `<jsp:include>` tag is encountered, control is passed to the included resource. Once the included resource's processing is complete, control is returned to the original JSP page and processing continues. In addition, includes can be nested infinitely deep. This means that included JSP pages can use the `jsp:include` action themselves to include other resources (and these resources can also use the `jsp:include` action). The syntax for the `<jsp:include>` tag looks like this:

```
<jsp:include page="local_url" flush="true"/>
```

The page attribute represents any local server resource that produces output. This attribute usually references a JSP page, servlet, CGI application, or static HTML document. The page attribute is specified using a relative URL (i.e., no protocol or hostname information). If the relative URL begins with a "/", the JSP container locates the page relative to the Web application's document root. Otherwise, the URL path is considered relative to the current JSP page's directory.

The flush attribute is required even though, currently, the only valid value is true. This attribute indicates that the output buffer will be flushed prior to transferring control to the included page. This fact is important to keep in mind because, as previously discussed, once the output buffer is flushed, HTTP headers can no longer be added or altered (including cookies) and control can no longer be forwarded to another page (not even the error page).

One extremely useful characteristic of the `jsp:include` action is the ability to dynamically set the value of its page attribute at request time using a standard JSP expression. For example, the following <jsp:include> tag's page attribute is dynamically set using a JSP expression.

```
<jsp:include page='<%= "greeting" + customerCode + ".jsp" %>'/>
```

In this example, the name of the included file is based on the customerCode variable that is evaluated at request time. This might be useful if each customer category is assigned a unique greeting. To illustrate, if the customerCode variable evaluates to 5, the <jsp:include> tag is replaced by the contents of a page called greeting5.jsp.

As previously discussed, the jsp:include action requests the included resource each time its JSP page is invoked. However, there may be times when a requested resource requires some request parameters that provide additional details regarding the information desired. For instance, imagine a servlet that calculates a customer's account balance based on the account number passed to it via a request parameter. Now imagine a JSP page that uses the jsp:include action to retrieve a customer's balance from this servlet. The only problem is that the JSP page must be able to pass a request parameter to the servlet indicating the customer's account number. Fortunately, request parameters can be added to the jsp:include action's request using the <jsp:param> tag. The syntax of the <jsp:include> tag, including <jsp:param> tags, is as follows:

```
<jsp:include page="local_url" flush="true">
  <jsp:param name="param_name1" value="param_value1"/>
  <jsp:param name="param_name2" value="param_value2"/>
  <jsp:param name="param_nameN" value="param_valueN"/>
</jsp:include>
```

Naturally, the <jsp:param> tag's name attribute represents the name of the request parameter and the value attribute contains the parameter value. And similar to the jsp:include action's page attribute, the <jsp:param> tag's value attribute supports dynamic request-time values. For example, the following <jsp:include> tag invokes the AccountBalance servlet and includes the account number specified by the accountNum variable as a request parameter.

```
<jsp:include page="/servlet/AccountBalance" flush="true">
  <jsp:param name="Account" value="<%= accountNum %>"/>
</jsp:include>
```

You might be wondering why JSP supports both the include directive and the jsp:include action. The answer is that these two elements behave very differently and are appropriate under different circumstances. For example, the include directive can include only static files (e.g., HTML or JSP pages) while the jsp:include action can include output produced by dynamic server resources, such as servlets or CGI scripts, in addition to static files. Futhermore, since the `include` directive inserts included files into the JSP page prior to the creation of the JSP page servlet, changes to the included files are not reflected automatically in the JSP page servlet's output (retranslation and recompilation of the page servlet are necessary in order to incorporate changes made to any files included with the `include` directive). On the other hand, since the `jsp:include` action includes server resources dynamically at request time, they are always current.

At this point, it may appear that the `jsp:include` action is far superior to the `include` directive. However, the `include` directive has some advantages of its own. For instance, the `include` directive requires less overhead than a `jsp:include` action because included files are processed only once rather than upon each request. In addition, since files included using the `include` directive are translated into the JSP page servlet, scripting code within these files can reference local variables defined within the page servlet's `_jspService()` method as well as instance and class variables. This is not possible using the `jsp:include` action. Lastly, since the `include` directive is processed when the JSP page is translated into a servlet rather than at request time, it does not require the output buffer to be flushed.

jsp:forward

The `jsp:forward` action forwards a request to another server resource. In contrast to the `jsp:include` action that temporarily transfers control, the `jsp:forward` action transfers control permanently to another resource. When control is transferred, the processing of the current page is terminated and any output generated by it is discarded. The syntax of the `<jsp:forward>` tag is as follows:

```
<jsp:forward page="local_url"/>
```

The page attribute represents any local server resource that produces output. This attribute usually references a JSP page, servlet, CGI application, or static HTML document. The page attribute is specified using a relative URL (i.e., no protocol or hostname information). If the relative URL begins with a "/", the JSP container locates the page relative to the Web application's document root. Otherwise, the URL path is considered relative to the current JSP page's directory.

Like the `jsp:include` action, the `jsp:forward` action's page attribute accepts dynamic request-time values. For example, the following sample code demonstrates how the page to which control should be forwarded can be generated dynamically at request time.

```
<% String nextPage;
   if (user.isVendor())
   {
     nextPage = "vendor.html";
   }
   else
   {
     nextPage = "customer.html";
   }
%>

<jsp:forward page="<%= nextPage %>"/>
```

Also similar to the `jsp:include` action, the `jsp:forward` action allows the JSP page developer to specify request parameters using the `<jsp:param>` tag. The syntax of the `<jsp:forward>` tag, including `<jsp:param>` tags, is as follows:

```
<jsp:forward page="local_url">
  <jsp:param name="param_name1" value="param_value1"/>
  <jsp:param name="param_name2" value="param_value2"/>
  <jsp:param name="param_nameN" value="param_valueN"/>
</jsp:forward>
```

Since the `jsp:forward` action terminates execution of the current page, this action is usually invoked conditionally. The following JSP code demonstrates how to implement a conditional forward.

```
<% if (!user.isLoggedIn())
   { %>

<%-- user is not logged in, forward to the login page --%>
<jsp:forward page="login.jsp" %>

<% } %>

<%-- user is logged in, continue processing this page --%>
```

In this example, a scriptlet tag is used to determine if the user has been authenticated (i.e., logged in). If not, the user is forwarded to the login page. Otherwise, processing of the page continues normally.

jsp:plugin

The `jsp:plugin` action is used to add Java 2 applet support to today's leading browsers—Netscape Navigator and Microsoft Internet Explorer. Since they currently support only JDK 1.02 or 1.1, Sun Microsystems has developed a browser plug-in that adds Java 2 support to both of these browsers. Once installed, it is possible to direct applets to use Sun's Java 2 Runtime Environment contained within the plug-in rather than the browser's default Java virtual machine. You can download the Java plug-in from the following URL:

http://java.sun.com/products/plugin/

Though the Java plug-in allows the Java 2 Runtime Environment to be used to run applets, instructing the browser to use the Java plug-in can be somewhat complex since the traditional <APPLET> tag cannot be used. This is due to the fact that when the <APPLET> tag is encountered, the browser automatically uses its own internal virtual machine to execute the applet. To overcome this problem, the Java plug-in from Sun takes advantage of each browser's proprietary extensions in order to provide an alternative method of running applets. Unfortunately, this involves replacing the simple <APPLET> tag with a long and complex <OBJECT> tag for Internet Explorer or an <EMBED> tag for Netscape. In addition, since you don't know which browser will be accessing your site, you will usually need to specify both the <OBJECT> tag and the <EMBED> tag for every applet (the <EMBED> tag can be included within the <OBJECT> tag's comment area). This can be a lot of work and is not something that you want to do by hand. Fortunately, the jsp:plugin action solves this problem by providing a simple and consistent syntax for defining applets on a JSP page. The jsp:plugin syntax is as follows:

```
<jsp:plugin type="applet|bean" code="applet_class_name"
    codebase="applet_directory" height="height" width="width"/>
```

For example, the following <jsp:plugin> tag specifies an applet named *SampleApplet.class* located in the */applets* directory on the server and having a height and width of 200 pixels.

```
<jsp:plugin type="applet" code="SampleApplet.class"
    codebase="/applets" height="200" width="200"/>
```

In addition to defining an applet, it is also possible to pass parameters to it using the <jsp:params> and <jsp:param> tags. The syntax for the <jsp:plugin> tag, including specifying parameters with the <jsp:params> and <jsp:param> tags, is as follows:

```
<jsp:plugin type="applet|bean" code="applet_class_name"
    codebase="applet_directory" height="height" width="width">
    <jsp:params>
        <jsp:param name="param_name1" value="param_value1"/>
        <jsp:param name="param_name2" value="param_value2"/>
        <jsp:param name="param_nameN" value="param_valueN"/>
    </jsp:params>
</jsp:plugin>
```

As an example, the following jsp:plugin action includes a parameter that specifies the stocks that should be displayed by a stock ticker applet.

```
<jsp:plugin type="applet" code="StockTicker.class"
  codebase="/applets" height="200" width="200">
  <jsp:params>
    <jsp:param name="stock1" value="sunw"/>
    <jsp:param name="stock2" value="ibm"/>
    <jsp:param name="stock3" value="novl"/>
    <jsp:param name="stock4" value="orcl"/>
    <jsp:param name="stock5" value="sybs"/>
  </jsp:params>
</jsp:plugin>
```

Lastly, the jsp:plugin action also allows the developer to specify a text message for browsers that do not support the <OBJECT> or <EMBED> tags. This message is specified using the <jsp:fallback> tag, like this:

```
<jsp:plugin type="applet" code="StockTicker.class"
  codebase="/applets" height="200" width="200">
  <jsp:fallback>
    The stock ticker applet will not run on your browser.
  </jsp:fallback>
</jsp:plugin>
```

Since this book's primary focus is on server-side programming (as opposed to client-side applet programming), this is all the time that we will spend on the jsp:plugin action. However, in case you are interested, Table 18.5 describes the jsp:plugin action's required attributes and Table 18.6 describes its optional attributes.

Table 18.5 Required Attributes of the jsp:plugin Action

Attribute	Description
type	Specifies the type of Java component to insert. Valid values are "applet" for applets and "bean" for JavaBeans.
code	Specifies the name of the component's class file or a serialized object. This attribute is analogous to the <APPLET> tag's CODE attribute.
height	Specifies the height, in pixels, of the component. This attribute is analogous to the <APPLET> tag's HEIGHT attribute.
width	Specifies the width, in pixels, of the component. This attribute is analogous to the <APPLET> tag's WIDTH attribute.

Table 18.6   Optional Attributes of the `jsp:plugin` Action

Attribute	Description
codebase	Specifies the directory on the server that contains the file specified by the code attribute. This attribute is analogous to the <APPLET> tag's CODEBASE attribute. Similarly, if this attribute is not specified, the location of the current JSP page is used as the default.
align	Specifies the horizontal or vertical alignment of the Java component within the page. Valid values include left, right, top, bottom, and middle. This attribute is analogous to the <APPLET> tag's ALIGN attribute.
hspace	Specifies the margin, in pixels, to reserve on the left and right sides of the component. This attribute is analogous to the <APPLET> tag's HSPACE attribute.
vspace	Specifies the margin, in pixels, to reserve above and below the component. This attribute is analogous to the <APPLET> tag's VSPACE attribute.
name	Assigns a logical name to the component in which it can be referenced by other components or through a scripting language like JavaScript. This attribute is analogous to the <APPLET> tag's NAME attribute.
title	Specifies a title that may be used as a tooltip. This attribute is analogous to the <APPLET> tag's TITLE attribute.
archive	Specifies a comma-delimited list of JAR files containing required component resources (e.g., classes, images, property files). This attribute is analogous to the <APPLET> tag's ARCHIVE attribute.
jreversion	Specifies the version of the Java Runtime Environment (JRE) that is required to execute the component. The default is JRE 1.1.
iepluginurl	Specifies the URL from which the Microsoft Internet Explorer plug-in can be downloaded.
nspluginurl	Specifies the URL from which the Netscape plug-in can be downloaded.

jsp:useBean, jsp:setProperty, *and* jsp:getProperty

To increase maintainability and reusability, JSP provides actions that tightly integrate with JavaBeans. A *JavaBean* is a discrete component that encapsulates behavior and data. Since JavaBeans are independent of other applications, they are easy to maintain and reuse. The developer needs only to publish the bean's interface in order to make it accessible to JSP page designers and other non-Java programmers. Using JSP's simple bean interface, the complexities of the bean's implementation are completely abstracted from the JSP page designer. And because the bean is totally self-contained, as long as its interface is not changed, its internal implementation can be altered and improved without affecting the applications that use it.

Before presenting the JSP actions that provide access to JavaBeans, let's start with a quick JavaBean primer. Simply put, JavaBeans are ordinary Java classes (they are not required to implement a certain interface or extend a particular class) that subscribe to published naming and design conventions as described in the JavaBeans specification. For the most part, these conventions require that all JavaBean properties be available through accessor methods. *Accessor methods* are `public` methods that provide access to the JavaBean's internal variables or functionality. JavaBeans should not expose internal variables as `public`, but rather should always provide accessor methods for them that allow their values to be *get* and *set* by external applications. Accessor methods use the get*Xxx*( ) format for reading property values and the set*Xxx*( ) format for setting property values (where Xxx is the name of the property). These methods are often referred to as *getter* and *setter* methods, respectively. Additionally, there is one more type of accessor method, assuming the form is*Xxx*( ), that returns a `boolean` value.

NOTE: Bean properties can be made read-only, write-only, or read/write by providing the appropriate combination of get*Xxx*( ) and set*Xxx*( ) methods. For instance, to create a read-only property, a bean may implement only the get*Xxx*( ) method without a set*Xxx*( ) method. Likewise, a property that implements only the set*Xxx*( ) method, without a get*Xxx*( ) method, is write-only.

Accessor methods allow JavaBeans to validate input before setting internal variables, format output before returning a value, or perform any other type of processing required when properties are get and set. For example, Listing 18.11 demonstrates a typical bean that validates input and formats output. Input validation consists of disallowing any grade-level value less than zero or greater than twenty. Output formatting consists of applying a currency format to the salary value (i.e., adding a dollar sign and comma separators, depending on the locale). In addition, the is`Manager`( ) method demonstrates an accessor method that returns a `boolean` value.

Listing 18.11 Simple JavaBean that validates input and formats output.

```
public class EmployeeBean
{
  private String name="";
  private int gradeLevel=0;
  private float salary=0;
  private boolean managerFlag=false;
```

```java
public String getName()
{
  return name;
}

public void setName(String name)
{
  this.name = name;
}

public int getGradeLevel()
{
  return gradeLevel;
}

public void setGradeLevel(int gradeLevel)
{
  if (gradeLevel < 0)
  {
    this.gradeLevel = 0;
  }
  else if (gradeLevel > 20)
  {
    this.gradeLevel = 20;
  }
  else
  {
    this.gradeLevel = gradeLevel;
  }
}

public String getSalary()
{
  java.text.NumberFormat currency =
    java.text.NumberFormat.getCurrencyInstance();

  return currency.format(salary);
}

public void setSalary(String salary)
{
  try
  {
    this.salary = Float.parseFloat(salary);
  }
  catch (NumberFormatException e)
  {
    this.salary = 0;
  }
}
```

```
public boolean isManager()
{
  return managerFlag;
}

public void setManager(boolean managerFlag)
{
  this.managerFlag = managerFlag;
}
}
```

NOTE: If a JSP JavaBean is both readable and writable, the setter method must accept the same data type as that returned by the property's getter method. For instance, if the `employee` bean's `getSalary()` method returns a `String`, the corresponding `setSalary()` method must accept a `String` as a parameter. Of course, additional `setSalary()` methods can be defined that accept integers or other data types but the JSP container will automatically call the `setSalary(String)` method when the `jsp:setProperty` action is invoked. This is because the JSP container uses the return value of the property's getter method to determine which setter method to call.

In addition to conforming to the accessor method naming conventions, JavaBeans must support an empty (no arguments) constructor. As demonstrated in Listing 18.11, this can be accomplished easily by not defining a constructor. If no constructors are defined, Java automatically provides a default, no-argument constructor. However, if you do define your own non-empty constructor, you must also provide a constructor that accepts no arguments. This is essential so that the JSP container can instantiate JavaBeans without knowing anything about them (other than the fact that they are beans).

Strictly speaking, the JavaBeans specification states that beans should implement the `serializable` interface. This interface does not define any methods and only serves as a flag to the Java virtual machine to indicate that the bean may be serialized. *Serialization* is the process of writing an object in its current state to persistent storage (in binary or text format). This data may then be *deserialized* later as it is converted back into a valid Java object in memory. Though the JavaBeans specification enforces it, JSP does not require beans to be serializable. This concludes our brief JavaBeans primer. For more information, see the JavaBeans specification, API documentation, and tutorials at the following URL:

http://java.sun.com/beans/docs/

JSP defines three actions for interacting with JavaBeans. The `jsp:useBean` action instantiates a bean and places it within a specified scope. The `jsp:get-Property` action retrieves the value of a JavaBean property and the `jsp:set-Property` method sets the value of a JavaBean property. The following sections describe each of these actions in detail.

jsp:useBean

The `jsp:useBean` action loads the specified bean and assigns it a logical name with which it can be referenced from within the JSP page. The process of *loading* a bean may involve instantiating it and placing it within the specified scope (e.g., page, request, session, application) or simply retrieving an existing bean from the designated scope. Therefore, the `jsp:useBean` action instantiates a new bean only if one does not already exist under the same name (i.e., `id`) and scope. The basic syntax for the `jsp:useBean` action looks like this:

```
<jsp:useBean id="bean_name" class="package.Class"/>
```

For example, the following `jsp:useBean` action instantiates the `com.inside-servlets.Employee` class and stores it under the name `employee` within the page scope. Notice that if the `scope` attribute is not specified, the default is page scope.

```
<jsp:useBean id="employee" class="com.insideservlets.Employee"/>
```

This action is actually equivalent to the following scriptlet. However, the `jsp:useBean` action uses an XML format that is easier to read and more accessible to page designers and HTML programmers.

```
<% Employee employee = new Employee(); %>
```

NOTE: There are a few naming restrictions regarding a bean's `id` (i.e., logical name) of which you should be aware. First, logical names must be unique to the page. That is, two `jsp:useBean` actions on the same page cannot use the same `id`. Second, bean names are case-sensitive. Last, bean names must begin with a letter and contain only letters, numbers, and underscores. Basically, a bean's `id` is subject to the same naming restrictions as Java variables.

The more advanced syntax for the `jsp:useBean` action looks like this:

```
<jsp:useBean id="bean_name" class="package.Class" scope="scope">
  initialization code
</jsp:useBean>
```

This syntax allows the user to specify the bean's scope as well as include initialization code that is executed only once when the bean is first instantiated. For example, the following `jsp:useBean` action instantiates a `com.insideservlets.Cart` object under the name `shoppingCart` and specifies a scope of `session` (i.e., the `shoppingCart` object is stored in the user's session). The `Cart` object is then initialized by setting its `maxItems` property to `10`.

```
<jsp:useBean id="shoppingCart" class="com.insideservlets.Cart"
  scope="session">
  <jsp:setProperty name="shoppingCart" property="maxItems"
    value="10"/>
</jsp:useBean>
```

In place of the `class` attribute, the `jsp:useBean` action can use the `beanName` attribute to designate either a bean class or a serialized object file. If the `beanName` specifies a serialized object file, the bean object is reinstantiated from the serialized file and stored under the specified name and scope. This attribute is usually used only if a bean is to be reconstructed from a serialized file.

Finally, the `jsp:useBean` also supports the `type` attribute. This attribute designates the class or interface to which the bean should be cast when it is retrieved. At times, this can be useful. For instance, if a bean implements a particular interface, you may choose to retrieve it as an instance of that interface rather than an instance of the bean class. To illustrate, assuming that the `shoppingCart` object instantiated previously implements the `Shoppable` interface, the following `jsp:useBean` action retrieves the `shoppingCart` object from the session as an instance of the `Shoppable` interface. Of course, if the `type` attribute is used as follows, the `shoppingCart` bean will support only the methods defined by the `Shoppable` interface.

```
<jsp:useBean id="shoppingCart" class="com.insideservlets.Cart"
  scope="session" type="com.insideservlets.Shoppable"/>
```

As you can see, the `jsp:useBean` action makes it quick and easy to instantiate beans from within a JSP page. In the following sections, we will learn that the `jsp:getProperty` and `jsp:setProperty` actions make it is just as easy to get and set a bean's properties.

jsp:getProperty

The `jsp:getProperty` action retrieves the value of a bean's property and inserts it into the JSP page. Unlike the `jsp:useBean` and `jsp:setProperty` actions, this action produces visible output on the JSP page. If necessary, the value is automatically converted into a String before it is inserted into the page (i.e., if the property returns a non-String value such as an integer). The syntax for the jsp:getProperty action is as follows:

```
<jsp:getProperty name="bean_name" property="property"/>
```

The name attribute specifies the bean whose property should be retrieved. This attribute's value corresponds to the logical name assigned to the bean by the jsp:useBean action's id attribute. Though it's easy to get them confused, remember that the <jsp:getProperty> tag specifies the bean using the name attribute and the <jsp:useBean> tag uses the id tag to assign the bean a name. To illustrate the jsp:getProperty action, the following tag is replaced with the value of the employee bean's salary property.

```
<jsp:getProperty name="employee" property="salary"/>
```

Though this action is equivalent to the following JSP expression, it is much easier to read and more accessible to those not skilled in Java programming.

```
<%= employee.getSalary() %>
```

You may be wondering what value is returned when a boolean property is requested. The answer is that the text representation (i.e., a String value) of the property's value is returned. Therefore, a boolean property returns either "true" or "false" String values. The following action illustrates a property that returns a boolean value. Remember that the accessor method for retrieving a boolean property usually assumes the form of isXxx() rather than getXxx(), as demonstrated in Listing 18.11. When a boolean property is requested, the JSP container first attempts to locate an isXxx() accessor method. If not found, the getXxx() method is used (if the getXxx() method is not found, an exception is thrown).

```
<jsp:getProperty name="employee" property="manager"/>
```

You may have noticed that the property specified by the <jsp:get-Property> tag often begins with a lowercase letter (e.g., salary) although the property within the accessor method to which it corresponds begins with a capital later (e.g., the getSalary() method). This, however, does not present a problem because the JSP container automatically capitalizes the first letter of the property before calling the getXxx() accessor method.

Dynamically setting attributes within HTML tags is one particularly useful application of the jsp:getProperty action. For example, Listing 18.12 presents a JSP page that displays an HTML form whose values are automatically populated by jsp:getProperty actions.

Listing 18.12   JSP page uses `jsp:getProperty` action to populate fields.

```
<jsp:useBean id="user" class="UserBean" scope="session"/>
<HTML>
<HEAD>
<TITLE>Update User Information</TITLE>
</HEAD>
<BODY>
<FORM METHOD="POST" ACTION="update.jsp">
<TABLE BORDER="0">
<TR>
<TD>Name: </TD><TD><INPUT TYPE="TEXT" NAME="name"
  VALUE="<jsp:getProperty name='user' property='name'/>"></TD>
</TR>
<TR>
<TD>Email Address: </TD><TD><INPUT TYPE="TEXT" NAME="email"
  VALUE="<jsp:getProperty name='user' property='email'/>"></TD>
</TR>
</TABLE>
<INPUT TYPE="SUBMIT" VALUE="Update">
</FORM>
</BODY>
</HTML>
```

jsp:setProperty

The `jsp:setProperty` action sets the value of a bean's property. Unlike `jsp:getProperty`, this bean does not produce visible output. The most basic syntax for this action is as follows:

```
<jsp:setProperty name="bean_name" property="property_name"
  value="value"/>
```

The `name` attribute specifies the bean whose property should be set. This attribute's value corresponds to the logical name assigned to the bean by the `jsp:useBean` action's `id` attribute. The `property` attribute designates the property to be set. The `value` attribute specifies the value to assign to the designated property. For example, the following `<jsp:setProperty>` tag sets the `gradeLevel` property of the `employee` bean to `10` (representing a position or salary grade level).

```
<jsp:setProperty name="employee" property="gradeLevel"
  value="10"/>
```

You may have noticed that the `employee` bean's `setGradeLevel()` method presented in Listing 18.11 is defined to accept only integer values. Fortunately, the JSP container automatically converts `String` values into the appropriate parameter type when necessary. This automatic conversion is provided for parameters that accept these data types: `boolean`, `Boolean`, `byte`, `Byte`, `char`,

Character, double, Double, int, Integer, float, Float, long, and Long. Similarly, JSP automatically converts any non-String return values into their String equivalents (e.g., it calls their toString() method).

The previous jsp:setProperty action is equivalent to the following scriptlet. However, the action uses an XML format that is easier to read and more accessible to page designers and HTML programmers.

```
<% employee.setGradeLevel(10); %>
```

Now that we've seen how to set a property using a literal String (e.g., 10), let's discuss how to set values based on request parameters. One way to set a bean's value based on a request parameter is to use a JSP expression like this:

```
<jsp:setProperty name="employee" property="salary"
   value='<%= request.getParameter("empSalary") %>'/>
```

This action retrieves the value of a request parameter named empSalary and uses it to set the employee bean's salary property. This request parameter can be passed to the JSP page from an HTML form submission or within a URL query string like this:

http://localhost:8080/employee.jsp?empSalary=50000

JSP expressions are effective, but there is a simpler way to associate request parameters to bean properties. The jsp:setProperty action's param attribute specifies the name of the request parameter whose value should be used to set the designated property. The param attribute is used in place of the value attribute to specify the property's value. The syntax for a <jsp:setProperty> tag using the param attribute looks like this:

```
<jsp:setProperty name="bean_name" property="property_name"
   param="request_param_name"/>
```

For example, the following action is equivalent to the previous one except the param attribute is used instead of a JSP expression. Notice how much simpler and more readable the tag becomes when the param attribute is used.

```
<jsp:setProperty name="employee" property="salary"
   param="empSalary"/>
```

To illustrate further how to tie request parameters to bean properties, Listing 18.13 demonstrates the jsp:setProperty action's param attribute.

Listing 18.13 Uses the param attribute to associate parameters and properties.

```
<jsp:useBean id="employee" class="EmployeeBean"/>
<jsp:setProperty name="employee" property="name"
  param="empName"/>
<jsp:setProperty name="employee" property="gradeLevel"
  param="empGrade"/>
<jsp:setProperty name="employee" property="salary"
  param="empSalary"/>
<jsp:setProperty name="employee" property="manager"
  param="empManager"/>
<HTML>
<HEAD>
<TITLE>View Employee Information</TITLE>
</HEAD>
<BODY>
<TABLE BORDER="0">
<TR>
<TD>Name: </TD><TD><B><jsp:getProperty name="employee"
  property="name"/></B></TD>
</TR>
<TR>
<TD>Grade Level: </TD><TD><B><jsp:getProperty name="employee"
  property="gradeLevel"/></B></TD>
</TR>
<TR>
<TD>Salary: </TD><TD><B><jsp:getProperty name="employee"
  property="salary"/></B></TD>
</TR>
<TR>
<TD>Is Manager: </TD><TD><B><jsp:getProperty name="employee"
  property="manager"/></B></TD>
</TR>
</TABLE>
</BODY>
</HTML>
```

Figure 18.8 displays the output generated by Listing 18.13 when invoked with the following URL (assuming that Listing 18.13 is stored in a file called *employee.jsp*).

http://localhost:8080/employee.jsp?empName=Tyler&empSalary=75750.50&
empGrade=12&empManager=true

NOTE: If the request parameter specified within the param attribute does not exist, no action is taken. That is, the bean property's set*Xxx*() method is not called.

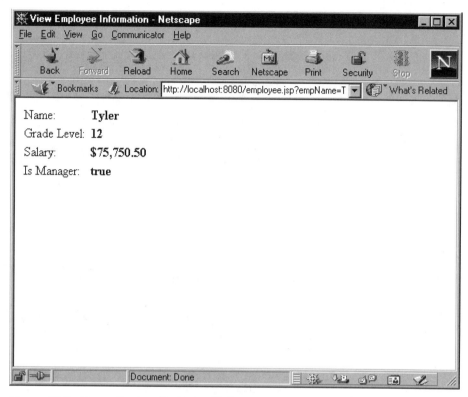

Figure 18.8   Output Produced by Listing 18.13

As we have seen, the param attribute greatly simplifies the process of asso-
ciating request parameters to bean properties. However, there is a quicker way
to accomplish this goal. If you are careful to give each request parameter the
exact name (including case) as the bean property to which it corresponds, you
can replace multiple <jsp:setProperty> tags with a single tag that specifies the
"*" wildcard for the property attribute. The "*" value indicates that each
request parameter should be associated to the bean property of the same name.
The syntax for this type of jsp:setProperty action is as follows:

```
<jsp:setProperty name="bean_name" property="*"/>
```

Using the "*" wildcard value, Listing 18.13 can be shortened to the JSP page
presented in Listing 18.14. Of course, the request parameters in the URL
must be renamed to correspond to their matching bean property names. For
example, Listing 18.14 produces the same output as illustrated in Figure 18.8
when the following URL is used:

> *http://localhost:8080/employee.jsp?name=Tyler&salary=75750.50&gradeLevel=12&*
> *manager=true*

Listing 18.14   Uses the "*" wildcard to associate parameters and properties.

```
<jsp:useBean id="employee" class="EmployeeBean"/>
<jsp:setProperty name="employee" property="*"/>
<HTML>
<HEAD>
<TITLE>View Employee Information</TITLE>
</HEAD>
<BODY>
<TABLE BORDER="0">
<TR>
<TD>Name: </TD><TD><B><jsp:getProperty name="employee"
   property="name"/></B></TD>
</TR>
<TR>
<TD>Grade Level: </TD><TD><B><jsp:getProperty name="employee"
   property="gradeLevel"/></B></TD>
</TR>
<TR>
<TD>Salary: </TD><TD><B><jsp:getProperty name="employee"
   property="salary"/></B></TD>
</TR>
<TR>
<TD>Is Manager: </TD><TD><B><jsp:getProperty name="employee"
   property="manager"/></B></TD>
</TR>
</TABLE>
</BODY>
</HTML>
```

Dynamic Attribute Values

Most of the attributes associated with JSP tags do not support dynamic values. That is, their values cannot be resolved at request time and must be specified within the JSP page using explicit static text. However, there are a handful of action tag attributes that do support request-time values, as documented in Table 18.7.

Table 18.7   JSP Action Tags and Attributes That Support Request-Time Values

JSP Action Tag	Dynamic Attribute
jsp:include	page
jsp:forward	page
jsp:useBean	beanName
jsp:setProperty	value
jsp:param	value

Attributes that support dynamic values can be set at request time using standard JSP expressions. For example, the following `jsp:include` action tag's page attribute is dynamically set using a JSP expression.

```
<jsp:include page='<%= "greeting" + customerCode + ".jsp" %>'/>
```

Custom Tag Libraries

Throughout this chapter, we have discussed the advantages of separating presentation from implementation. However, we have also presented scripting elements (e.g., scriptlets and JSP expressions) that essentially combine these two disciplines by embedding Java code in the HTML page. In fact, to this point, we have presented no other way to accomplish many common tasks, such as conditional or iterative output. Fortunately, JSP 1.1 provides a solution to this problem by allowing developers to define their own JSP tags. These tags, known as *custom tags,* assume the same XML-style format as JSP action tags and can be used to produce output, control program flow, or perform just about any other task that can be accomplished with scriptlets. However, since custom tags use the XML format, they are easier to read in the context of an HTML or XML document and are more accessible to page designers and other non-Java programmers.

When a custom tag is created, the developer is able to define just about every aspect of the tag's behavior including the manner in which the tag's attributes and body are interpreted. Custom tag development requires two main components—a tag library descriptor (TLD) file that describes the characteristics of the tag and a Java class, also called a *tag handler,* that is executed by the JSP container in order to perform the tag's behavior. Additionally, the JSP custom tag architecture supports an optional helper class, often called an *extra info class,* for each custom tag. This helper class must extend the `javax.servlet.jsp.tagext.TagExtraInfo` abstract class and may contain logic that performs complex tag validation and/or defines scripting variables that the tag should expose. After examining exactly how custom tags are processed, we will revisit TLDs, tag handlers, and extra info classes and describe how they are created.

A set of custom tags, usually performing similar or related functionality, can be grouped into a collection known as a *custom tag library.* Tag libraries allow the developer to package groups of custom tags neatly into libraries that are easy to reuse and simple to deploy. Since it cannot be referenced directly, every custom tag must belong to a tag library and can be referenced only via the `taglib` directive presented earlier. That is, any JSP page that includes a custom tag must also include a `taglib` directive.

Tag Library Descriptor

The taglib directive includes the prefix by which the tag library can be referenced within the page in addition to a URI that specifies the location of the tag library descriptor file. The descriptor file contains information about the tag library such as the name of each custom tag in the library, the attributes that it accepts, whether it supports body content (and the type of content), the name of the tag handler class that defines the tag's behavior, and (optionally) the name of a TagExtraInfo class that performs additional validation and/or introduces new scripting variables. Listing 18.15 presents a basic TLD file that defines five custom tags—dateTime, dateFormat, changeCase, loop, and forEach.

Listing 18.15   Tag library descriptor file that defines five custom tags.

```
<?xml version="1.0" encoding="ISO-8859-1" ?>
<!DOCTYPE taglib PUBLIC
  "-//Sun Microsystems, Inc.//DTD JSP Tag Library 1.1//EN"
  "http://java.sun.com/j2ee/dtds/web-jsptaglibrary_1_1.dtd">

<!-- a tag library descriptor -->

<taglib>
  <tlibversion>1.0</tlibversion>
  <jspversion>1.1</jspversion>
  <shortname>sample</shortname>
  <uri>http://www.insideservlets.com/tld/isspjp-taglib.tld</uri>
  <info>Inside Servlets Sample Tag Library</info>

  <!-- dateTime Custom Tag Definition -->
  <tag>
    <name>dateTime</name>
    <tagclass>DateTimeTag</tagclass>
    <bodycontent>EMPTY</bodycontent>
    <info>Display the Current Date and Time</info>
  </tag>

  <!-- dateFormat Custom Tag Definition -->
  <tag>
    <name>dateFormat</name>
    <tagclass>DateFormatTag</tagclass>
    <bodycontent>EMPTY</bodycontent>
    <info>Displays Current Date in the Specified Format</info>
    <attribute>
      <name>format</name>
      <required>false</required>
    </attribute>
  </tag>

  <!-- changeCase Custom Tag Definition -->
  <tag>
```

```
    <name>changeCase</name>
    <tagclass>ChangeCaseTag</tagclass>
    <bodycontent>JSP</bodycontent>
    <info>Converts Its Body Content to Upper or Lower Case</info>
    <attribute>
      <name>case</name>
      <required>false</required>
    </attribute>
  </tag>

  <!-- loop Custom Tag Definition -->
  <tag>
    <name>loop</name>
    <tagclass>LoopTag</tagclass>
    <bodycontent>JSP</bodycontent>
    <info>Repeats its Body Content a Specified # of Times</info>
    <attribute>
      <name>iterations</name>
      <required>true</required>
    </attribute>
  </tag>

  <!-- forEach Custom Tag Definition -->
  <tag>
    <name>forEach</name>
    <tagclass>ForEachTag</tagclass>
    <teiclass>ForEachTei</teiclass>
    <bodycontent>JSP</bodycontent>
    <info>Repeats Tag Body for Each Item in a Collection</info>
    <attribute>
      <name>id</name>
      <required>true</required>
    </attribute>
    <attribute>
      <name>collection</name>
      <required>true</required>
    </attribute>
  </tag>

</taglib>
```

Let's quickly review the TLD presented in Listing 18.15. [The root element for this XML file in which all other elements are nested is <taglib>.] The <taglib> element contains five elements that describe the tag library itself (as opposed to describing specific custom tags within the library). These elements are <tlibversion>, <jspversion>, <shortname>, <uri>, and <info>. The <tlibversion> element specifies the tag library's version number. The <jspversion> element indicates the JSP version with which the library is compatible. The <shortname> element contains a brief logical name by which the tag library can be referenced by the JSP container and JSP development tools. The <uri> element optionally specifies the location of a publicly available TLD file with which the current TLD can be validated. Finally, the <info> element contains a brief description of the tag library.

> **NOTE:** If, using Tomcat, you alter a specific custom tag's <tag> block within the TLD file, you may need to delete the corresponding compiled class files under the */jakarta-tomcat/work* directory before the changes will take effect.

Now that we've discussed the elements that describe the tag library as a whole, let's examine the elements that describe an individual custom tag. The custom tags in a tag library are defined using <tag> elements. The <tag> element contains nested elements that describe a particular custom tag. These elements include <name>, <tagclass>, <teiclass>, <bodycontent>, <info>, and <attribute>. The <name> element is the logical name by which the tag can be referenced from within a JSP page (along with the tag library's prefix like this: *<prefix: tag_name/>*). The <tagclass> element specifies the tag handler's fully qualified class name (including package information) and, optionally, the <teiclass> element declares the fully qualified class name of the custom tag's extra info class.

The <bodycontent> element indicates whether the tag supports body content and the type of body content supported, if any. Valid values for <bodycontent> include EMPTY, JSP, and TAGDEPENDENT. A value of EMPTY indicates that the custom tag does not support body content. Body content is the text between the beginning and ending tags (*<prefix: tag_name>body content</prefix: tag_name>*). An exception is thrown if a custom tag designated as EMPTY includes body content. A value of JSP indicates that the tag's body should be parsed and interpreted as standard JSP. Lastly, TAGDEPENDENT indicates that the tag's body should not be processed by the JSP container but, rather, the tag handler should interpret the body content. The <info> element includes a brief description of the custom tag.

The <attribute> element is the final element that may be included within the <tag> element. The <tag> element may include any number of <attribute> elements. Each <attribute> may include three elements—<name>, <required>, and <rtexprvalue>. Of these three elements, only <name> is mandatory and must be specified within the <attribute> element. The <name> element specifies the name by which the attribute can be referenced within the custom tag. For example, the following custom tag includes attributes named min and max.

```
<isspjp:showRandomNum min="0" max="10"/>
```

The optional <required> element indicates whether the attribute must be explicitly specified by the JSP page designer. Valid values for this element are true and false (if not specified, the default value is false). A value of false indicates that if the attribute is not specified, a default value will be used. An exception is thrown if a required attribute is not explicitly specified. Finally, the optional <rtexprvalue> element indicates whether the attribute can be set using a value that is calculated at request time. If true, the attribute supports request-time values. If false, the attribute's value can only be specified by using a static value.

NOTE: The JSP container usually looks for TLD files relative to the current Web application's document root. For example, if a JSP file within the *ROOT* Web application is requested, Tomcat will search the */jakarta-tomcat/webapps/ROOT* directory for the TLD file specified by the taglib directive's uri attribute.

Tag Handler

In addition to the TLD, a tag handler class is required. A tag handler is simply a Java class that implements either the javax.servlet.jsp.tagext.Tag or the javax.servlet.jsp.tagext.BodyTag interface. As we will see, custom tags usually implement one of these two interfaces by extending either the javax.servlet.jsp.tagext.TagSupport or the javax.servlet.jsp.tagext.BodyTagSupport class. As you may have guessed, the TagSupport class implements the Tag interface and the BodyTagSupport class implements the BodyTag interface. These classes provide default functionality that simplifies the process of creating custom tags. Primarily, these classes perform some basic initialization as well as provide a default (often empty) implementation of each method defined by their respective interfaces. In this way, custom tag developers are free to override only the methods they need without having to implement all of them.

The tag handler class is called by the JSP container whenever the custom tag is encountered on the JSP page. The handler then performs the action associated with the custom tag. The action associated with a tag (i.e., the tag's behavior) is prescribed by implementing methods defined by the Tag and BodyTag interfaces. The Tag interface (implemented by the TagSupport class) defines the doStartTag() and doEndTag() methods. The JSP container invokes these methods at the start and end of each tag. The BodyTag interface (implemented by the BodyTagSupport class) extends the Tag interface and defines additional methods useful for processing body content such as doInitBody()

and doAfterBody(). These methods are called before and after the tag's body is evaluated by the JSP container (i.e., before and after JSP tags are replaced with their appropriate values). The following skeleton code demonstrates the basic structure of a custom tag that extends the TagSupport class. Extending the TagSupport class is the simplest way to create custom tags that do not evaluate their body content.

```
import javax.servlet.jsp.*;
import javax.servlet.jsp.tagext.*;

public class ExampleTag extends TagSupport
{
  public int doStartTag()
  {
    //called when the start tag is processed
  }

  public int doEndTag()
  {
    //called when the end tag is processed
  }
}
```

Likewise, the following skeleton code demonstrates the basic structure of a custom tag that extends the BodyTagSupport class. Extending the BodyTag-Support class is the simplest way to create custom tags that evaluate their body content. Although custom tags that extend the TagSupport class can include body content, the body cannot be evaluated within the tag handler.

```
import javax.servlet.jsp.*;
import javax.servlet.jsp.tagext.*;

public class ExampleBodyTag extends BodyTagSupport
{
  public int doStartTag()
  {
    //called when the start tag is processed
  }

  public int doEndTag()
  {
    //called when the end tag is processed
  }

  public void doInitBody()
  {
    //if tag contains body content, called before body is
    //evaluated
  }
```

```
public int doAfterBody()
{
    //called after tag's body content is evaluated
}
}
```

Extra Tag Info

Although not required, an extra info class can perform additional validation
of a tag's attributes and define scripting variables that a tag should expose.
Of the sample tags, notice that only the forEach custom tag uses an extra
info class (see the <teiclass> element in Listing 18.15). As previously mentioned,   all   extra   info   classes   must   extend   the
javax.servlet.jsp.tagext.TagExtraInfo abstract class. The TagExtraInfo
class provides default implementations for two methods that can be overridden in order to provide additional attribute validation and to introduce new
scripting variables. The isValid() method provides tag validation beyond
that provided by the TLD and the getVariableInfo() method allows the
developer to make scripting variables available to the JSP page designer. Let's
examine in more detail these two methods and the functions they perform.

Tag Validation

The tag library descriptor provides only the most rudimentary validation of a
tag's attributes. Basically, the TLD allows the developer to specify only whether
each attribute is required. Any validation beyond a simple existence check
requires an extra info class. For this purpose, the TagExtraInfo class defines
the following method:

```
public boolean isValid(TagData data)
```

The isValid() method of a tag's extra info class is called when the JSP
page is translated into a servlet (usually occurring when the page is first
requested). The isValid() method performs tag-specific validation based on
the attribute values passed to it within the TagData parameter. TagData supports the following methods for retrieving attribute names and values:

```
public Object getAttribute(String name)
public String getAttributeString(String name)
public String getId()
public java.util.Enumeration getAttributes()
```

The getAttribute() and getAttributeString() methods return String objects containing the value of the named attribute. If the named attribute's value
consists of an expression that is evaluated at request time, these methods return

the TagData.REQUEST_TIME_VALUE constant. getId() is a convenience method that returns the value of the tag's "ID" attribute or null if it does not exist. Lastly, the getAttributes() method returns an Enumeration of String objects containing the names of the tag's attributes.

Though the TLD provides a simple way to validate attributes, the isValid() method can be used for more complex validation. For instance, an attribute may be required only when another attribute has been specified. Or perhaps a tag's attribute must contain a value from a finite set of valid values. For example, the changeCase sample tag defines an attribute named case for which "upper" and "lower" are the only valid values. The following isValid() method provides validation for the case attribute beyond that which is provided by the TLD.

```
public boolean isValid(TagData data)
{
  if (data.getAttributeString("case").equalsIgnoreCase("upper"))
  {
    return true;
  }

  if (data.getAttributeString("case").equalsIgnoreCase("lower"))
  {
    return true;
  }

  return false;
}
```

As you can see, the isValid() method returns true if the attribute is valid and false if it is not. The TagExtraInfo class's default implementation of this method always returns true. If the isValid() method returns false (i.e., the custom tag's attributes violate the validation rules), the JSP container will return an error message to the client when the page is requested. For example, if a custom tag's attributes are not valid, the Tomcat server returns an error like this:

```
org.apache.jasper.compiler.CompileException:
  C:\jakarta-tomcat\webapps\ROOT\case.jsp(7,0) Attributes are
  invalid according to TagInfo
```

Informing the JSP container that a custom tag uses an extra info class is extremely simple. This task is accomplished by simply adding a <teiclass> element to the appropriate custom tag's TLD declaration. The <teiclass> element specifies the extra info class's fully qualified class name. For instance, if the isValid() method demonstrated here were compiled into a file named *ChangeCaseTei.class,* the ChangeCaseTei extra info class could be associated with the changeCase custom tag by altering the custom tag's TLD declaration as follows:

```
<!-- changeCase Custom Tag Definition -->
<tag>
  <name>changeCase</name>
  <tagclass>ChangeCaseTag</tagclass>
  <teiclass>ChangeCaseTei</teiclass>
  <bodycontent>JSP</bodycontent>
  <info>Converts Its Body to Upper or Lower Case</info>
  <attribute>
    <name>case</name>
    <required>true</required>
  </attribute>
</tag>
```

Exposing Scripting Variables

Besides performing additional validation, extra info classes can be used to introduce scripting variables that are accessible within the JSP page. For this purpose, the TagExtraInfo class defines the following method:

```
public VariableInfo[] getVariableInfo(TagData data)
```

The getVariableInfo() method returns an array of VariableInfo objects that contain information about any scripting variables exposed by the custom tag. The VariableInfo class's constructor looks like this:

```
public VariableInfo(String varName, String className,
   boolean declare, int scope)
```

The VariableInfo class contains four important pieces of information that are used by the JSP container to resolve scripting variables that are introduced by the custom tag. This information includes the name of the scripting variable (i.e., the name by which the variable is referenced in the JSP page), the type of object represented by the variable (e.g., "java.lang.String"), a boolean value indicating whether the tag is declaring a new variable or assigning a value to an existing variable (true indicates a new variable), and an integer indicating the scope in which the variable is visible. The variable's scope is specified using one of the following three VariableInfo constants:

- VariableInfo.AT_BEGIN—indicates that the variable is in scope at the beginning of the start tag.
- VariableInfo.AT_END—indicates that the variable is in scope after the end tag.
- VariableInfo.NESTED—indicates that the variable is in scope only between the start and end tags.

To help illustrate how scripting variables can be exposed by an extra info class, let's take a look at a sample `getVariableInfo()` method. The following method creates a new variable of type `java.lang.Object` and assigns it the name specified by the custom tag's ID attribute. This is how the `forEach` sample custom tag exposes each object within a collection to the JSP page.

```java
public VariableInfo[] getVariableInfo(TagData data)
{
  VariableInfo nestedVariable = new VariableInfo(data.getId(),
    "java.lang.Object", true, VariableInfo.NESTED);

  return new VariableInfo[] { nestedVariable };
}
```

The JSP container extracts the value associated with a scripting variable from the JSP page's `PageContext` object. For all scripting variables that a custom tag exposes, the associated tag handler class is responsible for inserting corresponding values into the `PageContext` using the `PageContext.set-Attribute()` method. The attribute's name must be the same as the scripting variable's name. When the JSP container encounters a new scripting variable within the page, it retrieves its value using the `PageContext` object's `find-Attribute()` method (passing the scripting variable name as the method parameter). In this way, a custom tag can introduce new scripting variables as well as alter the value of existing variables.

`dateTime` *Custom Tag*

Now that you have a general idea of what a tag handler class looks like, let's learn how to build a working custom tag. We'll start by demonstrating an extremely basic tag handler. Listing 18.16 presents a tag handler class that simply outputs the current date and time. Notice that the `dateTime` tag referenced in Listing 18.15 specifies the following `DateTimeTag` class as its tag handler.

Listing 18.16   Simple custom tag handler class that displays the date/time.

```java
import javax.servlet.jsp.*;
import javax.servlet.jsp.tagext.*;

public class DateTimeTag extends TagSupport
{
  public int doStartTag()
  {
    try
    {
      JspWriter out = pageContext.getOut();
      out.print(new java.util.Date());
    }
```

```
      catch (java.io.IOException e)
      {
        System.out.println("Error in DataTimeTag: " + e);
      }

      return SKIP_BODY;
    }
  }
```

Since the `dateTime` tag does not evaluate body content, its tag handler class extends the `TagSupport` class rather than the `BodyTagSupport` class. The `doStartTag()` method is implemented in order to generate content that will replace the custom tag on the JSP page. The code within `doStartTag()` simply retrieves a reference to the `JspWriter` object and uses it to add content to the output buffer. In this case, the current date and time are added. If an exception occurs, the error is printed to standard out. Lastly, the `SKIP_BODY` value is returned indicating that any body content within the tag should be skipped. The `SKIP_BODY` value should always be returned by the `doStartTag()` method of any tag that has been designated as having an `EMPTY` body (see the <body-content> element in Listing 18.15). The other value that may be returned by the `doStartTag()` is `EVAL_BODY_INCLUDE`. In contrast to `SKIP_BODY`, the `EVAL_BODY_INCLUDE` constant indicates that the tag's body content should be included in the output.

Listing 18.17 demonstrates a JSP page that invokes the `dateTime` custom tag. This page assumes that Listing 18.15 has been written to a file called *isspjp-taglib.tld* and stored where the JSP container can find it (e.g., in the Web application's document root). It is also assumed that the `DateTimeTag` class presented in Listing 18.16 has been compiled and placed in the Web application's */WEB-INF/classes* directory. The JSP container looks in this directory for tag handler classes. Of course, if the tag handler resides within a Java package (i.e., the handler class uses the `package` statement to designate a Java package), the class file must be stored within the appropriate directory structure under the */WEB-INF/classes* directory. However, the tag handler examples presented in this chapter do not specify a Java package and, therefore, can simply be placed in the */WEB-INF/classes* directory.

Listing 18.17   JSP page that uses the dateTime tag to display the date.

```
<%@ taglib uri="isspjp-taglib.tld" prefix="isspjp" %>
<HTML>
<HEAD>
<TITLE>DateTimeTag Demo</TITLE>
</HEAD>
<BODY>
The current date and time is: <isspjp:dateTime/>
</BODY>
</HTML>
```

To test the `dateTime` custom tag, store the JSP page from Listing 18.17 in a text file and place it in a Web application's document root. For example, if using Tomcat's *ROOT* Web application, store Listing 18.17 in a file called *datetime.jsp* and store it in the */jakarta-tomcat/webapps/ROOT* directory. Once the *datetime.jsp* file is in the right location, you can invoke it like this:

http://localhost:8080/datetime.jsp

If everything is working properly, your browser should display the current date and time (see Figure 18.9).

And there you have it. You've built your first custom JSP tag. You might be starting to realize the power and utility of JSP's custom tag extensions. Before we move on to more complex custom tags, let's briefly discuss the `doEndTag()` method. The `doEndTag()` method is called by the JSP container when the tag's end tag is encountered. If an empty tag is used (e.g., `<isspjp:dateTime/>`), the `doStartTag()` method is called first followed by the `doEndTag()` method. The `doEndTag()` method is often used to evaluate whether the rest of the page

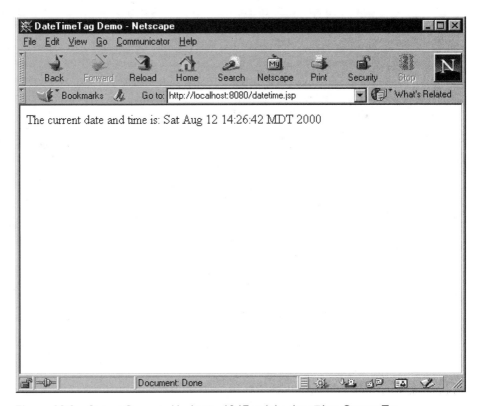

Figure 18.9 Output Generated by Listing 18.17 and the `dateTime` Custom Tag

should be processed. Depending on a conditional operation within the method, doEndTag() may return the SKIP_PAGE instruction or the EVAL_PAGE instruction. SKIP_PAGE indicates that the rest of the page should be skipped. In contrast, the EVAL_PAGE value indicates that page processing should continue. Additionally, the doEndTag() is useful for closing any open markup language tags that were generated by the doStartTag(). For instance, if the doStartTag() opens an HTML TABLE, the doEndTag() may be used to close the open <TABLE> tag by outputting the corresponding </TABLE> closing tag.

dateFormat *Custom Tag*

Now that you've built your first custom tag, let's dig a little deeper and look at a slightly more advanced tag. The <tag> block from Listing 18.15 indicates that the dateFormat custom tag uses the DateFormatTag handler class, includes no body content, and supports an optional attribute called format. Attribute values are passed to the tag handler class by way of traditional JavaBean setter methods. That is, the tag handler's corresponding setXxx() method is called for each specified attribute (where Xxx is the name of the attribute). For example, since the dateFormat tag supports an attribute named format, its tag handler class defines a method called setFormat() (the JSP container automatically capitalizes the attribute's name when calling its corresponding setXxx() method). The setFormat() method is called prior to the doStartTag() method to guarantee that the attribute value will be available when needed. Listing 18.18 presents the DateFormatTag handler class.

Listing 18.18 Tag handler class that supports the format attribute.

```
import javax.servlet.jsp.*;
import javax.servlet.jsp.tagext.*;
import java.text.SimpleDateFormat;

public class DateFormatTag extends TagSupport
{
  private String format = "M/d/yyyy h:mm:ss";

  public int doStartTag()
  {
    try
    {
      JspWriter out = pageContext.getOut();

      SimpleDateFormat formatter = new SimpleDateFormat(format);
      java.util.Date curDate = new java.util.Date();

      out.print(formatter.format(curDate));
    }
```

```
    catch (java.io.IOException e)
    {
      System.out.println("Error in DataFormatTag: " + e);
    }

    return SKIP_BODY;
  }


  public void setFormat(String format)
  {
    this.format = format;
  }
}
```

The purpose of the dateFormat tag is to allow the JSP page designer the
ability to specify the format of dates and times inserted into the page. The date
format is specified in the custom tag's format attribute using the
java.text.SimpleDateFormat formatting rules. Since the format attribute is
optional, a default format of "M/d/yyyy h:mm a" is provided. The default
format produces date and time output such as "8/12/2000 4:10 PM". If the
format attribute is not specifed, the default will be used. Listing 18.19 presents
a JSP page that uses the dateFormat custom tag to produce an HTML page
that includes multiple dates in varying formats (see Figure 18.10).

Listing 18.19   JSP page that uses the dateFormat tag to display date info.

```
<%@ taglib uri="isspjp-taglib.tld" prefix="isspjp" %>

<HTML>
<HEAD>
<TITLE>DateFormatTag Demo</TITLE>
</HEAD>
<BODY>
The default date format looks like this: <isspjp:dateFormat/>
<BR><BR>
The customized date format looks like this:
<isspjp:dateFormat format="MM-dd-yyyy"/>
<BR><BR>
Date elements can be separated like this: It is
<isspjp:dateFormat format="EEEE"/> in the month of
<isspjp:dateFormat format="MMMM"/> of the year
<isspjp:dateFormat format="yyyy"/>.
</BODY>
</HTML>
```

In order to test the dateFormat custom tag, save Listing 18.19 to a file
called *dateformat.jsp* and store it in the document root of the default Web
application. The TLD file shown in Listing 18.15 should also be stored in this
directory. Finally, compile the DateFormatTag class presented in Listing 18.18

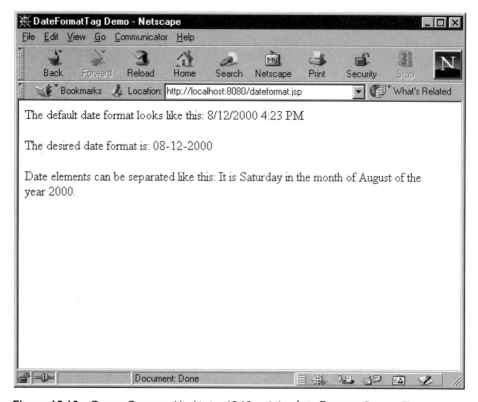

Figure 18.10   Output Generated by Listing 18.19 and the `dateFormat` Custom Tag

and place it in the Web applications /WEB-INF/*classes* directory. You should now be able to invoke the *dateformat.jsp* file like this (see Figure 18.10):

> *http://localhost:8080/dateformat.jsp*

changeCase *Custom Tag*

So far we have examined only custom tags that do not include body content. However, processing body content is one of the most useful functions performed by custom tags. As previously mentioned, custom tags that evaluate their body content should extend the `BodyTagSupport` class rather than the `TagSupport` class. Since it extends `TagSupport`, `BodyTagSupport` implements all of the `TagSupport` class's methods. In addition, the `BodyTagSupport` class implements the methods presented in Table 18.8.

The `BodyContent` object is an encapsulation of the tag's body content. This object can be used to access the tag's body content via a `String` or a `java.io.Reader` as well as retrieve the `JspWriter` associated with this tag. Table 18.9 documents the methods supported by the `BodyContent` object.

Table 18.8 Additional Methods Supported by the BodyTagSupport Class

Method	Description
doAfterBody()	Called after the tag's body content is evaluated by the JSP container. This method is not called for empty tags or tags that return SKIP_BODY within the doStartTag() method. doAfterBody() is initially invoked when the doStartTag() method returns EVAL_BODY_TAG and is called again each time doAfterBody() returns EVAL_BODY_TAG.
doInitBody()	Called before the JSP container evaluates the tag's body content. doInitBody() can be used to perform initialization prior to body content evaluation. This method is not invoked for empty tags.
getBodyContent()	Returns a BodyContent object representing the tag's body content.
getPreviousOut()	Returns the JSP writer used by the tag's parent.
setBodyContent()	JSP container calls this method prior to evaluating the body content in order to pass the BodyContent object to the tag.

Table 18.9 Methods Supported by the BodyContent Object

Method	Description
clearBody()	Discards the body content.
flush()	Flushes body content written to the specified output stream using the writeOut() method.
getEnclosingWriter()	Get a reference to the JspWriter currently associated with the tag (i.e., JspWriter used by the doStartTag() and doEndTag() methods).
getReader()	Returns the value of the tag's body content as a java.io.Reader object.
getString()	Returns the value of the tag's body content as a String.
writeOut()	Writes the value of the tag's body content to the specified java.io.Writer.

Now that we've covered the basic methods supported by the BodyTag-Support and BodyContent classes, let's put them to work. Listing 18.20 demonstrates the tag handler class specified for the changeCase tag (see Listing 18.15) that converts the tag's body content to upper- or lowercase. The case to which the body content should be converted can be specified by the JSP page designer using the changeCase tag's case attribute (the default is uppercase).

Listing 18.20   Tag handler that converts the body to upper- or lowercase.

```java
import javax.servlet.jsp.*;
import javax.servlet.jsp.tagext.*;
import java.text.SimpleDateFormat;

public class ChangeCaseTag extends BodyTagSupport
{
  private static final int UPPER_CASE = 1;
  private static final int LOWER_CASE = 2;

  private int caseFlag = 1; //default to upper case

  public int doAfterBody()
  {
    try
    {
      BodyContent body = getBodyContent();
      String bodyCase = body.getString();

      if (caseFlag == LOWER_CASE)
      {
        bodyCase = bodyCase.toLowerCase();
      }
      else
      {
        bodyCase = bodyCase.toUpperCase();
      }

      JspWriter out = body.getEnclosingWriter();
      out.print(bodyCase);
    }
    catch (java.io.IOException e)
    {
      System.out.println("Error in ChangeCaseTag: " + e);
    }

    //SKIP_BODY indicates that the body content should not be
    //evaluated again for this request
    return SKIP_BODY;
  }


  public void setCase(String caseString)
  {
    if (caseString.equalsIgnoreCase("lower"))
    {
      caseFlag = LOWER_CASE;
    }
    else
    {
      caseFlag = UPPER_CASE;
    }
  }
}
```

The ChangeCaseTag tag handler overrides the doAfterBody() method in order to process the tag's body after it has been evaluated by the JSP container but before it is returned to the client. To begin, the BodyContent object is acquired using the getBodyContent() method. The tag's body content is then retrieved as a String using the BodyContent object's getString() method. The tag handler then converts the body content to upper- or lowercase based on the value of the tag's case attribute. Notice that the tag handler implements the setCase() method in order to retrieve the value of the tag's case attribute. Next, the JspWriter associated with the current tag is acquired using the BodyContent object's getEnclosingWriter() method and is used to return the altered body content to the client. Lastly, the SKIP_BODY value is returned indicating that the body content should not be evaluated again.

NOTE: Actually, the call to the getBodyContent() method demonstrated in Listing 18.20 is usually not necessary. This is due to the fact that the BodyTagSupport class from which ChangeCaseTag extends exposes the BodyContent object as a protected variable named bodyContent (which is automatically visible within the ChangeCaseTag). Therefore, it is possible to reference the bodyContent variable directly instead of calling getBodyContent(). However, it is a good practice to always use the getBodyContent() method because this method is specified by the Servlet API and the name of the internal bodyContent variable is not (and, therefore, could vary between JSP implementations).

As we will see shortly, the EVAL_BODY_TAG value can be used to iterate through the tag's body content multiple times. This functionality can be very useful for building iterative tags that implement looping constructs within a JSP page (e.g., displaying rows within an HTML table). Listing 18.21 presents a simple JSP page that uses the changeCase tag to convert content to upper- and lowercase (see Figure 18.11). The valid values for the changeCase tag's case attribute are "upper" and "lower" (defaults to "upper").

Listing 18.21   JSP page uses the changeCase tag to uppercase body.

```
<%@ taglib uri="isspjp-taglib.tld" prefix="isspjp" %>

<HTML>
<HEAD>
<TITLE>ChangeCaseTag Demo</TITLE>
</HEAD>
<BODY>
<isspjp:changeCase case="upper">
```

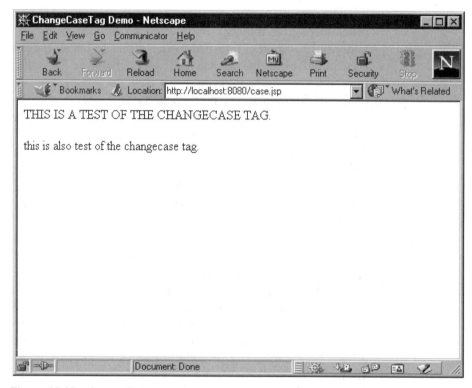

Figure 18.11   Output Generated by Listing 18.21 and the changeCase Custom Tag

```
This is a test of the changeCase tag.
</isspjp:changeCase>
<BR><BR>
<isspjp:changeCase case="lower">
This is also test of the changeCase tag.
</isspjp:changeCase>
</BODY>
</HTML>
```

loop *Custom Tag*

As previously mentioned, the doAfterBody() method can be used to process a custom tag's body content multiple times by returning EVAL_BODY_TAG. Each time the EVAL_BODY_TAG is returned, the tag's body content is reevaluated and the doAfterBody() method is called again. To end this cycle, the doAfter-Body() method must return SKIP_BODY, at which point the processing of the JSP page will continue immediately following the custom tag. The following custom tag demonstrates the iterative capabilities of the doAfterBody() method.

Listing 18.22 presents the LoopTag handler class specified in the TLD file from Listing 18.15.

Listing 18.22   Tag handler that displays the tag's body multiple times.

```
import javax.servlet.jsp.*;
import javax.servlet.jsp.tagext.*;
import java.text.SimpleDateFormat;

public class LoopTag extends BodyTagSupport
{
  private int iterations; //required attribute must be set by tag

  public int doAfterBody()
  {
    if (iterations-- > 0)
    {
      try
      {
        BodyContent body = getBodyContent();
        JspWriter out = body.getEnclosingWriter();
        out.println(body.getString());
        body.clearBody();
      }
      catch (java.io.IOException e)
      {
        System.out.println("Error in LoopTag: " + e);
      }

      //EVAL_BODY_TAG indicates that the body content should be
      //evaluated again and the doAfterBody() method called again
      return EVAL_BODY_TAG;
    }

    //SKIP_BODY indicates that the body content should not be
    //evaluated again for this request
    return SKIP_BODY;
  }


  public void setIterations(int iterations)
  {
    this.iterations = iterations;
  }
}
```

The LoopTag handler class allows for the iterative display of a tag's body content. To accomplish this, LoopTag implements the setIterations() method in order to retrieve the value of the tag's required iterations attribute. The handler class then iteratively writes the tag's body content to the output stream according to the value of the iterations attribute. During the looping cycle, EVAL_BODY_TAG is returned. After the body has been displayed the appropriate number of times, SKIP_BODY is returned to terminate the loop. Notice that the BodyContent object's clearBody() method is called at the end of each iteration. This is necessary because the BodyContent object is not automatically cleared between iterations. If not cleared, the body content will continue to grow as each iteration appends the tag's content to that previously stored in the Body-Content object. Listing 18.23 displays a JSP page that uses the loop tag to display its body content five times (see Figure 18.12).

Listing 18.23   JSP page that uses the loop tag to display content five times.

```
<%@ taglib uri="isspjp-taglib.tld" prefix="isspjp" %>

<HTML>
<HEAD>
<TITLE>LoopTag Demo</TITLE>
</HEAD>
<BODY>
<isspjp:loop iterations="5">
```

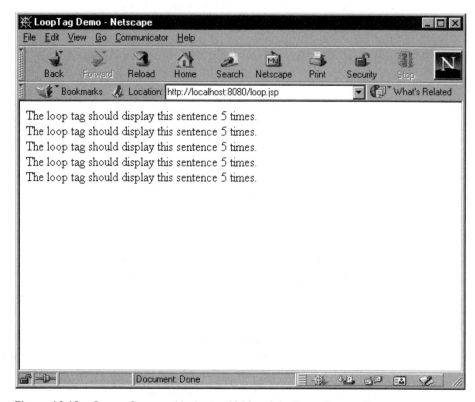

Figure 18.12   Output Generated by Listing 18.23 and the loop Custom Tag

```
The loop tag should display this sentence 5 times.<BR>
</isspjp:loop>
</BODY>
</HTML>
```

forEach *Custom Tag*

The forEach tag demonstrates how an extra info class can be used to expose scripting variables to the body of a custom tag. This tag defines two attributes—collection and id. The collection attribute specifies a collection (i.e., a List, Set, or Vector object or one of their derivatives) of JavaBean objects over which the tag should iterate, repeating its body content once for each object. The id attribute assigns a name by which the current object can be referenced within the body of the custom tag. Listing 18.24 presents the tag handler for the forEach custom tag.

Listing 18.24   Tag handler for the forEach custom tag.

```
import java.util.*;
import java.io.IOException;
import javax.servlet.jsp.*;
import javax.servlet.jsp.tagext.BodyTagSupport;

/**
 * ForEachTag repeats the tag's body for each item in a
 * collection and exposes the current item to its body content.
 */
public final class ForEachTag extends BodyTagSupport
{
  private Collection items = null;
  private String id = null;
  private Iterator iterator = null;
  private String collection = null;


  /**
   * Get the collection out of the request, session, or servlet
   * context. Then get an iterator and begin iterating over the
   * collection.
   *
   * @return Value that tells the JSP container how to proceed
   * @exception JspException is thrown if JSP error occurs
   */
  public int doStartTag() throws JspException
  {
    //find collection in request, session, or servlet context
    items = (Collection)pageContext.findAttribute(collection);

    if (items == null)
    {
      throw new JspException("Collection not found.");
    }
```

```
      iterator = items.iterator(); //get iterator for collection

      if (iterator.hasNext())
      {
         //store item using name specified by id attribute
         pageContext.setAttribute(id, iterator.next());

         return (EVAL_BODY_TAG); //tell container to evaluate body
      }
      else
      {
         return (SKIP_BODY); //no items in collection, skip body
      }
   }


   /**
    * After body has been evaluated, add the body content to the
    * output buffer. Next, determine if more items exist in the
    * collection and, if so, store the item in the PageContext and
    * instruct the JSP container to evaluate the body again.
    *
    * @return Value that tells the JSP container how to proceed
    * @exception JspException is thrown if JSP error occurs
    */
   public int doAfterBody() throws JspException
   {
      try
      {
         BodyContent body = getBodyContent();
         JspWriter out = body.getEnclosingWriter();
         out.println(body.getString());
         body.clearBody();
      }
      catch (IOException e)
      {
         throw new JspException("Error writing body content.");
      }

      if (iterator.hasNext())
      {
         //store item using name specified by id attribute
         pageContext.setAttribute(id, iterator.next());

         return (EVAL_BODY_TAG);
      }
      else
      {
         return (SKIP_BODY);
      }
   }
```

```
/**
 * Set the name of the scripting variable.
 *
 * @param id Name of the scripting variable
 */
public void setId(String id)
{
  this.id = id;
}


/**
 * Set the name of the collection as it is stored in the
 * request, session, or servlet context. This value is set by
 * the custom tag's collection attribute.
 *
 * @param collection Name specified by collection attribute
 */
public void setCollection(String collection)
{
  this.collection = collection;
}


/**
 * Release is called by the JSP container before discarding the
 * custom tag. Free resources here.
 */
public void release()
{
  super.release();

  items = null;
  id = null;
  iterator = null;
  collection = null;
}
}
```

The majority of the functionality implemented by the tag handler presented in Listing 18.24 is contained in two methods—doStartTag() and doAfterBody(). The doStartTag() method retrieves the collection specified by the custom tag's collection attribute from the page context, the request, the session, or the servlet context and creates an iterator from it. If the specified collection contains at least one bean, that bean is stored as a PageContext attribute (under the name specified by the id attribute) and the JSP container is instructed to process the custom tag's body content (i.e., the method returns EVAL_BODY_TAG). The body of the custom tag can include any number of <jsp:getProperty> tags that display the value of one or more properties from the current bean.

The `doAfterBody()` method adds the evaluated body content to the output buffer using the same technique previously demonstrated by the `changeCase` and `loop` tags. Next, this method uses the iterator's `next()` method to retreive the next bean from the collection and store it in the `PageContext`. The `doAfterBody()` method then returns the `EVAL_BODY_TAG` constant to instruct the JSP container to evaluate the custom tag's body again. This process continues for the remaining beans in the collection. Unlike the custom tag's `doStartTag()` method, which is called only once, `doAfterBody()` is called for every item in the collection (minus the first item that was retrieved within the `doStartTag()` method).

NOTE: Rather than write the body content to the output buffer within the `doAfterBody()` method, the custom tag could have let the generated body content accumulate with each iteration until it was flushed to the output stream in the `doEndTag()` method, like this:

```
public int doEndTag() throws JspException
{
  BodyContent body = getBodyContent();

  if (body != null)
  {
    try
    {
      getPreviousOut().print(body.getString());
    }
    catch (IOException e)
    {
      throw new JspException("Error writing content body.");
    }
  }

  return (EVAL_PAGE); //process the rest of the page
}
```

Notice that this method retrieves a `JspWriter` using `getPreviousOut()` and uses the writer's `print()` method to add the body content to the output buffer. The `getPreviousOut()` method rather than the `PageContext` object's `getOut()` method is used in case this tag is nested within another custom tag. If the tag is nested, then its output should be written to the outer tag's `BodyContent` (which extends `JspWriter`) in order to allow the outer tag to evaluate the content generated by the inner tag.

As previously discussed, custom tags require an extra info class in order to introduce new scripting variables. The `forEach` tag is no exception. Listing

18.25 presents the extra info class used by the forEach tag to expose each bean in the specified collection as a scripting variable (see the <teiclass> element in Listing 18.15). The VariableInfo object created within the getVariableInfo() method shows that the name of the scripting variable is specified by the custom tag's id attribute. It also indicates that a new variable of type java.lang.Object is being declared and should be visible only between the custom tag's begin and end tags (i.e., nested).

Listing 18.25 Extra info class for the forEach custom tag.

```
import javax.servlet.jsp.tagext.*;

/**
 * Tag extra info class used to introduce new scripting
 * variables.
 */
public class ForEachTei extends TagExtraInfo
{
  /**
   * Exposes a scripting variable using the name specified by the
   * custom tag's id property.
   *
   * @param data TagData object
   * @return Array of VariableInfo objects
   */
  public VariableInfo[] getVariableInfo(TagData data)
  {
    VariableInfo nestedVariable = new VariableInfo(data.getId(),
      "java.lang.Object", true, VariableInfo.NESTED);

    return new VariableInfo[] { nestedVariable };
  }
}
```

Now that we've reviewed the code behind the forEach tag handler and extra info class, let's examine how to use this new custom tag within a JSP page. Listing 18.26 presents a simple JSP page that uses the forEach custom tag in order to display the username and password for everyone in the users collection (see Figure 18.13). The users collection may contain any number of JavaBeans that implement the getUsername() and getPassword() methods. The custom tag, using the PageContext.findAttribute() method, will be able to locate this collection if it is stored in the page context, the request, the session, or the servlet context.

Listing 18.26 Simple JSP page that uses the forEach custom tag.

```
<%@ taglib uri="isspjp-taglib.tld" prefix="isspjp" %>

<HTML>
<HEAD>
```

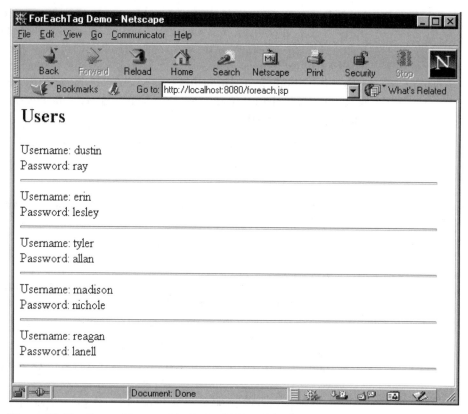

Figure 18.13   Output Generated by Listing 18.26 and the forEach Custom Tag

```
<TITLE>ForEachTag Demo</TITLE>
</HEAD>
<BODY>
<H2>Users</H2>
<isspjp:forEach id="user" collection="users">
Username: <jsp:getProperty name="user" property="username"/><BR>
Password: <jsp:getProperty name="user" property="password"/>
<HR>
</isspjp:forEach>
</BODY>
</HTML>
```

This concludes our discussion of JSP custom tags. As you can see, custom tags are an extremely powerful mechanism for building reusable components that page designers and HTML developers can use easily. In addition, custom tag libraries make Web applications simpler and easier to maintain by preserving a strict separation between an application's implementation code and the presentation of its content.

Using JSP and Servlets Together

Now that you realize the many advantages of JavaServer Pages, you might be wondering how this new technology relates to and cooperates with servlets. Fortunately, the answer is that JSP was designed specifically to work seamlessly with Java servlets as a complementary technology. Though application logic can be embedded in a JSP page, this task is often relegated to servlets while JSP is used for content presentation. This approach plays to the strengths of each technology. Servlets are very poor at providing a simple and maintainable user interface. However, they are extremely well suited for processing the business rules that drive an application. On the other hand, JSP is a poor choice for the implementation of application logic because this approach requires Java code to be embedded in the JSP page. However, JSP is perfectly adapted for building the presentation layer of an application. Obviously, servlets and JSP make a perfect combination upon which a clean, efficient, and easy-to-maintain application architecture can be built.

Servlets and JSP provide almost everything we need to build an effective Web application, but there is still one thing missing. We need a place to store application state and other program data. This role is usually filled by Java-Beans. As previously discussed, JavaBeans provide a simple and consistent API for the storage and retrieval of information. Encapsulating data in well-designed JavaBean objects greatly simplifies the sharing of information between servlets and JSP pages. In addition, business rules can be embedded in "smart" JavaBeans to allow much of an application's logic to reside in reusable components rather than in a single-purpose servlet.

An application architecture that uses JSP for presentation, servlets to control application flow, and JavaBeans for data storage and business logic is often referred to as the JSP Model 2 architecture. The JSP Model 2 architecture is an implementation of the Model-View-Controller (MVC) design pattern. This pattern defines a *model* to maintain state and perform business logic, a *view* to provide presentation, and a *controller* to process requests and drive the application flow. Therefore, according to the JSP Model 2 architecture, Java-Beans serve as the model, JSP as the view, and servlets as the controller (see Figure 18.14). In this model, JSP pages should not implement any application logic. Rather, they should only retrieve information from JavaBeans that are instantiated by the servlet and insert these values into the JSP page. Likewise, servlets should not generate presentation content (i.e., markup language). Rather, they should be used only to process incoming requests, instantiate and populate beans, and forward control to the appropriate servlet or JSP page. If control is forwarded to a servlet, it too will forward the request to either a servlet or a JSP page. This process continues until the request eventually arrives at a JSP page that returns the response to the client.

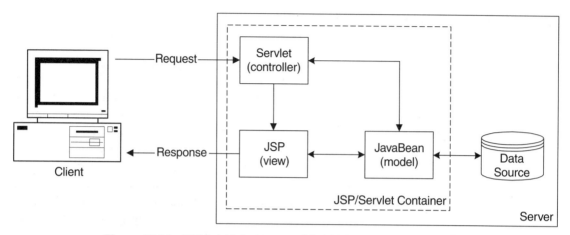

Figure 18.14   JSP Model 2 Architecture (Model-View-Controller Design Pattern)

To give you a better idea of how this architecture might work, let's discuss a concrete example. Authenticating a user using servlets, JSP, and JavaBeans is a typical example of the MVC design pattern. It works like this. Imagine that a user is attempting to view his bank account balance on the Web. The process begins when the user requests the login page (i.e., an HTML or JSP page). This page includes an HTML form that prompts the user for a username and password. After entering this information, the login page is submitted to a servlet that instantiates a special login bean and then asks it to validate the user's credentials. This login bean authenticates the user by requesting information from a database or directory server (using JDBC or JNDI). If the username and password are valid, a user bean is created and placed in the user's session to indicate that the user has been authenticated. Similarly, an account balance bean is populated with the user's account information and placed in the session. Finally, the servlet uses the `RequestDispatcher` object (presented in Chapter 15) to forward the request to a JSP page that references the account balance bean in order to display the user's balance. However, if the user's credentials are not valid, the servlet uses the `RequestDispatcher` object to forward control to a JSP page indicating that the username and password are incorrect (and no user or account balance beans are placed in the session).

NOTE: If you are interested in the JSP Model 2 architecture, you should evaluate the Apache Struts project. The goal of this project is to provide an open source framework based on servlets and JSP that encourages application architectures based on the Model-View-Controller design pattern (i.e., the JSP Model 2 architecture). You can find more information on the Struts project at *http://jakarta.apache.org/struts/*.

The JSP Model 2 architecture exploits the strengths of servlets, JavaServer Pages, and JavaBeans to create Web applications that are modular and easy to maintain. This architecture facilitates the division of labor between page designers and Java programmers by keeping presentation details in JSP pages and application logic in servlets and JavaBeans. Servlets, JavaServer Pages, and JavaBeans make a powerful combination.

Summary

This chapter presents a comprehensive introduction to JavaServer Pages. JSP provides a simple and efficient solution for separating application implementation from content presentation. Many advantages are realized when JSP is used as the presentation layer rather than embedding HTML directly within servlets. These advantages include improved code reuse and a strong division of labor between page designer and Java programmer. Finally, JSP provides a simple mechanism, known as custom tag libraries, through which Java developers can extend the collection of scripting tags supported by JSP.

This concludes our rather lengthy discussion on JavaServer Pages. In the next chapter, we will demonstrate how to build and deploy Web applications using Web application archive (WAR) files.

Chapter Highlights

- JSP is a server-side technology that allows dynamic Web applications to be created by adding special markup tags to a standard HTML document.

- All objects created in a JSP page are assigned a scope within which they are valid. JSP applications recognize four well-defined scopes: page, request, session, and application.

- *Implicit objects* are variables that are defined automatically by the JSP container and are available to the JSP page without having to declare them first.

- *Directives* are JSP tags that provide the JSP container with special instructions required to process the page. These instructions alter the structure of the servlet that is generated when the page is processed.

- *Scripting elements* allow code to be embedded in a JSP page. When the JSP page is processed, the embedded code is inserted into the appropriate places in the JSP page servlet.

- *Declarations* are used to insert code into the JSP page servlet at the class level, outside of existing methods.

- *Expressions* are JSP tags that contain a single valid scripting language expression that is evaluated for every request. The expression tag is then replaced with the expression's value.

- *Scriptlets* are used to insert arbitrary scripting code into the JSP page servlet.

- *Actions* are JSP tags that can transfer control to other server resources, generate output, or create and modify objects.

- The `jsp:include` action includes the output of a specified server resource (e.g., servlet, JSP page, CGI application) within a JSP page at request time.

- The `jsp:forward` action forwards a request to another server resource.

- The `jsp:plugin` action is used to add Java 2 applet support to today's leading browsers—Netscape Navigator and Microsof Internet Explorer.

- The `jsp:useBean` action loads the specified bean and assigns it a logical name with which it can be referenced from within the JSP page.

- The `jsp:getProperty` action retrieves the value of a bean's property and inserts it into the JSP page.

- The `jsp:setProperty` action sets the value of a bean's property.

- JSP 1.1 allows developers to define their own JSP tags. These tags, known as *custom tags*, assume the same XML-style format as JSP action tags and can be used to produce output, control program flow, or perform just about any other task that can be accomplished with scriptlets.

CHAPTER 19

Packaging and Deployment

This chapter discusses the packaging and deployment of Web applications. In previous versions of the Java Servlet Specification, the distribution of servlet-based Web applications was not a trivial task. Rather, it required the end user to follow detailed container-specific instructions regarding the proper placement of application files and changes to servlet configuration files. With the introduction of Servlet API 2.2 and Web application archives (WAR), distribution of servlet- and JSP-based applications has become much simpler and more portable. This is due to the fact that the distribution format has been standardized by the Java Servlet Specification. In this chapter, the following topics are covered.

- Building a Web application archive
- Deploying on Apache Tomcat
- Deploying on JRun™
- Deploying on ServletExec™

Building a Web Application Archive

Web applications were initially presented in Chapter 8. A brief discussion of Web applications is presented here but it might be a good idea to review the "Apache Tomcat" section of Chapter 8 to refresh your memory regarding Web applications.

Web Application Overview

All servlet containers that conform to version 2.2 (and later) of the Java Servlet Specification support the concept of a Web application. A *Web application*

consists of the hierarchy of directories and files that together make up an application. All Web applications use the same standard directory structure regardless of the server on which they are running. To illustrate, the following
directory structure shows a typical Tomcat installation that includes three Web
applications—*admin, examples,* and *ROOT.*

```
jakarta-tomcat
  |- bin
  |- conf
  |- doc
  |- lib
  |- logs
  |- src
  '- webapps
      |- admin
      |   |- contextAdmin
      |   |- META-INF
      |   '- WEB-INF
      |       '- classes
      |
      |- examples
      |   |- images
      |   |- jsp
      |   |- META-INF
      |   |- servlets
      |   '- WEB-INF
      |       |- classes
      |       '- jsp
      |
      '- ROOT
          |- docs
          |- javadoc
          |- META-INF
          '- WEB-INF
              |- classes
              '- lib
```

A Web application's top-level directory (e.g., *admin, examples, ROOT*) is
known as the Web application's *document root.* This is where the server looks
for HTML, JSP, and image files related to the Web application (or in directories under the document root, if specified in the request URL).

When deployed, each Web application is assigned a unique *context path* by
the system administrator. All requests to this context path are routed to the
appropriate Web application. For example, if the *admin* Web application is
assigned the context path of */admin,* then the following URL will display the
index.html file in the */jakarta-tomcat/webapps/admin* directory.

http://localhost:8080/admin/index.html

Creating the Deployment Descriptor

When building a Web application, creating the Web application deployment descriptor is one of the most important tasks. The descriptor file, named *web.xml*, resides in the Web application's */WEB-INF* directory and contains all of the application's configuration settings. Listing 19.1 presents a typical *web.xml* file containing the most common configuration elements (servlet, servlet-mapping, security-constraint, login-config, taglib).

Listing 19.1   Typical *web.xml* file (deployment descriptor).

```
<?xml version="1.0" encoding="ISO-8859-1"?>

<!DOCTYPE web-app PUBLIC "-//Sun Microsystems, Inc.//DTD
  Web Application 2.2//EN"
  "http://java.sun.com/j2ee/dtds/web-app_2.2.dtd">

<web-app>
  <servlet>
    <servlet-name>snoop</servlet-name>
    <servlet-class>SnoopServlet</servlet-class>
    <init-param>
      <param-name>foo</param-name>
      <param-value>bar</param-value>
    </init-param>
  </servlet>

  <servlet-mapping>
    <servlet-name>snoop</servlet-name>
    <url-pattern>/snoop</url-pattern>
  </servlet-mapping>

  <security-constraint>
    <web-resource-collection>
      <web-resource-name>Protected Area</web-resource-name>
      <url-pattern>/jsp/security/protected/*</url-pattern>
      <!-- Protected Methods -->
      <http-method>DELETE</http-method>
      <http-method>GET</http-method>
      <http-method>POST</http-method>
      <http-method>PUT</http-method>
    </web-resource-collection>
    <auth-constraint>
      <!-- These roles may access this area -->
      <role-name>tomcat</role-name>
      <role-name>role1</role-name>
    </auth-constraint>
  </security-constraint>
```

```
<login-config>
  <auth-method>BASIC</auth-method>
  <realm-name>Example Basic Authentication Area</realm-name>
</login-config>

<taglib>
  <taglib-uri>
    http://java.apache.org/tomcat/examples-taglib
  </taglib-uri>
  <taglib-location>
    /WEB-INF/jsp/example-taglib.tld
  </taglib-location>
</taglib>
</web-app>
```

Before creating the WAR file for any new Web application, you must first create a deployment descriptor like that shown in Listing 19.1. You can do this using any basic text editor. You simply have to name the descriptor file *web.xml,* follow the XML format as it is presented in Listing 19.1 and described in previous chapters, and copy it to your Web application's */WEB-INF* directory. Table 19.1 indicates the purpose of each element in the *web.xml* file and the chapter in which it was covered. For a detailed description of the *web.xml* file, see the deployment descriptor DTD in Appendix J.

Table 19.1   Typical *web.xml* Elements

Tag Name	Chapter	Description
`servlet`	8	Assigns servlet names (or aliases) as well as defines servlet initialization parameters.
`servlet-mapping`	8	Assigns a URL mapping to a servlet.
`security-constraint`	17	Secures directories relative to the Web application root by defining the roles required to access them. Assigning roles to users is a container-specific process (see Chapter 17 for Tomcat instructions).
`login-config`	17	Defines the authentication method used to secure the directories specified in the `<security-constraint>` element.
`taglib`	18	Maps a local URL to a remote tag library descriptor.

Creating the WAR File

All right, that's enough about Web applications and deployment descriptors. Let's talk about Web application archives. Simply put, a *Web application archive* (also known as a WAR file) is an archive file, created with the standard Java JAR utility, that contains the entire directory structure and files associated with a Web application (e.g., servlets, JSP and HTML pages, images, etc.). For example, to create a distributable WAR file for Tomcat's *examples* Web application, the entire directory structure under the */jakarta-tomcat/webapps/examples* directory must be stored in a single archive file, most likely called *examples.war*. The name of this archive file is very significant. First, all WAR files must use the .war extension if they are to be recognized as a Web application archive by the servlet container. Second, some servlet containers, such as Tomcat, use the name of the WAR file to assign the application a unique context path. That is, when the *examples.war* file is deployed on Tomcat, the application is automatically assigned a context path named examples. This allows a servlet within the deployed *examples.war* application to be invoked using a URL like this:

> *http://localhost:8080/examples/SnoopServlet*

Simply redeploying the application after changing the name of the *examples.war* file to *samples.war* would allow the same servlet to be invoked like this:

> *http://localhost:8080/samples/SnoopServlet*

However, on some servlet containers, such as JRun and ServletExec, the name of the WAR file is irrelevant since the administrator must manually assign the name of the context path (sometimes called an application URL) when the archive is deployed.

NOTE: You might be wondering why Web applications do not use the standard .jar extension. After all, they are created using the standard JAR utility. The answer is that a JAR file is meant to be placed within an application's CLASSPATH and contains classes and resource files that are loaded by the Java class loader. However, since a WAR file includes resources other than Java classes and resource files (e.g., images and HTML files), this file does not belong in the CLASSPATH and, therefore, it is not appropriate to name it using the .jar extension. Rather, the unique .war extension better conveys the purpose of the Web application archive file. In addition, a WAR file contains a */WEB-INF/web.xml* configuration file. JAR files do not have an equivalent configuration file.

Before describing deployment of a Web application archive using various servlet containers, let's examine exactly how to create this type of file. To demonstrate, we will create a WAR file containing Tomcat's *examples* Web application. Even if you are using another servlet container, you may wish to install Tomcat now so that you can follow along with this exercise.

To begin, start the Tomcat server in order to ensure that its sample WAR files have been deployed (see Chapter 8 for details). Next, delete the existing *examples.war* file in the */jakarta-tomcat/webapps*. Before creating the new *examples.war* file, move to the root of the Web application like this on Windows:

```
cd \jakarta-tomcat\webapps\examples
```

Or like this on UNIX:

```
cd /usr/local/jakarta-tomcat/webapps/examples
```

Once you're in the right directory, you can create the *examples.war* file using the Java JAR utility, like this (make sure the JAR utility, located in the */jdk/bin* directory, is in your path):

```
jar -cvf examples.war *
```

This command will create an *examples.war* file (in the current directory) that includes all directories and files under the */jakarta-tomcat/webapps/examples* directory (the JAR utility automatically recurses through all lower directories).

And that's all there is to it! You now have the entire *examples* Web application, including HTML pages, JSP templates, servlets, and images, within a single, self-contained archive file that's compact and easy to distribute. In addition, since servlet definitions and URL mappings are specified in the Web application's */WEB-INF/web.xml* file, all required servlet configuration settings are contained in the Web application archive and need not be set manually by the end user. That is, Web applications are fully configured as soon as they are deployed. In the following sections, we will demonstrate how easy it is to deploy the *examples.war* application using various servlet containers.

Deploying on Apache Tomcat

Deploying a Web application archive file on Tomcat involves only two simple steps. First, copy the WAR file to the */jakarta-tomcat/webapps* directory. Second, start the Tomcat server or, if already running, restart it. And that concludes the deployment process. It can't get much simpler than that. To try this process yourself, delete the */jakarta-tomcat/webapps/examples* directory, copy the *examples.war* file that you created in the previous section to the */jakarta-tomcat/webapps* directory, and start the Tomcat server, like this on Windows:

```
C:\> cd \jakarta-tomcat\bin
C:\jakarta-tomcat\bin> startup
```

Or like this on UNIX:

```
shell> cd /usr/local/jakarta-tomcat/bin
shell> ./startup.sh
```

Figure 19.1 shows the output produced by Tomcat when it starts. Notice that the examples context path is mapped to the */examples* directory (under the */webapps* directory). Also, if you examine the */jakarta-tomcat/webapps* directory, you should discover that the */examples* directory has been created. Tomcat automatically extracts and installs any WAR files that it finds in its */webapps* directory and assigns them a unique context path according to their filenames. You can verify that the *examples* application is installed properly with the following URL:

http://localhost:8080/examples/SnoopServlet

Figure 19.1 Output Produced by Tomcat at Startup

Deploying on JRun

Deploying a Web application archive on Allaire JRun is nearly as simple as it is on Tomcat. Begin by starting the JRun Admin Server and the JRun Default Server as demonstrated in Chapter 8. Next, log in to the *JRun Management Console* (JMC) from your browser using the following URL (use the admin username and password that you configured during installation):

   http://localhost:8000/security/login.jsp

Once you are logged in to the JMC application, click on the **JRun Default Server** link in the navigation tree displayed in the left-hand frame. This action will expand the **JRun Default Server** option and display the **Web Applications** link in both the navigation tree and the right-hand frame (see Figure 19.2). Click on either of these **Web Applications** links in order to be presented the options to edit, create, deploy, and remove Web applications (see Figure 19.3).

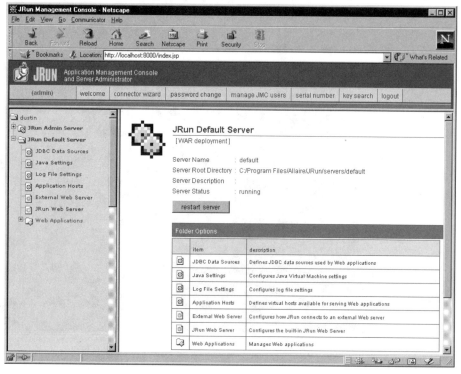

Figure 19.2   JMC JRun Default Server Options Screen

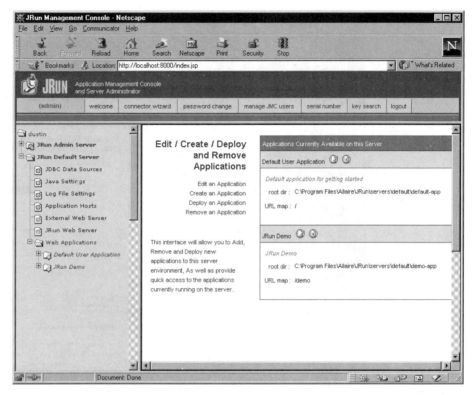

Figure 19.3   JMC Web Applications Management Screen

After selecting the **Web Applications** link, click the **Deploy an Application** link in the right-hand frame. To deploy the *examples.war* application, complete the form in the right-hand frame and click the **deploy** button (see Figure 19.4). The **Servlet War File or Directory** field contains the name and location of the WAR file to deploy. The **Application Name** field is an arbitrary name that is used to identify the application within the JRun administration tools. Lastly, the **Application URL** field specifies the name of the context path by which the deployed application can be referenced. After this form has been submitted, the **Deploy a Web Application** screen is displayed with a confirmation message indicating that the Web application has been deployed successfully (see Figure 19.5).

The final step in the deployment process is to restart the server. This can be done by selecting the **JRun Default Server** link in the navigation tree shown in the left-hand frame and clicking the **restart server** button that appears in the

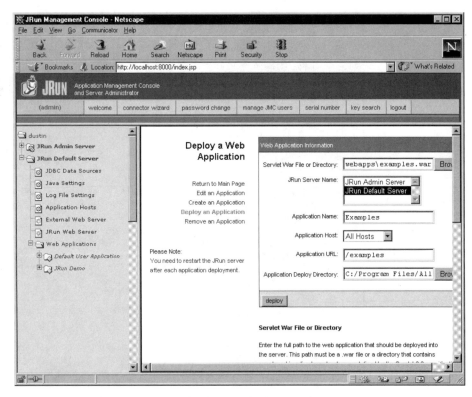

Figure 19.4   JMC Web Application Deployment Screen

right-hand frame (see Figure 19.2). At this point, the *examples* Web application should be fully deployed and accessible via the following URL:

http://localhost:8080/examples/SnoopServlet

Deploying on ServletExec

ServletExec, from New Atlanta Communications,[1] is another popular servlet container that makes quick work of deploying WAR files. Once you have ServletExec up and running according to the instructions presented in Chapter 8, invoke the ServletExec Administration Application using the following URL:

http://localhost/servlet/admin

1. New Atlanta Communications was acquired by Unify Corporation in early 2000. However, that acquisition was rescinded in late 2000. Therefore, the shortlived Unify eWave ServletExec product has been reinstated as ServletExec from New Atlanta Communications.

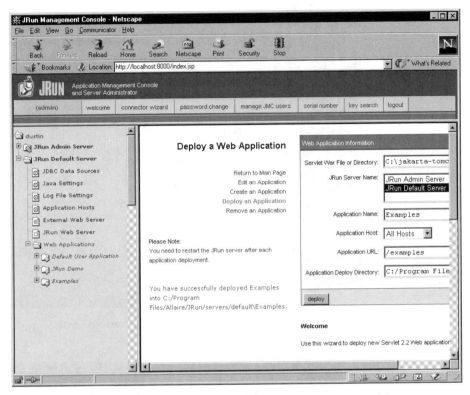

Figure 19.5 Confirmation That the Web Application Was Deployed Successfully

After invoking the Admin application, select the **configure** option under the **Web Applications** heading in the left-hand frame. This action will display the **Configure Web Applications** screen in the right-hand frame (see Figure 19.6).

Once the **Configure Web Applications** screen is visible, click the **Add Web Application...** button to display the **Add Web Application** screen (see Figure 19.7). This screen allows you to specify the information required to deploy a WAR file. The **Application Name** field contains the logical name by which the deployed application will be referenced within the ServletExec administration tools. The **URL Context Path** field specifies the unique context path by which this Web application can be invoked. Lastly, the **Location** field contains the full path and filename of the WAR file to be deployed. After completing this form, click the **Submit** button to deploy the application. If the Web application archive is deployed successfully, the **Configure Web Applications** screen will be displayed containing a confirmation message like that shown in Figure 19.8.

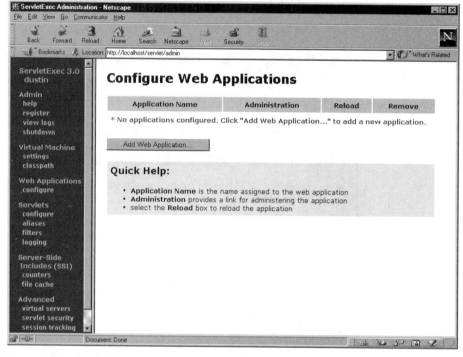

Figure 19.6 ServletExec **Configure Web Applications** Screen

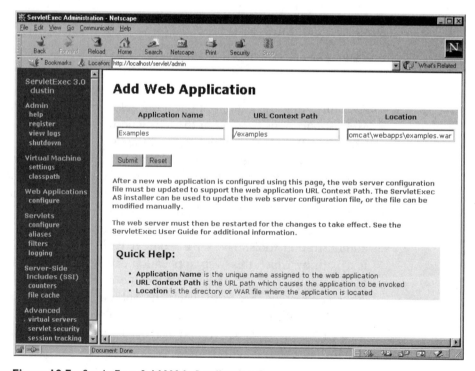

Figure 19.7 ServletExec **Add Web Application** Screen

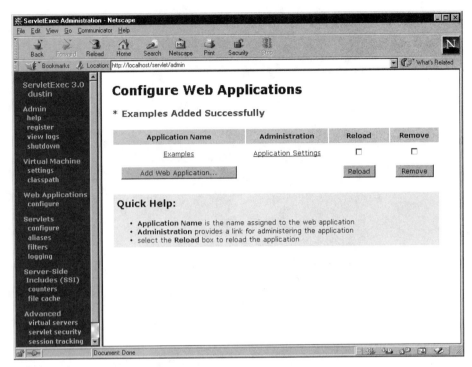

Figure 19.8 ServletExec **Configure Web Applications** Screen Confirms New Web Application.

After the WAR file has been successfully deployed, the final step is to modify the Web server's configuration file so that it will recognize the Web application's context path and pass Web application requests to the servlet container. The simplest way to do this is to run the ServletExec AS installer that you used to install ServletExec in the first place. When prompted by the installer for the type of installation, select **Install or Update a web server adapter** (see Figure 19.9).

After choosing to update a Web server adapter, select the Web server that you chose during the initial install (see Figure 19.10). The following screen will prompt you for the name of a ServletExec AS instance. Type the name of the instance that you previously installed (see Figure 19.11). Next, enter a comma-delimited list of all Web application URLs (i.e., context paths) that should be forwarded to the servlet container (see Figure 19.12). For this demonstration, you should choose the same URL context path that you chose when installing the *examples* Web application (see Figure 19.7). Finally, when asked whether or not the installer should update the Web server's configuration file, click **Yes** (see Figure 19.13). Once the Web server's configuration file has been updated,

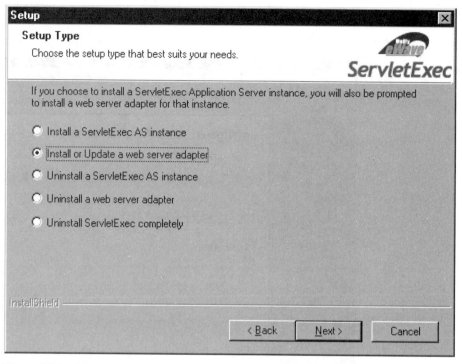

Figure 19.9 Select Type of Installation within ServletExec Installer.

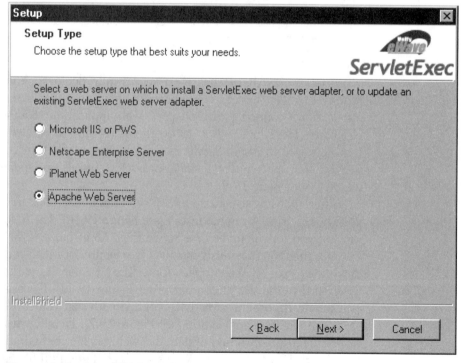

Figure 19.10 Select Web Server Type within ServletExec Installer.

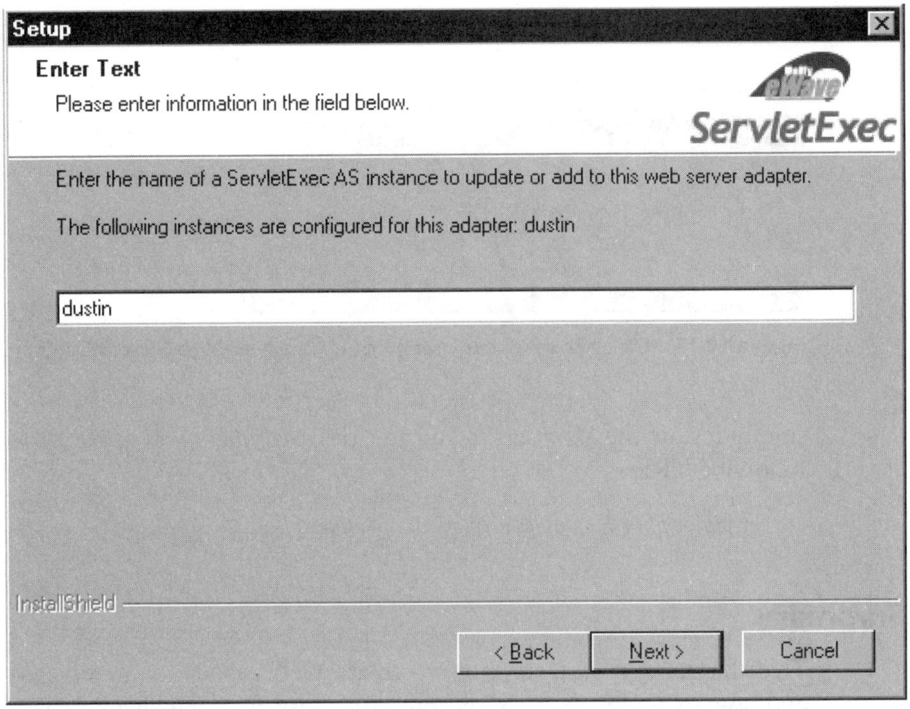

Figure 19.11 Select Instance Name to Update within the ServletExec Installer.

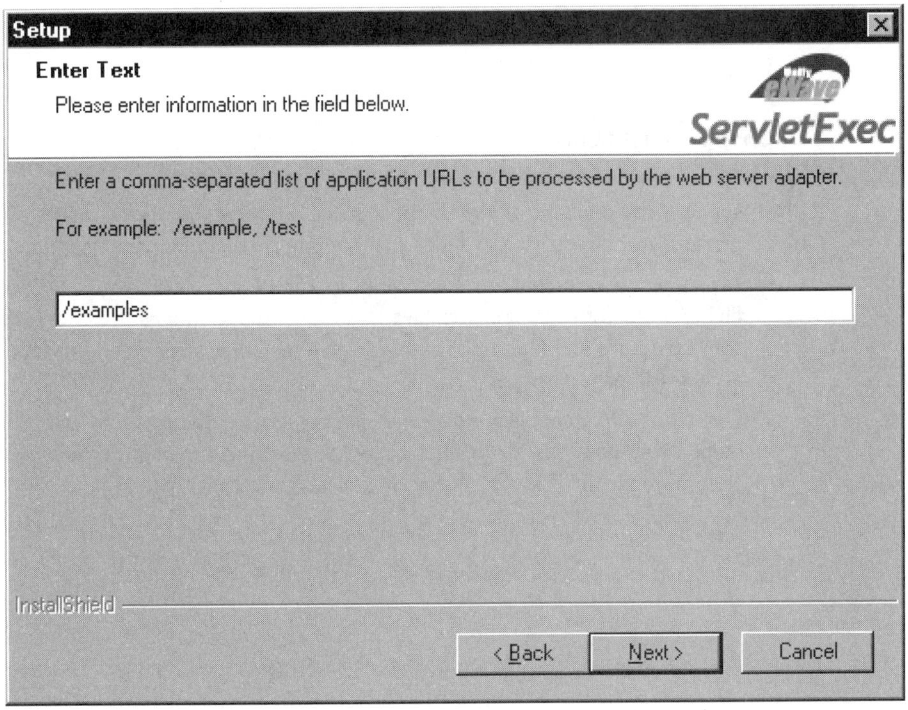

Figure 19.12 Specify the Application URLs (Context Paths) Used by This ServletExec Instance.

591

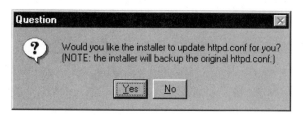

Figure 19.13   Dialog Box Prompts User about Updating the Web Server's Configuration File.

simply restart the Web server and test the *examples* Web application with the following URL:

http://localhost/examples/servlet/SnoopServlet

Summary

This chapter demonstrates how to create Web application archive (WAR) files and how to deploy them on several servers. As illustrated here, deploying WAR files is a quick and easy task on just about any J2EE-compatible server. In the next chapter, we will discuss how to troubleshoot servlets when things aren't working exactly as you expected.

Chapter Highlights

- All servlet containers that conform to the Servlet API 2.2 specification support the concept of a Web application. A *Web application* consists of the hierarchy of directories and files that together make up an application.

- Simply put, a *Web application archive* (also known as a WAR file) is an archive file, created with the standard Java JAR utility, that contains the entire directory structure and files associated with a Web application (e.g., servlets, JSP and HTML pages, images, etc.).

- Deploying a Web application archive file on Tomcat involves only two simple steps. First, copy the WAR file to the */jakarta-tomcat/webapps* directory. Second, start the Tomcat server or, if already running, restart it.

CHAPTER 20

Servlet Troubleshooting

Troubleshooting is a task that is required of every servlet developer from time to time. Even after a servlet is thoroughly debugged, subtle problems sometimes arise. Problems that do not surface during the debugging phase can often be uncovered by examining the application protocol layer. In this chapter, we will demonstrate how to evaluate the raw HTTP messages shared by the client and server in an effort to fully understand and troubleshoot servlet communications. In addition, a simple diagnostics servlet that displays the contents of the client request is presented. In summary, the following topics are covered:

- *Protocol Explorer* utility
- Diagnostics servlet

Protocol Explorer Utility

Protocol Explorer is a utility that allows you to examine the exact HTTP request sent by the client. It also provides the ability to examine the HTTP response returned by the server. Though we are concerned primarily with troubleshooting HTTP servlets, it should be noted that *Protocol Explorer* is also capable of communicating via most application-level protocols such as FTP, SMTP, POP3, and NNTP. The following sections demonstrate how to use the *Protocol Explorer* utility effectively to troubleshoot servlet HTTP communications. You can find *Protocol Explorer* on the accompanying CD or you can download the latest version from the following URL:

> *http://www.insideservlets.com/*

Receiving a Request from the Client

In order to troubleshoot communications between the client and the server, we must first be able to examine the client's request. Once we realize exactly what the client is saying to the server, we may then effectively analyze the other half of the conversation—the server's response. Therefore, let's begin by examining the client request. To do so, launch the *Protocol Explorer* application from the command line, like this:

```
java -jar ProtocolExporer.jar
```

Next, enter a number in the **Port** text field to indicate the port on which *Protocol Explorer* will listen for incoming connections. If this field is left empty, it defaults to port 80. For the purpose of this exercise, enter 8081 in the **Port** field. Finally, click the **Receive** button to begin listening for requests. At this point, you should see the "Listening on port 8081..." message in the **Hostname or IP** text field. *Protocol Explorer* is now ready to receive a request. To issue a request, type the following URL into your browser:

http://localhost:8081/examples/servlet/HelloWorldExample

This URL will invoke the HelloWorldExample servlet if directed to the Tomcat server instead of *Protocol Explorer.*

Upon receiving the request, *Protocol Explorer* echoes the request back to the client (see Figure 20.1). In addition to the client's browser, the request is displayed in the *Protocol Explorer's* **Request** window (see Figure 20.2). Finally, *Protocol Explorer's* response (containing the client's request plus some HTTP response headers) is displayed in the **Response** window. Once the client's request has been captured by *Protocol Explorer,* it is useful to forward that request immediately to the server in order to examine the server's response. The following section demonstrates how this can be accomplished.

Sending a Request to the Server

To begin, let's discuss how the client's request captured in the previous section can, in turn, be sent to the server in order to evaluate its response. If *Protocol Explorer* is still in receive mode, click the **Close** button to stop listening for requests. At this point, you should no longer see the message "Listening on port 8081..." in the **Hostname or IP** text field, but the client's request should still be visible in the **Request** field. Next, change the number in the **Port** text field to the port on which the server is listening. In this exercise, the Tomcat server is listening on port 8080. To follow along, start the Tomcat server according to the instructions in Chapter 8.

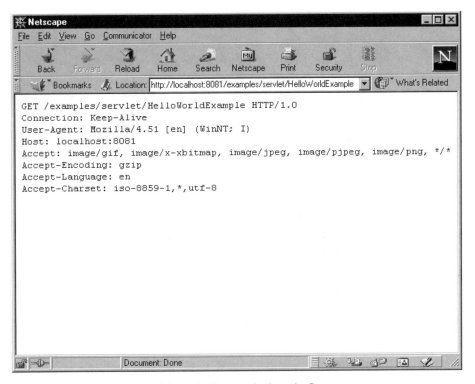

Figure 20.1 *Protocol Explorer* Echoes the Request back to the Browser.

To send the client's request to Tomcat, simply type `localhost` (or the name or IP number of the server on which Tomcat is running) into the **Hostname or IP** text field, enter the port number on which Tomcat is listening (e.g., `8080`) in the **Port** field, and click the **Send** button. The client's servlet request will be forwarded to the server and the servlet response, including all HTTP headers, will be displayed in the **Response** text field (see Figure 20.3). In this way, it is possible to examine the server's exact response to a particular client's request. Using *Protocol Explorer* as a "middleman" during client/server communications in this manner is a very useful troubleshooting technique.

Of course, capturing a client's request before communicating with a server is not required. If you wish, you may construct your own request by typing it directly into the **Request** text field. Once your request is ready to send, simply enter the server name or IP address in the **Hostname or IP** text field and the port on which it is listening in the **Port** field and click the **Send** button. The server's response to this request will be displayed in the **Response** field. For example, you can view and edit a sample request by clicking on the **HTTP**

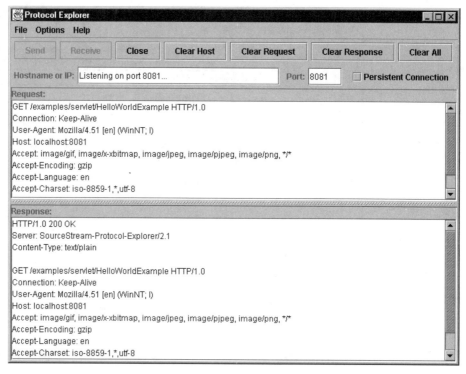

Figure 20.2   *Protocol Explorer* Displays the Client's Request.

Example option under the **Help** menu. When you are satisfied with the request, send it by clicking the **Send** button (see Figure 20.4).

NOTE: For complete *Protocol Explorer* instructions, click the **Instructions** option under the **Help** menu.

Protocol Explorer Source Code

The complete source code for the *Protocol Explorer* utility is presented here. In addition, you can find the *Protocol Explorer* JAR and source code on the accompanying CD. *Protocol Explorer* is composed of two classes—`ProtocolExplorer` and `ReceiveRequest`. The following text presents the source code for each of these classes.

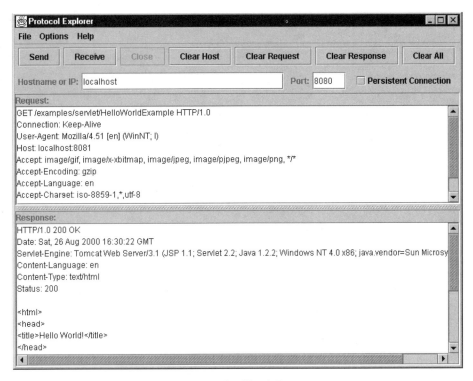

Figure 20.3   Tomcat Server's Response to the Client's Request

ProtocolExplorer Class

The `ProtocolExplorer` class is the primary class for this application. In addition to containing the `main()` method (i.e., the entry point to `Protocol-Explorer`), this class is responsible for displaying the user interface and implementing all functionality regarding sending requests and capturing the response. Listing 20.1 contains the complete source code for the `Protocol-Explorer` class.

Listing 20.1   Source code for the `ProtocolExplorer` class.

```
import javax.swing.*;
import java.awt.*;
import java.awt.event.*;
import java.net.*;
import java.io.*;

/**
 * ProtocolExplorer enables users to issue requests and view the
 * response from servers that implement many different protocols.
 * In addition, using the ReceiveRequest class, ProtocolExplorer
```

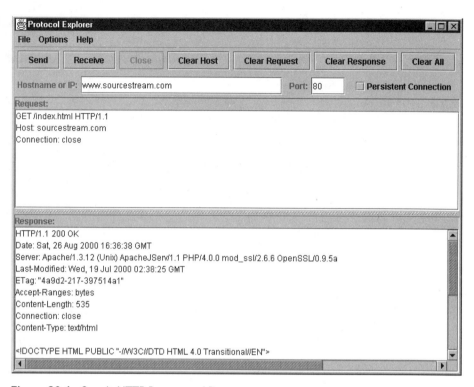

Figure 20.4   Sample HTTP Request and Response

```
 *  can listen for connections and display the request received
 *  from a client.
 *
 *  @author Dustin R. Callaway
 */
public class ProtocolExplorer implements Runnable
{
  //CONSTANTS
  public static final String APP_TITLE = "Protocol Explorer";
  public static final String ABOUT_TITLE =
    "Protocol Explorer 2.1";
  public static final String AUTHOR = "Dustin R. Callaway";
  public static final String EMAIL = "dustin@sourcestream.com";
  public static final String WEB = "http://www.sourcestream.com";
  public static final String COPYRIGHT =
    "Copyright (C) 2000, SourceStream. All Rights Reserved.";

  //INSTANCE VARIABLES
  Thread sendThread;
  Thread receiveThread;
  ReceiveRequest receiveRequest;
  JFrame frame;
```

```java
JDialog aboutBox;
JDialog instructBox;
JButton send;
JButton close;
JButton receive;
JButton clearHost;
JButton clearRequest;
JButton clearResponse;
JButton clearAll;
JTextField hostText;
JTextField portText;
JComboBox protocolCombo;
JComboBox commandsCombo;
JCheckBox persistentCheck;
JTextArea requestText;
JTextArea responseText;
JCheckBoxMenuItem menuCRLF;
JCheckBoxMenuItem menuNoCRLF;
Socket mySocket;
String linefeed = "\n";

/**
 * Called when ProtocolExplorer starts.
 *
 * @param args String array containing all command-line
 *   arguments
 */
public static void main(String[] args)
{
  ProtocolExplorer pe = new ProtocolExplorer();

  pe.init();
}


/**
 * Builds the Protocol Explorer window.
 */
private void init()
{
  frame = new JFrame(); //main Protocol Explorer frame

  //listen for window close command and exit
  frame.addWindowListener(new WindowAdapter()
  {
    public void windowClosing(WindowEvent e)
    {
      Window w = e.getWindow();
      w.setVisible(false);
      w.dispose();
      System.exit(0);
    }
  });
```

```
      frame.setTitle(APP_TITLE);

      buildMenuBar();            //add menu bar to frame
      buildToolBar();            //add tool bar to frame
      buildRequestResponseArea(); //add Request/Reponse area

      frame.pack(); //size frame based on size of all components

      //get dimensions of user's screen
      Dimension screenSize =
        Toolkit.getDefaultToolkit().getScreenSize();

      //get width and height of user's screen
      int x = new Double(screenSize.getWidth()).intValue();
      int y = new Double(screenSize.getHeight()).intValue();

      //center window on user's screen
      frame.setLocation((x - frame.getWidth())/2,
        (y - frame.getHeight())/2);
      frame.setVisible(true); //show the frame
    }


    /**
     * Builds the application menu bar.
     */
    private void buildMenuBar()
    {
      JMenuBar mb = new JMenuBar();

      JMenu menuFile = new JMenu("File"); //add File menu

      //add Exit menu item to File menu
      JMenuItem menuFileExit = new JMenuItem("Exit");
      menuFileExit.addActionListener(new ActionListener()
      {
        public void actionPerformed(ActionEvent e)
        {
          System.exit(0);
        }
      });
      menuFile.add(menuFileExit); //add Exit menu item
      mb.add(menuFile); //add File menu to menu bar

      JMenu menuOptions = new JMenu("Options"); //add Options menu

      //add CRLF option to Options menu
      menuCRLF = new JCheckBoxMenuItem("Add CRLF to HTTP Headers");
      menuOptions.add(menuCRLF);

      //add Remove CRLF option to Options menu
      menuNoCRLF = new JCheckBoxMenuItem(
        "Remove CRLF from Request");
```

```
menuOptions.add(menuNoCRLF);
mb.add(menuOptions); //add Options menu to menu bar

JMenu menuHelp = new JMenu("Help"); //add Help menu

//add Instructions menu item to Help menu
JMenuItem menuHelpInstruct = new JMenuItem("Instructions");
menuHelpInstruct.addActionListener(new ActionListener()
{
  public void actionPerformed(ActionEvent e)
  {
    showInstructions();  //show instructions
  }
});
menuHelp.add(menuHelpInstruct);

//add HTTP Example menu item to Help menu
JMenuItem menuHelpHttp = new JMenuItem("HTTP Example");
menuHelpHttp.addActionListener(new ActionListener()
{
  public void actionPerformed(ActionEvent e)
  {
    //create HTTP example
    hostText.setText("www.sourcestream.com");
    portText.setText("80");
    persistentCheck.setSelected(false);
    requestText.setText("GET /index.html HTTP/1.1" +
      linefeed + "Host: sourcestream.com" + linefeed +
      "Connection: close");
  }
});
menuHelp.add(menuHelpHttp);

//add FTP Example menu item to Help menu
JMenuItem menuHelpFtp = new JMenuItem("FTP Example");
menuHelpFtp.addActionListener(new ActionListener()
{
  public void actionPerformed(ActionEvent e)
  {
    //create FTP example
    hostText.setText("ftp.sourcestream.com");
    portText.setText("21");
    persistentCheck.setSelected(true);
    requestText.setText("USER anonymous" + linefeed +
      "PASS anonymous@emailaddress.com");
  }
});
menuHelp.add(menuHelpFtp);

//add POP3 Example menu item to Help menu
JMenuItem menuHelpPop3 = new JMenuItem("POP3 Example");
menuHelpPop3.addActionListener(new ActionListener()
{
```

```java
      public void actionPerformed(ActionEvent e)
      {
        //create POP3 example
        hostText.setText("sourcestream.com");
        portText.setText("110");
        persistentCheck.setSelected(true);
        requestText.setText("USER anonymous" + linefeed);
      }
    });
    menuHelp.add(menuHelpPop3);

    //add About... menu item to Help menu
    JMenuItem menuHelpAbout = new JMenuItem("About...");
    menuHelpAbout.addActionListener(new ActionListener()
    {
      public void actionPerformed(ActionEvent e)
      {
        showAboutBox();
      }
    });
    menuHelp.add(menuHelpAbout);

    mb.add(menuHelp); //add Help menu to menu bar

    frame.setJMenuBar(mb); //add menu bar to frame
}


/**
 * Build the application tool bar.
 */
private void buildToolBar()
{
  //create panel for toolbar
  JPanel toolbar = new JPanel(new BorderLayout());

  //create toolbar buttons
  JPanel toolbarButtons = new JPanel(new FlowLayout(
    FlowLayout.LEFT));
  send = new JButton("Send");
  close = new JButton("Close");
  close.setEnabled(false);
  receive = new JButton("Receive");
  clearHost = new JButton("Clear Host");
  clearRequest = new JButton("Clear Request");
  clearResponse = new JButton("Clear Response");
  clearAll = new JButton("Clear All");
  toolbarButtons.add(send);
  toolbarButtons.add(receive);
  toolbarButtons.add(close);
  toolbarButtons.add(clearHost);
  toolbarButtons.add(clearRequest);
  toolbarButtons.add(clearResponse);
```

```java
toolbarButtons.add(clearAll);
toolbar.add(toolbarButtons, BorderLayout.NORTH);

//add functionality to Send button
send.addActionListener(new ActionListener()
{
  public void actionPerformed(ActionEvent e)
  {
    sendRequest();
  }
});

//add functionality to Close button
close.addActionListener(new ActionListener()
{
  public void actionPerformed(ActionEvent e)
  {
    closeNow();
  }
});

//add functionality to Receive button
receive.addActionListener(new ActionListener()
{
  public void actionPerformed(ActionEvent e)
  {
    receiveRequest();

    portText.requestFocus();
  }
});

//add functionality to Clear Host button
clearHost.addActionListener(new ActionListener()
{
  public void actionPerformed(ActionEvent e)
  {
    hostText.setText("");

    hostText.requestFocus();
  }
});

//add functionality to Clear Request button
clearRequest.addActionListener(new ActionListener()
{
  public void actionPerformed(ActionEvent e)
  {
    requestText.setText("");

    requestText.requestFocus();
  }
});
```

```java
//add functionality to Clear Response button
clearResponse.addActionListener(new ActionListener()
{
  public void actionPerformed(ActionEvent e)
  {
    responseText.setText("");
  }
});

//add functionality to Clear All button
clearAll.addActionListener(new ActionListener()
{
  public void actionPerformed(ActionEvent e)
  {
    hostText.setText("");
    portText.setText("");
    requestText.setText("");
    responseText.setText("");

    hostText.requestFocus();
  }
});

//create hostname/port line
JPanel locationPort = new JPanel(new FlowLayout(
  FlowLayout.LEFT));
hostText = new JTextField();
hostText.setPreferredSize(new Dimension(300,25));
portText = new JTextField("");
portText.setPreferredSize(new Dimension(50,25));
persistentCheck = new JCheckBox("Persistent Connection",
  false);
locationPort.add(new JLabel("Hostname or IP:"));
locationPort.add(hostText);
locationPort.add(new JLabel("  Port:"));
locationPort.add(portText);
locationPort.add(new JLabel("  ")); //spacer
locationPort.add(persistentCheck);

//add buttons and Host/IP section to toolbar
toolbar.add(toolbarButtons, BorderLayout.NORTH);
toolbar.add(locationPort, BorderLayout.CENTER);

//add toolbar to frame
frame.getContentPane().setLayout(new BorderLayout());
frame.addWindowListener(new WindowAdapter()
{
  public void windowClosing(WindowEvent e)
  {
    Window w = e.getWindow();
    w.setVisible(false);
```

```
        w.dispose();
        System.exit(0);
      }
    });
    frame.getContentPane().add(toolbar, BorderLayout.NORTH);
  }


  /**
   * Build the response/request area of the window.
   */
  private void buildRequestResponseArea()
  {
    JSplitPane split = new JSplitPane(JSplitPane.VERTICAL_SPLIT);

    //request area on top
    JPanel topPanel = new JPanel(new BorderLayout());
    JLabel requestLabel = new JLabel("Request:");
    requestText = new JTextArea();
    requestText.setTabSize(2);
    JScrollPane topScroll = new JScrollPane(requestText);
    topScroll.setPreferredSize(new Dimension(600,150));
    topPanel.add(requestLabel, "North");
    topPanel.add(topScroll, "Center");
    split.setTopComponent(topPanel);

    //response area on bottom
    JPanel bottomPanel = new JPanel(new BorderLayout());
    JLabel responseLabel = new JLabel("Response:");
    responseText = new JTextArea();
    responseText.setTabSize(2);
    JScrollPane bottomScroll = new JScrollPane(responseText);
    bottomScroll.setPreferredSize(new Dimension(600,200));
    bottomPanel.add(responseLabel, "North");
    bottomPanel.add(bottomScroll, "Center");
    split.setBottomComponent(bottomPanel);

    frame.getContentPane().add(split, "Center");
  }


  /**
   * Displays the instructions dialog box.
   */
  private void showInstructions()
  {
    //create the instructions dialog box
    instructBox = new JDialog(frame,
      "Protocol Explorer Instructions", true);
    instructBox.getContentPane().setLayout(
      new BorderLayout());
    instructBox.getContentPane().add(new JLabel("  "),
      BorderLayout.NORTH); //indent top
```

```java
instructBox.getContentPane().add(new JLabel("  "),
  BorderLayout.WEST); //indent left
instructBox.getContentPane().add(new JLabel("  "),
  BorderLayout.EAST); //indent right

//create Close button
JButton closeInstructions = new JButton("Close");

//add functionality to Close button
closeInstructions.addActionListener(new ActionListener()
{
  public void actionPerformed(ActionEvent e)
  {
    instructBox.setVisible(false);
    instructBox.dispose(); //dispose of dialog box
  }
});

//add the close button to a panel so that it will be centered
JPanel closePanel = new JPanel(new FlowLayout());
closePanel.add(closeInstructions);

//add the close button to the bottom of the dialog box
instructBox.getContentPane().add(closePanel,
  BorderLayout.SOUTH);

//create the text area containing the instructions
JTextArea instructText = new JTextArea();
instructText.setLineWrap(true);
instructText.setWrapStyleWord(true);
JScrollPane instructScroll = new JScrollPane(instructText);
instructScroll.setPreferredSize(new Dimension(400,300));
instructText.setEditable(false);

//populate the text area with instructions and add it to the
//dialog box
instructText.setText(getInstructions());
instructBox.getContentPane().add(instructScroll,
  BorderLayout.CENTER);

//listen for window close command and exit
instructBox.addWindowListener(new WindowAdapter()
{
  public void windowClosing(WindowEvent e)
  {
    Window w = e.getWindow();
    w.setVisible(false);
    w.dispose();
  }
});

instructBox.pack(); //make dialog box fit its contents
```

```java
    //get dimensions of user's screen
    Dimension screenSize =
      Toolkit.getDefaultToolkit().getScreenSize();

    //get width and height of user's screen
    int x = new Double(screenSize.getWidth()).intValue();
    int y = new Double(screenSize.getHeight()).intValue();

    //center window on user's screen
    instructBox.setLocation((x - instructBox.getWidth())/2,
      (y - instructBox.getHeight())/2);

    instructBox.setVisible(true); //show instructions dialog box
  }


  /**
   * Displays the About dialog box.
   */
  private void showAboutBox()
  {
    //create the about dialog box
    aboutBox = new JDialog(frame, "About Protocol Explorer",
      true);
    aboutBox.getContentPane().setLayout(new BorderLayout());

    //create a panel to contain the about information
    JPanel aboutPanel = new JPanel(new GridLayout(7,1));
    JLabel title = new JLabel(ABOUT_TITLE);
    title.setFont(new Font(null, Font.BOLD, 20));
    aboutPanel.add(title);
    aboutPanel.add(new JLabel("By " + AUTHOR));
    aboutPanel.add(new JLabel("E-Mail: " + EMAIL));
    aboutPanel.add(new JLabel("Web: " + WEB));
    aboutPanel.add(new JLabel(""));
    JLabel copyRight = new JLabel(COPYRIGHT);
    copyRight.setFont(new Font(null, Font.PLAIN, 10));
    aboutPanel.add(copyRight);

    //create new panel using FlowLayout so button will not expand
    //the full width of the dialog box
    JPanel closePanel = new JPanel(new FlowLayout());
    JButton closeAbout = new JButton("Close"); //close button

    //add functionality to Close button
    closeAbout.addActionListener(new ActionListener()
    {
      public void actionPerformed(ActionEvent e)
      {
        aboutBox.setVisible(false);
        aboutBox.dispose(); //dispose of dialog box
      }
    });
```

```java
    closePanel.add(closeAbout); //add close button to close panel
    aboutPanel.add(closePanel); //add close panel to about panel

    aboutBox.getContentPane().add(new JLabel("  "),
      BorderLayout.WEST); //indent on left
    aboutBox.getContentPane().add(new JLabel("  "),
      BorderLayout.EAST); //indent or right
    aboutBox.getContentPane().add(aboutPanel,
      BorderLayout.CENTER);

    //listen for window close command and exit
    aboutBox.addWindowListener(new WindowAdapter()
    {
      public void windowClosing(WindowEvent e)
      {
        Window w = e.getWindow();
        w.setVisible(false);
        w.dispose();
      }
    });

    aboutBox.pack(); //shrink screen to fit components

    //get dimensions of user's screen
    Dimension screenSize =
      Toolkit.getDefaultToolkit().getScreenSize();

    //get width and height of user's screen
    int x = new Double(screenSize.getWidth()).intValue();
    int y = new Double(screenSize.getHeight()).intValue();

    //center window on user's screen
    aboutBox.setLocation((x - aboutBox.getWidth())/2,
      (y - aboutBox.getHeight())/2);

    aboutBox.setVisible(true); //show about dialog box
  }


  /**
   * Starts listening for a client request in a separate thread.
   */
  private void receiveRequest()
  {
    int port = 80; //default to port 80

    try
    {
      //get the port number from the port text box
      port = Integer.parseInt(portText.getText());
    }
```

```java
      catch (NumberFormatException e)
      {
        portText.setText("80");
      }

      requestText.setText("");
      responseText.setText("");

      //instantiate the ReceiveRequest object
      receiveRequest = new ReceiveRequest(hostText, requestText,
        responseText, send,close, receive, port, menuNoCRLF);
      receiveThread = new Thread(receiveRequest,
        "ProtocolExplorerReceive");
      receiveThread.start(); //start listening in a new thread
    }


    /**
     * Spawns a new thread in which to transmit the request to the
     * host.
     */
    private void sendRequest()
    {
      if (!checkHost()) //verify format of host string
      {
        return; //invalid host name
      }

      killThread(); //if a thread is currently running, stop it

      //start new thread to send request and listen for response
      sendThread = new Thread(this, "ProtocolExplorerSend");
      sendThread.start();

      //if a stateful protocol is being used, the send button
      //should always be on
      if (!persistentCheck.isSelected()) //stateless protocol
      {
        setButtons(false, true); //turn send button off, close on
      }
    }


    /**
     * closeNow stops the thread that is attempting to communicate
     * with the host and closes the socket connection.
     */
    private void closeNow()
    {
      setButtons(true, false); //turn send button on, close off

      killThread(); //if a thread is currently running, stop it
```

```
    try
    {
      if (mySocket != null)
      {
        mySocket.close();
        mySocket = null;
      }
    }
    catch (IOException ignored) {}
}


/**
 * Insures that the host string is in the proper format by
 * removing the opening "http://" string and moving any port
 * information to the port text box.
 */
private boolean checkHost()
{
  try
  {
    String search = "http://";
    String host = hostText.getText();

    //remove "http://" from host URL
    int pos = host.toLowerCase().indexOf(search);

    boolean emptyRequest = false;

    //determine if the request is empty
    if (requestText.getText().equals("")) //request is empty
    {
      //if request is empty, default to an HTTP GET request
      portText.setText("80");
      persistentCheck.setSelected(false);
      requestText.setText("GET / HTTP/1.1" + linefeed);
      emptyRequest = true;
    }

    if (pos != -1) //host URL does contain "http://"
    {
      //remove "http://" from host string
      host = host.substring(search.length());
    }

    //move resource path to request line
    pos = host.indexOf("/");

    if (pos != -1) //host URL contains a resource path
    {
      //move the resource path into the request
      String resourcePath = host.substring(pos);
```

```
        host = host.substring(0,pos);
        pos = requestText.getText().indexOf("/");

        String request = requestText.getText().substring(0,pos);
        pos = requestText.getText().indexOf(" ", pos);
        request = request + resourcePath +
          requestText.getText().substring(pos);
        requestText.setText(request);
      }

      //move port in URL to port text box
      if (host.indexOf(":") != -1)
      {
        portText.setText(host.substring(host.indexOf(":")+1));
        host = host.substring(0, host.indexOf(":"));
      }

      //determine if the request was empty
      if (emptyRequest) //request was empty
      {
        requestText.append("Host: " + host + linefeed +
          "Connection: close");
      }

      hostText.setText(host); //update host text box
    }
    catch (Exception e) //host string is not valid
    {
      setButtons(true, false); //turn send button on, close off

      responseText.setText("<< PROTOCOL EXPLORER MESSAGE: " +
        "Invalid hostname.\nDescription: " + e + " >>");

      return false;
    }

    return true;
  }


  /**
   * Kills any threads spawned to listen for reponses from the
   * host or to listen for requests from a client (if any such
   * threads currently exists).
   */
  private void killThread()
  {
    //determine if the send thread is running
    if (sendThread != null)
    {
      //setting sendThread to null serves as a semaphore
      //indicating the thread's run() method should be exited
      sendThread = null;
    }
```

```
        //determine if the receive thread is running
        if (receiveThread != null)
        {
          receiveRequest.closeSocket();
          receiveThread = null;
          hostText.setText("");
        }
      }


/**
 * Executes in a separate thread. This method opens a socket to
 * the specified host, sends the request, and receives the
 * response.
 */
public void run()
{
  InetAddress address = null;
  PrintWriter pw = null;
  BufferedReader br = null;
  int port = 80; //default to port 80

  String host = hostText.getText(); //get name of host or IP

  try
  {
    //get the port number from the port text box
    port = Integer.parseInt(portText.getText());
  }
  catch (NumberFormatException e)
  {
    portText.setText("80");
  }

  try
  {
    //create internet address from host string
    address = InetAddress.getByName(host);
  }
  catch (UnknownHostException e) //host string is not valid
  {
    setButtons(true, false); //turn send button on, close off

    responseText.setText("<< PROTOCOL EXPLORER MESSAGE: " +
      "Unknown host " + host + " when creating InetAddress." +
      "\nDescription: " + e + " >>");

    return;
  }
```

```
try
{
  //determine if socket has been set to null (it won't be for
  //persistent connections)
  if (mySocket == null)
  {
    mySocket = new Socket(address, port); //open socket
  }
}
catch (UnknownHostException e) //unable to locate the host
{
  setButtons(true, false); //turn send button on, close off

  responseText.setText("<< PROTOCOL EXPLORER MESSAGE: " +
    "Unknown host when opening socket...\nDescription: " +
    e.toString() + " >>");

  return;
}
catch (IOException e) //error opening socket
{
  setButtons(true, false); //turn send button on, close off

  responseText.setText("<< PROTOCOL EXPLORER MESSAGE: " +
    "IO Exception when opening socket...\nDescription: " +
    e.toString() + " >>");

  return;
}
catch(Exception e)
{
  setButtons(true, false); //turn send button on, close off

  responseText.setText("<< PROTOCOL EXPLORER MESSAGE: " +
    "An unexpected exception occurred...\nDescription: " +
    e.toString() + " >>");

  return;
}

try
{
  //open output stream to host
  pw = new PrintWriter(new OutputStreamWriter(
    mySocket.getOutputStream()));

  String request = requestText.getText().trim();

  //determine if a "\r\n" should be added to HTTP headers
  if (menuCRLF.getState())
  {
    request = addCR(request); //add "\r\n" to HTTP headers
  }
```

```
pw.print(request); //send request

//if request doesn't terminate with a linefeed, send one
if (!request.endsWith(linefeed))
{
  pw.print(linefeed); //send linefeed

  //if request is not persistent, send two linefeeds
  if (!persistentCheck.isSelected())
  {
    pw.print(linefeed);
  }
}

pw.flush(); //flush request to client

//open input stream to host
br = new BufferedReader(new InputStreamReader(
  mySocket.getInputStream()));

responseText.setText(""); //clear response box

String line = "";

//determine if we are using a persistent connection
if (!persistentCheck.isSelected()) //not persistent
{
  //read lines of information from client
  while ((line = br.readLine()) != null &&
    sendThread != null)
  {
    try
    {
      responseText.append(line);
      responseText.append(linefeed); //add linefeed

      //For some reason, if we don't sleep here the Close
      //button does not always respond to mouse clicks
      //(even though we're in a different thread).
      //Therefore, sleep here to insure that the Close
      //button will always work.
      Thread.sleep(1);
    }
    catch (InterruptedException i)
    {
      sendThread = null;
    }
  }
}
else //persistent connection
{
  setButtons(true, true); //turn send button on, close on
```

```
//read lines of information from client
while (sendThread != null)
{
  try
  {
    if (br.ready())
    {
      line = br.readLine();

      responseText.append(line);
      responseText.append(linefeed); //add linefeed
    }

    //looping through this infinite without sleeping can
    //effectively lock up the machine, so sleep between
    //iterations
    Thread.sleep(1);
  }
  catch (InterruptedException i)
  {
    sendThread = null;
  }
}
}
catch (IOException f)
{
  responseText.setText("<< PROTOCOL EXPLORER MESSAGE: " +
    "IOException when reading data from socket...\n" +
    "Description: " + f.toString() + " >>");

  return;
}
catch (Exception g)
{
  responseText.setText("<< PROTOCOL EXPLORER MESSAGE: " +
    "Unexpected exception occurred...\nDescription: " +
    g.toString() + " >>");

  return;
}
finally
{
  //if a persistent connection is not used, close the socket
  //after receiving response
  if (!persistentCheck.isSelected() & mySocket != null)
  {
    setButtons(true, false); //turn send button on, close off

    try
    {
      if (mySocket != null)
      {
```

```
            mySocket.close(); //close socket since not persistent
            mySocket = null;
          }
        }
        catch (IOException ignored) {}
      }
    }
}


/**
 * Adds a carriage return/linefeed to the end of each line in
 * the specified string. This method effectively changes all
 * linefeeds (\n) to a carriage return/linefeed pair (\r\n).
 * This is necessary since some servers require lines to be
 * terminated by a carriage return/linefeed rather than just a
 * linefeed.
 *
 * @param text String to which each line termination character
 *   should be changed to \r\n
 * @return String with every line terminated by \r\n
 */
private String addCR(String text)
{
  StringBuffer requestCR = new StringBuffer();

  try
  {
    //create a buffered reader from text to read line by line
    BufferedReader br = new BufferedReader(new StringReader(
      text));

    String line = br.readLine(); //get first line

    //add \r\n to end of all HTTP headers
    if (line.toLowerCase().indexOf("http/") > -1)
    {
      while (line != null && !line.trim().equals(""))
      {
        requestCR.append(line);
        requestCR.append("\r\n"); //terminate lines with \r\n

        line = br.readLine(); //read next line
      }

      requestCR.append("\r\n");
    }

    int x;
    char[] chars = new char[1024];
    while (br.ready() && (x = br.read(chars)) != -1)
    {
```

```
            requestCR.append(new String(chars, 0, x));
      }
    }
    catch (IOException ignored) {}

    return requestCR.toString(); //return altered text
}


/**
 * Set the send and close buttons to the proper state.
 */
private void setButtons(boolean sendOn, boolean closeOn)
{
  send.setEnabled(sendOn); //set Send button
  receive.setEnabled(sendOn); //set Receive button
  close.setEnabled(closeOn); //set Close button
}


/**
 * Populates a string with the application's instructions.
 */
private String getInstructions()
{
  //create the instructions to be placed in the text area
  StringBuffer iBuf = new StringBuffer();

  iBuf.append("Protocol Explorer is a utility that enables " +
      "the user to examine protocol communications between a " +
      "client and server. This program may be freely " +
      "distributed. To use this application in send mode, " +
      "follow these simple steps:\n\n");
  iBuf.append("1. Enter a resolvable hostname or IP address " +
      "in the 'Hostname or IP' text box. This value indicates " +
      "the server to which a connection will be established.\n");
  iBuf.append("2. Enter the port on which to make the " +
      "connection. If left empty or an invalid port number is " +
      "used, this setting will default to port 80.\n");
  iBuf.append("3. Select whether or not to use a persistent " +
      "connection by selecting or clearing the 'Persistent " +
      "Connection' checkbox. Protocols such as FTP, SMTP, and " +
      "NNTP (and even HTTP/1.1 using HTTP Keep-Alive) require " +
      "a persistent connection (that is, the same connection " +
      "is used for all requests). Traditional HTTP (i.e., " +
      "HTTP/1.0 and HTTP/1.1 when accompanied with a " +
      "Connection: Close header field) is connectionless and " +
      "requires new connection for each request.\n");
  iBuf.append("4. Type the exact request to send to the " +
      "server in the 'Request' text box.\n");
  iBuf.append("5. Click the 'Send' button to transmit the " +
      "request to the specified host server and listen for " +
      "the reply. The host's reply will be displayed in the " +
      "'Response' text box.\n\n");
```

```
iBuf.append("To use this application in receive mode, " +
  "follow these steps:\n\n");
iBuf.append("1. Enter the port on which you wish Protocol " +
  "Explorer to listen for incoming requests (in the Port " +
  "text box). If no port is specified, port 80 is used by " +
  "default.\n");
iBuf.append("2. Issue a request to Protocol Explorer from " +
  "a browser. For example, if Protocol Explorer is " +
  "listening on port 8080, request the URL " +
  "'http://localhost:8080' from your browser. The exact " +
  "client request will be displayed in Protocol Explorer " +
  "and returned to the browser.\n\n");
iBuf.append("The text below describes the function of " +
  "each element of the Protocol Explorer application.\n\n");
iBuf.append("[File]\nThe 'File' menu simply provides a " +
  "way to exit the application.\n\n");
iBuf.append("[Options]\nThe 'Options' menu provides a way " +
  "to tell Protocol Explorer to automatically add a CRLF " +
  "pair to the end of all HTTP header fields before the " +
  "request is sent (which some servers require) or to " +
  "remove the CRLF pair from the end of all lines after a " +
  "request is received.\n\n");
iBuf.append("[Help]\nThe 'Help' menu provides access to " +
  "this screen for instructions as well as sample " +
  "protocol requests and the about box.\n\n");
iBuf.append("[Send]\nThe 'Send' button transmits the text " +
  "in the 'Request' text box to the specified host and " +
  "port.\n\n");
iBuf.append("[Receive]\nThe 'Recieve' button starts " +
  "Protocol Explorer listening for a client request. When " +
  "received, the exact request is displayed in the " +
  "Response text box and returned to the client that " +
  "issued the request.\n\n");
iBuf.append("[Close]\nThe 'Close' button causes the " +
  "application to stop listening for a response and to " +
  "close the connection to the host server. If in receive " +
  "mode, it stops the server listening for a request.\n\n");
iBuf.append("[Clear Host]\nClears the 'Hostname or IP' " +
  "text box and sets focus to it.\n\n");
iBuf.append("[Clear Request]\nClears the 'Request' " +
  "text box and sets focus to it.\n\n");
iBuf.append("[Clear Response]\nClears the 'Response' " +
  "text box.\n\n");
iBuf.append("[Clear All]\nClears all text fields.\n\n");
iBuf.append("[Hostname or IP]\nThe hostname or IP address " +
  "of the server to which a connection will be " +
  "established.\n\n");
iBuf.append("[Port]\nThe port on which the connection to " +
  "the host server will be made.\n\n");
iBuf.append("[Persistent Connection]\nThe 'Persistent " +
  "Connection' checkbox indicates whether the protocol in " +
  "use requires a persistent connection (e.g., FTP or " +
  "SMTP) or should establish a new connection for each " +
  "request (e.g., HTTP).\n\n");
```

```
            iBuf.append("[Request]\nIn send mode, the 'Request' " +
              "text box contains the user-defined request that will be " +
              "sent to the host when the 'Send' button is clicked. In " +
              "receive mode, 'Request' contains the request received " +
              "from the client.\n\n");
            iBuf.append("[Response]\nIn send mode, the 'Response' " +
              "text box contains the reply returned from the host. In " +
              "receive mode, 'Response' contains the response that " +
              "Protocol Explorer returns to the client.\n\n");
            iBuf.append("Legal Disclaimer: This software is provided " +
              "\"AS IS\" and without warranty of any kind. The author " +
              "makes no claims regarding the suitability of this " +
              "application for any purpose. SourceStream and the " +
              "author shall not be liable for any harm resulting from " +
              "the use of this software.");

            return iBuf.toString();
    }
}
```

ReceiveRequest Class

ReceiveRequest is a helper class that listens for incoming requests and echoes
them back to the client. The ProtocolExplorer class invokes ReceiveRequest
when the user clicks the **Receive** button. Listing 20.2 contains the complete
source code for the ReceiveRequest class.

Listing 20.2   Source code for the ReceiveRequest class.

```
import javax.swing.*;
import java.net.*;
import java.io.*;

/**
 * ReceiveRequest works in conjunction with ProtocolExplorer to
 * allow the user to view incoming requests. This class, running
 * in its own thread, listens for incoming requests on a
 * specified port and returns the exact request to the client as
 * well as displaying the request in the ProtocolExplorer's
 * response box.
 *
 * @author Dustin R. Callaway
 */
public class ReceiveRequest implements Runnable
{
    //CONSTANTS
    public static final String SERVER =
        "SourceStream-Protocol-Explorer/2.1";

    //INSTANCE VARIABLES
    ServerSocket serverSocket; //gets client connection
    JTextField hostText;
```

```
JTextArea requestText;
JTextArea responseText;
JButton send;
JButton close;
JButton receive;
JCheckBoxMenuItem menuNoCRLF;
int port;


/**
 * ReceiveRequest constructor accepts the Protocol Explorer
 * user interface elements that should be updated by this
 * class.
 *
 * @param hostText Host text box
 * @param requestText Request text box
 * @param responseText Response text box
 * @param send Send button (so it can be disabled when
 *   listening starts)
 * @param close Close button (so it can be enabled when
 *   listening starts)
 * @param receive Receive button (so it can be disabled when
 *   listening starts)
 * @param port Port number on which to start listening for
 *   incoming requests
 * @param menuNoCRLF Checkbox that indicates whether or not to
 *   remove all CRLF pairs from an incoming request
 */
public ReceiveRequest(JTextField hostText,
  JTextArea requestText, JTextArea responseText, JButton send,
  JButton close, JButton receive,int port,
  JCheckBoxMenuItem menuNoCRLF)
{
  this.hostText = hostText;
  this.requestText = requestText;
  this.responseText = responseText;
  this.send = send;
  this.close = close;
  this.receive = receive;
  this.port = port;
  this.menuNoCRLF = menuNoCRLF;
}


/**
 * Allows ProtocolExplorer to close the server socket when
 * receive mode is disabled.
 */
public void closeSocket()
{
  try
  {
```

```
      if (serverSocket != null)
      {
        serverSocket.close();
        serverSocket = null;
      }
    }
    catch (IOException ignored) {}
  }


  /**
   * Listens for incoming requests using a specified port number
   * while executing within a separate thread.
   */
  public void run()
  {
    String line;
    Socket socket = null;
    PrintWriter out = null;
    StringBuffer response;

    try
    {
      //create ServerSocket
      serverSocket = new ServerSocket(port);
    }
    catch (IOException e)
    {
      requestText.setText("<< PROTOCOL EXPLORER MESSAGE: " +
        "IOException occurred when creating server socket...\n" +
        "Description: " + e.toString() + " >>");
      return;
    }

    hostText.setText("Listening on port " + port + "...");
    send.setEnabled(false);    //disable send button
    close.setEnabled(true);    //enable close button
    receive.setEnabled(false); //disable receive button

    while (serverSocket != null) //receive requests until stopped
    {
      try
      {
        socket = serverSocket.accept(); //block until connection
        socket.setSoTimeout(250); //set timeout to 1/4 second

        requestText.setText("");
        responseText.setText("");

        //open input stream
        BufferedReader in = new BufferedReader(
          new InputStreamReader(socket.getInputStream()));
```

```
      responseText.append("HTTP/1.0 200 OK\r\n");
      responseText.append("Server: " + SERVER + "\r\n");
      responseText.append("Content-Type: text/plain\r\n\r\n");

      int x; //stores number of bytes returned with each read
      char[] chars = new char[1024]; //stores request
      try
      {
        if (menuNoCRLF.isSelected()) //remove CRLF from lines
        {
          while ((line = in.readLine()) != null)
          {
            requestText.append(line);
            requestText.append("\n");
            responseText.append(line);
            responseText.append("\n");
          }
        }
        else //display lines exactly as received
        {
          while ((x = in.read(chars)) > -1)
          {
            String req = new String(chars, 0, x);
            requestText.append(req); //add to Request text box
           responseText.append(req); //add to Response text box
          }
        }
      }
      catch (InterruptedIOException ignored) {}

      //open output stream
      out = new PrintWriter(socket.getOutputStream());

      //send response to client
      out.print(responseText.getText());
    }
    catch (Exception e)
    {
      break;
    }
    finally
    {
      try
      {
        out.flush();    //flush output stream
        out.close();    //close output stream
      }
      catch (Exception ignored) {}

      try
      {
        socket.close(); //close socket connection
      }
```

```
                    catch (Exception ignored) {}
                }
            }
        }
    }
```

Diagnostics Servlet

Similar to *Protocol Explorer*, the Diagnostics servlet presented here may serve as a helpful troubleshooting tool as well as a useful programming reference. This servlet uses many Servlet API methods to reveal information concerning an HTTP request and the server environment in which the servlet is executing. Much of this information may be useful to the servlet developer when debugging and troubleshooting HTTP communications.

The following list enumerates some of the information revealed by the Diagnostics servlet:

- Requested resource
- HTTP method used by request (GET, POST, etc.)
- Request query string
- Server and servlet information (name, IP address, port, initialization parameters, etc.)
- Request HTTP headers
- Request parameters (Web variables)

This information, particularly the request's HTTP headers and Web variables, may be very useful when building servlets that respond to client requests. Figure 20.5 shows a screen shot of the servlet responding to a typical HTTP request.

Listing 20.3 provides the full source code for the Diagnostics servlet. Inline documentation provides further information regarding the code.

Listing 20.3   Source code for the Diagnostics servlet.

```java
import java.io.*;
import java.util.*;
import javax.servlet.*;
import javax.servlet.http.*;

/**
 * Diagnostics servlet. Displays various information concerning
 * the client's request and the state of the servlet
 * environment. This information includes init parameters,
 * request HTTP method, request parameters, and request headers.
 * This servlet is useful when troubleshooting.
 *
 * @author Dustin R. Callaway
 */
```

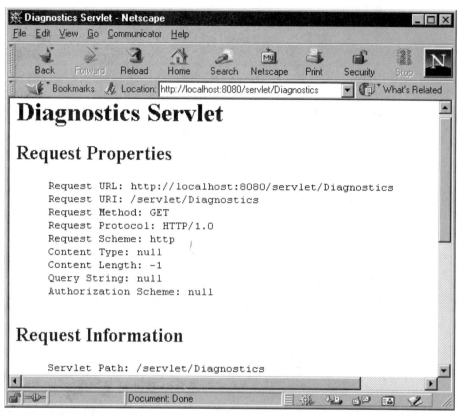

Figure 20.5   Response Generated by the Diagnostics Servlet

```
public class Diagnostics extends HttpServlet
{
  /**
   * Called in response to any request to this servlet
   */
  public void service(HttpServletRequest request,
    HttpServletResponse response) throws ServletException,
    IOException
  {
    response.setContentType("text/html"); //HTML output

    //get handle to output stream
    PrintWriterout = response.getWriter();

    //generate HTML to return to client
    out.println("<HTML>");
    out.println("<HEAD>");
    out.println("<TITLE>Diagnostics Servlet</TITLE>");
    out.println("</HEAD>");
```

```
out.println("<BODY>");
out.println("<H1>Diagnostics Servlet</H1>");

//REQUEST PROPERTIES
out.println("<H2>Request Properties</H2>");
out.println("<BLOCKQUOTE><PRE>");
out.println("Request URL: " +
  HttpUtils.getRequestURL(request).toString());
out.println("Request URI: " + request.getRequestURI());
out.println("Request Method: " + request.getMethod());
out.println("Request Protocol: " + request.getProtocol());
out.println("Request Scheme: " + request.getScheme());
out.println("Content Type: " + request.getContentType());
out.println("Content Length: " +
  request.getContentLength());
out.println("Query String: " + request.getQueryString());
out.println("Authorization Scheme: " +
  request.getAuthType());
out.println("</PRE></BLOCKQUOTE><BR>");

//REQUEST INFORMATION
out.println("<H2>Request Information</H2>");
out.println("<BLOCKQUOTE><PRE>");
out.println("Servlet Path: " + request.getServletPath());
out.println("Path Information: " + request.getPathInfo());
out.println("Path Translated: " +
  request.getPathTranslated());
out.println("Server Name: " + request.getServerName());
out.println("Server Port: " + request.getServerPort());
out.println("Remote User: " + request.getRemoteUser());
out.println("Remote Address: " + request.getRemoteAddr());
out.println("Remote Host: " + request.getRemoteHost());
out.println("Character Encoding: " +
  request.getCharacterEncoding());
out.println("</PRE></BLOCKQUOTE><BR>");

//REQUEST HEADERS
//create Enumeration of headers
Enumeration headers = request.getHeaderNames();
if (headers.hasMoreElements()) //check for headers
{
  out.println("<H2>Request Headers</H2>");
  out.println("<BLOCKQUOTE><PRE>");
  //iterate through header names
  while (headers.hasMoreElements())
  {
    //get header name
    String header = (String)headers.nextElement();
    //generate HTML to display header name and value
    out.println(header + ": " + request.getHeader(header));
  }
  out.println("</PRE></BLOCKQUOTE><BR>");
}
```

```java
//REQUEST PARAMETERS (web variables)
//create Enumeration of parameter names
Enumeration paramNames = request.getParameterNames();
if (paramNames.hasMoreElements()) //check for param names
{
  out.println("<H2>Request Parameters</H2>");
  out.println("<BLOCKQUOTE><PRE>");
  while (paramNames.hasMoreElements()) //iterate thru params
  {
    //get parameter name
    String paramName = (String)paramNames.nextElement();
    //get parameter value
    String paramValues[] =
      request.getParameterValues(paramName);
    if (paramValues != null)
    {
      //print parameter name and first value
      out.print(paramName + ": " + paramValues[0]);
      //print remaining parameter values (if any)
      for (int i = 1; i < paramValues.length; i++)
      {
        out.print(", " + paramValues[i]);
      }
      out.println("");
    }
  }
  out.println("</PRE></BLOCKQUOTE><BR>");
}

//INITIALIZATION PARAMETERS
//create Enumeration of initialization parameters
Enumeration initParams =
  getServletConfig().getInitParameterNames();
if (initParams.hasMoreElements()) //check for init params
{
  out.println("<H2>Initialization Parameters</H2>");
  out.println("<BLOCKQUOTE><PRE>");
  while (initParams.hasMoreElements()) //iterate thru params
  {
    //get param name
    String initParam = (String) initParams.nextElement();
    //generate HTML to display init parameter name and value
    out.println(initParam + ": " +
      getInitParameter(initParam));
  }
  out.println("</PRE></BLOCKQUOTE><BR>");
}

out.println("</BODY>");
out.println("</HTML>");
out.close(); //close output stream
}
```

```
/**
 * Allows server to identify this servlet
 */
public String getServletInfo()
{
  return "Servlet returns various request information.";
}
}
```

Summary

This chapter demonstrates a few useful techniques for troubleshooting servlet HTTP communications. We learned that the *Protocol Explorer* tool is capable of both receiving a client's request and forwarding it to a server. In this manner, the *Protocol Explorer* user is able to examine the client's exact request and the server's response to this request. Similarly, the Diagnostics servlet presented in this chapter is useful for troubleshooting client/server conversations by returning extensive information about the request back to the client.

Chapter Highlights

- *Protocol Explorer* is a utility that allows you to examine the exact HTTP request sent by the client. In addition, it also provides the ability to examine the HTTP response returned by the server.

- Similar to *Protocol Explorer*, the Diagnostics servlet may serve as a helpful troubleshooting tool as well as a useful programming reference. This servlet utilizes many Servlet API methods to reveal information concerning an HTTP request and the server environment in which the servlet is executing.

This chapter concludes the Advanced Servlet Concepts part of the book. The next part, Sample Servlets, offers several useful servlet examples.

PART IV

Sample Servlets

CHAPTER 21

Form Mailer Servlet

The Form Mailer servlet provides a convenient way to e-mail information entered on an HTML form. This servlet extracts the required e-mail data (e.g., sender, recipient, subject, message) from a basic HTML form, opens a socket to the mail server, and transmits the message via the SMTP protocol. After the message is sent, the client is redirected to a page specified by a hidden field on the HTML form. Likewise, the client may be redirected to a different page if an error occurs and the send operation fails. This servlet can be used by any number of HTML forms concurrently.

The successful operation of the Form Mailer servlet depends on the proper naming of the HTML form elements. Table 21.1 shows the correct names of each HTML form element. The naming of each element is critical because when the servlet extracts the mail information from the form, it queries for these parameters by name.

The simple HTML document shown in Listing 21.1 uses the naming conventions described in Table 21.1 and works well with the Form Mailer servlet. Notice the hidden fields in the HTML form that instruct the server where to redirect the client after the mail has been sent (i.e., NextPage and ErrorPage) as well as which mail server to use. Be sure to alter the value of the MailServer hidden field to point to a valid SMTP mail server. Figure 21.1 shows how Listing 21.1 looks when rendered by a browser.

Listing 21.1 HTML form that invokes the Form Mailer servlet.

```
<HTML>
<HEAD>
<TITLE>Mail Form</TITLE>
</HEAD>
```

Table 21.1   HTML Form Element Naming Scheme Required by the Form Mailer Servlet

HTML Form Element	Element Name
Mail recipient (**To** field)	To
Carbon copy recipient (**CC** field)	CC
Blind carbon copy recipient (**BCC** field)	BCC
Mail sender (**From** field)	From
Subject text	Subject
Message text	Message
Success URL (page to which client is redirected if mail is sent successfully)	NextPage
Error URL (page to which client is redirected if mail operation fails)	ErrorPage
Mail server (SMTP server used to send mail)	MailServer

```
<BODY>
<H1>Mail Form</H1>
<FORM ACTION="http://localhost:8080/servlet/FormMailer"
  METHOD="POST">

<P>To: <INPUT TYPE="TEXT" NAME="To" SIZE="50"></P>
<P>CC: <INPUT TYPE="TEXT" NAME="CC" SIZE="50"></P>
<P>BCC: <INPUT TYPE="TEXT" NAME="BCC" SIZE="50"></P>
<P>From: <INPUT TYPE="TEXT" NAME="From" SIZE="25"></P>
<P>Subject: <INPUT TYPE="TEXT" NAME="Subject" SIZE="25"></P>
<P>Message:<BR>
<TEXTAREA NAME="Message" ROWS="5" COLS="65"></TEXTAREA></P>

<INPUT TYPE="HIDDEN" NAME="NextPage" VALUE="/mailsent.html">
<INPUT TYPE="HIDDEN" NAME="ErrorPage" VALUE="/mailerror.html">
<INPUT TYPE="HIDDEN" NAME="MailServer" VALUE="localhost">

<P><INPUT TYPE="SUBMIT" NAME="Submit" VALUE="Submit">
<INPUT TYPE="RESET" NAME="Reset" VALUE="Reset"></P>

</FORM>
</BODY>
</HTML>
```

Now that we've seen the HTML form, let's take a look at the `FormMailer` servlet. Contrary to its name, this simple servlet does not actually send the mail. Rather, it collects the information submitted by the HTML form and then invokes the `SmtpMail` class to send the mail using an SMTP server. Separating the mail functions into another class improves reusability by allowing the `SmtpMail` class to be used by other servlets and Java applications. Listing

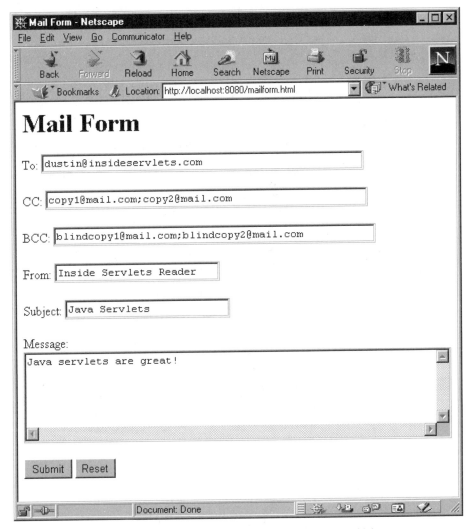

Figure 21.1 Browser's Rendering of the Mail Form Presented in Listing 21.1

21.2 contains the full source code for the FormMailer servlet. In-line documentation is provided within the code.

Listing 21.2 FormMailer servlet source code.

```
import javax.servlet.*;
import javax.servlet.http.*;
import java.io.*;

/**
 * Form mailer servlet. Accepts input from an HTML form and
 * e-mails it to the specified recipient(s). The form should
```

```
 * contain a hidden variable specifying the page to which the
 * client should be redirected after the mail is sent. This
 * servlet requires the SmtpMail class.
 */
public class FormMailer extends HttpServlet
{
  static final String DEFAULT_MAIL_SERVER = "localhost";


  /**
   * doPost processes the information submitted by the client.
   * The to, cc, and bcc addresses may consist of a comma or
   * semi-colon delimited list of e-mail addresses.
   *
   * @param request Client's request to this servlet.
   * @param response Response object.
   * @throws IOException thrown in case of an IO error.
   */
  public void doPost(HttpServletRequest request,
    HttpServletResponse response) throws IOException
  {
    //extract parameter information from HTML form
    String heloHost = request.getServerName(); //local server
    String from = request.getParameter("From");
    String to = request.getParameter("To");
    String cc = request.getParameter("CC");
    String bcc = request.getParameter("BCC");
    String subject = request.getParameter("Subject");
    String message = request.getParameter("Message");
    String nextPage = request.getParameter("NextPage");
    String errorPage = request.getParameter("ErrorPage");
    String mailServer = request.getParameter("MailServer");

    if (mailServer == null) //MailServer parameter was not passed
    {
      mailServer = DEFAULT_MAIL_SERVER; //use default mail server
    }

    //instantiate SMTP mail class
    SmtpMail mail = new SmtpMail(mailServer);

    mail.setMailFrom(from); //mail sender

    mail.setMailTo(to); //mail recipient(s)

    if (cc != null)
    {
      mail.setMailCC(cc); //carbon copy recipient(s)
    }
```

```
      if (bcc != null)
      {
        mail.setMailBCC(bcc); //blind copy recipient(s)
      }

      mail.setMailSubject(subject); //subject of message

      mail.setMailMessage(message); //message body

      mail.setHeloHost(heloHost); //host name used for handshaking

      if (mail.send())
      {
        //mail was sent successfully, redirect client
        response.sendRedirect(nextPage);
      }
      else //mail NOT sent successfully
      {
        //mail was not sent due to error, redirect to error page
        response.sendRedirect(errorPage);
      }
    }


    /**
     * Allows server to identify this servlet.
     *
     * @return Brief description of servlet.
     */
    public String getServletInfo()
    {
      return "Servlet sends e-mail based on info from HTML form";
    }
  }
```

As you can see from Listing 21.2, the FormMailer servlet relies on the SmtpMail class to perform the mail operation. The FormMailer servlet's function is to collect the information submitted by the mail form, instantiate the SmtpMail class, and then call the SmtpMail object's methods in order to transmit the mail. Table 21.2 describes some of the common methods implemented by the SmtpMail class.

Note that the setMailTo(), setMailCC(), and setMailBCC() methods all support multiple e-mail addresses separated by semicolons or commas. Therefore, the **To, CC,** and **BCC** mail form fields may include multiple e-mail addresses (see Figure 21.1). Of course, the SmtpMail class will send a copy of the mail message to all specified addresses. Listing 21.3 presents the complete source code for the SmtpMail class. In-line documentation is provided within the code. Additionally, both the FormMailer servlet and the SmtpMail class are provided on the accompanying CD.

Table 21.2   Common Methods Implemented by the `SmtpMail` Class

Method	Description
`setMailFrom()`	Sets the value that should be displayed in the **From** field of the recipient's mail client.
`setMailTo()`	Sets the e-mail address(es) to which the message should be sent. This field accepts multiple addresses as semicolon- or comma-delimited lists.
`setMailCC()`	Sets the e-mail address(es) to which a carbon copy (CC) of the message should be sent. This field accepts multiple addresses as semicolon- or comma-delimited lists.
`setMailBCC()`	Sets the e-mail address(es) to which a blind carbon copy (BCC) of the message should be sent. This field accepts multiple addresses as semicolon- or comma-delimited lists.
`setMailSubject()`	Sets the subject that should be displayed in the **Subject** field of the recipient's mail client.
`setMailMessage()`	Sets the body of the mail message.
`setHeloHost()`	Sets the name of the host machine that wishes to communicate with the SMTP server.
`send()`	Sends the e-mail message.

NOTE: This chapter presents a custom SMTP mail class in order to educate the reader about the SMTP protocol. This class is simple, functional, and appropriate for many e-mail applications. Note, however, that a standard Java e-mail package, known as JavaMail, is available from Sun Microsystems. This package provides industrial-strength messaging functionality, including implementations of both the IMAP and SMTP protocols. You can learn more about JavaMail at *http://java.sun.com/products/javamail/*.

Listing 21.3   `SmtpMail` class source code.

```java
import java.io.*;
import java.net.*;
import java.util.*;

/**
 * SmtpMail is a simple implementation of the SMTP protocol used
 * to send electronic mail.
 *
 * @author Dustin R. Callaway
 */
```

```java
public class SmtpMail
{
  private static final int DEFAULT_MAIL_PORT = 25;
  private static final int MAX_LINE_LENGTH = 80;

  private int mailPort = DEFAULT_MAIL_PORT;

  private String mailServer = "";
  private String mailFrom = "";
  private String mailMessage = "";
  private String mailSubject = "";
  private String heloHost = "";
  private String errorMessage = "";

  private Vector mailTo = null;
  private Vector mailCC = null;
  private Vector mailBCC = null;

  private BufferedReader readSocket;
  private PrintWriter writeSocket;
  private Socket socket = null;


  /**
   * Default constructor.
   */
  public SmtpMail()
  {
    mailTo = new Vector();
    mailCC = new Vector();
    mailBCC = new Vector();

    try
    {
      //determine name of the local machine for HELO handshake
      heloHost = InetAddress.getLocalHost().toString();
    }
    catch (UnknownHostException e)
    {
      //if unable to determine name, default to localhost
      heloHost = "localhost";
    }
  }


  /**
   * Constructor requires the resolvable hostname or IP address
   * of the SMTP mail server.
   *
   * @param mailServer Resolvable hostname or IP address of an
   *  SMTP mail server.
   */
```

```java
public SmtpMail(String mailServer)
{
  this();

  this.mailServer = mailServer;
}


/**
 * Returns the hostname or IP address of the mail server.
 *
 * @return Hostname or IP address of the mail server.
 */
public String getMailServer()
{
  return mailServer;
}


/**
 * Sets the location of the mail server.
 *
 * @param mailServer Hostname or IP address of the mail server.
 */
public void setMailServer(String mailServer)
{
  this.mailServer = mailServer;
}


/**
 * Returns the port on which the mail server is listening.
 *
 * @return Port number on which the mail server is listening.
 */
public int getMailPort()
{
  return mailPort;
}


/**
 * Sets the mail port on which the mail server is listening.
 *
 * @param mailPort Port number on which the mail server is
 *  listening.
 */
public void setMailPort(int mailPort)
{
  this.mailPort = mailPort;
}
```

```
/**
 * Returns the sender's e-mail address.
 *
 * @return Sender's e-mail address.
 */
public String getMailFrom()
{
  return mailFrom;
}


/**
 * Sets the sender's e-mail address.
 *
 * @param mailFrom Sender's e-mail address.
 */
public void setMailFrom(String mailFrom)
{
  this.mailFrom = mailFrom;
}


/**
 * Returns a vector containing e-mail addresses of all
 * recipients.
 *
 * @return Vector containing e-mail addresses of all
 *    recipients.
 */
public Vector getMailTo()
{
  return mailTo;
}


/**
 * Adds a single e-mail address to list of recipients.
 *
 * @param address E-mail address to add to list of recipients.
 */
public void addMailTo(String address)
{
  mailTo.add(address);
}


/**
 * Populates the recipients list from either a single e-mail
 * address or a comma-delimited list of addresses.
 *
 * @param address E-mail address or comma-delimited list of
 *    addresses to add to recipient list.
 */
```

```java
public void setMailTo(String address)
{
  String delimiter = ",";

  if (address.indexOf(";") != -1)
  {
    delimiter = ";";
  }

  StringTokenizer addressTokens = new StringTokenizer(address,
    delimiter);

  //iterate through all of the addresses in the comma-delimited
  //list adding each one to the recipients Vector
  while (addressTokens.hasMoreTokens())
  {
    addMailTo(addressTokens.nextToken());
  }
}


/**
 * Clears the recipient list.
 */
public void clearMailTo()
{
  mailTo.clear();
}


/**
 * Returns a vector containing e-mail addresses of all carbon
 * copy recipients.
 *
 * @return Vector containing e-mail addresses of all carbon
 *   copy recipients.
 */
public Vector getMailCC()
{
  return mailCC;
}


/**
 * Adds a single e-mail address to list of carbon copy
 * recipients.
 *
 * @param address E-mail address to add to list of carbon copy
 *   recipients.
 */
public void addMailCC(String ccAddress)
{
```

```
      mailCC.add(ccAddress);
    }


    /**
     * Populates the carbon copy recipients list from either a
     * single e-mail address or a comma-delimited list of
     * addresses.
     *
     * @param address E-mail address or comma-delimited list of
     *   addresses to add to the carbon copy recipient list.
     */
    public void setMailCC(String ccAddress)
    {
      String delimiter = ",";

      if (ccAddress.indexOf(";") != -1)
      {
        delimiter = ";";
      }

      StringTokenizer ccAddressTokens = new StringTokenizer(
        ccAddress, delimiter);

      //iterate through all of the cc addresses in the comma-
      //delimited list adding each one to the recipients Vector
      while (ccAddressTokens.hasMoreTokens())
      {
        addMailCC(ccAddressTokens.nextToken());
      }
    }


    /**
     * Clears the carbon copy recipient list.
     */
    public void clearMailCC()
    {
      mailCC.clear();
    }


    /**
     * Returns a vector containing e-mail addresses of all blind
     * carbon copy recipients.
     *
     * @return Vector containing e-mail addresses of all blind
     *   carbon copy recipients.
     */
    public Vector getMailBCC()
    {
      return mailBCC;
    }
```

```
/**
 * Adds a single e-mail address to list of blind carbon copy
 * recipients.
 *
 * @param address E-mail address to add to list of blind carbon
 *   copy recipients.
 */
public void addMailBCC(String bccAddress)
{
  mailBCC.add(bccAddress);
}


/**
 * Populates the blind carbon copy recipients list from either
 * a single e-mail address or a comma-delimited list of
 * addresses.
 *
 * @param address E-mail address or comma-delimited list of
 *   addresses to add to the blind carbon copy recipient list.
 */
public void setMailBCC(String bccAddress)
{
  String delimiter = ",";

  if (bccAddress.indexOf(";") != -1)
  {
    delimiter = ";";
  }

  StringTokenizer bccAddressTokens = new StringTokenizer(
    bccAddress, delimiter);

  //iterate through all of the bcc addresses in the comma-
  //delimited list adding each one to the recipients Vector
  while (bccAddressTokens.hasMoreTokens())
  {
    addMailBCC(bccAddressTokens.nextToken());
  }
}


/**
 * Clears the recipient list.
 */
public void clearMailBCC()
{
  mailBCC.clear();
}


/**
 * Returns the subject of the current message.
 *
```

```
  * @return Subject of the current message.
  */
public String getMailSubject()
{
  return mailSubject;
}


/**
 * Sets the subject of the current message.
 *
 * @param mailSubject Subject of the current message.
 */
public void setMailSubject(String mailSubject)
{
  this.mailSubject = mailSubject;
}


/**
 * Gets the current mail message.
 *
 * @return Current mail message.
 */
public String getMailMessage()
{
  return mailMessage;
}


/**
 * Sets the current mail message.
 *
 * @param mailMessage Current mail message.
 */
public void setMailMessage(String mailMessage)
{
  this.mailMessage = mailMessage;
}


/**
 * Returns the name of this machine.
 *
 * @return Name of this machine sent in the HELO handshake.
 */
public String getHeloHost()
{
  return heloHost;
}
```

```
/**
 * Sets the name of this server to send in HELO SMTP handshake.
 *
 * @param heloHost Name of this server used in HELO handshake.
 */
public void setHeloHost(String heloHost)
{
  this.heloHost = heloHost;
}


/**
 * Returns an error message in case an exception is thrown.
 *
 * @return Error message.
 */
public String getErrorMessage()
{
  return errorMessage;
}


/**
 * Sends the mail message using the current settings.
 */
public boolean send()
{
  return sendMessage();
}


/**
 * Sends the specified message using the current settings.
 *
 * @param mailMessage Message to send.
 */
public boolean send(String mailMessage)
{
  this.mailMessage = mailMessage;

  return sendMessage();
}


/**
 * Sends a mail message using the current settings.
 *
 * @return True indicates success.
 */
private boolean sendMessage()
{
  errorMessage = "";
```

```java
      if (mailServer.equals(""))
      {
        errorMessage = "SmtpMail Error: No mail server";

        return false;
      }

      try
      {
        openSocket();         //open socket to mail server
        getInputStream();     //get handle to input stream
        getOutputStream();    //get handle to output stream
        connect();            //SMTP handshaking
        sendEnvelope();       //send addressing information
        sendData();           //send message content
        disconnect();         //end SMTP session
      }
      catch(Exception e)
      {
        errorMessage = e.toString();
      }
      finally
      {
        closeOutputStream();
        closeInputStream();
        closeSocket();

        return (errorMessage == ""); //return true if no errors
      }
  }


  /**
   * Opens a socket connection to the mail server.
   *
   * @throws Exception if unable to open socket to mail server.
   */
  private void openSocket() throws Exception
  {
    socket = new Socket(mailServer, mailPort);
  }


  /**
   * Closes the socket connection with the mail server.
   */
  private void closeSocket()
  {
    if (socket != null)
    {
      try
      {
        socket.close();
      }
```

```
        catch (IOException e)
        {
        }
      }
  }


  /**
   * Opens an input stream from the mail server.
   *
   * @throws Exception if there is a problem opening the input
   *   stream from the mail server.
   */
  private void getInputStream() throws Exception
  {
    readSocket = new BufferedReader(new InputStreamReader(
      socket.getInputStream()));
  }


  /**
   * Closes the input stream from the mail server.
   */
  private void closeInputStream()
  {
    if (readSocket != null)
    {
      try
      {
        readSocket.close();
      }
      catch (IOException e)
      {
      }
    }
  }


  /**
   * Opens the output stream to the mail server.
   *
   * @throws Exception if there is a problem opening the output
   *   stream to the mail server.
   */
  private void getOutputStream() throws Exception
  {
    writeSocket = new PrintWriter(socket.getOutputStream(),
      true);
  }


  /**
   * Closes the output stream to the mail server.
   */
```

```java
private void closeOutputStream()
{
  if (writeSocket != null)
  {
    writeSocket.close();
  }
}


/**
 * Initiates SMTP session with initial handshaking.
 *
 * @throws Exception if mail server returns an unexpected
 *   response.
 */
private void connect() throws Exception
{
  getResponse("220");
  sendCommand("HELO " + heloHost, "250");
}


/**
 * Ends the SMTP session
 *
 * @throws Exception if mail server returns an unexpected
 *   response.
 */
private void disconnect() throws Exception
{
  sendCommand("QUIT", "221");
}


/**
 * Sends addressing information for this message to the mail
 * server.
 *
 * @throws Exception if mail server returns an unexpected
 *   response.
 */
private void sendEnvelope() throws Exception
{
  String value = "";

  if (mailTo.isEmpty())
  {
    throw new Exception("SmtpMail Error: No recipients");
  }

  sendCommand("MAIL FROM: " + getEmail(mailFrom), "250");
```

```
      //send list of recipients
      Enumeration enum = mailTo.elements();
      while (enum.hasMoreElements())
      {
        value = getEmail((String)enum.nextElement());

        sendCommand("RCPT TO: " + value, "250");
      }

      //send list of carbon copy recipients
      enum = mailCC.elements();
      while (enum.hasMoreElements())
      {
        value = getEmail((String)enum.nextElement());

        sendCommand("RCPT TO: " + value, "250");
      }

      //send list of blind carbon copy recipients
      enum = mailBCC.elements();
      while (enum.hasMoreElements())
      {
        value = getEmail((String)enum.nextElement());

        sendCommand("RCPT TO: " + value, "250");
      }
    }


    /**
     * Parses out the email portion of an address in the following
     * format: Dustin Callaway <dustin@sourcestream.com>
     * This format allows a mail client to display the user's name
     * in the From and To fields rather than email addresses.
     *
     * @param address Name/email of a to, cc, or bcc recipient.
     * @return Email portion of the name/email string.
     */
    private String getEmail(String address)
    {
      int beginEmail = address.indexOf("<");

      if (beginEmail != -1)
      {
        int endEmail = address.indexOf(">");

        if ((endEmail == -1) && (endEmail < beginEmail))
        {
          address = address.substring(beginEmail + 1);
        }
        else
        {
```

```
      address = address.substring(beginEmail + 1, endEmail);
    }
  }

  return address;
}


/**
 * Sends the message content to the mail server. Send Date,
 * From, To, CC, and Subject headings to allow mail client to
 * display them.
 *
 * @throws Exception if mail server returns an unexpected
 *   response.
 */
private void sendData() throws Exception
{
  String value = "";

  sendCommand("DATA", "354");
  writeSocket.println("Date: " + new Date());
  writeSocket.println("From: " + mailFrom);

  //send list of recipients
  Enumeration enum = mailTo.elements();
  while (enum.hasMoreElements())
  {
    value = (String)enum.nextElement();

    writeSocket.println("To: " + value);
  }

  //send list of carbon copy recipients
  enum = mailCC.elements();
  while (enum.hasMoreElements())
  {
    value = (String)enum.nextElement();

    writeSocket.println("CC: " + value);
  }

  writeSocket.println("Subject: " + mailSubject);
  writeSocket.println();

  //wrap all lines in message that exceed MAX_LINE_LENGTH
  mailMessage = wordWrap(mailMessage, MAX_LINE_LENGTH);

  //create a buffered reader to read message one line at a time
  BufferedReader messageReader = new BufferedReader(
    new StringReader(mailMessage));

  String line = "";
```

```
  //send each line of the message to the mail server
  while((line = messageReader.readLine()) != null)
  {
    if (line.equals("."))
    {
      line = ".."; //prevents user from ending message
    }

    writeSocket.println(line);
  }

  writeSocket.println();    //send blank line
  sendCommand(".", "250"); //end message with single period
}


/**
 * Sends a command to the mail server and receives a reply.
 *
 * @param command Command to send to mail server.
 * @param expectedResponse Response expected from mail server
 *   if no errors occur.
 * @throws Exception if mail server returns an unexpected
 *   response.
 */
private String sendCommand(String command, String
  expectedResponse) throws Exception
{
  writeSocket.println(command);

  return getResponse(expectedResponse);
}


/**
 * Receives a response from the mail server.
 *
 * @param expectedResponse Value expected from mail server in
 *   response to prior command.
 * @return Response from mail server.
 * @throws Exception if mail server returns an unexpected
 *   response.
 */
private String getResponse(String expectedResponse) throws
  Exception
{
  String response = readSocket.readLine(); //read response

  //if response is not what we expected, throw exception
  if (!response.startsWith(expectedResponse))
  {
    errorMessage = "SmtpMail Error: " + response;
    throw new Exception(errorMessage);
  }
```

```
      //discard the rest of the valid response lines
      while(response.startsWith(expectedResponse + "-"))
      {
        response = readSocket.readLine();
      }

      return response;
  }


  /**
   * Wraps message lines longer than specified length.
   *
   * @param message Message to wrap.
   * @param lineLength Maximum length of line before wrapping.
   */
  private String wordWrap(String message, int lineLength)
  {
    String word;
    int column=0;
    int length;

    StringBuffer messageBuffer = new StringBuffer();

    //tokenize the message by spaces (break into single words)
    StringTokenizer words = new StringTokenizer(message, " ");

    while (words.hasMoreTokens()) //iterate through each word
    {
      word = words.nextToken();

      length = word.length();

      //word exceeds line length, print on next line
      if (column > 0 && (column + length) > lineLength)
      {
        messageBuffer.append("\n" + word + " ");
        column = length + 1;
      }
      else if (word.endsWith("\n")) //word ends current line
      {
        messageBuffer.append(word);
        column = 0;
      }
      else //word does not exceed line length or end line
      {
        messageBuffer.append(word + " ");
        column += length + 1;
      }
    }

    return messageBuffer.toString(); //return wrapped message
  }
}
```

CHAPTER 22

File Upload Servlet

The File Upload servlet enables the client to upload files to the server via a simple HTML form. This servlet requires a Web browser that supports the form-based upload specification documented in RFC 1867. Fortunately, the current versions of Netscape Navigator and Microsoft Internet Explorer both support form-based file uploads.

Let's start by briefly reviewing form-based uploads. An HTML form can specify that a file is to be uploaded to the server by indicating an encoding type of `multipart/form-data` and including an `INPUT` HTML element of type `FILE`. The following HTML demonstrates a simple form that facilitates file uploads.

```
<FORM ENCTYPE="multipart/form-data"
  ACTION="http://localhost:8080/servlet/UploadServlet"
  METHOD="POST">

<B>File Name: </B>
<INPUT TYPE="FILE" NAME="Filename" MAXLENGTH=255><P>
<INPUT TYPE="SUBMIT" Value="Upload">

</FORM>
```

Notice that the form's encoding type (`ENCTYPE`) is set to `multipart/form-data`. This encoding type tells the browser that the data corresponding to each form element should be separated within the request (see Listing 22.2). The data corresponding to each form element is separated by a unique string known as a *boundary marker*. This marker allows the server to parse the request and extract the data from each element. Also notice the new `FILE` form element. This `INPUT` element is similar to a normal text box except that a **Browse** button is displayed to its immediate right (see Figure 22.1). The **Browse** button displays a standard file dialog box. After the user chooses a file, the text box portion of the `FILE` element is populated with the path and

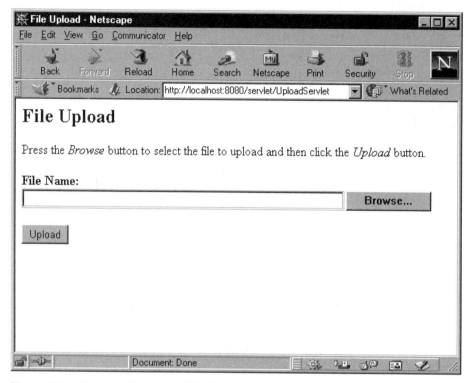

Figure 22.1   Browser's Rendering of File Upload Servlet's Generic Upload Form

filename of the selected file. Finally, when the form is submitted, the browser packages the data that correspond to each form element into separate sections (or parts) within the request and sends the request to the server (see Listing 22.2). The data that comprise the selected file are included in one of these sections.

NOTE: The browser will package each section of the multipart request in the order that the form elements appear on the HTML page. However, the order of these elements is not critical and does not affect the operation of the Form Upload servlet.

To provide maximum flexibility, several File Upload servlet options can be set by servlet initialization parameters. This allows the servlet to be customized without recompiling. Table 22.1 describes each File Upload servlet initialization parameter.

Table 22.1 Names and Descriptions of File Upload Servlet Initialization Parameters

Element Name	Description
SaveDirectory	Specifies the directory to which the uploaded file should be written. The value of this element should always end with a file separator (e.g., "/") but not begin with one (e.g., "temp/"). If this initialization parameter is not set, uploaded files will be written to the root of the file system by default (i.e., "/").
SuccessMessage	Specifies the message that should be returned to the client in the event that the upload operation succeeds.
ErrorMessage	Specifies the message that should be returned to the client in the event that the upload operation fails.

In addition to the initialization parameters described in Table 22.1, the File Upload servlet can also be customized through a hidden field on the HTML form. That is, a hidden field named SuccessPage can be used to specify the page to which the client should be redirected after the upload operation succeeds. The SuccessPage variable may consist of an absolute or relative URL. If no SuccessPage parameter is passed by the HTML form, the text specified by the SuccessMessage initialization parameter is returned to the client.

The File Upload servlet can stand alone or be used in conjunction with a customized file upload HTML form. This is because the File Upload servlet generates its own generic upload HTML form in response to any HTTP GET request (see Figure 22.1). Therefore, it is possible to retrieve a basic upload form by simply issuing a request directly to the upload servlet from a browser. The generic upload form returned by the servlet is preconfigured to post the form data back to the servlet. Once the form is posted, the servlet container will invoke the servlet's doPost() method in order to process the upload. This generic form includes a SuccessPage hidden variable having a value of /success.html. This hidden variable conveys to the servlet that upon completion of the upload the client should be redirected to the success.html file located in the server's document root.

In addition to the generic form provided by the File Upload servlet, a custom file upload HTML document may be used. For example, Listing 22.1 provides a sample HTML form that implements form-based file uploads. The HTML form within this document is posted to the UploadServlet (see the <FORM> tag's ACTION attribute). Also, notice the SuccessPage hidden variable that tells the servlet where to redirect the client when the upload is complete. Figure 22.2 illustrates how this document is rendered by a browser.

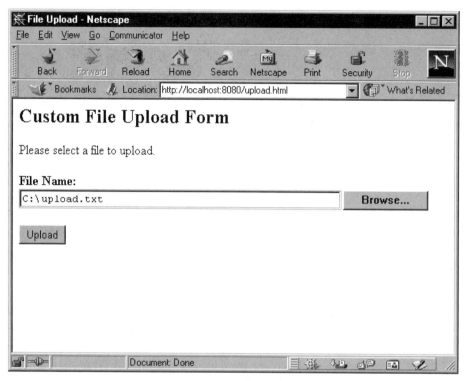

Figure 22.2   Browser's Rendering of Listing 22.1 after a File Has Been Selected

Listing 22.1   HTML document that implements form-based file uploads.

```
<HTML>
<HEAD>
<TITLE>File Upload</TITLE>
</HEAD>
<BODY>
<H2>Custom File Upload Form</H2>
<FORM ENCTYPE="multipart/form-data"
  ACTION="http://localhost:8080/servlet/UploadServlet"
  METHOD="POST">

Please select a file to upload.<P>
<B>File Name:</B> <INPUT TYPE="FILE" NAME="Filename" SIZE="50"
  MAXLENGTH="255"><P>
<INPUT TYPE="SUBMIT" VALUE="Upload">
<INPUT TYPE="HIDDEN" NAME="SuccessPage" VALUE="/continue.html">

</FORM>
</BODY>
</HTML>
```

Now that we have seen how form-based file uploads are accomplished from the HTML side, let's take a look at the format of the `multipart/form-data` request constructed by the browser. Listing 22.2 shows the request generated by the browser when the HTML form presented in Listing 22.1 is submitted (including the HTTP headers).

Listing 22.2   Format of the `multipart/form-data` request.

```
POST /servlet/UploadServlet HTTP/1.0
Connection: Keep-Alive
User-Agent: Mozilla/4.51 [en] (WinNT; I)
Host: localhost:8080
Accept: image/gif, image/x-xbitmap, image/jpeg, image/pjpeg, */*
Accept-Encoding: gzip
Accept-Language: en
Accept-Charset: iso-8859-1,*,utf-8
Content-type: multipart/form-data; boundary=--------------------
      -------7763320785010
Content-Length: 425


----------------------------7763320785010
Content-Disposition: form-data; name="Filename"; file-
   name="C:\upload.txt"
Content-Type: text/plain

This text comprises the entire contents of the sample upload file
   called "upload.txt" read from the "C:\" directory.
----------------------------7763320785010
Content-Disposition: form-data; name="SuccessPage"

/continue.html
----------------------------7763320785010--
```

Listing 22.2 should give you a good idea of how the browser packages a file upload request. The file information is stored in the first part of this request immediately following the first boundary marker (since the `FILE` element appears first on the page). The following part contains the name and value of the HTML form's hidden variable. Also, keep in mind that the upload file could have just as easily been composed of binary data rather than ASCII text.

The boundary marker is identified in the `Content-Type` HTTP header field following the "boundary=" text. The boundary marker for this request is:

```
----------------------------7763320785010
```

This marker is used by the File Upload servlet to find the beginning and end of the upload file and to extract the values of hidden variables or other form elements.

NOTE: Uploading data can be taxing on server resources. For this reason, the sample servlet presented here prevents clients from uploading files bigger than 1MB. However, this setting can be configured by changing the MAX_SIZE variable. It is wise to limit uploaded files to a reasonable size based on server resources.

The bulk of the file upload process is not actually performed by the File Upload servlet. Rather, the File Upload servlet instantiates a utility class called MultipartRequestParser. It is this class that receives the uploaded file and writes it to disk. In fact, the functionality provided by the File Upload servlet consists primarily of checking the length of the uploaded file, instantiating the MultipartRequestParser to handle the upload operation, and forwarding the user to the correct location when the upload is complete. Moving the upload implementation into the MultipartRequestParser class improves reusability by making this functionality accessible to other servlets. Listing 22.3 contains the full source code for the File Upload servlet. In-line documentation is provided within the code.

Listing 22.3   Complete source code for the File Upload servlet.

```java
import javax.servlet.*;
import javax.servlet.http.*;
import java.io.*;
import java.util.*;

/**
 * Upload servlet works in conjunction with a browser's form-
 * based file upload capability to allow the client to transfer
 * a file (binary or ASCII) to the server which is then stored
 * in the server's file system. This servlet uses the
 * MultipartRequestParser class to parse the upload request and
 * store the file.
 *
 * @author Dustin R. Callaway
 */
public class UploadServlet extends HttpServlet
{
    //indicates the action to take if the upload file is too large
    // 0 - throw IOException
    // 1 - send MAX_SIZE_MSG to client
    // 2 - redirect client to MAX_SIZE_REDIRECT
    private static final int MAX_SIZE_ACTION = 0;
    private static final String MAX_SIZE_MSG =
        "Sorry, that file exceeds the maximum file size limit.";
    private static final String MAX_SIZE_REDIRECT = "/TooBig.html";
```

```
//default maximum allowable file size is 1MB
private static final int MAX_SIZE = 1024 * 1024;

//names of initialization and web parameters
private static final String SAVE_DIRECTORY = "SaveDirectory";
private static final String SUCCESS_MESSAGE = "SuccessMessage";
private static final String ERROR_MESSAGE = "ErrorMessage";
private static final String SUCCESS_PAGE = "SuccessPage";

String fileSeparator;
String saveDirectory;
String successMessage;
String errorMessage;


/**
 * Called when the first time the servlet loads. This method
 * initializes the saveDirectory, successMessage, and
 * errorMessage variables using either an initialization
 * parameter (if it exists) or a hard-coded default.
 *
 * @exception ServletException
 */
public void init() throws ServletException
{
  //get the file separator for the current operating system
  fileSeparator = System.getProperty("file.separator");

  //get the directory to which to save files
  saveDirectory = getInitParameter(SAVE_DIRECTORY);
  if (saveDirectory == null)
  {
    saveDirectory = fileSeparator; //default to root directory
  }

  //Get message to display when upload is complete. Used only
  //if a success redirect page is not supplied by upload form.
  successMessage = getInitParameter(SUCCESS_MESSAGE);
  if (successMessage == null)
  {
    //default success message
    successMessage = "File upload complete!";
  }

  //Get message to display when an error occurs.
  errorMessage = getInitParameter(ERROR_MESSAGE);
  if (errorMessage == null)
  {
    //default error message
    errorMessage = "File upload failed. Error: ";
  }
}
```

```java
/**
 * Handles all HTTP GET requests. The upload servlet returns a
 * generic upload HTML form in response to all GET requests.
 * Upon success, this form indicates that the servlet should
 * redirect to a file called "/success.html" located at the web
 * server's root. Though this form may be used, in most cases a
 * custom upload form should be created that posts to this
 * servlet.
 *
 * @param request HttpServletRequest
 * @param response HttpServletResponse
 * @exception ServletException
 * @exception IOException
 */
public void doGet(HttpServletRequest request,
  HttpServletResponse response) throws ServletException,
  IOException
{
  response.setContentType("text/html");

  PrintWriter out = new PrintWriter(
    response.getOutputStream());

  out.println("<HTML>");
  out.println("<HEAD><TITLE>File Upload</TITLE></HEAD>");
  out.println("<BODY>");
  out.println("<H2>File Upload</H2>");

  //the encoding type is multipart/form-data for file uploads
  out.println("<FORM ENCTYPE=\"multipart/form-data\" ");
  out.println("METHOD=\"POST\">");

  out.println("Press the <I>Browse</I> button to select the ");
  out.println("file to upload and then click the ");
  out.println("<I>Upload</I> button.<P>");

  //these lines add the file box and browse button to the form
  out.println("<B>File Name:</B> <INPUT TYPE=\"FILE\" ");
  out.println("NAME=\"Filename\" SIZE=\"50\" ");
  out.println("MAXLENGTH=\"255\"><P>");

  out.println("<INPUT TYPE=\"SUBMIT\" VALUE=\"Upload\">");

  //these lines indicate where to redirect in case of success
  out.println("<INPUT TYPE=\"HIDDEN\" NAME=\"SuccessPage\" ");
  out.println("VALUE=\"/success.html\">");

  out.println("</FORM></BODY></HTML>");
  out.close();
}
```

```
/**
 * Process all HTTP POST requests. This method makes sure that
 * the POSTed request is of type multipart/form-data and that
 * the uploaded file is not too large. It then instantiates the
 * MultipartRequestParser to parse the request and write the
 * file to the file system. It then either displays a success
 * message or redirects the user to the success HTML page
 * submitted by the upload HTML form.
 *
 * @param request HttpServletRequest
 * @param response HttpServletResponse
 * @exception ServletException
 * @exception IOException
 */
public void doPost(HttpServletRequest request,
  HttpServletResponse response) throws ServletException,
  IOException
{
  response.setContentType("text/html");
  PrintWriter out = response.getWriter();

  try
  {
    String contentType = request.getContentType();

    //make sure content type is multipart/form-data
    if(contentType != null && contentType.startsWith(
      "multipart/form-data"))
    {
      int contentLength = request.getContentLength();

      //make sure request is not larger than max upload size
      if (contentLength > MAX_SIZE)
      {
        if (MAX_SIZE_ACTION == 0) //throw exception
        {
          //Upload file is too large. We cannot return a
          //message to the client until we have read the entire
          //request. Since we don't want to waste resources
          //reading the entire request, simply throw an
          //IOException.
          throw new IOException("File too large to upload.");
        }
        else if (MAX_SIZE_ACTION == 1) //return message
        {
          //get handle to request's input stream
          ServletInputStream in = request.getInputStream();

          //read and discard the entire request
          in.skip(contentLength);
```

```
          //send a brief error message to the client
          out.println(MAX_SIZE_MSG);
          out.flush();
        }
        else //redirect client
        {
          //redirect to the MAX_SIZE_REDIRECT URL
          response.sendRedirect(MAX_SIZE_REDIRECT);
        }

        return; //stop processing request
      }

      //instantiate class to parse multipart/form-data request
      MultipartRequestParser mrp = new MultipartRequestParser(
        request, saveDirectory);

      mrp.parseRequest(); //parse the request

      //get hashmap containing all web variables from request
      HashMap webVars = mrp.getWebVars();

      //get success page URL from web variables
      String successPage = (String)webVars.get(SUCCESS_PAGE);

      if (successPage == null)
      {
        //no success page variable, send default message
        out.println(successMessage);
      }
      else
      {
        //success page variable exists, redirect to page
        response.sendRedirect(successPage);
      }
    }
    else //request is not multipart/form-data
    {
      //send error message to client
      out.println("<H2>Request not multipart/form-data.</H2>");
    }
  }
  catch (Exception e)
  {
    out.println(errorMessage + e);
    log("UploadServlet Error: " + e);
  }
  finally
  {
    out.close();
  }
}
```

```
/**
 * Returns information about this servlet to the server.
 *
 * @return Brief description of this servlet
 */
public String getServletInfo()
{
  return "UploadServlet allows the client to upload files.";
}
}
```

As you can see from Listing 22.3, the `MultipartRequestParser` class is extremely easy to use. This class's constructor accepts two arguments—a `ServletRequest` object and a `String` specifying the directory to which the upload file should be written. Therefore, the `MultipartRequestParser` can be instantiated from within the `service()`, `doGet()`, or `doPost()` method, like this:

```
MultipartRequestParser mrp = new MultipartRequestParser(request,
  "/home/upload");
```

Fortunately, the `MultipartRequestParser` is just as easy to use as it is to create. To perform the upload operation, call the `parseRequest()` method, like this:

```
mrp.parseRequest();
```

This method parses the multipart request, writes the uploaded file to disk, and creates a `HashMap` containing the names and values of all Web variables passed by hidden fields or other form elements. To retrieve this `HashMap`, call the `getWebVars()` method, like this:

```
HashMap webVars = mrp.getWebVars();
```

Listing 22.4 contains the complete source code for the `MultipartRequest-Parser` class. In-line documentation is provided within the code.

Listing 22.4 Source code for the `MultipartRequestParser` class.

```
import java.io.*;
import javax.servlet.*;
import javax.servlet.http.*;
import java.util.*;

/**
 * MultipartRequestParser reads a multipart/form-data HTTP
 * request, writes any files to disk, and stores all web
 * variables in a hashmap.
 *
 * @author Dustin R. Callaway
 */
```

```java
public class MultipartRequestParser
{
  private static final int BUFFER_SIZE = 8 * 1024; //8K buffer

  private ServletRequest request;
  private ServletInputStream in;
  private MultipartStreamReader msr;
  private String saveDirectory = "";
  private String boundary;
  private String fileSeparator;
  private HashMap webVars;


  /**
   * Constructor that initializes all instance variables.
   *
   * @param request ServletRequest
   * @param saveDirectory Directory to which to save files
   * @exception IOException
   */
  public MultipartRequestParser(ServletRequest request,
    String saveDirectory) throws IOException
  {
    this.request = request;
    this.saveDirectory = saveDirectory;
    in = request.getInputStream();
    msr = new MultipartStreamReader();
    fileSeparator = System.getProperty("file.separator");

    //instantiate hashmap to store web variables
    webVars = new HashMap();
  }


  /**
   * Returns the web variables hashmap.
   *
   * @return HashMap containing all of the web variables.
   */
  public HashMap getWebVars()
  {
    return webVars;
  }


  /**
   * Gets the boundary marker, moves past the first boundary,
   * and calls processParts() to process each part of the
   * request.
   *
   * @exception Exception
   */
```

```
public void parseRequest() throws Exception
{
  String contentType = request.getContentType();

  //make sure the request is multipart/form-data
  if (!contentType.startsWith("multipart/form-data"))
  {
    throw new Exception("Request not multipart/form-data.");
  }

  //get the boundary marker
  boundary = getBoundary(contentType);

  findNextBoundary(); //move past first boundary

  processParts(); //process each part of the multipart request
}


/**
 * Processes each part of the multipart/form-data request.
 *
 * @exception Exception
 */
private void processParts() throws Exception
{
  //get the web variable name and filename from the request
  ContentDisposition disposition = getDisposition();

  //loop through all of the parts of the request
  while (!disposition.getName().equals(""))
  {
    if (disposition.getFilename().equals(""))
    {
      //if filename is empty, this part must be a web variable
      storeVariable(disposition.getName());
    }
    else
    {
      //filename exists so this part is a file being uploaded
      storeFile(disposition);
    }

    //get name of next web variable and filename
    disposition = getDisposition();
  }
}


/**
 * Reads the name and value of the web variable and places it
 * in the web variable hashmap.
 *
```

```
 * @param name String containing the name of the variable to
 *   store
 * @exception IOException
 */
private void storeVariable(String name) throws IOException
{
  findEmptyLine(); //move past empty line

  webVars.put(name, msr.readLine()); //add variable to hashmap

  findNextBoundary(); //move past next boundary
}


/**
 * Reads a file from the multipart/form-data request and writes
 * it to the file system.
 *
 * @param disposition ContentDisposition object containing the
 *   name of the web variable and filename
 */
private void storeFile(ContentDisposition disposition) throws
  IOException
{
  FileOutputStream fileOut = null;

  try
  {
    //create file object and output stream for writing file
    File file = new File(saveDirectory +
      disposition.getFilename());
    fileOut = new FileOutputStream(file);

    findEmptyLine(); //move past empty line

    int bytesRead = 0;

    boolean rnAddFlag = false;

    byte[] bytes = new byte[BUFFER_SIZE];

    //read entire upload file from request in 8K chunks
    while ((bytesRead = in.readLine(bytes, 0, BUFFER_SIZE))
      != -1)
    {
      //pre-check for boundary marker
      if (bytes[0] == '-' && bytes[1] == '-' && bytes[2] == '-'
        && bytesRead < 500)
      {
        //this may be boundary marker, get string to make sure
        String line = new String(bytes, 0, bytesRead,
          "ISO8859_1");
```

```
        if (line.startsWith(boundary))
        {
          //we're at the boundary marker so we're done reading
          break;
        }
      }

      //we read a \r\n from the previous iteration that needs
      //to be written to the file
      if (rnAddFlag)
      {
        fileOut.write('\r');
        fileOut.write('\n');
        rnAddFlag = false;
      }

      //since ServletInputStream adds its own \r\n to the last
      //line read, don't write it to the file until we're sure
      //that this is not the last line
      if (bytesRead > 2 && bytes[bytesRead-2] == '\r' &&
        bytes[bytesRead-1] == '\n')
      {
        bytesRead = bytesRead - 2;
        rnAddFlag = true;
      }

      fileOut.write(bytes, 0, bytesRead); //write data to file
    }
  }
  finally
  {
    fileOut.close();
  }
}


/**
 * Returns the boundary marker from the Content-Type header.
 *
 * @param contentType The value passed in the Content-Type
 *  header
 * @return String containing the boundary marker
 */
private String getBoundary(String contentType)
{
  String boundaryMarker = "boundary=";

  int boundaryIndex = contentType.indexOf(boundaryMarker) +
    boundaryMarker.length();

  //the boundary in the Content-Type lacks a leading "--"
  boundaryMarker = "--" + contentType.substring(boundaryIndex);
```

```
    return boundaryMarker;
}


/**
 * Moves past the next boundary marker.
 *
 * @exception IOException
 */
private void findNextBoundary() throws IOException
{
  String line = msr.readLine();

  //keep reading until the end of stream or boundary marker
  while (line != null && !line.startsWith(boundary))
  {
    line = msr.readLine();
  }
}


/**
 * Reads the name of web variable and filename from the
 * Content-Disposition header and stores it in a new
 * ContentDisposition object.
 *
 * @return ContentDisposition object with name of web variable
 *   and filename
 * @exception Exception
 */
private ContentDisposition getDisposition() throws Exception
{
  //read first line of this part of the multipart request
  String line = msr.readLine();

  //find the Content-Disposition header
  while (line != null && !line.equals("") &&
    !line.toLowerCase().startsWith("content-disposition:"))
  {
    line = msr.readLine();
  }

  ContentDisposition disposition = new ContentDisposition();

  if (line == null || !line.toLowerCase().startsWith(
    "content-disposition:"))
  {
    //we're at the end of the stream or the part doesn't
    //contain a Content-Disposition header, return empty object
    return disposition;
  }
```

```
    //get name of web variable and filename
    String name = getDispositionName(line);

    disposition.setName(name);

    //get filename from Content-Disposition if it exists
    String filename = getDispositionFilename(line);

    disposition.setFilename(filename);

    return disposition;
}


/**
 * Returns the web variable name from the Content-Disposition
 * header.
 *
 * @param line String containing the Content-Disposition header
 * @return String containing the name of the web variable
 */
private String getDispositionName(String line)
{
    String search = "name=\"";

    int nameIndex = line.toLowerCase().indexOf(search);

    if (nameIndex == -1)
    {
        return "";
    }

    nameIndex += search.length();

    String dispositionName = line.substring(nameIndex,
        line.indexOf("\"", nameIndex+1));

    return dispositionName;
}


/**
 * Returns the filename from the Content-Disposition header.
 *
 * @param line String containing the Content-Disposition header
 * @return String containing the filename if it exists
 */
private String getDispositionFilename(String line)
{
    String search = "filename=\"";

    int filenameIndex = line.toLowerCase().indexOf(search);
```

```
          if (filenameIndex == -1)
          {
            return "";
          }

          filenameIndex += search.length();

          String filename = line.substring(filenameIndex,
            line.indexOf("\"", filenameIndex));

          filename = filename.substring(
            filename.lastIndexOf(fileSeparator)+1);

          return filename;
        }


        /**
         * Moves past the next empty line in the input stream.
         *
         * @exception IOException
         */
        private void findEmptyLine() throws IOException
        {
          String line = msr.readLine();

          //loop until end of stream or empty line
          while (line != null && !line.equals(""))
          {
            line = msr.readLine();
          }
        }


        /**
         * MultipartStreamReader is an inner class that contains a
         * single readLine() method. This method returns a single line
         * from the request input stream.
         */
        class MultipartStreamReader
        {
          /**
           * Reads a single line (up to 1K in length) from the input
           * stream. The line is limited to 1K in length since this
           * method is for reading HTTP headers and web variable
           * values, not files.
           *
           * @return String containing a single line from the input
           *   stream
           * @exception IOException
           */
```

```java
public String readLine() throws IOException
{
  String line = "";

  byte[] bytes = new byte[1024]; //1K buffer

  int bytesRead = in.readLine(bytes, 0, BUFFER_SIZE);

  if (bytesRead == -1)
  {
    return null; //no line to read so return null
  }
  else
  {
    //convert byte array to a string
    line = new String(bytes, 0, bytesRead, "ISO8859_1");
  }

  if (line.endsWith("\r\n"))
  {
    //remove the trailing \r\n
    line = line.substring(0, line.length()-2);
  }

  return line;
}
}


/**
 * ContentDisposition is an inner class that encapsulates the
 * properties of the Content-Disposition HTTP header.
 * Specifically, this class stores the name of the web variable
 * and the filename.
 */
class ContentDisposition
{
  private String name = "";
  private String filename = "";


  /**
   * Returns the name of the web variable extracted from the
   * Content-Disposition header.
   *
   * @return Name of web variable
   */
  String getName()
  {
    return name;
  }
```

```java
/**
 * Sets the name of the web variable.
 *
 * @param name String containing the name of the web
 *  variable
 */
void setName(String name)
{
  this.name = name;
}


/**
 * Returns the filename extracted from the Content-
 * Disposition header.
 *
 * @return String containing the filename
 */
String getFilename()
{
  return filename;
}


/**
 * Sets the filename value.
 *
 * @param filename String containing the name of the file
 */
void setFilename(String filename)
{
  this.filename = filename;
}
  }
}
```

CHAPTER 23

Servlet Template Framework

As discussed in Chapter 18, JavaServer Pages, many advantages can be gained by separating content presentation from application logic. These advantages include improved reusability, simplified maintenance, and division of labor. A *template framework* (also known as a *template engine*) is an application architecture, like JSP, that facilitates the separation of presentation and implementation. This separation is accomplished by encapsulating presentation logic within templates and application code within servlets, JavaBeans, or other Java classes. Basically, a template is a text file that contains standard markup language (e.g., HTML) in addition to special tags that are interpreted by the template framework each time the template is requested. In this way, the page designer can work with familiar markup languages, having to learn only a few new tags, and the Java developer can focus on developing reusable objects without regard to presentation details.

There are many template frameworks available free of charge on the Internet. WebMacro and FreeMarker are two popular examples (see *http://www.webmacro.org/* and *http://freemarker.sourceforge.net/* for more information). In fact, Apache Tomcat also falls into this category because of its support for JavaServer Pages. In this chapter, we will examine a servlet-based template framework, developed by the author, that is freely available to use, copy, modify, and distribute according to the terms of the GNU General Public License (GPL). This open source framework is called the SourceStream Template Server (STS) and is available on the accompanying CD or at the following URL:

http://www.sourcestream.com/

After our lengthy discussion regarding JavaServer Pages, you may be wondering why an alternative technology is being presented here. The purpose of this chapter is twofold. First, it is meant to give you an idea of the many types of applications that can be created with servlets. In this case, servlets are used to build a framework that makes it faster and easier to write Web applications. Second, this chapter is meant to educate you on how to build a basic template framework. This knowledge can be very useful if you decide to customize a framework or to build your own from scratch. Additionally, the SourceStream Template Server is compatible with JDK 1.1+ and Servlet API 2.0+, which allows it to be used in older environments that may not support JSP.

Due to the size of this program, the SourceStream Template Server source code is not presented in this chapter. Rather, this chapter focuses on how to build Web applications using the template server. The complete source code for this product can be found on the accompanying CD or downloaded from SourceStream's Web site. The source code contains comprehensive in-line documentation. If, after reading this chapter, you have additional questions about the STS, please consult the documentation within the source code. The following sections describe how the SourceStream Template Server works and how to use it.

Building a Web Application

Project Properties File

Each SourceStream Template Server (STS) project includes a properties file that conveys information about the application to the template server. The template server searches for this properties file in the root of the CLASSPATH or in the directory specified by the project servlet's `PropertiesFile` initialization parameter (the project servlet is discussed in the next section). Listing 23.1 illustrates a sample project properties file.

Listing 23.1   Sample project properties file.

```
# SourceStream Template Server
#
# Sample Project Properties

ProjectName=SampleProject
FileRoot=/dev/webpages/sample
DefaultPackage=com.sourcestream.sample
DebugMode=true
DbDriver=org.gjt.mm.mysql.Driver
DbURL=jdbc:mysql://localhost/sample
DbUsername=
DbPassword=
```

A typical project properties file includes project information such as the name of the project, the document root where the project's HTML files are located, the Java package in which the project's classes are stored, and whether the project should be run in debug mode (adding more verbose output). In addition to the standard project properties just mentioned, each project can add project-specific information to the properties file. In Listing 23.1, database information was added to the properties file because the project to which it belongs requires database connectivity. When the project servlet is first invoked, the template server automatically loads the information contained in the project's properties file into a public instance variable called `project`. This operation is performed within the `BaseServlet` object's `init()` method. The `project` object extends `java.util.Hashtable` and, therefore, can store all types of information as name/value pairs. This is how the `DbDriver`, `DbURL`, `DbUsername`, and `DbPassword` portions of Listing 23.1 are stored within the `project` object.

Base Servlet

The first step in creating a Web application that runs under the SourceStream Template Server is to write a Java class, known as an STS *project servlet*, that extends `com.sourcestream.template.BaseServlet`. `BaseServlet` extends `javax.servlet.http.HttpServlet` and provides default implementations of the Servlet API's `init()` and `service()` methods. These methods are inherited by all project servlets. In this way, project servlets are only required to override particular methods in order to add project-specific functionality. However, a project class should never override the `service()` method. It is the Base-Servlet object's default `service()` implementation that performs the bulk of the template server's functionality (e.g., template and module processing). Listing 23.2 demonstrates a basic project servlet that overrides the `BaseServlet` object's `init()` and `initSession()` methods in order to add project-specific functionality. In this case, a database connection pool is created in the `init()` method and a user object is added to the session in the `initSession()` method.

Listing 23.2   Sample project servlet.

```
package com.sourcestream.sample;

import com.sourcestream.template.*;
import com.sourcestream.database.*;
import javax.servlet.*;
import javax.servlet.http.*;
import java.io.*;
import java.util.*;
```

```
/**
 * SampleServlet extends BaseServlet and is the entry point to
 * the Sample application.
 */
public class SampleServlet extends BaseServlet
{
  /**
   * init() initializes the project by creating a database
   * connection pool and adding it to the project object.
   *
   * @param config ServletConfig object
   */
  public void init(ServletConfig config) throws ServletException
  {
    ConnectionPool connectionPool = null;

    //call BaseServlet's init() to populate the project object
    super.init(config);

    try
    {
      //create a connection pool object
      connectionPool = new ConnectionPool(
        (String)project.get("DbDriver"),
        (String)project.get("DbURL"),
        (String)project.get("DbUsername"),
        (String)project.get("DbPassword"));

      connectionPool.setInitialConnections(3);
      connectionPool.setIncrementalConnections(1);
      connectionPool.setMaxConnections(20);

      connectionPool.createPool();
    }
    catch (Exception e)
    {
      System.out.println("Error: " + e);
    }

    //store the connection pool in the project object
    project.put(ConnectionPool.NAME, connectionPool);
  }


  /**
   * initSession is called each time a new session is created.
   * The code here performs the necessary initialization for this
   * project. The initSession method of its parent class is
   * called first.
   *
   * @param session HttpSession object that was just created and
   *   ready to be initialized
   */
```

```
public void initSession(HttpSession session)
{
    //perform server-level initialization before project-level
    super.initSession(session);

    //instantiate fictitious User object and store it in session
    session.setAttribute("user", new User());
}
}
```

Once the project servlet is compiled and deployed, HTML files stored in the project's document root (specified within the project properties file) can be requested through the project servlet, like this:

http://localhost:8080/servlet/SampleServlet/index.html

This URL requests the *index.html* file located in the project's document root. Since it is requested by invoking `SampleServlet`, the *index.html* file will be processed by the template server before it is returned to the client. In addition to just requesting a template, a query string can be added to any URL in order to invoke methods on objects that exist in the session. For example, the following URL requests the *index.html* page and simultaneously sets the `User` bean's `NewUser` property (i.e., calls its `setNewUser()` method).

http://localhost:8080/servlet/SampleServlet/index.html?User.setNewUser=true

Any parameters submitted by an HTML form, as opposed to those submitted within a URL query string, are processed similarly.

Substitution Tags

From the Web application developer's perspective, the SourceStream Template Server is very simple. Basically, HTML content is dynamically generated by inserting special substitution tags into an HTML template. These tags are called "substitution tags" because they are evaluated by the template framework and replaced with the resulting value (i.e., the value is substituted for the literal tag). A basic substitution tag looks like this:

```
<% Customer.getName() %>
```

When this tag is processed, the STS retrieves the `Customer` object from the user's session, calls the object's `getName()` method (using Java reflection), and then replaces the tag with the method's return value. If the method does not return a `String`, the framework automatically calls the returned object's `toString()` method in order to convert it to a `String`. This example is a good illustration of how all substitution tags are processed by the STS. That is, all objects referenced in substitution tags must already exist in the user's session. Thus, in the case of this example, an object that implements the `getName()` method must have already been instantiated and placed in the user's session under the name `Customer`. If the object referenced by a substitution tag does not exist in the session, the tag is simply ignored. A little later we will learn how special Java classes called modules can be used to instantiate objects and place them in the session.

In addition to no-argument method calls, substitution tags can include parameters within method invocations. However, only `String` parameters can be passed from within a template substitution tag. For example, the following substitution tag calls a method that accepts two `String` parameters and returns a value based on these parameters.

```
<% Weather.getTemperature("Farenheit", "Salt Lake City UT US") %>
```

This substitution tag calls the `Weather` session object's `getTemperature()` method in order to retrieve Salt Lake City's current temperature in Farenheit. Similarly, the following code demonstrates how a JavaBean's property can be set using a substitution tag.

```
<% Customer.setType("Corporate") %>
```

Notice that this tag does not actually return a value. If a tag only performs an operation (such as setting a property) without returning a value, the template server produces no visible output on the HTML page on behalf of the tag. Lastly, it is possible to nest tags within other tags like this:

```
<% Customer.setOrderTotal("<% Orders.getTotal() %>") %>
```

Just remember that all of the objects referenced by these tags (e.g., `Weather`, `Customer`, `Orders`) must have already been instantiated and placed in the session. Also, empty parentheses are optional if a method does not accept parameters. For instance, both of the following tags are perfectly legal and perform identically.

```
<% Orders.getTotal() %>
<% Orders.getTotal %>
```

In addition to object method calls, substitution tags may reference an object without specifying a method. In this case, the named session object will be converted to a `String` (if necessary) and displayed in place of the tag. For example, if a `String` exists in the session under the name `Greeting`, the following substitution tag will be replaced with the `String` object's value.

```
<% Greeting %>
```

In addition to substitution tags, there is another way to set an object's properties. Properties can also be set by appropriately naming input elements in an HTML form. That is, whenever an HTML form is submitted to the template server, all form elements are evaluated and their associated object methods, if any, are called. For example, if an <INPUT> element named `Customer.setFirstName` is submitted, the template server will attempt to retrieve an object called `Customer` from the session and call its `setFirstName()` method. The value entered into the <INPUT> field by the user will be passed to the `setFirstName()` method as a parameter. In this way, JavaBeans stored in the user's session can be dynamically populated when an HTML form is submitted by simply using the appropriate element-naming conventions. The following sample HTML form, Listing 23.3, demonstrates this concept.

Listing 23.3   HTML form that sets the `Customer` object's properties.

```
<HTML>
<HEAD>
<TITLE>Customer Form</TITLE>
</HEAD>
<BODY>
<H2>Customer Form</H2>
<FORM NAME="CustomerForm" METHOD="POST"
  ACTION="/servlet/ProjectServlet/welcome.html">
<INPUT TYPE="HIDDEN" NAME="Customer.setStatus" VALUE="New">
<INPUT TYPE="TEXT" NAME="Customer.setFirstName"><BR>
<INPUT TYPE="TEXT" NAME="Customer.setLastName"><BR>
<INPUT TYPE="TEXT" NAME="Customer.setPhone"><BR>
<INPUT TYPE="TEXT" NAME="Customer.setAddress"><BR>
<INPUT TYPE="TEXT" NAME="Customer.setCity"><BR>
<INPUT TYPE="TEXT" NAME="Customer.setState"><BR>
<INPUT TYPE="TEXT" NAME="Customer.setCountry"><BR>
<INPUT TYPE="SUBMIT" VALUE="Save New Customer Record">
</FORM>
</BODY>
</HTML>
```

If Listing 23.3 were submitted to a project servlet, the template server would automatically call the `Customer` object's `setStatus()`, `setFirstName()`, `setLastName()`, `setPhone()`, `setAddress()`, `setCity()`, `setState()`, and `setCountry()` methods. After invoking these methods, the template server would process the *welcome.html* file (replacing any substitution tags with dynamic values) and return it to the client. If the specified object does not exist in the session or the object in the session does not support the specified method, the field's value is simply discarded and no action is performed.

The main *Implicit Object*

As presented in the previous section, object method calls are the primary function supported within templates. In keeping with this convention, a great deal of server-based functionality can be invoked using a template-based object method call. This server-based functionality is accessible through an implicit session object called main. The main object is said to be implicit because it is automatically accessible from within any template. Table 23.1 describes the methods supported by the implicit main object.

Now that we've learned a little about what the main object can do, let's look at a couple of examples. First, the template code presented in Listing 23.4 creates a Customer object and places it in the session if the object does not already exist. The HTML form that follows the object creation then populates

Table 23.1   Methods Supported by the main Implicit Object

Method	Description
addCookie()	Instructs the client browser to store a cookie of the specified name and value and return it with all future requests.
createObject()	Instructs the template server to create the specified object and place it in the session under the specified name. If an object already exists in the session under that name, it is replaced.
createStringObject()	Instructs the template server to create the specified String and place it in the session under the specified name. If an object already exists in the session under that name, it is replaced.
destroyObject()	Removes the specified object from the session.
forward()	Forwards the request to another template or a module.
include()	Includes output from another template.
preserveObject()	Instructs the template server to create the specified object and place it in the session under the specified name but only if an object of that name does not already exist in the session.
preserveStringObject()	Instructs the template server to create the specified String and place it in the session under the specified name but only if an object of that name does not already exist in the session.

the `Customer` object. The first parameter of the `preserveObject()` method specifies the name under which the object should be stored in the session and the second parameter specifies the name of the class that should be instantiated. If the class does not reside in the default package specified in the project properties file, it must be fully qualified (i.e., full package information included).

Listing 23.4   `main` object instantiates a class and places it in the session.

```
<% main.preserveObject("Customer", "util.ebiz.Customer") %>

<HTML>
<HEAD>
<TITLE>Customer Form</TITLE>
</HEAD>
<BODY>
<H2>Customer Form</H2>
<FORM NAME="CustomerForm" METHOD="POST"
  ACTION="/servlet/ProjectServlet/welcome.html">
<INPUT TYPE="HIDDEN" NAME="Customer.setStatus" VALUE="New">
<INPUT TYPE="TEXT" NAME="Customer.setFirstName"><BR>
<INPUT TYPE="TEXT" NAME="Customer.setLastName"><BR>
<INPUT TYPE="TEXT" NAME="Customer.setPhone"><BR>
<INPUT TYPE="TEXT" NAME="Customer.setAddress"><BR>
<INPUT TYPE="TEXT" NAME="Customer.setCity"><BR>
<INPUT TYPE="TEXT" NAME="Customer.setState"><BR>
<INPUT TYPE="TEXT" NAME="Customer.setCountry"><BR>
<INPUT TYPE="SUBMIT" VALUE="Save New Customer Record">
</FORM>
</BODY>
</HTML>
```

`include` is another common `main` method. This method inserts the contents of another template into the current template. The snippet of HTML and template code in Listing 23.5 inserts the contents of the *greeting.html* file (located at the document root specified by the project properties file) into the current template.

Listing 23.5   The `main` object includes another file within this template.

```
<HTML>
<HEAD>
<TITLE>Greeting Page</TITLE>
</HEAD>
<BODY>
<H3><% main.include("greeting.html") %></H3>
Thank you for visiting!
</BODY>
</HTML>
```

The main object implements significant functionality and can be very useful when building Web applications. For additional information regarding the methods supported by main, please see the SourceStream Template Server JavaDocs or the source code for the main object (within the *main.java* file) contained on the accompanying CD or downloadable from the SourceStream Web site.

Directives

In SourceStream Template Server terminology, a *directive* is a special template tag that does not produce visible output. Rather, a directive is meant to control program flow or provide other specialized functionality that does not generate output or directly invoke an object's method. Currently, three directives are supported by the STS—If, List, and Comment. Each of these directives will be discussed shortly. First, let's examine the syntax of an STS directive. The following If directive is used to produce conditional output.

```
<%# If Customer.getType == "Corporate" %>
  Welcome Corporate Customer, <% Customer.getCompanyName() %>!
<%# /If %>
```

You should immediately notice several significant differences between directives and substitution tags. First, unlike substitution tags, directive tags begin with "<%#" and, like substitution tags, end with "%>". The "#" symbol following the leading "<%" indicates to the template server that the tag should be processed as a directive rather than as a substitution tag. Second, a directive does not include an object name followed by a method call. Rather, each directive defines its own syntax. Last, unlike substitution tags that can be embedded anywhere in an HTML document, directives must exist on a line by themselves. That is, the line on which a directive resides should not include other text or tags.

If Directive

An If directive is used to generate conditional output based on a boolean comparison. This directive uses the following syntax:

```
<%# If Object[.method] == "string_value" %>
  If expression evaluates to true, show this text
<%# Else %>
  If expression evaluates to false, show this text.
<%# /If %>
```

Similarly, the If expression can check for a "not equal to" condition, like this:

```
<%# If Object[.method] != "string_value" %>
  The object method call did not equal the specified value.
<%# /If %>
```

To illustrate, the following If directives produce conditional output.

```
<%# If Customer.getCountry() == "USA" %>
  Customer is from the United States.
<%# Else %>
  Customer is from outside the United States.
<%# /If %>

<%# If Greeting != "" %>
  Show greeting. <% Greeting %>
<%# Else %>
  Show default greeting. Hello!
<%# /If %>
```

Notice that the expression on the left side of the operator (== or !=) is assumed to be an object in the session and the right side is assumed to be a literal String or a tag that evaluates to a String. For example, the following If expression uses a dynamic conditional. If the object's method call returns a String that equals the specified value (case insensitive), the expression evaluates to true.

```
<%# If Customer.getName() == "<% RaffleWinner.getName() %>" %>
  Congratulations! You won a $20 gift certificate.
<%# /If %>
```

In addition, the If expression does not require a value at all. For example, the following If expression evaluates to true if the specified object exists and does not equal the string false or an empty string. This can be very useful for checking for the existence of an object before calling it. You can also prepend an exclamation point (!) to the object name in order to negate the expression.

```
<%# If Customer %>
  The Customer object exists. Hello, <% Customer.getName %>.
<%# Else %>
  There is no Customer object in the session.
<%# /If %>

<%# If !Customer %>
  There is no Customer object in the session.
<%# Else %>
  The Customer object exists in the session.
<%# /If %>
```

Likewise, if an object method call is made within the If expression, the expression evaluates to true if the return value is not an empty string or the string false. That is, an expression that returns a value evaluates to false only if the value is an empty string or the string false.

```
<%# If Customer.getName() %>
  The Customer has a name. Hello, <% Customer.getName %>.
<%# Else %>
  The Customer does not have a name.
<%# /If %>

<%# If !Customer.getName() %>
  The Customer does not have a name.
<%# Else %>
  The Customer has a name.
<%# /If %>
```

Now that you have a feel for how the If directive is used, let's look at a concrete example. Listing 23.6 demonstrates an HTML form that is automatically filled based on the properties of a JavaBean stored in the session.

Listing 23.6 Template uses If directive to produce conditional output.

```
<% main.preserveObject("Customer", "util.ebiz.Customer") %>

<HTML>
<HEAD>
<TITLE>Customer Form</TITLE>
</HEAD>
<BODY>
<H2>Customer Form</H2>
<%# If Customer.getName() != "" %>
Hello, <% Customer.getName() %>
<%# /If %>

<FORM NAME="CustomerForm" METHOD="POST"
  ACTION="/servlet/ProjectSerylet/greeting.html">
<INPUT TYPE="HIDDEN" NAME="Customer.setStatus"
  VALUE="<% Customer.getStatus() %>">
<INPUT TYPE="TEXT" NAME="Customer.setFirstName"
  VALUE="<% Customer.getFirstName() %>"><BR>
<INPUT TYPE="TEXT" NAME="Customer.setLastName"
  VALUE="<% Customer.getLastName() %>"><BR>
<INPUT TYPE="TEXT" NAME="Customer.setPhone"
  VALUE="<% Customer.getPhone() %>"><BR>
<INPUT TYPE="TEXT" NAME="Customer.setAddress"
  VALUE="<% Customer.getAddress() %>"><BR>
<INPUT TYPE="TEXT" NAME="Customer.setCity"
  VALUE="<% Customer.getCity() %>"><BR>
<INPUT TYPE="TEXT" NAME="Customer.setState"
  VALUE="<% Customer.getState() %>"><BR>
<INPUT TYPE="TEXT" NAME="Customer.setCountry"
  VALUE="<% Customer.getCountry() %>"><BR>
```

```
Please select your gender:
<SELECT NAME="Customer.setGender">
<OPTION
<%# If Customer.getGender() == "Male" %>
 SELECTED
<%# /If %>
 VALUE="M">Male</OPTION>
<OPTION
<%# If Customer.getGender() == "Female" %>
 SELECTED
<%# /iF %>
 VALUE="F">Female</OPTION>
</SELECT><BR>

<INPUT TYPE="SUBMIT" VALUE="Save Customer Record">
</FORM>
</BODY>
</HTML>
```

List Directive

The List directive is used to iterate through collections of objects in order to generate HTML tables or other repeating constructs. The syntax for the List directive looks like this:

```
<%# List collection="collection" items="item1,item2,..." %>
  Repeated content here.
<%# /List %>
```

The List directive consists of two attributes—collection and items. The collection attribute specifies the name of a java.util.Vector object stored in the session. The List directive iterates through the specified Vector and repeats the template code between the beginning and ending List tags for each object in the Vector. The items attribute specifies the name by which the current item can be referenced within each iteration. For example, if a Vector containing Customer objects is stored in the session under the name Customers, the following List directive references the current Customer object using the name specified by the items attribute.

```
<%# List collection="Customers" items="Customer" %>
  <% Customer.getLastName() %>, <% Customer.getFirstName() %><BR>
<%# /List %>
```

In addition to a single value, the items attribute may contain a comma-delimited list of item names. When multiple item names are specified, the first name is assigned to the first item in the iteration, the second name to the second item, and so on. This functionality can be extremely useful for creating tables that use alternating colors, as demonstrated in Listing 23.7.

Listing 23.7   HTML page that uses the List directive to show customers.

```
<HTML>
<HEAD>
<TITLE>Customer List</TITLE>
</HEAD>
<BODY>
<H2>Customer List</H2>
<TABLE BORDER="0" CELLSPACING="3" CELLPADDING="5">
<TR BGCOLOR="#888888">
  <TH>Last Name</TH><TH>First Name</TH>
</TR>
<%# List collection="Customers" items="Customer1,Customer2" %>
<TR BGCOLOR="#FFFFFF">
  <TD><% Customer1.getLastName() %></TD>
  <TD><% Customer1.getFirstName() %></TD>
</TR>
<TR BGCOLOR="#E0E0E0">
  <TD><% Customer2.getLastName() %></TD>
  <TD><% Customer2.getFirstName() %></TD>
</TR>
<%# /List %>
</TABLE>
</BODY>
</HTML>
```

You may be wondering what happens when the items attribute includes an even number of item names and the Vector specified by the collection attribute contains an odd number of objects. In this case, the second item will not exist during the final iteration. Any method calls on a nonexistent object are simply ignored. However, though the object calls are ignored, the HTML will still be included in the output and, thus, produce a blank row at the end of the table. To suppress the blank row at the end, you can use the If directive to check for the existence of the second object before displaying the final row, like this:

```
<TABLE BORDER="0" CELLSPACING="3" CELLPADDING="5">
<TR BGCOLOR="#888888">
  <TH>Last Name</TH><TH>First Name</TH>
</TR>
<%# List collection="Customers" items="Customer1,Customer2" %>
<TR BGCOLOR="#FFFFFF">
  <TD><% Customer1.getLastName() %></TD>
  <TD><% Customer1.getFirstName() %></TD>
</TR>
<%# If Customer2 %>
<TR BGCOLOR="#E0E0E0">
  <TD><% Customer2.getLastName() %></TD>
  <TD><% Customer2.getFirstName() %></TD>
</TR>
<%# /If %>
<%# /List %>
</TABLE>
```

In addition to simply listing items, the List directive supports some advanced list management functionality. This functionality includes breaking the list into small portions that can be displayed on separate screens, identifying the user's location within the list and the total number of items in the list, and allowing the user to move forward and backward within the list. To take advantage of this functionality, the collection attribute must specify an object that extends the com.sourcestream.template.STSList class. This class extends java.util.Vector and adds functionality that supports incremental traversal of the list. When the collection attribute references an STSList object, it is possible to designate the maximum number of rows to show per page using the List tag's maxrows attribute. Lastly, the STSList object's move method can be used to move through the list and the getStartPosition(), getEndPosition(), and getTotalRows() methods indicate the list's size and position. Listing 23.8 demonstrates the list management functionality built into the STSList class by allowing the user to move through the list five customers at a time (see Figure 23.1).

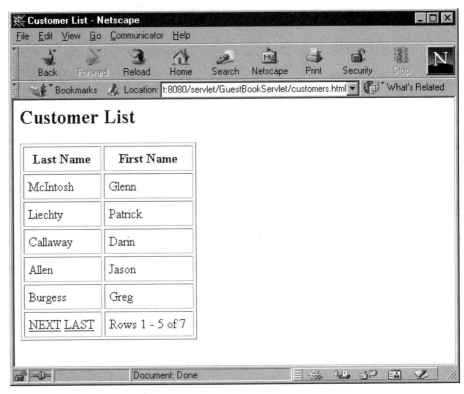

Figure 23.1 Customer List That Uses the STSList Object's List Management Features

Listing 23.8   An STSList object is used to track the user's list traversal.

```
<HTML>
<HEAD>
<TITLE>Customer List</TITLE>
</HEAD>
<BODY>
<H2>Customer List</H2>
<TABLE BORDER="1" CELLSPACING="3" CELLPADDING="5">
<TR>
  <TH>Last Name</TH><TH>First Name</TH>
</TR>
<%# List collection="Customers" items="Customer" maxrows="5" %>
<TR>
  <TD><% Customer.getLastName() %></TD>
  <TD><% Customer.getFirstName() %></TD>
</TR>
<%# /List %>
<TR>
  <TD>
    <%# If !Customers.isFirstRowDisplayed() %>
    <A HREF="/servlet/ProjectServlet/cust.html?Customers.move=
      first">FIRST</A>
    <A HREF="/servlet/ProjectServlet/cust.html?Customers.move=
      prev">PREV</A>
    <%# /If %>
    <%# If !Customers.isLastRowDisplayed() %>
    <A HREF="/servlet/ProjectServlet/cust.html?Customers.move=
      next">NEXT</A>
    <A HREF="/servlet/ProjectServlet/cust.html?Customers.move=
      last">LAST</A>
    <%# /If %>
  </TD>
  <TD ALIGN="RIGHT">
    Rows <% Customers.getStartPosition() %> -
         <% Customers.getEndPosition() %> of
         <% Customers.getTotalRows() %>
  </TD>
</TR>
</TABLE>
</BODY>
</HTML>
```

Comment Directive

The Comment directive is a simple tag that allows comments to be inserted into a template. These comments differ from standard HTML comments in that they are removed from the page when it is processed and are never returned to the client. Therefore, unlike HTML comments, the user is unable to view comments inserted into the template using the Comment directive (even when viewing the HTML source). The Comment directive supports two syntax styles. The first style is useful for brief, single-line comments. The second style is useful for more descriptive template documentation. Notice that the single-line style is terminated with "/%>".

```
<%# Comment: This is a brief, single-line comment /%>

<%# Comment %>
   This is a multi-line comment. Like all Comment directives, this
   comment will not be included in the response.
<%# /Comment %>
```

Modules

SourceStream Template Server *modules* are Java classes that can be instantiated and executed by the template framework. These modules perform the business logic associated with a project. Modules can be used to perform various functions, including accessing a database or directory server, instantiating objects and storing them in the session, communicating across the network, controlling application flow, and much more. Modules are the real workhorses behind the STS.

STS modules can be invoked from a template by specifying the module name followed by the .mod extension within a hyperlink or within the ACTION attribute of a <FORM> tag. The .mod extension tells the template framework that the request is referencing a module rather than a template. To illustrate, the following hyperlink invokes the ForwardToRandomPage module.

```
<A HREF="/servlet/ProjectServlet/ForwardToRandomPage.mod">
   Click here to go to a random page.
</A>
```

Because no package information is included, the previous hyperlink assumes that the ForwardToRandomPage module is contained in the default package. If this module existed outside the default package, it would have to be fully qualified (i.e., its package would have to be specified). For example, if this module existed in the com.sourcestream.stuff package, it could be invoked in either of these two ways:

```
<A HREF="/servlet/ProjectServlet/com.sourcestream.stuff.
   ForwardToRandomPage.mod">
   Click here to go to a random page.
</A>

<A HREF="/servlet/ProjectServlet/com/sourcestream/stuff/
   ForwardToRandomPage.mod">
   Click here to go to a random page.
</A>
```

In addition to hyperlinks, HTML forms can request modules. The HTML form presented in Listing 23.9 invokes the `LoginModule` module.

Listing 23.9 HTML page that submits login credentials to a login module.

```
<HTML>
<HEAD>
<TITLE>Login Form</TITLE>
</HEAD>
<BODY>
<H2>Login Form</H2>
<FORM NAME="LoginForm" METHOD="POST"
  ACTION="/servlet/ProjectServlet/LoginModule.mod">
User Name: <INPUT TYPE="TEXT" NAME="setUserName"><BR>
Password: <INPUT TYPE="PASSWORD" NAME="setPassword"><BR>
<INPUT TYPE="SUBMIT" VALUE="Login">
</FORM>
</BODY>
</HTML>
```

When the template server receives a request for a module, it first attempts to retrieve the specified module out of the session. If the module is not already in the session under the specified name, it is automatically instantiated by the framework. It should be noted, however, that modules instantiated by the framework do not persist between requests. To use the same module instance across requests, instantiate it from within the project servlet or another module and place it in the session (this can also be accomplished from within a template using the `main.createObject()` method).

Once it has a reference to the module object, the framework attempts to invoke the module's methods based on the name of the submitted form elements. For instance, if the form contains an `<INPUT>` tag named `setUserName` and a `<PASSWORD>` tag named `setPassword`, the framework will automatically call the module's `setUserName()` and `setPassword()` methods, if they exist. On the other hand, if an object is specified within the form element name, that object's method, rather than the module's method, is called. For example, if the form contains an element named `Customer.setName`, the `Customer` object's `setName()` method, not the module's `setName()` method, will be invoked.

After calling all methods that match parameter names, the module's `process()` method is invoked. The module performs any required functionality within its `process()` method and then forwards control to a template or to another module. The `process()` method is defined by the `com.source-stream.template.Module` interface, which all modules must implement. For example, Listing 23.10 demonstrates a basic module that validates a user's login credentials and then, based on whether the credentials are valid, forwards the user to either the application's main menu or back to the login page.

Listing 23.10   Module that validates a user's login credentials.

```
package com.sourcestream.guestbook;

import com.sourcestream.template.*;
import com.sourcestream.database.*;
import javax.servlet.*;
import javax.servlet.http.*;
import java.sql.*;
import java.util.*;

/**
 * LoginModule processes the login page.
 */
public class LoginModule implements Module
{
  private String username;
  private String password;


  /**
   * process() accepts a Helper object and processes the client's
   * login request.
   *
   * @param Helper object containing request and response info
   */
  public void process(Helper helper) throws Exception
  {
    HttpSession session = helper.getSession();
    HttpServletRequest req = helper.getRequest();

    DataQuery dataQuery = null;

    try
    {
      Project project = helper.getProject();
      ConnectionPool pool =
        (ConnectionPool)project.get(ConnectionPool.NAME);

      dataQuery = new DataQuery(pool);

      String sql = "select * from USERS where USERNAME = '" +
        username + "' and PASSWORD = '" + password + "'";

      ResultSet set = dataQuery.executeQuery(sql);

      if (set.next())
      {
        helper.forward("mainmenu.html");
        return;
      }
    }
```

```
      catch (SQLException e)
      {
        helper.log(e);
      }
      finally
      {
        dataQuery.close(); //return connection to pool
      }

      helper.forward("login.html");
    }


    public void setUsername(String username)
    {
      this.username = username;
    }


    public void setPassword(String password)
    {
      this.password = password;
    }
  }
```

You may have noticed the Helper object that is referenced several times in Listing 23.10. This object is passed to the module's process() method and it contains a wealth of useful functionality and object references. For instance, the Helper object provides access to the Project, HttpServletRequest, HttpServletResponse, HttpSession, ServletInputStream, ServletOutputStream, and PrintWriter objects. Additionally, it implements handy functionality such as forwarding and logging features. Table 23.2 documents the methods supported by the Helper class.

This chapter has presented the most essential elements of the SourceStream Template Server. A wide array of Web applications can be built quickly and efficiently using a framework of project servlets, templates, and modules. If you have further questions regarding the STS, please see the JavaDocs or the extensive in-line documentation within the source code. You can find both the JavaDocs and the source code on the accompanying CD or on the Web at *http://www.sourcestream.com/*.

Inside the Template Server

In this section, we will examine the implementation of the SourceStream Template Server. This exercise will consist of a review of all classes contained in the

Table 23.2 Methods Implemented by the `Helper` Class

Method	Description
`forward()`	Forwards control to the specified module or template.
`getInputStream()`	Retrieves the `ServletInputStream` for the current request.
`getOutputStream()`	Retrieves the `ServletOutputStream` for the current request.
`getProject()`	Retrieves the `Project` object for the current application.
`getRequest()`	Retrieves the `HttpServletRequest` object.
`getResponse()`	Retrieves the `HttpServletResponse` object.
`getSession()`	Retrieves the `HttpSession` object for the current user.
`getWriter()`	Retrieves the `PrintWriter` for the current request.
`include()`	Includes the output generated by another module or servlet in the current module's output.
`log()`	Performs event and error logging.
`processModule()`	Transfers control to another module. Under most circumstances, use the `forward()` method.
`processTemplate()`	Transfers control to a template. Under most circumstances, use the `forward()` method.
`sendLine()`	Writes a line of text to the output stream.

`com.sourcestream.template` package and an illustration of how the template server processes a request.

Template Server Classes

The classes that comprise the SourceStream Template Server reside in the `com.sourcestream.template` package. Currently, this package contains 15 classes that, together, implement the functionality supported by the STS. Table 23.3 describes the purpose of each class. See the JavaDocs or source code for more information.

In addition to the classes in the `com.sourcestream.template` package, two other classes are used by the SourceStream Template Server—Tag and TagParser. Both of these tags reside in the `com.sourcestream.util` package. The TagParser class parses a markup language tag or template tag and returns a populated Tag object that encapsulates the tag's information, such as the tag

Table 23.3   SourceStream Template Server Classes

Class	Description
BaseServlet	Class from which all project servlets extend. It provides default functionality that accepts requests, determines if a template, module, or image is being requested, and appropriately services the request.
Constants	Interface that contains numerous STS constants such as the start and end delimiters for substitution tags and directives, the name of the error and event logs, and the default extension used to indicate a module request (i.e., .mod).
DirectiveTagParser	Class used to parse directive tags.
Helper	Class that contains essential objects related to the current request and project and that performs functionality such as request forwarding and error/event logging.
IfDirective	Class that processes an If directive.
ListDirective	Class that processes a List directive.
Main	Implicit class available from within all templates. This class provides functionality such as request forwarding, server-side includes, adding cookies, and instantiating objects.
Module	Interface that must be implemented by all modules. This interface defines a single process() method that is automatically called by the template server when the module is invoked.
ModuleAction	Class that processes a module request.
ProcessDirective	Class that processes all directives.
ProcessInclude	Class that processes server-side include operations.
ProcessLine	Class that is used to evaluate a line of text. This evaluation includes replacing all substitution tags with their appropriate values.
Project	Class that extends java.util.Hashtable that is used to store project-specific information such as the application's document root and default package.
STSList	Class that extends java.util.Vector and implements list management functionality such as the ability to track a user's position within the list.
TemplateAction	Class that processes template requests.

type and all tag attributes. And finally, many STS projects also use several of the classes provided in the com.sourcestream.database package. This package includes classes, such as a database connection pool class, that make database access easier and more efficient.

Template Server Architecture

The SourceStream Template Server processes a template or module each time it is requested. The flow chart presented in Figure 23.2 demonstrates how the

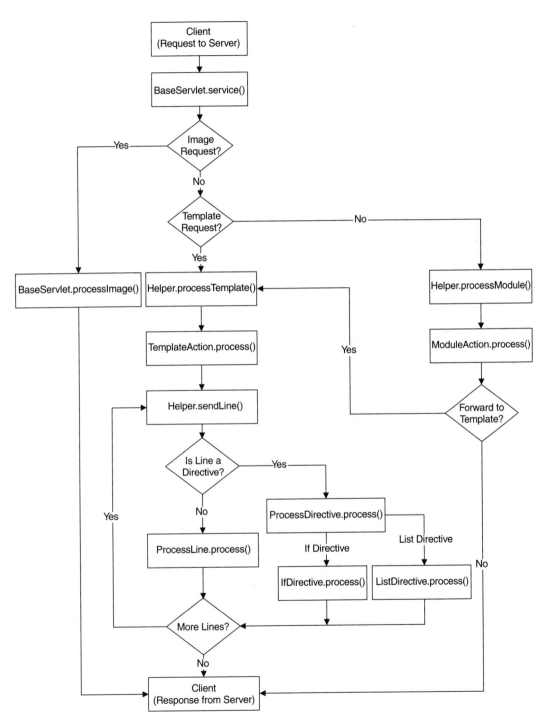

Figure 23.2 How a Request Is Processed by the SourceStream Template Server

template server processes each request by illustrating the flow of control through the STS classes.

Guest Book Sample Application

The Guest Book application is a simple program that keeps a record of clients that visit a Web site by allowing visitors to "sign" a guest book (i.e., submit their names and e-mail addresses to the server), as well as allowing the clients to view the guest book. This is an extremely simple demonstration of the SourceStream Template Server, but it should give you a pretty good idea of how this framework simplifies the Web application development process. The following sections describe each step required to develop an STS application, including creating a project properties file, writing the project servlet that extends BaseServlet, creating the project database, developing the JavaBeans that the program will use, writing the modules that implement business logic and functionality, and creating the templates that produce the user interface.

Project Properties File

The project properties file conveys important information about the project to the template server. The properties file, presented in Listing 23.11, specifies the name of the project, the document root location where templates are stored, the default Java package, the debug mode, and information required to establish a database connection to the guest book database. This information is read automatically by the template server and stored in the com.sourcestream.template.Project object. The Project object is accessible from the Helper object that is passed to each module's process() method.

The Project object includes properties that store the project's name, document root, default package, and more. Table 23.4 documents all of the properties exposed by the Project object (the Project object contains a getXxx() and setXxx() method for each property where Xxx is the property's name). In addition, since the Project object extends java.util.Hashtable, it can store any project-specific information required by a particular project. For instance, the properties DbDriver, DbURL, DbUsername, and DbPassword are not properties defined by the Project class. Rather, these values are stored within the Project object's Hashtable.

Listing 23.11   Sample project properties file.

```
# SourceStream Template Server
#
# Guest Book Project Properties
```

Table 23.4 Properties Defined by the `Project` Object

Property	Description
DebugMode	Boolean value indicating whether the project should be run in debug mode. Debug mode produces verbose output to standard out and includes descriptive HTML comments in the output sent to the client.
DefaultFile	Name of file template to process if no file is specified in request. Default is *index.html*.
DefaultPackage	Name of package in which to search for unqualified objects (e.g., modules and JavaBeans) referenced within a template. Fully qualified objects (i.e., references that include full package information) do not use this property.
ErrorRedirect	Name of file to which the client should be redirected in the case of an uncaught error.
FileRoot	Root location (i.e., document root) of the project's templates. All template references are relative to the `FileRoot` property.
NotFoundRedirect	Name of file to which the client should be redirected when the requested resource is not found.
ProjectName	Name of the current project.

```
ProjectName=GuestBook
FileRoot=/dev/webpages/guestbook
DefaultPackage=com.sourcestream.guestbook
DebugMode=true
DbDriver=org.gjt.mm.mysql.Driver
DbURL=jdbc:mysql://localhost/guestbook
DbUsername=
DbPassword=
```

Project Servlet

The project servlet extends `com.sourcestream.template.BaseServlet`. Although `BaseServlet` provides the default functionality required to process templates and modules, the project servlet can override the `BaseServlet` class's `init()` and `initSession()` methods in order to perform project-specific initialization. For instance, the project servlet for the Guest Book application requires database access so it creates a database connection pool within its `init()` method. Listing 23.12 presents the project servlet for the Guest Book application.

Listing 23.12   Guest Book application project servlet.

```java
package com.sourcestream.guestbook;

import com.sourcestream.template.*;
import com.sourcestream.database.*;
import javax.servlet.*;
import javax.servlet.http.*;
import java.io.*;

/**
 * GuestBookServlet extends BaseServlet and is the entry point
 * to the Guest Book application.
 */
public class GuestBookServlet extends BaseServlet
{
  /**
   * init() initializes the project by creating a database
   * connection pool and adding it to the project object.
   *
   * @param config ServletConfig object
   */
  public void init(ServletConfig config) throws ServletException
  {
    ConnectionPool connectionPool = null;

    //call BaseServlet's init() to populate the project object
    super.init(config);

    try
    {
      //create a connection pool object
      connectionPool = new ConnectionPool(
        (String)project.get("DbDriver"),
        (String)project.get("DbURL"),
        (String)project.get("DbUsername"),
        (String)project.get("DbPassword"));

      connectionPool.setInitialConnections(3);
      connectionPool.setIncrementalConnections(1);
      connectionPool.setMaxConnections(20);

      connectionPool.createPool();
    }
    catch (Exception e)
    {
      System.out.println("Error: " + e);
    }

    //store the connection pool in the project object
    project.put(ConnectionPool.NAME, connectionPool);
  }
```

```
/**
 * initSession is called each time a new session is created.
 * The code here performs the necessary initialization for this
 * project. The initSession method of its parent class is
 * called first.
 *
 * @param session HttpSession object that was just created and
 *   ready to be initialized
 */
public void initSession(HttpSession session)
{
  //perform server-level initialization before project-level
  super.initSession(session);
}
}
```

Notice that the `init()` method was used to build a connection pool. The connection pool properties were acquired from the `Project` object's `Hashtable`. Although this project servlet does not perform additional initialization in the `initSession()` method, this method is demonstrated to illustrate where project-specific session initialization can be performed (e.g., objects can be instantiated and placed in the session). The `initSession()` method is automatically called by the template server whenever a new session is created.

Project Database

The simple database used for this project consists of a single table that contains four columns. The information stored in the database includes a unique ID for each guest as well as the guest's first name, last name, and e-mail address. Listing 23.13 presents the My SQL database script that creates the guest book database.

Listing 23.13   Guest Book application database.

```
CREATE TABLE GUEST (
  GUEST_ID    int NOT NULL AUTO_INCREMENT PRIMARY KEY,
  FIRST_NAME  varchar(30) NOT NULL,
  LAST_NAME   varchar(30) NOT NULL,
  EMAIL       varchar(200) NULL
);
```

JavaBeans

The state of an STS application is usually stored in JavaBeans that have been placed in the user's session. As we have seen, a JavaBean's properties can be set automatically by a template if the HTML form elements are named appropriately. The Guest Book application uses the `Guest` bean to write information to and retreive it from the database. That is, the `Guest` bean is populated by the *signbook.html* template in order to insert a guest into the database (see Listing 23.18). Likewise, when each row is read from the database (each row represents a different guest), a Guest bean is instantiated and populated with the information read from the database. After the Guest bean is created, it is added to a java.util.Vector object that is placed in the session (see Listing 23.16). This Vector object can then be referenced from a template to display a list of guests (see Listing 23.19). Listing 23.14 presents the code for the Guest bean.

Listing 23.14   Guest JavaBean used to store a guest's information.

```java
package com.sourcestream.guestbook;

/**
 * Guest class is a JavaBean that represents a single guest.
 */
public class Guest
{
  private String firstName;
  private String lastName;
  private String email;

  public void setFirstName(String firstName)
  {
    this.firstName = firstName;
  }

  public String getFirstName()
  {
    return firstName;
  }

  public void setLastName(String lastName)
  {
    this.lastName = lastName;
  }

  public String getLastName()
  {
    return lastName;
  }

  public void setEmail(String email)
  {
    this.email = email;
  }

  public String getEmail()
  {
    return email;
  }
}
```

Modules

Modules implement the bulk of the functionality performed by the Guest Book application. This functionality includes inserting guests into the database as well as retrieving information from the database in order to create a collection of Guest beans. The SignBookModule and ViewBookModule implement this functionality.

SignBookModule

The SignBookModule retrieves a populated Guest bean from the session and uses it to insert a row into the database. The Guest bean is populated by the *signbook.html* template. After inserting a row into the database, the module forwards control to the *mainmenu.html* template. Listing 23.15 presents the SignBookModule module.

Listing 23.15   SignBookModule inserts a guest into the database.

```
package com.sourcestream.guestbook;

import com.sourcestream.template.*;
import com.sourcestream.database.*;
import javax.servlet.*;
import javax.servlet.http.*;
import java.sql.*;

/**
 * SignBookModule writes the guest's information to the database.
 */
public class SignBookModule implements Module
{
  /**
   * process() accepts a Helper object and processes the client's
   * login request.
   *
   * @param Helper object containing request and response info
   */
  public void process(Helper helper) throws Exception
  {
    HttpSession session = helper.getSession();
    HttpServletRequest req = helper.getRequest();

    DataQuery dataQuery = null;

    try
    {
      Guest guest = (Guest)session.getAttribute("Guest");

      if (guest == null)
      {
```

```
          helper.log(new ServletException("No Guest Bean"));
          return; //exit here since no Guest bean is in the session
        }

        Project project = helper.getProject();
        ConnectionPool pool =
          (ConnectionPool)project.get(ConnectionPool.NAME);

        dataQuery = new DataQuery(pool);

        String sql = "insert into GUEST (FIRST_NAME, LAST_NAME, " +
          "EMAIL) values ('" + guest.getFirstName() + "', '" +
          guest.getLastName() + "', '" + guest.getEmail() + "')";

        dataQuery.executeUpdate(sql);
      }
      catch (SQLException e)
      {
        helper.log(e);
      }
      finally
      {
        dataQuery.close(); //return connection to pool
      }

      helper.forward("mainmenu.html");
    }
  }
```

ViewBookModule

The ViewBookModule reads each row out of the database, creates a Guest bean
for each row, adds all Guest beans to a java.util.Vector object, stores the
Vector in the user's session, and forwards control to the *viewbook.html* template. The template then references the Vector object in the session in order to
display a list of guests. Listing 23.16 presents the code for the ViewBookModule.

Listing 23.16 ViewBookModule creates a collection of guests.

```
package com.sourcestream.guestbook;

import com.sourcestream.template.*;
import com.sourcestream.database.*;
import javax.servlet.*;
import javax.servlet.http.*;
import java.sql.*;

/**
 * ViewBookModule populates a Vector containing a Guest object
 * for each guest in the database.
 */
```

```java
public class ViewBookModule implements Module
{
  /**
   * process() accepts a Helper object and processes the client's
   * login request.
   *
   * @param Helper object containing request and response info
   */
  public void process(Helper helper) throws Exception
  {
    HttpSession session = helper.getSession();
    HttpServletRequest req = helper.getRequest();

    DataQuery dataQuery = null;

    try
    {
      Project project = helper.getProject();
      ConnectionPool pool =
        (ConnectionPool)project.get(ConnectionPool.NAME);

      dataQuery = new DataQuery(pool);

      String sql = "select * from GUEST";

      ResultSet set = dataQuery.executeQuery(sql);

      java.util.Vector guests = new java.util.Vector();

      while (set.next())
      {
        Guest guest = new Guest();
        guest.setFirstName(set.getString("FIRST_NAME"));
        guest.setLastName(set.getString("LAST_NAME"));
        guest.setEmail(set.getString("EMAIL"));

        guests.add(guest);
      }

      session.setAttribute("Guests", guests);
    }
    catch (SQLException e)
    {
      helper.log(e);
    }
    finally
    {
      dataQuery.close(); //return connection to pool
    }

    helper.forward("viewbook.html");
  }
}
```

Templates

Templates are used to construct the application's user interface. The Guest Book application consists of three templates—*mainmenu.html*, *signbook.html*, and *viewbook.html*. Each of these templates is presented in the following sections.

mainmenu.html

The *mainmenu.html* template simply provides a menu that presents two options—**Sign Guest Book** and **View Guest Book** (see Figure 23.3). The **Sign Guest Book** hyperlink requests the *signbook.html* template. In contrast, the **View Guest Book** hyperlink issues a request to ViewGuestModule, which populates the Guests collection before forwarding control to the *viewbook.html* template. The *mainmenu.html* template can be referenced through the Guest-BookServlet using a URL, like this:

http://localhost:8080/servlet/GuestBookServlet/mainmenu.html

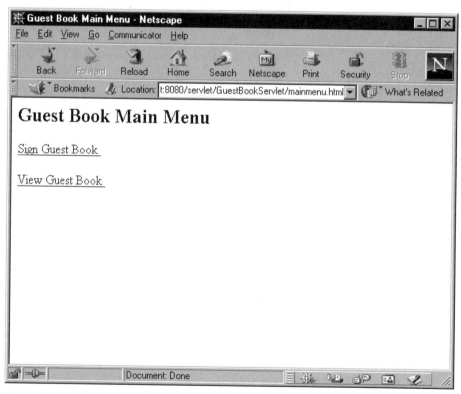

Figure 23.3   Main Menu for the Guest Book Application

Listing 23.17 presents the *mainmenu.html* template.

Listing 23.17   The *mainmenu.html* template presents choices to the user.

```
<HTML>
<HEAD>
<TITLE>Guest Book Main Menu</TITLE>
</HEAD>
<BODY>
<H2>Guest Book Main Menu</H2>
<A HREF="/servlet/GuestBookServlet/signbook.html">
Sign Guest Book
</A>
<BR><BR>
<A HREF="/servlet/GuestBookServlet/ViewBookModule.mod">
View Guest Book
</A>
</BODY>
</HTML>
```

signbook.html

The *signbook.html* template presents a simple HTML form that allows the user to "sign" the guest book by entering his or her first name, last name, and e-mail address (see Figure 23.4). Notice that this template uses the following line to instantiate a Guest bean and place it in the session under the name Guest.

```
<% main.createObject("Guest", "Guest") %>
```

The first Guest represents the name under which the object will be stored in the session and the second Guest indicates the name of the class to instantiate. Since the Guest class resides in the default package (as specified by the project properties file), no package information need be specified.

The <FORM> tag in the *signbook.html* template submits its values to SignBookModule. This module retrieves the populated Guest bean from the session and uses its values to insert a row into the database. The form elements are named so that the template server will automatically set the Guest bean's values when the form is submitted. Listing 23.18 presents the *signbook.html* template.

Listing 23.18   The *signbook.html* template allows the user to sign book.

```
<% main.createObject("Guest", "Guest") %>

<HTML>
<HEAD>
<TITLE>Sign the Guest Book</TITLE>
</HEAD>
<BODY>
```

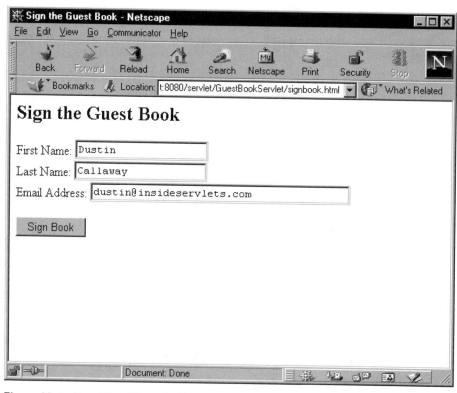

Figure 23.4   Form That Allows the User to Sign the Guest Book

```
<H2>Sign the Guest Book</H2>
<FORM METHOD="POST" ACTION="SignBookModule.mod">
First Name:
  <INPUT TYPE="TEXT" NAME="Guest.setFirstName" SIZE="20"><BR>
Last Name:
  <INPUT TYPE="TEXT" NAME="Guest.setLastName" SIZE="20"><BR>
Email Address:
  <INPUT TYPE="TEXT" NAME="Guest.setEmail" SIZE="40">
<BR><BR>
<INPUT TYPE="SUBMIT" VALUE="Sign Book">
</FORM>
</BODY>
</HTML>
```

viewbook.html

The *viewbook.html* template displays a list of all visitors who have signed the guest book (see Figure 23.5). This template uses the List directive to create an HTML table that displays all guests in the Guests collection (created by View-BookModule). The List directive's items attribute specifies Guest1 and Guest2 to

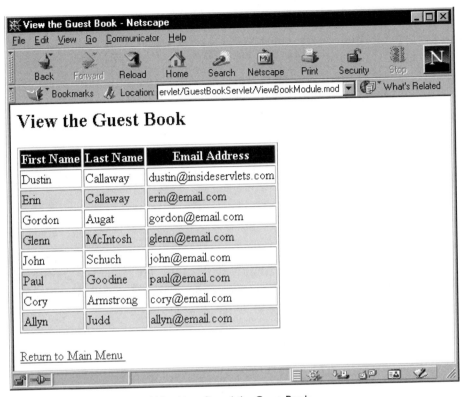

Figure 23.5 List of Visitors Who Have Signed the Guest Book

produce rows of alternating colors. Listing 23.19 presents the *viewbook.html* template.

Listing 23.19 The *viewbook.html* template displays all guests.

```
<HTML>
<HEAD>
<TITLE>View the Guest Book</TITLE>
</HEAD>
<BODY>
<H2>View the Guest Book</H2>
<TABLE BORDER="1">
<TR BGCOLOR="#000000">
<TH><FONT COLOR="WHITE">First Name</FONT></TH>
<TH><FONT COLOR="WHITE">Last Name</FONT></TH>
<TH><FONT COLOR="WHITE">Email Address</FONT></TH>
</TR>
<%# List collection="Guests" items="Guest1,Guest2" %>
<TR BGCOLOR="#FFFFFF">
<TD><% Guest1.getFirstName() %></TD>
<TD><% Guest1.getLastName() %></TD>
```

```
<TD><% Guest1.getEmail() %></TD>
</TR>
<%# If Guest2 %>
<TR BGCOLOR="#E0E0E0">
<TD><% Guest2.getFirstName() %></TD>
<TD><% Guest2.getLastName() %></TD>
<TD><% Guest2.getEmail() %></TD>
</TR>
<%# /If %>
<%# /List %>
</TABLE>
<BR>
<A HREF="/servlet/GuestBookServlet/mainmenu.html">
Return to Main Menu
</A>
</BODY>
</HTML>
```

This concludes the presentation of the SourceStream Template Server. If you are interested in how this pure Java template framework is implemented, please review the source code available on the accompanying CD or on the Web at *http://www.sourcestream.com/*.

PART V

Servlet API Quick Reference

CHAPTER 24

javax.servlet Package

The javax.servlet package contains interfaces and classes used to build generic servlets. Unlike the javax.servlet.http package, this package does not contain protocol-specific functionality and can be used to implement any standard or custom protocol. The javax.servlet package contains the interfaces and classes shown in Table 24.1.

Table 24.1   Interfaces and Classes of the javax.servlet Package

Interfaces	RequestDispatcher
	Servlet
	ServletConfig
	ServletContext
	ServletRequest
	ServletResponse
	SingleThreadModel
Classes	GenericServlet
	ServletInputStream
	ServletOutputStream
	ServletException
	UnavailableException

Interface RequestDispatcher

```
javax.servlet.RequestDispatcher
```

Definition

```
public interface RequestDispatcher
```

Serves as a "wrapper" around a server resource and provides request forwarding and server-side include functionality. Use the getRequestDispatcher() method of the ServletContext object to get a RequestDispatcher object.

Methods

forward()

```
public void forward(ServletRequest request, ServletResponse
    response) throws ServletException, java.io.IOException
```

Forwards a request from a servlet to another server resource (known as the delegate). Since the delegate servlet must generate all content, the servlet that calls the forward() method should not acquire a reference to the output stream (i.e., use the getWriter() or getOutputStream() methods) or attempt to set HTTP headers (i.e., use the setHeader() or setStatus() methods). This allows the first servlet to perform preliminary processing and the second to generate the response. This method must be called before the response is committed.

include()

```
public void include(ServletRequest request, ServletResponse
    response) throws ServletException, java.io.IOException
```

Allows the output generated by another server resource to be included in the servlet's response. The included servlet should not attempt to set the response status code or any HTTP headers (i.e., use the setStatus() or setHeader() methods). Setting response codes and headers is the responsibility of the calling servlet.

Interface Servlet

> javax.servlet.Servlet

Definition

```
public interface Servlet
```

The Servlet interface defines the methods that every servlet must implement. That is, every servlet must implement the Servlet interface. Typically, most servlets implement the Servlet interface by extending GenericServlet or HttpServlet (which implement Servlet). Most notably, the Servlet interface defines the lifecycle methods init(), service(), and destroy().

Methods

destroy()

```
public void destroy()
```

Called by the servlet container immediately before the servlet is unloaded. Should be used to free any resources held by the servlet. Returns nothing.

getServletConfig()

```
public ServletConfig getServletConfig()
```

Returns a ServletConfig object, which contains servlet initialization parameters and other server configuration settings.

getServletInfo()

```
public String getServletInfo()
```

Returns a String that contains a brief description of the servlet.

init()

```
public void init(ServletConfig config) throws ServletException
```

Called exactly once when the servlet is first loaded. One-time initialization should be performed here. This method is guaranteed to be called before the service() method is invoked. Returns nothing.

service()

```
public void service(ServletRequest request, ServletResponse
    response) throws ServletException, java.io.IOException
```

Called in response to each request. The servlet container passes objects that represent the client's request and the server's response to this method. Returns nothing.

Interface ServletConfig

> javax.servlet.ServletConfig

Definition

```
public interface ServletConfig
```

The ServletConfig interface is implemented by an object that the servlet container passes to the servlet during initialization. This object contains configuration information, including initialization parameters and the ServletContext object. This interface is also implemented by GenericServlet. A Servlet-Config object is passed to the servlet's init() method.

Methods

getInitParameter()

```
public String getInitParameter(String name)
```

Returns a String that contains the value of the specified initialization parameter or null if the parameter does not exist.

getInitParameterNames()

```
public java.util.Enumeration getInitParameterNames()
```

Returns an Enumeration of String objects that contain the names of the servlet's initialization parameters or an empty Enumeration if no initialization parameters exist.

getServletContext()

```
public ServletContext getServletContext()
```

Returns a ServletContext object that contains information about the environment in which the servlet is running.

getServletName()

```
public String getServletName()
```

Returns a String object that contains the name of this servlet instance. This name can be assigned by the servlet container or from within the Web application deployment descriptor. For an unregistered (and therefore unnamed) servlet, this method returns the servlet's class name.

Interface ServletContext

> javax.servlet.ServletContext

Definition

```
public interface ServletContext
```

The ServletContext interface defines methods that allow a servlet to communicate with the servlet container in order to log events and obtain information about the servlet's environment. A handle to a ServletContext object may be obtained using the getServletContext() method of the ServletConfig object or GenericServlet (which implements the ServletConfig interface).

Methods

getAttribute()

```
public Object getAttribute(String name)
```

Returns an Object of the specified name that has been stored in the servlet context or null if the attribute does not exist. An object can be stored in the context using the setAttribute() method. Objects stored in the servlet context endure as long as the servlet container is running. This method can be used to pass objects between servlets within the same context.

getAttributeNames()

```
public java.util.Enumeration getAttributeNames()
```

Returns an Enumeration of String objects that contain the names of the attributes available within this servlet context. If the context contains no attributes, an empty Enumeration is returned.

getContext()

```
public ServletContext getContext(String uripath)
```

Returns a ServletContext object related to a given URI path or null if there is no ServletContext associated with this path (or if disallowed by security policies). The specified URI path must be an absolute path (i.e., it must begin with a "/") that is interpreted relative to the server's document root.

getInitParameter()

```
public String getInitParameter(String name)
```

Returns a `String` that contains the value of the specified initialization parameter or `null` if the parameter does not exist.

getInitParameterNames()

```
public java.util.Enumeration getInitParameterNames()
```

Returns an `Enumeration` of `String` objects that contain the names of the servlet's initialization parameters or an empty `Enumeration` if no initialization parameters exist.

getMajorVersion()

```
public int getMajorVersion()
```

Returns the major version number of the Servlet API supported by this servlet container.

getMimeType()

```
public String getMimeType(String file)
```

Returns a `String` that describes the MIME type of the specified file or `null` if unknown. MIME types depend on server configuration and may be set from within the Web application deployment descriptor file.

getMinorVersion()

```
public int getMinorVersion()
```

Returns the minor version number of the Servlet API supported by this servlet container.

getNamedDispatcher()

```
public RequestDispatcher getNamedDispatcher(String name)
```

Returns a `RequestDispatcher` object that corresponds to the specified servlet name. The servlet name can be retrieved using the `ServletConfig` or `Generic-Servlet` object's `getServletName()` method.

getRealPath()

    public String getRealPath(String path)

Returns a String that describes the physical (file system) path corresponding to the specified virtual path. Returns null if the translation fails for any reason (such as if the requested resource resides within a .war file).

getRequestDispatcher()

    public RequestDispatcher getRequestDispatcher(String path)

Returns a RequestDispatcher object associated with the given path. This object provides request forwarding and server-side include functionality. The path must be an absolute path (i.e., it must begin with a "/") that is interpreted relative to the servlet context root.

getResource()

    public java.net.URL getResource(String path) throws
      java.net.MalformedURLException

Returns a URL object that provides access to the specified resource or null if the resource is not found. The path must be an absolute path (i.e., it must begin with a "/") that is interpreted relative to the servlet context root.

getResourceAsStream()

    public java.io.InputStream getResourceAsStream(String path)

Returns an input stream to the specified resource or null if the resource is not found. The path must be an absolute path (i.e., it must begin with a "/") that is interpreted relative to the servlet context root.

getServerInfo()

    public String getServerInfo()

Returns a String that contains the servlet container's name and version in the form *name/version*.

log()

    public void log(String msg)

Writes the specified message to the servlet log file. Returns nothing.

    public void log(String message, Throwable throwable)

Writes the specified message and the stack trace to the servlet log file. Useful for logging exceptions. Returns nothing.

removeAttribute()

```
public void removeAttribute(String name)
```

Removes the attribute bound to the specified name within the current servlet context. Returns nothing.

setAttribute()

```
public void setAttribute(String name, Object object)
```

Binds the specified `Object` to the specified name within the current servlet context. The object can be retrieved using the `getAttribute()` method. This method can be used to pass objects between servlets within the same context. Returns nothing.

Interface ServletRequest

> javax.servlet.ServletRequest

Definition

```
public interface ServletRequest
```

The ServletRequest interface encapsulates information pertaining to a client request. An object that implements this interface is created by the server and passed as a parameter to the servlet's service() method. Some of the request information contained in the ServletRequest object includes content length, content type, and protocol. In addition, the ServletRequest object provides a handle to the client's input stream. Although ServletRequest is protocol independent, other interfaces may extend this interface to provide better support for a specific protocol. For instance, the HttpServletRequest interface extends ServletRequest and provides additional HTTP information and services.

Methods

getAttribute()

```
public Object getAttribute(String name)
```

Returns an Object stored within the request that corresponds to the specified attribute name or null if the attribute does not exist. This method is used to obtain information about the request that is not already provided by another method or to retrieve objects stored in the request by another servlet. The naming convention for attributes should be the same as packages. Servlet containers may add container-specific information to the request in the form of request attributes. For example, Table 24.2 describes three request attributes provided by some servlet containers that contain information regarding a secure SSL connection. This method can be used to pass objects between servlets. It is typically used in conjunction with the forward() and include() methods of the RequestDispatcher interface.

Table 24.2   Secure SSL Connection Request Attributes Provided by Some Containers

Attribute Name	Attribute Object Type
javax.net.ssl.cipher_suite	String
javax.net.ssl.peer_certificates	javax.security.cert.X509Certificate array
javax.net.ssl.session	javax.net.ssl.SSLSession

getAttributeNames()

```
public java.util.Enumeration getAttributeNames()
```

Returns an Enumeration of String objects that contain the names of the attributes included in the request. If the request contains no attributes, an empty Enumeration is returned.

getCharacterEncoding()

```
public String getCharacterEncoding()
```

Returns a String description of the request's character set encoding (e.g., ISO-8859-1). That is, this method specifies the character-encoding method used to encode the body of the request. This method returns null if the request does not specify a character encoding.

getContentLength()

```
public int getContentLength()
```

Returns an integer that indicates the size of the request's data portion in bytes or -1 if unknown. For HTTP requests, the content length is specified by the Content-Length HTTP header.

getContentType()

```
public String getContentType()
```

Returns a String that describes the MIME type of the request's data portion or null if unknown. For HTTP requests, the content type is specified by the Content-Type HTTP header.

getInputStream()

```
public ServletInputStream getInputStream() throws
    java.io.IOException
```

Returns an input stream to the request's data portion as a ServletInputStream object. This input stream should be used to read binary data. The getReader() method should be used to read text information.

getLocale()

```
public java.util.Locale getLocale()
```

Returns a Locale object that indicates the client's preferred locale based on the Accept-Language HTTP header. If the request does not include an Accept-Language header, the server's default locale is returned.

getLocales()

```
public java.util.Enumeration getLocales()
```

Returns an Enumeration that contains Locale objects in order of the client's preference according to the Accept-Language HTTP header. If the request does not include an Accept-Language header, this method returns an Enumeration containing the server's default locale.

getParameter()

```
public String getParameter(String name)
```

Returns the String value of the specified parameter or null if the parameter does not exist. For HTTP requests, this method can be used to retrieve a Web variable passed in a query string or in the body of a POST request. Use this method only when you wish to retrieve a single value. For parameters that may contain multiple parameters, use getParameterValues().

getParameterNames()

```
public java.util.Enumeration getParameterNames()
```

Returns an Enumeration of String objects that contain the names of all parameters passed in this request. If no parameters exist, an empty Enumeration is returned.

getParameterValues()

```
public String[] getParameterValues(String name)
```

Returns a String array that contains all values of the specified parameter or null if the parameter does not exist. For HTTP requests, this method can be used to retrieve the values of a Web variable passed in a query string or in the body of a POST request.

getProtocol()

```
public String getProtocol()
```

Returns a String that describes the name and version of the protocol used by the request. The protocol is displayed in this format:

protocol/major_version.minor_version

getReader()

```
public java.io.BufferedReader getReader() throws
    java.io.IOException
```

Returns a BufferedReader object for reading text information from the data portion of the request. When necessary, character set translation is handled automatically. This method should be used only for text information. For reading binary data, use the getInputStream() method.

getRemoteAddr()

```
public String getRemoteAddr()
```

Returns a String that contains the client's IP address.

getRemoteHost()

```
public String getRemoteHost()
```

Returns a String that contains the client's fully qualified hostname or, if the hostname cannot be determined, the client's IP address.

getRequestDispatcher()

```
public RequestDispatcher getRequestDispatcher(String path)
```

Returns a RequestDispatcher object associated with the given path. This object provides request forwarding and server-side include functionality. The difference between this method and the getRequestDispatcher() method implemented by ServletContext is that this method accepts both absolute and relative paths (i.e., they may or may not begin with a "/"). Though relative paths are allowed, they must reference resources within the current servlet context.

getScheme()

```
public String getScheme()
```

Returns a String that describes the scheme indicated in the requested URL. The scheme usually describes the requested protocol. For example, http, https, ftp, and telnet are common schemes.

getServerName()

```
public String getServerName()
```

Returns a String that contains the hostname of the server that received the request.

getServerPort()

```
public int getServerPort()
```

Returns an integer that indicates the port on which the server received the request.

isSecure()

```
public boolean isSecure()
```

Returns a boolean value that indicates whether the request was received over a secure connection, such as HTTPS. This method returns true if the connection was secure; otherwise, it returns false.

removeAttribute()

```
public void removeAttribute(String name)
```

Removes the named attribute from the request. This method is rarely used because objects stored in the request are automatically released after the request is processed.

setAttribute()

```
public void setAttribute(String name, Object o)
```

Stores an Object in the request and binds it to the specified name. The object can be retrieved using the getAttribute() method. Request attributes are reset with each new request. This method is useful for passing objects between servlets. It is often used in conjunction with the forward() and include() methods of the RequestDispatcher interface. Returns nothing.

Interface ServletResponse

javax.servlet.ServletResponse

Definition

```
public interface ServletResponse
```

The ServletResponse interface encapsulates information pertaining to the server's response. An object that implements this interface is created by the servlet container and passed as a parameter to the servlet's service() method. The ServletResponse object provides a handle to the output stream and allows the servlet to specify the content length and content type of the response. Although ServletResponse is protocol independent, other interfaces may extend this interface to provide better support for a specific protocol. For instance, the HttpServletResponse interface extends ServletResponse and provides additional HTTP services.

Methods

flushBuffer()

```
public void flushBuffer()
```

Flushes the output buffer to the client and commits the response (i.e., the HTTP status code and headers are sent).

getBufferSize()

```
public int getBufferSize()
```

Returns the size of the response buffer in bytes. If no buffer is used, this method returns zero (0).

getCharacterEncoding()

```
public String getCharacterEncoding()
```

Returns a String description of the character set encoding used by the data portion of the response. If no character set has been assigned, ISO-8859-1 is assigned by default.

getLocale()

```
public java.util.Locale getLocale()
```

Returns a `Locale` object that indicates the locale assigned to this response.

getOutputStream()

```
public ServletOutputStream getOutputStream() throws
    java.io.IOException
```

Returns a handle to the output stream as a `ServletOutputStream` object. This output stream should be used when sending binary data. For text information, use the `getWriter()` method.

getWriter()

```
public java.io.PrintWriter getWriter() throws
    java.io.IOException
```

Returns a `PrintWriter` object for writing text information to the output stream. Use the `getOutputStream()` method to send binary data.

isCommitted()

```
public boolean isCommitted()
```

Returns a `boolean` value that indicates whether the response has been committed (i.e., the HTTP status code and headers have been sent). This method returns `true` if the response has been committed; otherwise, it returns `false`.

reset()

```
public void reset()
```

Clears all information in the response buffer, including the HTTP status code and any headers. If the response has already been committed, this method throws an `IllegalStateException`.

setBufferSize()

```
public void setBufferSize(int size)
```

Sets the minimum buffer size to be used when buffering the response. The actual size of the buffer used by the server can be retrieved with the `getBufferSize()` method. The server may choose a larger buffer but cannot use a buffer smaller than that specified by this method. A larger buffer sends information in larger chunks, which may be more efficient. A larger buffer also allows more time to set the HTTP status code and headers before the response is committed. On the other hand, a smaller buffer reduces demand for server resources (e.g., memory) and returns information to the client more quickly.

setContentLength()

```
public void setContentLength(int len)
```

Sets the content length of the response. For an HTTP response, this method sets the value of the Content-Length header. Returns nothing.

setContentType()

```
public void setContentType(String type)
```

Sets the content type of the response. For an HTTP response, this method sets the value of the Content-Type header. Returns nothing.

setLocale()

```
public void setLocale(java.util.Locale loc)
```

Sets the locale for the response. This method sets the appropriate headers in order to communicate the locale to the client. For an HTTP response, this method sets the character-encoding portion of the Content-Type header. If no locale is specified, the default server locale is used.

Interface SingleThreadModel

> javax.servlet.SingleThreadModel

Definition

```
public interface SingleThreadModel
```

The SingleThreadModel interface defines no methods and serves only as a flag that conveys to the server that the servlet should run in a single thread. The SingleThreadModel interface guarantees that no two threads will execute this servlet concurrently. That is, threads that execute the servlet's service() method will never run concurrently when servicing requests. The SingleThreadModel is the simplest way to ensure thread safety within a servlet.

To help offset the performance penalty incurred by executing only a single thread, a pool of servlet instances is usually created for each SingleThreadModel servlet. As requests arrive for a servlet that implements the SingleThreadModel interface, the request is routed to a free servlet instance. Keep in mind that this method of enforcing thread safety requires additional server resources.

Class GenericServlet

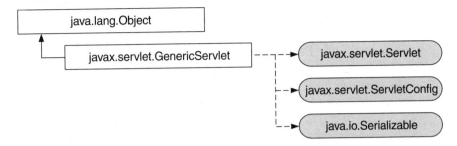

Definition

```
public class GenericServlet implements Servlet, ServletConfig,
    Serializable
```

The GenericServlet class implements the Servlet and ServletConfig interfaces. This class is provided to give the servlet developer a basic framework from which to start. The GenericServlet class implements the init() and destroy() methods as well as the methods defined by ServletConfig. It also provides a log() method for logging significant events. By extending the GenericServlet class, a functional servlet can be built by simply overriding the service() method. However, it is always a good practice to override the get-ServletInfo() method as well in order to provide a brief description of the servlet to the servlet container. This class is protocol independent but it may be extended to add protocol-specific functionality. For example, HttpServlet extends GenericServlet and adds HTTP-specific functionality.

Constructors

GenericServlet()

```
public GenericServlet()
```

Default constructor. Performs no work.

Methods

destroy()

```
public void destroy()
```

Called automatically by the server when the servlet is unloaded. This method can be used to free any resources held by the servlet. The servlet destruction is noted in the log file. This method is called immediately before the servlet is removed from service (after all requests have been processed by the `service()` method).

getInitParameter()

```
public String getInitParameter(String name)
```

Returns a `String` that contains the value of the specified initialization parameter or `null` if the parameter does not exist. This is a convenience method that simply calls the `ServletConfig` object's `getInitParameter()` method.

getInitParameterNames()

```
public java.util.Enumeration getInitParameterNames()
```

Returns an `Enumeration` of `String` objects that contain the names of the servlet's initialization parameters or an empty `Enumeration` if no initialization parameters exist. This is a convenience method that simply calls the `ServletConfig` object's `getInitParameterNames()` method.

getServletConfig()

```
public ServletConfig getServletConfig()
```

Returns a `ServletConfig` object that provides access to servlet initialization parameters and other server configuration settings.

getServletContext()

```
public ServletContext getServletContext()
```

Returns a `ServletContext` object that contains information about the environment in which the servlet is running. This is a convenience method that simply calls the `ServletConfig` object's `getServletContext()` method.

getServletInfo()

```
public String getServletInfo()
```

Returns a `String` object that contains a brief description of the servlet. If not overridden, this method returns an empty string by default.

getServletName()

```
public String getServletName()
```

Returns a String object that contains the name of this servlet instance. This name can be assigned by the servlet container or from within the Web application deployment descriptor. For an unregistered (and therefore unnamed) servlet, this method returns the servlet's class name. This is a convenience method that simply calls the ServletConfig object's getServletName() method.

init()

```
public void init(ServletConfig config) throws ServletException
```

Method defined by the Servlet interface that is called by the servlet container when the servlet is first loaded. Performs servlet initialization tasks and notes the servlet initialization in the log file. Returns nothing. This method stores the ServletConfig object for future reference. When overriding this method, call super.init(config) in order to store the ServletConfig object.

```
public void init() throws ServletException
```

Convenience method that frees the developer from having to store the ServletConfig object (and implement the getServletConfig() method) or call super.init(config) (to pass the ServletConfig object to the parent class). This method is actually called by the GenericServlet object's implementation of the init(ServletConfig) method previously described. Returns nothing. When overriding init(), the ServletConfig object can be retrieved using getServletConfig().

log()

```
public void log(String msg)
```

Writes the name of the servlet and the specified message to the servlet log file. The name and location of this file are server specific. Returns nothing.

```
public void log(String message, Throwable t)
```

Writes the name of the servlet, the specified message, and the stack trace to the servlet log file. The name and location of this file are server specific. Returns nothing.

service()

```
public abstract void service(ServletRequest request,
    ServletResponse response) throws ServletException,
    java.io.IOException
```

Called for each client request. The servlet container passes objects that represent the client's request and the server's response to this method. Returns nothing. This method is declared abstract so classes that extend Generic-Servlet, such as HttpServlet, must implement this method.

Class ServletInputStream

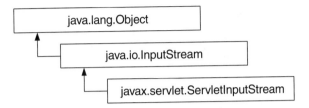

Definition

```
public abstract class ServletInputStream extends
   java.io.InputStream
```

The ServletInputStream class is an abstract class that is implemented by the servlet container. Subclasses of this class must implement the read() method defined by the InputStream object. ServletInputStream provides an input stream for reading binary data from the request as well as a readLine() method that allows servlets to read data from the client request one line at a time.

Constructors

ServletInputStream()

```
protected ServletInputStream()
```

Default constructor. Performs no work.

Methods

readLine()

```
public int readLine(byte b[], int off, int len) throws
   java.io.IOException
```

Returns an integer value that indicates the number of bytes read or -1 if the end of the stream was reached. Starting at the offset (off), this method reads the specified number of bytes (len) into a byte array (b). It stops reading when the end of the stream is reached or a linefeed character ("\n") is encountered (the linefeed character is read into the array).

Class ServletOutputStream

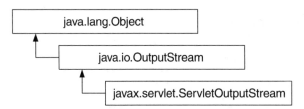

Definition

```
public abstract class ServletOutputStream extends
    java.io.OutputStream
```

The ServletOutputStream class is an abstract class that is implemented by the servlet container. This class provides an output stream for sending binary data to the client. ServletOutputStream implements many variations of print() and println() methods used for writing data to the output stream.

Constructors

ServletOutputStream()

```
protected ServletOutputStream()
```

Default constructor. Performs no work.

Methods

print()

```
public void print(boolean b) throws java.io.IOException
```

Writes a boolean value to the output stream. Returns nothing.

```
public void print(char c) throws java.io.IOException
```

Writes a character value to the output stream. Returns nothing.

```
public void print(double d) throws java.io.IOException
```

Writes a double value to the output stream. Returns nothing.

```
public void print(float f) throws java.io.IOException
```

Writes a float value to the output stream. Returns nothing.

```
public void print(int i) throws java.io.IOException
```

Writes an integer value to the output stream. Returns nothing.

```
public void print(long l) throws java.io.IOException
```

Writes a `long` value to the output stream. Returns nothing.

```
public void print(String s) throws java.io.IOException
```

Writes a `String` value to the output stream. Returns nothing.

println()

```
public void println() throws java.io.IOException
```

Writes a carriage return/linefeed (CRLF) to the output stream. Returns nothing.

```
public void println(boolean b) throws java.io.IOException
```

Writes a `boolean` value followed by a CRLF to the output stream. Returns nothing.

```
public void println(char c) throws java.io.IOException
```

Writes a character value followed by a CRLF to the output stream. Returns nothing.

```
public void println(double d) throws java.io.IOException
```

Writes a `double` value followed by a CRLF to the output stream. Returns nothing.

```
public void println(float f) throws java.io.IOException
```

Writes a `float` value followed by a CRLF to the output stream. Returns nothing.

```
public void println(int i) throws java.io.IOException
```

Writes an integer value followed by a CRLF to the output stream. Returns nothing.

```
public void println(long l) throws java.io.IOException
```

Writes a `long` value followed by a CRLF to the output stream. Returns nothing.

```
public void println(String s) throws java.io.IOException
```

Writes a `String` value followed by a CRLF to the output stream. Returns nothing.

Class ServletException

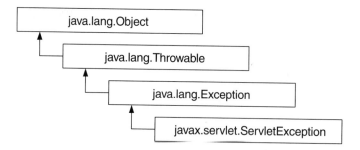

```
java.lang.Object
    java.lang.Throwable
        java.lang.Exception
            javax.servlet.ServletException
```

Definition

> javax.servlet.ServletException extends Exception

The ServletException exception is thrown by the servlet to indicate a problem. The problem should be described by the message parameter passed to the ServletException object's constructor.

Constructors

ServletException()

> public ServletException()

Constructs a new ServletException object.

> public ServletException(String message)

Constructs a new ServletException object using the specified message.

> public ServletException(String message, Throwable rootCause)

Constructs a new ServletException object using the specified message and an exception that represents the "root cause" of the ServletException's being thrown.

> public ServletException(Throwable rootCause)

Constructs a new ServletException object using an exception that represents the "root cause" of the ServletException's being thrown.

Methods

getRootCause()

> public Throwable getRootCause()

Returns the exception that caused the ServletException to be thrown.

Class UnavailableException

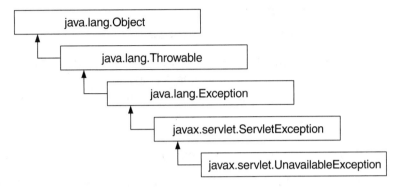

Definition

```
public class UnavailableException extends ServletException
```

A servlet throws an UnavailableException exception to indicate that it is not available for some reason. The servlet may be permanently unavailable (e.g., the servlet is misconfigured or contains an error) or temporarily unavailable (e.g., network traffic is too high or server load is too great). The problem should be described by the message parameter passed to the UnavailableException object's constructor.

Constructors

UnavailableException()

```
public UnavailableException(String msg)
```

Constructs a new UnavailableException that includes a description of the problem that makes the servlet permanently unavailable.

```
public UnavailableException(String msg, int seconds)
```

Constructs a new UnavailableException that includes a description of the problem that makes the servlet temporarily unavailable as well as an estimate of how long, in seconds, it will be unavailable (zero or negative no estimate is available).

Methods

getUnavailableSeconds()

```
public int getUnavailableSeconds()
```

Returns an integer that indicates the number of seconds the servlet estimates it will be unavailable. If no estimate is available or the servlet is permanently unavailable, a negative number is returned.

isPermanent()

```
public boolean isPermanent()
```

Returns a boolean value to indicate whether the server is permanently unavailable. This method returns true if the servlet is permanently unavailable; otherwise, it returns false. A permanently unavailable condition requires some administrative action to correct the problem.

CHAPTER 25

javax.servlet.http Package

The javax.servlet.http package contains interfaces and classes that simplify the process of writing servlets that use the HTTP protocol. This package defines and implements much of the functionality required to communicate via HTTP. Cookie, HTTP redirect, and session management support are just a few examples of the functionality provided by the javax.servlet.http package. The javax.servlet.http package contains the interfaces and classes shown in Table 25.1.

Table 25.1   Interfaces and Classes of the javax.servlet.http Package

Interfaces	HttpServletRequest
	HttpServletResponse
	HttpSession
	HttpSessionBindingListener
Classes	Cookie
	HttpServlet
	HttpSessionBindingEvent
	HttpUtils

Interface HttpServletRequest

Definition

> public interface HttpServletRequest extends ServletRequest

The HttpServletRequest interface encapsulates vital information pertaining to an HTTP service request. Much of its functionality is inherited from the ServletRequest interface, which it extends. An object that implements the HttpServletRequest interface is created by the servlet container and passed as a parameter to the servlet's service(), doGet(), and doPost() methods.

Some of the request information contained in the HttpServletRequest object includes HTTP header information, requested URL, content type, content length, Web variables, and cookies. In addition, the HttpServletRequest object provides a handle to the client's input stream via the getReader() or getInputStream() method inherited from ServletRequest.

Methods

getAuthType()

> public String getAuthType()

Returns a String object describing the authentication scheme used by this request (e.g., BASIC, DIGEST, SSL) or null if no authentication is used.

getContextPath()

> public String getContextPath()

Returns a String object that contains the context path portion of the request URL. The context path indicates the Web application in which the resource is stored. The context path begins with a "/" character but does not end with one. If the requested resource resides within the default (or root) context, this method returns an empty string (""). For example, this method returns the value /examples for the following request:

http://localhost:8080/examples/index.html

getCookies()

    public Cookie[] getCookies()

Returns an array of Cookie objects. Returns a Cookie object for every cookie included in the request or null if the requested does not contain cookies.

getDateHeader()

    public long getDateHeader(String name)

Returns a long that represents the date value of the specified HTTP header field. If the specified header cannot be converted to a date, an Illegal-ArgumentException is thrown. A -1 is returned if the specified header field does not exist. The name parameter is not case-sensitive. This method can be used with any header fields that contain dates, such as the If-Modified-Since HTTP header.

getHeader()

    public String getHeader(String name)

Returns the String value of the specified HTTP header field. A null is returned if the specified header does not exist. The name parameter is not case-sensitive.

getHeaderNames()

    public java.util.Enumeration getHeaderNames()

Returns an Enumeration of String objects that contain the names of each HTTP header field in the request. If the request does not contain headers, an empty Enumeration is returned.

getHeaders()

    public java.util.Enumeration getHeaders(String name)

Returns an Enumeration of String objects that contain all of the values of the specified HTTP header field. If the request does not contain any headers, an empty Enumeration is returned.

getIntHeader()

    public int getIntHeader(String name)

Returns the integer value of the specified HTTP header. If the specified header cannot be converted to an integer, a NumberFormatException is thrown. If the specified header does not exist, a -1 is returned. The name parameter is not case-sensitive.

getMethod()

```
public String getMethod()
```

Returns a String object that describes the HTTP method used by this request (e.g., GET, POST, PUT, HEAD).

getPathInfo()

```
public String getPathInfo()
```

Returns a String object that represents the portion of the URL path immediately following the servlet path but prior to the query string. Returns null if no extra path information exists in the URL.

getPathTranslated()

```
public String getPathTranslated()
```

Converts the portion of the URL path immediately following the servlet path but prior to the query string to a real path (as it exists in the file system) and returns the real path as a String. Returns null if no extra path information exists in the URL.

getQueryString()

```
public String getQueryString()
```

Returns a String object that contains the query string portion of the URL. Returns null if the URL does not contain a query string.

getRemoteUser()

```
public String getRemoteUser()
```

Returns a String object that contains the name of the user that issued this request if the user was authenticated. The name is contained in the HTTP authentication header field. Returns null if the user has not been authenticated or the name is not available for any other reason.

getRequestedSessionId()

```
public String getRequestedSessionId()
```

Returns a `String` object containing the session ID in this request. If the request contains an invalid session ID, this method creates a new session and returns the new session ID. Returns `null` if the request is not associated with a session.

getRequestURI()

```
public String getRequestURI()
```

Returns a `String` object containing the complete URI, excluding the query string.

getServletPath()

```
public String getServletPath()
```

Returns a `String` consisting of the portion of the URL that contains the servlet path.

getSession()

```
public HttpSession getSession()
```

Returns an `HttpSession` object representing the current valid session. If the request is not associated with a valid session, a new session is created and returned.

```
public HttpSession getSession(boolean create)
```

Returns an `HttpSession` object representing the current valid session. If the request is not associated with a valid session and the `create` parameter is `true`, a new session is created and returned. If `create` is `false` and no valid session exists, `null` is returned.

getUserPrincipal()

```
public java.security.Principal getUserPrincipal()
```

Returns a `Principal` object containing information about the currently authenticated user. If the user is not authenticated, `null` is returned.

isRequestedSessionIdFromCookie()

```
public boolean isRequestedSessionIdFromCookie()
```

Returns a `boolean` value indicating whether the request's session ID was passed in a cookie. Returns `true` if a cookie was used; otherwise, returns `false`.

isRequestedSessionIdFromURL()

```
public boolean isRequestedSessionIdFromURL()
```

Returns a boolean value indicating whether the request's session ID was passed as part of the URL. Returns `true` if the session ID was passed in the URL; otherwise, returns `false`.

isRequestedSessionIdValid()

```
public boolean isRequestedSessionIdValid()
```

Returns a boolean value indicating whether the request's session ID is valid. An invalid session ID usually indicates that the session has expired. Returns `true` if the session ID is valid; otherwise, returns `false`.

isUserInRole()

```
public boolean isUserInRole(String role)
```

Returns a boolean value indicating whether the current authenticated user is included in the specified role. If the current user has not been authenticated, this method returns `false`. Roles can be created and assigned to users within the Web application deployment descriptor.

Interface HttpServletResponse

Definition

```
public interface HttpServletResponse extends ServletResponse
```

The HttpServletResponse interface encapsulates information and functionality pertaining to an HTTP response. Many of the methods that it defines are inherited from the ServletResponse interface, which it extends. The Http-ServletResponse interface is implemented by the server and passed as a parameter into the servlet's service(), doGet(), and doPost() methods. Some of the functionality implemented by the HttpServletResponse object includes adding cookies, sending redirects, setting headers, and retrieving a handle to the output stream (in order to return data to the client).

Methods

addCookie()

```
public void addCookie(Cookie cookie)
```

Adds the specified cookie to the server response. This method adds a Set-Cookie HTTP header to the response. Returns nothing.

addDateHeader()

```
public void addDateHeader(String name, long date)
```

Adds a new header to the response according to the specified name and given date value. The date is expressed as a long that represents the number of milliseconds since January 1, 1970 GMT. This number can be retrieved from a java.util.Date object using its getTime() method. This method allows multiple values to be specified for a single header field. Returns nothing.

addHeader()

```
public void addHeader(String name, String value)
```

Adds a new header to the response according to the specified name and given value. This method allows multiple values to be specified for a single header field. Returns nothing.

addIntHeader()

```
public void addIntHeader(String name, int value)
```

Adds a new header to the response according to the specified name and given integer value. This method allows multiple values to be specified for a single header field. This method returns nothing.

containsHeader()

```
public boolean containsHeader(String name)
```

Returns a `boolean` value that indicates whether the response contains the specified header. Returns `true` if the header exists; otherwise, `false`.

encodeRedirectURL()

```
public String encodeRedirectURL(String url)
```

Returns a `String` object that encodes the specified URL to include the session ID for use with the `sendRedirect()` method. If no encoding is necessary, this method returns the URL unchanged.

encodeURL()

```
public String encodeURL(String url)
```

Returns a `String` object that encodes the specified URL to include the session ID. If no encoding is necessary, this method returns the URL unchanged.

sendError()

```
public void sendError(int sc) throws
   java.io.IOException
```

Generates an error response using the specified status code and a default message. If the response has already been committed, this method throws an `IllegalStateException`. Returns nothing.

```
public void sendError(int sc, String msg) throws
   java.io.IOException
```

Generates an error response using the specified status code and message. If the response has already been committed, this method throws an `IllegalState-Exception`. Returns nothing.

sendRedirect()

```
public void sendRedirect(String location) throws
    java.io.IOException
```

Generates a temporary redirect response using the specified redirect location. This method accepts both relative and absolute URLs. If a relative URL is specified, the servlet container automatically converts it to an absolute URL. If the response has already been committed, this method throws an `Illegal-StateException`. Returns nothing.

setDateHeader()

```
public void setDateHeader(String name, long date)
```

Adds or replaces the named response header using the given date value. The date is expressed as a `long` that represents the number of milliseconds since January 1, 1970 GMT. This number can be retrieved from a `java.util.Date` object using its `getTime()` method. If a header field having this name already exists, it is replaced with the new value. Returns nothing.

setHeader()

```
public void setHeader(String name, String value)
```

Adds or replaces the named response header using the given value. If a header field having this name already exists, it is replaced with the new value. Returns nothing.

setIntHeader()

```
public void setIntHeader(String name, int value)
```

Adds or replaces the named response header using the given integer value. If a header field having this name already exists, it is replaced with the new value. Returns nothing.

setStatus()

```
public void setStatus(int sc)
```

Sets the response status code. This method should be used when the response is processed without error (e.g., returns `SC_OK` or `SC_MOVED_TEMPORARILY`). If an error occurs, use `sendError()` instead. Returns nothing.

Variables

SC_ACCEPTED

```
public static final int SC_ACCEPTED
```

Integer variable representing HTTP status code 202. Indicates that the request has been received and is being processed.

SC_BAD_GATEWAY

```
public static final int SC_BAD_GATEWAY
```

Integer variable representing HTTP status code 502. Indicates that the server received an invalid response from a gateway to which it forwarded the request.

SC_BAD_REQUEST

```
public static final int SC_BAD_REQUEST
```

Integer variable representing HTTP status code 400. Indicates that the request used invalid syntax and should not be repeated without modification.

SC_CONFLICT

```
public static final int SC_CONFLICT
```

Integer variable representing HTTP status code 409. Indicates that the request cannot be serviced because of a resource conflict.

SC_CONTINUE

```
public static final int SC_CONTINUE
```

Integer variable representing HTTP status code 100. Indicates that the client may continue to make requests.

SC_CREATED

```
public static final int SC_CREATED
```

Integer variable representing HTTP status code 201. Indicates that the request was fulfilled successfully and resulted in the creation of a new resource.

SC_EXPECTATION_FAILED

```
public static final int SC_EXPECTATION_FAILED
```

Integer variable representing the HTTP status code 417. Indicates that the server could not satisfy the request based on the expectation specified in the Expect HTTP request header.

SC_FORBIDDEN

```
public static final int SC_FORBIDDEN
```

Integer variable representing HTTP status code 403. Indicates that the server understood the request but refuses to fulfill it.

SC_GATEWAY_TIMEOUT

```
public static final int SC_GATEWAY_TIMEOUT
```

Integer variable representing HTTP status code 504. Indicates that the server did not receive a timely response from a server to which it forwarded the request.

SC_GONE

```
public static final int SC_GONE
```

Integer variable representing HTTP status code 410. Indicates that the requested resource is no longer available.

SC_HTTP_VERSION_NOT_SUPPORTED

```
public static final int SC_HTTP_VERSION_NOT_SUPPORTED
```

Integer variable representing HTTP status code 505. Indicates that the server does not support the HTTP version used by the request.

SC_INTERNAL_SERVER_ERROR

```
public static final int SC_INTERNAL_SERVER_ERROR
```

Integer variable representing HTTP status code 500. Indicates that the server encountered an unexpected condition that prevented it from fulfilling the request.

SC_LENGTH_REQUIRED

```
public static final int SC_LENGTH_REQUIRED
```

Integer variable representing HTTP status code 411. Indicates that the request cannot be serviced unless a Content-Length header is included in the request.

SC_METHOD_NOT_ALLOWED

```
public static final int SC_METHOD_NOT_ALLOWED
```

Integer variable representing HTTP status code 405. Indicates that the method defined by the Request-Line header cannot be performed on the requested resource.

SC_MOVED_PERMANENTLY

```
public static final int SC_MOVED_PERMANENTLY
```

Integer variable representing HTTP status code 301. Indicates that the resource has been moved permanently.

SC_MOVED_TEMPORARILY

```
public static final int SC_MOVED_TEMPORARILY
```

Integer variable representing HTTP status code 302. Indicates that the resource has been moved temporarily.

SC_MULTIPLE_CHOICES

```
public static final int SC_MULTIPLE_CHOICES
```

Integer variable representing HTTP status code 300. Indicates that the resource is available from multiple locations.

SC_NO_CONTENT

```
public static final int SC_NO_CONTENT
```

Integer variable representing HTTP status code 204. Indicates that the server has fulfilled the request but there is no new information to return.

SC_NON_AUTHORITATIVE_INFORMATION

```
public static final int SC_NON_AUTHORITATIVE_INFORMATION
```

Integer variable representing HTTP status code 203. Indicates that the meta information sent in the client's request was not created by the server.

SC_NOT_ACCEPTABLE

```
public static final int SC_NOT_ACCEPTABLE
```

Integer variable representing HTTP status code 406. The requested resource consists of a format that the client's request did not include in the Accepts header.

SC_NOT_FOUND

```
public static final int SC_NOT_FOUND
```

Integer variable representing HTTP status code 404. Indicates that no resource matching the requested URL exists on the server.

SC_NOT_IMPLEMENTED

```
public static final int SC_NOT_IMPLEMENTED
```

Integer variable representing HTTP status code 501. Indicates that the server does not implement the functionality required to fulfill the request.

SC_NOT_MODIFIED

```
public static final int SC_NOT_MODIFIED
```

Integer variable representing HTTP status code 304. Indicates that the Web client issued a GET request with an If-Modified-Since header and the resource has not changed since the specified date.

SC_OK

```
public static final int SC_OK
```

Integer variable representing HTTP status code 200. Indicates that the request succeeded.

SC_PARTIAL_CONTENT

```
public static final int SC_PARTIAL_CONTENT
```

Integer variable representing HTTP status code 206. Indicates that the request was partially fulfilled.

SC_PAYMENT_REQUIRED

```
public static final int SC_PAYMENT_REQUIRED
```

Integer variable representing HTTP status code 402. Reserved for future use.

SC_PRECONDITION_FAILED

```
public static final int SC_PRECONDITION_FAILED
```

Integer variable representing HTTP status code 412. The precondition defined in one or more of the request header fields failed when evaluated by the server.

SC_PROXY_AUTHENTICATION_REQUIRED

```
public static final int SC_PROXY_AUTHENTICATION_REQUIRED
```

Integer variable representing HTTP status code 407. Indicates that the client must first be authenticated by the proxy server.

SC_REQUEST_ENTITY_TOO_LARGE

```
public static final int SC_REQUEST_ENTITY_TOO_LARGE
```

Integer variable representing HTTP status code 413. Indicates that the server refuses to service the request because the requested resource is too large.

SC_REQUEST_TIMEOUT

```
public static final int SC_REQUEST_TIMEOUT
```

Integer variable representing HTTP status code 408. Indicates that the client did not issue a request within a predefined timeout period.

SC_REQUEST_URI_TOO_LONG

```
public static final int SC_REQUEST_URI_TOO_LONG
```

Integer variable representing HTTP status code 414. Indicates that the server refuses to service the request because the requested URI is too long.

SC_REQUESTED_RANGE_NOT_SATISFIABLE

```
public static final int SC_REQUESTED_RANGE_NOT_SATISFIABLE
```

Integer representing the HTTP status code 416. Indicates that the server cannot service a request within the requested byte range.

SC_RESET_CONTENT

```
public static final int SC_RESET_CONTENT
```

Integer variable representing HTTP status code 205. Indicates that the client should reset the document view.

SC_SEE_OTHER

```
public static final int SC_SEE_OTHER
```

Integer variable representing HTTP status code 303. Indicates that the resource can be located at a different location.

SC_SERVICE_UNAVAILABLE

```
public static final int SC_SERVICE_UNAVAILABLE
```

Integer variable representing HTTP status code 503. Indicates that the server is temporarily unable to fulfill the request.

SC_SWITCHING_PROTOCOLS

```
public static final int SC_SWITCHING_PROTOCOLS
```

Integer variable representing HTTP status code 101. Indicates that the server is changing protocols as declared in the Upgrade header.

SC_UNAUTHORIZED

```
public static final int SC_UNAUTHORIZED
```

Integer variable representing HTTP status code 401. Indicates that authorization, such as username and password, is required to access this resource.

SC_UNSUPPORTED_MEDIA_TYPE

```
public static final int SC_UNSUPPORTED_MEDIA_TYPE
```

Integer variable representing HTTP status code 415. Indicates that the server is refusing to service the request because the body of the request is in a format that is not supported by the requested resource.

SC_USE_PROXY

```
public static final int SC_USE_PROXY
```

Integer variable representing HTTP status code 305. Indicates that the requested resource can be accessed only through the proxy server described by the Location header.

Interface HttpSession

> javax.servlet.http.HttpSession

Definition

```
public interface HttpSession
```

The HttpSession interface encapsulates information pertaining to an HTTP session. An object that implements this interface is created by the servlet container and returned when the getSession() method of HttpServletRequest is called. The HttpSession object provides methods to read, add, and remove various session data as well as methods to view session information such as the session identifier, creation time, and the time the session was last accessed.

Methods

getAttribute()

```
public Object getAttribute(String name)
```

Returns the session object bound to the specified name or null if the named object does not exist.

getAttributeNames()

```
public java.util.Enumeration getAttributeNames()
```

Returns an Enumeration of String objects containing the names of all attributes currently stored in the session.

getCreationTime()

```
public long getCreationTime()
```

Returns a long representing the time this session was created. The time is expressed as the number of milliseconds since January 1, 1970 GMT.

getId()

```
public String getId()
```

Returns a String object containing the unique session ID used to identify this session. This identifier is created by the servlet container and is specific to each implementation.

getLastAccessedTime()

```
public long getLastAccessedTime()
```

Returns a `long` representing the time the client last issued a request that contained this session's ID. The time is expressed as the number of milliseconds since January 1, 1970 GMT.

getMaxInactiveInterval()

```
public int getMaxInactiveInterval()
```

Returns the maximum number of seconds that a session is guaranteed to be valid without a request from the client. After the maximum inactive interval expires, the session may be expired by the servlet container. A -1 is returned for sessions that never expire.

getValue()

```
public Object getValue(String name)
```

Deprecated. Use `getAttribute()` instead.

getValueNames()

```
public String[] getValueNames()
```

Deprecated. Use `getAttributeNames()` instead.

invalidate()

```
public void invalidate()
```

Invalidates (i.e., expires) this HTTP session and releases any objects bound to it. Returns nothing.

isNew()

```
public boolean isNew()
```

Returns a `boolean` value indicating whether this session is new, meaning that it was just created by the server and has not yet been returned to the client.

putValue()

```
public void putValue(String name, Object value)
```

Deprecated. Use `setAttribute()` instead.

removeAttribute()

```
public void removeAttribute(String name)
```

Removes the named attribute from the session. If the named attribute does not exist, no work is performed. Returns nothing.

removeValue()

```
public void removeValue(String name)
```

Deprecated. Use removeAttribute() instead.

setAttribute()

```
public void setAttribute(String name, Object value)
```

Stores an object in the session under the specified name. If an object already exists in the session under the specified name, it is replaced with the new value. Returns nothing.

setMaxInactiveInterval()

```
public void setMaxInactiveInterval(int interval)
```

Sets the maximum number of seconds that a session is guaranteed to be valid without a request from the client. After the maximum inactive interval expires, the session may be expired by the servlet container.

Interface HttpSessionBindingListener

Definition

```
public interface HttpSessionBindingListener extends
    java.util.EventListener
```

The HttpSessionBindingListener interface is implemented by objects that wish to be notified when they are being bound or unbound to an HTTP session. HttpSessionBindingListener extends EventListener.

Methods

valueBound()

```
public void valueBound(HttpSessionBindingEvent event)
```

Notifies the listening object that it is being bound to an HTTP session. Returns nothing.

valueUnbound()

```
public void valueUnbound(HttpSessionBindingEvent event)
```

Notifies the listening object that it is being unbound from an HTTP session. Returns nothing.

Class Cookie

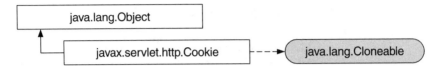

Definition

```
public class Cookie implements Cloneable
```

The Cookie class represents a cookie as originally defined by Netscape in addition to the updated cookie specification, RFC 2109. Cookies are used to store small amounts of state information on the client in the form of name/value pairs. This state information is returned to the server with every client request. Once a Cookie object is created, it is passed to the client using the HttpServletResponse object's addCookie() method.

Constructors

Cookie()

```
public Cookie(String name, String value)
```

Constructor that creates a Cookie object using the specified name and value.

Methods

clone()

```
public Object clone()
```

Returns an Object that is an exact copy of this cookie.

getComment()

```
public String getComment()
```

Returns a String object containing a comment that describes the purpose of this cookie. If no comment exists, returns null.

getDomain()

```
public String getDomain()
```

Returns a String object containing the domain to which this cookie will be returned.

getMaxAge()

```
public int getMaxAge()
```

Returns an integer value indicating the maximum age (in seconds) that this cookie remains valid. A negative value indicates that the cookie expires when the client agent is closed.

getName()

```
public String getName()
```

Returns a String object containing the name of this cookie.

getPath()

```
public String getPath()
```

Returns a String object containing all URL prefixes to which this cookie is valid.

getSecure()

```
public boolean getSecure()
```

Returns a boolean value indicating if this cookie should be returned only across a secure connection. A true value indicates that the cookie should be returned only if the connection is secure; otherwise, false is returned.

getValue()

```
public String getValue()
```

Returns a String object containing the value of this cookie.

getVersion()

```
public int getVersion()
```

Returns an integer value indicating the version of the cookie protocol currently in use. A zero (0) value indicates this cookie is using the original cookie specification defined by Netscape. A one (1) value indicates this cookie is using the updated cookie specification defined by RFC 2109.

setComment()

```
public void setComment(String purpose)
```

Adds a comment to this cookie that describes its purpose to the client agent. If the client's browser has been configured to issue a warning when cookies are received, this comment will be displayed to the user. Returns nothing.

setDomain()

```
public void setDomain(String pattern)
```

Sets the domain pattern for which this cookie is valid. This cookie should be returned only to domains that match the specified pattern. For more information on the syntax of this pattern, see RFC 2109. Returns nothing.

setMaxAge()

```
public void setMaxAge(int expire)
```

Sets the maximum age, specified in seconds, that this cookie is valid. A negative value indicates the Cookie object's default behavior—the cookie expires when the client agent is closed. Setting a zero (0) value indicates that the cookie should be deleted by the client. Returns nothing.

setPath()

```
public void setPath(String uri)
```

This cookie should be returned only when the requested resource begins with the specified URI. Returns nothing.

setSecure()

```
public void setSecure(boolean flag)
```

Indicates whether the cookie should be returned only across a secure connection. A true value indicates that the cookie should be returned only if the connection is secure. Returns nothing.

setValue()

```
public void setValue(String newValue)
```

Sets the cookie's value. Returns nothing.

setVersion()

```
public void setVersion(int v)
```

Sets the version of the cookie protocol used by this cookie. A zero (0) value indicates this cookie is using the original cookie specification defined by Netscape. A one (1) value indicates this cookie is using the updated cookie specification defined by RFC 2109. Returns nothing.

Class HttpServlet

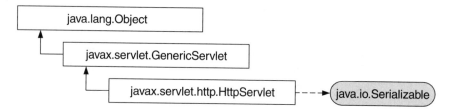

Definition

```
public abstract class HttpServlet extends GenericServlet
    implements java.io.Serializable
```

HttpServlet is an abstract class that can be extended and implemented by servlet developers. This class simplifies servlet development by providing a framework for supporting the HTTP protocol. HttpServlet extends the GenericServlet class.

Constructors

HttpServlet()

```
public HttpServlet()
```

Default constructor. Performs no work.

Methods

doDelete()

```
protected void doDelete(HttpServletRequest request,
    HttpServletResponse response) throws ServletException,
    java.io.IOException
```

Called in response to an HTTP DELETE request. The DELETE operation allows the client to request that a resource be removed from the server. Returns nothing.

doGet()

```
protected void doGet(HttpServletRequest request,
    HttpServletResponse response) throws ServletException,
    IOException
```

Called in response to an HTTP GET request. The GET operation requests a server resource. Returns nothing.

doOptions()

```
protected void doOptions(HttpServletRequest request,
    HttpServletResponse response) throws ServletException,
    java.io.IOException
```

Called in response to an HTTP OPTIONS request. The OPTIONS operation allows the client to request the HTTP methods that are supported by the requested resource. The supported methods are returned in the Allow header field. Returns nothing.

doPost()

```
protected void doPost(HttpServletRequest request,
    HttpServletResponse response) throws ServletException,
    java.io.IOException
```

Called in response to an HTTP POST request. The POST operation allows the client to transmit information to the server and specify the resource that should process this data. Returns nothing.

doPut()

```
protected void doPut(HttpServletRequest request,
    HttpServletResponse response) throws ServletException,
    java.io.IOException
```

Called in response to an HTTP PUT request. The PUT operation requests that a new resource be created on the server at the specified URL using the data included in the request. Typically used for file uploads. Returns nothing.

doTrace()

```
protected void doTrace(HttpServletRequest request,
    HttpServletResponse response) throws ServletException,
    java.io.IOException
```

Called in response to an HTTP TRACE request. The TRACE operation returns the request to the client for debugging purposes, and thus allows the client to see the request received by the server at the end of the calling chain. This information can be useful for testing or diagnostic purposes. Returns nothing.

getLastModified()

```
protected long getLastModified(HttpServletRequest request)
```

Returns a long indicating when the specified resource was last updated. This information is useful for caching information on the client. Often used in conjunction with the If-Modified-Since header. A negative value indicates that a last modified time is not available.

service()

```
protected void service(HttpServletRequest request,
    HttpServletResponse response) throws ServletException,
    java.io.IOException
```

Called in response to any request directed to this servlet by way of the HttpServlet object's service(ServletRequest, ServletResponse) method. The parameters passed to this method are HTTP specifc. Returns nothing.

```
public void service(ServletRequest request, ServletResponse
    response) throws ServletException,
    java.io.IOException
```

Called in response to any request directed to this servlet. This method overrides the basic service() method defined by the GenericServlet class. This method casts the ServletRequest and ServletResponse objects to their HTTP equivalents and then calls the HttpServlet object's service(HttpServletRequest, HttpServletResponse) method.

Class HttpSessionBindingEvent

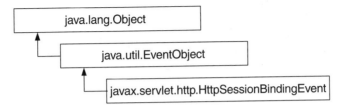

Definition

```
public class HttpSessionBindingEvent extends
    java.util.EventObject
```

The HttpSessionBindingEvent object is passed to an HttpSessionBinding-Listener whenever the listener is bound to or unbound from a session using the setAttribute() and removeAttribute() methods of the HttpSession object. The HttpSessionBindingEvent class extends EventObject.

Constructors

HttpSessionBindingEvent()

```
public HttpSessionBindingEvent(HttpSession session, String name)
```

Constructor that creates a new HttpSessionBindingEvent object using the specified HttpSession and name.

Methods

getName()

```
public String getName()
```

Returns a String object containing the name of the object to which the listener is being bound or unbound. Returns nothing.

getSession()

```
public HttpSession getSession()
```

Returns the HttpSession object to which the listener is being bound or unbound. Returns nothing.

Class HttpUtils

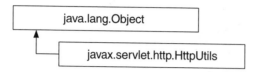

Definition

    public class HttpUtils

The HttpUtils class consists of three static utility methods.

Constructors

HttpUtils()

    public HttpUtils()

Default constructor. Performs no work.

Methods

getRequestURL()

    public static StringBuffer getRequestURL(HttpServletRequest
        request)

Returns a StringBuffer containing the URL requested by the client, excluding
any query string.

parsePostData()

    public static java.util.Hashtable parsePostData(int len,
        ServletInputStream in)

Returns a Hashtable containing the name/value pairs posted to the server. The
parameters indicate the length of the request's data (len) and the input stream
from which the data can be read (in).

parseQueryString()

    public static java.util.Hashtable parseQueryString(String s)

Returns a Hashtable containing the name/value pairs transmitted to the server
in the query string. The parameter specifies the query string to be parsed.

CHAPTER 26

Servlet API 2.3 Update

Servlet API 2.3 is the API defined by the latest version of the Java Servlet Specification. Version 2.3 deviates from version 2.2 in several significant ways. The purpose of this chapter is to document the differences between versions 2.2 and 2.3 of the Servlet API. Specifically, the following topics are discussed:

- Filtering
- Application lifecycle events
- Shared library dependencies
- New error and security attributes
- Welcome files
- New classes, interfaces, and methods

As discussed previously, Tomcat 3.*x* is the official reference implementation for Servlet API 2.2 and JSP 1.1. Likewise, Tomcat 4.*x* is the reference implementation for Servlet API 2.3 and JSP 1.2. At the time of this writing, a beta version of Tomcat 4.0 is available at *http://jakarta.apache.org/tomcat/*. However, since the final release was not ready at publication time, Tomcat 4.0 is not included on the accompanying CD.

NOTE: This chapter is based on information provided in the Java Servlet Specification 2.3 Proposed Final Draft. Though the authors of this specification do not anticipate significant changes between the proposed final draft and the final specification, it should be noted that changes are possible. Therefore, the information contained in this chapter cannot be guaranteed 100% accurate. For the latest Servlet API 2.3 slifecyclepecification, see *http://java.sun.com/products/servlet/*.

Filtering

Filters are one of the most significant new features introduced in version 2.3 of the Servlet API. Filtering provides a mechanism for performing dynamic transformations of requests and/or responses. This mechanism allows a request to be altered prior to reaching the requested resource. Likewise, the filtering framework allows servlet-generated or static content to be altered before it is returned to the client.

What Is a Filter?

A *filter* is a reusable piece of code that is capable of altering a request or reponse including any header information. Unlike servlets, filters do not usually generate a response. Rather, filters are used to adapt a request or response before it reaches its intended destination (the destination being the requested resource or the client, respectively). A filter may be applied to a single servlet, multiple servlets, or static resources. Similarly, multiple filters can be assigned to a single servlet. Filters are capable of performing the following tasks:

- Intercept the invocation of a servlet or static resource and examine the request body and headers
- Intercept the invocation of a servlet or static resource and modify the request body or headers using a request wrapper such as `ServletRequestWrapper` or `HttpServletRequestWrapper`
- Intercept a servlet or static resource response and examine the response body and headers
- Intercept a servlet or static resource response and modify the response body or headers using a response wrapper such as `ServletResponseWrapper` or `HttpServletResponseWrapper`

Now that you know what filters can do, you might be wondering when you would use them. Here are just a few examples of useful filters.

- Data compression filters
- Encryption filters
- Image conversion filters
- Logging and auditing filters
- Security authentication filters
- XSL/T filters (to transform XML to HTML, WML, XHTML, etc.)

NOTE: Filter classes are distributed in the same manner as servlet classes. That is, filters are included in a Web application within the */WEB-INF/classes* directory. Additionally, filters may also be included within a JAR file located in the */WEB-INF/lib* directory.

Filter Syntax

A filter is a Java class that implements the `javax.servlet.Filter` interface. This class must provide a public constructor that takes no arguments. When a filtered resource is invoked, the container automatically calls the filter's `doFilter()` method. This method is defined by the `Filter` interface and must be implemented by the filter. The signature for the `doFilter()` method looks like this:

```
public void doFilter(ServletRequest request,
    ServletResponse response, FilterChain chain)
```

As you can see, the container passes the `ServletRequest` and `Servlet-Response` objects to the filter. This allows the filter to examine and modify the request and response objects. In addition, the container passes a `FilterChain` object to the filter via the `doFilter()` method. The `FilterChain` object implements its own `doFilter()` method that allows the `Filter` to pass the request and response to the next filter in the chain or to the resource at the end of the chain. The signature for the `FilterChain` class's `doFilter()` method looks like this:

```
public void doFilter(ServletRequest request,
    ServletResponse response)
```

Any code implemented in the filter's `doFilter()` method prior to calling `FilterChain.doFilter()` is executed before the destination resource is invoked. Similarly, all code following the filter's call to `FilterChain.doFilter()` is executed after the destination resource has responded. Therefore, a request can be altered prior to the resource's being invoked by placing the modifying code before the call to `FilterChain.doFilter()`. Likewise, the response from the requested resource can be altered by code that follows the call to `Filter-Chain.doFilter()`. Additionally, a filter can prevent a request from being serviced altogether by simply not calling `FilterChain.doFilter()` from within its `doFilter()` method. In this case, the filter must generate the response that should be returned to the client.

In addition to doFilter(), the Filter interface also defines the setFilterConfig() and getFilterConfig() methods. The setFilterConfig() method is called automatically by the servlet container in order to make the FilterConfig object available to the filter. FilterConfig provides access to the servlet context as well as filter initialization parameters. When passed to it within the setFilterConfig() method, the filter is responsible for storing the FilterConfig object and making it available through the getFilterConfig() method.

Filter Configuration

A filter is defined in the Web application deployment descriptor (i.e., *web.xml*) using the <filter> and <filter-mapping> elements. The <filter> element defines the filter name, the filter class, and any initialization parameters that should be passed to the filter within the FilterConfig object. The syntax for the <filter> element looks like this:

```
<filter>
  <filter-name>FILTER_NAME</filter-name>
  <filter-class>FILTER_CLASS</filter-class>
  <init-param>
    <param-name>PARAMETER_NAME_1</param-name>
    <param-value>PARAMETER_VALUE_1</param-value>
  </init-param>
  <init-param>
    <param-name>PARAMETER_NAME_2</param-name>
    <param-value>PARAMETER_VALUE_2</param-value>
  </init-param>
</filter>
```

For example, the following XML demonstrates a typical <filter> element within the *web.xml* file.

```
<filter>
  <filter-name>Timer Filter</filter-name>
  <filter-class>TimerFilter</filter-class>
  <init-param>
    <param-name>language</param-name>
    <param-value>english</param-value>
  </init-param>
</filter>
```

Just as the <filter> element defines a filter, the <filter-mapping> element defines the resources to which the filter is mapped. These resources can be designated by name or by URL pattern. For example, the following <filter-mapping> element maps a filter named Timer Filter to the AuthorizeCredit-Card servlet.

```
<filter-mapping>
  <filter-name>Timer Filter</filter-name>
  <servlet-name>AuthorizeCreditCard</servlet-name>
</filter-mapping>
```

Similarly, a filter can be mapped to any number of resources according to a specified URL pattern. The following `<filter-mapping>` element maps the `Timer Filter` to all incoming requests.

```
<filter-mapping>
  <filter-name>Timer Filter</filter-name>
  <url-pattern>/*</url-pattern>
</filter-mapping>
```

Now let's put these configurations together. The following XML demonstrates a typical deployment descriptor entry that combines the `Timer Filter` definition with some filter mappings.

```
<web-app>
  <filter>
    <filter-name>Timer Filter</filter-name>
    <filter-class>TimerFilter</filter-class>
  </filter>
  <filter-mapping>
    <filter-name>Timer Filter</filter-name>
    <servlet-name>AuthorizeCreditCard</servlet-name>
  </filter-mapping>
  <filter-mapping>
    <filter-name>Timer Filter</filter-name>
    <url-pattern>/servlet/*</url-pattern>
  </filter-mapping>
</web-app>
```

The servlet container builds a chain of filters based on the filters and filter mappings defined in a Web application's deployment descriptor. These filters are added to the chain in a specified order. First, filters that match the URL pattern specifed within the `<url-pattern>` element are added to the chain in the order that they appear in the deployment descriptor. Second, filters that match the servlet name specified within the `<servlet-name>` element are added to the chain in the order that they appear in the deployment descriptor.

Filter Lifecycle

Whenever a resource is requested, the servlet container must evaluate the request against a list of filters and their associated URL patterns specified in the Web application's deployment descriptor. If the request maps to one or more filters, the container must instantiate each filter and call its `setFilterConfig()`

method. The `FilterConfig` object (containing the filter name, a reference to the servlet context, and any filter initialization parameters) is created by the container and passed to the filter via the `setFilterConfig()` method. The container must create only one instance of a filter for each `<filter>` declaration within the deployment descriptor. Once the filter has been instantiated and its `setFilterConfig()` method has been called, the container calls the filter's `doFilter()` method in order to allow the filter to perform its function. The container calls the `doFilter()` method of only the first filter in the filter chain. If there are multiple filters assigned to a servlet, the first filter is responsible for calling the next filter's `doFilter()` method. To illustrate, the following eight steps describe the filter's lifecycle.

1. The container receives a resource request.
2. The container compares the requested URL with a list of filters contained within the application deployment descriptor.
3. If it does not map to a filter, the resource is invoked and its output is returned to the client in the usual manner. Otherwise, each filter to which the resource maps is instantiated and its `setFilterConfig()` method is called followed by its `doFilter()` method.
4. Prior to calling `FilterChain.doFilter()`, filter code in the `doFilter()` method may examine and modify the request data and headers before the request is processed by the resource at the end of the chain. The filter may alter the request by wrapping it in a `ServletRequestWrapper` or `HttpServletRequestWrapper` object. In addition, the filter may block the request at this point by not calling the `FilterChain.doFilter()` method and, instead, use the response object to generate a response of its own.
5. Once the `FilterChain.doFilter()` method is called, control is passed to the next filter in the chain or, if at the end of the chain, to the requested resource. If another filter exists in the chain, this process begins again at step 4. If no further filters exist in the chain, the requested resource is invoked. This resource may be a servlet, JSP page, image, or some other dynamic or static content. The resource generates output in the usual manner without any knowledge that its request has been filtered (or that its response might be).
6. After calling `FilterChain.doFilter()` (i.e., after the requested resource has been invoked), filter code in the `doFilter()` method may examine and modify the response data and headers generated by the requested resource. The filter may alter the response by wrapping it in a `ServletResponse-Wrapper` or `HttpServletResponseWrapper` object. Alternatively, the filter may throw an exception, indicating that there was an error processing the request.

7. Once the filter's `doFilter()` method finishes execution, the response is returned to the client. Neither the client nor the requested resource is aware that their communication was filtered.

8. Finally, before a filter is taken out of service, the container must call the filter's `setFilterConfig()` method, passing it a `null`, to indicate that the filter is being removed from service.

NOTE: The thread safety concerns for filters are the same as for standard servlets. A filter can execute simultaneously within multiple threads. It is up to the developer to insure thread safety within the filter. See Chapter 11 for instructions on writing thread-safe code.

Sample Filter

Now that we've discussed the creation and configuration of filters, let's conclude our filter discussion with a sample filter. Listing 26.1 presents a filter that records the amount of time required by the requested resource, including any remaining filters in the filter chain, to process the request. With each request, the time calculation is written to a file.

Listing 26.1 Timer filter records the requested resource's response time.

```
import javax.servlet.*;
import java.io.*;

/**
 * Timer filter measures the amount of time required for the
 * requested resource to process the request. The timing results
 * are written to disk.
 */
public class TimerFilter implements Filter
{
  private FilterConfig filterConfig = null;

  /**
   * Records the time necessary to execute the requested resource
   * as well as any filters remaining in the filter chain.
   */
  public void doFilter(ServletRequest request, ServletResponse
    response, FilterChain chain) throws IOException,
    ServletException
  {
    long start = System.currentTimeMillis(); //get start time
```

```
                //pass the request and response along the filter chain
                chain.doFilter(request, response);

                long stop = System.currentTimeMillis(); //get stop time

                long responseTime = stop - start; //get total time

                FileWriter fileOut = null;

                try
                {
                  //append results to the timer.txt text file
                  fileOut = new FileWriter("timer.txt", true);
                  PrintWriter out = new PrintWriter(fileOut);
                  out.println("Time: " + responseTime + " milliseconds");
                }
                finally
                {
                  fileOut.close(); //close file output stream
                }
              }


              /**
               * Returns the FilterConfig object.
               */
              public FilterConfig getFilterConfig()
              {
                return filterConfig;
              }


              /**
               * Stores the FilterConfig object.
               */
              public void setFilterConfig(FilterConfig filterConfig)
              {
                this.filterConfig = filterConfig;
              }
            }
```

Application Lifecycle Events

Application lifecycle events are another significant addition to the Servlet API. These events give the application developer greater control over each servlet context and each HTTP session. Using the new application event framework, the developer can create classes that "listen" for specific application events. When a particular event occurs, the servlet container notifies all corresponding listener classes. A class indicates its desire to be notified when particular events occur by implementing specific interfaces defined by Servlet API 2.3 and registering itself within the Web application deployment descriptor. Table 26.1

Table 26.1   Application Event Listener Interfaces

Listener Interface	Description
`javax.servlet.ServletContextListener`	Listener objects notified when the servlet context to which they belong is created or destroyed.
`javax.servlet.ServletContextAttributesListener`	Listener objects notified when the servlet context attributes are added, removed, or replaced.
`javax.servlet.http.HttpSessionListener`	Listener objects notified when an HTTP session is created and when a session is invalidated or timed out.
`javax.servlet.http.HttpSessionAttributesListener`	Listener objects notified when HTTP session attributes are added, removed, or replaced.

presents the listener interfaces that allow classes to be notified when specific events occur.

Application Event Listeners

Application event listeners are Java classes that implement one or more of the event-specific interfaces documented in Table 26.1. These classes must be included in the Web application archive (WAR) when the application is distributed. All application event listener classes must exist either in the */WEB-INF/classes* directory or in a JAR file in the */WEB-INF/lib* directory.

ServletContextListener

Classes that implement the `javax.servlet.ServletContextListener` interface are notified when the servlet context to which they belong is created or destroyed. A servlet context is destroyed when the server is shut down or the Web application to which it belongs is removed from service. This interface defines the following two methods:

```
public void contextDestroyed(ServletContextEvent event)
public void contextInitialized(ServletContextEvent event)
```

The container passes a `ServletContextEvent` object to the methods defined by the `ServletContextListener` interface. This event object defines the `getServletContext()` method in order to provide access to the servlet context that is being created or destroyed.

ServletContextAttributesListener

Classes that implement the `javax.servlet.ServletContextAttributes-Listener` interface are notified when servlet context attributes are added, removed, or replaced. This interface defines the following three methods:

```
public void attributeAdded(ServletContextAttributeEvent event)
public void attributeRemoved(ServletContextAttributeEvent event)
public void attributeReplaced(ServletContextAttributeEvent
  event)
```

The container passes a `ServletContextAttributeEvent` object to the methods defined by the `ServletContextAttributesListener` interface. This event object defines the `getName()` and `getValue()` methods in order to provide access to the name and value of the attribute that was added, removed, or replaced.

HttpSessionListener

Classes that implement the `javax.servlet.http.HttpSessionListener` interface are notified when an HTTP session is created or destroyed. A session is destroyed when the session expires or is programmatically invalidated or when the server shuts down. This interface defines the following two methods:

```
public void sessionDestroyed(HttpSessionEvent event)
public void sessionCreated(HttpSessionEvent event)
```

The container passes an `HttpSessionEvent` object to the methods defined by the `HttpSessionListener` interface. This event object defines the `getSession()` method in order to provide access to the HTTP session that is being created or destroyed.

HttpSessionAttributesListener

Classes that implement the `javax.servlet.http.HttpSessionAttributes-Listener` interface are notified when HTTP session attributes are added, removed, or replaced. Like `ServletContextAttributesListener`, this interface defines the following three methods:

```
public void attributeAdded(HttpSessionBindingEvent event)
public void attributeRemoved(HttpSessionBindingEvent event)
public void attributeReplaced(HttpSessionBindingEvent event)
```

The container passes an `HttpSessionBindingEvent` object to the methods defined by the `HttpSessionAttributesListener` interface. This event object defines the getSession(), getName(), and getValue() methods in order to provide access to the session that changed as well as the name and value of the attribute that was added, removed, or replaced.

Application Event Listener Configuration

In addition to including the appropriate class files in the WAR file, application event listeners must be registered within the application's deployment descriptor. When an event occurs, the servlet container will invoke the appropriate event listeners in the order they appear in the deployment descriptor. Application event listeners are defined within the deployment descriptor using the <listener> and <listener-class> elements like this:

```
<web-app>
  <listener>
    <listener-class>com.insideservlets.Logging</listener-class>
  </listener>
  <listener>
    <listener-class>com.insideservlets.Alerts</listener-class>
  </listener>
</web-app>
```

These sample deployment descriptor settings define two classes, Logging and Alerts, that implement one or more of the application event listener interfaces. Each class must implement the interfaces that correspond to the events for which they wish to be notified. In this example, events will be logged by the Logging class before any alerts are sent by the Alerts class because Logging appears first in the deployment descriptor.

HttpSessionActivationListener

The javax.servlet.http.HttpSessionActivationListener interface is also new with version 2.3 of the Servlet API. However, this listener is slightly different from those discussed previously. A class that implements the HttpSessionActivationListener need not be registered within the application's deployment descriptor. Rather, all classes stored within an HTTP session that implement this interface are automatically notified when the container is about to passivate or activate the session to which they belong. This event notification can be very useful if classes within the session hold resources that must be released when the session is passivated and recovered when the session is activated. For instance, if a session object maintains an open database connection, this connection can be released when the object's session is passivated and reestablished when the session is activated. The `HttpSessionActivation-Listener` interface defines the following two methods:

```
public void sessionDidActivate(HttpSessionEvent event)
public void sessionWillPassivate(HttpSessionEvent event)
```

The container passes an `HttpSessionEvent` object to the methods defined by the `HttpSessionActivationListener` interface. This event object defines the `getSession()` method in order to provide access to the session that is being passivated or activated.

A similar type of listener interface named `HttpSessionBindingListener` was introduced in an earlier version of the Servlet API. Though similar to `HttpSessionActivationListener`, rather than notify objects when their session is about to be passivated or activated, objects that implement the `HttpSessionBindingListener` are notified whenever they are added to or removed from an HTTP session. See Chapter 14 for more information about the `HttpSessionBindingListener` interface.

Shared Library Dependencies

It is not uncommon for a servlet or WAR file to require specific code libraries or other resources to be available at the time they are installed. These resources are usually made available to servlets or WAR files containerwide, thus alleviating the developer from having to include all library classes within each independent WAR file. However, to efficiently use common code libraries, the servlet must be able to determine which shared code is available in a particular container configuration. In addition, the container must be able to determine the libraries upon which a servlet or WAR file is dependent. Fortunately, Servlet API 2.3 addresses both of these issues.

First, Servlet API 2.3 indicates that all servlet containers should include a mechanism that allows any application running within the container to discover which library files are available to it. This recommendation may be implemented in a container-specific manner. See the documentation that accompanied the servlet container for more information. Second, a WAR file may specify code libraries or other dependencies in its */META-INF/MANIFEST.MF* file. The manifest file can even specify which version of the library to use. The format of this file must follow the standard JAR manifest format. For detailed information regarding the JAR manifest format, see the following URL:

http://java.sun.com/j2se/1.3/docs/guide/extensions/versioning.html

Second, Servlet API 2.3 specifies that servlet containers should be sensitive to dependencies specified in a WAR file's manifest file or in the manifest files of any included JAR files. If the container is unable to satisfy all application dependencies, it should reject the WAR file and indicate which required libraries are missing.

New Error and Security Attributes

Servlet API 2.3 introduces several new error and security attributes. These attributes can be retrieved using the `getAttribute()` method of the `Http-ServletRequest` object that is passed to the servlet's `service()`, `doGet()`, and `doPost()` methods. For example, the `javax.servlet.error.message` attribute returns a `String` that can be retrieved like this:

```
String uri = (String)request.getAttribute(
  "javax.servlet.error.message");
```

Error Attributes

Within the *web.xml* deployment descriptor file, it is possible to specify the page to which a request should be forwarded when a particular error occurs. For instance, the deployment descriptor may designate that whenever a requested resource cannot be found, the servlet container should return the *notfound.html* page or, if a client authentication error occurs, the request should be forwarded to the `LoginServlet`. Similarly, this portion of the *web.xml* file may dictate that when a particular Java exception is thrown, the request should be forwarded to a specific URL. For example, the container may be instructed to forward the request to the *unavailable.html* page whenever a `javax.servlet.UnavailableException` error occurs. The following XML demonstrates these instructions.

```
<web-app>
  <error-page>
    <error-code>
      404
    </error-code>
    <location>
      /notfound.html
    </location>
  </error-page>
  <error-page>
    <error-code>
      401
    </error-code>
    <location>
      /servlet/LoginServlet
    </location>
```

```
    </error-page>
    <error-page>
      <exception-type>
        javax.servlet.UnavailableException
      </exception-type>
      <location>
        /servlet/LoginServlet
      </location>
    </error-page>
  </web-app>
```

Servlet API 2.2 introduced three error attributes—`javax.servlet.error.status_code`, `javax.servlet.error.exception_type`, and `javax.servlet.error.message`. Servlet API 2.3 defines two additional attributes—`javax.servlet.error.exception` and `javax.servlet.error.request_uri`. Table 26.2 describes each of these attributes.

Security Attributes

Servlet API 2.3 adds two request attributes that may be of interest when the servlet is responding across a secure connection. For instance, the servlet may reject requests for secure data if the encryption algorithm is not of sufficient strength (i.e., key size). When a request is received via HTTPS, the container makes the following two request attributes available:

- `javax.servlet.request.cipher_suite`—A `String` indicating the cipher suite used by the secure connection
- `javax.servlet.request.key_size`—An `Integer` indicating the key size of the algorithm used to encrypt the transmission

Table 26.2   Error Attributes Defined by Servlet API 2.2 and 2.3

Attribute Name	Description
`javax.servlet.error.status_code`	An `Integer` indicating the error status code, if any
`javax.servlet.error.exception_type`	A `Class` representing the type of exception that caused the error, if any
`javax.servlet.error.message`	A `String` containing the exception's error message
`javax.servlet.error.exception`	A `Throwable` object representing the exception that was thrown (new with Servlet API 2.3)
`javax.servlet.error.request_uri`	A `String` containing the URI of the resource in which the error occurred (new with Servlet API 2.3)

Welcome Files

Welcome files were supported in version 2.2 of the Java Servlet Specification, but their function has been clarified and expanded in version 2.3. Welcome files allow the developer to indicate a default file to return in response to a request that does not indicate a specific resource. For instance, the most common welcome file is *index.html*. If a request does not reference a specific resource, the *index.html* file is often returned by default. Version 2.2 of the Java Servlet Specification added support for developer-defined welcome files within the Web application deployment descriptor. Within this descriptor, the developer is able to define an ordered list of partial URIs that will be appended to each nonspecific request. Consider, for example, the welcome files defined in this portion of a deployment descriptor.

```
<welcome-file-list>
  <welcome-file>index.html</welcome-file>
  <welcome-file>default.jsp</welcome-file>
  <welcome-file>pub/index.html</welcome-file>
</welcome-file-list>
```

According to this descriptor, if the client were to issue a request to *http://www.insideservlets.com/order/*, the container would attempt to locate resources in this order:

1. *http://www.insideservlets.com/order/index.html*
2. *http://www.insideservlets.com/order/default.jsp*
3. *http://www.insideservlets.com/order/pub/index.html*

The first resource that existed would be served to the client. If none of these resources could be found, the container could respond as it saw fit. For some containers, this might involve invoking a default file servlet, generating a directory listing, or returning an HTTP 404 (Not Found) error.

New Classes, Interfaces, and Methods

Servlet API 2.3 introduces a number of new classes, interfaces, and methods. The new methods are not very substantial, but the new classes and interfaces add significant functionality to the Servlet API. All of these classes and interfaces contribute to either the new application event listeners or the filtering features.

Method ServletContext.getResourcePaths()

```
public java.util.Set getResourcePaths()
```

Returns a collection of paths that represent all of the resources in the current Web application. The paths are stored in a java.util.Set object as String objects. All resource paths begin with a "/" and are relative to the root of the Web application.

Method ServletContext.getServletContextName()

```
public String getServletContextName()
```

Returns the name of this Web application according to its corresponding <display-name> element within the deployment descriptor or null if no name is specified.

Method ServletRequest.getParameterMap()

```
public java.util.Map getParameterMap()
```

Returns a java.util.Map object containing the request parameters. Parameter names are stored as map keys and parameter values are stored as map values. This method replaces the parsing functionality provided by the HttpUtils class (deprecated as of Servlet API 2.3).

Method ServletResponse.resetBuffer()

```
public void resetBuffer()
```

Clears the information in the response buffer without resetting the HTTP status code or any headers. If the response has already been committed, this method throws an IllegalStateException.

Method ServletRequest.setCharacterEncoding()

```
public void setCharacterEncoding(String enc)
```

Currently, many browsers do not specify character encoding within the request's Content-Type header. If not specified, the container does not know the character-encoding scheme used to encode the body of the request. In this case, the servlet container usually chooses the JVM default encoding (usually

ISO-8859-1). However, if the container uses the wrong character encoding, the servlet will be unable to interpret the contents of the request.

To remedy this problem, the `setCharacterEncoding()` method has been added to the `ServletRequest` interface. The `String` parameter (enc) represents the name of the encoding scheme used to encode the body of the request, such as ISO-8859-1. The `setCharacterEncoding()` method allows a servlet to override the character encoding selected by the container. This method must be called prior to reading any data from the request. The character encoding cannot be changed once any input has been read from the request.

Method `HttpServlet.doHead()`

```
protected void doHead(HttpServletRequest request,
   HttpServletResponse response)
```

The `doHead()` method is called in response to HTTP HEAD requests. Although it can be useful at times, this method is rarely overridden. This is because implementing the `doGet()` method provides automatic support for HTTP HEAD requests as long as the `doHead()` method is not overridden. "Automatic support" means that if the `doGet()` method is implemented, no other special coding is required to support HEAD requests. No special coding is necessary because the default implementation of `doHead()` automatically calls the `doGet()` method and allows it to generate the proper HTTP header fields. Any output generated by `doGet()` other than header fields is discarded.

Actually, the `doHead()` method is not new to Servlet API 2.3. This method was supported by early versions of the Servlet API until it was removed in version 2.2. However, after much feedback from the Java community, the `doHead()` method has been reinstated in version 2.3.

Method `HttpServletRequest.getRequestURL()`

```
public StringBuffer getRequestURL()
```

Returns a `StringBuffer` containing the URL that the client used to make the request. This URL includes the protocol, server name, port number, and server path, but does not contain the query string. In Servlet API 2.2, this method resided in the `HttpUtils` class (`HttpUtils` is deprecated in Servlet API 2.3).

Interface `Filter`

javax.servlet.Filter

Definition

```
public interface Filter
```

The `javax.servlet.Filter` interface defines the methods that must be implemented by any Java class that wishes to filter the request or response.

Methods

`doFilter()`

```
public void doFilter(ServletRequest request, ServletResponse
    response, FilterChain chain)
```

This method is called by the container each time a filterable request is received.
The `doFilter()` method is implemented by the filter class in order to perform
any desired request or response filtering.

`getFilterConfig()`

```
public FilterConfig getFilterConfig()
```

Returns a `FilterConfig` object containing initialization parameters for this
filter as well as the filter name and a reference to the servlet context.

`setFilterConfig()`

```
public void setFilterConfig(FilterConfig filterConfig)
```

When the filter is instantiated, the container calls this method and passes it a
`FilterConfig` object. The container again calls this method before the filter is
destroyed, passing it a `null`.

Interface `FilterChain`

javax.servlet.FilterChain

Definition

```
public interface FilterChain
```

The `javax.servlet.FilterChain` interface defines a method that allows the
filter class to pass the request and response to the next filter in the chain or to

the resource at the end of the chain. The container passes a `FilterChain` object to the filter via the filter's `doFilter()` method.

Methods

doFilter()

```
public void doFilter(ServletRequest request, ServletResponse
    response)
```

This method passes control to the next filter in the chain or to the resource at the end of the chain (if there are no more filters in the filter chain).

Interface FilterConfig

> javax.servlet.FilterConfig

Definition

```
public interface FilterConfig
```

The container passes an object that implements the `javax.servlet.Filter-Config` interface to the filter via the filter's `setFilterConfig()` method. This interface provides methods to retrieve the initialization parameters for the filter as well as the filter's name and a reference to the servlet context.

Methods

getFilterName()

```
public String getFilterName()
```

Returns the `String` containing the name of the filter as specified by the `<filter-name>` element within the deployment descriptor.

getInitParameter()

```
public String getInitParameter(String name)
```

Returns a `String` containing the value of the named initialization parameter or `null` if the parameter does not exist.

getInitParameterNames()

```
public java.util.Enumeration getInitParameterNames()
```

Returns an `Enumeration` of `String` objects containing the names of initialization parameters or an empty `Enumeration` if no initialization parameters exist.

getServletContext()
```
public ServletContext getServletContext()
```

Returns a ServletContext object containing information about the environment in which the servlet is running.

Interface ServletContextAttributesListener

Definition
```
public interface ServletContextAttributesListener extends
    java.util.EventListener
```

Objects that implement the javax.servlet.ServletContextAttributes-Listener interface are notified by the container when servlet context attributes are added, removed, or replaced.

Methods

attributeAdded()
```
public void attributeAdded(ServletContextAttributeEvent event)
```

This method is called by the container after a servlet context attribute is added. The ServletContextAttributeEvent object passed to this method describes the attribute that was added.

attributeRemoved()
```
public void attributeRemoved(ServletContextAttributeEvent event)
```

This method is called by the container after a servlet context attribute is removed. The ServletContextAttributeEvent object passed to this method describes the attribute that was removed.

attributeReplaced()
```
public void attributeReplaced(ServletContextAttributeEvent
    event)
```

This method is called by the container after a servlet context attribute is replaced. The ServletContextAttributeEvent object passed to this method describes the attribute that was replaced.

Interface `ServletContextListener`

Definition

```
public interface ServletContextListener extends
    java.util.EventListener
```

Objects that implement the `java.servlet.ServletContextListener` interface are notified by the container when the servlet context to which they belong is created or destroyed.

Methods

`contextDestroyed()`

```
public void contextDestroyed(ServletContextEvent event)
```

This method is called by the container just before the class's servlet context is shut down. The `ServletContextEvent` object passed to this method provides a reference to the servlet context that is about to be destroyed.

`contextInitialized()`

```
public void contextInitialized(ServletContextEvent event)
```

This method is called by the container immediately after the class's servlet context is created and ready to accept requests. The `ServletContextEvent` object passed to this method provides a reference to the servlet context that was just created.

Interface `HttpSessionActivationListener`

```
javax.servlet.http.HttpSessionListener
```

Definition

```
public interface HttpSessionActivationListener
```

Objects that implement the `java.servlet.HttpSessionActivationListener` interface and are bound to a session are notified by the container when their session is activated or passivated.

Methods

sessionDidActivate()

```
public void sessionDidActivate(HttpSessionEvent event)
```

This method is called by the container immediately after the session is activated. The HttpSessionEvent object passed to this method provides a reference to the session that was just activated.

sessionWillPassivate()

```
public void sessionWillPassivate(HttpSessionEvent event)
```

This method is called by the container just before the session is passivated. The HttpSessionEvent object passed to this method provides a reference to the session that will be passivated.

Interface HttpSessionAttributesListener

java.util.EventLListener

javax.servlet.http.HttpSessionAttributesListener

Definition

```
public interface HttpSessionAttributesListener extends
    java.util.EventListener
```

Objects that implement the javax.servlet.http.HttpSessionAttributes-Listener interface are notified by the container when session attributes within this Web application are added, removed, or replaced.

Methods

attributeAdded()

```
public void attributeAdded(HttpSessionBindingEvent event)
```

This method is called by the container after a session attribute has been added. The HttpSessionBindingEvent object passed to this method describes the attribute that was added.

attributeRemoved()

```
public void attributeRemoved(HttpSessionBindingEvent event)
```

This method is called by the container after a session attribute has been removed. The HttpSessionBindingEvent object passed to this method describes the attribute that was removed.

attributeReplaced()

```
public void attributeReplaced(HttpSessionBindingEvent event)
```

This method is called by the container after a session attribute has been replaced. The HttpSessionBindingEvent object passed to this method describes the attribute that was replaced.

Interface HttpSessionListener

```
javax.servlet.HttpSessionListener
```

Definition

```
public interface HttpSessionListener
```

Objects that implement the javax.servlet.http.HttpSessionListener interface are notified when HTTP sessions in this Web application are created or destroyed.

Methods

sessionCreated()

```
public void sessionCreated(HttpSessionEvent event)
```

This method is called by the container immediately after a new HTTP session is created. The HttpSessionEvent object passed to this method provides a reference to the new session.

sessionDestroyed()

```
public void sessionDestroyed(HttpSessionEvent event)
```

This method is called by the container after a session has been invalidated. The HttpSessionEvent object passed to this method provides a reference to the session that was invalidated.

Class ServletContextEvent

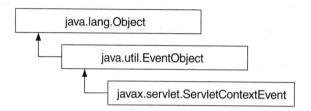

Definition

    public class ServletContextEvent extends java.util.EventObject

The javax.servlet.ServletContextEvent class encapsulates information about a servlet context event. When a servlet context is created or destroyed, a ServletContextEvent object is passed to all objects that implement the ServletContextListener interface.

Constructors

ServletContextEvent()

    public ServletContextEvent(ServletContext source)

Constructs a new ServletContextEvent object from the specified servlet context.

Methods

getServletContext()

    public ServletContext getServletContext()

Returns a ServletContext object representing the servlet context that was created or destroyed.

Class ServletContextAttributeEvent

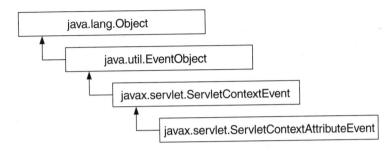

Definitions

```
public class ServletContextAttributeEvent extends
    ServletContextEvent
```

The javax.servlet.ServletContextAttributeEvent class encapsulates information about a servlet context attribute event such as the name and value of the modified attribute. When a servlet context attribute is added, removed, or replaced, a ServletContextAttributeEvent object is passed to all objects that implement the ServletContextAttributesListener interface.

Constructors

ServletContextAttributeEvent()

```
public ServletContextAttributeEvent(ServletContext source,
    String name, Object value)
```

Constructs a new ServletContextAttributeEvent object from the specified servlet context, attribute name, and attribute value.

Methods

getName()

```
public String getName()
```

Returns a String object containing the name of the servlet context attribute that was modified.

getValue()

```
public Object getValue()
```

Returns a String object containing the value of the servlet context attribute that was modified. If the attribute was replaced, this method returns the value of the old attribute.

Class ServletRequestWrapper

Definition

```
public class ServletRequestWrapper implements ServletRequest
```

The javax.servlet.ServletRequestWrapper class implements the Servlet-Request interface and provides a default implementation of all of its methods. This class can be used to wrap the ServletRequest object created by the container. The ServletRequestWrapper class's default implementation simply calls the corresponding method on the ServletRequest object that it wraps. In this way, any of the default ServletRequest methods can be overridden before the request is passed along the filter chain (using the FilterChain.doFilter() method).

Constructors

ServletRequestWrapper()

```
public ServletRequestWrapper(ServletRequest request)
```

Creates a new ServletRequestWrapper object using the given ServletRequest.

Methods

getAttribute()

```
public Object getAttribute(String name)
```

The default implementation of this method calls the wrapped request object's getAttribute() method.

getAttributeNames()

```
public java.util.Enumeration getAttributeNames()
```

The default implementation of this method calls the wrapped request object's getAttributeNames() method.

getCharacterEncoding()

```
public String getCharacterEncoding()
```

The default implementation of this method calls the wrapped request object's getCharacterEncoding() method.

getContentLength()
```
public int getContentLength()
```
The default implementation of this method calls the wrapped request object's getContentLength() method.

getContentType()
```
public String getContentType()
```
The default implementation of this method calls the wrapped request object's getContentType() method.

getInputStream()
```
public ServletInputStream getInputStream()
```
The default implementation of this method calls the wrapped request object's getInputStream() method.

getLocale()
```
public java.util.Locale getLocale()
```
The default implementation of this method calls the wrapped request object's getLocale() method.

getLocales()
```
public java.util.Enumeration getLocales()
```
The default implementation of this method calls the wrapped request object's getLocales() method.

getParameter()
```
public String getParameter(String name)
```
The default implementation of this method calls the wrapped request object's getParameter() method.

getParameterMap()
```
public java.util.Map getParameterMap()
```
The default implementation of this method calls the wrapped request object's getParameterMap() method.

getParameterNames()
```
public java.util.Enumeration getParameterNames()
```
The default implementation of this method calls the wrapped request object's getParameterNames() method.

getParameterValues()

```
public String[] getParameterValues(String name)
```

The default implementation of this method calls the wrapped request object's getParameterValues() method.

getProtocol()

```
public String getProtocol()
```

The default implementation of this method calls the wrapped request object's getProtocol() method.

getReader()

```
public java.io.BufferedReader getReader()
```

The default implementation of this method calls the wrapped request object's getReader() method.

getRealPath()

```
public String getRealPath(String path)
```

The default implementation of this method calls the wrapped request object's getRealPath() method.

getRemoteAddr()

```
public String getRemoteAddr()
```

The default implementation of this method calls the wrapped request object's getRemoteAddr() method.

getRemoteHost()

```
public String getRemoteHost()
```

The default implementation of this method calls the wrapped request object's getRemoteHost() method.

getRequest()

```
public ServletRequest getRequest()
```

Returns the wrapped ServletRequest object.

getRequestDispatcher()

```
public RequestDispatcher getRequestDispatcher(String path)
```

The default implementation of this method calls the wrapped request object's getRequestDispatcher() method.

getScheme()
```
public String getScheme()
```

The default implementation of this method calls the wrapped request object's getScheme() method.

getServerName()
```
public String getServerName()
```

The default implementation of this method calls the wrapped request object's getServerName() method.

getServerPort()
```
public int getServerPort()
```

The default implementation of this method calls the wrapped request object's getServerPort() method.

isSecure()
```
public boolean isSecure()
```

The default implementation of this method calls the wrapped request object's isSecure() method.

removeAttribute()
```
public void removeAttribute(String name)
```

The default implementation of this method calls the wrapped request object's removeAttribute() method.

setAttribute()
```
public void setAttribute(String name, Object o)
```

The default implementation of this method calls the wrapped request object's setAttribute() method.

setCharacterEncoding()
```
public void setCharacterEncoding(String enc)
```

The default implementation of this method calls the wrapped request object's setCharacterEncoding() method.

setRequest()
```
public void setRequest(ServletRequest request)
```

Sets the ServletRequest object being wrapped.

Class ServletResponseWrapper

Definition

```
public class ServletResponseWrapper implements ServletResponse
```

The `javax.servlet.ServletResponseWrapper` class implements the Servlet-Response interface and provides a default implementation of all of its methods. This class can be used to wrap the `ServletResponse` object created by the container. The `ServletResponseWrapper` class's default implementation simply calls the corresponding method on the `ServletResponse` object that it wraps. In this way, any of the default `ServletResponse` methods can be over-ridden before the request is passed along the filter chain (using the `Filter-Chain.doFilter()` method).

Constructors

ServletResponseWrapper()

```
public ServletResponseWrapper(ServletResponse request)
```

Creates a new `ServletResponseWrapper` object using the given `Servlet-Response`.

Methods

flushBuffer()

```
public void flushBuffer()
```

The default implementation of this method calls the wrapped response object's `flushBuffer()` method.

getBufferSize()

```
public int getBufferSize()
```

The default implementation of this method calls the wrapped response object's `getBufferSize()` method.

getCharacterEncoding()
```
public String getCharacterEncoding()
```
The default implementation of this method calls the wrapped response object's getCharacterEncoding() method.

getLocale()
```
public java.util.Locale getLocale()
```
The default implementation of this method calls the wrapped response object's getLocale() method.

getOutputStream()
```
public ServletOutputStream getOutputStream()
```
The default implementation of this method calls the wrapped response object's getOutputStream() method.

getResponse()
```
public ServletResponse getResponse()
```
Returns the wrapped ServletResponse object.

getWriter()
```
public java.io.PrintWriter getWriter()
```
The default implementation of this method calls the wrapped response object's getWriter() method.

isCommitted()
```
public boolean isCommitted()
```
The default implementation of this method calls the wrapped response object's isCommitted() method.

reset()
```
public void reset()
```
The default implementation of this method calls the wrapped response object's reset() method.

resetBuffer()
```
public void resetBuffer()
```
The default implementation of this method calls the wrapped response object's resetBuffer() method.

setBufferSize()
```
public void setBufferSize(int size)
```

The default implementation of this method calls the wrapped response object's setBufferSize() method.

setContentLength()
```
public void setContentLength(int len)
```

The default implementation of this method calls the wrapped response object's setContentLength() method.

setContentType()
```
public void setContentType(String type)
```

The default implementation of this method calls the wrapped response object's setContentType() method.

setLocale()
```
public void setLocale(java.util.Locale loc)
```

The default implementation of this method calls the wrapped response object's setLocale() method.

setResponse()
```
public void setResponse(ServletResponse response)
```

Sets the ServletResponse object being wrapped.

Class HttpServletRequestWrapper

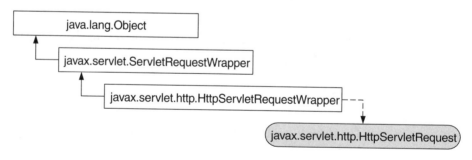

Definition
```
public class HttpServletRequestWrapper extends
    ServletRequestWrapper implements HttpServletRequest
```

The javax.servlet.http.HttpServletRequestWrapper class implements the HttpServletRequest interface and provides a default implementation of all of its methods. This class can be used to wrap the `HttpServletRequest` object created by the container. The `HttpServletRequestWrapper` class's default implementation simply calls the corresponding method on the `HttpServlet-Request` object that it wraps. In this way, any of the default `HttpServlet-Request` methods can be overridden before the request is passed along the filter chain (using the `FilterChain.doFilter()` method).

Constructors

HttpServletRequestWrapper()

```
public HttpServletRequestWrapper(HttpServletRequest request)
```

Creates a new `HttpServletRequestWrapper` object using the given `HttpServletRequest`.

Methods

getAuthType()

```
public String getAuthType()
```

The default implementation of this method calls the wrapped request object's `getAuthType()` method.

getContextPath()

```
public String getContextPath()
```

The default implementation of this method calls the wrapped request object's `getContextPath()` method.

getCookies()

```
public Cookie[] getCookies()
```

The default implementation of this method calls the wrapped request object's `getCookies()` method.

getDateHeader()

```
public long getDateHeader(String name)
```

The default implementation of this method calls the wrapped request object's `getDateHeader()` method.

getHeader()

```
public String getHeader(String name)
```

The default implementation of this method calls the wrapped request object's `getHeader()` method.

getHeaderNames()

```
public java.util.Enumeration getHeaderNames()
```

The default implementation of this method calls the wrapped request object's getHeaderNames() method.

getHeaders()

```
public java.util.Enumeration getHeaders(String name)
```

The default implementation of this method calls the wrapped request object's getHeaders() method.

getIntHeaders()

```
public int getIntHeader(String name)
```

The default implementation of this method calls the wrapped request object's getIntHeaders() method.

getMethod()

```
public String getMethod()
```

The default implementation of this method calls the wrapped request object's getMethod() method.

getPathInfo()

```
public String getPathInfo()
```

The default implementation of this method calls the wrapped request object's getPathInfo() method.

getPathTranslated()

```
public String getPathTranslated()
```

The default implementation of this method calls the wrapped request object's getPathTranslated() method.

getQueryString()

```
public String getQueryString()
```

The default implementation of this method calls the wrapped request object's getQueryString() method.

getRemoteUser()

```
public String getRemoteUser()
```

The default implementation of this method calls the wrapped request object's getRemoteUser() method.

getRequestedSessionId()

```
public String getRequestedSessionId()
```

The default implementation of this method calls the wrapped request object's getRequestedSessionId() method.

getRequestURI()

```
public String getRequestURI()
```

The default implementation of this method calls the wrapped request object's getRequestURI() method.

getRequestURL()

```
public StringBuffer getRequestURL()
```

The default implementation of this method calls the wrapped request object's getRequestURL() method.

getServletPath()

```
public String getServletPath()
```

The default implementation of this method calls the wrapped request object's getServletPath() method.

getSession()

```
public HttpSession getSession()
public HttpSession getSession(boolean create)
```

The default implementation of this method calls the wrapped request object's corresponding getSession() method.

getUserPrincipal()

```
public java.security.Principal getUserPrincipal()
```

The default implementation of this method calls the wrapped request object's getUserPrincipal() method.

isRequestedSessionIdFromCookie()

```
public boolean isRequestedSessionIdFromCookie()
```

The default implementation of this method calls the wrapped request object's isRequestedSessionIdFromCookie() method.

isRequestedSessionIdFromURL()

```
public boolean isRequestedSessionIdFromURL()
```

The default implementation of this method calls the wrapped request object's isRequestedSessionIdFromURL() method.

isRequestedSessionIdValid()

```
public boolean isRequestedSessionIdValid()
```

The default implementation of this method calls the wrapped request object's isRequestedSessionIdValid() method.

isUserInRole()

```
public boolean isUserInRole(String role)
```

The default implementation of this method calls the wrapped request object's isUserInRole() method.

Class HttpServletResponseWrapper

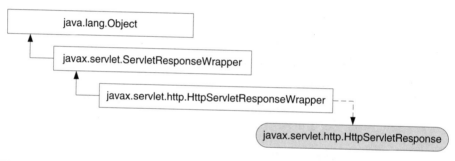

Definition

```
public class HttpServletResponseWrapper extends
    ServletResponseWrapper implements HttpServletResponse
```

The javax.servlet.http.HttpServletResponseWrapper class implements the HttpServletResponse interface and provides a default implementation of all of its methods. This class can be used to wrap the HttpServletResponse object created by the container. The HttpServletResponseWrapper class's default implementation simply calls the corresponding method on the HttpServlet-Response object that it wraps. In this way, any of the default HttpServlet-Response methods can be overridden before the request is passed along the filter chain (using the FilterChain.doFilter() method).

Constructors

HttpServletResponseWrapper()

```
public HttpServletResponseWrapper(HttpServletResponse response)
```

Creates a new HttpServletResponseWrapper object using the given Http-ServletResponse.

Methods
addCookie()
```
public void addCookie(Cookie cookie)
```
The default implementation of this method calls the wrapped response object's addCookie() method.

addDateHeader()
```
public void addDateHeader(String name, long date)
```
The default implementation of this method calls the wrapped response object's addDateHeader() method.

addHeader()
```
public void addHeader(String name, String value)
```
The default implementation of this method calls the wrapped response object's addHeader() method.

addIntHeader()
```
public void addIntHeader(String name, int value)
```
The default implementation of this method calls the wrapped response object's addIntHeader() method.

containsHeader()
```
public boolean containsHeader(String name)
```
The default implementation of this method calls the wrapped response object's containsHeader() method.

encodeRedirectURL()
```
public String encodeRedirectURL(String url)
```
The default implementation of this method calls the wrapped response object's encodeRedirectURL() method.

encodeURL()
```
public String encodeURL(String url)
```
The default implementation of this method calls the wrapped response object's encodeURL() method.

sendError()

```
public void sendError(int sc)
public void sendError(int sc, String msg)
```

The default implementation of this method calls the wrapped response object's corresponding sendError() method.

sendRedirect()

```
public void sendRedirect(String location)
```

The default implementation of this method calls the wrapped response object's sendRedirect() method.

setDateHeader()

```
public void setDateHeader(String name, long date)
```

The default implementation of this method calls the wrapped response object's setDateHeader() method.

setHeader()

```
public void setHeader(String name, String value)
```

The default implementation of this method calls the wrapped response object's setHeader() method.

setIntHeader()

```
public void setIntHeader(String name, int value)
```

The default implementation of this method calls the wrapped response object's setIntHeader() method.

setStatus()

```
public void setStatus(int sc)
public void setStatus(int sc, java.lang.String sm)
```

The default implementation of this method calls the wrapped response object's corresponding setStatus() method.

Class HttpSessionEvent

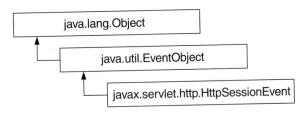

Definition

        public class HttpSessionEvent extends java.util.EventObject

The java.servlet.http.HttpSessionEvent class encapsulates information about an HTTP session event. When an HTTP session is created or destroyed, an HttpSessionEvent object is passed to all objects that implement the HttpSessionListener interface.

Constructors

HttpSessionEvent()

        public HttpSessionEvent(HttpSession source)

Creates a new HttpSessionEvent object using the given HttpSession.

Methods

getSession()
        public HttpSession getSession()

Returns the HttpSession object that was created or destroyed.

PART VI

Appendices

APPENDIX A

Common Well-Known Port Assignments

Table A.1   Common Well-Known Port Assignments

Name	Port	Description
echo	7	Echo is used to test the connection between hosts. Any data sent to port 7 is echoed back to the sender.
daytime	13	Responds to any connection with the time of day on the server.
ftp	21	Used to transfer files.
telnet	23	Allows remote login to a host machine.
smtp	25	Simple Mail Transport Protocol for sending e-mail.
whois	43	A directory service for looking up names of users on a remote server.
finger	79	Displays information about a user or all users logged in to a server.
http	80	Responds to HyperText Transfer Protocol requests. HTTP is the protocol used to communicate on the World Wide Web.
pop3	110	Post Office Protocol 3 allows users to retrieve stored e-mail messages.
nntp	119	Network News Transfer Protocol provides access to thousands of newsgroups for the exchange of information. Commonly known as USENET.
https	443	Secure HTTP protocol. This is the HTTP protocol running on top of the Secure Sockets Layer (SSL) for encrypted HTTP transmissions.

APPENDIX B

Java Port Scanner

The Java Port Scanner scans a range of TCP/IP ports on a remote host and indicates whether a server is responding on each port. The *Port Scanner* program accepts the IP address or hostname as a command-line parameter or, if absent, defaults to the localhost.

```java
import java.io.*;
import java.net.*;

/**
 * Port Scanner
 *
 * Scans for servers listening on a range of ports.
 */
public class PortScanner
{
  final static int LOW_RANGE = 0; //scan reserved ports
  final static int HIGH_RANGE = 1023;

  public static void main(String[] args)
  {
    Socket connect=null;
    String host = "localhost"; //defaults to local host

    if (args.length > 0)
    {
      host = args[0]; //sets host to command-line parameter
    }
    for (int iCount = LOW_RANGE; iCount < HIGH_RANGE; iCount++)
    {
      System.out.print("Checking port " + iCount + "...");
      try
      {
```

```
        connect = new Socket(host, iCount);
        System.out.println("Server responding on port " +
          iCount + " of " + host);
      }
      catch (UnknownHostException e)
      {
        System.err.println("Host is invalid.");
        break;
      }
      catch (IOException e)
      {
        System.out.println("No server found");
      }
      finally
      {
        try
        {
          connect.close(); //close socket connection
        }
        catch (Exception e) {}
      }
    }
  }
}
```

This small portion of the output shows a server listening on port 7.

```
C:\>java PortScanner
Checking port 0...No server found
Checking port 1...No server found
Checking port 2...No server found
Checking port 3...No server found
Checking port 4...No server found
Checking port 5...No server found
Checking port 6...No server found
Checking port 7...Server found on port 7 of localhost
Checking port 8...No server found
Checking port 9...No server found
Checking port 10...No server found
```

APPENDIX C

The Internet Standardization Process

Who is responsible for managing the Internet standardization process? In t
past, that was a difficult question to answer. However, today the answer is t
Internet Engineering Task Force (IETF) and the Internet Engineering Steeri
Group (IESG). The IETF is a self-organized volunteer group with represent
tives from around the world. It describes itself as "the principal body engag
in the development of new Internet standard specifications." The IETF is p
marily responsible for providing a forum for discussion of standards and su
mission of standards proposals to the IESG.

The IESG, on the other hand, is responsible for overseeing the activities
the IETF and the standards process. The IESG "is directly responsible for t
actions associated with entry into and movement along the Internet 'standar
track,' including final approval of specifications as Internet Standards." F
more information on the IETF and the IESG, see:

http://www.ietf.org/

Before a new standard is proposed, a working document called an *Intern
Draft* (ID) is prepared and placed in the IETF's *internet-drafts* directory (*ftp.
ftp.ietf.org/internet-drafts/*). Placing the document in this directory does n
"publish" it, but rather makes it available for informal review and comment b
interested parties. The Internet Draft is a "working document" because it
constantly evolving as the specification is developed. Due to its inform
nature, an ID should never be quoted or referenced in a formal document. A
unrevised Internet Draft remains in the *internet-draft* directory for a maximur
of six months. This policy ensures that an ID is constantly being refined an
does not grow stale. Eventually, every Internet Draft either will be promoted t
an RFC or it will be deleted.

When those involved in developing the new specification agree that it is complete, the document is submitted to the IESG. If approved, the document becomes an official Internet RFC (*Request for Comment*). The IESG then determines whether to place the document on the Standards Track, the Non-Standards Track, or to reject the document. Within the two tracks, each RFC is designated as being at a particular stage, or *maturity level*, in the standardization process.

For the Standards Track the stages include "Proposed Standard," "Draft Standard," and "Standard." As the specification is refined, it may garner additional community support and move through the stages until it becomes a Standard. However, chances are good that it will never get past the Proposed Standard stage or perhaps even be retracted from the Standards Track. Many popular protocols are still Proposed Standards or not even on the Standards Track.

For the Non-Standards Track, the levels are "Prototype," "Experimental," "Informational," and "Historic." Although it may seem that Non-Standards Track RFCs would not be very useful, there are many extremely important protocols relegated to this track. For instance, the RFC specification for HTTP/1.0 (the protocol supported by practically every Web browser in existence) is designated as Informational! Not only is it not an Internet Standard, it is not even on the Standards Track. This is due to the fact that when the original HTTP specification was developed, it did not follow the accepted Internet standardization process. On the other hand, its successor, HTTP/1.1, followed the process and is currently designated as a Proposed Standard. For a detailed description of the entire standardization process, see RFC 1602 entitled "The Internet Standards Process."

APPENDIX D

URL Syntax for Common Protocols

Table D.1 shows the URL format for many common protocols. For mo detailed information, see RFC 1738.

Table D.1 URL Syntax for Common Protocols

Protocol	Default Port	URL Syntax and Description
http	80	`http://host[:port]/path/filename[#section]` `[?query_string]` HyperText Transfer Protocol for communicating with Web servers.
ftp	21	`ftp://username:password@host[:port]/path` File transfer protocol for transferring files to and from an FTP server.
gopher	70	`gopher://host[:port]/gopher_path` The Gopher protocol used for document retrieval.
mailto		`mailto:email_address` Sends mail to the specified e-mail address (address must conform to the format specified in RFC 822).
news		`news:newsgroup_name` Used to access USENET newsgroups as specified in RFC 1036.
nntp	119	`nntp://host[:port]/newsgroup_name/article_number` Used to access USENET news on NNTP servers.
telnet	23	`telnet://[user:password@]host[:port]/` Used to establish remote login sessions.

Table D.1   URL Syntax for Common Protocols

Protocol	Default Port	URL Syntax and Description
wais	210	`wais://host[:port]/database` Used to access databases on WAIS servers.
file		`file://host/path/filename` Specifies a file accessible from the local machine (such as a file on the local hard drive).
prospero	1525	`prospero://host[:port]/object_name` Specifies resources accessed via the Prospero Directory Service. Prospero is used by Archie to search FTP archives.

APPENDIX E

Meaning of URL Special Characters

Table E.1 describes the meaning of each of the special characters in the URL specification. For more information, see RFC 1738.

Table E.1   URL Special Characters

Character	Meaning/Examples

:	`http://www.awl.com`
	Separates the protocol (or scheme) from the rest of the URL.
	`http://www.sourcestream.com:80`
	Separates the port from the host.
	`ftp://guest:password@ftp.sun.com/`
	Separates the username from the password.

//	`http://www.awl.com` The double slash indicates that the URL uses the Common Internet Scheme Syntax defined in RFC 1738.
@	`ftp://guest:password@ftp.sun.com/` The "at" symbol is used to separate the host from the name and password.

/	`http://www.awl.com/index.html`
	Separates the host and port from the path.
	`http://www.awl.com/documents/public_html/index.html`
	Separates directories and the filename in a resource path.

%	`http://www.awl.com/Inside%20Servlets` Indicates the beginning of a URL-encoded character.

Table E.1   URL Special Characters

Character	Meaning/Examples
+	`http://www.awl.com/Inside+Servlets` Used in place of spaces.

?	`http://www.webcrawler.com/cgi-bin/WebQuery?searchText=`
	    `servlets`
	Separates a query string from the rest of the URL.

=	`http://www.webcrawler.com/cgi-bin/WebQuery?searchText=`
	    `servlets`
	Used in a query string to separate the key and the value.

&	`http://www.mysearch.com?searchText=servlets&order=`
	    `Ascending`
	Used in query strings to separate key/value pairs.

~	`http://www.isp.com/~dustin` Normally used to indicate the user's home directory.

APPENDIX F

US-ASCII Encoding for Unsafe URL Characters

Table F.1 shows the US-ASCII encoding for many unsafe or unprintable URL characters. (See Chapter 2 for information about URL encoding.)

Table F.1 US-ASCII Encoding for Unsafe URL Characters

Hex	Character	Hex	Character	Hex	Character	Hex	Character
08	Backspace	26	&	3A	:	5E	^
09	Tab	27	'	3B	;	5F	_
0A	Linefeed	28	(	3C	<	60	`
0D	Carriage Return	29	)	3D	=	7B	{
20	Space	2A	*	3E	>	7C	|
21	!	2B	+	3F	?	7D	}
22	"	2C	,	40	@	7E	~
23	#	2D	-	5B	[	7F	.
24	$	2E	.	5C	\		
25	%	2F	/	5D	]		

APPENDIX G

Java HTTP Server

The following code implements a generic HTTP server. This simple server supports only GET and HEAD requests from the client and returns HTML files and image data. Adding a "-v" command-line parameter enables verbose mode, which displays all connections in the HTTP server's console window.

```java
import java.io.*;
import java.net.*;
import java.util.StringTokenizer;
import java.util.Date;

/**
 * Java HTTP Server
 *
 * This simple HTTP server supports GET and HEAD requests.
 *
 * @author Dustin R. Callaway
 */
public class HttpServer implements Runnable
{
  //static constants
  //HttpServer root is the current directory
  static final File WEB_ROOT = new File(".");
  static final String DEFAULT_FILE = "index.html";
  static final int PORT = 8080; //default port

  //static variables
  static boolean verbose=false;

  //instance variables
  Socket connect;
```

```java
//constructor
public HttpServer(Socket connect)
{
  this.connect = connect;
}


/**
 * main method creates a new HttpServer instance for each
 * request and starts it running in a separate thread
 */
public static void main(String[] args)
{
  ServerSocket serverConnect=null;

  if (args.length > 0)
  {
    if (args[0].equals("-v") || args[0].equals("-verbose"))
    {
      verbose = true; //print status to standard out
    }
    else if (args[0].equals("-?") || args[0].equals("-help"))
    {
      //print instructions to standard out
      String instructions =
        "usage: java HttpServer [-options]\n\n" +
        "where options include:\n" +
        "    -? -help\t print out this message\n" +
        "    -v -verbose\t turn on verbose mode";

      System.out.println(instructions);
      return;
    }
  }

  try
  {
    serverConnect = new ServerSocket(PORT); //listen on port
    System.out.println("\nListening for connections on port "
      + PORT + "...\n");
    while (true) //listen until user halts execution
    {
      HttpServer server = new HttpServer(
        serverConnect.accept()); //instantiate HttpServer
      if (verbose)
      {
        System.out.println("Connection opened. (" +
          new Date() + ")");
      }
      //create new thread
      Thread threadRunner = new Thread(server);
      threadRunner.start(); //start thread
    }
  }
```

```
      catch (IOException e)
      {
        System.err.println("Server error: " + e);
      }
  }


  /**
   * run method services each request in a separate thread
   */
  public void run()
  {
    try
    {
      //get character input stream from client
      BufferedReader in = new BufferedReader(new
        InputStreamReader(connect.getInputStream()));
      //get character output stream to client (for headers)
      PrintWriter out = new PrintWriter(
        connect.getOutputStream());
      //get binary output stream to client (for requested data)
      BufferedOutputStream dataOut = new BufferedOutputStream(
        connect.getOutputStream());

      //get first line of request from client
      String input = in.readLine();
      //create StringTokenizer to parse request
      StringTokenizer parse = new StringTokenizer(input);
      //parse out method
      String method = parse.nextToken().toUpperCase();
      //parse out file requested
      String fileRequested = parse.nextToken().toLowerCase();

      //methods other than GET and HEAD are not implemented
      if (!method.equals("GET") && !method.equals("HEAD"))
      {
        if (verbose)
        {
          System.out.println("501 Not Implemented: " + method +
            " method.");
        }

        //send Not Implemented message to client
        out.println("HTTP/1.0 501 Not Implemented");
        out.println("Server: HttpServer 1.0");
        out.println("Date: " + new Date());
        out.println("Content-Type: text/html");
        out.println(); //blank line between headers and content
        out.println("<HTML>");
        out.println("<HEAD><TITLE>Not Implemented</TITLE>" +
          "</HEAD>");
        out.println("<BODY>");
        out.println("<H2>501 Not Implemented: " + method +
          " method.</H2>");
```

```
      out.println("</BODY></HTML>");
      out.flush();
      out.close(); //close output stream
      connect.close(); //close socket connection

      if (verbose)
      {
        System.out.println("Connection closed.\n");
      }

      return;
    }

    //If we get to here, request method is GET or HEAD

    if (fileRequested.endsWith("/"))
    {
      //append default file name to request
      fileRequested += DEFAULT_FILE;
    }

    try
    {
      //create file object
      File file = new File(WEB_ROOT, fileRequested);
      //get length of file
      int fileLength = (int)file.length();

      //get the file's MIME content type
      String content = getContentType(fileRequested);

      //generate HTTP headers
      out.println("HTTP/1.0 200 OK");
      out.println("Server: HttpServer 1.0");
      out.println("Date: " + new Date());
      out.println("Content-type: " + content);
      out.println("Content-length: " + file.length());
      out.println(); //blank line between headers and content
      out.flush(); //flush character output stream buffer

      //if request is a GET, send the file content
      if (method.equals("GET"))
      {
        //open input stream from file
        FileInputStream fileIn = new FileInputStream(file);
        //create byte array to store file data
        byte[] fileData = new byte[fileLength];
        //read file into byte array
        fileIn.read(fileData);
        fileIn.close(); //close file input stream
```

```
            dataOut.write(fileData,0,fileLength); //write file
            dataOut.flush(); //flush binary output stream buffer
        }

        if (verbose)
        {
          System.out.println("File " + fileRequested +
              " of type " + content + " returned.");
        }

        out.close(); //close character output stream
        dataOut.close(); //close binary output stream
        connect.close(); //close socket connection
        if (verbose)
        {
          System.out.println("Connection closed.\n");
        }
      }
      catch (IOException e)
      {
        //inform client file doesn't exist
        fileNotFound(out, fileRequested);

        out.close();
        connect.close();
        if (verbose)
        {
          System.out.println("Connection closed.\n");
        }
      }
    }
    catch (IOException e)
    {
      System.err.println("Server Error: " + e);
    }
  }


  /**
   * fileNotFound informs client that requested file does not
   * exist.
   *
   * @param out Client output stream
   * @param file File requested by client
   */
  private void fileNotFound(PrintWriter out, String file)
    throws IOException
  {
    out.println("HTTP/1.0 404 File Not Found");
    out.println("Server: HttpServer 1.0");
    out.println("Date: " + new Date());
    out.println("Content-Type: text/html");
    out.println();
```

```
out.println("<HTML>");
out.println("<HEAD><TITLE>File Not Found</TITLE></HEAD>");
out.println("<BODY>");
out.println("<H2>404 File Not Found: " + file + "</H2>");
out.println("</BODY>");
out.println("</HTML>");
if (verbose)
{
  System.out.println("404 File Not Found: " + file);
}
}


/**
 * getContentType returns the proper MIME content type
 * according to the requested file's extension
 *
 * @param fileRequested File requested by client
 */
private String getContentType(String fileRequested)
{
  if (fileRequested.endsWith(".htm") ||
    fileRequested.endsWith(".html"))
  {
    return "text/html";
  }
  else if (fileRequested.endsWith(".gif"))
  {
    return "image/gif";
  }
  else if (fileRequested.endsWith(".jpg") ||
    fileRequested.endsWith(".jpeg"))
  {
    return "image/jpeg";
  }
  else if (fileRequested.endsWith(".class") ||
    fileRequested.endsWith(".jar"))
  {
    return "applicaton/octet-stream";
  }
  else
  {
    return "text/plain";
  }
}
}
```

APPENDIX H

HTTP Response Status Codes

Table H.1 describes the meaning behind the various HTTP status code ranges. For more information, see RFC 1945. Table H.2 describes the status codes defined by HTTP/1.0.

Table H.1   HTTP Status Code Ranges

Code Range	Category	Description
1xx	Informational	A provisional status code for use only in experimental applications. HTTP/1.0 does not define any Informational status codes; however, HTTP/1.1 does.
2xx	Successful	The request was received, understood, and accepted.
3xx	Redirection	The server is requesting the Web client to redirect to another URL. The Web client can automatically redirect only in response to a GET or HEAD request. Redirection of a POST request requires user confirmation. A client should never automatically redirect more than five times.
4xx	Client Error	The request is formatted improperly or cannot be fulfilled. Unless responding to a HEAD request, the server should return information describing the error and whether it is a temporary or permanent condition in the response body. The client must immediately stop sending requests to the server.
5xx	Server Error	A valid request was received but the server cannot fulfill it. Unless responding to a HEAD request, the server should return information describing the error and whether it is a temporary or permanent condition in the response body.

Table H.2 HTTP/1.0 Status Codes

Status Code	Description
200 OK	The request succeeded. The information returned in the response depends on the request method, as follows:
	GET—Returns the information corresponding to the requested resource.
	HEAD—Response contains header information only. The body portion of the response is empty.
	POST—A message describing the results of the action is returned.
201 Created	The request was fulfilled successfully and resulted in the creation of a new resource. The URL to the new resource is specified in the body portion of the response. Of the HTTP/1.0 methods, only a POST request can create a resource. (There is, however, another method specified in HTTP/1.1 that can create a resource. For more information, see the PUT method described in Chapter 3.)
202 Accepted	A noncommittal response conveying that the request has been received and is being processed. The body of the response should indicate the current status of the request and either an estimate of when the processing will be complete or a pointer to a status monitor.
204 No Content	The server has fulfilled the request but there is no new information to return. The client should maintain its current view. If desired, additional meta information can be included in the response headers.
300 Multiple Choices	Indicates that the resource is available from multiple locations. The body of the response should include a list of locations where the resource can be found. If a particular location is preferred, the server can specify a URL in the Location header of the response. The Web client may automatically redirect to this new location.
301 Moved Permanently	The resource has been moved permanently. The Location header field specifies the new location. The Web client should automatically redirect to the new URL and update any bookmarks pointing to the old location. Unless a HEAD request has been issued, the body of the response should include a short message explaining the move and a hyperlink to the new location. This message is useful for older browsers that do not automatically redirect. If received in response to a request using the POST method, the Web client must confirm the redirection request with the user.
302 Moved Temporarily	The requested resource has moved temporarily. The Location header field specifies the temporary location. The Web client should automatically redirect to the new URL but bookmarks should not be updated. Unless a HEAD request has been issued, the body of the response should include a short message explaining the temporary move and a hyperlink to the temporary location. This message is useful for older browsers that do not automatically redirect. If received in response to a request using the POST method, the Web client must confirm the redirection request with the user.

Table H.2 HTTP/1.0 Status Codes

Status Code	Description
304 Not Modified	Returned if the Web client issued a GET request with an If-Modified-Since header and the resource has not changed since the specified date. The body of the response is empty and the page should be loaded from the browser's cache.
400 Bad Request	The request used invalid syntax and should not be repeated without modification.
401 Unauthorized	Authorization, such as username and password, is required to access this resource. A WWW-Authenticate header field containing an authorization challenge is returned with the response. Normally, upon receiving this challenge, the Web browser displays a username/password dialog box to the user. If the request has already included authorization information, this response indicates that authorization has been refused for those credentials. If authorization is denied a second time for the same credentials, the browser should display the body of the response. This may help the user diagnose the problem.
403 Forbidden	The server understood the request but refuses to fulfill it. Authorization will not help and the same request should not be repeated. If the request was not HEAD and the server chooses to explain the refusal, it may include an explanation in the body of the response.
404 Not Found	No resource matching the requested URL exists on the server. If the server does not wish to divulge the absence of a resource, it may choose to respond with status code 403 instead.
500 Internal Server Error	The server encountered an unexpected condition that prevented it from fulfilling the request.
501 Not Implemented	The server does not implement the functionality required to fulfill the request. Returned if the server does not recognize the method in the request or is not capable of servicing the request method.
502 Bad Gateway	The server received an invalid response from a gateway to which it forwarded the request.
503 Service Unavailable	The server is temporarily unable to service the request, possibly because of overloading or maintenance.

APPENDIX I

Common HTTP Request Header Fields

The HTTP/1.0 and 1.1 specifications define many header fields that are val in an HTTP request. These fields convey a wide variety of information and/ instructions to the server. The syntax of all HTTP request headers consists the header name, followed immediately by a colon (":"), a single space, and th field value as illustrated here:

HEADER: *VALUE*

Table I.1 shows many common request headers. For more information, se RFC 1945.

Table I.1   Common HTTP Request Header Fields

Header	Description
Allow	Communicates to the client the HTTP methods that are supported by the requested resource. See example: `Allow: GET, HEAD`
Authorization	Contains authentication information required by the server.
Content-Encoding	Indicates the encoding scheme that was used, in addition to the MIME encoding to package the data. See example: `Content-Encoding: x-tar`
Content-Length	Indicates the length of the request's data portion. See example: `Content-Length: 1234`

Table I.I   Common HTTP Request Header Fields

Header	Description
Content-Type	Indicates the MIME type of the request's data. See example: `Content-Type: text/html`
Date	Indicates the date and time the request was generated. See example: `Date: Sat, 05 Aug 2000 11:35:15 GMT`
Expires	Indicates the date after which the resource should be considered invalid. See example: `Expires: Sat, 05 Aug 2000 11:35:15 GMT`
From	Indicates the Internet e-mail address of the client generating the request. See example: `From: dustin@insideservlets.com`
If-Modified-Since	Indicates that the requested resource should be returned only if it has been modified since the date contained in this header field. See example: `If-Modified-Since: Sat, 05 Aug 2000 11:35:15 GMT`
Last-Modified	Indicates the date and time the requested resource was last modified. See example: `Last-Modified: Sat, 05 Aug 2000 11:35:15 GMT`
Location	Indicates the location of a server resource. Used in conjunction with $3xx$ responses to redirect the client to a different URL. See example: `Location: www.insideservlets.com/index.html`
Pragma	Communicates implementation directives to the client. This example informs the client that the response should not be cached. `Pragma: no-cache`
Referer	Indicates the address that contained the reference (or hyperlink) to the currently requested resource. In essence, this header indicates the HTML page that referred the client to the requested resource. Useful for determining where the client came from. See example: `Referer: http://www.insideservlets.com/login.html`
Server	Indicates the name and version of the server software. See example: `Server: Apache/1.2.5`
User-Agent	Indicates the type and version of the user's browser. See example: `User-Agent: Mozilla/4.03 [en] (Win95; I)`

APPENDIX J

Deployment Descriptor DTD

The Document Type Definition (DTD) for the Web application deployme
descriptor file (i.e., the *web.xml* file) is presented here. The primary configur
tion areas that are referenced within this DTD are as follows:

- Servlet context initialization parameters
- Session configuration
- Servlet/JSP definitions
- Servlet/JSP mappings
- Mime type mappings
- Welcome file list
- Error pages
- Security

The following DTD defines the XML grammar for a Web applicatio
deployment descriptor (based on Java Servlet Specification 2.2).

```
<!--
The web-app element is the root of the deployment descriptor fo
a web application
-->
<!ELEMENT web-app (icon?, display-name?, description?,
   distributable?,
context-param*, servlet*, servlet-mapping*, session-config?,
mime-mapping*, welcome-file-list?, error-page*, taglib*,
resource-ref*, security-constraint*, login-config?, security-
   role*,
env-entry*, ejb-ref*)>

<!--
The icon element contains a small-icon and a large-icon element
which specify the location within the web application for a small an
```

```
large image used to represent the web application in a GUI tool.
  At a
minimum, tools must accept GIF and JPEG format images.
-->
<!ELEMENT icon (small-icon?, large-icon?)>


<!--
The small-icon element contains the location within the web
application of a file containing a small (16x16 pixel) icon
  image.
-->
<!ELEMENT small-icon (#PCDATA)>


<!--
The large-icon element contains the location within the web
application of a file containing a large (32x32 pixel) icon
  image.
-->
<!ELEMENT large-icon (#PCDATA)>


<!--
The display-name element contains a short name that is intended
to be displayed by GUI tools
-->
<!ELEMENT display-name (#PCDATA)>


<!--
The description element is used to provide descriptive text about
the parent element.
-->
<!ELEMENT description (#PCDATA)>


<!--
The distributable element, by its presence in a web application
deployment descriptor, indicates that this web application is
programmed appropriately to be deployed into a distributed serv-
  let
container
-->
<!ELEMENT distributable EMPTY>


<!--
The context-param element contains the declaration of a web
application's servlet context initialization parameters.
-->
<!ELEMENT context-param (param-name, param-value, description?)>


<!--
The param-name element contains the name of a parameter.
-->
<!ELEMENT param-name (#PCDATA)>


<!--
```

The param-value element contains the value of a parameter.
-->
<!ELEMENT param-value (#PCDATA)>

<!--
The servlet element contains the declarative data of a
servlet. If a jsp-file is specified and the load-on-startup
  element is
present, then the JSP should be precompiled and loaded.
-->
<!ELEMENT servlet (icon?, servlet-name, display-name?,
  description?,
(servlet-class|jsp-file), init-param*, load-on-startup?,
  security-role-ref*)>

<!--
The servlet-name element contains the canonical name of the
servlet.
-->
<!ELEMENT servlet-name (#PCDATA)>

<!--
The servlet-class element contains the fully qualified class name
of the servlet.
-->
<!ELEMENT servlet-class (#PCDATA)>

<!--
The jsp-file element contains the full path to a JSP file within
the web application.
-->
<!ELEMENT jsp-file (#PCDATA)>

<!--
The init-param element contains a name/value pair as an
initialization param of the servlet
-->
<!ELEMENT init-param (param-name, param-value, description?)>

<!--
The load-on-startup element indicates that this servlet should be
loaded on the startup of the web application. The optional
  contents of
these element must be a positive integer indicating the order in
  which
the servlet should be loaded. Lower integers are loaded before
  higher
integers. If no value is specified, or if the value specified is
  not a
positive integer, the container is free to load it at any time in
  the
startup sequence.
-->

```
<!ELEMENT load-on-startup (#PCDATA)>

<!--
The servlet-mapping element defines a mapping between a servlet
and a url pattern
-->
<!ELEMENT servlet-mapping (servlet-name, url-pattern)>

<!--
The url-pattern element contains the url pattern of the
mapping. Must follow the rules specified in Section 10 of the
  Servlet
API Specification.
-->
<!ELEMENT url-pattern (#PCDATA)>

<!--
The session-config element defines the session parameters for
this web application.
-->
<!ELEMENT session-config (session-timeout?)>

<!--
The session-timeout element defines the default session timeout
interval for all sessions created in this web application. The
specified timeout must be expressed in a whole number of minutes.
-->
<!ELEMENT session-timeout (#PCDATA)>

<!--
The mime-mapping element defines a mapping between an extension
and a mime type.
-->
<!ELEMENT mime-mapping (extension, mime-type)>

<!--
The extension element contains a string describing an
extension. example: "txt"
-->
<!ELEMENT extension (#PCDATA)>

<!--
The mime-type element contains a defined mime type. example:
"text/plain"
-->
<!ELEMENT mime-type (#PCDATA)>

<!--
The welcome-file-list contains an ordered list of welcome files
elements.
-->
<!ELEMENT welcome-file-list (welcome-file+)>
```

```
<!--
The welcome-file element contains file name to use as a defaul
welcome file, such as index.html
-->
<!ELEMENT welcome-file (#PCDATA)>

<!--
The taglib element is used to describe a JSP tag library.
-->
<!ELEMENT taglib (taglib-uri, taglib-location)>

<!--
The taglib-uri element describes a URI, relative to the locatic
of the web.xml document, identifying a Tag Library used in the
  Web
Application.
-->
<!ELEMENT taglib-uri (#PCDATA)>

<!--
the taglib-location element contains the location (as a resourc
relative to the root of the web application) where to find the
  Tag
Libary Description file for the tag library.
-->
<!ELEMENT taglib-location (#PCDATA)>

<!--
The error-page element contains a mapping between an error code
or exception type to the path of a resource in the web
  application
-->
<!ELEMENT error-page ((error-code | exception-type), location)>

<!--
The error-code contains an HTTP error code, ex: 404
-->
<!ELEMENT error-code (#PCDATA)>

<!--
The exception type contains a fully qualified class name of a
Java exception type.
-->
<!ELEMENT exception-type (#PCDATA)>

<!--
The location element contains the location of the resource in the
web application
-->
<!ELEMENT location (#PCDATA)>
```

```
<!--
The resource-ref element contains a declaration of a Web
Application's reference to an external resource.
-->
<!ELEMENT resource-ref (description?, res-ref-name, res-type,
  res-auth)>


<!--
The res-ref-name element specifies the name of the resource
factory reference name.
-->
<!ELEMENT res-ref-name (#PCDATA)>


<!--
The res-type element specifies the (Java class) type of the data
source.
-->
<!ELEMENT res-type (#PCDATA)>


<!--
The res-auth element indicates whether the application component
code performs resource signon programmatically or whether the
container signs onto the resource based on the principle mapping
information supplied by the deployer. Must be CONTAINER or
  SERVLET
-->
<!ELEMENT res-auth (#PCDATA)>


<!--
The security-constraint element is used to associate security
constraints with one or more web resource collections
-->
<!ELEMENT security-constraint (web-resource-collection+,
auth-constraint?, user-data-constraint?)>


<!--
The web-resource-collection element is used to identify a subset
of the resources and HTTP methods on those resources within a web
application to which a security constraint applies. If no HTTP
  methods
are specified, then the security constraint applies to all HTTP
methods.
-->
<!ELEMENT web-resource-collection (web-resource-name,
  description?,
url-pattern*, http-method*)>


<!--
The web-resource-name contains the name of this web resource
collection
-->
<!ELEMENT web-resource-name (#PCDATA)>
```

```
<!--
The http-method contains an HTTP method (GET | POST |...)
-->
<!ELEMENT http-method (#PCDATA)>

<!--
The user-data-constraint element is used to indicate how data
communicated between the client and container should be protect
-->
<!ELEMENT user-data-constraint (description?, transport-
   guarantee)>

<!--
The transport-guarantee element specifies that the communicatic
between client and server should be NONE, INTEGRAL, or
CONFIDENTIAL. NONE means that the application does not require
   any
transport guarantees. A value of INTEGRAL means that the
   application
requires that the data sent between the client and server be sent
   in
such a way that it can't be changed in transit. CONFIDENTIAL
   means
that the application requires that the data be transmitted in a
fashion that prevents other entities from observing the contents
   of
the transmission. In most cases, the presence of the INTEGRAL o
CONFIDENTIAL flag will indicate that the use of SSL is required
-->
<!ELEMENT transport-guarantee (#PCDATA)>

<!--
The auth-constraint element indicates the user roles that shoul
be permitted access to this resource collection. The role used
   here
must appear in a security-role-ref element.
-->
<!ELEMENT auth-constraint (description?, role-name*)>

<!--
The role-name element contains the name of a security role.
-->
<!ELEMENT role-name (#PCDATA)>

<!--
The login-config element is used to configure the authenticatior
method that should be used, the realm name that should be used
   for
this application, and the attributes that are needed by the form
   login
mechanism.
-->
```

```
<!ELEMENT login-config (auth-method?, realm-name?, form-login-
  config?)>

<!--
The realm name element specifies the realm name to use in HTTP
Basic authorization
-->
<!ELEMENT realm-name (#PCDATA)>

<!--
The form-login-config element specifies the login and error pages
that should be used in form based login. If form based
  authentication
is not used, these elements are ignored.
-->
<!ELEMENT form-login-config (form-login-page, form-error-page)>

<!--
The form-login-page element defines the location in the web app
where the page that can be used for login can be found
-->
<!ELEMENT form-login-page (#PCDATA)>

<!--
The form-error-page element defines the location in the web app
where the error page that is displayed when login is not
  successful
can be found
-->
<!ELEMENT form-error-page (#PCDATA)>

<!--
The auth-method element is used to configure the authentication
mechanism for the web application. As a prerequisite to gaining
  access
to any web resources which are protected by an authorization
constraint, a user must have authenticated using the configured
mechanism. Legal values for this element are "BASIC", "DIGEST",
"FORM", or "CLIENT-CERT".
-->
<!ELEMENT auth-method (#PCDATA)>

<!--
The security-role element contains the declaration of a security
role which is used in the security-constraints placed on the web
application.
-->
<!ELEMENT security-role (description?, role-name)>

<!--
The role-name element contains the name of a role. This element
must contain a non-empty string.
-->
```

```
<!ELEMENT security-role-ref (description?, role-name, role-
    link)>
```

```
<!--
The role-link element is used to link a security role referenc
to a defined security role. The role-link element must contain
    the
name of one of the security roles defined in the security-role
elements.
-->
<!ELEMENT role-link (#PCDATA)>
```

```
<!--
The env-entry element contains the declaration of an
application's environment entry. This element is required to be
honored on in J2EE compliant servlet containers.
-->
<!ELEMENT env-entry (description?, env-entry-name, env-entry-
    value?,
env-entry-type)>
```

```
<!--
The env-entry-name contains the name of an application's
environment entry
-->
<!ELEMENT env-entry-name (#PCDATA)>
```

```
<!--
The env-entry-value element contains the value of an
application's environment entry
-->
<!ELEMENT env-entry-value (#PCDATA)>
```

```
<!--
The env-entry-type element contains the fully qualified Java typ
of the environment entry value that is expected by the
    application
code. The following are the legal values of env-entry-type:
java.lang.Boolean, java.lang.String, java.lang.Integer,
java.lang.Double, java.lang.Float.
-->
<!ELEMENT env-entry-type (#PCDATA)>
```

```
<!--
The ejb-ref element is used to declare a reference to an
enterprise bean.
-->
<!ELEMENT ejb-ref (description?, ejb-ref-name, ejb-ref-type,
    home,
remote,
ejb-link?)>
```

```
<!--
The ejb-ref-name element contains the name of an EJB
reference. This is the JNDI name that the servlet code uses to
  get a
reference to the enterprise bean.
-->
<!ELEMENT ejb-ref-name (#PCDATA)>


<!--
The ejb-ref-type element contains the expected java class type of
the referenced EJB.
-->
<!ELEMENT ejb-ref-type (#PCDATA)>


<!--
The ejb-home element contains the fully qualified name of the
EJB's home interface
-->
<!ELEMENT home (#PCDATA)>


<!--
The ejb-remote element contains the fully qualified name of the
EJB's remote interface
-->
<!ELEMENT remote (#PCDATA)>


<!--
The ejb-link element is used in the ejb-ref element to specify
that an EJB reference is linked to an EJB in an encompassing
  Java2
Enterprise Edition (J2EE) application package. The value of the
ejb-link element must be the ejb-name of and EJB in the J2EE
application package.
-->
<!ELEMENT ejb-link (#PCDATA)>


<!--
The ID mechanism is to allow tools to easily make tool-specific
references to the elements of the deployment descriptor. This
  allows
tools that produce additional deployment information (i.e
  information
beyond the standard deployment descriptor information) to store
  the
non-standard information in a separate file, and easily refer
  from
these tools-specific files to the information in the standard
  web-app
deployment descriptor.
-->
<!ATTLIST web-app id ID #IMPLIED>
<!ATTLIST icon id ID #IMPLIED>
<!ATTLIST small-icon id ID #IMPLIED>
```

```
<!ATTLIST large-icon id ID #IMPLIED>
<!ATTLIST display-name id ID #IMPLIED>
<!ATTLIST description id ID #IMPLIED>
<!ATTLIST distributable id ID #IMPLIED>
<!ATTLIST context-param id ID #IMPLIED>
<!ATTLIST param-name id ID #IMPLIED>
<!ATTLIST param-value id ID #IMPLIED>
<!ATTLIST servlet id ID #IMPLIED>
<!ATTLIST servlet-name id ID #IMPLIED>
<!ATTLIST servlet-class id ID #IMPLIED>
<!ATTLIST jsp-file id ID #IMPLIED>
<!ATTLIST init-param id ID #IMPLIED>
<!ATTLIST load-on-startup id ID #IMPLIED>
<!ATTLIST servlet-mapping id ID #IMPLIED>
<!ATTLIST url-pattern id ID #IMPLIED>
<!ATTLIST session-config id ID #IMPLIED>
<!ATTLIST session-timeout id ID #IMPLIED>
<!ATTLIST mime-mapping id ID #IMPLIED>
<!ATTLIST extension id ID #IMPLIED>
<!ATTLIST mime-type id ID #IMPLIED>
<!ATTLIST welcome-file-list id ID #IMPLIED>
<!ATTLIST welcome-file id ID #IMPLIED>
<!ATTLIST taglib id ID #IMPLIED>
<!ATTLIST taglib-uri id ID #IMPLIED>
<!ATTLIST taglib-location id ID #IMPLIED>
<!ATTLIST error-page id ID #IMPLIED>
<!ATTLIST error-code id ID #IMPLIED>
<!ATTLIST exception-type id ID #IMPLIED>
<!ATTLIST location id ID #IMPLIED>
<!ATTLIST resource-ref id ID #IMPLIED>
<!ATTLIST res-ref-name id ID #IMPLIED>
<!ATTLIST res-type id ID #IMPLIED>
<!ATTLIST res-auth id ID #IMPLIED>
<!ATTLIST security-constraint id ID #IMPLIED>
<!ATTLIST web-resource-collection id ID #IMPLIED>
<!ATTLIST web-resource-name id ID #IMPLIED>
<!ATTLIST http-method id ID #IMPLIED>
<!ATTLIST user-data-constraint id ID #IMPLIED>
<!ATTLIST transport-guarantee id ID #IMPLIED>
<!ATTLIST auth-constraint id ID #IMPLIED>
<!ATTLIST role-name id ID #IMPLIED>
<!ATTLIST login-config id ID #IMPLIED>
<!ATTLIST realm-name id ID #IMPLIED>
<!ATTLIST form-login-config id ID #IMPLIED>
<!ATTLIST form-login-page id ID #IMPLIED>
<!ATTLIST form-error-page id ID #IMPLIED>
<!ATTLIST auth-method id ID #IMPLIED>
<!ATTLIST security-role id ID #IMPLIED>
<!ATTLIST security-role-ref id ID #IMPLIED>
<!ATTLIST role-link id ID #IMPLIED>
<!ATTLIST env-entry id ID #IMPLIED>
<!ATTLIST env-entry-name id ID #IMPLIED>
<!ATTLIST env-entry-value id ID #IMPLIED>
```

```
<!ATTLIST env-entry-type id ID #IMPLIED>
<!ATTLIST ejb-ref id ID #IMPLIED>
<!ATTLIST ejb-ref-name id ID #IMPLIED>
<!ATTLIST ejb-ref-type id ID #IMPLIED>
<!ATTLIST home id ID #IMPLIED>
<!ATTLIST remote id ID #IMPLIED>
<!ATTLIST ejb-link id ID #IMPLIED>
```

APPENDIX K

Common MIME Types

Table K.1 describes the main areas into which MIME types are categorized as well as specific subtypes. The format of the MIME content type identifier is *type/subtype*. For instance, the MIME type for an HTML document is text/html, and for a JPEG file, it is image/jpeg.

Table K.1 Common MIME Types

Type	Subtype	Description
application		Binary data that is read or executed by another program
	java	Java bytecode file (.class)
	mac-binhex40	Binary Macintosh file
	msword	Microsoft Word document
	octet-stream	Arbitrary binary data that can be executed or used in another program (sometimes used for Java .class files)
	pdf	Adobe Acrobat file
	postscript	Adobe PostScript file
	rtf	Rich Text Format document
	x-compress	UNIX compress file
	x-dvi	Device-independent file
	x-framemaker	FrameMaker document
	x-gtar	GNU tar archive file
	x-gzip	Compressed UNIX gzip file
	x-latex	LaTeX document
	x-mif	FrameMaker MIF document
	x-sd	Session directory announcement for MBONE events

Table K.1   Common MIME Types

Type	Subtype	Description
	x-shar	Self-extracting UNIX shell file
	x-tar	UNIX tar archive file
	x-tcl	Tool Command Language program
	x-tex	TeX document
	x-texinfo	GNU texinfo document
	x-troffv	UNIX troff document
	x-wais-source	Wide Area Information Servers source file
	zip	Compressed zip file
audio		Sound file that can be played by another program
	basic	Standard audio format used by .au and .snd files
	x-aiff	AIFF audio format
	x-wav	Microsoft WAV format
image		Picture file that can be displayed by another program
	gif	GIF image
	jpeg	JPEG image
	tiff	TIFF image
	x-bitmap	Bitmap image
	x-fits	Flexible Image Transport System image used by the astronomy community
	x-macpict	Macintosh PICT image
	x-pict	Macintosh PICT image
	x-pbm	Portable bitmap image
	x-pgm	PGM image
	x-portable-bitmap	Portable bitmap image
	x-portable-greymap	Portable greymap image
	x-portable-pixmap	Portable pixmap image
	x-xbitmap	X Window bitmap image
	x-xpixmap	X Window pixmap image
message		Encapsulated mail message
	external-body	Headers of an e-mail message with a reference to the message body located elsewhere
	news	News article

(continued)

Table K.1 Common MIME Types *(continued)*

Type	Subtype	Description
	`partial`	Part of a fragmented message
	`rfc822`	RFC822-compliant e-mail message
`multipart`		Data consisting of multiple, possibly heterogenous, parts
	`alternative`	Multiple formats of the same message (allows the client to choose)
	`digest`	Message formed by merging many e-mail messages
	`mixed`	Mixed formats in the same message
	`parallel`	Multipart message containing parts that should be viewed simultaneously
`text`		Data consisting of printable text
	`html`	Hypertext Markup Language document
	`plain`	Plain ASCII text without formatting
	`richtext`	Rich Text Format document (includes formatting codes in standard ASCII text)
	`tab-separated-values`	Popular file format for exchanging data between spreadsheets and databases. Fields are separated by tabs and records are separated by carriage return/linefeeds.
`video`		Video file that can be played by another program
	`mpeg`	Moving Pictures Experts Group video file
	`quicktime`	Apple QuickTime video file
	`x-msvideo`	Microsoft AVI (Audio Video Interleave) video file
	`x-sgi-movie`	Silicon Graphics video file
`x-world`		Experimental data types
	`x-vrml`	Virtual Reality Markup Language document

APPENDIX L

printStackTrace() *to* String

The printStackTrace() method of the java.lang.Exception object (inherited from the Throwable object) is a very useful debugging function. This method prints the stack trace to standard error or to a specified output stream (PrintStream or PrintWriter). However, there may be times when you would prefer to write the stack trace to an error log or send it to the client. Unfortunately, it is not immediately apparent how the output produced by the printStackTrace() method can be converted to a String for easy use. The following code demonstrates how this can be accomplished.

```
catch (Exception e)
{
  StringWriter swError = new StringWriter();
  PrintWriter pwError = new PrintWriter(swError);
  e.printStackTrace(pwError);
  String sError = swError.toString();

  // The printStackTrace() output is stored in the String
  // variable, sError, and can now be written to a file
  // or returned to the client.
}
```

APPENDIX M

Servlet API Class Hierarchy Diagram

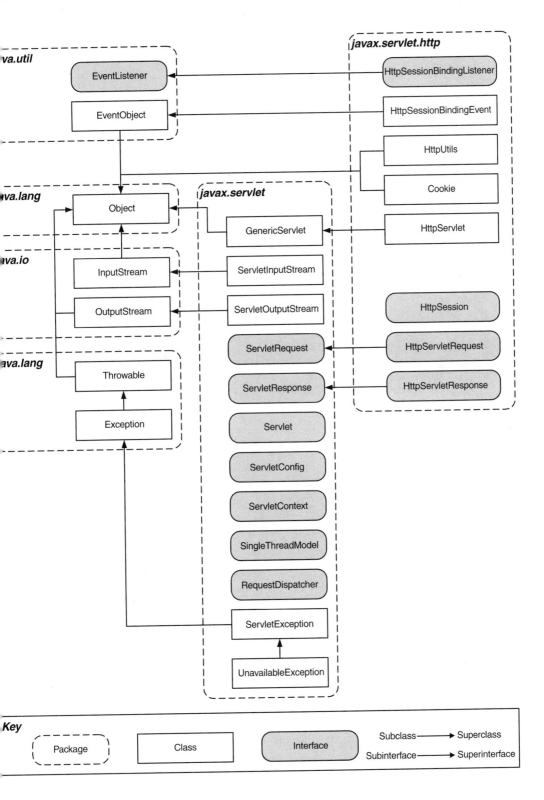

java.util

EventListener

EventObject

javax.servlet.http

HttpSessionBindingListener

HttpSessionBindingEvent

HttpUtils

Cookie

HttpServlet

java.lang

Object

javax.servlet

GenericServlet

java.io

InputStream

ServletInputStream

OutputStream

ServletOutputStream

HttpSession

ServletRequest

HttpServletRequest

ServletResponse

HttpServletResponse

java.lang

Throwable

Exception

Servlet

ServletConfig

ServletContext

SingleThreadModel

RequestDispatcher

ServletException

UnavailableException

Key

Package   Class   Interface   Subclass ────▶ Superclass
                              Subinterface ────▶ Superinterface

847

INDEX

Note: Italicized page locators indicate tables/figures.

Java™ Technology from Addison-Wesle

ISBN 0-201-70720-9

ISBN 0-201-70421-8

ISBN 0-201-70429-3

ISBN 0-201-60446

ISBN 0-201-61646-7

ISBN 0-201-72588-6

ISBN 0-201-71501-5

ISBN 0-201-59614-

ISBN 0-201-30972-6

ISBN 0-201-67491-2

ISBN 0-201-48543-5

http://www.aw.com/cseng   ⋀ Addison-Wesley